A List of Geographical Atlases

in the Library of Congress

VOLUME 9

Comprehensive Author List

Compiled by

CLARA EGLI LEGEAR

Geography and Map Division

LIBRARY OF CONGRESS • WASHINGTON • 1992

Library of Congress Cataloging-in-Publication Data

(Revised for vol. 9)

Library of Congress. Geography and Map Division.
  A list of geographical atlases in the Library of
Congress, with bibliographical notes.

  At head of title, v. 1–4: Library of Congress.
  Vols. 1–4, compiled under the direction of P. L.
Phillips, chief, Division of Maps and Charts: v. 5–6,
by C. E. LeGear, Map Division (v. 7–9, Geography and
Map Division)
  Supt. of Docs. no.: LC 5.2:G29
  Contents: v. 1–2. Titles 1–3265: Atlases; Author
list, Index.—v. 3. Titles 3266–4087.—[etc.]—
v. 9. Comprehensive author list.
  1. Library of Congress. Geography and Map Division.
2. Atlases—Bibliography—Catalogs. I. Phillips,
Philip Lee, 1857–1924. II. Le Gear, Clara Egli.
III. Library of Congress. Geography and Map Division.
IV. Title. V. Title: Geographical atlases in the
Library of Congress.
Z6028.U56 [GA 300]   016.912   09-35009
ISBN 0-8444-0117-X

For sale by the Superintendent of Documents, U. S. Government Printing Office, Washington, D.C. 20402

Contents

Preface

"THAT ATLASES have not received the consideration in bibliography due to their importance in literature and as contributions to knowledge is shown by the paucity of works on the subject. No exhaustive study of them has been attempted, and the available sources consist merely of a few monographs and some scattered information to be found only after much research in many out of the way places."

In establishing the rationale for compiling *A List of Geographical Atlases*, Philip Lee Phillips noted in the preface of the first volume (1909) that there was a lack of literature on the atlas. This observation was made over eighty years ago. Since that time, however, the atlas has been evolving into a variety of specialized formats, including the latest advances in computerized CRT displays and data bank printouts. All this, however, postdates the material included in the present volume. No doubt future compilations of this sort will have the advantage of advanced computer technologies and techniques.

Although there has been no comprehensive study of the atlas as a cartographic format, there have been several studies in the past few years which deal with the different types of atlases. Thus, there is a growing corpus of literature on the history of the atlas in all its varied formats and area-subject content. One can cite, as an excellent introduction, David Woodward's "The Techniques of Atlas Making," *The Map Collector*, no. 18, March 1982, pp. 2–11, in which he discusses the history, format, fabric, editing, bibliographic citation, engraving and printing, use of color, and inks and binding. A thorough albeit brief exposition, he also includes explanatory diagrams and illustrations and a glossary of technical terms. Additionally, the variety and depth of papers presented at the Library of Congress 1984 symposium "Images of the World: The Atlas Through History,"

which focused attention on the atlas as a distinct publishing and cartographic format and as a social and economic force, showed an increasingly sophisticated and scholarly approach to the history of the genre. A major exhibit of over three hundred atlases from the division's collections was mounted in the Library's Madison Hall at the time and generated a great deal of interest.

Undoubtedly this multivolume bibliography of atlases has been utilized to some degree in historical research, but the full extent of its influence cannot be measured without an extensive survey of pertinent footnotes. More important in measuring the significance of this work, perhaps, is the growing number of comparable comprehensive atlas lists of all types that have been initiated since the beginning of the twentieth century. It is possible to identify approximately a dozen similarly important bibliographies which utilize a variety of temporal, geographic, and institutional approaches and, of course, limitations.

Some of these atlas bibliographies, such as the Phillips-LeGear listing, provide a list of the atlases in an individual collection or repository. For example, atlases in the major Polish libraries are described by Marian Lodynski in *Centralny katalog zbiorow kartograficznych w Polsce*, vols. 1–4, *Katalog atlasow i dziei geograficznych* (Warszawa: Instytut Geografii, Polska Akademia Nauk and Biblioteka Narodowa, 1961–68), while a selection of atlases found among the cartographic holdings of the National Archives of Canada are described by Lou Seboek in *Atlases Published in the Netherlands in the Rare Atlas Collection* (Ottawa: Public Archives of Canada, National Map Collection, 1973), and *French Atlases in the Rare Atlas Collection* (Ottawa: Public Archives of Canada, National Map Collection, 1974). A smaller atlas collection held by the Servicio Geografico of the

Spanish Army is listed in *Catalog de Atlas* (Madrid: Servicio Geografico de Ejercito, 1962). Similarly, the atlases included in what was originally a private collection are described by Ann-Mari Mickwitz and Leena Miekkavaara in *The A.E. Nordenskiold Collection in the Helsinki University Library: Annotated Catalogue of Maps Made up to 1800*, vols. 1–2, *Atlases* (Helsinki: Helsinki University Press, 1979–1981).

Several other atlas bibliographies have focused only on those atlases published within an individual country. Cornelis Koeman lists the atlases (and their contents) published in the Netherlands in his exemplary *Atlantes Neerlandici: Bibliography of Terrestrial, Maritime and Celestial Atlases and Pilot Books Published in the Netherlands up to 1880* (5 vols., Amsterdam: Theatrum Orbis Terrarum, 1967), and *Atlantes Neerlandici: A Supplement to the Volumes I–V and a Bibliography of Geographical, Celestial and Thematic Atlases Published in the Netherlands between 1880 and 1940* (Alphen aan den Rijn: Canaletto, 1985). Similarly, Mireille Pastoureau has begun to list French atlases with *Les Atlases français XVIe-XVIIe siècles: répertoire bibliographique et étude* (Paris: Bibliothèque Nationale, 1984).

More specialized bibliographies have focused on those atlases depicting a particular country or pertaining to a specific topic. Before Clara LeGear continued her work on Phillips's list, she compiled a list of atlases of the United States and the individual states, counties, and cities in *United States Atlases: A List of National, State, County, and Regional Atlases in the Library of Congress* (2 vols., Washington, D.C.: Library of Congress, 1950–53). Atlases of Great Britain and its administrative subdivisions have been listed in three separate publications: Thomas Chubb, *The Printed Maps in the Atlases of Great Britain and Ireland: A Bibliography, 1579–1820* (London: Homeland Association, 1927); Raleigh Ashlin Skelton, *County Atlases of the British Isles, 1579–1850: A Bibliography*, vol. 1, *1579–1703* (London: Carta Press, 1970); and Donald Hodson,

County Atlases of the British Isles Published after 1703: A Bibliography, vol. 1, *Atlases Published 1704 to 1742 and Their Subsequent Editions* (Tewin, Welwyn, Hertfordshire: Tewin Press, 1984). An example of a topical atlas bibliography is Astrid Badziag and Petra Mohs's listing of German school atlases, entitled *Schulatlanten in Deutschland und benachbarten Landern vom 18. Jahrhundert bis 1950: ein bibliographisches Verzeichnis* (Munich: K. G. Saur, 1982).

Whether or not the atlas bibliographies mentioned were inspired by the inaugural efforts of Phillips or, perhaps, were conceived independently, the growing international data base represented by their combined efforts attests to the perceived importance of this type of bibliographic information and the importance of continued efforts to compile such lists. The advent of computerized cataloging and data base printouts shared nationally and internationally may limit the need for formal publication of institutional listings such as this one. However, the new techniques will certainly facilitate the production of regional, temporal, and topical atlas bibliographies.

It is unlikely that the Library of Congress will again undertake such an ambitious task as listing the individual plates from such a large number of atlases or, indeed, of updating the present volumes. This comprehensive author list, therefore, is offered as a conclusion to the preceding eight volumes. It will, of course, make the earlier works easier to use and will also serve as an important additional source of biographical data for scores of important and some less important atlas makers. More importantly, it will stand as a memorial to the dedicated and meticulous work of Philip Lee Phillips, who initiated the project, and more particularly to Clara Egli LeGear, who persisted in bringing it to a satisfactory conclusion in her ninetieth year. While Mrs. LeGear was responsible for the initial compilation of this comprehensive author list, Ronald E. Grim and Kathryn L. Engstrom of the division's Reference and Bibliography Section and Iris Newsom of the

Library's Publishing Office took on the assignment of supervising, coordinating, and proofreading the final production of this volume.

JOHN A. WOLTER
Chief
Geography and Map Division

Introduction

THIS VOLUME contains a Comprehensive Author List for the 18,435 geographical atlases described in the *List of Geographical Atlases in the Library of Congress*, 8 volumes (1909–1974). This list includes the full name and birth and death dates, if known, of the principal authors or compilers (main entry) of each atlas. Authors of the various atlas plates and names of publishers, other than principal compiler, are not included. This biographical data is followed by a listing of abbreviated atlas titles and their dates of publication. Index numbers refer to individual entries which are numbered consecutively throughout the six primary volumes of bibliographical descriptions.

About the Bibliography

Before the publication of the present volume, *A List of Geographical Atlases* consisted of eight volumes, with a publication history spanning some sixty-five years and two compilers, Philip Lee Phillips and Clara Egli LeGear. The publication style and format were established with the issuance of the first two volumes in 1909. The first volume consisted of a bibliographical listing of atlases acquired by the Geography and Map Division up to 1909. The geographical coverage was comprehensive with bibliographical descriptions grouped according to the geographical hierarchy: World, Europe, Asia, Africa, Polar Regions, and Americas, and within each of these broad categories by country, state, province, or lesser geographical area. The second volume provided an author index and an extensive subject index to the first volume.

This publication program was continued with the issuance of a third volume in 1914. It listed atlases of all geographical areas acquired between 1909 and 1914. It also included a comprehensive author list for volumes 1 and 3,

while its subject index pertained only to volume 3. Similarly, a fourth volume was issued in 1920, covering accessions up to 1920. Again, the coverage was worldwide. This volume concluded with a comprehensive author list to volumes 1, 3, and 4, while the subject index was confined to those bibliographical descriptions found only in volume 4.

The first four volumes were prepared under the direction of Mr. Phillips, the first chief of the Map Division. Subsequently, four volumes were compiled by Mrs. LeGear, beginning with the fifth volume, published in 1958. Volume 5, limited to bibliographical descriptions for world atlases acquired between 1920 and 1955, also included an author list and subject index. Volume 6, which was published in 1963, listed atlases of Europe, Asia, Africa, Oceania, and the Polar Regions acquired between 1920 and 1960. It also contained an author list and subject index. Volume 7, published in 1973, described atlases of the Americas acquired between 1920 and 1969, but included none dated after 1967. This volume included an author list, but the subject index was issued separately as volume 8, which was published in 1974. The contents of the eight volumes are summarized in the table below.

Long recognized as a basic reference tool for the study of atlases, the utility of this work has been hampered by the lack of a comprehensive author list and subject index. The present volume remedies one of these deficiences. It provides a comprehensive author list for the 18,435 titles listed in volumes 1, 3, 4, 5, 6, and 7. This author list was compiled by Clara LeGear from cards generated during the indexing of the earlier volumes. She integrated the files from the separate volumes into one alphabetical listing. Similarly, the six separate subject indexes have been integrated into one alphabetical file, but it is not likely that this file will be published in the near future because of its size and the expense of preparing manually such a sizeable index for publication.

Consequently, this volume provides an index to the primary authors for over 18,000 atlases listed in the earlier volumes. Unfortunately, the various geographical coverages do not end with a common date. Volume 9, therefore, indexes world atlases acquired by the Library to 1955, Eastern Hemisphere atlases acquired to 1960, and Western Hemisphere atlases acquired to 1969. Although it would be desireable to have all atlases acquired before 1969 included in this multivolume publication, the unlisted atlases

are still accessible. These atlases, cataloged in the 1950s and 1960s, were described in a systematic cataloging effort. The resulting bibliographic descriptions were made available through the Library's card cataloging program and are now accessible in one of the Library's data bases, PRE-MARC. Those atlases acquired and cataloged after 1968, have been described according to Anglo-American Cataloging Rules and are accessible through the Library's main data base, MARC (which is available outside the Library in either computer tape format or National Union Catalog microfiche).

| Volume | Title Numbers | Date of Publication | Geographical Coverage | | | Index Coverage | |
			World	Europe Asia, Etc.	America	Author List for Volumes	Subject Index for Volumes
1	1–3,265	1909	Up to 1909	Up to 1909	Up to 1909		
2	Index to volume 1	1909				1	1
3	3,266–4,087	1914	1909–14	1909–14	1909–14	1, 3	3
4	4,088–5,324	1920	1914–20	1914–20	1914–20	1, 3, 4	4
5	5,325–7,623	1958	1920–55			5	5
6	7,624–10,254	1963		1920–60		6	6
7	10,255–18,435	1973			1920–69	7	
8	Index to volume 7	1974					7
9		1991				1, 3, 4, 5, 6, 7	

About the Compiler

While 1914 marks the year in which the third volume (i.e., the first supplement) of *A List of Geographical Atlases in the Library of Congress* was published, it was also the year that Clara Egli joined the staff of the Library of Congress. She was born in Hoboken, New Jersey, May 2, 1896. Her father Henry Egli emigrated to the United States from Canton Zurich, Switzerland, in 1883, while her mother Bertha Laubinger came to the United States from Baden, Germany, in 1892. After her father's death in 1914, Clara and her mother and older sister moved to Washington, D.C., where her mother's brother worked as a bookbinder in the Library of Congress. In Washington, Clara attended secretarial

school for several months before obtaining a position at the Library of Congress in December 1914. After a two-week assignment typing headings on catalog cards for books to be exhibited at the Panama Pacific Exposition in San Francisco, she worked in the Library's cataloging divison, answering telephones, writing book numbers on catalog cards, and alphabetizing cards. Eleven months later in November 1915, she transferred to the Division of Maps, then under the direction of Philip Lee Phillips, chief of the division since its creation in 1897.

Although she began as a typist, her active career in the Division of Maps, now the Geography and Map Division, spanned forty-six years and involved almost all aspects of map librarianship—cataloging, reference, acquisitions, bibliography, and administration. During her first thirty-five years she served in a variety of positions including cataloger, reference librarian, assistant chief (1931–1945), and librarian in charge of cartographic acquisitions. During that time she also continued her education. In 1930 she received an A.B. degree with a major in Library Science from the George Washington University. She obtained a Master's degree in 1936, from the same institution, majoring in Library Science and minoring in Geology. She also completed several courses in cartography and editing at the U.S. Department of Agriculture Graduate School.

After World War II, she relinquished her administrative duties in order to devote full time to writing and bibliographic activities. Her first major publication was a manual on the care and preservation of cartographic materials, *Maps: Their Care, Repair and Preservation in Libraries* (1949), which quickly became a standard reference work in the field of map librarianship. With the official designation of Bibliographer she resumed work on Phillips's bibliography of atlases. This bibliographic activity resulted in several publications: *United States Atlases* (2 vols., 1950–1953) and *A List of Geographical Atlases in the Library of Congress* (vol. 5, 1958). She also continued work on the division's card file of bibliographic citations to cartographic literature which was eventually published as *The Bibliography of Cartography* (5 vols., Boston: G. K. Hall, 1973). In 1959 she was appointed head of the division's Reference and Bibliography Section.

Upon her retirement in 1961, after forty-seven years of service, she was appointed Honorary Consultant in Historical Cartography. She served in this capacity for eleven years and completed volumes 6, 7, and 8 of *A List of Geographical Atlases*. She also continued compiling the *Bibliography of Cartography* until a full-time bibliographer was appointed in 1969. Although she concluded her official association with the division in 1972 after fifty-eight years with the Library, she returned to the division on a periodic basis, completing this comprehensive author list, an index for the entire *A List of Geographical Atlases*.

Throughout her career, Clara Egli LeGear has been active in a number of professional organizations including the Special Libraries Association, Society of Women Geographers, Association of American Geographers, and American Geographical Society. Of her various professional associations, her most significant contributions were made to the Geography and Map Division of the Special Libraries Association. She was one of the individuals involved in founding the division, which was the first such professional organization for map librarians in the United States. The division had its origins in the smaller Geography and Map Group of the Washington, D.C., Chapter of the Special Libraries Association, which she had helped to organize in October 1941. She served as the first chair of this local group and also as the first chair of the division when it attained national status within the Special Libraries Association in 1944.

Clara and her husband Russell LeGear, who was a descriptive cataloger in the Library of Congress for thirty-four years, have been married since 1938. They have travelled extensively throughout the United States, the Americas, and Europe, often visiting other map libraries and acquiring maps for the division's collections.

As a result of her long and productive career, which is partially reflected in the attached bibliography of published works, she has received extensive national and international recognition. Her contributions to the fields of map librarianship and cartographic bibliography have been noted by several professional organizations. In 1943, she was elected to membership in the Association of American Geographers. This was at a time when membership in that organization was honorary (based on contributions to the field) rather than voluntary. She also received the Association's Meritorious Achievement Award in 1952, most particularly for her work in compiling *United States Atlases* (1950). That same year she was appointed as the U.S. member to the International Geographical

Union's "Commission pour la Bibliographie des Cartes Anciennes," a committee composed of internationally recognized authorities on the identification and bibliographic control of historical maps. In 1957, she received the Honors Award of the Special Libraries Association's Geography and Map Division. In the citation for this award she was recognized "as the first Chairman of the Geography and Map Division...; as patron saint to anyone interested in historical cartography; as a source of advice and counsel to all; as author or editor of many of the bibles of the profession...; and especially ... for the very gracious modesty with which all of these things have [been] accomplished." Two years after her 1961 retirement, she received the Distinguished Service Award from the Library of Congress. During that same year she was also honored by the American Library Association as the first recipient of the C. S. Hammond Company Library Award. Five years later in 1968 she was designated an Honorary Fellow of the American Geographical Society of New York. In 1984 she received special recognition at the international symposium, "Images of the World: The Atlas Through History," held at the Library of Congress. This international gathering of scholars interested in the history of cartography gave her a standing ovation, after formally recognizing her many valuable contributions to the bibliographic description of atlases and the history of cartography.

Chronological List of Publications by Clara Egli LeGear

1929
(With Lawrence Martin). *Noteworthy Maps.* No. 2: *Accessions 1926–27.* Washington, D. C.: Library of Congress, Division of Maps, 1929.

1930
(With Lawrence Martin). *Noteworthy Maps.* No. 3: *Accessions 1927–28.* Washington, D.C.: Library of Congress, Division of Maps, 1930.

1935
"Southack, Cyprian (Mar. 25, 1662–Mar. 27, 1745)." In *Dictionary of American Biography*, vol. 17, pp. 408–409. Edited by Dumas Malone. New York: Charles Scribner's Sons, 1935.

1939
"The Division of Maps at the Library of Congress." *Education*, vol. 60, no. 4 (December 1939), pp. 220–224.

1944
"Map Making by Primitive Peoples." *Special Libraries*, vol. 35, no. 3 (March 1944), pp. 79–83.

1947
"Cyprian Southack, An Early American Map Maker." *Annals of the Association of American Geographers*, vol. 37, no. 1 (March 1947), pp. 42–43.

1948
"The Hotchkiss Map Collection." *Library of Congress Quarterly Journal of Current Acquisitions*, vol. 6, no 1 (November 1948), pp. 16–20. Reprinted as "The Hotchkiss Collection of Confederate Maps," in *A La Carte: Selected Papers on Maps and Atlases*, compiled by Walter W. Ristow (Washington, D.C.: Library of Congress, 1972), pp. 183–188.

1949
Maps: Their Care, Repair and Preservation in Libraries. Washington, D.C.: Library of Congress, 1949. Reprinted, 1950; revised edition, 1956.

"The Sixteenth-Century Maps Presented by Mr. Lessing J. Rosenwald." *Library of Congress Quarterly Journal of Current Acquisitions*, vol. 6, no. 3 (May 1949), pp.

18–22. Reprinted as "Rosenwald Gift of 16th-Century Map," in *A La Carte* (1972), pp. 39–44.

1950

"Maps of Early America." *Library of Congress Quarterly Journal of Current Acquisitions*, vol. 8, no. 1 (November 1950), pp. 44–53. Reprinted in *A La Carte* (1972), pp. 78–90.

"Mercator's Atlas of 1595." *Library of Congress Quarterly Journal of Current Acquisitions*, vol. 7, no. 3 (May 1950), pp. 9–13. Reprinted as "Gerardus Mercator's Atlas of 1595," in *A La Carte* (1972), pp. 45–50.

United States Atlases: A List of National, State, County, City, and Regional Atlases in the Library of Congress. Washington, D.C.: Library of Congress, 1950. Reprinted by Arno Press, New York, 1971.

1951

The Hotchkiss Map Collection: A List of Manuscript Maps, Many of the Civil War Period by Major Jed. Hotchkiss, and Other Manusript and Annotated Maps in His Possession. Foreword by Willard Webb. Washington, D.C.: Library of Congress, 1951. Reprinted by Sterling Press, Fairfax, Va., 1977.

1953

"The Evaluation of Old Maps." [New York]: Special Libraries Association, Geography and Map Division, May 1953.

United States Atlases: A Catalog of National, State, County, City, and Regional Atlases in the Library of Congress and Cooperating Libraries. Washington, D.C.: Library of Congress, 1953.

1954

(With Walter W. Ristow). *A Guide to Historical Cartography: A Selected, Annotated List of References on the History of Maps and Map Making*. Washington, D.C.: Library of Congress, 1954. Revised edition, 1960; reprinted 1962.

"The New England Coasting Pilot of Cyprian Southack." *Imago Mundi*, vol. 11 (1954), pp. 137–144.

1958

A List of Geographical Atlases in the Library of Congress. Vol. 5: Titles 5325–7623. Washington, D.C.: Library of Congress, 1958.

"The Melville Eastham Gift of Atlases." *Library of Congress Quarterly Journal of Current Acquisitions*, vol. 15, no. 4 (August 1958), pp. 219–227. Reprinted as "Sixteenth-Century Atlases Presented by Melville Eastham," in *A La Carte* (1972), pp. 51–61.

1963

A List of Geographical Atlases in the Library of Congress. Vol. 6: Titles 7624–10254. Washington, D.C.: Library of Congress, 1963.

1969

"Early Years in the Map Division, Library of Congress." In *Federal Government Map Collecting: A Brief History*, pp. 20–28. Edited by Richard W. Stephenson. Washington, D.C.: Special Libraries Association, Washington, D.C. Chapter, Geography and Map Group, 1969.

1971

"Obituary [of] Ena Laura Yonge (1895–1971)." *Imago Mundi*, vol. 25 (1971), pp. 85–86.

1973

A List of Geographical Atlases in the Library of Congress. Vol. 7: Titles 10255–18435. Washington, D.C.: Library of Congress, 1973.

1974

A List of Geographical Atlases in the Library of

Congress. Vol. 8: *Index to Volume 7.* Washington, D.C.: Library of Congress, 1974.

RONALD E. GRIM
Head
Reference and Bibliography Section
Geography and Map Division

Comprehensive Author List

NUMBERS REFER TO MAIN ENTRIES

Aa, Pieter van der, 1659–1733.
Atlas nouveau et curieux. [1714]   96, 170, 3329
Cartes des itineraires & voïages modernes.
[1707]   5482
Galerie agréable du monde. [1729]   3485
Nouvel atlas. [1714]   4277
Représentation. [1730?]   55

Aakerman, Andreas, 1723–1778.
Atlas juvenalis. [1789?]   4185

Abendanon, Eduard Cornelius, 1878–
Midden-Celebes-expeditie. Atlas. [1916]   9756

Abich, Hermann, 1806–1886.
Atlas zu den geologischen Forschungen in den
Kaukasischen Ländern. [1882]   3119, 3180, 9282
Atlas zu den geologischen Fragmenten aus
dem Nachlasse Hermann Abich's. [1887]   9283

Ablancourt, Nicolas Perrot d', 1606–1664.
See Perrot d' Ablancourt, Nicolas, 1606–
1664.

**Academia Republicii Populare Romîne. *Institutul de
Lingvistică*.**
Micul atlas lingvistic Romîn. 1956.   9206

Académie Royale des Sciences d' Outre-mer.
Atlas général du Congo et du Ruanda-
Urundi. 1948–54.   10114

Accumulatoren-Fabrik AG.
Varta Auto-Atlas, mit Ravensteins Deutschen
Autokarten. [1950]   8624
—— [3. Aufl.] 1952.   8636

Achával, Luis, 1870–
See Rio, Manuel E., 1872– *and* Achával,
Luis, 1870–

Action Business Service.
City map and street directory. A complete set
of maps of the streets and roads in the Pikes
Peak region. 1961.   11674

Adair Realty and Trust Company.
Pocket map and street guide of Atlanta [Ga.]
and suburbs. 1926.   11957

Adams, Daniel, 1773–1864.
Atlas to Adams' Geography. 1814.   6035
School atlas to Adams' Geography. 1823.   6050

Adams, James Truslow, 1878–1949.
Atlas of American history. 1943.   10594

Adams, John Quincy, and Company.
New international atlas of the world. 1914.   4402

Adams Engineering and Blue Printing Company.
Atlas of Oklahoma. 1913.   4998

Adinegoro, Djamaludin, 1904–
Atlas Indonesia dan dunia untuk sekolah
rakjat. Tjetakan 2. 1953.   7541
Tanah air dan dunia. [1951]   7438

Adler, C.
Handatlas. 6. Aufl. [1870?]   6171
Supplement zu C. Adler's Atlas f. Volks– &
Bürgerschulen. [1870]   5730

Administrative div [isions of Iran] [1955?]   9763

Aerial Map Industries.
Aerial atlas of Los Angeles County [Calif.]
1965.   11420
Aerial atlas of Orange County [Calif.] 1966.   11442

Aerial Surveyors.
Aero-map ... of Winston-Salem and all of
Forsyth County [N.C. 1958]   16244
Scaled street map of the metropolitan Atlanta
[Ga.] area. [1959]   11961

Aerial Surveys.
Aero-map ... of Winston-Salem and all of
Forsyth County [N.C. 1963]   16247

Aero Surveys.
Metropolitan Atlanta. Aero atlas. [1963]   11965
Scaled street map of the metropolitan Atlanta
[Ga.] area. [1961]   11962
Street guide of Atlanta, Ga. [1963]   11964

Afferden, Francisco de, 1653–1709.
Atlas abreviado. 3. ed. 1709.   4275
—— 1711.   5965
—— 3. ed. 1725.   3483

Agnese, Battista, 1514–1564.
[Portolan atlas. ca. 1544] *ms.*   5914

Agostini, Federico de.
Twenty centuries of Catholicism. 1950.   5398
Zwanzig Jahrhunderte der Kirche. 1950.   5399

Alaska Railroad.
Alaskan Engineering Commission. Maps.
[1916]   11235

Alaskan Boundary Tribunal.
Appendix to the case of His Majesty's government. v. 2. Atlas. 1903.   1192
Atlas of award. 1904.   10484
British case. Atlas. 1903.   1261
Case of the United States. Atlas. 1903.   1193, 1259
Counter case of the United States. Atlas. 1903.   1194, 1260
Proceedings. Atlas. 1904.   1452

Alaskan-Canadian Boundary Commission.
Alaskan boundary atlas. 1895.   10482
Photographs of topographic surveys of the United States Commission. [1898]   10483

Alaskan Map Service.
Anchorage area maps. 1953.   11237

Alberta and British Columbia Boundary Commission.
Report of the Commission ... Atlas. 1917–55.   10380

Alberta-Northwest Territories Boundary Commission.
Report of the Commission ... Atlas. 1956.   10381

Album geográfico ilustrado de la República Argentina.
[1933]   18204

Albuquerque Blue Print Company.
Albuquerque zoning atlas. 1954.   15818

Alcedo, Antonio de, 1736–1812.
See Arrowsmith, Aaron, 1750–1823. Atlas to Thompson's Alcedo. 1816–[17]

Alden, John Berry, 1847–1924.
Home atlas. 1887.   936
Home atlas of the world. 1888.   6239

Alden, Ogle and Company.
Plat book of Fayette County, Ill. 1891.   1531
Plat book of Macon County, Ill. 1891.   1549
Plat book of Marshall and Putnam Counties, Ill. 1890.   1553, 1561

Alden Publishing Company.
Standard atlas of Barnes County, N.Dak. 1910.   3855
Standard atlas of Fillmore County, Nebr. 1905.   2110
Standard atlas of Lyon County, Iowa. 1911.   3748
Standard atlas of Norman County, Minn. 1910.   3813
Standard atlas of Ramsey County, N.Dak. 1909.   16308

Standard atlas of Richland County, N.Dak. 1910.   3863
Standard atlas of Towner County, N.Dak. 1909.   16334
Standard atlas of Walsh County, N.Dak. 1910   3867

Alexandria, *Va. Dept. of City Planning*.
Assessment map, city of Alexandria, Va. 1958.   17364

Alexandria, *Va. Dept. of Planning and Urban Renewal*.
Real estate atlas of Alexandria, Va. [1964]   17365

Alexandria Drafting Company.
Northern Virginia area map. 1961.   17337
Street map of Montgomery County [Md.] 1966.   14360
Street map of northern Virginia. 1964.   17338
——— 1965.   17339
——— 1966.   17340
——— 1967.   17342

Alford, Newell Gilder, 1887–
Map appendix to Report on strippable coal reserves in southern Venago County, Pa. 1955.   16804

Algeria. *Service Cartographique*.
Atlas d' Algérie et de Tunisie. [1923–37]   10108

Algérie; altas historique, géographique et économique.
1934.   10109

Alinot, Paul.
Petit atlas de la Cochinchine. [1906]   10083

Alison's History of Europe. Atlas. 1848.   7685
——— 1850.   7686

Allain, Maurice, *d.* 1947.
Atlas universel Quillet. 2 v. [1923–25]   6537
——— v. 2. 1929.   6697
——— 2 v. 1951.   7440

Allan, Ian.
Railway map of England & Wales and Scotland. 1948.   8027

Allard, Carolus, 1648–1709.
Atlas minor. [1696?]   523
Magnum theatrum belli. [1702]   538
Orbis habitabilis oppida et vestitus. [1698?]   5385

Allegany County, *N.Y. Dept. of Highways*.
Towns of Allegany County, State of New York. [1962]   15855

Allen, C. R.
Illustrated atlas of Harrison County, Iowa. 1884.   1668

Illustrated atlas of Pottawattamie County,
Iowa. 1885.   1692

Allen, Daniel B.
New atlas of the city and vicinity of Peoria,
Ill. 1903.   12701

Allen, Fawcett, 1876–1961.
Atlas of commercial geography. 1913.   4107

Allen, Thomas.
Canada and the new world. 1920.   6405

Allgemeiner Deutscher Automobil-Club.
Auto-Atlas. [1950–51]   8629
Durchfahrtspläne für 150 Deutsche Städte.
[193–]   8524

Allied Forces. *Southwest Pacific Area.*
Road folder for Luzon (Philippine series)
1944.   10069

Allodi, Pietro, *fl.* **1859–1878.**
See Naymiller, Filippo, *and* Allodi, Pietro, *fl.*
1859–1878.

Alm, B. C., *and* **Henry, F.**
Plat book of Price County, Wis. [1920]   17885

Almagià, Roberto, 1884–1962.
Monumenta Italiæ cartographica. 1929.   8966
See also Vatican. Biblioteca Vaticana.

Almeyda Arroyo, Elías, *and* **Sáez Solar, Fernando.**
Recopilación de datos climáticos de Chile.
1958.   18319

Alnwick, Herbert.
Picture atlas of the British Isles. [1937]   8078
See also Bartholomew, John, 1890– *and*
Alnwick, Herbert.

Alphen, Pieter van.
Nieuwe Zee-atlas. 1682.   491

Alting, Menso, 1637–1713.
See Schotanus à Sterringa, Bernardus, *and*
Alting, Menso, 1637–1713.

Amapá, *Brazil (Ter.)*
Atlas do Amapá. 1966.   18301

Amaya Topete, Jesús.
Atlas mexicano de la conquista. [1958]   18065
Atlas mexicano del siglo XVI. 1956.   18064

Ambrosius, Ernst, 1866–1940.
Velhagen & Klasings Kleiner Handatlas. 4.
Aufl. 1924.   6538
—— 5. Aufl. 1928.   6667

Ambrosius, Ernst, *and* **Frenzel, Konrad, 1902–**
Bild der Erde. Ein neuer Atlas. 1930.   6719

Ambrosius, Ernst, *and* **Tänzler, Karl, 1858–1944.**
Velhagen & Klasings Taschenatlas für Eisen-
bahnreisende. 1925.   8590
—— 2., verb. Aufl. 1927.   8591
—— 4., verb. Aufl. 1930.   8592
—— 5., unveränderte Aufl. 1933.   8593

American Aerial Atlas and Allied Services.
Aerial photographic tourist's guide from
Washington, D.C. to Richmond, Va.
[1947]   17328

American Association of Port Authorities.
Maps relating to reclaimed tide and sub-
merged lands. [194–]   10693

American Atlas Company.
Atlas and directory of Lorain County, Ohio.
1896.   16429
Altas and directory of Madison County, Ind.
1901.   1617
Atlas of the city of Buffalo, N.Y. 1894.   15951
Plat book of Coles County, Ill. 1893.   1525
Plat book of Fulton County, Ill. 1895.   1533
Plat book of Hillsdale County, Mich. 1894.   1972
Plat book of Morgan County, Ill. 1894.   1555

American Automobile Association.
AAA members' guide to New York City &
vicinity. [1948]   16074
—— [1950]   16076
—— [1951]   16078
—— [1953]   16081
—— [1954]   16083
—— [1955]   16088
—— [1956]   16091
—— [1960]   16097
—— [1962]   16101
—— [1964]   16105
—— [1967]   16110
[Caribbean area. 1946]   18158
Motor maps. [New York State] 1906.   15844
Motor maps; official maps and routes. 1905
–1906.   10769

American Baptist Foreign Mission Society.
Missionary atlas. 1908.   3337

American Baptist Missionary Union.
See American Baptist Foreign Mission
Society.

American Board of Commissioners for Foreign Missions.
Maps of missions. 1898.   5400

American Dental Association. *Bureau of Economic Research and Statistics.*
Map supplement; distribution of dentists in
the United States. 1956.   10698
—— 1961.   10699

American Education Press.
War geography atlas. [1942]   5854

American Exporter.
Concise atlas of the world. [1912]   4382

American Express Company.
Note book and atlas. 1889.   948
Tourist's pocket atlas. 1881.   893

American Heritage.
Pictorial atlas of United States history.
[1966]   10595

American Home.
Localizers: Localizing the national sales effort ... of the 43 top metropolitan markets
in the United States. [1953?]   10533

American Hotel Register Company.
Leahy's Hotel guide and railway distance
maps of America. 1916.   4467

American Institute of Pacific Relations.
Preliminary collection of maps of the Pacific
area. [1931]   10253

American Map Company.
Cleartype business control atlas of the United
States. [1962]   11083
Cleartype general atlas of the world. 1943.   7123
Cleartype junior world atlas. [1943]   7124
Cleartype transcontinental highway atlas;
United States. [1950?]   10878
Colorprint atlas of New York City, five
boroughs. [1960]   16098
Itinerary and diary atlas of Western Europe.
1955.   7813

American Tract Society.
Bible atlas and gazetteer. [1862]   79

Ames Engineering and Testing Service.
Marshall County [Iowa] plat book. [1951]   13710
Story County [Iowa] plat book. [1950]   13952

Ammann, Hektor, 1984–   and Schib, Karl, 1898–
Historischer Atlas der Schweiz. 1951.   9430

Amorim Girão, Aristides de, 1895–
Atlas de Portugal. 1941.   9190
—— 2. ed. [1957–59]   9191

Ancelin, —— and Le Grand, ——
Atlas général et élémentaire de l'Empire de
toutes les Russies. 1795.   4061

Ancessi, Victor Antoine, 1844–1878.
Atlas géographique et archéologique ... de
l'Ancien et du Nouveau Testament. 1885.   5341

Anderson, A. H.
Plat book of Redwood County, Minn. 1898.   15085

Anderson and Goodwin Company.
Standard historical atlas of Plymouth Coun-
ty, Iowa. 1907.   1690
Standard historical atlas of Sioux County,
Iowa. 1908.   1695
Standard historical atlas of Winneshiek
County, Iowa. 1905.   1708

Anderson Map Company.
Plat book of Kitsap County, Wash. 1909.   17472
Plat book of Whitman County, Wash. 1910.   17541

Anderson Publishing Company.
Atlas and farm directory ... of Plymouth
County, Iowa. 1914.   13832
Atlas of Adams County, Nebr. 1919.   15344
Atlas of Allamakee County, Iowa. 1917.   4621
Atlas of Andrew County, Mo. 1926.   15210
Atlas of Atchison County, Kans. 1925.   14146
Atlas of Atchison County, Mo. 1921.   15212
Atlas of Audubon County, Iowa. 1921.   13060
Atlas of Benton County, Iowa. 1917.   4623
Atlas of Black Hawk County, Iowa. 1926.   13085
Atlas of Bon Homme County, S.Dak. 1925.   17016
Atlas of Boone County, Iowa. 1918.   4624
Atlas of Boone County, Nebr. 1920.   15350
Atlas of Bremer County, Iowa. 1927.   13104
Atlas of Buena Vista County, Iowa. 1923.   13128
Atlas of Buffalo County, Nebr. 1919.   15356
Atlas of Burt County, Nebr. 1922.   15362
Atlas of Butler and Polk Counties, Nebr.
1918.   4878, 4901
Atlas of Butler County, Iowa. 1917.   4626
Atlas of Carroll County, Iowa. 1923.   13163
Atlas of Cass County, Iowa. 1917.   4627
Atlas of Cass County, Nebr. 1918.   4879
Atlas of Cedar County, Iowa. 1916.   4628
Atlas of Cerro Gordo County, Iowa. [1912]   3744a
Atlas of Cherokee County, Iowa. 1923.   13213
Atlas of Clay and Union Counties, S.Dak.
1924.   17022
Atlas of Clay County, Iowa. 1919.   4630a
Atlas of Clinton County, Iowa. 1925   13268
Atlas of Colfax County, Nebr. 1925.   15388
Atlas of Cottonwood County, Minn. 1926.   14960
Atlas of Crawford County, Iowa. 1920.   13279
Atlas of Cuming County, Nebr. 1918.   4883
Atlas of Dallas County, Iowa. 1916.   4632
Atlas of Dawson County, Nebr. 1919.   15406
Atlas of Dixon and Dakota Counties, Nebr.
1925   15414
Atlas of Dodge County, Nebr. 1918.   4885
Atlas of Doniphan County, Kans. 1927.   14160
Atlas of Douglas and Sarpy Counties, Nebr.
1920.   15426
Atlas of Fayette County, Iowa. 1927.   13375
Atlas of Fillmore County, Nebr. 1918.   4887
Atlas of Floyd County, Iowa. 1913.   4637
Atlas of Fremont County, Iowa. 1920.   13407
Atlas of Grundy County, Iowa. 1924.   13429
Atlas of Hancock County, Iowa. 1914.   4641
Atlas of Harrison County, Iowa. 1922.   13479
Atlas of Iowa County, Iowa. 1917.   4643
Atlas of Knox County, Nebr. 1920.   15492

Atlas of Kossuth County, Iowa. 1913.	4646
Atlas of Lancaster County, Nebr. 1921.	15496
Atlas of Marshall County, Iowa. 1924.	13708
Atlas of Marshall County, Kans. 1922.	14184
Atlas of Mills County, Iowa. 1921.	13721
Atlas of Monona County, Iowa. 1919.	4651
Atlas of Montgomery County, Iowa. 1919.	13768
Atlas of Murray County, Minn. 1926.	15054
Atlas of Muscatine County, Iowa. 1916.	4652
Atlas of Nemaha County, Kans. 1922.	14188
Atlas of Nemaha County, Nebr. 1922.	15521
Atlas of Nicollet County, Minn. 1927.	15056
Atlas of Nobles County, Minn. 1926.	15059
Atlas of Nodaway County, Mo. 1925.	15241
Atlas of O'Brien County, Iowa. 1924.	13789
Atlas of Olmsted County, Minn. 1928.	15066
Atlas of Otoe County, Nebr. 1922.	15533
Atlas of Page County, Iowa. 1920.	13812
Atlas of Platte County, Nebr. 1923.	15552
Atlas of Plymouth County, Iowa. 1921.	13833
Atlas of Pocahontas County, Iowa. 1918.	4654
Atlas of Pottawattamie County, Iowa. 1919.	13867
Atlas of Richardson County, Nebr. 1924.	15564
Atlas of Saline County, Nebr. 1918.	4903
Atlas of Saunders County, Nebr. 1916.	4905
Atlas of Shelby County, Iowa. 1921.	13925
Atlas of Sibley County, Minn. 1926.	15101
Atlas of Sioux County, Iowa. 1913.	4659
—— 1923.	13939
Atlas of Tama County, Iowa. 1916.	4660
—— 1926.	13961
Atlas of Taylor County, Iowa. 1923.	13971
Atlas of Washington County, Nebr. 1920.	15613
Atlas of Webster County, Iowa. 1923.	14046
Atlas of Winnebago County, Iowa. 1913.	4664
Atlas of Woodbury County, Iowa. 1917.	4666
Atlas of Yankton County, S.Dak. 1925.	17062
Atlas of York County, Nebr. 1924.	15630
Standard historical atlas of Chickasaw County, Iowa. 1915.	4629
Standard historical atlas of Mills and Fremont Counties, Iowa. 1910.	3746, 3749
Standard historical atlas of Mitchell County, Iowa. 1911.	3750
Standard historical atlas of Nodaway County, Mo. 1911.	3819
Standard historical atlas of Worth County, Iowa. 1913.	4667

Andō, Rikinosuke.

Saishin chōsa Dai Nihon bunken chizu. [Prefectural atlas of Japan based on the latest survey. 1920]	9807
—— [1930]	9808
—— [1931]	9809

Andreas, Alfred Theodore, 1839–1900.

Atlas map of Peoria County, Ill. 1873.	12438
Atlas map of Richland County, Ohio. 1873.	2411
Atlas map of Vigo County, Ind. 1874.	3740
Historical atlas of Dakota. 1884.	2339, 2572
Illustrated historical atlas of Hancock County, Ill. 1874.	12258

Illustrated historical atlas of the State of Iowa. 1875.	1639
Illustrated historical atlas of the State of Minnesota. 1874.	2007

Andreas and Baskin.

Illustrated historical atlas of Lucas and part of Wood Counties, Ohio. 1875	16434

Andreas, Lyter and Company.

Atlas map of Adams County, Ill. 1872.	12077
Atlas map of Knox County, Ill. 1870–[71]	12321
Atlas map of Morgan County, Ill. 1872.	1554
Atlas map of Pike County, Ill. 1872.	1559
Atlas map of Schuyler County, Ill. 1872.	12494
Atlas map of Scott County, Ill. 1873.	1565
Atlas map of Tazewell County, Ill. 1873.	1571
Atlas of Fulton County, Ill. 1871.	12242

Andree, Karl Theodor, 1808–1875.

See Lange, Henry, *i.e.,* Karl Julius Henry, 1821–1893. Kartenwerk zu Dr. Karl Andree's Nord-Amerika. 1854.	1231

Andree, Richard, 1835–1912.

Allgemeiner Handatlas. 1881.	6205
—— Supplement zur 1. Aufl. 1887.	6233
—— 2. Aufl. 1887.	6232
—— 3. Aufl. 1893.	6262
—— 3. Aufl. 2. Abdr. 1896.	6274
—— 4. Aufl. 1899.	1031
—— 4. Aufl. 2. Abdr. 1900.	1047
—— 4. Aufl. 3. Abdr. 1901.	6295
—— 4. neubearb. Aufl. 1904.	1089a
—— 5. Aufl. 1906.	6320
—— 5. Aufl. 2. Abdr. 1907.	6323
—— 5. neubearb. Aufl. 1907.	1112b
—— 2. Aufl. 3. Abdr. 1912.	6348
—— 6. Aufl. 1914.	6367
—— 7. Aufl. 1921.	6433
—— 8. Aufl. 1922.	6474
—— 8. Aufl. 2. Abdr. 1924.	6539
—— 8. Aufl. 3. Abdr. 1924.	6571
—— 8. Aufl. 4. Abdr. 1928.	6668
—— 8. Aufl. 5. Abdr. 1930.	6720
Allgemeiner Schul-Atlas. 44. Aufl. Ausg. B. 1898.	265
Altas manuel de géographie moderne. 1883.	6214
—— 1884.	6216
Berliner Schul–Atlas. 28. Aufl. 1927.	6640
Bonniers Världsatlas. [1919–24]	6401
Handatlas. 1937.	6902
—— [1938]	6937
Neuer allgemeiner und Österreichisch-Ungarischer Handatlas. 1910.	3599, 3993
Stora handatlas. 3. nordiska uppl. [1907]	6324

Andree, Richard, *and* Peschel, Oscar Ferdinand, 1826–1874.

Physikalisch statistischer Atlas des Deutschen Reichs. 1878.	3026

Andree, Richard, *and* Putzger, Friedrich Wilhelm, 1849–
Gymnasial- und Realschulatlas. 1880.   3359

Andrews, J. D., and Son.
Atlas of the suburbs of greater Nashville, Tenn. 1906.   2588

Andrews, John, 1736–1809.
Collection of plans of the capital cities. 2 v. 1771.   5386
Collection of plans of the most capital cities. 1772.   3291
—— [1792?]   56
Geographical atlas of England. 1809.   8124
Plans of the principal cities. [1792?]   57

Andriveau–Goujon, Eugene, 1832–1897.
Atlas de choix. [1841–62]   6093

Andriveau-Goujon, J.
Atlas classique et universel. 1843–[44]   791
Atlas de géographie ancienne et moderne. [1856]   6123
See also Soulier, E., *and* Andriveau-Goujon, J.

Anesi, José.
Atlas geográfico de Chile. 1946.   18337
Atlas geográfico escolar. 1936.   18217
—— 1937.   18218
Nuevo atlas geográfico de la Argentina. 1. ed. 1943.   18224
—— 2. ed. 1947.   18226
—— 5. ed. 1958.   18230
—— 6. ed. 1962.   18232
Nuevo atlas geográfico de las Américas. 1. ed. 1943.   10273
—— 2. ed. 1945.   10274
Nuevo atlas geográfico metódico universal. 7. ed. 1942.   7081
—— 8. ed. 1943.   7125
—— 10. ed. 1951.   7441

Anglers Atlas Company.
Anglers atlas of California. 1948.   11335

Anglo-American Oil Company.
Pratt's Road atlas of England and Wales. 1905.   8103
—— 1929.   8104

Anglo-South American Bank, *London*.
Atlas of Latin America. [1922?]   18048

Angot, Pierre, 1902–
See Bichelonne, Jean, 1904–1944, *and* Angot, Pierre, 1902–

Anich, Peter, 1723–1766, *and* Hueber, Blasius, 1735–1814.
Atlas Tyrolensis. 1774.   7918

Ann Arbor, *Mich.*
Assessor's maps, city of Ann Arbor. 1964.   14841

Année cartographique.
Supplément annuel. 1891–1913.   3572, 4370

Annuaire Almanach du Commerce.
See Bottin.

Anrick, Carl Julius, 1895– *and* Lundqvist, Magnus.
STF:s Lilla atlas över Sverige. [1949]   9377

Ansted, David Thomas, 1814–1880, *and* Nicolay, Charles Grenfell.
Atlas of physical and historical geography. [1852–59]   211

Anthoine, Édouard, 1847–1919.
See Schrader, Franz, 1844–1924, Prudent, Ferdinand Pierre Vincent, 1835–1915, *and* Anthoine, Édouard, 1847–1919.

Antillón y Marzo, Isidoro de, 1778–1814.
[Atlas of the world. 1804]   4305

Antropov, Petr Aleksandrovich.
Финансово-статистическій атласъ Россіи. [Financial-statistical atlas of Russia] 1898.   9267

Anville, Jean Baptiste Bourguignon d', 1697–1782.
Atlas and geography of the antients. 1815.   4
Atlas antiquus. 1798–[99]   5586
Atlas antiqvvs. 1784.   3268
Atlas général. 1727–80.   571
—— 1727–86.   572
—— 1743–80.   599
Atlas of antient geography. [1821?]   5588
Atlas to the ancient geography. 1814.   5587
Complete body of ancient geography. [1771?]   3267
—— 1775.   2
—— 1795.   3266
—— 1801.   3270
—— 1806.   3
—— 1818.   5589
Géographie ancienne abrégée. Nouv. éd. 1769.   1
Nouvel atlas de la Chine. 1737.   3189
Twelve maps of antient geography. 1750.   3266

Aomori-ken Nōji Shikenjō, *Kuroishi, Japan*.
Aomori-ken no nōgyō zusetsu. [Agricultural atlas of Aomori Prefecture] 1954.   9851

Apenes, Ola, 1898–1943.
Mapas antiguos del Valle de México. 1947.   18116

Applebaum, William, 1906– *and* Schapker, Bernard L.
Atlas of business centers, Cincinnati ... Ohio. [1956]   16492

Appleton, D., and Company.
Atlas of the United States. 1888.   11049

General atlas of the world.   1872.   862
Hand atlas.   1891.   963
Library atlas of modern geography.   1892.   969
—— 1895.   6271
Map of Manhattan Borough.   1899.   15996

Appleton's Modern school atlas.   [1928]   6680

Appleton's Standard school atlas.   [1932]   6785

Approved Atlas and Maps, Ltd.
Approved subdivision and zoning atlas of
   Miami Beach, Fla.   [1948]   11906
Approved subdivision and zoning atlas of
   town of Miami Springs ... Fla.   [1948]   11910
Subdivision and zoning atlas of Hialeah, Fla.
   [1947]   11876

**Après de Mannevillette, Jean Baptiste Nicolas
Denis d', 1707–1780.**
East-India pilot.   [1795]   3169
Neptune oriental.   1745.   3163
—— 1775.   3165
—— [1775–81]   3166, 3167
Supplément au Neptune oriental.   1781.   3168, 3231

Aragon, Anne Alexandrine, b. 1798.
See Perrot, Aristide Michel, 1793–1879, *and*
   Aragon, Anne Alexandrine, b. 1798.

Araújo, Orestes, 1853–1916.
Atlas escolar de la república oriental del
   Uruguay.   [1910?]   3961

Arbingast, Stanley Alan, 1910–
Atlas of Texas.   1963.   17123
—— 1967.   17124
Texas resources and industries.   1955.   17121
—— 1958.   17122

Arena, Luis.
Atlas de la geografia argentina.   1940.   18222
Atlas de la República Argentina.   [194–]   18219

Argentine Republic.
Argentine-Chilian boundary.   Report presented to the tribunal.   Atlas.   1900.   2730

**Argentine Republic. *Comision Argentina Demar-
cadora de Limites con el Brasil.***
[Planos topográficos. Islas del Rio Uruguay
   ... Islas del Rio Iguazú.   1900–1904]   5133

**Argentine Republic. *Departamento de Agromete-
orologia.***
Atlas agroclimático argentino.   1953.   18200

**Argentine Republic. *Dirección General de Nave-
gación e Hidrografia.***
Cartas náuticas.   [1946]   18203
Cartas y gráficos.   1948.   18227
—— [1950]   18228

**Argentine Republic. *Dirección General de Nave-
gación, Hidrografia, Faros y Balizas.***
Atlas, evoluciones tipo del tiempo.   1944.   18201

Argentine Republic. *Dirección Nacional de Vialidad.*
Atlas vial argentino.   [1938]   18210

Argentine Republic. *Instituto de Suelos y Agrotecnia.*
[Zona de erosión eólica de la región pampeana.
   1948]   18257

Argentine Republic. *Instituto Geográfico Militar.*
Atlas de la República Argentina.   1953.   18229
—— 2. ed.   1959.   18231
—— 3. ed.   1962.   18233
Planchetas de la Provincia de Buenos Aires.
   [1924]   18237

**Argentine Republic. *Ministerio de Relaciones Exte-
riores y Culto.***
Frontera argentino-chilena.   [1908]   18199

Argentine Republic. *Servicio de Hidrográfia Naval.*
Croquis de los ríos.   [1963]   18207

Argentine Republic. *Servicio Hidrográfico.*
Atlas ... del derrotero argentino de los Ríos
   Paraná, Paraguay, y Uruguay.   1932.   18208

**Argentine Republic. *Servicio Meteorológico Na-
cional.***
Atlas climático de la República Argentina.
   [1962]   18202

**Arizona. *Highway Dept. Photogrammetry and Map-
ping Division.***
Atlas of Cochise County.   1966.   11252
Atlas of Gila County.   1961.   11253
Atlas of Graham County.   1965.   11254
Atlas of Greenlee County.   1965.   11255
Atlas of Maricopa County.   1960.   11259
Atlas of Pima County.   1963.   11261
Atlas of Pinal County.   1964.   11262
Atlas of Santa Cruz County.   1961.   11263
Atlas of Yuma County.   1964.   11264

Arizona. *State Bureau of Mines.*
Folio of geologic and mineral maps of
   Arizona.   1962.   11244

Arizona Highway Planning Survey.
State of Arizona.   1939.   11248

Arkansas. *Industrial Development Commission.*
Economic atlas of Arkansas.   1961.   11282

**Arkansas. *Resources and Development Commis-
sion.***
Industrial prospectus of Arkansas.   [1950]   11283
—— [1952]   11284

Arkansas. *State Geologist.*
[Atlases to accompany the 4th and 5th annual
   reports for 1890 and 1892.   1893–1900]   11286

Arkansas. *State Highway Commission.*
General highway and transportation maps.
[1940] 11287
—— 1947. 11288

Arkansas. *State Highway Dept.*
Arkansas highway facts and figures. [1950] 11289

Arkansas. University. *City Planning Division.*
Lepanto, Ark. 1960. 11309
Look at Paris, Ark. [1960] 11316

Arledge, Thomas J.
"Arledge" portfolio abstract maps [East
Texas area. 1932] 17141

Arlington County, *Va. Dept. of Real Estate Assessments.*
Real estate atlas of Arlington County, Va.
[1961] 17347

Armbruester, J. Rud.
Pocket atlas and guide of Buffalo, N.Y.
1909. 3844
—— 1910. 3845

Arms, Walter F., *and others.*
Caldwell's Illustrated historical atlas of
Adams County, Ohio, 1797–1880. [1880?] 2352

Armstrong, Le Roy, *i.e.,* **Dwight Le Roy, 1854–1927.**
Pictorial atlas illustrating the Spanish-American War. [1898] 1357, 10687, 10688

Armstrong, Mostyn John, *fl.* **1770–1791.**
Actual survey of the great post road between
London and Dover. 1777. 8097
Actual survey of the great post-roads between
London and Edinburgh. 3d ed. 1777. 8028
Scotch atlas. 1787. 8205
—— 1794. 8206

Arnal, Pedro.
Atlas escolar de Venezuela. 1950. 18425
—— [2. ed. 1956] 18429

Arnberger, Erik, 1917–
Atlas von Niederösterreich (und Wien).
1951–58. 7913

Arnois, Spielmann and Company.
Insurance map of the city of Hoboken [N.J.]
1868. 15758

Arnold Engineering Company.
Map of village of Briarcliff Manor, N.Y. 1907. 15937
Map of village of Ossining, N.Y. 1907. 16142

Arnout, Jules.
Paris, vues et monuments. [1855?] 5231

Arnz, J.
Atlas der Alten Welt. [1829] 5590

Arquiza, Jacobo de.
Mapa general de las almas ... en estas islas
Filipinas. 1845. 5305

Arrowsmith, Aaron, 1750–1823.
Atlas of South India. 1822. 9698
Atlas to Thompson's Alcedo. 1816–[17] 1174
New general atlas. 1817. 730, 3543
Nouvel atlas universel–portatif. 1811. 6030
Pilot from England to Canton. 1806. 5685

Arrowsmith, Aaron, *and* **Lewis, Samuel, 1754?–1822.**
New and elegant general atlas. 1804. 702
—— 1805. 708
—— 1812. 718
—— 1819. 734

Arrowsmith, Aaron, *Jr.*
Comparative atlas. 1830. 6064
New general atlas of America. 1829. 10268
Orbis terrarum veteribus noti descriptio.
1828. 98, 266
Outlines of the world. 1828. 6059

Arrowsmith, Aaron, *Jr., and* **Arrowsmith, Samuel.**
[Comparative atlas. 1829] 4110

Arrowsmith, John, 1790–1873.
London atlas. [1832–46] 764
—— 1840. 4322
—— 1842–[50] 789
—— 1842–[53] 790
—— 1858. 4339

Arrowsmith, Samuel, *d.* **1839.**
Bible atlas. 1835. 4113

Art Craft Reproduction Company.
Electric utility loose leaf atlas of the United
States. [1928] 10571

Art-Line Company.
Chicago expressways. [1961] 12664

Artcraft Company.
Adams County, Ill. atlas. 1946. 12080
Atlas of the county of Rock Island, Ill. 1947. 12477
Lee County, Iowa, atlas. 1946. 13623
Marion County, Mo. atlas. [1946] 15237
Monroe County, Mo. atlas. [1946] 15240
Muscatine County, Iowa, atlas. 1947. 13778
Plat map of the city of Moline, Ill. [1947?] 12695
Plat map of the city of Rock Island, Ill.
[1947?] 12709
Ralls County, Mo. atlas. [1946] 15244
Standard atlas of Adams County, Ill. 1958. 12082

Artero y González, Juan de la Gloria.
Atlas histórico-geográfico de España. 1879. 3138

Artists and Writers Press.
Holiday Inn travel guide & road atlas.
[1961] 10930

Asbury Park, *N.J. Common Council.*
Sectional atlas of the district annexed to the
city of Asbury Park ... N.J. 1910.   3835

Asche, Albert.
Harms Heimatatlas Hannover. [1956]   8862

Asensio, José, *b.* 1759.
See Martínez de la Torre, Fausto, *and* Asensio,
José, *b.* 1759.

Asher, Adams and Higgins.
New topographical atlas and gazetteer of
Indiana. 1870–71.   1598

Asher and Adams.
New Columbian railroad atlas. 1875.   1300
New commercial and statistical atlas ... of the
United States. 1872.   1271
New commercial and statistical gazetteer of
the United States. [1875]   1274
New commercial, topographical and statisti-
cal atlas ... of the United States. [1872]   1270
—— [1873]   1272
—— [1874]   1273
New statistical and topographical atlas of the
United States. [1872]   11031
—— [1873]   1329, 11032
—— [1874]   11033
New topographical atlas and gazetteer of New
York. [1870]   2209
—— [1871]   15847
New topographical map of New York.
[1869]   2208

Asociación de Automovilistas de Santiago.
Cartilla geográfica de turismo. 1925.   18325

Asociación Nacional Automovilística (*México*)
Atlas, rutas de México. 2. ed. [1962?]   18077
—— 3. ed. [1965]   18080

Assam.
Road & railway map of Assam. [1st ed.]
1940.   9708
Road and railway maps of Assam. 1943–44.   9709

Associated Map Company.
Atlas of Florida. 1926.   11797

Associated Press.
First six months of war. [1940]   5855

Association of American Railroads.
Railroads of America. [1963]   10726

Astigarraga, José Pedro, 1896–
Historia de la división política de la República
Oriental del Uruguay, 1828–1945. [195–]   18399

Asunción. Colegio de San José.
Mapas corográficos del Paraguay. [1946]   18372

Atlanta. *Metropolitan Planning Commission.*
Metropolitan Atlanta, a factual inventory.
1950.   11960

Atlante dell'America. 1777.   1167

Atlante geografico. 1788–1800.   669

Atlante tascabile. 1804.   703

Atlantic Neptune.
Copy no. 1.   [1774–81]   1198
Copy no. 2.   [1774–81]   1199
Copy no. 3.   [1774–81]   1200
Copy no. 4.   [1774–81]   1201
Copy no. 5.   [1774–81]   1202
Copy no. 6.   [1774–81]   1203
Copy no. 7.   [1776–81]   1204
Copy no. 8.   [1775–81]   1205
Copy no. 9.   [1775–81]   3658
Copy no. 10. [1774–81]   3654
Copy no. 11. [1774–81]   3655
Copy no. 12. [1774–81]   3656
Copy no. 13. [1774–81]   3657
Copy no. 14. [1775–81]   3659
Copy no. 15. [1774–81]   4473
Copy no. 16. [1775–80]   4474
Copy no. 17. 1780–81.   10323
Copy no. 18. 1777–80.   10317
Copy no. 19. 1779–80.   10320
Copy no. 20. 1780.   10321
1780. *facsim.* [1966]   10322
Sea coast of Nova Scotia. [1775–78]   1250

Atlantic Refining Company of Africa.
Union of South Africa ... road maps. [195–]   10164

Atlantik-Verlag Paul List.
Berliner Grundschulatlas. [1953]   8844
Berliner Heimatatlas. [1950]   8841
Bremer Heimatatlas. [1950]   8852
—— [1952]   8853
Harms Heimatatlas Mannheim. [1958]   8866
List's Taschenatlas der Welt. [1953]   7544
Münchner Heimatatlas. [1958]   8872
Schulatlas für den Regierungsbezirk Stade.
[1951]   7442

Atlas aï mejmua khartat resm al-arz. 1835.   768

Atlas de géographie militaire. Nouv. éd. 1902.   176

Atlas ... de l'histoire ancienne et moderne. MS.
[1840?]   97

**Atlas de las Comunicaciones de la República Argen-
tina.** 1932–33.   18213

Atlas del Perú. [1934?]   18387
—— [1940]   18388
—— [1941?]   18390
—— 5. ed. [1943]   18391
—— 8. ed. [1946?]   18392

—— 24. ed. 1962–63.	18394
—— 26. ed. 1965–66.	18396

Atlas des enfans. 1760.	3504

Atlas des Königreichs Preussen. 1831.	8762

[Atlas détaillé de l'Allemagne et de Prusse] [1759–1890]	8680

Atlas du Cameroun. [1946–48]	10136

Atlas elementar. 1786.	5730a
—— 1795.	5730b

Atlas geográfico del Peru. [1955]	18393

Atlas géographique et statistique des départemens de la France et de ses colonies. 1832.	4022

Atlas geographus. 1711–17.	557

Atlas historique. 3 v. 1936–37.	5483
—— v. 1–2. 1948–51.	5484

Atlas historyczny Polski. 1930–58.	9142

Atlas maritimus & commercialis. 1728.	3298

Atlas moderne. [1762]	629
—— [1771–83]	646, 5986
—— 1787–[91]	664

[Atlas of Germany, Prussia, and Poland. 1763–1809]	8681

Atlas of the United States of North America. 1832.	3691

[Atlas of the world] [1375]	4251

Atlas of Western, Northwestern, and middle Western States. [1905]	1301

Atlas permanent. 1940–43.	7039

Atlas photographique des formes du relief terrestre. 1914.	4170

Atlas Publishing Company.

Illustrated atlas and Columbian souvenir of Branch County, Mich. 1894.	14621
Illustrated atlas and directory of … Calhoun County, Mich. 1894.	14626
Illustrated atlas and directory of Erie County, Ohio. 1896.	2374
Universal atlas. 1893.	3574

Атласъ: Картъ, плановъ и схемъ къ описанію военныхъ дѣйствій въ Китаѣ, 1900–1901 ГГ.

[Atlas of maps, plans and sketches to accompany the description of the military operations in China, 1900–1901] 1905.	9516

Атласъ Россійской Имперій.

[Atlas of the Russian Empire] 1794.	9280

Attinger, Victor, 1856–1927.

Pochette routière de la Suisse. [191–]	9431

Atwood, Elmer Bagby, 1906–

Survey of verb forms in the eastern United States. 1953.	10694

Atwood, Holmes and Read.

Pocket atlas of the United States. 1884.	1420
—— 1888.	1425

Aubin, Hermann, 1885–1969.

Geschichtlicher Handatlas der Rheinprovinz. 1926.	8770

Audubon County, *Iowa*.

[Atlas of Audubon County, Iowa. 194–]	13061

August, Oskar, 1911–
See Schlüter, Otto, 1872–1959, *and* August, Oskar, 1911–

Augustana Evangelical Lutheran Church.

Augustana atlas of the world. [1924?]	6540

Austin, William V., and Associates.

Ventura County [Calif.] property guide. 1966.	11500

Austin Road atlas of Great Britain. [1955]

	8061
—— 3d ed. [1956]	8063
—— 4th ed. [1957]	8065

Australia. *Bureau of Meteorology*.

Climatological atlas of Australia. [1940]	10170

Australia. *Commonwealth Forestry Bureau*.

Distribution of the more important timber trees of the genus eucalyptus. [1947]	10174

Australia. *Ministry of National Development*.

Atlas of Australian resources. [1953–58]	10172

Australia. *News and Information Bureau*.

Maps of Australia. [194–]	10173

Austria. *Ackerbau-Ministerium*.

Atlas der Urproduction Oesterreichs. [1877]	2860, 2862
Forste der … stehenden Staats- und Fondsgüter. 1885.	2858
Geologisch-bergmännische Karte mit Profilen von Joachimsthal. 1891.	2868

Austria. *Bundesamt für Eich- und Vermessungswesen*.

Amstetten. [1951]	7921
Bruck a. d. Leitha. [1951]	7922
Eisenstadt. [1948]	7923
Moedling. [194–]	7924
St. Pölten. [1946]	7925

Straszen-Übersichtskarte von Österreich.
[1949]   7905
Wiener Neustadt. [1948]   7933

Austria. *Bundesministerium für Handel und Verkehr.*
Karte der Österreichischen Donau. [1930]   7837

Austria. *Kartographisches Institut.*
Offizieller Strassenatlas von Österreich.
[1930?]   7899

Austria. *Militärgeographisches Institut.*
Carta di cabottaggio del Mare Adriatico.
[1822–24]   2802

Austro-Hungarian Monarchy. *Kriegs-Archiv.*
Graphische Beilagen zum I–VIII Band des
Oesterreichischen Erbfolgekrieges 1740–
1748. [1896–1905]   7895

**Austro-Hungarian Monarchy. *Reichskriegsminis-
terium.***
Feldzüge des Prinzen Eugen von Savoyen.
[1876–92]   2812
Oesterreichischer Erbfolge-Krieg, 1740–1748.
[1896–1905]   2863
Karte der gefürsteten Grafschaft Tyrol nebst
Vorarlberg. [1823]   7919

Autokarten- und Reiseführer-Verlag.
Neue Auto-Strassen-Atlas. [1952]   8637

Autokarten-Vertrieb.
Lux-Auto-Karte Rheinland. [192–]   8774

Automobil-Club der Schweiz.
Schweiz. [1934]   9432
—— [1935]   9433

Automobil Club Regal Român.
Ghidul drumurilor din România. 1928.   9208

Automobile Association.
Road book of England and Wales. [1951]   8106

Automobile Blue Book Publishing Company.
Detail road maps covering New England.
1913.   10771

Automobile Club d'Italia.
Atlante automobilistico d'Europa. [1958?]   7773
Attraversamenti di 124 città. [1938]   8938
Attraversamenti di 130 città italiane. [1950]   8939
Attraversamenti di 150 città italiane. [1955]   8940
Carta dello stato delle strade. [1936]   8941
Italia: Atlante automobilistico. [1957]   8977
Piantine di attraversamento delle città ca-
poluoghi di provincia. [1937]   8942

Automobile Club di Milano.
Atlante delle strade d'Europa. 2. ed.
[1930]   7762
Atlante delle strade d'Italia. [1930]   8969
—— 1931.   8970

Automobile Club of Southern California.
Los Angeles [Calif.] & vicinity freeway system. [1954]   11550
Mex. 15, Mex. 45, Mex. 85 . . . with important
connecting routes. 1956.   18076
National old trails road to Southern California. 1916.   10772
Orange County. A comprehensive street and
recreation guide. [1967]   11444

Automobile Legal Association.
New England States in detail. 1920.   10773
Road maps of Ohio. 1923.   16369

Automóvil Club Argentino.
Provincia de Buenos Aires. 1953.   18238
—— 1954.   18239

Averill and Hagar.
New and concise geographical and historical
description of Clinton County, N.Y.
1879.   2220

Avity, Pierre d', *sieur de Montmartin, 1573–1635.*
Neuwe archontologia cosmica. [1646?]   58, 456
Newe archontologia cosmica. 1646.   4104

Ayala Z., Alfredo.
Atlas económico de Bolívia. 1954.   18258
Atlas escolar de Bolívia. 1943.   18261
—— 1953.   18262
—— 1956–[60]   18265

Ayers, Stuart.
World histri-ography combined with Hammond's Self-revising world atlas and gazetteer. 1941.   7041

Ayrouard, Jacques.
Recüeil de plusieurs plans des ports et rades
. . . de la Mer Mediterranée. 1732–46.   187, 7862

Azara, Félix de, 1746–1821.
Voyages dans l'Amérique Méridionale.
1809.   3952

B. R. V. Engineering Associates.
Detailed planimetric maps of Kansas. 1955.   14144

Baalsrud, Andreas, 1872–
Kart over riks- og fylkesveier i Norge. 1942.   9111

Babinet, Jacques, 1794–1872.
Atlas universel. [1861]   834

Bach, John.
Road map from Manila to Baguio. 1926.   10068

Bachiene, Willem Albert, 1712–1783.
Atlas. 1785.   657

Bachiller, Doroteo, *d. 1866.*
Atlas de España. 1852–[53]   9324

Bachmann, Friedrich, 1860–1947.
Alte Deutsche Stadt, ein Bilderatlas. 1941–
49.   8525

Backhoff, A. E. T.
Karta öfver kanal-vägen mellan Stockholm
och Göteborg. [1873]   9420

Backhouse, Thomas.
New pilot for the southeast coast of Nova
Scotia. 1798.   1251

Bacon, G. W., and Company.
All essentials school atlas. [1947]   7253
Atlas of Great Britain and Ireland. [1938]   8079
Australian contour atlas. [192–]   6402
Contour atlas. [1915]   6375
County atlas of England and Wales. [1924]   8137
Excelsior contour-relief atlas. [1913?]   4182
—— [1913–14]   4111
New handy atlas. 1901.   1061
Physical atlas. [1921]   6434
Physical atlas of Europe. [1927]   7744
Physical atlas of the British Isles. [1927]   8026
Pocket atlas of London. [1916?]   5211
Road atlas of Scotland. [192–]   8202
School and college atlas. [1914]   4186

Bacon, George Washington, 1830–1921.
Commercial and library atlas. 1908.   3580
Complete atlas. 1890.   956
Cycling and touring pocket atlas of the Brit-
ish Isles. 1898.   2887
[Excelsior memory maps. 1889?]   4366
Large scale atlas of London. [1916]   5210
—— [1929]   8172
New general atlas. 1912.   4383
New large-scale atlas of London and suburbs.
1905.   8159
New large scale ordnance atlas of the British
Isles. [1884]   2899
Pocket atlas of London. [1905?]   5209
—— [1907]   8161
Up-to-date pocket atlas of London. [1948]   8180

Bacon's Biblical atlas. 1926.   5367

**Baden (Grand Duchy). Centralbureau für Meteoro-
logie und Hydrographie.**
Rheinstrom und seine wichtigsten Nebenflüsse. 1889.   7881

Baden. Topographisches Bureau.
Topographischer Atlas des Grossherzogthums
Baden. 1875–[1901]   3038

Badeslade, Thomas, 1718–1750.
Chorographia Britanniæ. 1742.   2916
—— 2d ed. 1745.   8115

Badhy, S.
Atlas pulau Djawa, naskah dan pertanjaan.
[1953]   9759

Baeck, Elias, 1679–1747.
Atlas geographicus. [1710]   555

Bäggli, Walter.
Atlas der Schweizerischen Landwirtschaft.
[1954]   9421

Bär, Joseph Christoph, 1789–1848.
See Stülpnagel, Johann Friedrich von, 1786–
1865, and Bär, Joseph Christoph, 1789–
1848.

Bagley, Edward Orick.
Map of the city of Jacksonville, Ark. 1961.   11308

Bagley, Helen C.
Map of the city of Little Rock ... Ark.
[1962]   11315

Bagrow, Leo, 1888–1957, and Köhlin, Harald.
Maps of the Neva River. 1953.   9297

Bahamas.
Maps of the Bahama Islands. 1926.   18161

Bailly-Bailliere é hijos.
Atlas de las cinco partes. [1900?]   1046
Mapas de las cuarenta y nueve provincias de
España. 1904.   3139

Baist, George William, 1859–1927.
Atlas of Camden, N.J. 1886.   2175
Atlas of Long Branch, N.J. 1886.   2186
Atlas of Philadelphia. 1888.   2535
Atlas of properties along the Pennsylvania
R.R. ... from Overbrook to Malvern Sta.
1887.   16891
Atlas of properties along the Schuylkill Valley
from Philadelphia to Norristown. 1886.   2447
Atlas of the city of Lancaster, Pa. 1886.   5022
Atlas of the city of Richmond, Va. 1889.   5071
Atlas of the 1st, 26th & 30th wards, Philadel-
phia. 1886.   16856
Atlas of the properties in the north-west
suburbs of Philadelphia. 1893.   16892
Atlas of West Philadelphia, 24th and 27th
wards. 1886.   16857
Atlas of Wilmington, Del. 1887.   1494
Plat book of the city of Detroit and suburbs,
Mich. 1916.   4771
Property atlas of Birmingham, Ala. 1902.   1450
Property atlas of Camden, N.J. 1902.   2176
Property atlas of Milwaukee and vicinity,
Wis. 1898.   2676
Real estate atlas of surveys of Columbus and
vicinity, Ohio. 1910.   3881
—— 1920.   16518
Real estate atlas of surveys of Denver, Colo.
1905.   3708
Real estate atlas of surveys of Detroit, Mich.
1906.   2004
Real estate atlas of surveys of Detroit and
Highland Park, Mich. 1911.   3809

Real estate atlas of surveys of Detroit and
  suburbs, Mich. 1915.   4770
—— 1918.   4772
—— 1923.   14852
—— 1926–30.   14853
Real estate atlas of surveys of Indianapolis
  and vicinity, Ind. 1908.   1638
—— 1916.   4619
—— 1927.   12979
—— 1941.   12980
Real estate atlas of surveys of Los Angeles,
  Cal. 1905.   3706
—— 1910.   3707
—— 1914.   4540
—— 1921.   11533
—— 1923.   11534
Real estate atlas of surveys of Omaha, Nebr.
  1910.   3831
—— 1918.   4913
Real estate atlas of surveys of Seattle, Wash.
  1905.   2626
—— 1908.   2626a
—— 1912.   3929
Real estate atlas of surveys of Toledo, Ohio.
  1904.   16565
Real estate atlas of surveys of Washington,
  D.C. 1903.   1505
—— 1907.   1506
—— 1909–11.   3716
—— 1913–15.   4550
—— 1919–21.   4552, 11775
—— 1924–28.   11776
—— 1931–36.   11778
—— 1937–43.   11779
—— 1945–50.   11782
—— 1954–59.   11785
—— 1960–67.   11786

Baist, Robert Harrison, 1919–
Atlas of surveys of Detroit and suburbs, Mich.
  1955.   14863

Baker, Brookes.
Map of Fort Worth, Tex. 1924.   17235
—— 1949.   17238

Baker, Charles E.
[Atlas of Langlade County, Wis. 1927] 17814

Baker, John Norman Leonard, 1893–1971.
Atlas of the war. [1939]   5856
—— [1940]   5857

Baker, Marion M.
Historical geography maps of the United
  States. [1914]   4504

Baker, Oliver Edwin, 1883–1949.
See Finch, Vernor Clifford, 1883–1959, *and*
Baker, Oliver Edwin, 1883–1949.

Baker, Simon, 1924–   *and* McCleneghan,
Thomas J.
Arizona economic and historic atlas. 1966. 11243

Baker and Tilden.
Atlas of Hartford City and County [Conn.]
  1869.   1478, 1487

Balcar, Antonín, 1847–1888, *and* Kameniček,
František, 1856–1930.
Historicko–zeměpisný atlas školní. [1923] 5485

Baldwin, Cecilia Brewster, 1893–
Land maps of New Canaan, Conn. [1938] 11733

Baldwin, M. C.
Popular atlas. 1885.   4362

Balen, C. L. van, *d.* 1943.
See Bos, Pieter Roelof, 1847–1902, *and* Balen,
  C. L. van, *d.* 1943.

Balen, Willem Julius van, 1890–
Atlas van Zuid-Amerika. 1957.   18191

Ballester y Castell, Rafael, 1872–
Geografía-atlas. 1. ed. 1931.   6735

Ballino, Giulio, *fl.* 1560–1569.
Disegni delle piv illvstri città, et fortezze del
  mondo. 1569.   5387

Baltimore. *Topographical Survey.*
Atlas of the city of Baltimore, Md. 1897. 14378
—— 1914.   4711
Baltimore, Md. Topographic maps ... added
  to the city by the Act of 1918. 1923. 14381

Banco de la República, *Bogotá.*
Atlas de economía colombiana. 1959–64. 18342

Bankasha, *Nagoya.*
Nagoya-shi kubun chizu. [Nagoya ward
  atlas. 1956]   9926

Bankes, Thomas, Blake, Edward Warren, *and*
Cook, Alexander.
New royal ... system of universal geography.
  1787–[1810?]   665

Bannock Title Company.
Map of city of Pocatello, Idaho. [1954] 12064

Banque Nationale pour le Commerce et l'Industrie,
Paris.
Algérie, touristique et routière. [1949] 10106
France routière et touristique. [1948] 8434
Tunisie, touristique et routière. [1949] 10157

Bansemer, Jan Marcin, 1802–1840, *and* Zaleski
Falkenhagen, Piotr, 1809–1883.
Atlas, containing ten maps of Poland. 1837. 5276

Baquol, Jacques, 1813–1856, *and* Schnitzler,
Johann Heinrich, 1802–1871.
Atlas historique et pittoresque. 1860.   99
—— 1861–64.   100
—— 1884–85.   4128

Baralle, Alphonse.
  See Fayard de la Brugère, Jean Arthême, and
  Baralle, Alphonse.

Baranovskii, Stepan Ivanovich, b. 1817.
  Географическій атласъ древняго мір—
  Geographical atlas of the ancient world.
  2d ed. 1845.   5591

Baratta, Mario, 1868–1935.
  Atlante storico. [1923–24]   5486

Baratta, Mario, and Fraccaro, Plinio, 1883–
  Piccolo atlante storico. 2 v. [1928–32]   5489

Baratta, Mario, and others.
  Atlante storico. [1940–41]   5487
  —— [1942–54]   5488

Baratta, Mario, and Visintin, Luigi, 1892–1958.
  Atlante delle Colonie Italiane. [1928]   8952
  Atlante della produzione e dei commerci.
  [1922]   5420
  —— 2a ed. [1929]   5421
  —— 3a ed. [1933]   5422
  Atlante geografico universale. 5. ed. 1942.   7082
  Atlas historico universal. [1929]   5490
  —— [1933]   5491
  Grande atlante geografico. [1922]   6475
  —— 2. ed. [1924]   6541
  —— 3. ed. [1927]   6641
  —— 4. ed. [1938]   6938
  —— 4. ed. [1943]   7126

Barbié du Bocage, Jean Denis, 1760–1825.
  See Barthélemy, Jean Jacques, 1716–1795.

Barcelona. Servicio del Plano de la Ciudad.
  Plano de Barcelona. 1949.   9345

Barendsz, Willem, 1560?–1597.
  Description de la Mer Méditerranée. 1607.   188

Barkemeyer, Johann Bernhard.
  Taschenatlas der Bayerischen Alpen. [1926]   8729

Barlow, Hammond, and Haun Geologists.
  Denver and Raton Basins map folio. 1958.   11635
  Eastern Utah, western Colorado map folio.
  1958.   17292
  Montana map folio. 1958.   15310
  North and South Dakota map folio. 1958.   16248
  Wyoming map folio. 1958.   18033

Barnes, Rowland H., and Beal, Henry F.
  Atlas of city of Newton, Mass. 1929.   14507

Barnes and Farnham.
  Atlas of Berkshire County, Mass. 1904.   1809

Barral, Jean Augustin, 1819–1879.
  Atlas du cosmos. 1867.   212
  —— 1882.   5775

Barreiros, Eduardo Canabrava.
  Atlas da evolução urbana da cidade do Rio de
  Janeiro; ensaio. 1565–1965. 1965.   18316

Barrineau Map Service.
  Atlas of Pensacola, Fla. [1955]   11920

Barron y Cadena.
  [Atlas geográfico de los Estados Unidos Mex-
  icanos] 1897.   18087

Barron County, Wis.
  Atlas, Barron County, Wis. 1942.   17658, 17659

Barthel, Otto, and others.
  Atlas of the city of Wheeling, W.Va. 1901.   2630
  See also Kiser, Ellis, and Barthel, Otto.

Barthélemy, Jean Jacques, 1716–1795.
  Atlas des ÔEuvres complètes. 1822.   8886
  Maps, plans, views … of the Travels of An-
  acharsis the Younger in Greece. 1791.   8891
  —— 1796.   8892
  —— 5th ed. 1817.   8893
  —— 6th ed. 1825.   8894
  Recueil de cartes géographiques, plans, vues
  … de l'ancienne Grèce, relatifs au voyage
  du jeune Anacharsis. 2. éd. 1789.   8887
  —— 1791.   3049, 8888
  —— Nouv. éd. [1798–1811]   8889
  —— 1817.   8890
  Voyage du jeune Anacharsis en Grèce. 1822–
  [30]   8895

Bartholomew, John, 1831–1893.
  Atlas of the world. [1913]   6355
  Black's General atlas, supplement. 1858.   826
  Black's General atlas. 1860.   829
  Black's School atlas for beginners. 1860.   6138
  Collegiate atlas. [1872]   6178
  Handy atlas. 1871.   6174
  Handy reference atlas of the world. 1890.   6251
  —— 9th ed. 1912.   6349
  —— 10th ed. 1923.   6513
  —— 11th ed. 1928.   6669
  —— 12th ed. 1933.   6790
  —— 13th ed. 1935.   6832
  —— 14th ed. 1940.   7000
  —— 14th ed. 1941.   7042
  —— 15th ed. 1949.   7335
  Library reference atlas. 1890.   957
  Philips' Handy atlas of the counties of Ireland.
  [1881]   2939
  Philips' Handy atlas of the counties of Scot-
  land. 1898.   2942
  Philips' Handy atlas of the counties of Wales.
  1889.   2944
  Philips' Handy general atlas. 1874.   6185
  Philips' Handy general atlas of America.
  [1879]   1184, 1233, 1403
  Pocket atlas. 1887.   937
  Student's atlas. 1875.   6189
  —— [188–]   6202, 6203
  Zell's Desciptive hand atlas. 1871.   860

Reference atlas of Greater London. 7th ed.
1940.   8176
—— 8th ed. 1948.   8181
—— 9th ed. 1954.   8192
—— 10th ed. 1957.   8194
Royal atlas of England and Wales. [1900?]   2931
School economic atlas. 1910.   3360
—— Rev. ed. 1912.   4122
—— 3d ed. 1915.   4123
—— 5th ed. 1921.   5426
Survey atlas of England & Wales. 1903–
[1904]   2932
—— 2d ed. 1939.   8139
Survey atlas of Scotland. 1912.   4015a
Tourists' atlas-guide to the continent of
Europe. [1896]   2811
XXth century citizen's atlas. [1903]   1081
—— [1908?]   1127
See also Robertson, *Sir* Charles Grant, 1869–
1948, *and* Bartholomew, John George.

**Bartholomew, John George, *and* Cramp, Karl
Reginald, 1878–**
Australasian school atlas. 1915.   5317

**Bartholomew, John George, *and* Herbertson,
Andrew John, 1865–1915.**
Atlas of meteorology. 1899.   213

Bartholomew, John George, *and* Jefford, Edward.
Paris pour tous; atlas. [1919]   8497

Bartholomew, John George, *and* others.
Atlas of zoogeography. 1911.   5378
Physical atlas. 1899–1911.   3345
Royal Scottish Geographical Society's Atlas
of Scotland. 1895.   2941

Bartholomew, John, and Son.
Birmingham [England] pocket atlas and guide.
1945.   8145
—— 1952.   8146
Central London atlas-guide. 1951.   8185
Edinburgh atlas-guide. 1950.   8214
—— 1955.   8215
Excel atlas of the world. [1943]   7129
—— [1947]   7255
London pocket atlas. 1946.   8178
Map of Norway. [193–]   9117
Pocket atlas and guide to Birmingham [Eng-
land] 1933.   8144
Pocket atlas and guide to Liverpool. 1928.   8154
Pocket atlas and guide to Manchester. 1927.   8196
Pocket atlas of the world and gazetteer.
[1940]   7003
Road atlas of Great Britain. [1943]   8041
—— 9th ed. 1952.   8056
Roadmaster motoring atlas of Great Britain.
1958.   8066

Barthos, Indár, *Albisi, and* Kurucz, György.
Történelmi atlasz Magyarország. [1926]   8918

Bartlett, Fred E.
See Stewart, John L., *and* Bartlett, Fred E.

Bartlett, S. M.
County atlas of Monroe, Mich. 1876.   1988

Bartolommeo *da li Sonetti, fl.* 1485.
[Isolario; ossia, Carte del mare Egeo. 1485?]   5170a

Barton, William.
Map of the city of Troy, West Troy, and Green
Island, N.Y. 1869.   2285, 2330, 2334

Bartram, Frances P.
Easy-read street directory, with maps, Colorado
Springs & environs. [1959]   11673

Basch, L., and Company.
Atlas of the settled counties of New South
Wales. [1873]   3255

Bashore, Frederick William, 1831–1902.
See Morrow, Oliver, *and* Bashore, Frederick
William, 1831–1902.

Baskin, Forster and Company.
Illustrated historical atlas of the state of In-
diana. 1876.   1599

Bastert, A., *and* Enthoffer, Joseph, 1818–1901.
Map of the city of Washington [D.C.] 1872.   11768

Battisti, Cesare, 1875–1916.
Venezia Giulia. 1920.   8998

**Battlefield maps of the war in Germany from 1757
to 1762.** [1782–1800]   7698

Bauer, Jacob L.
Atlas of Union County, N.J. 1906.   15722

Bauer, Karl, *and* Scheuerlein, H.
Harms Heimatatlas Regensburg. [1958]   8874

Baughman, Robert Williamson, 1907–
Kansas in maps. 1961.   14139

Baum, Frank George, 1870–
Atlas of U.S.A. electric power industry.
1923.   10572

Baur, Carl Friedrich.
Atlas für Handel u. Industrie. 1857.   5427

**Bavaria. *Heer. Generalstab. Topographisches
Bureau.***
[Topographischer Atlas vom Königreich
Bayern. 1812–67]   5251

Bavaria. *Statistisches Landesamt.*
Bayerland und seine lebendigen Kräfte.
[1951]   8720

Bavio, Ernesto A., 1860–1916.
Atlas escolar de la República Argentina. 11.
ed. [191–?]   5134

Bayer, Herbert, 1900–
World geo-graphic atlas. 1953.   7549

Bayerischer Schulbuch–Verlag.
Grosser historischer Weltatlas. 1953.   5492

Baylor, Henry B.
See Latham, E. B., and Baylor, Henry B.

Bazeley, Charles William.
New juvenile atlas. 1815.   4310

Bazewicz, J. M.
Atlas geograficzny wszystkich części świata.
Wyd. 5. [192–]   6403
Atlas historyczny Polski. Wyd. 4. 1920.   9143

Beach, Harlan Page, 1854–1933.
Geography and atlas of Protestant missions.
1903.   178

Beal, Henry F.
See Barnes, Rowland H., and Beal, Henry F.

Beale, Allan S.
Town of Wareham [Mass.] 1942.   14536

Beard, Frank.
Township plats, Clark County, Mo. 1962.   15222
—— 1964.   15223

Beardsley, Robert S.
Gulf beaches, Pinellas Co. [Fla. 1956]   11846
Township[s], Pinellas County [Fla. 1956]   11847

Beaty, John Owen, 1890– and Foscue, Edwin Jay, 1899–
Outline maps for English literature. 1930.   5731

Beaulieu, Sébastien de, sieur de Pontault, 1613–1674.
Plans & profils avec les descriptions des principales villes & places fortes de France.
[1694?]   2963

Beauman, Guy.
20th century atlas of Jefferson County, Ark.
1905.   1453
20th century atlas of Pulaski County, Ark.
1906.   1454

Beaumont, Tex. Chamber of Commerce.
Ownership and occupancy map, central business district, Beaumont, Tex. 1961.   17199

Beaurain, Jean, chevalier de, 1696–1772.
Carte d'Allemagne. 1765.   2813

Beautemps-Beaupré, Charles François, 1766–1854.
Atlas du voyage de Bruny-Dentrecasteaux.
1807.   5318

Beauvais, ——
Atlas ecclésiastique, littéraire, civil, politique
... de la France et du globe. 1783.   3523

Bechler, Gustavus R.
Atlas showing battles ... connected with the
campaigns in Virginia. [1864]   1348, 2606

Becker, Edward P.
Hessen, das chattische Stammland. 1932.   8748

Becker, Fridolin, 1854–1922, and Imhof, Eduard, 1895–
Neuer schweizerischer Volksschulatlas. 1924.   6545

Becker, George Ferdinand, 1847–1919.
Atlas to accompany a monograph on the geo-
logy of the quicksilver deposits of the Paci-
fic slope. 1887.   1282
Geology of the quicksilver deposits of the
Pacific slope. 1888.   1458

Becker, Henry Floyd, 1898– and Christensen, David E.
Florida reference atlas. [1960]   11801

Becker, William H., Engineering Company.
Compiled recorded plats of Maricopa Coun-
ty, Ariz. 1926.   11256
—— 1940.   11258
View of Salt River Valley, Maricopa County,
Ariz. 1932.   11257

Beckmann, Otto.
Welt-Atlas. 1932.   6772

Becquet, Charles.
Sécurité française (Atlas historique). [1949]   8403

Bee Publishing Company.
Atlas of Douglas, Sarpy and Washington
counties, Nebraska, and Mills and Pottawattamie counties, Iowa. 1913.
                         4650, 4655, 4886, 4904, 4910
Atlas of Greene County, Iowa. 1942.   13417

Beek, Anna van Westerstee, 1657–1718?
[Collection of plans of fortifications and battles. 1684–1709]   5152

Beekman, Anton Albert, 1854–1947.
Nieuwe schoolatlas van Nederland. 1911.   9088

Beekman, Anton Albert, and Schuiling, Roelof, 1854–1936.
Schoolatlas van de geheele aarde. 3. druk.
[1903]   267
—— 7. druk. [1921]   6435
—— 8. druk. [1927]   6642
Schoolatlas van Nederland. [1903]   3074

Beers, D. G., and Company.

Atlas of Allegany County, N.Y.   1869.   2213

Atlas of Bourbon, Clark, Fayette, Jassamine
and Woodford Counties, Ky.   1877.

1748, 1752, 1753, 1759, 1768

Atlas of Cattaraugus County, N.Y.   1869.   2214

Atlas of Columbia County, N.Y.   1873.   2221

Atlas of Essex County, Mass.   1872.   1812

Atlas of Franklin County, N.Y.   1876.   15878

Atlas of Oneida County, N.Y.   1874.   2241

Atlas of Steuben County, N.Y.   1873.   3841

Atlas of the State of Rhode Island and Providence Plantations.   1870.   16949

Atlas of Wayne Co., N.Y.   1874.   4933

Beers, Daniel G.

Atlas of Luzerne County, Pa.   1873.   2482

Atlas of Northampton County, Pa.   1874.   2492

Atlas of the state of Delaware.   1868.   1492

Atlas of Union & Snyder Counties, Pa.   1868.

5019, 5020

See also Beers, S.N., *and* Beers, Daniel G.

Beers, Daniel G., *and* **Lanagan, J.**

Atlas of Jefferson and Oldham Counties, Ky.
1879.   1758, 1762

Beers, F. W., and Company.

Atlas of the counties of Lamoille and Orleans,
Vt.   1878.   5069, 5070

Illustrated historical atlas of Erie Co., N.Y.
1880.   2226

Illustrated historical atlas of the county of
Chautauqua, N.Y.   1881.   2217

Beers, Frederick W.

Atlas of Calhoun County, Mich.   1873.   1965

Atlas of Cumberland County, Me.   1871.   1775

Atlas of Cumberland County, Pa.   1872.   2472

Atlas of Douglas County, Kans.   1873.   1719

Atlas of Franklin and Grand Isle Cos., Vt.
1871.   2598, 2599

Atlas of Genesee County, Mich.   1873.   1968

Atlas of Hunterdon Co., N.J. 1873.   2163

Atlas of Indiana Co., Pa.   1871.   2478

Atlas of Ionia Co., Mich.   1875.   1974

Atlas of Kalamazoo Co., Mich.   1873.   1978

Atlas of Lapeer Co., Mich.   1874.   1982

Atlas of Livingston Co., Mich.   1875.   1986

Atlas of Livingston Co., N.Y.   1872.   2235

Atlas of Long Island, N.Y.   1873.   2202

Atlas of Monmouth Co., N.J.   1873.   2166

Atlas of Monroe Co., N.Y.   1872.   2237

Atlas of New Haven County, Conn.   1868.   1481

Atlas of New London County, Conn.   1868.   1482

Atlas of of Oakland Co., Mich.   1872.   1994

Atlas of Otsego Co., N.Y.   1868.   2247

Atlas of Shawnee Co., Kans.   1893.   1739

Atlas of Somerset Co., N.J.   1873.   2170

Atlas of Staten Island, Richmond Co., N.Y.
1874.   2203

Atlas of Susquehanna Co., Pa.   1872.   2496

Atlas of the city of Newton, Mass.   1874.   1913

Atlas of the county of Orange, Vt.   1877.   2600

Atlas of the Hudson River Valley from New
York City to Troy.   1891.   2201

Atlas of Wayne Co., Pa.   1872.   2499

Atlas of Windham Co., Vt.   1869.   2603

County atlas of Bedford, Pa.   1877.   2460

County atlas of Berkshire, Mass.   1876.   1807

County atlas of Caledonia, Vt.   1875.   2596

County atlas of Carbon, Pa.   1875.   2467

County atlas of Cayuga, N.Y.   1875.   2215

County atlas of Hampshire, Mass.   1873.   1817

County atlas of Ingham, Mich.   1874.   1973

County atlas of Lebanon, Pa.   1875.   2480

County atlas of Litchfield, Conn.   1874.   1479

County atlas of Middlesex, Conn.   1874.   1480

County atlas of Monroe, Pa.   1875.   2486

County atlas of Muskegon, Mich.   1877.   1990

County atlas of Orange, N.Y.   1875.   2244

County atlas of Rensselaer, N.Y.   1876.   2249

County atlas of Rockland, N.Y.   1876.   2250

County atlas of Shiawassee Co., Mich.
1875.   1999

County atlas of Somerset, Pa.   1876.   2495

County atlas of Sullivan, N.Y.   1875.   2256

County atlas of Ulster, N.Y.   1875.   2259

County atlas of Warren, N.J.   1874.   2171

County atlas of Warren, N.Y.   1876.   2260

County atlas of Washington, Vt.   1873.   2602

Illustrated atlas of the city of Richmond [Va.
1877]   2621

New York City from official records and surveys.   1876–85.   2296

State atlas of New Jersey.   1872.   2144

Beers, Frederick W., *and* **Cochran, A. B.**

County atlas of Schuylkill, Pa.   1875.   2494

Beers, Frederick W., *and* **Cramer, Louis H.**

Combination atlas of Saratoga and Ballston
[N.Y.]   1876.   2270, 2324

Beers, Frederick W., Fulmer, F. S., *and others.*

Atlas of Rutland Co., Vt.   1869.   2601

**Beers, Frederick W., Leavenworth, A., Warner,
George E.,** *and others.*

Atlas of Delaware Co., Ohio.   1866.   2372

Beers, Frederick W., Nichols, Beach, *and others.*

Atlas of Licking Co., Ohio.   1866.   2393

Atlas of Muskingum Co., Ohio.   1866.   2405

Beers, Frederick W., Peet, W. S., *and others.*

Atlas of Addison Co., Vt.   1871.   2594

Beers, Frederick W., Prindle, A. B., *and others.*

Atlas of Morris Co., N.J.   1868.   2167

Atlas of New York [City] and vicinity.   1868. 2292

Beers, Frederick W., Sanford, G. P., *and others.*

Atlas of Bennington Co., Vt.   1869.   2595

Atlas of Bradford Co., Pa.   1869.   2463

Atlas of Chemung Co., N.Y.   1869.   2218

Atlas of Chittenden Co., Vt.   1869.   2597

Atlas of Clinton Co., N.Y.   1869.   2219

Atlas of Stark County, Ohio. 1870.	2415
Atlas of Tioga Co., N.Y. 1869.	2257
Atlas of Windsor Co., Vt. 1869.	2604

Beers, Frederick W., Warner, George E., *and others*.
Atlas of Greene County, N.Y. 1867.	2229
Atlas of Jefferson Co., Ohio. 1871.	2389
Atlas of New York [City] and vicinity. 1867.	2290

Beers, Frederick W., *and others*.
Atlas of Bristol Co., Mass. 1871.	1810
Atlas of Delaware Co., N.Y. 1869.	2223
Atlas of Erie County, Pa. 1865.	2475
Atlas of Franklin Co., Mass. 1871.	1814
Atlas of Hampden Co., Mass. 1870.	1815
Atlas of Jamestown, N.Y. 1888.	2287
Atlas of the city of Worcester, Mass. 1870.	1958
Atlas of the oil region of Pennsylvania. [1865]	2441
Atlas of Worcester County, Mass. 1870.	1826
County atlas of Middlesex, Mass. 1875.	1818

Beers, J. B., and Company.
Atlas of Staten Island, Richmond Co., N.Y. 1887.	2204
Atlas of the city of Newton, Mass. 1886.	1915
County atlas of Westchester, N.Y. 1872.	2261

Beers, J. H., and Company.
Atlas of Decatur Co., Ind. 1882.	1602
Atlas of De Kalb Co., Ind. 1880.	1603
Atlas of Franklin Co., Ind. 1882.	1605
Atlas of Hendricks Co., Ind. 1878.	12812
Atlas of Kankakee Co., Ill. 1883.	1542
Atlas of Montgomery Co., Ind. 1878.	12861
Atlas of Putnam Co., Ind. 1879.	1623
Atlas of Shelby Co., Ind. 1880.	1627
Atlas of Union Co., Ind. 1884.	1630
Historical atlas of Ford County, Ill. 1884.	1532
Illustrated historical atlas of the County of Ontario, Ont. 1877.	10420

Beers, S. N., *and* Beers, Daniel G.
New topographical atlas of Jefferson Co., N.Y. 1864.	2231
New topographical atlas of St. Lawrence Co., N.Y. 1865.	2252
New topographical atlas of Saratoga Co., N.Y. 1866.	15901
New topographical atlas of Schoharie Co., N.Y. 1866.	2254
New topographical atlas of the counties of Albany and Schenectady. N.Y. 1866.	
	2212, 2253

Beers, Ellis and Company.
Atlas of Columbia County, N.Y. 1888.	2222
Atlas of Oil City, Pa. 1887.	2515
Atlas of the city of Birmingham and suburbs, Ala. 1887–88.	1449

Beers, Upton and Company.
Atlas of Niagara and Orleans Counties, N.Y. 1875.	4927, 4929

Behner, Hermann.
Atlas der Funktelegraphie und Seekabel im Weltverkehr. [1922]	5796

Behrmann, Walter, 1882–1955, *and* Maull Otto, 1887–1957.
Rhein-Mainischer Atlas für Wirtschaft, Verwaltung und Unterricht. 1929.	8550

Beirne, James P.
Atlas of the garden spots of Berkshire: Stockbridge, Lennox and Lee, Mass. [1894?]	
	4722, 4723, 4725

Beke, László.
Besten Anbaugebiete landwirtschaftlicher Ausfuhrartikel Ungarns. [193–]	8906

Bélanger, Marcel.
Agriculture du Québec. 1965.	10427

Belavin, Aleksei Fedorovich, 1890–
Атлас Союза Советских Социалистических Республик. [Atlas of the Union of Soviet Socialist Republics.] 1928.	9281

Belcher Abstract and Title Company.
Atlas of Humboldt Co., Cal. [1921–22]	11386

Belden, H., and Company.
[Illustrated] historical atlas of Milwaukee County, Wis. 1876.	17842
Illustrated historical atlas of the counties of Hastings and Prince Edward, Ont. 1878.	10417
Illustrated historical atlas of the counties of Northumberland and Durham, Ont. 1878.	10419
Illustrated historical atlas of the county of Carleton ... Ont. 1879.	10414
Illustrated historical atlas of the county of Huron, Ont. 1879.	10418
Illustrated historical atlas of the county of Kent, Mich. 1876.	1979
Illustrated historical atlas of the county of Wayne, Mich. [1875] Repub. 1967.	14829
—— 1876.	2001

Belgium. *Administration de la Marine*.
Hydrografie, Mer du Nord. Cartes synoptiques des courants devant ... Ostende. [1937]	7981
Hydrografie, Noordzee. Synoptische kaarten der stroomen ... van Zeebrugge. 1935.	7982

Belgium. *Administration des Ponts et Chaussées*.
Album du développement progressif du réseau des routes ... 1830 à 1880. [1881]	2871

Belgium. *Administration des Voies Hydrauliques*.
Kaarten van de dijken. [1953?]	7943

Belgium. *Direction des Travaux Hydrauliques*.
Album des dépenses et des recettes ... de 1830 à 1880. [1881]	2872

Belgium. *Institut Cartographique Militaire.*
Atlas d'histoire militaire. 1912. 4216
Carte topographique de la Belgique. [1899]
2875, 2876, 2877

Belgium. *Ministère de l'Agriculture.*
Statistique de la Belgique ... Atlas. 1899. 2869

Belgium. *Ministère de l'Agriculture, de l'Industrie et des Travaux Publics.*
Carte agricole administrative. 1884. 7940

Belgium. *Office du Travail.*
Atlas statistique du recensement général des industries et des métiers. (31 octobre 1896). 1903. 5188

Belgium. *Service du Survey National.*
Atlas du Survey National. [1954–59] 7969a

Belgium. *Service Historique de l'Armée.*
Campagne de mai 1940. [1945?] 7948

Belgrad. Vojno-Istoriski Institut.
Historical atlas of the liberation war of the peoples of Yugoslavia, 1941–1945. 1957. 9465
Istoriski atlas oslobodilačkog rata naroda Jugoslaviie. 1941–1945. 1952. 9466

Bell, Allan, and Company.
New general atlas. 1837–38. 6082

Bell, James, 1769–1833.
[Maps of England and Wales. 1836] 8129

Bell Telephone Company of Pennsylvania.
Line maps, eastern Pennsylvania exchange and base rate areas. 1956. 16764

Bellasis, George Hutchins.
Views of Saint Helena. 1815. 5193

Bellin, Jacques Nicolas, 1703–1772.
Atlas de l'Isle de Corse. [1769] 4029
Atlas maritime. 1751. 172, 613
—— 1801. 697
Description des débouquements qui sont au nord de l'Isle de Saint Domingue. 1768. 3949
—— 1773. 3950
Description géographique des Isles Antilles. 1758. 3940
Description géographique du Golfe de Venise et de la Morée. 1771. 3973
Petit atlas maritime. 1764. 638, 3508
Teatro della guerra marittima. 1781. 348
See also Rocque, Jean, *and* Bellin, Jacques Nicolas, 1703–1772.

Bellin, Jacques Nicolas, *and others.*
Hydrographie françoise. [1737–72] 587
—— [1737–91] 588
—— [1737–94] 589
—— [1737–1807] 590
—— [1750–84] 4288

Bellingshausen, Faddeï Faddeevich, 1779–1852.
Атласъ къ путешествію капитана Беллинс-гаузена въ южномъ Ледовитомъ океанъ. [Atlas to the voyage of Captain Bellingshausen in the Antarctic Ocean] 1831. 10210

Bellue, Pierre.
Atlas ou Neptune des cartes de la Mer Méditerranée. 1830–[34] 189

Belmas, Jacques Vital, 1792–1864.
Journaux des sièges faits ou soutenus par les français dans la Péninsule de 1807 à 1814. 1836. 2964

Beltrán Frías, Roberto.
Atlas de la República Mexicana, 1967. [1966] 18108
Atlas de México. 1966. 18081
Atlas geográfico de comunicaciones de la República Mexicana. 1964. 18078

Bement, Alburto, 1862–
Peabody atlas; shipping mines and coal railroads in ... the United States. 1906. 10507

Bemporat, *firm, publishers.*
Atlas Bemporat de la República Argentina. 2. ed. [1941?] 18220

Ben-Eliyahu, Ephraim.
Atlas li-yedi'at Erets-Yisrael veha-TaNaKH. [Atlas for the understanding of Israel and the Old Testament. 1957–58] 9772

Benazech, Peter, *engraver.*
See Pownall, Thomas. Six remarkable views in the provinces of New-York, New-Jersey, and Pennsylvania, in North America. 1761.

Benians, Ernest Alfred, 1880– *and* Knight, Thomas Harold.
Historical atlas. 1908. 2880a

Bennet, Roelof Gabriel, 1774–1829, *and* Wijk Roelandszoon, Jacobus van, 1781–1847.
Verhandeling over de nederlandsche ontdekkingen in Amerika, Australië, de Indiën en de Poollanden. Atlas. 1827. 1134, 3072a, 3252

Bennet, John, *d.* 1787.
See Sayer, Robert, 1725–1794, *and* Bennett, John, *d.* 1787.

Bennett, L. G., *and* Smith, A. C.
Map of Winona County, Minn. 1867. 2046

Bennett, William Donald, 1906–
Logging atlas of eastern Canada. 1958–[61] 10341

Benson, Noel Milton, 1930–
Dickinson County [Kans.] atlas. 1950. 14159

Benzie Soil Conservation District.
Plat book, Benzie County, Mich. [1965]   14616

Benziger und Companie.
Kleiner Führer und Atlas der Walfahrtsstätten Italiens. 1950.   8990

Berecz, Antal, 1836–1905.
See Erödi, Béla, 1846–1936, Berecz, Antal, 1836–1905, *and* Brózik, Károly, 1849–1911.

Berg, Alfred Willi, 1876–
Universal-Atlas. [1908]   6325

Berger-Levrault et Cie.
Atlas-index de tous les théâtres de la guerre. 3v. [1915–]   5814
Front. 1915.   5815

Berghaus, Heinrich Karl Wilhelm, 1797–1884.
Atlas von Asia. 1832–43.   3175
Kleiner geographisch-statistischer Atlas der Preüssischen Monarchie. 1842.   8763
Physikalischer Atlas. 1850–51.   215
—— 2. Aufl. 1852.   216
—— 3. Ausg. 1892.   217
Physikalischer Schul-Atlas. 1850.   214

Berghaus, Hermann, 1828–1890.
Schul-Atlas der Österreichischen Monarchie. 1855.   2861
See also Stieler, Adolf, 1775–1836, *and* Berghaus, Hermann, 1828–1890.

Bergsträsser, Gotthelf, 1886–1933.
Sprachatlas von Syrien und Palästina. 1915.   10074

Bergvalls nya skolatlas. [1952]   7524

Berlandier, Luis, *d.* 1851, *and others*.
Voyage au Mexique. Vues diverses. MS. 1827–31.   5117

Berlin. Deutsches Pädagogisches Zentralinstitut.
Abteilung Erdkunde.
Vom Bild zur Karte: Ausg. Brandenburg. [1951]   8737
—— Ausg. Mecklenburg. [1951]   8755
—— Ausg. Sachsen. [1951]   8787
—— Ausg. Sachsen-Anhalt. [1951]   8788
—— Ausg. Thüringen. [1951]   8817

Berliner Morgenpost
Berlin in der Tasche. [1929]   8833
—— [193–]   8834
—— [1940]   8838
—— [1950]   8842
—— [1952]   8843
—— [1954]   8845
—— [1956]   8847
Weltkarten der Berliner Morgenpost. [1927]   6643
1000 Wege um Berlin. [1930]   8835
—— [1936]   8836

Bermejo Rodríguez, José, *and* Villarroya San Mateo, Antonio.
Atlas de geografía postal universal. [193–?]   5783

Bernard, Guillaume.
See Barendsz, Willem. 1560?–1597.

Bernhard, Hans Ulrich, 1888–1942.
Landwirtschaftlicher Atlas des Kantons Zürich. 1925.   9456

Berry, Leonard, 1930–
See Tregear, Thomas R., *and* Berry, Leonard, 1930–

Berry, Maurice Edward, 1904–
Lot and block atlas of Fort Lauderdale, Fla. 1940.   11870
Official atlas, Hallandale, Fla. [1948]   11875

Berry, William, *fl.* 1669–1708.
[Collection of maps of the world. 1680–89]   3442

Berson, Arthur, 1859–1942
See Gross, H., *and* Berson, Arthur, 1859–1942.

Bertelsmann, C.
Weltatlas. [1954]   7589

Berthaut, Henri Marie Auguste, 1848–1937.
Principes de stratégie ... Atlas. 1881.   7727

Bertius, Petrus, 1565–1629.
Beschreibung der gantzen Welt. 1650.   5942
Commentariorvm rervm Germanicarvm libri tres. 1616.   8526
Geographie racourcie. 1618.   5925
Geographischer eyn oder zusammengezogener Tabeln. 1612.   3413
Tabvlarvm geographicarvm. 1616.   5924
Tabvlarvm geographicvm. Ed. 2a. 1602.   414
—— Ed. 3a. 1606.   3409
[Variæ orbis universi. 1628?]   5592

Bertsch, Fred.
See Moessinger, George, *and* Bertsch, Fred.

Berwick, Jacobo María del Pilar Carlos Manuel Stuart Fitz-James, *10. duque* de, 1878–
Mapas españoles de América, siglos XV–XVII. 1951.   10257

Beskovnyï, L. G.
Атлас карт и схем по русской военной истории. [Atlas of maps and diagrams of Russian military history] 1946.   9221

Betka, Bernard.
Lake County [Mich.] plat book. [1958]   14707
—— [1965]   14708

Bettencourt, Emiliano Augusto de.
Atlas pecuario de Portugal. [1870]   3095

Bevan, George Phillips, 1829?–1889.
Royal relief atlas. 2d ed. [1881]   5776
—— 3d ed. 1885.   245
Sonnenschein & Allen's Royal relief atlas.
[1880]   3352
Statistical atlas of England, Scotland and Ire-
land. 1882.   2890

Beyer, Carlos.
Atlas general de la República Argentina. 6. ed.
1893.   5135
See also Biedma, José Juan, 1864–1933, and
Beyer, Carlos.

Beyin, Faik Sabri.
Coğrafya defterleri, orta mektepler için.
1934.   5732

Bhavani Shanker Rao, U.
See Srinivas Kini, K., and Bhavani Shanker
Rao, U.

Bianco, Andrea, 15th cent.
[Facsimile dell' Atlante di Andrea Bianco
dell'anno 1436. 1869]   3356
—— 1879.   247

Biblical atlas. 2d ed. 1936.   5342

Bibliographisches Institut, Leipzig.
Auto-Atlas "Neues Deutschland." 1951.   8630
—— 1953.   8644
—— 1954.   8649
—— 1955.   8655
—— 1956.   8662
—— 1957.   8667
—— 1958.   8671
Grosse Weltatlas. 1933.   6792
—— 3. Aufl. 1935.   6835
—— 6. Aufl. 1939.   6970
—— 6. Aufl. 1940.   7004
Meyers Physikalischer Handatlas. 1916.   5777
Soldaten-Atlas. 1941.   7045
Weltatlas. [1952]   7496
Werden Grossdeutschlands im Kartenbild,
1786–1939. [1939]   8557

**Bibliothek des Geographischen Lexikons der
Schweiz.**
Atlas géographique, économique, historique
de la Suisse. [1908]   9447
Geographischer, volkswirtschaftlicher, ge-
schichtlicher Atlas der Schweiz. [1908]   9448

**Bichelonne, Jean, 1904–1944, and Angot, Pierre,
1902–**
Formation ferrifère Lorraine ... Atlas.
[1939]   8488

Bickmore, David Pelham, 1917–
Oxford travel atlas of Britain. 1953.   8080

Bickmore, David Pelham, and Cook, K. F.
Concise Oxford atlas. 1952.   7497

Biddenback, H. J.
City atlas of La Crosse, Wis. 1898.   5111

Biedma, José Juan, 1864–1933, and Beyer, Carlos.
Atlas histórico de la República Argentina.
1909.   3955

Biel, E. R.
See Landsberg, Helmut, 1906–   and Biel,
E. R.

Bielenstein, August Johann Gottfried, 1826–1907.
Atlas der ethnologischen Geographie des ...
Lettenlandes. 1892.   4055

Bien, Joseph Rudolph.
Atlas of New York. 1895.   2211
Atlas of Pennsylvania. 1900.   2456
—— 1901.   2457
Atlas of Westchester County, N.Y. 1893.   2262

**Bien, Joseph Rudolph, and Vermeule, Cornelius
Clarkson.**
Atlas of the metropolitan district and adjacent
country ... in ... New York ... and New
Jersey. 1891.   2150, 2210

**Bier, James Allen, 1927–   and Raup, Henry A.,
1933–**
Campground atlas of the United States and
Canada. [1960]   10295
—— [1962]   10296
—— [1964]   10297
—— [1966]   10298

Bihar, India (State)
Bihar community projects; map and list of
villages. 1953.   9713

Billerica, Mass.
Town of Billerica, 1960; assessors map.
[1964]   14415

Bins, P., and others.
Heimatatlas Rheinland-Pfalz. [1953]   8775

Birch, William, 1755–1834.
Country seats of the United States. 1808.   4516a

Birch, William, and Birch, Thomas, 1779–1851.
City of Philadelphia. 1800.   2516
Eleven of the principal views of Birch's Phila-
delphia. [1800–27]   2517

Bird, John H.
Compact atlas of the world. [1910]   3600

Birdseye Abstract Company.
Ownership map of Vernon County, Mo.
1954.   15248

Birkett, Walter Snowden, *and* Lewis, George Gregory.
Evans' Atlas, Australia and abroad. 3d ed. [1941]   5428
Pupils's empire atlas. 5th ed. 1926.   7984

Bischoff, Karl, 1905–
Studien zur Dialektgeographie des Elbe-Saale-Gebietes. 1935.   8580

Bishop, H. G.
Atlas of Keokuk County, Iowa. 1895.   1680

Bishop, Mildred Catherine, 1886– *and* Robinson, Edward Kilburn, 1883–
Practical map exercises and syllabus in American history. 1922.   10596
Practical map exercises and syllabus in European history to 1714. 1923.   7732a
Practical map exercises and syllabus in European history since 1714. 1923.   7733

Bisiker, William.
British Empire and Japan. 1909.   4008, 4076

Bitner, Fred H.
Arizona rock trails. 1957.   11251

Bjørnbo, Axel Anthon, 1874–1911, *and* Petersen, Carl Sophus, 1873–
Anecdota cartographica septentrionalis. 1908.   2798a

Black, Adam, 1784–1874, *and* Black, Charles.
Atlas of Australia with all the gold regions. [1853]   10175
Atlas of North America. 1856.   1232, 1385
General atlas. 1840.   777
—— 1841.   779
—— 1844.   793
—— 1851.   4328
—— New ed. 1852.   4330
—— New ed. 1853.   4332
—— New ed. 1854.   4334
—— Supplement. 1858.   826
—— 1860.   829
—— 1867.   849
—— American ed. 1876.   3565
—— New and rev. ed. 1890.   4368
—— 1898.   1021
General atlas of the world. 1856.   6124
—— 1870.   6172
—— 1885.   6221

Blackie, Walter Graham, 1816–1906.
Imperial atlas of modern geography. 1860.   3556

Black's School atlas for beginners. 1860.   6138

Blackwood, William, and Sons.
Atlas of Scotland. 1838.   8209
—— 1839.   8210

Blaeu, Joan, 1596–1673.
Atlas maior. Latin ed. [1662–65]   3430
—— [1662–72]   4263
Atlas mayor. Spanish ed. [1659–72]   4262
Grand atlas. French ed. [1667]   479
Grooten atlas. Dutch ed. 1664–65.   471
Nieuw stede boek van Italie. 1704–1705.   5260
Nieuw vermeerderd en verbeterd groot stede-boek van Piemont en van Savoye. 1725.   8944
Nouveau théâtre d'Italie. 1704.   3053
—— 1724.   8945
Nouveau théâtre du Piémont et de la Savoye. 1725.   3055
Novum Italiæ theatrum. 1705.   8943
—— 1724.   3054
Novvm ac magnvm theatrvm vrbivm Belgicæ. [1649]   9030
Theatrvm civitatvm et admirandorvm Italiæ. 1663.   4039
Toonneel der steden van de Vereenighde Nederlanden. [1649]   3076
See also Blaeu, Willem Janszoon, 1571–1638, *and* Blaeu, Joan, 1596–1673.

Blaeu, Willem Janszoon, 1571–1638.
Flambeau de la navigation. 1620.   2829
Light of navigation. 1622.   5177
Zeespiegel. 1643–44.   7725

Blaeu, Willem Janszoon, *and* Blaeu, Joan, 1596–1673.
Novvs atlas. 2 v. 1635.   5933
—— German ed. 3 v. 1641–42.   5936
Théâtre du monde. French ed. 2 v. 1635.   3420
—— 3 v. 1638–40.   3421
—— 2d part. 1644.   455
—— French ed. 3 v. 1645.   5938
Theatrvm orbis terrarvm. Latin ed. v. 4. 1646.   5939
—— 5 v. 1648–54.   5941
Toonneel des aerdriicx, ofte Nievwe atlas. Dutch ed. 2 v. 1635.   448
—— 3d part. 1642.   454
—— 6 v. 1648–58.   460

Blaeu, Willem Janszoon, *and* others.
[Collection of maps of Europe. 1645?–1670?]   7784

Blair, John, *d.* 1782.
Chronology and history of the world. 1768.   3305

Blaisdell, F. L.
Atlas of Arkansas counties. 1919.   11290

Blake, Edward Warren.
See Bankes, Thomas, Blake, Edward Warren, *and* Cook, Alexander.

Blake, John Lauris, 1788–1857.
Geographical, chronological, and historical atlas. 1826.   747

Blanchard, F. S., and Company.
"Pilot" sectional road maps of New England
and Hudson River district. 1908.   1325a
—— 1909.   10770

Blanchet, Adrien, 1866–1957.
Carte archéologique de la Gaule Romaine.
1931–44.   8381

Blanco, Manuel.
Mapa general de las almas que administran
los pp. Augustinos calzados en estas Islas
Filipinas. 1845.   5305

Blancquaert, Edgard, 1894–
Dialect-atlas van Klein Brabant. [1925]   7950
—— 2. uitg. 1950–52.   7951
Dialect-atlas van Noord-Oost Vlaanderen.
[1935]   7952
See also Pée, Willem, 1903–   and Blancquaert, Edgard, 1894–

Blancquaert, Edgard *and* Meertens, Pieter Jacobus, 1899–
Dialect-atlas van de Zeeuwsche eilanden.
[1940]   9047

Blancquaert, Edgard, *and* Vangassen, Hendrik Frans, 1896–
Dialect-atlas van Zuid-Oost-Vlaanderen.
[1931]   7953

Blegen, John, 1842–1927.
Veileder og verdens-atlas. [1892]   970

Bloch, Oscar, 1877–
Atlas linguistique des Vosges méridionales.
1917.   8418

Block, Maurice, 1816–1901.
Puissance comparée des divers états de l'-
Europe. 1862.   2808

Blome, Richard, *d.* 1705.
Britannia. 1673.   8074

Blondel la Rougery, Édouard.
Plan de Paris-atlas. [1912–13]   5237

Blondel la Rougery, Max, 1913–
Atlas Blondel. 1947.   7256

Blondel la Rougery, Éditions.
Atlas Simca des routes de France. [1950]   8437
—— [1952]   8440
Europe ... routes. [1952]   7770
Guide des grandes routes de France. [193–] 8430
—— [1950]   8438

Bludau, Alois, 1861–1913.
Schwann'scher Schul-Atlas. [1914?]   4188

Blum, George W.
Cyclers' guide and road book of California.
[1895]   11340

Blum's Commercial Map Publishing Company.
Commercial atlas. [1918]   4495

Blunt, Edmund March, 1770–1862, *and* Blunt, George William, 1802–1878.
Charts of the North and South Atlantic oceans.
1830.   3661

Bobrik, Hermann, 1814–1845.
Atlas zur Geographie des Herodot. 1838.   5593

Bock, George J.
Atlas of Coshocton County, Ohio. 1910.   16395

Bock, Richard Ernst, 1899–
Atlas of magnetic declination of Europe for
epoch 1944.5. [1951]   7775

Bodenehr, Gabriel, 1664–1758.
Atlas curieux. [1704?]   545
Curioses Staats und Kriegs Theatrum.
[1710–30?]   2814
Dritter Theil des Tractats genandt Europens
Pracht. [1737?]   3962
Europens Pracht und Macht. [172–?]   7634

Bodenehr, Hans Georg, 1631–1704.
Sac. Imperii Romano Germanici geographica
descriptio. 1677.   5250
—— 1682.   3033

Bodo, Fritz, 1895–
Burgenland (1921–1938). 1941.   7911

Böeseken, A. J., *and others.*
Geskiedenis-atlas vir Suid-Afrika. 2. uitg.
[1953]   5495

Böhm, Wilhelmine, 1901– *and* Deuerlein, Ernst, 1893–
Welt im Spiegel der Geschichte. Geschichtsatlas. [4. Aufl. 1952]   5493
—— [5. Aufl. 1952]   5494

Boer, Michiel George de, 1867–   *and* Hettema, Hette Hettes, 1868–
Kleine schoolatlas der vaderlandse en alge-
mene geschiedenis. 8e verb. druk. 1949.   9040

Boerman, Willem Everhard, 1889–1965 *and* Ver-schueren, Joseph, 1889–
Leopold's Wereldatlas. 1939.   6971
—— [1947?]   7257

Boesch, Hans Heinrich, 1911–
Wirtschafts-geographischer Atlas der Welt.
[1951]   5429

Bogart, James P.
See Scofield, Horace G., *and* Bogart, James P.

Bogdanov, A. A., *and* **Moskvin, M. M.**
Атлас учебных геологических карт. [Atlas of school geological maps.] 1955.   9272

Bogue, John J.
Plats of subdivisions of the city of Washington, D.C. 1883.   11770

Bohinec, Valter.
See Roglić, Josip C., *and* Bohinec, Valter.

Bohn, Henry George, 1796–1884.
Standard library atlas of classical geography. 1861.   5

Boisseau, Jean, *fl.* **1637–1658.**
Trésor des cartes géographiqves. 1643.   3424

Boissevin, Louis, *fl.* **1652–1658.**
Trésor des cartes géographiqves. 1653.   462

Boiste, Pierre Claude Victoire, 1765–1824.
Dictionnaire de géographie universelle. Atlas. 1806.   710

Bokshchanin, A. G.
Атлас по истории древнего мира. [Atlas of the history of the ancient world.] 3d ed. [1953]   5593a
—— [1954]   5593b

Bolis, Ed.
Atlante delle regioni d'Italia. [1950]   8991

Bolivia. *Ministerio de Justicia e Industria.*
[Atlas of geological, mineralogical and industrial maps of Bolivia. 1913?]   5139

Bolkestein, G. W., *and* **Eggink, H.**
Werkbladen bij het Aardrijkskundig leerboek voor de middelbare scholen. 4. druk. [1951]   5733

Bollo, Luis Cincinato, 1862–
Atlas geográfico ... de la República Oriental del Uruguay. 1896.   2774

Boloña, Nicanor.
Nuevo mappa de Chile. 1904.   2758a

Большой советский атлас мира.—
Great Soviet world atlas. 1937–39.   6936a

Bombay (*Presidency***).** *Dept. of Land Records and Agriculture.*
Statistical atlas of the Bombay Presidency. 3d ed. 1925.   9715

Bombay (*Province***).** *Bureau of Economics and Statistics.*
Statistical atlas of Bombay State. Rev. ed. 1950.   9716

Bonacci, Giovanni.
Albo per esercizi cartografici. 9. ed. 1921.   6436

Bone, Frank A.
Complete atlas of Warren County, Ohio. 1891.   16459

Bonnange, Ferdinand, 1830–
Atlas graphique et statistique du commerce de la France. 1878.   2962

Bonne, Rigobert, 1727–1794.
Atlas de toutes les parties connues du globe terrestre. [1780]   652
Atlas maritime. [1762]   2988
Petit tableau de la France. 1764.   2989
Recueil de cartes sur la géographie ancienne. 1783.   3271

Bonne, Rigobert, *and* **Desmarest, Nicolas, 1725–1815.**
Atlas encyclopédique. 1787–88.   666, 667

Bonnier, *firm.*
Automobil karta: Södermanland-Uppland specialen. 1923.   9359
Automobil kartor: Norrköping-Karlskrona specialen. 1924.   9360
Hela Sverige för 1 : 50. 2. uppl. [1914]   9358

Bonniers Stora världsatlas. [1951]   7487

Bonniers Världsatlas. [1919–24]   6401

Bont, A. L. de.
Kleine schoolatlas der algemene en vaderlandse geschiedenis. 7. druk. 1948.   5496

Boom, Henry, *and* **Boom, T.**
Atlas françois. [1667]   5223

Boom-Ruijgrok, N. V., Uitgevers- en Drukkersbedrijf.
Zenith automobielkaart van Nederland. [1931]   9058

Booth, R. C., Enterprises.
Adair County, Iowa, TAM service. 1951.   13020
—— 1953.   13022
—— 1955.   13023
Adams County, Ill., TAM service. 1954.   12081
Adams County, Iowa, TAM service. 1951.   13032
—— 1953.   13033
—— 1955.   13034
Adams County, Nebr., TAM service. 1951.   15346
—— 1953.   15347
—— 1955.   15348
Allamakee County, Iowa, TAM service. 1952.   13043
—— 1954.   13044
—— 1956.   13046
Appanoose County, Iowa, TAM service. 1952.   13053

—— 1954.	13054	Atlas of Crawford County, Iowa. [1946]	13281
—— 1956.	13056	—— [1963]	13292
Atlas of Adair County, Iowa. [1946]	13018	Atlas of Cuming County, Nebr. [1948]	15394
—— [1958]	13027	—— 1965.	15398
—— [1963]	13030	Atlas of Custer County, Nebr. [1950]	15399
Atlas of Adams County, Iowa. 1963.	13040	Atlas of Dakota County, Nebr. [1948]	15401
Atlas of Adams County, Nebr. [1948]	15345	—— [1965]	15405
Atlas of Allamakee County, Iowa. [1949]	13042	Atlas of Dallas County, Iowa. [1946]	13293
Atlas of Antelope County, Nebr. [1948]	15349	Atlas of Davis County, Iowa. [1946]	13303
Atlas of Appanoose County, Iowa. [1946]	13052	Atlas of Davison County, S.Dak. [1949]	17028
Atlas of Atchison County, Kans. [1949]	14147	Atlas of Dawson County, Nebr. [1948]	15407
Atlas of Atchison County, Mo. 1957.	15214	—— [1958]	15411
Atlas of Audrain County, Mo. 1964.	15215	Atlas of Delaware County, Iowa. [1947]	13319
Atlas of Audubon County, Iowa. [1946]	13062	Atlas of Des Moines County, Iowa. [1949]	13331
—— [1967]	13075	Atlas of Dixon County, Nebr. [1948]	15415
Atlas of Beadle County, S.Dak. [1949]	17014	—— [1963]	15419
Atlas of Benton County, Iowa. [1946]	13076	Atlas of Dodge County, Nebr. [1947]	15421
Atlas of Black Hawk County, Iowa. [1947]	13086	Atlas of Doniphan County, Kans. [1949]	14161
Atlas of Bon Homme Co., S.Dak. 1957.	17017	Atlas of Douglas County, Nebr. [1948]	15427
Atlas of Boone County, Iowa. [1965]	13103	—— [1957]	15432
Atlas of Boone County, Nebr. [1948]	15351	Atlas of Emmet County, Iowa. [1957]	13369
Atlas of Boyd County, Nebr. [1948]	15354	—— [1967]	13374
—— [1957]	15355	Atlas of Fayette County, Iowa. [1946]	13376
Atlas of Bremer County, Iowa. [1952–53]	13106	—— [1964]	13386
Atlas of Brown County, Kans. [1956]	14151	Atlas of Fillmore County, Nebr. [1948]	15434
Atlas of Buchanan County, Iowa. [1947]	13118	—— [1967]	15438
Atlas of Buena Vista County, Iowa. [1946]	13129	Atlas of Floyd County, Iowa. [1949]	13388
—— [1967]	13139	Atlas of Franklin County, Iowa. [1964]	13406
Atlas of Buffalo County, Nebr. [1948]	15357	Atlas of Franklin County, Nebr. [1948]	15439
—— [1953]	15358	Atlas of Fremont County, Iowa. [1946]	13408
—— [1957]	15361	Atlas of Frontier County, Nebr. [1948]	15440
Atlas of Burt County, Nebr. [1948]	15363	Atlas of Furnas County, Nebr. [1948]	15442
—— [1963]	15366	Atlas of Gage County, Nebr. [1946]	15446
Atlas of Butler County, Iowa. [1954]	13141	Atlas of Garfield County, Nebr. [1948]	15451
—— [1964]	13149	Atlas of Gosper County, Nebr. [1948]	15453
Atlas of Butler County, Nebr. [1947]	15367	—— [1957]	15454
—— [1967]	15370	Atlas of Greeley County, Nebr. [1948]	15457
Atlas of Calhoun County, Iowa. [1946]	13151	Atlas of Greene County, Iowa. [1946]	13418
—— [1964]	13162	Atlas of Guthrie County, Iowa. [1946]	13438
Atlas of Carroll County, Iowa. [1946]	13164	Atlas of Hall County, Nebr. 1948.	15458
—— [1956]	13170	Atlas of Hamilton County, Iowa. [1946]	13448
—— [1967]	13177	—— [1964]	13457
Atlas of Cass County, Iowa. [1946]	13178	Atlas of Hamilton County, Nebr. 1948.	15464
Atlas of Cass County, Nebr. [1947]	15372	—— [1957]	15468
Atlas of Cedar County, Iowa. [1949]	13191	Atlas of Hancock County, Iowa. 1966.	13467
—— [1964]	13202	Atlas of Hanson County, S.Dak. [1949]	17036
Atlas of Cedar County, Nebr. [1948]	15376	Atlas of Hardin County, Iowa. [1947]	13469
—— [1963]	15380	—— [1964]	13478
Atlas of Cerro Gordo County, Iowa. [1964]	13212	Atlas of Harlan County, Nebr. [1953]	15470
Atlas of Cherokee County, Iowa. [1946]	13214	Atlas of Harrison County, Iowa. [1946]	13480
—— [1963]	13225	Atlas of Henry County, Iowa. [1949]	13490
Atlas of Chickasaw County, Iowa. [1954]	13227	—— [1964]	13501
Atlas of Clarke County, Iowa. [1963]	13243	Atlas of Howard County, Nebr. [1948]	15473
Atlas of Clay County, Iowa. [1946]	13244	Atlas [of] Humboldt County, Iowa. [1967]	13520
—— [1964]	13254	Atlas of Ida County, Iowa. [1946]	13521
Atlas of Clay County, Nebr. [1948]	15384	Atlas of Iowa County, Iowa. [1946]	13531
Atlas of Clay County, S.Dak. [1948]	17023	—— [1964]	13541
Atlas of Clayton County, Iowa. [1946]	13255	Atlas of Jasper County, Iowa. [1946]	13554
—— [1958]	13263	—— [1966]	13562
Atlas of Clinton County, Iowa. [1949]	13269	Atlas of Jefferson County, Iowa. [1946]	13563
—— [1967]	13278	—— [1964]	13575
Atlas of Codington County, S.Dak. [1949]	17024	Atlas of Jefferson County, Nebr. [1947]	15477
Atlas of Colfax County, Nebr. [1947]	15389	—— [1967]	15481
—— [1958]	15393	Atlas of Jewell County, Kans. [1957]	14174

Atlas of Johnson County, Iowa. [1946]	13578
—— [1966]	13589
Atlas of Johnson County, Nebr. [1947]	15482
Atlas of Jones County, Iowa. [1949]	13591
Atlas of Kearney County, Nebr. [1948]	15487
Atlas of Keokuk County, Iowa. [1946]	13602
—— [1964]	13612
Atlas of Knox County, Nebr. [1948]	15493
Atlas of Kossuth County, Iowa. [1946]	13614
Atlas of Lancaster County, Nebr. [1947]	15497
—— [1957]	15501
Atlas of Lincoln County, Nebr. [1948]	15503
—— [1958]	15504
Atlas of Lincoln County, S.Dak. [1949]	17042
Atlas of Linn County, Iowa. [1946]	13633
Atlas of Lyon County, Iowa. [1950]	13663
—— [1967]	13673
Atlas of Madison County, Nebr. [1948]	15505
Atlas of Mahaska County, Iowa. [1946]	13687
—— [1964]	13697
Atlas of Marion County, Iowa. [1946]	13698
Atlas of Marshall [County] Iowa. [1949]	13709
Atlas of Marshall County, Kans. [1957]	14185
Atlas of Merrick County, Nebr. [1948]	15510
—— [1965]	15514, 15515
Atlas of Mills County, Iowa. [1946]	13722
—— 1958.	13730
—— [1963]	13733
Atlas of Minnehaha County, S.Dak. [1949]	17047
Atlas of Mitchell County, Iowa. [1946]	13734
—— [1964]	13744
Atlas of Monona County, Iowa. [1946]	13745
—— [1963]	13756
Atlas of Monroe County, Iowa. [1946]	13759
Atlas of Montgomery County, Iowa. [1946]	13769
Atlas [of] Muscatine County, Iowa. [1966]	13787
Atlas of Nance County, Nebr. [1948]	15519
Atlas of Nemaha County, Kans. [1949]	14189
—— [1957]	14190
Atlas of Nemaha County, Nebr. [1948]	15522
—— [1957]	15526
Atlas of Nuckolls County, Nebr. [1948]	15527
—— [1957]	15531
Atlas of O'Brien County, Iowa. [1946]	13790
Atlas of Osceola County, Iowa. [1950]	13801
—— [1964]	13811
Atlas of Otoe County, Nebr. [1947]	15534
—— [1967]	15538
Atlas of Page County, Iowa. [1946]	13813
—— [1957]	13820
—— [1965]	13824
Atlas of Pawnee County, Nebr. [1947]	15539
—— [1957]	15543
Atlas of Phelps County, Nebr. [1948]	15546
Atlas of Pierce County, Nebr. [1948]	15548
Atlas of Platte County, Nebr. [1948]	15553
Atlas of Plymouth County, Iowa. [1946]	13834
—— [1957]	13840
—— [1963]	13844
Atlas of Pocahontas Co., Iowa. [1957]	13851
Atlas of Polk County, Iowa. [1946]	13855
—— [1963]	13865
—— [1966]	13866
Atlas of Polk County, Nebr. [1948]	15556

Atlas of Pottawattamie County, Iowa. [1946]	13868
—— [1957]	13874
—— [1963]	13880
Atlas of Poweshiek County, Iowa. [1946]	13881
Atlas of Red Willow County, Iowa. [1948]	15561
—— [1957]	15562
Atlas of Richardson County, Nebr. [1946]	15565
—— [1967]	15569
Atlas of Ringgold County, Iowa. [1946]	13891
—— [1963]	13899
Atlas of Sac County, Iowa. [1956]	13905
—— [1964]	13910
Atlas of Saline County, Nebr. [1947]	15570
—— [1957]	15574
Atlas of Sarpy County, Nebr. [1947]	15575
—— [1957]	15579
Atlas of Saunders County, Nebr. [1947]	15580
—— [1967]	15585
Atlas of Scott County, Iowa. [1966]	13923
Atlas of Scotts Bluff County, Nebr. [1949]	15587
Atlas of Seward County, Nebr. [1947]	15589
—— [1967]	15593
Atlas of Shelby County, Iowa. [1946]	13926
Atlas of Sherman County, Nebr. [1948]	15595
Atlas of Sioux County, Iowa. [1946]	13940
Atlas of Stanton County, Nebr. [1948]	15596
Atlas of Story County, Iowa. [1947]	13951
—— [1963]	13960
Atlas of Tama County, Iowa. [1946]	13962
—— [1964]	13970
Atlas of Taylor County, Iowa. [1946]	13972
Atlas of Thayer County, Nebr. [1947]	15600
—— [1957]	15604
—— [1967]	15605
Atlas of Thurston County, Nebr. [1948]	15607
Atlas of Turner County, S.Dak. [1949]	17058
Atlas of Union County, Iowa. [1946]	13982
Atlas of Union County, S.Dak. [1949]	17061
Atlas of Valley County, Nebr. [1948]	15611
Atlas of Van Buren County, Iowa. [1946]	13991
—— [1964]	14001
Atlas of Wapello County, Iowa. [1946]	14003
—— [1964]	14014
Atlas of Warren County, Iowa. [1949]	14016
—— [1966]	14025
Atlas of Washington County, Iowa. [1946]	14026
Atlas of Washington County, Nebr. [1948]	15614
Atlas of Wayne County, Iowa. [1951]	14037
Atlas of Wayne County, Nebr. [1948]	15620
Atlas of Webster County, Iowa. [1946]	14047
—— [1967]	14056
Atlas of Webster County, Nebr. [1948]	15624
—— [1967]	15628
Atlas of Wheeler County, Nebr. [1948]	15629
Atlas of Winnebago County, Iowa. [1952]	14058
—— [1967]	14067
Atlas of Woodbury County, Iowa. [1946]	14079
Atlas of Worth County, Iowa. [1964]	14097
Atlas of Yankton County, S.Dak. [1948]	17063
Atlas of York County, Nebr. [1947]	15631
Audubon County, Iowa, TAM service. 1951.	13064
—— 1953.	13066
—— 1955.	13067
Benton County, Iowa, TAM service. 1952.	13077

—— 1954.	13078
—— 1956.	13080
Black Hawk County, Iowa, TAM service. 1952.	13087
—— 1954.	13088
—— 1956.	13090
Boone County, Iowa, TAM service. 1951.	13096
—— 1953.	13097
—— 1955.	13098
Bremer County, Iowa, TAM service. 1952.	13105
—— 1954.	13107
—— 1956.	13109
Brown County, Ill., TAM service. 1954.	12098
Buchanan County, Iowa, TAM service. 1952.	13119
—— 1954.	13120
—— 1956.	13122
Buena Vista County, Iowa. [1947]	13130
Buena Vista County, Iowa, TAM service. 1951.	13131
—— 1953.	13132
—— 1955.	13133
Buffalo County, Nebr., TAM service. 1953.	15359
—— 1955.	15360
Bureau County, Ill., TAM service. 1954.	12103
Burt County, Nebr., TAM service. 1953.	15364
—— 1955.	15365
Butler County, Iowa, TAM service. 1952.	13140
—— 1954.	13142
—— 1956.	13144
Butler County, Nebr., TAM service. 1953.	15368
—— 1955.	15369
Calhoun County, Iowa, TAM service. 1951.	13153
—— 1953.	13155
—— 1955.	13156
Carroll County, Ill., TAM service. 1954.	12111
Carroll County, Iowa, TAM service. 1951.	13166
—— 1953.	13167
—— 1955.	13168
Cass County, Iowa, TAM service. 1951.	13181
—— 1953.	13182
—— 1955.	13183
Cass County, Nebr., TAM service. 1951.	15373
—— 1953.	15374
—— 1955.	15375
Cedar County, Iowa, TAM service. 1952.	13192
—— 1954.	13193
—— 1956.	13195
Cedar County, Nebr., TAM service. 1951.	15377
—— 1953.	15378
—— 1955.	15379
Cerro Gordo County, Iowa, TAM service. 1952.	13204
—— 1954.	13205
—— 1956.	13207
Cherokee County, Iowa. [1947]	13215
Cherokee County, Iowa, TAM service. 1951.	13216
—— 1953.	13218
—— 1955.	13219
Chickasaw County, Iowa, TAM service. 1952.	13226
—— 1954.	13228
—— 1956.	13230
Clarke County, Iowa, TAM service. 1951.	13236

—— 1953.	13237
—— 1955.	13238
Clay County, Iowa. [1947]	13245
Clay County, Iowa, TAM service. 1951.	13246
—— 1953.	13247
—— 1955.	13248
Clay County, Nebr., TAM service. 1951.	15385
—— 1953.	15386
—— 1955.	15387
Clayton County, Iowa, TAM service. 1952.	13257
—— 1954.	13258
—— 1956.	13260
Clinton County, Iowa, TAM service. 1952.	13270
—— 1954.	13271
—— 1956.	13273
Colfax County, Nebr., TAM service. 1951.	15390
—— 1953.	15391
—— 1955.	15392
Crawford County, Iowa, TAM service. 1951.	13282
—— 1953.	13283
—— 1955.	13284
Cuming County, Nebr., TAM service. 1951.	15395
—— 1953.	15396
—— 1955.	15397
Dakota County, Nebr., TAM service. 1951.	15402
—— 1953.	15403
—— 1955.	15404
Dallas County, Iowa, TAM service. 1951.	13295
—— 1953.	13296
—— 1955.	13297
Davis County, Iowa, TAM service. 1952.	13304
—— 1954.	13305
—— 1956.	13307
Dawson County, Nebr., TAM service. 1951.	15408
—— 1953.	15409
—— 1955.	15410
Decatur County, Iowa, TAM service. 1951.	13311
—— 1953.	13312
—— 1955.	13313
Delaware County, Iowa, TAM service. 1952.	13322
—— 1954.	13323
—— 1956.	13326
Des Moines County, Iowa, TAM service. 1952.	13332
—— 1954.	13333
—— 1956.	13335
Dickinson County, Iowa. [1947]	13343
Dickinson County, Iowa, TAM service. 1951.	13344
—— 1953.	13345
—— 1955.	13346
Dixon County, Nebr., TAM service. 1951.	15416
—— 1953.	15417
—— 1955.	15418
Dodge County, Nebr., TAM service. 1951.	15422
—— 1953.	15423
—— 1955.	15424
Douglas County, Nebr., TAM service. 1951.	15429
—— 1953.	15430
—— 1955.	15431
Dubuque County, Iowa, TAM service. 1952.	13354
—— 1954.	13355
—— 1956.	13357
Emmet County, Iowa, TAM service. 1951.	13364

—— 1953.	13365
—— 1955.	13366
Fayette County, Iowa, TAM service. 1952.	13378
—— 1954.	13379
—— 1956.	13381
Fillmore County, Nebr., TAM service. 1951.	15435
—— 1953.	15436
—— 1955.	15437
Floyd County, Iowa, TAM service. 1952.	13389
—— 1954.	13390
—— 1956.	13392
Franklin County, Iowa, TAM service. 1952.	13398
—— 1954.	13399
—— 1956.	13401
Fremont County, Iowa, TAM service. 1951.	13410
—— 1953.	13411
Fulton County, Ill., TAM service. 1954.	12246
Gage County, Nebr., TAM service. 1951.	15447
—— 1953.	15448
—— 1955.	15449
Greene County, Iowa, TAM service. 1951.	13420
—— 1953.	13421
—— 1955.	13422
Grundy County, Iowa, TAM service. 1952.	13430
—— 1954.	13431
—— 1956.	13433
Guthrie County, Iowa, TAM service. 1951.	13440
—— 1953.	13441
—— [1955]	13442
Hall County, Nebr., TAM service. 1951.	15459
—— 1953.	15460
—— 1955.	15461
Hamilton County, Iowa, TAM service. 1951.	13449
—— 1953.	13450
—— 1955.	13451
Hamilton County, Nebr., TAM service. 1951.	15465
—— 1953.	15466
—— 1955.	15467
Hancock County, Ill., TAM service. 1954.	12261
Hancock County, Iowa, TAM service. 1951.	13458
—— 1953.	13460
—— 1955.	13461
Hardin County, Iowa, TAM service. 1952.	13470
—— 1954.	13471
—— 1956.	13473
Harrison County, Iowa, TAM service. 1951.	13481
—— 1953.	13482
—— [1955]	13483
Henderson County, Ill., TAM service. 1954.	12269
Henry County, Ill., TAM service. 1954.	12273
Henry County, Iowa, TAM service. 1952.	13491
—— 1954.	13492
—— 1956.	13494
Howard County, Iowa, TAM service. 1952.	13502
—— 1954.	13503
—— 1956.	13505
Howard County, Nebr., TAM service. 1951.	15474
—— 1953.	15475
—— 1955.	15476
Humboldt County, Iowa, TAM service. 1951.	13511
—— 1953.	13512
—— 1955.	13513

Ida County, Iowa, TAM service. 1951.	13523
—— 1953.	13524
—— 1955.	13525
Iowa County, Iowa, TAM service. 1952.	13532
—— 1954.	13534
—— 1956.	13536
Jackson County, Iowa, TAM service. 1952.	13544
—— 1954.	13545
—— 1956.	13547
Jasper County, Iowa, TAM service. 1952.	13555
—— 1954.	13556
—— [1956]	13558
Jefferson County, Iowa, TAM service. 1952.	13564
—— 1954.	13565
—— 1956.	13567
Jefferson County, Nebr., TAM service. 1951.	15478
—— 1953.	15479
—— 1955.	15480
Jo Daviess County, Ill., TAM service. 1954.	12298
Johnson County, Iowa, TAM service. 1952.	13579
—— 1954.	13580
—— 1956.	13582
Johnson County, Nebr., TAM service. 1951.	15483
—— 1953.	15484
—— 1955.	15485
Jones County, Iowa, TAM service. 1952.	13593
—— 1954.	13594
—— 1956.	13596
Kearney County, Nebr., TAM service. 1953.	15488
—— 1955.	15489
Keokuk County, Iowa, TAM service. 1952.	13603
—— 1954.	13604
—— 1956.	13606
Knox County, Ill., TAM service. 1954.	12325
Kossuth County, Iowa, TAM service. 1951.	13615
—— 1953.	13616
—— 1955.	13617
Lancaster County, Nebr., TAM service. 1951.	15498
—— 1953.	15499
—— 1955.	15500
Lee County, Ill., TAM service. 1954.	12346
Lee County, Iowa, TAM service. 1952.	13624
—— 1954.	13625
—— 1956.	13627
Linn County, Iowa, TAM service. 1952.	13634
—— 1954.	13635
—— 1956.	13637
Louisa County, Iowa, TAM service. 1952.	13643
—— 1954.	13644
—— 1956.	13646
Lucas County, Iowa, TAM service. 1951.	13653
—— 1953.	13654
—— 1955.	13655
Lyon County, Iowa. [1947]	13662
Lyon County, Iowa, TAM service. 1951.	13664
—— 1953.	13665
—— 1955.	13666
McDonough County, Ill., TAM service. 1954.	12361
Madison County, Iowa, TAM service. 1951.	13676
—— 1953.	13678
—— 1955.	13679
Madison County, Nebr., TAM service. 1951.	15506

—— 1953.	15507
—— 1955.	15508
Mahaska County, Iowa, TAM service. 1952.	13688
—— 1954.	13689
—— [1956]	13691
Marion County, Iowa, TAM service. 1952.	13699
—— 1954.	13700
—— 1956.	13702
Marshall County, Ill., TAM service. 1954.	12396
Marshall County, Iowa, TAM service. 1952.	13711
—— 1954.	13712
—— 1956.	13714
Mercer County, Ill., TAM service. 1954.	12413
Merrick County, Nebr., TAM service. 1951.	15511
—— 1953.	15512
—— 1955.	15513
Mills County, Iowa, TAM service. 1951.	13724
—— 1953.	13725
—— 1955.	13726
Mitchell County, Iowa, TAM service. 1952.	13735
—— 1954.	13736
—— 1956.	13738
Monona County, Iowa. [1947]	13746
Monona County, Iowa, TAM service. 1951.	13747
—— 1953.	13748
—— 1955.	13749
Monroe County, Iowa, TAM service. 1952.	13760
—— 1954.	13762
—— 1956.	13764
Montgomery County, Iowa, TAM service. 1951.	13770
—— 1953.	13771
—— 1955.	13772
Muscatine County, Iowa, TAM service. 1952.	13779
—— 1954.	13780
—— 1956.	13782
Nemaha County, Nebr., TAM service. 1951.	15523
—— 1953.	15524
—— 1955.	15525
Nuckolls County, Nebr. [1967]	15532
Nuckolls County, Nebr., TAM service. 1951.	15528
—— 1953.	15529
—— 1955.	15530
O'Brien County, Iowa. [1947]	13791
O'Brien County, Iowa, TAM service. 1951.	13792
—— 1953.	13793
—— 1955.	13794
Ogle County, Ill., TAM service. 1954.	12436
Osceola County, Iowa. [1947]	13800
Osceola County, Iowa, TAM service. 1951.	13802
—— 1953.	13803
—— 1955.	13805
Otoe County, Nebr., TAM service. 1951.	15535
—— 1953.	15536
—— 1955.	15537
Page County, Iowa, TAM service. 1951.	13815
—— 1953.	13816
—— [1955]	13817
Palo Alto County, Iowa, TAM service. 1951.	13825
—— 1953.	13826
—— 1955.	13827
Pawnee County, Nebr., TAM service. 1951.	15540

—— 1953.	15541
—— 1955.	15542
Peoria County, Ill., TAM service. 1954.	12442
Pierce County, Nebr., TAM service. 1951.	15549
—— 1953.	15550
—— 1955.	15551
Plat book of Knox County, Nebr. 1957.	15494
—— [1963]	15495
Platte County, Nebr., TAM service. 1953.	15554
—— 1955.	15555
Plymouth County, Iowa, TAM service. 1951.	13835
—— 1953.	13836
—— 1955.	13837
Pocahontas County, Iowa. [1947]	13845
Pocahontas County, Iowa, TAM service. 1951.	13846
—— 1953.	13847
—— 1955.	13848
Polk County, Iowa, TAM service. 1951.	13856
—— 1953.	13857
—— 1955.	13859
Polk County, Nebr., TAM service. 1951.	15557
—— 1953.	15558
—— 1955.	15559
Pottawattamie County, Iowa, TAM service. 1951.	13869
—— 1953.	13870
—— 1955.	13871
Poweshiek County, Iowa, TAM service. 1952.	13882
—— 1954.	13883
—— 1956.	13885
Putnam County, Ill., TAM service. 1954.	12467
Richardson County, Nebr., TAM service. 1951.	15566
—— 1953.	15567
—— 1955.	15568
Ringgold County, Iowa, TAM service. 1951.	13892
—— 1953.	13893
—— 1955.	13894
Rock Island County, Ill., TAM service. 1954.	12479
Rural directory, Adair County, Iowa. 1947.	13019
Rural directory, Adams County, Iowa. 1947.	13031
Rural directory, Audubon County, Iowa. 1947.	13063
Rural directory, Boone County, Iowa. 1947.	13095
Rural directory, Calhoun County, Iowa. 1947.	13152
Rural directory, Carroll County, Iowa. 1947.	13165
Rural directory, Cass County, Iowa. 1947.	13179
Rural directory, Dallas County, Iowa. [1947]	13294
Rural directory, Fremont County, Iowa. 1947.	13409
Rural directory, Greene County, Iowa. 1947.	13419
Rural directory, Guthrie County, Iowa. 1947.	13439
Rural directory, Ida County, Iowa. [1947]	13522
Rural directory, Madison County, Iowa. [1947]	13675
Rural directory, Mills County, Iowa. [1947]	13723
Rural directory of Shelby County [Iowa. 1946]	13927
Rural directory, Page County, Iowa. [1947]	13814

Rural directory, Sac County, Iowa. [1947] 13900
Rural directory, Taylor County, Iowa. [1947] 13973
Rural directory, Union County, Iowa. [1947] 13983
Rural directory, Webster County, Iowa.
  [1947] 14048
Sac County, Iowa, TAM service. 1951. 13901
—— 1953. 13902
—— 1955. 13903
Saline County, Nebr., TAM service. 1951. 15571
—— 1953. 15572
—— 1955. 15573
Sarpy County, Nebr., TAM service. 1951. 15576
—— 1953. 15577
—— 1955. 15578
Saunders County, Nebr., TAM service.
  1951. 15581
—— 1953. 15582
—— 1955. 15583
Schuyler County, Ill., TAM service. 1954. 12497
Scott County, Iowa, TAM service. 1952. 13912
—— 1954. 13914
—— [1956] 13916
Seward County, Nebr., TAM service. 1951. 15590
—— 1953. 15591
—— 1955. 15592
Shelby County, Iowa, TAM service. 1951. 13928
—— 1953. 13929
—— [1955] 13930
Sioux County, Iowa. [1947] 13941
Sioux County, Iowa, TAM service. 1951. 13942
—— 1953. 13943
—— 1955. 13944
Stanton County, Nebr., TAM service. 1951. 15597
—— 1953. 15598
—— 1955. 15599
Stark County, Ill., TAM service. 1954. 12508
Story County, Iowa, TAM service. 1952. 13953
—— 1954. 13954
—— 1956. 13956
Tama County, Iowa, TAM service. 1952. 13963
—— 1954. 13964
—— 1956. 13966
Taylor County, Iowa, TAM service. 1951. 13974
—— 1953. 13975
—— 1955. 13976
Tazewell County, Ill., TAM service. 1954. 12516
Thayer County, Nebr., TAM service. 1951. 15601
—— 1953. 15602
—— 1955. 15603
Thurston County, Nebr., TAM service.
  1951. 15608
—— 1953. 15609
—— 1955. 15610
Union County, Iowa, TAM service. 1951. 13984
—— 1953. 13985
—— 1955. 13986
Van Buren County, Iowa, TAM service.
  1952. 13992
—— 1954. 13993
—— 1956. 13995
Wapello County, Iowa, TAM service. 1952. 14004
—— 1954. 14005
—— 1956. 14007
Warren County, Ill., TAM service. 1954. 12535

Warren County, Iowa, TAM service. 1952. 14018
—— 1954. 14019
—— 1956. 14021
Washington County, Iowa, TAM service.
  1952. 14027
—— 1954. 14028
—— 1956. 14030
Washington County, Nebr., TAM service.
  1951. 15615
—— 1953. 15616
—— 1955. 15617
Wayne County, Iowa, TAM service. 1951. 14038
—— 1953. 14039
—— 1955. 14040
Wayne County, Nebr., TAM service. 1951. 15621
—— 1953. 15622
—— 1955. 15623
Webster County, Iowa, TAM service. 1951. 14049
—— 1953. 14050
—— 1955. 14051
Webster County, Nebr., TAM service. 1951. 15625
—— 1953. 15626
—— 1955. 15627
Whiteside County, Ill., TAM service. 1954. 12551
Winnebago County, Iowa, TAM service.
  1951. 14057
—— 1953. 14060
—— 1955. 14061
Winneshiek County, Iowa, TAM service.
  1952. 14070
—— 1954. 14071
—— 1956? 14073
Woodbury County, Iowa, TAM service.
  1951. 14080
—— 1953. 14081
—— 1955. 14082
Woodford County, Ill., TAM service. 1954. 12578
Worth County, Iowa, TAM service. 1952. 14088
—— 1954. 14089
—— 1956. 14091
Wright County, Iowa, TAM service. 1951. 14099
—— 1953. 14100
—— 1955. 14101
York County, Nebr., TAM service. 1951. 15632
—— 1953. 15633
—— 1955. 15634

Bootsma, Cartografisch Instituut.
  See Cartografisch Instituut Bootsma.

Borchert, John R., 1918–
  Reconnaissance atlas of Minnesota agriculture. 1958. 14906

Bordón, F. Arturo.
  See Jaeggli, Alfredo L., *and* Bordón, F. Arturo.

Bordone, Benedetto, 1460–1531.
  Isolario. 1534. 163
  —— 1547. 164
  —— [1560?] 165
  Libro. 1528. 162

Borel, Maurice.
    Atlas cantonal, politique et économique de la
      Suisse. [1913]   9450
    Politisch-Wirtschaftlicher Atlas der Schweiz
      nach Kantonen. [1913]   9451

Borghi, Bartolommeo, 1750–1821.
    Atlante generale. 1819.   735

Bory de St. Vincent, Jean Baptiste Geneviève Mar-
cellin, *Baron*, 1778–1846.
    See Desmarest, Nicolas, 1725–1815, *and* Bory
    de St. Vincent, Jean Baptiste Geneviève
    Marcellin, *Baron*, 1778–1846.

Bos, Pieter Roelof, 1847–1902.
    Atlas voor de volksschool. 23. druk. [1908]   3361
    Schoolatlas der geheele aarde. 16. druk.
      1904.   268

Bos, Pieter Roelof, *and* Balen, C. L. van. *d.* 1943.
    Atlas der geheele aarde. 4. druk. [1924]   6546
    Kleine schoolatlas der gehele aarde. 42.
      druk. 1948.   7293

Bos, Pieter Roelof, *and* Niermeyer, Jan Frederik,
1866–1923.
    Schoolatlas der geheele aarde. 31. druk.
      1927.   6644
    —— 32. druk. 1929.   6698
    —— 34. druk. 1934.   6808
    —— 35. druk. 1936.   6868
    —— 36. druk. 1939.   6972
    —— 37. druk. 1947.   7258
    —— 38. druk. 1951.   7445

Bos, R.
    Atlas der geheele aarde. 23. druk. 1926.   6604
    —— 24. druk. 1928.   6671
    —— 28. druk. 1940.   7005
    —— 30. druk. 1950.   7385
    Schoolatlas van Nederland. 14. druk.
      1925.   9089
    —— 17. druk. 1949.   9092

Bos, R., *and* Zeeman, K.
    Atlas seluruh dunia, untuk sekolah landjutan.
      Tjetakan 2. 1954.   7590
    Economische atlas der geheele aarde. 2.
      druk. 1924.   5430

Bosch, Johannes, *Graaf* van den, 1780–1844.
    Atlas der overzeesche bezittingen van zyne
      majesteit den koning der Nederlanden.
      1818.   3072

Bosch, *firm*.
    Atlas elemental de España, geográfico y
      estadístico. [1950]   9338
    Mapa de España. [1953]   9340

Boschini, Marco, 1613–1678.
    Regno tvtto di Candia delineatio à parte.
      1651.   3160, 8902

Bosman, H. W.
    Atlas van de Nederlandsche bezittingen in
      Oost-Indië. [1908]   9740

Bossi, Luigi, 1758–1835.
    Nuovo atlante universale. 1824.   743

Boston. *Board of Aldermen*.
    City of Boston voting precincts. 1896.   14426

Boston. *City Surveyor*.
    City of Boston voting precincts. [1886]   14423
    —— [1890]   14425

Bostwick, Henry, 1787–1836?
    Historical and classical atlas. 1828.   3306

Botero, Giovanni, 1540–1617.
    Mvndvs imperiorvm. 1602.   3405
    Theatrum, oder Schawspiegel. 1596.   3402

Bottiglioni, Gino, 1887–
    Atlante linguistico etnografico italiano della
      Corsica. 1933–42.   8419

Bottin.
    Atlas du Bottin. [1943]   8475
    —— [1947]   8478
    —— 1950.   8479
    —— 1951.   8480

Bouché-Leclercq, Auguste, 1842–1923.
    Atlas pour servir à l'histoire grecque de E.
      Curtius. 1888.   8896

Boucher, André, 1879–
    Petit atlas des missions catholiques. 2e éd.
      1933.   5401

Boudinot, E. S.
    Atlas of Vermilion County, Ill. 1907.   1573

Bougainville, Hyacinthe Yves Philippe Potentien,
**** *Baron* **de, 1781–1846.**
    Journal de la navigation autour du globe.
      Atlas. 1837.   204, 3243

Bougard, R.
    Little sea torch. 1801.   2852
    Petit flambeau de la mer. 4. éd. 1709.   5163
    —— 1752.   2841
    —— 1763.   7649

Bouguereau, Maurice, *fl.* 1588–1596.
    Theatre Francois. 1594.   8451

Bouillet, Marie Nicolas, 1798–1864.
    Atlas universel. 1865.   5497
    —— 3. éd. 1877.   101, 882

Bourdon, Jean, 1602–1668.
    Plans of the first French settlements on the
      Saint Lawrence, 1635–1642. 1958.   10429

Bourgoing, Jean François, *Baron* de, 1750–1811.
Atlas pour servir au tableau de l'Espagne
    moderne. 1807.   3134

Bousquet, J. G.
See Gruner, Édouard, 1849–   *and* Bous-
    quet, J. G.

Boussard, Jacques.
Atlas historique et culturel de la France.
    [1957]   8404

Boutruche, A.
Atlas chronologique et synchronique d'his-
    toire universelle. 1837.   5498

Bowen, B. F., and Company.
Automobile and sportsmen's guide for In-
    diana. 1917.   12728
Automobile and sportsmen's guide for Michi-
    gan. [1916]   14577
Indiana State atlas. 1917.   4605
Michigan State atlas. 1916.   4731

Bowen, Emanuel, *d.* 1767, *and* Bowen, Thomas.
Atlas anglicanus. [1777?]   2919
Complete atlas. 1752.   614

Bowen, Emanuel, *and others*.
Large English atlas. 1767–[96]   4004
—— [1777?]   8120
Royal English atlas. [1778]   2920, 2921

Bowen, Emily, *and* Lobaugh, Doris.
Rural ownership atlas of Washington County
    [Kans.] 1957.   14207

Bower, Robert A.
New handy atlas of the United States and
    Canada. 1884.   1415
New handy family atlas of the United States
    and Canada. 1885.   1421

Bowles Carington, 1724–1793.
New medium English atlas. 1785.   8121
Post-chaise companion. 1782.   2904

Bowles's Universal atlas. [1775–80]   5988

Bowman, Samuel W.
Atlas of Norfolk, Portsmouth, and Berkley,
    Va. 1900.   2616, 2618, 2620

Boy Scouts of America.
Road atlas and guide to overnight camping.
    1964.   10747

Boyer, Abel, 1667–1729.
Draughts of the most remarkable fortified
    towns of Europe. 1701.   5166

BP Benzin- und Petroleum-Gesellschaft.
Dieselatlas Deutschland. [195–]   8623

Braakman, Adriaan, 1664–1720.
Atlas minor. 1706.   3466

Bracey, Hugh Laurence, 1893–
Block maps of the city of Austin [Tex.] 1957.   17195
Block maps of the city of Corpus Christi and
    vicinity [Tex.] 1951.   17202
—— 2d ed. 1956.   17203
—— 3d ed. 1961.   17205
—— 4th ed. 1965.   17207
Block maps of the city of Dallas. 1st ed. 1935. 17213
—— 3d ed. 1942.   17214
—— 4th ed. 1949.   17216
—— 5th ed. 1954.   17219
—— 6th ed. 1958.   17225
Block maps of the city of Houston [Tex.]
    1919.   17248
—— 6th ed. 1929.   17250
—— 1942.   17253
—— 1946.   17255
—— 1950.   17256
—— 1953.   17257
Block maps of the north half of San Antonio,
    Tex. 1962.   17280
Houston [Tex.] sectional map. [1939] 17252
Plat book of Harris County, Tex. 1944. 17172
Plat book of the county of Dallas [Tex.]
    1959.   17157
—— 1964.   17159
—— 1967.   17161

Bradford, Thomas Gamaliel, 1802–1887.
Atlas designed to illustrate the abridgment of
    Universal geography. 1835.   769
Comprehensive atlas. 1835.   770
Illustrated atlas. [1838]   1381, 11028

Bradford, Thomas Gamaliel, *and* Goodrich, Samuel
Griswold, 1793–1860.
Universal illustrated atlas. 1842.   783

Bradford, Tom.
Soils map of Yolo County, Calif. 1960.   11504

Bradley, William M., and Brother.
Atlas of the world. 1885.   923
—— 1893.   980

Bradley, William M., and Company.
Atlas of the world. 1886.   6227, 6228
—— 1889.   6244
—— 1896.   6275

Bradshaw, George, 1801–1853.
Plans of the most important cities and towns
    of continental Europe. [1872]   7637
—— 1905.   7638
—— 1906.   7639
Plans of towns to accompany ... Continental
    railway guide. [1860?]   7636
Plans of towns to accompany ... General
    handbook. [185–?]   7635
Railway companion ... Great Britain and Ire-
    land. 1844.   8088

Railway time tables ... with illustrative maps
& plans. 1839.　　　　　　　　　　　8087

Bradstreet Company.
Pocket atlas for the use of commercial trave-
lers. 1878.　　　　　　　　　　　1400
Pocket atlas of the United States. 1880.　11039

Bramsen, Bo.
Gamle Danmarkskort; en historisk oversigt.
1952.　　　　　　　　　　　　　8262

Branch, Ernest W.
Atlas of the city of Quincy ... Mass. 1907.　1926
—— 1923-[31]　　　　　　　　　14514

Brandis, Gerrit Brender a', 1751–1802.
Nieuwe natuurgeschieden handelkundige
zak-en reis-atlas. [1787?]　　　　　660

Braun, Franz, 1884– *and* Ziegfeld, Arnold Hil-
len, 1894–
Geopolitischer Atlas zur Deutschen
Geschichte. 1934.　　　　　　　8558
Geopolitischer Geschichtsatlas. 1930.　5499
—— 2. Aufl. 1934.　　　　　　　5500

Braun, Georg, 1541–1622.
Civitates orbis terrarvm. [1612–18]　59, 3292
Théâtre des cites dv monde. [1564–1620]　4105

Braun, Georg, *and* Hogenberg, Franz, *d.* 1590?
Alte Europäische Städte-Bilder. [1954]　7640
Old European cities. [1955]　　　7641
Old German cities. [1938]　　　8527

Bravo, Francisco Javier.
Atlas de cartas géográficas de los países de la
América Meridional. 1872.　　　2723

Brazil.
Maps of the 22 states of Brazil. [194–?]　18288
Statement submitted by the United States of
Brazil to the President of the United States
of America as arbitrator ... between Brazil
and the Argentine Republic. 1894.　18272

Brazil. *Commissão de Exploração do Rio Araguay.*
Commission brésilienne d'exploration du
haut Araguay. 1896. [1899]　　5143

Brazil. *Commissão Hydrographica.*
Primeiros traços geraes de carta particular
do Rio Amazonas no curso Brazileiro.
[1866?]　　　　　　　　　　5130

Brazil. *Conselho Nacional de Geografía.*
Atlas climatológico do Brasil. 1955–56.　18273
Atlas nacional do Brasil. 1966.　　18297
Carta do Brasil ao milionésimo. 1960.　18293

Brazil. *Conselho Nacional de Geografía. Divisão de
Geografía.*
Atlas do Brasil (geral e regional). 1959.
　　　　　　　　　　　18290–18292
—— 1960.　　　　　　　　　　18294

Brazil. *Departamento Nacional da Produção Mineral. Divisão de Geologia e Mineralogia.*
Atlas geológico do Brasil. 1939.　18281

Brazil. *Departamento Nacional de Estradas de
Rodagem.*
Roteiro da Br. [196–]　　　　18286
Roteiro rodoviário do estado de Alagôas.
1951.　　　　　　　　　　18300
Roteiro rodoviário do estado do Ceará.
1951.　　　　　　　　　　18304

Brazil. *Departamento Nacional de Obras contra as
Sêcas.*
Atlas pluviometrico do nordéste do Brasil.
1923–24.　　　　　　　　　18274

Brazil. *Departamento Nacional do Café.*
Atlas corográfico da cultura cafeeira.
[1941–43]　　　　　　　　18267

Brazil. *Diretoria de Hidrografía e Navegação.*
Cartas de correntes de maré, pôrto de Madre
de Deus. 1963.　　　　　　18315
Miniaturas de cartas náuticas. [1924–59]　18277

Brazil. *Divisão de Aguas.*
Atlas pluviométrico de Brasil (1914–1938)
1948.　　　　　　　　　　18275

Brazil. *Inspectoria Federal de Portos, Rios e Canaes.*
Portos do Brasil. Atlas. 1923.　18282

Brazil. *Ministerio da Agricultura.*
Atlas económico de Minas Gerais. 1938.　18308
Descripção topographica do mappa da Pro-
vincia de Santa Catharina. 1873.　2752
Inspectoria geral das terras e colonisação.
Mappa topographico da Provincia do
Esperito Santo. 1878.　　　2750
Mappa topographico da Provincia do Paraná.
1877.　　　　　　　　　　2751

Brazil. *Ministerio da Agricultura. Serviço de
Informações.*
[Atlas do Brazil. 1908]　　　5140

Brazil. *Ministerio de Educação e Cultura.*
Atlas histórico e geográfico brasileiro. [1962]　18283
—— [1966]　　　　　　　　18284

Brazil. *Servico Nacional de Recenseamento.*
Atlas censitário industrial do Brasil. [1965]　18278

Brazil. *Treaties, etc., 1894–1898 (Moraes Barros)*
[Frontières du Brésil et de la Guyane Anglaise.
Atlas. 1903]　　　　　2721, 2740

Frontières entre le Brésil et la Guyane
Française. Atlas. 1899. 2720, 2741
—— 1899–1900. 2719, 2739

Breasted, James Henry, 1865–1935, *and* **Huth, Carl Frederick, 1883–**
Ancient history atlas. [1920] 5595

Breasted, James Henry, *and others.*
Ancient and European history atlas. [1916–
20] 7666
Ancient, European and American history
atlas. [1924] 5594
Atlas de historia Europea. [1946] 7669
European history atlas. 3d rev. ed. [1929] 7667
—— [5th rev. ed. 1937] 7668
—— 7th rev. ed. 1947. 7670
—— 9th rev. ed. 1951. 7671
—— [10th rev. ed. 1954] 7673
—— Student ed. [1st ed. 1951] 7672

Breese, Samuel, 1802–1873.
See Morse, Sidney Edwards, 1794–1871, *and*
Breese, Samuel, 1802–1873.

Bremond, Laurent.
See Michelot, Henri, *and* Bremond, Laurent.

Brenier, Henri, 1867–
Essai d'atlas statistique de la XIe région
économique. 1927. 8396

Brennan, John Edward, 1880–1942.
Urban markets and retail sales. [1938] 10534

Brentano's Record atlas of the World War. 1918. 4224

Breou, Forsey.
See Wolverton, Chester, *and* Breou, Forsey.

Breou, Forsey, and Company.
Property and insurance atlas of the City of
Reading ... Pa. 1884. 2554

Bretschneider, Carl Anton, 1808–1878.
Historisch-geographischer Wand-Atlas nach
Karl von Sprunner. 1856. 102, 2786a
See also Spruner von Merz, Karl, *and* Bret-
schneider, Carl Anton.

Bretschneider, Emilii Vasil'evich, 1833–1901.
Map of China. 1898. 3192
—— 1900. 3193

Brette, Armand, 1848–1912.
Recueil de documents relatifs à la convocation
des états généraux en 1789. 1904. 2956

Breuning, Verlag Arbeitsgemeinschaft.
See Verlag Arbeitsgemeinschaft Breuning.

Brewer, James McMillen, 1903–
Commercial and residential Philadelphia.
[1934] 16873

Brewster Mapping Service.
1960 census tracts ... for Los Angeles County
and Orange County [Calif.] 1960. 11413
Plat book of the Palos Verdes Peninsula
[Calif.] 1958. 11618

Bridgens, H. F.
Atlas of Lancaster County, Pa. 1864. 5017

Bridgens, H. F., Witmer, A. R., *and others.*
Atlas of Chester County, Pa. 1873. 2468

Bridwell, W. E., Map and Engineering Company.
Street guide with sectional maps of Greater
Los Angeles. [194–] 11539

Brief, relating to the central Florida cross state highway. [1941] 11795

Brigham, John C., *and* **Morse, Sidney Edwards, 1794–1871.**
Nuevo sistema de geografía. 1827–28. 4316

Brigham, William Tufts, 1841–1926.
Index to the islands of the Pacific Ocean.
1900. 3248

Brink, H. ten.
Nieuwe zak-atlasje van Nederland. 2le
druk. [1931?] 9059
—— 27e druk. [194–?] 9062
—— 32e druk. [1947] 9064
—— 34e druk. [1949] 9067
—— 35e druk. [1954] 9071
Reisatlas van Nederland. [14. druk. 192–] 9054
—— [24. druk. 193–] 9056
—— 32ste druk. [1947] 9065
—— 34ste druk. [1948] 9066
—— 35ste druk. [1954] 9072

Brink, McCormick and Company.
Illustrated atlas map of Sangamon County,
Ill. 1874. 12490
Illustrated encyclopedia and atlas map of
Madison County, Ill. 1873. 12384

Brink, McDonough and Company.
Illustrated historical atlas map of Carroll
County, Mo. 1876. 2072
Illustrated historical atlas map of Jefferson
County, Mo. 1876. 15234

Brink, W. R., and Company.
Illustrated atlas map of Iroquois County, Ill.
1884. 4571
Illustrated atlas map of Mason County, Ill.
1874. 12399
Illustrated atlas map of Menard County, Ill.
1874. 12406
Illustrated atlas map of St. Charles County,
Mo. 1875. 15245
Illustrated historical atlas map of Douglas
County, Ill. 1875. 12191

Illustrated historical atlas map of Vermilion
County, Ill. 1875.   12523

Brion de la Tour, Louis, *fl.* 1756–1823.
Atlas ecclésiastique. 1766.   80
Atlas, et tables élémentaires. 1777.   5989
Atlas général. 1766.   3509
—— 1767.   640
—— 3. ed. 1790–[98]   5999
Atlas itinéraire, portatif, de l'Europe, adapté,
quant à la France. 1776–[77]   8427
Coup d'oeil général sur la France. 1765.   2990

Brion de la Tour, Louis, *fils.*
[Cartes des departements de la France.
1789?]   8457

Briscoe, John D'Auby, *and others.*
Mapbook of English literature. [1936]   8020

British Columbia Natural Resources Conference.
British Columbia atlas of resources. 1956.   10383

British Honduras. *Lands and Survey Dept.*
Atlas of British Honduras. 1939.   18123

Britton, Robert Leevern, 1907–
See Clagg, Sam Edward, 1920–   *and*
Britton, Robert Leevern, 1907–

Broadhead, Garland Carr, 1827–1912.
See Missouri. *Geological Survey.*

Broadway Subway Advertising Company.
Guide to the world's greatest market, New
York City and suburbs. [1925]   16021

Brock and Company.
Standard atlas of Barnes County, N.Dak.
1928.   16255
Standard atlas of Bottineau County, N.Dak.
1929.   16261
Standard atlas of Champaign County, Ill.
1929.   12117
Standard atlas of Crawford County, Wis.
1930.   17700
Standard atlas of Grand Forks County,
N.Dak. 1927.   16282
Standard atlas of Grant County, S.Dak.
1929.   17031
Standard atlas of Kingsbury County, S.Dak.
1929.   17038
Standard atlas of Marshall County, Minn.
1928.   15032
Standard atlas of Marshall County, S.Dak.
1929.   17045
Standard atlas of Miami County, Kans.
1927.   14186
Standard atlas of Nelson County, N.Dak.
1928.   16300
Standard atlas of Norman County, Minn.
1927.   15063
Standard atlas of Piatt County, Ill. 1927.   12452

Standard atlas of Ramsey County, N.Dak.
1928.   16309
Standard atlas of Rawlins County, Kans.
1928.   14194
Standard atlas of St. Joseph County, Mich.
1930.   14805
Standard atlas of Sargent County, N.Dak.
1930.   16323
Standard atlas of Steele County, N.Dak.
1928.   16329
Standard atlas of Stutsman County, N.Dak.
1930.   16332
Standard atlas of Thomas County, Kans.
1928.   14205
Standard atlas of Towner County, N.Dak.
1928.   16335
Standard atlas of Traill County, N.Dak.
1927.   16339
Standard atlas of Walsh County, N.Dak.
1928.   16340
Standard atlas of Wood County, Wis. 1928.   17991

Brockhaus, *firm.*
Brockhaus Atlas. 1937.   6903
Grossdeutschland in Bild und Karte. 1939.   8700

Brockhaus' Reise-Atlas. 1857.   8685

Broekman, Gerardo van M.
Lago del Yeso … Atlas. [1912]   5148

Bromley, G. W., and Company.
Atlas of the borough of Manhattan, city of
New York. 1916.   4950
Atlas of the city of New York, borough of
Manhattan. 1930.   16034
—— 1957–60.   16095
Atlas of the city of New York, borough of the
Bronx. 1938–42.   16116
Atlas of the entire city of Brooklyn, N.Y.
1880.   2274
Atlas of the entire city of New York. 1879.
                                                        4942, 15989
Atlas of the 19th & 22nd wards, city of New
York. 1880.   2298
Atlas of the 23rd ward, city of New York.
1882.   4943
Atlas of Westchester County, N.Y. 1881.   15917
—— 1915.   4934
Bronx land book … of the city of New York.
1960–65.   16117
Manhattan land book. City of New York.
1934.   16041
—— 1955.   16089

Bromley, George Washington, *and* Bromley, Walter Scott.
Atlas of Baltimore County, Md. 1898.   1785
—— 1915.   4709
Atlas of Bergen County, N.J. 1912–13.   15682
Atlas of Boston. 1888.   1860
Atlas of properties on mainline, Pennsylvania
R.R. from Overbrook to Paoli. 1926.   16894

Atlas of the city of Baltimore, Md.   1896.   1797
—— 1906.   1798
Atlas of the city of Boston.   6 v.   1883–85.
                                    1859, 4716, 14421
Atlas of the city of Boston.   4 v.   1888–90.
                                           1860, 14424
Atlas of the city of Boston.   v. 5 (Dorches-
   ter).   1898.   14428
Atlas of the city of Boston, Boston proper and
   Back Bay.   1908.   1861a
—— 1912.   4719
Atlas of the city of Boston, city proper and
   Roxbury.   1890.   4717
Atlas of the city of Boston, Roxbury.   1899.   14429
Atlas of the city of Chelsea and the towns of
   Revere and Winthrop [Mass.]   1886.
                                        4721, 4724, 4726
Atlas of the city of New York, borough of
   Manhattan.   1908.   15998
—— 1913.   3852a
—— 1913–15.   4947
Atlas of the city of New York, borough of
   Richmond.   1917.   4953
Atlas of the city of New York, borough of the
   Bronx.   1900.   16113
—— 1911–13.   3852, 16115
Atlas of the city of New York, Manhattan
   Island.   1891.   2309
Atlas of the city of New York, 23rd & 24th
   wards.   1893.   16112
Atlas of the city of Newton, Mass.   1895.   14505
Atlas of the city of Philadelphia.   1885–94.
                                    2536, 5027, 16855
—— 2d ed.   1894.   16858
—— 1895.   16859
—— 1901.   16860
—— 23rd & 35th wards.   1894.   5032
Atlas of the town of Brookline ... Mass.
   1888.   14445
—— 1900.   14446
—— 1907.   14447
—— 1913.   14448
Atlas of Westchester County, N.Y.   1901.   2263
—— 1911.   3843
Owners names of the city of New York, bor-
   ough of Manhattan.   1910.   3848

Bromley, Walter Scott.
   See Bromley, George Washington, *and* Bromley, Walter Scott.

Bromme, Traugott, 1802–1866.
   Atlas zu Alex. v. Humboldt's Kosmos.
   [1851–53]   218
   Illustrirter Hand-Atlas.   1862.   3557

Brookline, *Mass.*
   Town of Brookline, Mass., assessors' plans.
   1937.   14451

Brooks, Charles Franklin, 1891–1958, *and others*.
   Climatic maps of North America.   1936.   10282

Broome County, *N.Y.*
   Assessment map, town of Vestal, Broome
   County, N.Y.   [1937]   15871
   Town of Barker, Broome County, N.Y.
   1941.   15858
   Town of Binghamton, Broome County, N.Y.
   [1938]   15859
   Town of Chenango, Broome County, N.Y.
   1940.   15860
   Town of Colesville, Broome County, N.Y.
   [1940]   15861
   Town of Conklin, Broome County, N.Y.
   [1938]   15862
   Town of Dickinson, Broome County, N.Y.
   [1938]   15863
   Town of Fenton, Broome County, N.Y.
   [1938]   15864
   Town of Kirkwood, Broome County, N.Y.
   [1938]   15865
   Town of Lisle, Broome County, N.Y.   1941.   15866
   Town of Maine, Broome County, N.Y.   1941.   15867
   Town of Nanticoke, Broome County, N.Y.
   1941.   15868
   Town of Sanford, Broome County, N.Y.
   [1939]   15869
   Town of Triangle, Broome County, N.Y.
   1941.   15870
   Town of Windsor, Broome County, N.Y.
   [1939]   15872

Brothers of the Christian Schools.
   Atlas de Chile.   [194–]   18335

Brouckner, Isaac, 1686–1762.
   Erste Preussische Seeatlas.   1749.   [Reprint]
   1912.   4146
   Nieuwe atlas, of, Zee en weereld beschryving.
   1759.   5686
   Nouvel atlas.   1749.   612

Brown, Ernest Francis, 1903–
   War in maps.   1942.   5858
   —— [2d ed.]   1943.   5859
   —— [3d ed.]   1944.   5860
   —— [4th ed.]   1946.   5861

Brown, H. O., and Company.
   Illustrated atlas of Racine and Kenosha
   Counties, Wis.   1887.   17889

Brown, Martha Walker.
   Bartlesville, Okla.   1947.   16622

Brown, Mary Ross.
   Illustrated genealogy of the counties of Maryland and the District of Columbia.   [1967]   14336

Brown, Milton R.
   Continental atlas.   1889.   949, 1428

Brown, Richard H.
   RiKon Texas Panhandle atlas.   1957.   17145

Brown, Robert Harold, 1921– *and* **Tideman,**
Philip L., 1926–
Atlas of Minnesota occupancy. 1961.   14908
—— Rev. ed. 1966.   14909

Brown, Thomas.
General atlas. 1801.   6019

Brown, W. S., *and* **Foote, Charles M., 1848–1899.**
See Foote, Charles M., 1848–1899, *and*
Brown, W. S.

Brown, William Ernest, *and* **Coysh, Arthur Wilfred.**
Map approach to modern history, 1789–1914.
[1935]   5658

Brown and Bigelow.
Automobile Travl-map road atlas. [1950]   10879
Travl-map road atlas. [1951]   10881

Brown County, Wis. Board of Supervisors.
Plat book of Brown County, Wis. [1936]   17668

Brown-Scoville Publishing Company.
Plat book of Cass County, Nebr. 1905.   15371

Browne, C. H.
Atlas adapted for the eighth, Seventh …
grammar grades. 1883.   270
Butler's atlas. 1883.   269

Browne, Lewis, 1897–
Graphic Bible. 1928.   5343
—— 1932.   5344

Brózik, Károly, 1849–1911.
Nagy magyar atlasz. 1906.   6321
See also Erödi, Bela, 1846–1936, Berecz,
Antal, 1836–1905, *and* Brózik, Károly,
1849–1911.

Brué, Adrien Hubert, 1786–1832.
Atlas. [1826]   3546
Atlas classique de géographie. 2. éd. 1830–
[32]   6
Atlas géographique, historique, politique et
administratif de la France. 1820–[28]   8405
Atlas universel. 2. éd.   1830–[34]   758
—— 2. éd.   1838–[39]   4321
Grand atlas universel. 1816.   726

Brückner, Isaak, 1686–1762.
See Brouckner, Isaac, 1686–1762.

Brüning, Kurt, 1897–1961.
Atlas Niedersachsen. [1934]   8795
—— 1950.   8796

Brüning, Kurt, *and others.*
Karte der nutzbaren Lagerstätten und Ges-
teine Niedersachsens. 1952.   8791
Kreisraumordnungsplan für den Kreis Grafschaft Diepholz (Provinz Hannover). 1944.   8743

Bruhns, Karl Christian, 1830–1881.
See Kiepert, Heinrich, 1818–1899, Gräf, Carl,
Gräf, A., *and* Bruhns, Karl Christian,
1830–1881.

Brunamonti, G.
See Gibelli, Giuseppe, 1831–1898, Brunamonti,
G., *and* Danesi, C.

Brunclík, Josef, 1850–1929.
Atlas zeměpisný pro školy měšťanské. 6.
vydání. [1930]   6721
Zeměpisný atlas pro školy střední. 7. vydání.
1938.   6940

Brunel, Georges, 1861–
Atlas universel de géographie.   [1936]   6869

Brunner, Anton, *and* **Voigt, L.**
Deutscher   Handelsschul-Atlas.   3.   Aufl.
[1913]   4189
—— 4. Aufl.   [1920]   6407

Brunswick (City). Handelskammer.
Industrieatlas vom Verwaltungsbezirk Braunschweig. 1949.   8740

Brush, Charles B.
Insurance maps of Hudson County, N.J.
1885–87.   15707

Brussels. Institut Royal Colonial Belge.
See   Academie   Royale   des   Sciences
d'Outre-mer.

Brust, G.
See Pohle, Robert *and* Brust, G.

Bryan, Edwin Horace, 1898–
Pacific war atlas. [1942]   10188
—— [3d rev. ed. 1943]   10189
—— [4th rev. ed. 1944]   10190
Sectional map of Honolulu and rural Oahu.
1950.   11990
—— [1957]   11993
Sectional maps of Honolulu and the Hawaiian
Islands. 1959.   11994
—— 1960.   11995
—— 1961.   11996
—— 1964.   11998

Bryant Literary Union.
Panorama of the Hudson. 1888.   3838

Bryce, James, 1806–1877, Collier, William Francis,
and **Schmitz, Leonard, 1807–1890.**
Comprehensive atlas. [1882]   6209
International atlas. [1880?]   891
Library atlas. [1876]   6193
—— [188–]   6204

Buache, Philippe, 1700–1773.
Considérations géographiques et phisiques
sur les nouvelles découvertes au nord-est de

l'Asie et au nord-ouest de l'Amérique.
1781.   10252

Considérations géographiques ... sur les
nouvelles découvertes au nord de la Grande
Mer. 1753–[54]   3342

See also Delisle, Guillaume, 1675–1726, *and*
Buache, Philippe, 1700–1773.

Buch, Leopold, *Freiherr* von, 1774–1853.
Atlas zur physicalischen Beschreibung der
Canarischen Inseln. 1825.   9347

Buchenau, Franz Georg Philipp, 1831–1906.
Atlas ... für die Schulen Bremens. 4. Aufl.
1870.   8851

Buchon, Jean Alexandre C., 1789–1846.
Atlas géographique ... des Amériques. 1825.   1176

**Buchon, Jean Alexandre C., *and* Tastu, Joseph,
1787–1849.**
[Atlas Catalan. 1375]   4251

Buck, John Lossing, 1890–
Land utilization in China. Atlas. [1937]   9505

Buck, Nathaniel.
See Buck, Samuel, 1696–1779, *and* Buck,
Nathaniel.

Buck, Samuel, 1696–1779, *and* Buck, Nathaniel.
Perspective views of near one hundred cities
... in England and Wales. 1774.   8083

Buck, Thaddeus E.
Atlas of Morrow County, Ohio. 1901.   2404

**Budapest. Vizgazdálkodási Tudományos Kutató
Intézet.**
Magyarország hidrológiai atlasza. 1953–56.   8921

**Buenos Aires (*Province*). Ministerio de Asuntos
Agrarios.**
Atlas de condiciones de los suelos. [1965?]   18240
—— [1966?]   18241

Büring, H.
Harms Nordrhein-Westfalen in Karte, Bild
und Wort. [1956]   8825

Bulifon, Antoine, *b.* 1649.
Accuratissima e nuova delineazione del Regno
di Napoli. [1692]   3067

Bullard Company.
Red road book for all New England and eastern New York. 1914.   4516

Bulleit, F. A.
Illustrated atlas and history of Harrison
County, Ind. 1906.   1610

Bullock, William *fl.* 1808–1828.
Atlas historique pour servir au Mexique en
1823. 1824.   3936

Bureau d'Aménagement de l'Est du Québec.
Atlas régional du Bas-St-Laurent, de la
Gaspésie, et des Îles-de-la-Madeleine.
1966.   10435

Burgdörfer, Friedrich, 1890–
Welt-Bevölkerungs-Atlas. [1954]   5782

Burgess complete radio atlas of the world. [1923]   5797

Burgett, H. W., and Company.
Illustrated topographical and historical atlas
of the State of Vermont. 1876.   2593

Burke, Mark Parnell, 1887–
Township plats of the oil fields in north central Oklahoma. [1917]   5000

Burma. *Land Records Dept.*
Atlas of the Province of Burma. 1923.   9501

Burn, George.
See Stephenson, John, *and* Burn, George.

Burn, Walter P., and Associates.
Radio broadcasting atlas. [1938]   10718

Burpee, Lawrence Johnstone, 1873–1946.
Historical atlas of Canada. 1927.   10344

Burr, David H., 1803–1875.
American atlas. [1839]   4525
Atlas of New York. 1838.   2207
Atlas of the State of New York. 1829.   2206
New universal atlas. [1835?]   771, 1379a

Burrill, Meredith F., 1902–
Socio-economic atlas of Oklahoma. [1936]   16585

Burrow, Ed. J., and Company.
Directional pointer guide-map of Hudders-
field. [1936]   8151
Pointer guide map of Coventry. 5th ed.
[194–]   8148
Pointer guide map of Croydon. [1948]   8150
Pointer guide map of Wolverhampton. 2d ed.
[1948]   8198

Bury, John Bagnell, 1861–1927.
Atlas to the historical geography of Europe.
1903.   2787

Bush, Lee M., and Company.
Plat book of Oklahoma City and vicinity.
1948.   16628

Business Services, *West Columbia, Tex.*
Historical Brazoria County. [1961]   17149

Bussell, Charles E.
Atlas of the city of Eau Claire, Wis. 1888.   2672

Bussell and Holway.
Map of the county of Marathon, Wis. [1881]   17826

Bussy, J. H., de.
Atlas van Nederlandsch Oost-Indië. 1919.   9745
—— 2de druk. 1922.   9746

Butler, George, 1819–1890.
Public schools atlas of ancient geography. 1893.   3272
Public schools atlas of modern geography. 1886.   3362
—— 1901.   3363

Butler, Samuel, *bishop of Lichfield and Coventry*, 1774–1839.
Atlas of antient geography. 1831.   4089
—— 1832.   7
—— 1834.   4090
—— 1838.   8
—— 1839.   9
—— 1841.   10
—— 1843.   4091
—— 1844.   11
—— 1855.   4092
—— 1868.   3273
Atlas of modern geography. 1844.   792
—— 1871.   861

Buy de Mornas, Claude, *d*. 1783.
Atlas méthodique et élémentaire. 1761–62.   628
—— 1783.   656

Byck, A. D., and Company.
Subdivision atlas [of Savannah, Ga. 1958]   11982

Byland-Fritschy, C. F.
Atlas universal americano. [1926]   6605

Bylandt Palstercamp, A., *comte* de.
Cabinet atlas. 1830.   3548
Théorie des volcans. Atlas. 1836.   347

Byrne, Joseph James.
Maps of the estate of Charles Lionel Kirwan Esqre. in the counties of Mayo and Galway. 1852. MS.   8235

Byrnes, Clara.
Block sketches of New York City. [1917?]   16007

C***
See Chatelain, Henri Abraham, 1684–1743.

Cacciatore, Leonardo, 1775–1830.
Nuovo atlante istorico. 4. ed. 1832–33.   103

Cadillac Evening News.
See Standard Map Company.

Cadwell, George B., and Company.
Atlas of Lenawee County, Mich. 1893.   14714

Caldwell, John W.
See Halfpenny, H. E., *and* Caldwell, John W.

Caldwell, Joseph A.
Atlas of Ashland Co., Ohio. 1874.   16380
Atlas of Harrison County, Ohio. 1875.   2383
Atlas of Knox County, Ohio. 1896.   2391
Atlas of Monroe County, Ohio. 1898.   2402
Atlas of Wayne Co., and the city of Wooster, Ohio. 1873.   16461
Atlas of Wayne County, Ohio. 1897.   16462
—— 1908.   3879
Illustrated, historical, centennial atlas of Beaver County, Pa. 1876.   16771
Illustrated, historical, centennial atlas of Washington Co., Pa. 1876.   16805
Illustrated, historical, combination atlas of Cambria County, Pa. 1890.   2466
Illustrated, historical, combination atlas of Clarion County, Pa. 1877.   16776
Illustrated, historical, combination atlas of Clearfield County, Pa. 1878.   2470

Caldwell, Joseph A., *and* Gould, Hueston T.
Atlas of Franklin Co., and the city of Columbus, Ohio. 1872.   2376, 2431

Caldwell, Joseph A., *and* Starr, J. W.
Atlas of Knox County, Ohio. 1871.   2390

California.
California political subdivision maps. [195-]   11321
—— [1961]   11322

California. *Dept. of Natural Resources. Div. of Mines.*
Geology and mineral deposits of an area north of San Francisco Bay, Calif. 1949.   11328

California. *Division of Highways.*
Highway transportation survey of 1934. [1935]   11341
San Diego traffic flow. 1966.   11582

California. *Public Utilities Commission.*
Distance table 6: Book of maps. [1967]   11352

California. *State Earthquake Investigation Commission.*
Atlas of maps and seismograms accompanying the report ... of April 18, 1906. 1908.   3703

California. *State Mining Bureau.*
Petroleum industry of California. 1914.   4538

California. University. *Scripps Institution of Oceanography, La Jolla.*
Word atlas of sea surface temperatures. 1944.   5391

California Block Book and Map Company.
100 vara San Francisco, Cal. [1906]   11586

California Land Directory Company.
San Francisco plat map book. 1964.   11597
Santa Clara County plat map book. 1965.   11484

Calleja, Fernandez Saturnio.
Atlas de geografía universal. [1911]   3610a

Caltex (Africa)
Motorist's fishing guide. [195–]   10165

Caltex (Philippines)
Road maps of the Philippines. 1957.   10066

Caltex Oil AB., *Stockholm.*
Med Caltex genom Sverige. [1950]   9380
—— [1952]   9381
—— [2.uppl. 1952]   9382
Med Texaco genom Sverige. [1938]   9367

Camacho Elizondo, Rodrígo.
Geografía gráfico de Costa Rica. 1962.   18126
Historia de Costa Rica. [1959]   18125

Camacho Lara, René R.
Atlas de Bolivia. 1958.   18263
Atlas escolar de Bolivia. 1958.   18264

Cambridge modern history atlas. 1912.   4129
—— 2d ed. 1924.   5501

Cameron, Frank Kenneth, 1869–1958.
Potash from kelp . . . Kelp groves of the Pacific
coast . . . of the United States. 1914.   10288

Camocio, Giovanni Francesco, *d.* 1575?
Isole famose porti, fortezze e terre maritime
sottoposte alla ser.^{ma} sig.^{ria} di Venetia.
[1574]   2815, 3975, 7855

Campbell, James Donald, 1884–
See Lewis, *Sir* Clinton Gresham, 1885–
and Campbell, James Donald, 1884–

Campbell, Robert Allen.
New atlas of Missouri. 1873.   2061

Campbell, Robert Allen, *and* Walling, Henry Francis, 1825–1888.
New atlas of the state of Illinois. 1870.   1511

Campbell, *Calif.*
Topographic survey of Campbell. 1961.   11514

Campini, Ugo.
Atlante stradale . . . Italia. [1946]   8973

Canada. *Advisory Commission on the Development of Government in the Northwest Territories.*
Atlas of the Northwest Territories, Canada.
1966.   10404

Canada. *Bureau of Statistics.*
Agriculture, climate and population of the
Prairie Provinces. 1931.   10336

Canada. *Dept. of Agriculture.*
Atlas du Canada. 1913.   10364
Atlas of Canada. 1914.   4483

Canada. *Dept. of Citizenship and Immigration.*
Canada: Descriptive atlas. 1951.   10375

Canada. *Dept. of Crown Lands.*
Maps of Canada. 1857.   10356

Canada. *Dept. of Immigration and Colonization.*
Canada: Descriptive atlas. 1922.   10368
—— [1936]   10371

Canada. *Dept. of Mines and Technical Surveys. Geographical Branch.*
Atlas du Canada. 1957–[58]   10378
Atlas of Canada. 1957–[58]   10377

Canada. *Dept. of Mines and Technical Surveys. Surveys and Mapping Branch.*
Nova Scotia, New Brunswick, Prince Edward
Island, Newfoundland: Federal electoral
district maps. 1953.   10376
Topographical maps of Canada. [1965]   10350

Canada. *Dept. of Public Works.*
Georgian Bay Ship Canal survey. [1909]   10438

Canada. *Dept. of the Interior.*
Atlas of Canada. 1906.   1249
—— [1908?]   10361
—— 1910.   10362
—— 1912.   10363
—— Rev. and enl. ed. [1915]   10365
—— 1916.   10367
Atlas of western Canada. 1901.   10359
—— 1902.   1245
—— [1903]   1246
Beschreibender Atlas des westlichen Canada.
1899.   1242
Concise school atlas of the Dominion of
Canada. 1900.   1243
Descriptive atlas to western Canada. [1899]   1241
—— 1900.   1244
Electoral atlas of the Dominion of Canada.
1915.   10366
Electoral district[s of the Dominion of Canada. 1902?]   10360

Canada. *Dept. of the Interior. Natural Resources Intelligence Branch.*
Canada from two viewpoints. [1929]   10370

Canada. *Geological Survey.*
Plans of various lakes and rivers. 1857.   4479
Report of progress from its commencement to
1863. Atlas. 1865.   10342

Canada. *Hydrographic Service.*
Athabasca and Slave Rivers. 1962.   10437
Kootenay Lake and River. 1st ed. 1964.   10389
Slave River; Fort Smith to Great Slave Lake.
1962.   10439

Canada. *Meteorological Branch.*
Maps of upper winds over Canada. 1957.   10338

Canada. *Post Office Dept.*
Postal map of the province of Ontario, with
adjacent counties of the province of Quebec.
1883.   4484, 4488
Postal map of the province of Quebec. 1880.   4489

Canada. *Surveys and Mapping Branch.*
British Columbia, Alberta and the electoral
district of Yukon—Mackenzie River.
1948.   10384
British Columbia, Alberta, Northwest Territories and Yukon Territory. Federal electoral district maps. 1953.   10385
Manitoba, Saskatchewan. Dominion electoral district maps. 1948.   10393
Manitoba, Saskatchewan. Federal electoral
district maps. 1953.   10394
Ontario. Dominion electoral district maps.
1948.   10411
Ontario. Federal electoral district maps.
1953.   10412
Québec: Cartes des districts électoraux du
Dominion. 1948.   10430
Québec: Cartes des districts électoraux féd-
éraux. 1953.   10431

Canada. *Surveys and Mapping Bureau.*
Nova Scotia, New Brunswick, Prince Edward
Island: Dominion electoral district maps.
1948.   10373

Canada. *Tidal and Current Survey.*
Tidal current charts, Vancouver Harbour,
British Columbia. [2d ed. 1953]   10387

Canadian National Railways.
Maps ... issued as aids to the development of
the mineral resources along the Canadian
National Railways. 1926.   10343

Canet Alvarez, Gerardo A., 1911–
Atlas de Cuba. 1949.   18166

Cantwell Printing Company.
Standard historical atlas of Dane County,
Wis. 1911.   3930

Capitol Title Company.
Ada County [Idaho] book of plats. 1958.   12007

Cappelens atlas. 1953.   7553

Cappelens Atlas [for folkeskolen] 1951.   7459

Capper Farm Press.
Study in circulations. [1920]   10535

Capper Publications.
Counties of the United States classified by
farm income quality groups. [194–]   10446

Caraci, Giuseppe, 1893–
Tabulae geographicae vetustiores in Italia
adservatae. 3 v. 1926–32.   5787

Carafa, Giovanni, *Duca di Noia,* **1715–1768.**
Mappa topografica della citta di Napoli.
1775.   9007

Cardiff, *Wales. City Surveyor's Dept.*
City of Cardiff, Town and country planning
act, 1947. 1953.   8224

Carey, Henry Charles, 1793–1879, *and* **Lea, Isaac,**
1792–1886.
Complete historical, chronological, and geographical American atlas. 1822.   1373a
—— 1823.   3660a, 4464
—— 1827.   1177, 1227, 1379, 2728
Family cabinet atlas. 1832.   762
—— 1834.   767

Carey, Mathew, 1760–1839.
American atlas. 1795.   1172, 1213, 1362
—— 1809.   1173, 1222, 1369
American pocket atlas. 1796.   1364
—— 1801.   1367
—— 1805.   1368, 3690
—— 4th ed. 1813.   4523
—— 1814.   1370
General atlas. 1796.   683, 1365
—— 1802.   3535
—— 1804.   6021
—— [1814?]   721, 1371
—— 1814.   722, 1372
—— 1817.   4311
—— 1818.   732, 1373
General atlas for the present war. 1794. 6003
Minor American atlas. 1802.   11022
Minor atlas. 1810.   11023
Scripture atlas. 1817.   3274

Carey, Mathew, and Son.
Picturesque views of American scenery.
1820.   4518

Carls, Norman, 1907–   *and* **Sorenson, Frank**
England, 1903–
[Air-route maps from Neighbors across the
seas. 1950]   5328
[Plates I-XVI from Neighbors across the seas.
1950]   7386

Carpenter, Benjamin D.
Map of the real estate in the county of
Washington, D.C. 1881.   4549

Carrez, Louis, 1833–1920.
    Atlas geographicus Societatis Jesu. 1900.   5402

Carrillo Escribano, Alejandro.
    See Hernández Millares, Jorge, *and* Carrillo
    Escribano, Alejandro.

Carrington, Henry Beebee, 1824–1912.
    Battle maps and charts of the American Rev-
    olution. [1881]   1336

Carroll, S. S., and Company.
    Atlas of Ralls County, Mo. 1904.   2091

**Carroll County, *Md. Board of County Commis-
sioners.***
    Photogrammetric map[s] of Carroll County,
    Md.: Westminster area. 1964.   14391

Carson Map Company.
    Aerial platbook of the county of Dallas, Tex.
    1966.   17160
    Becker County [Minn.] plat book. 1961.   14927
    City of Albuquerque [N.Mex.] 1966.   15821
    City of Topeka [Kans.] plat maps. [1961]   14221
    Denver City and County plat book. 1963.   11683
    Kansas City, Mo. & Kansas City, Kans. met-
    ropolitan street atlas. 1965.   15259
    Plat book of Cheyenne [Wyo.] and suburban
    area. 1961.   18037
    Plat book of Colorado Springs, Colo. 1963.   11675
    Plat book of Dubuque, Iowa. 1961.   14128
    Plat book of Duluth, Minn. 1964.   15146
    Plat book of the city of Milwaukee ... Wis.
    1962.   18014
    Plat book of the city of St. Paul [Minn.]
    1960.   15167
    Plat book of the city of Wichita Falls, Tex.
    1963.   17290
    Plat book of Waco, Tex. and suburban area.
    1964.   17287
    Platbook of Fond du Lac County, Wis.
    1966.   17742
    Platbook of the city of Dallas, Tex. 1964.   17228
    Platbook of Topeka, Kans. 1962.   14222
    Suburban Minot [N.Dak.] plat book. 1961.   16353
    Wayne County [Mich.] plat book. 1967.   14834

Cartée, Cornelius Sowle, 1806–1885.
    School atlas of physical geography. 1856.   219

Carter, Henry John.
    Atlas to geoglical papers on western India.
    1857.   3198

Cartes et plans de l'Amérique. 1745.   10267

Cartografisch Instituut Bootsma.
    Autokaart Nederland, met alle verharde
    wegen. [1952]   9070

Cartografisch Instituut P. Mantnieks, *Brussels.*
    Atlas classique. 2. éd. [1951]   7446
    Schoolatlas. [1950]   7387

Cary, John, ca. 1754–1835.
    Actual survey of the country fifteen miles
    round London. 1786.   2933
    New and correct English atlas. 1787.   8122
    —— 1793.   5207
    —— 1809.   8125
    —— 1818.   8126
    New universal atlas. 1808.   714
    —— 1811–[12]   6031
    —— 1813.   6033
    —— 1819.   736
    —— 1824–[25]   745
    Survey of the high roads from London. 1790.   5202
    Traveller's companion ... England and Wales.
    1791–[92]   4012
    —— 1806.   8098
    —— 1810.   8099
    —— 1814.   2905
    —— 1817.   8100

Cary, John, *and* Stockdale, John, 1749?–1814.
    New British atlas. 1805.   8075

Case, O. D., and Company.
    Bible atlas. 1877.   5345
    —— 1878.   4114

Caspar, C. N., Company.
    Official quarter sectional atlas of the city of
    Milwaukee. 1907.   5112
    —— Supplement. 1914.   5113
    —— 1915.   5114

Cass County, *Ind. Surveyor's Office.*
    Cass County, Ind. 1960.   12752

Cass County Land and Abstract Company.
    Personal ownership map of Cass County [Tex.]
    1927.   17152

Cassell's Atlas. 1910.   6334

Cassell's New atlas. [1921]   6452
    —— 6th ed. [1932]   6784

Cassini, Giovanni Domenico, 1625–1712, *and others.*
    Hydrographia Galliae. [1685?]   2987

Cassini, Giovanni Maria.
    Nuovo atlante geografico universale. 1792–
    1801.   670

Cassini de Thury, César François, 1714–1784.
    Atlas topographique, minéralogique et statis-
    tique de la France. 1818.   2996

**Castillo Cordero, Clemente, *and* García O., Juan
Alfredo.**
    Atlas politico-administrativo de ... Guatemala.
    1953.   18131

Castillo Marin, Guillermo José.
Atlas de Centro-América, especial de Nicaragua. [1947] 18138
—— 3. ed. 1961. 18139

Castro, João de, 1500–1548.
Roteiro de Goa a Dio. [1538–39] Facsim. 1843. 9686
[Roteiro em que se contem a viagem que fizeram os Portuguezes no anno de 1541 ... Atlas. 1833] 9500

Catalan atlas. 1375. 4251

Catholic Church. *Congregatio de Propaganda Fide.*
Atlante delle missioni cattoliche. [1947] 5403

Cave Research Foundation.
Flint Ridge cave system, Mammouth Cave National Park, Ky. 1966. 14264

Cayo, Roberto Manuel.
Atlas argentino y americano. [1966] 10281

Čechoslovák, *London.*
Czechoslovakia in maps and statistics. [1944] 8248

Cedar Rapids, *Iowa. City Engineer's Office.*
Map of Cedar Rapids, Iowa. 1960. 14111

Cellarius, Andreas, *fl.* **1656–1708.**
Harmonia macrocosmica. 1661. 469
—— 1708. 4274

Cellarius, Christoph, 1638–1707.
Geographia antiqua. 1817. 5596
—— 1819. 5597
See also Keller, Christoph, 1638–1707.

Cellarius, Frederick Julius, 1865–1953.
Atlas of the city of Dayton, Ohio. 1907. 2432
—— 1918. 4996
—— 1931. 16530
Map of Dayton, Ohio. 1908. 4995

Centennial Atlas Association.
Centennial atlas of Warren County, Ohio. 1903. 16460

Centennial Atlas Company.
Plat book of Monroe County, Ill. 1916. 4582

Central Atlas Company.
Standard atlas of Dodge County, Minn. 1937. 14973
Standard atlas of Jackson County, Minn. 1936. 15012
Standard atlas of Martin County, Minn. 1936. 15038
Standard atlas of Rock County, Minn. 1935. 15094
Standard atlas of Steele County, Minn. 1937. 15108
Standard atlas of Waseca County, Minn. 1937. 15124

Central Map Survey and Publishing Company.
Chicago suburban maps, Cook County, Ill. 1891. 1526

Insurance maps of Chicago. 1892. 1588
Union stock yards and packing houses, Chicago, Ill. 1891. 1584

Central Publishing Company.
Standard historical and pictorial atlas ... of Blue Earth County, Minn. 1895. 14937
Standard township map and gazetteer of Wright County, Minn. 1894. 2048

Centre d'Information et de Documentation du Congo Belge et du Ruanda-Urundi.
Cartes géographiques du Congo Belge. 2. éd. 1953. 10116
—— 3. éd. 1954. 10117

Century atlas of the world. [1914]
See also Smith, Benjamin Eli, 1857–1913.

Century Map Company.
New century atlas, Erie County, N.Y. 1909. 4924
New century atlas of Cayuga County, N.Y. 1904. 2216
New century atlas of Herkimer County, N.Y. 1906. 15881
New century atlas of Livingston County, N.Y. 1902. 2236
New century atlas of Montgomery and Fulton Counties, N.Y. 1905. 15886
New century atlas of Orleans County, N.Y. 1913. 15898
New century atlas of Otsego County, N.Y. 1903. 2248
New century atlas of Wyoming County, N.Y. 1902. 2265
New century atlas, Oneida County, N.Y. 1907. 2242

Česka Akademie Věd a Uměni, *Prague.*
Atlas Republiky Československé. [1931–35] 8247

Chabert-Ostland, Clément Casimir de.
See Gallois, Lucien Louis Joseph, 1857–1941, *and* Chabert-Ostland, Clément Casimir de.

Chace, Henry Richmond, 1838–
Maps of Providence, R.I. 1650–1765–1770. 1914. 5054
Owners and occupants of the lots, houses and shops in the town of Providence, Rhode Island, in 1798. [1914] 5055

Chadwick, Clifton William, 1889–
Farm atlas of Cass County, Ind. 1916. 4608
Farm atlas of Gratiot County, Mich. 1914. 4743
Farm atlas of Huron County, Mich. [1913] 4745
Farm atlas of Ingham County, Mich. 1914. 4746
Farm atlas of Lapeer County, Mich. 1915– [16] 4750
Farm atlas of Montcalm County, Mich. 1913. 4759
Farm atlas of Osceola County, Mich. 1916. 4761
Farm atlas of Sanilac County, Mich. 1916. 4765
—— 1917. 14808

[Michigan manual maps of railroads, congressional, senatorial, and representative districts. 1931]   14548
—— [1933]   14549
—— [1935]   14550
—— [1937]   14551
Michigan State manual maps. [1917]   14547
Plat book of Greater Chattanooga District ... Tenn. 1928.   17092
Plat book of Lucas County, Ohio. 1924.   16435
Plat book of the city of Toledo ... Ohio. 1930.   16567

Chalmers, John West.
Philips' Historical atlas of Canada. 1966.   10345

Chaloupka, William Franklin.
Land ownership plat, Morrill County, Nebr. 1951.   15516
Oil and mineral lease plat, Morrill County, Nebr. 1951.   15517

Chamberlain, Ernest Lorenz, 1884–
Plat book, Renville County, Minn. 1926.   15088

Chambers, William, 1800–1883, and Chambers, Robert, 1802–1871.
Atlas to accompany Chambers's Encyclopedia. 1869.   4351a
Handy atlas. 1877.   833

Chambre Syndicale des Forces Hydrauliques, de l'Électrométallurgie, de l'Électrochimie, et des Industries qui s'y Rattachent.
Atlas hydroélectrique de France. [1945]   8401

Champion Map Corp.
Lake Norman [N.C.] 5***** atlas. [1963]   16212
Metropolitan Columbia [S.C.] atlas. [1963]   17004

Chandler Engraving Company.
U.S. Oregon National forest maps. 1950.   16640

Chang, Hsien-ch'iu, and others.
Ecological crop geography atlas of China. 1948.   9506

Chang, Jên-chün.
Kuang-hsi yü ti ch'üan t'u. [Complete geographical atlas of Kwangsi. 1907]   9653
Kuang-tung yü ti ch'üan t'u. [Complete geographical atlas of Kwangtung. 1897]   9656

Chang, Yüan-ch'i, 1865–
Fêng-t'ien ch'üan shêng ti fang tzŭ chih ch'ü yü t'u. [Atlas of local autonomous districts of Fêng-t'ing (i.e., Liaoning) Province. 1911]   9659

Chang, Yung-ju.
Hsin Chung-kuo ti t'u. [New atlas of China] 1950.   9590

Chanlaire, Pierre Grégoire, 1758–1817.
Atlas national de la France. 1810–[12]   4024
See also Dumez, ——, *and* Chanlaire, Pierre Grégoire.
See also Mentelle, Edme, 1730–1815, *and* Chanlaire, Pierre Grégoire.

Chanlaire, Pierre Grégoire, and Herbin de Halle, P. Etienne, 1772–
Tableau de la division des six nouveaux départemens ... de la France. 1803.   8462
Tableau général de la nouvelle division de la France. 1802.   8461

Chanzy, Antoine Eugène Alfred, 1823–1883.
Campagne de 1870–1871. La deuxième armée de la Loire. Atlas. 1871.   8410

Chapeaurouge, Carlos de.
Atlas del plano catastral de la República Argentina. 1901–[25]   18215
—— 1905.   3957

Chappe d'Auteroche, Jean, 1728–1769.
[Voyage en Sibérie, fait par ordre du roi en 1761. 1768]   9243

Charcot, Jean Baptiste Auguste Étienne, 1867–1936.
Deuxième expédition Antarctique Française (1908–1910). 1912.   5324

Chardonnet, Jean, 1913–
Atlas de l'Europe occidentale. [1953]   7651

Charity Organization Society of the City of New York.
District maps. 1898.   15995

Charle, J. B. L.
Nouvel atlas national de la France. 1833.   2998

Charlotte, N.C. Engineering Dept.
City of Charlotte, N.C., topographic maps. 1958.   16229

Charras, Jean Baptiste Adolphe, 1810–1865.
Campagne de 1815. Waterloo. 1858.   3996

Châtelain, Henri Abraham, 1684–1743.
Atlas historique. 1705–20.   548
—— 1732–39.   579

Chatterjee, Shiba Prasad, 1903–
Bengal in maps. [1949]   9711

Chaturvedi, Baij Nath, 1916–
Descriptive atlas of Hyderabad State. 1956.   9718

Chauchard, Capt.——
General map of the Empire of Germany, Holland ... 1800.   7791

Chekiang, *China (Province). Yü t'u tsung chü.*
Chê-chiang ch'üan shêng yü t'u ping shui lu tao li chi. [Complete provincial atlas of Chekiang, with waterway and road distances. 1894]   9630

Ch'en, Chêng-hsiang.
Atlas of land utilization in Taiwan. 1950.   9672

Ch'ên, Pao-chên, 1831–1900.
Hu-nan ch'üan shêng yü ti t'u, piao. [Complete atlas of Hunan Province. 1896].   9638

Ch'ên, To.
Hsin chih Chung-kuo ti t'u, piao chieh shuo ming. [New atlas of China, with tables and explanations. 1934]   9566a

Chenault, Dwight Edwin.
Atlas of rural routes in Arizona. 1941.   11246
—— 1945–47.   11247
Rural routes of El Paso, Tex. 1948.   17231

Cherry County, *Nebr. Farm Bureau.*
Atlas of Cherry County, Nebr. 1938.   15383

Chesnutt, John Martin.
Plat book, atlas and directory, McDonough County, Ill. [1948]   12360
Plat book, Fulton County, Ill. 1948.   12244

Chevalier, Michel, 1806–1879.
Historie et description des voies de communication aux États-Unis. 1841.   1266

Chevalier, Stanislas, 1852–1930.
Atlas du Haut Yang-tse, de I-Tchang Fou à P'ing-Chan Hien. [1899]   3196

Chia, Tan-yüeh.
See P'ei, Hsiu-t'ang, *and* Chia, Tan-yüeh.

Chiang, Kuo-chang, *fl.* 1899.
Hsia chiang t'u k'ao. [Yangtze River gorges between Ichang and Chungking. 1899]   9671

[Chiang-hsi shêng Kuei-ch'i hsien ti t'u. Atlas of Kuei-ch'i hsien, Kiangsi Province] MS. [18—]   9667

Chías y Carbó, Benito.
Atlas de España. [1931]   9329
Atlas geográfico ibero-americano, Perú. [1907]   18385
Atlas Geográfico pedagógico de España. [192–]   9326

Chicago. *Dept. of City Planning.*
City of Chicago. [1957]   12659
Reference atlas ... city of Chicago. [1st ed.] 1958.   12661
—— [2d ed. 1961]   12665

Chicago. *Dept. of Subways and Superhighways.*
Comprehensive superhighway system. [1940]   12648

Chicago. *Dept. of Subways and Traction.*
Comprehensive plan for the extension of the subway system of Chicago. 1939.   12646

Chicago. *Ordinances, etc.*
Chicago zoning ordinance. [1924]   12624
—— [1927?]   12633
—— [1945]   12653

Chicago. *Plan Commission.*
Survey of vacant land suitable for residential use. 1949.   12654

Chicago. *University. Institute of Meteorology.*
Preliminary climatic atlas of the Mediterranean region. 1942.   7856

Chicago and North Western Railway.
Sites for munitions industries. [1941?]   10536

Chicago Chronicle.
Unrivalled atlas. 1899.   1032

Chicago Evening American.
Working manual for sales control of the Chicago market. 1929.   12639
—— 1930.   12642
—— 1934.   12643

Chicago Real Estate Index Company.
Atlas and ownership index ... Chicago. v. 11–15. 1912–13.   4596
Book of valuations of the central business district of Chicago. 1915.   4598
1911 to 1914 Book of valuations for the heart of Chicago. 1911.   12611
1919–1922 Book of valuations of the central business district of Chicago. 1920.   12616
1923–1926 Book of valuations of the central business districts of Chicago. 1924.   12625
1927–1930 Book of valuations of the central business districts of Chicago. 1928.   12635
1939–1942 Book of valuations of the central business districts of Chicago. 1940.   12649

Chicago Regional Planning Association.
Maps of the region of Chicago. 1928.   12636

Chicago Transit Authority.
Gorand's street map of Chicago and suburbs. 1951.   12656

Chicago Tribune.
Salesman's guide map of Chicago, Evanston and Oak Park. 1919.   12614

Chichester, Francis.
Map & guide of London. [1952]   8191
—— [1958?]   8195
Pocket map & guide of the British Isles. [1956]   8062

Ch'ien-lung Huang-ho hsia yu cha pa t'u. [Atlas of the embankments along the lower reaches of the Hwaing-ho] MS. [17—]   9670

Chigaku Kyōkai.
Dai Nagoya-shi zensangyō jūtaku annai zuchō. [Real estate atlas of Nagoya. 1957]   9927

Chih-li Tung san-shêng yü ti t'u. [Atlas of Chih-li and the Three Eastern Provinces. 1899?]   9636

Chiiki Keizai Kenkyūjo, *Tokyo.*
Hokkaidō shakai keizai zufu. Graphical approach to Hokkaido economics. 1953.   10030

Childs, Cephas Grier, 1792–1871.
Views in Philadelphia. [1830]   5023

Chile. *Ejército.*
Cartografía hispano colonial de Chile. II atlas. 1952.   18324

Chile. *Inspección General de Colonización e Inmigración.*
Carta general de colonización de la Prov'a de Cautín. 1916.   18340

Chile. *Inspección General de Ferrocarriles.*
Atlas de la monografia de lineas ferreas fiscales. 1910.   5145

Chile. *Inspección General de Geografía.*
Cartografía hispano colonial de Chile. Atlas. 1924.   18323
Chile. Edición económica. [1925]   18334
Chile, red caminera. [1925]   18326
Mapa de Chile, con red caminera. [1928]   18327

Chile. *Instituto Geográfico Militar.*
Atlas de la República de Chile. [1966]   18339
Carta nacional. 1945.   18336
Colección de mapas esquemáticos de las provincias de Chile. 1930.   18322

Chile. *Ministerio de Instrucción Pública.*
Mapa escolar de Chile. 1911.   5146

Chile. *Oficina de Mensura de Tierras.*
Mapa de Chile. [1911]   18330
—— [1913]   18331
—— 1919.   18332

Chile *and* **Argentina.**
Esposicion que por parte de Chile i en respuesta a la esposicion Arjentina. 1902.   2756a

Chin, Ch'ing-yü.
Chung-hua jên min kung ho kuo fên shêng ching t'u. [Detailed provincial atlas of the People's Republic of China. Popular ed.] 1951.   9594
Chung-hua jên min kung ho kuo fên shêng ti t'u. [Provincial atlas of the People's Republic of China. 4th ed.] 1951.   9595

Chung-kuo fên shêng ching t'u. [Detailed provincial atlas of China. 1st rev. ed. 1947]   9583
Hsiu chên Chung-hua jên min kung ho kuo fên shêng ching t'u. [Detailed pocket atlas of the People's Republic of China.] 1950.   9591
—— [Popular ed.] 1951.   9596
Hsiu chên Chung-kuo fên shêng ching t'u. [Detailed pocket atlas of China. 14th rev. ed. 1947]   9584

Chin, Tê-hung, *fl.* **1874.**
Wu hsien t'u t'u. [Atlas of Wu hsien (i.e. Soochow district) 1874]   9648

China. *Directorate General of Posts.*
China postal album. [2d ed.] 1919.   9529
China postal atlas. [3d ed.] 1933.   9530
—— [4th ed.] 1936.   9531

China. *Inspectorate General of Customs.*
China postal album. 1907.   9532

China. *K'ung chün tsung chih hui pu. Ts'an mou ch'u.*
[Chung-kuo Jih-pên chi Tung-nan Ya kuo chia hang hsing ti t'u. Aeronautical atlas of China, Japan and Southeast Asia. 1942]   9475

China Foundation for the Promotion of Education and Culture, *Peking.*
See Chung-hua chiao yü wên hua chi chin tung shih hui pien i wei yüan hui, *Peking.*

China provincial atlas and geography. [1934]   9567

Chinese Eastern Railway. *Economic Bureau.*
Экономический атлас Китая и Маньчжурии. [Economic atlas of China and Manchuria] 1932–34.   9509

Ch'ing Kao-tsung, *Emperor of China,* **1711–1799.**
Ch'ien-lung ching ch'êng ch'üan t'u. [Complete atlas of the Capital City [Peking] in the Ch'ien-lung period. 18th cent. 1940]   9668a
Ch'ing Ch'ien-lung nei fu yü t'u. [Imperial palace atlas of Ch'ien-lung's reign. 1760. Repr. 1932]   9549
Ch'ing nei wu fu ts'ang ching ch'êng ch'üan t'u. [Complete atlas of the Capital City [Peking] in the (collections of the) Imperial Palace. 1736. 1940]   9668

Ch'ing Shêng-tsu, *Emperor of China,* **1654–1722.**
Man Han ho pi nei fu i t'ung yü ti pi t'u. [Imperial palace atlas of the Ch'ing dynasty in Manchu and Chinese. 1718. Repr. 1929]   9547

Chiquet, Jacques.
Nouveau atlas françois. [1719]   5224
Nouveau et curieux atlas géographique et historique. [1719]   4279

Chiri Chōsajo, *Chiba.*
Chiri Chōsajo no chizuchō Nihon. [Atlas of

Japan by the Geographical Survey Institute. 1948]   9818

Chiriquí Land Company.
District farms. [1947–48]   18149

Chisholm, George Goudie, 1850–1930.
Longmans' New atlas political and physical. 1889.   3364
Longmans' New five-shilling atlas. 1893.   3365

Chisholm, George Goudie, *and* Leete, Charles Henry, 1857–
Longmans' New school atlas. New ed. 1901.   271
—— 1912.   4190

Chizu Shuppan Kabushiki Kaisha, *Tokyo*.
See Tōkyō Chizu Shuppan Kabushiki Kaisha.

[Chŏlla-do chido. Atlas of Cholla Province, Korea]
MS. [18—]   10052

Cholley, André, 1886–
See Seive, Fleury Marius, 1896–   *and*
Cholley, André, 1886–

Cholnoky, Jenő, 1870–1950.
Földrajzi és statisztikai atlasz. 2. kiad. 1929.   6699

[Chosŏn chido. Atlas of Korea]   MS. [1850–93]
10046–10047

Chou Jên-chi, *fl.* 1755.
[Liang Chê yü t'u. Atlas of Chekiang. 1755]   9629

Chou, Li-san, *and others*.
Ssu-ch'uan ching chi ti t'u chi. [Economic atlas of Szechuan. 1946]   9663

Christchurch Press Company.
Press sectional maps of Christchurch. [1958?]   10203

Christensen, Carl Christian, 1860–1935, *and* Krogsgaard, Anders Meinert Rindom, 1869–
Atlas for folkeskolen. 22. udg. 1950.   7388
Atlas for mellemskolen og højere skoler. 13. udg. 1944.   7169
—— 16. udg. 1948.   7294
Atlas uden navne. 2 v. 1948.   7295
—— v. l. 13. udg. 1950.   7389

Christensen, David E.
See Becker, Henry Floyd, 1898–   *and*
Christensen, David E.

Christian and Missionary Alliance.
Missionary atlas. [1936]   5404

Chrussachi, Matthew George.
See Mills, John Saxon, *d.* 1929, *and* Chrussachi, Matthew George.

Chu, K'o-pao, 1845–1903.
Chiang-su ch'üan shêng yü t'u. [Complete atlas of Kiangsu Province. 1895]   9649

Chu, Ssŭ-pen, 1273–*ca.* 1335.
Kuang yü t'u. [Enlarged terrestrial atlas of China. 1558]   9538
—— [1579]   9539
—— [162–]   9543

Ch'üan shêng yü ti t'u. [Complete provincial atlas of China] MS. [16—]   9540

Chung-hua chiao yü wên hua chi chin tung shih hui pien i wei yüan hui, *Peking*.
Chung-kuo fên shêng t'u. [Provincial atlas of China. 1934]   9568
—— [Rev. ed. 1936]   9572
—— [Rev. 4th ed. 1938]   9574

Chung-kuo chih t'u shê, *Pei-p'ei*.
Chung-kuo fên shêng ti t'u. [Provincial atlas of China. 1st ed. 1945]   9581

Chung-kuo k'o hsüeh yüan. *Ti chih yen chiu so, Nanking*.
Chung-kuo ku ti li t'u. [Paleogeographic maps of China] 1955.   9514

Chung-kuo ko shêng ti t'u. [Provincial atlas of China 18—]   9550

Chung-kuo shih ti t'u piao pien tsuan shê, *Shanghai*.
Chung-kuo fên shêng hsin ti t'u. [New provincial atlas of China. 1st ed. 1947]   9584a
Chung-kuo hsin ti t'u. [New atlas of China. 4th rev. ed. 1947]   9585

Chūō Chizu Kenkyūjo, *Tokyo*.
Shizuoka-ken bōka kenchikutari zōsei keikaku zu. [Planning maps for fireproof building zones in Shizuoka Prefecture. 1957]   9860
Yokohama-shi gosenbun no ichi chikeizu. [Topographical atlas of Yokohama. 1958]   10026

Church Missionary Society.
Church Missionary atlas. New ed. (6th) 1879.   5405
—— New ed. (8th) 1896.   179

Churchill, William, 1859–1920.
Pacific colonies of Germany. [1918]   10187

Cincinnati Commercial Tribune.
Unrivalled atlas. 1899.   1033

Cincinnati Gas and Electric Company.
Service area, file number 202. [Cincinnati, Ohio. 1960]   16493

Cisneros, Carlos B.
Atlas del Perú. [1903]   2772

—— [1667?]   3432
—— 1676.   3439
—— 1697.   4270
—— 1729.   573

Clurg, George.
History in the open, its outdoor sites and land-
marks, graphic American and world history. [1948]   10597
Open-air and wide horizons; graphic American history, historical atlas and touring
guide. 1939.   10598

Cobbe, Rosser W.
See Willard, Constance Beatrice, *and* Cobbe,
Rosser W.

Cochran, A. B.
See Beers, Frederick W. *and* Cochran, A. B.

Cochrane, Thomas, 1866–1953.
Atlas of China in provinces. 1913.   9559

**Codazzi, Agostini, *i.e.*, Giovanni Battista Agostino,
1793–1859.**
Atlas físico y político de la República de Vene-
zuela. 1840.   2775
Atlas geográfico é histórico de la República de
Colombia. 1889–[90]   2761

**Coello de Portugal y Quesada, Francisco, 1820–
1898.**
Atlas de España y sus posesiones de ultramar.
[1848–69]   3137, 9323

Coffman, Ferris La Verne.
Atlas of treasure maps. [1957]   10262

Coggeshall Publishing Company.
Ad-a-page map of Corpus Christ, Tex., and
vicinity. [1960]   17204

Cohen, L., and Eggink, H.
Aardrijkskundig werkschrift, met vragen-
boek. 8. druk. v. 1 [1950]   5734

Cohrs, Edvard, 1858–1934.
Atlas öfver Sverige. 8. uppl. 1908.   9392
—— 9. uppl. [1913]   9393
—— 10. uppl. [1916]   9394
—— 11. uppl. [1920]   9396

Coil, Rollie A., *and* Cleland, Samuel.
Complete survey and atlas of Noble County,
Ind. 1914.   4614

Colart, L. S.
Histoires de France et d'Angleterre com-
parées. 1841.   4010, 4018

Colbeck, Charles.
Public schools historical atlas. 2d ed. 1885.   104
—— 8th ed. 1907.   4131

Colby, C. J., 1840–
Illustrated centennial sketches, map and directory of Union County, Iowa. 1876.   3754

Colby, Charles Galusha, 1830–1866.
Diamond atlas. 1857.   1180, 4338
World in miniature. 1857.   820
—— 1861.   1181

Colby, George N.
Atlas of Hancock County, Maine. 1881.   14311
Atlas of the State of Maine. 1885.   14305
See also Roe, Frederick B., 1845–1905, *and*
Colby, George N.

Colby, George N., and Company.
Atlas of Piscataquis County, Maine. 1882.   14314
Atlas of Somerset County, Me. 1883.   3764
Atlas of the state of Maine. 1884.   1773
Atlas of Washington County, Me. 1881.   3765

Cole, Donald B.
Atlas of American history. [1963]   10599
—— [1967]   10600

**[Collection of canals and proposed canals in Great
Britain 1780–96]**   7991

**[Collection of MS. col. maps of various islands of the
world 1810?]**   4145

**Collection of maps, charts, drawings, surveys, etc.
1843.**   1384

**[Collection of maps of various parts of Europe]
[1760?]**   5181

Collegiate Special Advertising Agency.
Collegiate salesman ... College town maps.
[1924]   10537

Colles, Christopher, 1738–1816.
Survey of the roads of the United States.
1789.   1326
—— 1789. Facsim. 1961.   10768

Collier, James E.
Agricultural atlas of Missouri. 1955.   15204

Collier, P. F., and Son.
New encyclopedic atlas and gazetteer of the
world. [1907]   1113
—— [1909]   3588
—— [1911]   3622
—— [1914]   4416
—— [1915]   6376
—— 1917.   4434
—— 1918.   4447
New world atlas and gazetteer. [1919]   6391
—— [1920]   6408
—— [1921]   6437
—— [1922]   6478
—— [1923]   6515
—— [1924]   6547

Colorado. *Water Conservation Board.*
Basic maps of Colorado and history of changes
in county boundaries. 1931.   11634

Colorcraft Art Company.
Boston and Suffolk County street guide map.
1945.   14434

Colton, George Woolworth, 1827–1901.
Atlas of America. 1856.   10269
—— 1864.   1182, 1386
Atlas of the world. 1855.   6116
—— 2 v. 1856.   816, 6125
General atlas. 1857.   6129
—— 1858.   827
—— 1864.   6148
—— 1866.   6155
—— 1868.   4348
—— 1870.   856
—— 1872.   6179
—— 1873.   866
—— 1874.   3564, 4354
—— 1876.   879
—— 1877.   6195
—— 1878.   886
—— 1880.   4357
—— 1881.   4359
—— 1883.   911
—— 1884.   6217
—— 1888.   3570
Illustrated cabinet atlas. 1859.   4341

Colton, G. W. and C. B., and Company.
Complete ward atlas of New York City.
1892.   2310, 4944
Stand atlas of Bible geography. 1891.   4115

Colton, Joseph Hutchins, 1800–1893.
Condensed octavo atlas of the Union. 1864.   1387
—— 1865.   11029
General atlas. 1860.   4342
Quarto atlas. 1865.   845

Columbia standard illustrated world atlas. [1942]   7090

Columbian Correspondence College, *Washington, D.C.*
Columbian atlas of two wars. [1900]   3226

Columbiana County Map and Atlas Company.
Atlas of surveys of Columbiana County,
Ohio. 1902.   16394

Columbus Verlag, Paul Oestergaard KG.
Auto-Atlas für Reise, Verkehr und Handel.
[7. Aufl. 1950]   8625
Verkehrs und Strassen Atlas. [1948]   8619

Comisión Técnica de Demarcación de la Frontera entre Honduras y Guatemala.
Mapas que acompañan al Informe detallado.
[1936]   18128

Comissão Interestadual da Bacia Paraná-Uruguai.
Brasil: Alto-Paraná, cartas hidrográficas.
1957.   18195

Comité de Géographie du Maroc.
Atlas du Maroc. [1954–58]   10150

Comité de Rapprochement Belgo-Néerlando-Luxembourgeois.
Officiële auto en motor encyclopaedie der
Benelux landen. [195–]   9069

Comité National de Géographie *(Belgium)*
Atlas de Belgique. [1950–58]   7969

Comité National Français de Géographie.
Atlas de France. [1933–45]   8472
—— [2. éd. 1951–58]   8481

Comité Spécial du Katanga.
Atlas du Katanga. [1929]–52.   10120

Commercial Drafting Service.
Outline desk maps. [1941]   5735
Outline map set for history 4–B. 1940.   5736

Commercial Intelligence. *London.*
Atlas of the world's chief industries. 1905.   71

Commercial Survey Company.
Official street atlas of Akron, Summit and
Portage Counties [Ohio. 1957]   16477
Official street atlas of Ashtabula County
[Ohio. 1958]   16381
Official street atlas of Cleveland and Cuyahoga
County [Ohio. 1953]   16512
Official street atlas of Lake and Geauga
Counties [Ohio. 1953]   16426
Official street atlas of Lorain and Medina
Counties [Ohio. 1955]   16431
Revised official street atlas of Akron and
Summit County [Ohio. 1950]   16476
Revised official street atlas of Cleveland and
Cuyahoga County [Ohio. 1949]   16507
—— [1950]   16508

Commissie voor den Geschiedkundigen Atlas van Nederland.
Geschiedkundige atlas van Nederland. 1913–
38.   9045

Commission de Délimitation de la Frontière Germano-Belge.
Atlas frontière Germano-Belge. [1922]   8522

Commission Dominicano-Haïtienne de Délimitation de Frontières.
Ligne[s] frontière[s]. 194–]   18168

Commission Européenne du Danube. *Galatz, 1856–*
Cartes du delta du Danube. 1887.   2800

Commissione Italo—S. H. S. per la Delimitazione dei Confini del Regno d'Italia e del Regno—S. H. S. Verso lo Stato di Fiume.
Rilievo della linea di confine dello Stato di Fiume. 1922.   8994

Commonwealth Institute of Entomology, *London.*
Distribution maps of insect pests. [1951–52]   5379

Compagnie Française Atlas.
Atlas du monde. 1936.   6871, 6872

Compagnie Nouvelle du Canal de Panama.
Notes techniques concernant l'exposé des dispositions ... Atlas. 1899.   2692

Compañía Hulera Euzkadi.
Caminos de México. [1964]   18079
—— [3. ed. 1967]   18082

Compañía Shell de Venezuela.
Carreteras de Venezuela. 3. ed. [1960?]   18421

Compañía Suramericana de Seguros.
Atlas de Colombia. [1963?]   18346
—— [1965]   18348

Compleat geographer. 4th ed. 1723.   566

Complete set of maps ... relating to ... the canal & rail-road, from the Point of Rocks to Harpers Ferry. MS. 1830.   1778

Complete system of geography. 1747.   603

Compton, Richard J.
Pictorial St. Louis. 1876.   15266

Concentrated farm buying power. [1939]   10538

Conclin, George.
New river guide. 1849.   1308
—— 1850.   1309
—— 1851.   1310
—— 1855.   1311

Condeminas Mascaró, Francisco, 1890–
See Aguado Bleye, Pedro, 1884–   *and* Condeminas Mascaró, Francisco, 1890–

Confédération Nationale des Hôteliers et Restaurateurs.
Belles routes de France. 1. éd. 1932.   8431

Conklin, George W.
Handy manual of useful information and world's atlas. 1889.   4367

Conn Engineering Company.
City of Atmore, Ala. [1962]   11208

Connecticut. *State Highway Dept.*
General highway map[s] 1938.   11694

Connecticut. *State Planning Board.*
Compendium of studies and maps, Connecticut. 1937.   11691

Connecticut State-Wide Highway Planning Survey.
County traffic flow maps. [1940]   11695

Consolidated Edison Company of New York.
Survey of the New York City market. 1945.   16061

Consolidated Publishing Company.
Plat book of Cheboygan County, Mich. 1902.   4739

Constable, Archibald, and Company.
Hand atlas of India. 1893.   3202

Continental Gummi-Werke AG.
Atlas für Kraftfahrer. Deutschland. 9 verb. Aufl. [1930]   8602
—— 11. Aufl. [1932]   8604
Atlas für Mittel-Europa. 8. verb. Aufl. [1924]   7758
—— 9. verb. Aufl. [1925]   7759
Atlas Polski Continental. [193–]   9155
Conti Atlas für Kraftfahrer. Deutschland. 1. (13.) Aufl. [1935]   8609
—— 2. (14.) Aufl. [1935?]   8610
Continental Atlas. 26. Aufl. [1956]   8663
—— 27. Ausg. [1957]   8668
—— 28. Ausg. [1958]   8672
Grosse Conti Atlas für Kraftfahrer. Deutsches Reich. 17. Aufl. [1938]   8615
—— 18. Aufl. [1938]   8616
Grosse Continental Atlas. 20. Aufl. [1950]   8626
—— 21. Aufl. [1951]   8631
—— 22. Aufl. [1951]   8632
—— 23. Aufl. [1952]   8638
—— 24. Aufl. [1953]   8645
—— 25. Aufl. [1955]   8656
Grosser Continental Atlas für Kraftfahrer. Deutschland und Grenzgebiete. [1931]   8603
Landstrassen-Atlas für Mittel-Europa. [1907]   7756
—— 2. verb. Aufl. [1910]   7757

Continental Oil Company.
Touraide. [1959]   10917
—— [1960]   10924

Contra Costa County Title Company.
Map of lands from Pinole thru San Pablo to North Richmond [Calif.] 1955.   11379

Converse, M. S.
City atlas of Elmira, N. Y. 1876.   2283

Cook, Alexander.
See Bankes, Thomas, Blake, Edward Warren, *and* Cook, Alexander.

Cook, Elsie K.
Macmillan's English-Sinhalese wall atlas of Ceylon. [1927]   9504

Cook, James, 1728–1779.
Reizen rondom de waereld. 1797–1809. 648

Cook, James, Lane, Michael, *and others.*
Collection of charts of the coasts of New
foundland and Labrador. [1765–69]
1254, 1256, 10402
James Cook ... collection of charts of the
coasts of Newfoundland and Labrador.
1769–70. *Facsim.* 1965. 10403
Pilote de Terre-Neuve. 1784. 4490

Cook, K. F.
See Bickmore, D. P., *and* Cook, K. F.

Cook County, *Ill. Highway Dept.*
Township maps of Cook County and city of
Chicago. 1935. 12144
—— 1939. 12146
—— 1944. 12148
—— 1952. 12150
—— 1956. 12151
—— 1962. 12159
Township maps of Cook County, Ill. 1958. 12152
—— 1959. 12155
—— 1960. 12156
—— 1961. 12157
—— 1962. 12158
—— 1964. 12160
—— 1965. 12161
—— 1966. 12163
—— 1967. 12164

Cook County, *Ill. Office of Assessor.*
Aer-o-plat atlas of Worth Township, Cook
County, Ill. [1956] 12174

Cookingham, E. R.
Atlas of Sanilac County, Mich. 1894. 1998

Cooperative Well Velocity Surveying Group.
Index of wells surveyed for velocity in California. 1952. 11334

Copenhagen. *Stadskonduktørens Direktorat.*
Kort over København—Frederiksberg.
[1954] 8313

Coppens, P.
[Atlas de géographie de la Belgique. 1852] 7964

Coral State Engineering Company.
[Atlas of Duval County, Fla.] 1926. 11820

Cordier, Henri, 1849–1925.
Description d'un atlas Sino-Coréen. 1896. 3212

Cornell, Sarah S.
Companion atlas to Cornell's High school
geography. 1859. 6134
—— 1864. 273

Cornish, George Augustus, 1872–
Canadian school atlas. 1922. 6479
—— 1925. 6574

Cornish, Vaughan, 1862–1948.
Singapore and naval geography. 1925. 5687

Coronelli, Vincenzo, 1650–1718.
Atlante Veneto. 2 v. 1691–96 [i.e., 1697] 5950
—— 1695–[97] 521
Collection de vues des villes et des plans dans
les pays-Bas. [1697?] 5268
Conquiste della ser. Republica di Uenezia.
1686. 8996
Corso geografico universale. 1692–[94] 5951
Historical and geographical account of the
Morea, Negropont, and the maritime
places, as far as Thessalonica. 1687. 3050, 8900
Memorie istoriografiche delli regni della
Morea, e Negroponte. 1686. 8899

Corréard, Joseph, 1792–1870.
Atlas du guide maritime et stratégique dans la
Mer Noire. 1854. 2816

**Cortambert, Eugène, *i.e.,* Pierre François Eugène,
1805–1881.**
Nouvel atlas de géographie. [1865?] 6152
Nouvel atlas de géographie moderne. [1873?] 4353
Petit atlas de géographie ancienne. [1865?] 5598

Costa Rica.
Costa Rica-Panama arbitration. Maps
annexed to the answer of Costa Rica ...
1914. 5124

**Costa Rica. *Dirección General de Estadística y
Censos.***
Atlas estadístico de Costa Rica. 1953. 18124

Coudreau, Henri Anatole, 1859–1899.
France Équinoxiale. Études et voyage a travers
les Guyanes et l'Amazonie. Atlas. 1887. 18367

Coulier, Philippe Jean.
Atlas général des phares et fanaux. 1850. 95

Council of Social Agencies, *Rochester, N.Y.*
Rochester, New York, 1940. Atlas of population variables. 1943. 16158

County Atlas Company.
Ada County [Idaho] atlas & rural directory.
1967. 12008
Canyon County [Idaho] atlas & rural directory. 1967. 12024

County Map Company.
Official Crystal Lake, Algonquin ... street
and road guide. 1966. 12670
Official McHenry, Wonder Lake ... [Ill.]
street and road guide. 1966. 12693

County Plat and Directory Company.

Dane County, Wis., official farm plat book and directory. [1966]	17712
Delaware County, Ind., official farm plat book. [1966]	12772
Dodge County, Wis., official farm plat book and directory. [1966]	17720
Fulton County, Ind., official farm plat book and directory. [1966]	12792
Fulton County, Ohio, official farm plat book. [1967]	16411
Grant County, Ind., official farm plat book and directory. [1966]	12799
Holmes County, Ohio, official farm plat book. [1965]	16422
Huron County, Mich., official farm plat book and directory. [1965]	14675
Pulaski County, Ind. [1966]	12892
Randolph County, Ind., official farm plat book and directory. [1966]	12896
St. Clair County, Mich., official farm plat book and directory. [1965]	14802
San Joaquin County, Calif., official plat book. [1966]	11469
Starke County, Ind., official farm plat book and directory. [1966]	12916
Tuscola County, Mich., official farm plat book and directory. [1965]	14818
Wabash County, Ind., official farm plat book and directory. [1967]	12942
Wayne County, Ohio, official farm plat book and directory. [1966]	16464

Courtalon, *L'abbé*

Atlas élémentaire. 1774.	3036

Cousté, T. Désire.

Atlas contenant toutes les pieces de terre ... situées sur les communes Arcueil, Cachan, etc. 1851. MS.	8490

Coutans, Guillaume, *b.* 1724.

Atlas topographique en xvi feuilles des environs de Paris. 1800.	3015

Covarrubias, Miguel, 1904–1957.

Pageant of the Pacific. [1940]	10254

Cóvens, Johannes, 1697–1774, *and* Mortier, Cornelis, 1699–1783.

Atlas nouveau. [1683–1761]	3448
[Mappe monde ou globe terrestre—Europe—Asie—Afrique—Amérique. 1703?]	4273
Nieuwe atlas. 1730–[39]	576
—— [1740–1817]	595
Nouvel atlas. [1735?]	3488
Veteris orbis tabulae geographicae. [1714?]	3275

Covert, Walter.

See Palmer, *Sir* Thomas, *and* Covert, Walter.

Covington, C. C., *and* Morse, E. D.

Map of Houston, Tex. 1929.	17251

Cowell, Robert G.

Plat book, Alger County, Mich. [1965]	14594

Cowles, Calvin Duvall, 1849–

See U.S. *War Dept.* Atlas of the War of the Rebellion. 1892.	1349

Coysh, Arthur Wilfred.

See Brown, William Ernest, *and* Coysh, Arthur Wilfred.

Craig, George A.

Atlas of Spencer Town, Mass. 1884.	1939

Cram, de Gruyter und Company.

Elfha-Stadtatlas Hamburg. [1956]	8861

Cram, George F., Company.

Auto trails and commercial survey of the United States. [1922]	10778
Burgess Complete radio atlas of the world. [1923]	5797
Commercial atlas. [1928]	6673
Descriptive review ... of Pennsylvania. 1916.	5012
—— 1917.	5013
Easy reference business-man's atlas of the United States. [1942]	11067
—— [2d ed. 1945]	11070
—— [3d ed. 1947]	11072
—— [4th ed. 1952]	11076
—— [5th ed. 1962]	11084
Europe and the world today. 1920.	7803
Global war atlas. [1944]	7172
Good roads atlas of the United States. [1921]	10775
Historical atlas of Europe past and present. 1916.	7674
Historical war atlas of Europe. 1917.	4220
History-atlas. "Story of the Great War." 1919.	4220a
Home-library world atlas. [1927]	6646
Ideal reference atlas of the world. 1916.	4425
—— [1926]	6607
—— 1931.	6737
International atlas. 1922.	6480
—— [1927]	6647
International radio atlas. 1925–1926 ed. [1925]	5798
Maps of the Bible Lands. 1950.	5347
Modern reference atlas. 1917.	4435
—— 1918.	6380
Modern reference atlas of the world. 1922.	6481
—— 1924.	6548
Modern reference world atlas. [1929]	6700
Official highway map-atlas of Chicago and vicinity. [1928]	12637
Official highway map-atlas of Indiana. [1928]	12729
Official highway map-atlas of Ohio. [1928]	16370
Official paved road atlas of the United States. [1925]	10784

Official paved road atlas of the United States
and Canada. [1929]					10805
—— [1930]						10810
Official paved road atlas of the United States
and Lower Canada. [1927]				10793
—— [1928]						10798
Popular atlas of the world. 1941.			7047
Quick reference atlas of the world. [1950]		7392
Road atlas of the United States, Canada,
Mexico. 1958.					10912
—— [1960]						10925
Story of the Great War. 1918.			5816
Student–quick reference atlas of the world.
[1954]						7592
United States at war. 1918.			4222
Unrivaled atlas of the world. 1916.		4132
—— 1917.						4436

Cram, George F., and Company.
Atlas of the war in Europe. 1914.			4218
Historical atlas of Europe. 1916.			5156
United States at war—American war atlas.
1917.						4221

Cram, George Franklin, 1841–1928.
Agricultural and industrial review of Minne-
sota with world atlas. [1913]		4391, 4773
American readers atlas. 1911.			3611
Army and Navy edition of Cram's Quick ref-
erence atlas. [1907]				1114
—— [1912]						3635
Atlas of Cuyahoga County and the city of
Cleveland, Ohio. 1892.			2368, 2425
Atlas of the war in Europe. 1915.			4219
Atlas of the world. 1902.				1074
—— [1907]						1115
Bankers' and brokers' railroad atlas. 1899.	236
—— 1900.						237
—— 1913.						4181
Complete atlas. 1903.				1082
Descriptive review of ... New York. [1914]	4922
Handy reference atlas. 1903.			1083
Ideal reference atlas. 1902.			1075
—— 1907.						1116
—— 1911.						3615
—— 1913.						4393
—— 1914.						4404
Illustrated atlas. 1885.				924
Illustrated family atlas. [1882]			901
Junior atlas of the world. 1911.			3612
—— 1912.						4385
—— [1923]						6516
Modern atlas. 1907.				1117
—— 1908.						1129
Modern new census atlas of the United States
and world. 1911.				3613
—— 1912.						4386
—— 1914.						6368
Quick reference atlas of the world. [1906]	1109
—— [1922]						6482
Standard American atlas of the world. [1887]	938
—— [1889]						950
Standard American railway system atlas of
the world. [1891]				3349

—— 1892.						238
—— 1897.						239
—— 1898.						240
—— 1899.						241
—— 1900.					4180, 4509
—— 1902.					3350, 3679
—— 1903.						242
—— 1904.						243
—— 1905.					244, 1302
—— 1907.					1118, 1303
—— 1908.					1130, 1304
—— 1909.					3351, 3680
—— 1910.						3601
Success handy reference atlas and gazetteer of
the world. 1902.				6303
—— 1904.						1090
Superior reference atlas of California, Ne-
vada, and the world. 1908	1131, 1459, 2134
Superior reference atlas of Illinois and the
world. 1906.				1110, 1514
Superior reference atlas of Iowa and the
world. 1907.				1119, 1641
Superior reference atlas of Kansas and the
world. 1907.				1120, 1711
Superior reference atlas of Michigan and the
world. 1908.				1131a, 1960a
Superior reference atlas of Minnesota and the
world. 1907.				1121, 2009
Superior reference atlas of Missouri and the
world. 1908.				1131b, 2065
Superior reference atlas of Nebraska and the
world. 1908.				1131c, 2107a
Superior reference atlas of No. and So. Dakota
and the world. 1908.			2340a, 2573a
Superior reference atlas of Oklahoma and the
world. 1908.				1131d, 2436a
Superior reference atlas of Wisconsin and the
world. 1908.				1131e, 2634a
Travelers' atlas of the United States. [1912]	4529
Unabridged atlas. [1907]				1122
Universal atlas. [1896?]				4374
—— [1899]						4376
—— [1900]						6293
Unrivaled atlas of the world. [18th ed.] 1887.	939
—— [23d ed.] 1888.				6240
—— [1891]						6256
—— 1911.						3614
—— 1913.						4392
—— [37th ed.] 1920.				6409
—— 1921.						6438
—— 1927.						6648
—— 62d ed. 1931.				6738
—— 63d ed. 1941.				7048
—— 1952.						7500
Unrivaled family atlas of the world. [1883]	912
—— [1885]						6222
—— [10th ed. 1885]				6223

Cram, George Franklin, and Stebbins, Henry S.
Imperial office directory and reference atlas of
the United States. 1889.				11050

Cram Atlas Company.
New commercial atlas of the United States.
[1875]   1275

Cramer, Louis H.
See Beers, Frederick W., *and* Cramer, Louis
H.

Cramer, Zadok, 1773–1813.
Navigator.   1806.   1312
—— 1808.   1313
—— 1811.   1314
—— 1814.   1315
—— 1817.   1316
—— 1818.   1317
—— 11th ed.   1821.   11098

Cramp, Karl Reginald, 1878–
See Bartholomew, John George, 1860–1920,
and Cramp, Karl Reginald, 1878–

Crane, A. O.
New geography.   [1944]   7173

Crawford, D. C.
Atlas of Ionia County, Mich.   1891.   1975

Crawford, James Ludovic Lindsay, *26th earl of*, 1847–1913.
Bibliotheca Lindesiana. Atlas.   1898.   248

Creutzburg, Nikolaus, 1893–
Atlas der Freien Stadt Danzig.   1936.   9185

Crevaux, Jules Nicolas, 1847–1882.
Fleuves de l'Amérique du Sud, 1877–1879.
1883.   2725

Crevier, Jean Baptiste Louis, 1693–1765.
Atlas de géographie ancienne.   1819.   5599

Crews, Bill D.
Plat book, Williamson County, Ill.   1959.   12567

Crinò, Sebastiano, 1877–
Atlante di geografia moderna.   [1943]   7132

Crisler, Robert Morris, 1921–
See Thomas, Lewis Francis, *and* Crisler,
Robert Morris, 1921–

Crisscross Directory Publishers Company.
Marion County [Ind.] rural route maps.
1937.   12850

Croes, John James Robertson, 1834–1906.
Additions to, and revisions of the West Side
atlas   [of New York City.   1879]   2297

Croes and Van Winkle.
West Side of the city of New York.   [1873]   2294

Croscup, George Edward, 1851–1917.
History made visible: A synchronic chart and

statistical tables of United States history.
1910.   4505
History made visible: United States history
with   synchronic   charts.   National   ed.
1911.   4506

Crowell and Kirkpatrick Company.
New people's atlas.   1901.   1062
New popular atlas.   1900.   1048
Twentieth century peerless atlas.   1901.   1063
Twentieth century pictorial atlas.   1901.   1064
Twentieth century popular atlas.   1901.   1065

Crowell Publishing Company.
National markets and national advertising.
1922.   10539
Twentieth century peerless atlas.   1902.   1076
—— 1903.   1084
—— 1905.   1099

Croydon Natural History and Scientific Society.
Regional survey atlas of Croydon.   1936.   8149

Crull, Richard.
Mecklenburg, Werden und Sein eines Gaues.
[1938]   8754

Cruls, Luiz, 1848–1908.
Commissão exploradora do planalto central
do Brazil.   1894.   2744

Cruquius, Jacob.
See Cruquius, Nicolaas Samuel, 1678–1754,
and Cruquius, Jacob.

Cruquius, Nicolaas Samuel, 1678–1754, *and* Cruquius, Jacob.
Hooge heemraedschap van Delflant.   1712.   9099

Crutwell, Clement, 1743–1808.
Atlas to Cruttwell's gazetteer.   [1799]   692
—— [1808]   715

Cruys, Cornelius, 1657–1727.
Nieuw pas-kaart boek, behelsende de groote
rivier Don of Tanais.   [1703 or 4]   9296

Cuba. *Dirección General del Censo.*
Censo de 1943.   [Atlas. 1945]   18165

Cuba. *Gobierno y Capitania General.*
Planos de bolsillo de la Isla de Cuba.   1842.   2712

Cuba. *Ministerio de Gobernación.*
Plano general de la isla de Cuba.   [1908]   18164

Cuba. *Oficina Nacional de los Censos Demográfico y Electoral.*
Atlas censo 1953.   [1958?]   18167

Cuba. *Secretaría de Obras Públicas.*
Planos indicando el plan general de carreteras.
[1925]   18163

Cumberland, Kenneth Brailey.
Whitcombe's Atlas of geography for New
Zealand and Australian schools. 3d ed.
[1943]   7133
—— 4th ed. [1946]   7227

Cumings, Samuel.
Western navigator. 1822.   1318
Western pilot. 1825.   1319
—— 1829.   3681
—— 1832.   1320
—— 1834.   1321
—— 1838.   1322
—— 1840.   4513
—— 1843.   4514
—— 1848.   3682
—— 1854.   4515

Cumming, William Patterson, 1900–
North Carolina in maps. 1966.   16204

Cummings, J. Q.
See Derr, C. W., and Cummings, J. Q.

Cummings, Jacob Abbot, 1773–1820.
School atlas. 4th ed. [1817]   274
—— [1818]   6040
—— 7th ed. [1820]   275
—— 8th ed. [1821]   276, 740

Cummings, Robert A., Jr., and Associates.
Allegheny County [Pa.] maps. [1954]   16769

**Cunetto's Street and sectional guide map of St.
Louis and St. Louis County [Mo. 1959]**   15290
—— [1961]   15292
—— [1963]   15294

Cunill Grau, Pedro.
Atlas histórico de Chile. 2. ed. 1961.   18321

Cunningham, R. S., and Company.
Atlas of Schenectady, N. Y. 1892.   2326

Curlux Map Company.
Atlas of Florida. 1926.   11798

Current Events.
Map supplement. 1941.   5862
Maps and facts for world understanding.
[1950]   7393

Curtice, David L.
Revised atlas of the city of St. Paul. 1908.   2058a
Standard atlas of the city of St. Paul. [1887]   2057

Curtis, J. R.
Great State, Ohio. [Darke County. 1951]   16404

Curtis Publishing Company.
National market; a series of maps. 1947.   10540
Sales quotas by counties and by cities. 1925.   10541

**Curtius, Ernst, 1814–1896, and Kaupert, Johann
August, 1822–1899.**
Atlas von Athen. 1878.   4038
Karten von Attika. 1904.   3052

Cutch, India. Statistics Dept.
Statistical atlas of Kutch. 1954.   9717

Cutter, James W.
Puget Sound and Northwest waterways.
[1953]   17593

Cvijić, Jovan, 1865–1927.
Велика језера Балканскоіа полуострва:
Језера Македоније, Старе Србије и
Епира. [Large lakes of the Balkan Penin-
sula: Lakes of Macedonia, Old Serbia and
Epirus] 1902.   7821
Геолошки атлас. [Geological atlas of Mace-
donia.] 1903.   3161

**Cyclopaedia; or, Universal dictionary of arts, sci-
ences ... Ancient and modern atlas.** [1806]   711
—— 1820.   4312a

**Czechoslovak Republic. Ústředni Správa Geodesie a
Kartografie.**
Automapa ČSR. [1. vyd.] 1957.   8244
Lesnický a myslivecký atlas. [1. vyd.] 1955.   8239
Spojené státy americké. 1962.   11085
—— [2. vyd.] 1965.   11088
Střední Amerika. 1966.   18054
Vodácká a rybářská mapa Lužnice. [1. vyd.
1957]   8254
Vodácká mapa Vltavy. [1. vyd. 1955]   8255

**Czoernig von Czernhausen, Karl, Freiherr, 1804–
1889.**
Ethnographische Karte der Oesterreichischen
Monarchie. 1855.   3990

Dagnino Pastore, Lorenzo.
Atlas ajustado al texto de geografía. [194-]   6994
Cuaderno de trabajos practicos de geografia.
[1940?]   5737

Dahl, Peter M.
Plat book of Hennepin County, Minn. 1898.   2020
Plat book of Ramsey County, Minn. 1898.   2036

Dai Nihon Chiri Gakkai.
Dai Nihon fukembetsu chizu narabini chimei
taikan. [Prefectural atlas of Japan with
comprehensive gazetteer. 1944]   9817

Daiichi Jūtaku Kyōkai, Fuse, Japan.
Kameoka-shi [jūtaku annai zuchō. Kameoka
real estate atlas. New ed. 1959]   9889

Daily Express, London.
Road book and gazetteer of Great Britain.
[1950]   8052

Daily News key atlas to a reconstructed world.
1922. 6489

Daily Telegraph victory atlas of the world. [1920] 6410
—— [1921] 6440

Dainelli, Giotto, 1878–1968.
Atlante fisico economico d'Italia. 1940. 8953
Dalmazia. 1918. 5186a

Dairyman-Gazette Company.
Plat book, Waupaca County, Wis. 1939. 17978

Dale, W., and Rennard, T. A.
Historical atlas for South African schools.
[195–?] 5502

Dallas. *Dept. of City Planning.*
Thoroughfares: Dallas metropolitan area.
1957. 17223

Dalrymple, Alexander, 1737–1808, and others.
Charts and plans. 1703–1807. 543, 544

Danckerts, Justus, 1635–1701.
Atlas. [1703?] 540, 541
—— [1710?] 3470

Danckwerth, Caspar, d. 1672.
Newe Landesbeschreibung der zweij Hert-
zogthümer Schleswich und Holstein.
1652. 8804

Dane County Atlas Company.
New atlas of Dane County, Wis. 1926. 17707

Danesi, C.
See Gibelli, Giuseppe, 1831–1898, Brunamonti, G., and Danesi, C.

Dansk Shell.
Automobil-kort over Danmark. 1947. 8270

Danske Pertroleums Aktieselskab.
Danmarkskort med oplysninger for auto-
mobilister. [194–] 8269

Danske Videnskabernes Selskab, Copenhagen.
Atlas over Kongeriget Danmark og
Hertugdömmet Slesvig. [1956] 8263

Dantín Cereceda, Juan, 1881–1943, and Loriente
Cancio, V.
Atlas histórico de la América Hispano-Portu-
guesa. 1936. 18042

Danysz-Fleszarowa, Regina.
See Romer, Eugeniusz, 1871–1954, and
Danysz-Fleszarowa, Regina.

Danz, Caspar Friedrich, 1796–1881, and Fuchs,
Caspar Friedrich, 1803–1874.
Acht Tafeln zur physisch-medicinischen To-

pographie des Kreises Schmalkalden.
1848. 3041

Darbishire, Benard Vernon, 1865–
School Bible atlas. [1914] 4116
War atlas. 1915. 4223

Dardano, Achille, 1870–1938, and Riccardi,
Riccardo, 1897–
Atlante d'Africa. 1936. 10098

Darton, William, *fl.* 1810–1837.
New miniature atlas ... of England & Wales.
[1820] 8128
Union atlas. 1812–[14] 719

Davidson, C. Wright.
Atlas of the city of Minneapolis ... Minn.
1887. 2054

Davidson, Samuel.
[Plat book of land in the District of Columbia.
1809] 11762

Davies, Cuthbert Collin, 1896–
Historical atlas of the Indian peninsula.
1949. 9690
—— [1953] 9691
—— 2d ed. 1959. 9692

Davies, Margaret.
Wales in maps. 1951. 8221
—— 1958. 8223

Davies, Thomas.
See Nelson, Thomas, 1822–1892, *and* Davies,
Thomas.

Davis, Ellis A.
Commercial encyclopedia. British Columbia,
Alberta, Saskatchewan, and Manitoba.
1910. 3671
Commercial encyclopedia. California, Ne-
vada, Utah, and Arizona. 1910.
3694, 3701, 3705, 3832, 3923
Standard encyclopedia. Montana, Idaho,
Alaska, Washington, and Oregon. 1910.
3695, 3700, 3717, 3823, 3886, 3924

Davis, F. A.
Illustrated historical atlas of Berks County,
Pa. 1876. 2461
New illustrated atlas of Lehigh County, Pa.
1876. 2481

Davis, F. A., and Company.
Combination atlas map of Rockland County,
N.Y. 1876. 2251

Davis, J. E.
Township plat book of Delaware County,
Iowa. 1894. 13318

Davis, William Morris, 1850–1914.
Atlas for practical exercises in physical geography. 1908. — 3346
New England states. 1895. — 1441

Davity, Pierre.
See Avity, Pierre d', *Sieur de Montmartin,* 1573–1635.

Daya, Parameshwar, 1920–
Bihar in maps. 1953. — 9714

Dayton, A. W.
See Lathrop, J. M., *and* Dayton, A. W.

De Agostini, Giovanni, 1863–1941.
See Agostini, Giovanni De, 1863–1941.

Dean, James, 1777–1849.
Alphabetical atlas, or Gazetteer of Vermont. 1808. — 2592

Deaner, Otto Percival, 1886–
Abstract plats of Panola County, Tex. 1946. — 17182
Abstract plats of Shelby County, Tex. 1949. — 17183

Debes, Ernst, 1840–1923.
Columbus Hausatlas. [1952] — 7501
Columbus–Volksatlas. 1938. — 6943
—— 3. Aufl. 1941. — 7049
Columbus Weltatlas. 1935. — 6837
—— 1937. — 6908
—— [1950] — 7394, 7395
Elementar-Atlas. 1906. — 3366
Neuer Handatlas. 1895. — 4372
—— 1900. — 1049
—— 1905. — 1099a
—— 1911–12. — 3634a
—— 4. verm. und verb. Aufl. 1913. — 4394
—— 4. verm. und verb. Aufl. 2. Abdr. 1914. — 4405
Schul–Atlas. [1901] — 277
—— 1904. — 3367
Schul–Atlas für die mittleren Unterrichtsstufen. 53. Aufl. [1901] — 6296
Schul–Atlas für die Oberklassen höherer Lehranstalten. 11. Aufl. 1893. — 6264
Schulatlas für die unteren und mittleren Unterrichtsstufen. 90. Aufl. [1908] — 6326
—— 95. Aufl. 1913. — 6356
Schul–Atlas für Ober– und Mittelklassen höherer Lehranstalten. 48. Aufl. 1905. — 6317
—— 53. Aufl. 1908. — 6327

Debes, Ernst, *and* Schlee, Paul, 1868–
Brandenburger Schulatlas. 70. Aufl. 1925. — 6575
Grosser Schulatlas. 70. Aufl. 1925. — 6576
—— 75. Aufl. 1931. — 6739
Hamburger Schulatlas. 70. Aufl. 1925. — 6577
Kölner Schulatlas. 71. Aufl. 1926. — 6608
Rheinischer Schulatlas. 70. Aufl. 1925. — 6578
Schlesischer Schulatlas. 71. Aufl. 1926. — 6609
Schulatlas für Bremen und das Unterwesergebiet. 107. Aufl. 1925. — 6579

Debes, Ernst, *and* Schmidt, Max Georg, 1870–
Westfälischer Schulatlass. 71. Aufl. 1926. — 6610

De Boeck, Albert.
Petit atlas du Congo Belge. [1911?] — 5312
—— [1912?] — 4083a

De Brahm, John Gerar William, 1717–*ca.* 1799.
Atlantic pilot. 1772. — 1197

Deets, Edward Henderson, 1888–1958, *and* Maddox, Charles J.
Real estate atlas of the part of Montogomery County, Maryland, adjacent to the District of Columbia. 1917. — 4710

De Fee, Larry.
Aero-map ... of Winston-Salem and all of Forsyth County [N.C. 1962] — 16246

Defenders of the world, United States and her allies. [1917] — 5817

Deharme, ——
Plan de la ville et fauxbourgs de Paris. 1766. — 3014

De Kalb County Abstract Company.
Atlas of De Kalb County, Ill. [1956] — 12185

De Kalb Daily Chronicle, *De Kalb, Ill.*
Plat book of De Kalb County, Ill. [1920?] — 12182

De Krafft, Frederick C.
Plan of the city of Washington. MS. 1824. — 11764
[Plats of Washington. MS. 1824?] — 11765

De Krafft, John W.
Copy of the original squares in the city of Washington [D.C.] MS. 1832. — 11766

Delachaux, Enrique A. S., 1864–1908.
Atlas meteorológico de la República Argentina. 1901. — 2736

Delagrave, *firm.*
Proche Orient. [1937] — 9491

Delamarche, Alexandre, *i.e.* Francois Alexandre, 1815–1884.
Atlas de géographie ancienne, du moyen âge, et moderne. 1850. — 3554, 6110

Delamarche, Charles Francois, 1740–1817.
Atlas élémentaire. 1816. — 727
Institutions géographiques, ou Description générale du globe terrestre. [1795] — 6005

Delamarche, Félix.
Atlas de la géographie ancienne, du moyen âge, et moderne. 1827. — 6058
Atlas de la géographie ancienne et moderne. [1820] — 4317, 6044

De La Valette, John.
Atlas of the progress in Nawanagar State. [1932]   9726

Delaware. *State Highway Dept.*
Incorporated towns of Delaware. [1950]   11750
—— [1955]   11751
—— [1959]   11752

De-Lazari, Aleksandr Nikolaevich, 1880–
Альбомсхем по истории гражданской войны в СССР (1917–1922 ГГ.) [Book of Plans on the history of the civil war in USSR.] 1939.   9238

Déléage, André.
Vie économique et sociale de la Bourgogne dans le haut moyen âge. 1941.   8487

Delesse, Achille Ernest Oscar Joseph, 1817–1881.
Lithologie du fond des mers ... Atlas. 1872.   4161

Delgadillo, Daniel, 1872–
Atlas geográfico escolar de la República Mexicana. [1910]   18088

Delisle, Guillaume, 1675–1726.
Atlante novissimo. 1740–50.   594
[Atlas de géographie] 1700–12.   533
Atlas nouveau. 1730.   3486
—— 1733.   580, 581, 3487
—— [1741?]   596
[Collection of maps of the world] 1722–74.   565

Delisle, Guillaume, *and* **Buache, Philippe, 1700–1773.**
Atlas géographique de la France. [1794]   8459
Atlas géographique des quatre parties du monde. [1769–99]   3512
—— [1780–1824]   5993
—— [1789?]   671
—— [1831?]   759
[Atlas géographique et universel. 1700–63]
                                       535, 636, 3456
Atlas géographique et universel. 1781–[84]   655
Cartes et tables de la géographie physique. 1754–[57]   220

Delisle, Guillaume, *and others.*
Atlas géographique et universel. 1789–[90]   3525

Delisle, Joseph Nicolas, 1688–1768, *and others.*
See Akademiia Nauk SSSR.

Delkeskamp, Friedrich Wilhelm, 1794–1872.
Atlas pittoresque du Rhin. 1847–[48]   7880
Relief pittoresque du sol classique de la Suisse. [1830]   9443

Delphi Journal, *and* **Hoosier Democrat.**
See Kenyon Company.

Denaix, Maxime Auguste, *d.* **1844.**
Atlas physique, politique et historique de la France. 1855.   4019
Atlas physique, politique et historique de l'Europe. 1855.   3965
—— 1860.   3966

Denis, Louis, 1725–1795.
Atlas géographique. [1764?]   3299
Empire des Solipses. 1764.   81
See also Pasquier, Jacques Jean, 1718–1785, *and* Denis, Louis, 1725–1795.

Denison, Charles, 1845–1909.
Annual and seasonal climatic charts of the United States. 1888.   10499
Climates of the United States in colors. 1893.   10500

Denison Bulletin, *Denison, Ia.*
County map and township plat book of Crawford County, Iowa. [1940?]   13280

Denmark, L. Polk.
See Warren, Jule Benjamin, 1887– *and* Denmark, L. Polk.

Denmark. *Geodǣtisk Institut.*
Generalstabens kort, Danmark i 1:160,000. 1916–29.   8274
Generalstabens kort, Danmark i 1:320,000. 3. udg. 1923.   8276
—— 4. udg. 1929.   8278
Generalstabskort, Danmark i 1:100,000. 1928–55.   8277
Gennemkørselskort for 177 Danske byer. 1933.   8256
Hjemstavnskort over København. [1932]   8297
Kort, Danmark i 1:200,000. 1931.   8279
—— 2. udg. 1935.   8280
—— 4. udg. 1938.   8281
—— 5. udg. 1942.   8282
—— 6. udg. 1945.   8283
—— 7. udg. 1946.   8284
—— 7. udg. 3. opl. 1947.   8285
—— 13. udg. 1. opl. 1955.   8287
—— 14. udg. 1. opl. 1956.   8288
Uppdráttur Íslands. [1936–45]   8933
—— 1945.   8934

Denmark. *Hǣren. Generalstaben. Topografiske Afdeling.*
Amtskort over Danmark. [1904]   8272

Denmark. *Statens Ligningsdirektorat.*
Grundvǣrdikort over Aalborg købstad. 1951.   8292
Grundvǣrdikort over Aarhus købstad. 1951.   8293
—— 1957.   8294
Grundvǣrdikort over Esbjerg købstad. 1951.   8320
—— 1957.   8321

Grundvaerdikort over Farum kommune. 1952. 8322

Grundvaerdikort over Fredericia købstad.
1951. 8323
—— 1957. 8324

Grundvaerdikort over Gentofte kommune.
1957. 8325

Grundvaerdikort over Glostrup og Brønd-byernes kommuner. 1957. 8326

Grundvaerdikort over Helsingør købstad.
1951. 8327
—— 1957. 8328

Grundvaerdikort over Herlev kommune.
1952 8329
—— 1957. 8330

Grundvaerdikort over Himmelev kommune.
1952. 8331

Grundvaerdikort over Høje Taastrup kom-mune. 1951. 8332
—— 1957. 8333

Grundvaerdikort over Hørsholm kommune.
1951. 8334
—— 1957. 8335

Grundvaerdikort over Horsens købstad.
1951. 8336
—— 1957. 8337

Grundvaerdikort over Hvedstrup-Fløng kommune. 1952. 8338

Grundvaerdikort over Hvidovre kommune.
1951. 8339
—— 1957. 8340

Grundvaerdikort over København og Frederiksberg. 1951. 8307
—— 1957. 8317

Grundvaerdikort over købstaeder i Bornholms Amt. 1953. 8289

Grundvaerdikort over købstaeder i Maribo Amt. 1953. 8291

Grundvaerdikort over købstaeder i Svend-borg, Odense og Assens amter. 1953. 8257

Grundvaerdikort over købstaeder i Vejle, Ringkøbing, Ribe. 1954. 8258

Grundvaerdikort over Kolding købstad.
1951. 8341
—— 1957. 8342

Grundvaerdikort over Lynby-Taarbaek kom-mune. 1951. 8343
—— 1957. 8344

Grundvaerdikort over Odense købstad.
1951. 8345
—— 1957. 8346

Grundvaerdikort over Randers købstad.
1951. 8347
—— 1957. 8348

Grundvaerdikort over Rødovre kommune.
1951. 8349
—— 1957. 8350

Grundvaerdikort over Søllerød kommune.
1951. 8351
—— 1957. 8352

Grundvaerdikort over Store Magleby.
1951. 8353
—— 1957. 8354

Grundvaerdikort over Taarnby kommune.
1957. 8355

Grundvaerdikort over Torslunde-Ishøj og Vallensbaek kommuner. 1952. 8356
—— 1957. 8357

Grundvaerdikort over Vejle købstad. 1951. 8358
—— 1957. 8359

Denoyer, Levinus Philippus, 1875–1964.
Abridged elementary school atlas. [1944] 7174
—— [1952] 7502
School atlas. 1947. 7260
Student atlas. 1949. 7339

Denoyer-Geppert Atlas of American history.
[1957] 10641

Denoyer–Geppert Company.
Desk outline maps, $8\frac{1}{2} \times 11$ [inch] size.
[1945] 5738
—— 11 × 16 [inch] size. [1945] 5739
—— 16 × 22 [inch] size. [1945] 5740

Dent, J. M., and Sons.
Atlas of ancient & classical geography.
[1909] 5600
—— [1933] 5601
—— [1935?] 5602
Everyman's Atlas of ancient and classical geography. [1952] 5603

Denver Weekly Post.
Atlas containing ... maps [of] Colorado, Utah, Wyoming. 1914. 4531
Atlas of the Rocky Mountains and national forests. [1911] 3697

De Pue and Company.
Illustrated atlas and history of Yolo County, Cal. 1879. 11503

De Puy, William Harrison, 1821–1901.
People's atlas. [1885] 925
Universal guide and gazetteer. 1887. 940

Derok, D. J.
Атлас кръевина србијс. [Atlas of Serbia.]
1911. 4063a

Derr, C. W., and Cummings, J. Q.
Atlas of Winnebago county, Ill. 1947. 12571

Derr Map Studio.
Atlas of Walworth County, Wis. 1966. 17956
Atlas of Waukesha County, Wis. 1964. 17973
Plat book, Branch County, Mich. 1958. 14624
Plat book, Dodge County, Wis. 1958. 17719
Plat book, Jefferson County, Wis. 1959. 17787
Plat book, Jersey County, Ill. 1958. 12294
Plat book, Lafayette County, Wis. 1958. 17810
Plat book, Marshall & Putnam Counties, Ill.
1959. 12397
Plat book, Pike County, Ill. 1958. 12459
Plat book, Winnebago County, Ill. 1960. 12573

Derrick, Paul E., Advertising Agency.
Marketing maps of Gt. Britain & Eire.
[1949]   8002

Des Barres, Joseph Frederick Wallet, 1721–1824.
See Atlantic Neptune.

Desbuissons, L. E., b. 1827 and others.
Nouvel atlas illustré. 1891.   964

Descripcion de plazas, prendos y fuertes de las Filipinas [1777?]   5304

Deseret News, Salt Lake City.
Deseret News atlas. 1914.   11052

Desert Engineering Company.
Hesperia [Calif.] 1957.   11525
Lucerne Vallery [Calif.] and vicinity 1957.   11556

Desmarest, Nicolas, 1725–1815.
See Bonne, Rigobert, 1727–1794, *and* Desmarest, Nicolas, 1725–1815.

Desmarest, Nicolas, and Bory de St. Vincent, Jean Baptiste Geneviève Marcellin, baron, 1778–1846.
Atlas encyclopédique. 1827.   221

Desmond, John T.
Atlas of Haverhill and Bradford, Mass.
1892.   1863, 1891

Desnos, Louis Charles, fl. 1750–1770.
Almanach géographique. 1770.   644
Atlas chorographique, historique, et portatif des élections du Royaume. 1763–[66]   5225
Atlas de la France. 1775.   8455
Atlas général. 1767–[69]   5985
—— 1790–[92]   5998
Nouvel atlas d'Angleterre. 1767.   2918
Nouvel itinéraire général. 1768.   5162
Tableau analytique de la France. 1766.   2993

Despont, J.
Nouvel atlas des missions. 1951.   5406

Detroit. Board of Assessors.
Land valuation maps of the city of Detroit.
[1928]   14854
—— [1929]   14855
—— [1950]   14859
—— [1951]   14862

Deuerlein, Ernst, 1893–
See Böhm, Wilhelmine, 1901–   *and*
Deuerlein, Ernst, 1893–

Deutsche Arbeitsfront. Arbeitswissenschaftliches Institut.
Karten zur Struktur der UdSSR. 1941.   9214

Deutsche Buch-Gemeinschaft, Berlin.
Kleiner Weltatlas. [1938]   6944

Deutsche Kolonialgesellschaft.
Deutscher Kolonialatlas. 1905.   8533
—— 1906.   8534
—— 1908.   8535
—— 1910.   8536
—— 1911.   8537
—— 1912.   8538
—— 18. Jahrg. 1914.   8539
—— 19. Jahrg. 1918.   8540
—— 20. Jahrg. 1936.   8541
Kleiner Deutscher Kolonialatlas. 1896.   8542
—— 2. durchgesehene und verm. Ausg.
1898.   8543
—— 1899.   8544
—— 1900.   3018
Wirtschafts Atlas der Deutschen Kolonien.
[1908]   3019

Deutsche Kolonialgesellschaft. Kolonial-Wirthschaftliches Komitee.
Wirtschafts-Atlas der Deutschen Kolonien.
2. verb. Aufl. [1907]   8545

Deutsche Reichsbahn.
Wegkarten (Leitungswege) für die besetzten Westgebiete nach und von Bahnhöfen der Deutschen Reichsbahn. [1944]   8594

Deutsche Viscobil Öl Gesellschaft.
Viscobil Auto Tourenkarte. 1953.   8646

Deutscher Kraftverkehr.
Wirschafts- und Verkehrsatlas Rheinisch-Westfälisches Industriegebiet. [1952]   8820

Deutscher Sprachatlas. 1926–52.   8581

Deutscher Wetterdienst in der US Zone.
Klima-Atlas von Bayern. 1952.   8719
Klima-Atlas von Hessen. 1950.   8745

Deutscher Zentralverlag.
Strassen Atlas von Deutschland. 2. verb.
Aufl. [1948]   8620
—— 3. verb. Aufl. [1952]   8639

Deutschland und die Welt. Atlas für Beruf und Haus. 1934.   6809

Developing Urban Detroit Area Research Project.
Emergence and growth of ... urban Detroit
area. 1966.   14558

Deventer, Jacobus van, ca. 1500–1575.
Atlas des villes de la Belgique au XVIe siècle.
1884–1924.   2870, 3995, 5187, 7941
Kaarten van de Nederlandsche Provinciën in de zestiende eeuw. 1941.   9080
Nederlandsche steden in de 16e eeuw. 1916–
23.   5269, 9031

Devert, B. A. H., and others.
See Plan de Paris. [1830?]

Devlin and Company.
Metropolis explained. 1871.   2293

Dewey, James H.
Map of the city of Benton Harbor and vicinity ... Mich. 1916.   14847

Dheulland, Guillaume, 1700–1770.
Carte nouvelle du Duché de Brabant et partie de la Hollande. [1747]   4050

Diamond State Telephone Company.
Line maps, New Castle County [Del.] exchange and base rate areas. 1957.   11754

Díaz de Villegas y Bustamante, José.
Atlas general de España. 1946.   9337

Diccionario geográfico universal. Atlas. [1830–34]   4318

Dickerson Map Service.
Scott County, Iowa, plat book. 1941.   13911

Dickson, George K.
See Riniker, H., Hagnauer, Robert, *and* Dickson, George K.

Diercke, Carl, 1842–1913.
Schul-Atlas. 44. Aufl. 1908.   278
Schulatlas für die unteren Klassen höherer Lehranstalten. 1923.   6517
Schul–Atlas für höhere Lehranstalten. 37. Aufl. 2. Abdr. 1901.   6297
—— 44. Aufl. 2. Abdr. 1908.   6328
—— 52. Aufl. 2. Abdr. 1918.   6381
—— 63. Aufl. 1926.   6611
—— 68. Aufl. 1929.   6701
—— 70. Aufl. 1930.   6722
—— 78. Aufl. [1937 i.e., 1938]   6935
—— 79. Aufl. 2. Abdr. [1939]   6974
—— 81. Aufl. [1942]   7091
Welt Atlas. 83. Aufl. [1950]   7396
—— 86. Aufl. [1952]   7503
See also Lange, Henry, 1821–1893, *and* Diercke, Carl, 1842–1913.

Diercke, Paul, 1874–1937.
Schulatlas für höhere Lehranstalten. Mittelausg. 1. Aufl. 1914.   4191

Diercke, Paul, *and* Reicke, Erich, 1884–
Reichswehr–Atlas. 1923.   6518
—— 2. Aufl. 1924.   6549

Dietrich, Bruno, 1886–
Natural border of the north-east districts of Upper-Silesia. [1921]   8810

Digby, Charles Eckler.
Crowley County, Colo. [1947]   11655
Pueblo County, Colo. land ownership. 1947.   11667

Dilich, Wilhelm [Schäffer] *called*, d. 1655.
Landtafeln Hessischer Ämter zwischen Rhein und Weser. 1927.   8747

Dipti Printing and Binding Works, *Calcutta*.
Map of Calcutta. [195–]   9727

Dirwaldt, Joseph.
Allgemeiner Hand–Atlas. 1816.   6037

Dispatch atlas. 1863.   839

District of Columbia. *Board of Commissioners*.
City of Washington ... Statistical maps. [1880]   11769

District of Columbia. *Highway Dept*.
Sectional maps of the District of Columbia. [1942]   11780

Dittmar, Heinrich, 1792–1866.
Historischer Atlas. 4. Aufl. [1856?]   4133

Diversified Map Corportion.
Complete Abercrombie & Fitch vacation atlas for all North America. 1965.   10954
Interstate atlas. [1967]   10970
New Grosset road atlas of the United States, Canada and Mexico. 1967.   10971
Road atlas. 1967.   10972
This Week Magazine's Vacation planner and speedy flip-out road atlas. [1965]   10955

Diversity Shop.
Plat book, Delaware County [Ohio] 1964.   16407

Dixon Evening Telegraph.
Lee County, Ill., farm plat book. [1949]   12345

Djakarta. Magnetisch en Meteorologisch Observatorium.
Regenval in Nederlandsch-Indië. 1925.   9757
Uitkomsten der regenwaarnemingen op Java. 1915.   9758

Dodd, Mead and Company.
Universal atlas. 1892.   971, 971a

Dodge, Robert Perly, 1817–1887.
Plats of the 131 squares in West Washington. 1883.   1502

Doerre, Edmund.
Fishing maps [Wisconsin, Minnesota, and Iowa] 1951.   10748

Dollfus, Jean.
Atlas mondial. [1948]   7302

Dolph, Frank Bernard, 1897–
Land ownership atlas of Polk County, Fla. [1946]   11849
Miami Beach to Golden Beach, Fla. [1944]   11905

Dolph, Frank B., Company.
Acreage atlas of Dade County, Fla.   [1956]   11816
Atlas, Florida's southeast coast cities.   [1947]   11790
Land atlas of Broward County, Fla.   [1956]   11807
Land atlas of Hillsborough County, Fla. 1946.   11827
Land atlas of Martin County, Fla.   [1956]   11835
Land atlas of St. Lucie County, Fla.   [1956]   11853
Land atlas of Sarasota County, Fla.   1956.   11854
Lot, block and subdivision atlas of Fort Lauderdale, Fla.   [1957]   11872
Lot, block and subdivision atlas of Lakeland, Fla.   1958.   11890
Street and pictorial atlas of Broward County, Fla.   1958.   11808
Subdivision atlas, Deerfield Beach [Fla.] and vicinity.   [1957]   11868
Subdivision atlas, Pompano Beach [Fla.] and vicintiy.   [1956]   11921

Dolph and Stewart.
Acreage ownership atlas of Dade County, Fla. [1937]   11815
Atlas of Fairfield County, Conn.   [1933]   11697
Atlas of Hartford County, Conn.   [1931]   11702
Atlas of New Haven County, Conn.   [1931]   11706
Atlas of Suffolk County, N.Y.   [1929]   15905
Atlas of Westchester County, N.Y.   [1942]   15919
Lot and block atlas of the city of Savannah, Ga.   1927.   11980
Map of Palm Beach County, Fla.   1937.   11843
Street and pictorial atlas of Brooklyn [N.Y.] 1942.   15947
Street and pictorial atlas of Queens Borough, New York City.   [1941]   16122
Street, land ownership and pictorial atlas of Fairfield County, Conn.   1942.   11699
Street, road and land ownership atlas of Nassau County ... N.Y.   [1940]   15890

Dolph Map Company.
Street & pictorial atlas of Orange County, Fla.   [1948]   11837
Street atlas of eastern Palm Beach County, Fla.   1964.   11844

Dolph-Stewart atlas of Jacksonville ... Fla.   1938.   11884

Dolph-Stewart lot and block atlas of Jacksonville, Fla.   1940.   11885
—— 1942.   11886

Dominican Republic. *Dirección General de Estadistica y Censos.*
Republica Dominicana.   1944.   18169

Donald, Guy D.
Map of San Pedro [Calif.   1946]   11604

Doncker, Hendrik, 1626–1699.
Zee-atlas.   1660–[61]   468
—— 1665.   472
—— 1666.   5688

See also Jacobsz, Theunis, Doncker, Hendrik, *and* Goos, Hendrik.

Donnelley, Reuben Hamilton, 1864–1929.
Atlas of the city of St. Paul, Minn.   1892.   2058, 15161
Sectional atlas of the city of Chicago.   1905.   1590

Donohue, Jerry, 1885–
Atlas of Sheboygan County, Wis.   [1916]   5104

Donohue, Jerry, Engineering Company.
Geographical and historical atlas of Sheboygan County, Wis.   [1941]   17929

Dorn Seiffen, Isaac, 1818–1898.
Atlas van Nederlandsch Oost- en West Indië. [1901]   2715, 3217

Douglas County, *Oreg. Forest Appraisal Dept.*
Central & southern Douglas County, Oreg. [1954]   16678

Dow, Earle Wilbur, 1868–1946.
Atlas of European history.   1907.   2788

Dower, John, *fl.* **1838.**
New general atlas.   1831.   3549
—— 1835.   772
—— 1838.   6083
—— 1842.   6094
—— [1854]   812

Doyle, Joseph B.
See Barthel, Otto, Halfpenny, H. E., Hasson, Thomas W., *and* Doyle, Joseph B.

Draper Brothers Company.
Atlas of American papermaking.   1947.   10705

Drexel, Albert, 1889–
Atlas linguisticus.   [1934]   5682

Drioux, Claude Joseph, 1820–1898, *and* **Leroy, Charles.**
Atlas universel et classique de géographie. 1867.   3562
—— 1879.   889
—— 1882.   3567
—— 1887.   940a
—— 1890.   6253
—— 1892.   6260
—— [192–]   6404

Dripps, Mathew.
Atlas of New Utrecht [Brooklyn, N.Y. 1887]   4940
Map of the city of Brooklyn, N.Y.   1869.   2273
Plan of New York City from the Battery to Spuyten Duyvil Creek.   1867.   2291

Droysen, Gustav, 1838–1908.
Allgemeiner historischer Handatlas.   1886.   105

Drury, Luke, *d.* **1845.**
  Geography for schools.   1822.   279

Dubail, Yvon, *i.e.* **Augustin Yvon Edmond, 1851–1934.**
  Atlas de l'Europe militaire.   1880.   2817

Dubois, Edmond Marcel, 1856–1916, *and* **Sieurin, E.**
  Cartes d'étude pour servir à l'enseignement de la géographie. 7. éd.   1905.   2857
  Cartes d'étude pour servir à l'enseignement de la géographie ... Amérique. 9. éd.   1905.   281
  Cartes d'étude pour servir à l'enseignement de la géographie ... Asie, Insulinde, Afrique. 9. éd.   1905.   280
  Cartes d'étude pour servir à l'enseignement de la géographie. France et colonies. 9. éd. 1905.   3009
  Cartes d'étude pour servir à l'enseignement de l'histoire et de la géographie. 13. éd.   1912.   7675
  —— 14. éd.   1912.   8406

Du Caille, Louis Alexandre.
  Étrennes géographiques.   1760.   3505, 3506
  —— 1760–61.   626

Dudley, *Sir* **Robert,** *styled Duke of Northumberland and Earl of Warwick,* **1574–1649.**
  Arcano del mare.   1661.   3428
  Dell'arcano del mare.   1646–47.   457, 458

Duflot de Mofras, Eugène, 1810–1884.
  Exploration du territoire de l'Orégon, des Californies et de la mer Vermeille exécutée pendant les années 1840, 1841 et 1842. Atlas.   1844.   1457, 2437

Dufour, Auguste Henri, 1798–1865.
  Atlas de geografia.   [1858]   6131
  Atlas de géographie numismatique.   1838.   5604
  Atlas géographique dressé pour l'histoire ... de l'Église Catholique.   1861.   3300
  Atlas universel.   1860–[61]   833
  —— [1868]   852
  Globe; Atlas classique universel.   [1835]   6076
  Grand atlas universel.   [1881]   894

Dufour, Auguste Henri, *and* **Duvotenay, Thunot, 1796–1875.**
  France. Atlas des 86 départements et des colonies françaises.   [1860?]   5227
  Globo. Atlas historico universal de Geografia.   1852.   4331
  Terre. Atlas historique et universel.   [1864]   6149

Dufour, Guillaume Henri, 1787–1875.
  Topographische Karte der Schweiz.   1833–63.   3156
  —— [1864]   9445
  —— [1890]   9446

Dufrénoy, *firm.*
  Atlas des 20 arrondissements de Paris. [193–]   8501
  —— [1945]   8503

Dugout, Henry.
  Atlas philologique élémentaire.   [1910]   5683

Dulaure, Jacques Antoine, 1755–1835.
  Histoire physique civile et morale de Paris. 1829.   3010, 4030

Dumas, Mathieu, *i.e.,* **Guillaume Mathieu,** *Comte,* **1753–1837.**
  Précis des événémens militaires ... Campagnes de 1799 à 1807.   [1816–26]   2819, 7705

Dumbarton Land and Improvement Company.
  Property on San Francisco Bay.   [1914]   4541

Dumez, —— *and* **Chanlaire, Pierre Grégoire, 1758–1817.**
  Atlas national de France.   [1793]   8458
  Atlas national portatif de la France.   1792.   2995

Dumolin, Maurice, 1868–1935.
  Précis d'histoire militaire; Révolution et Empire. [Atlas.   1906–13]   7706

Dumont, Maurice E.
  Gent, een stedenaardrijkskundige studie. 1951.   7979

Dumont d'Urville, Jules Sébastien César, 1790–1842.
  Voyage au Pole Sud et dans l'Océanie sur les corvettes l'Astrolabe et Zélée ... Atlas. 1842–48.   3244
  Voyage de la corvette l'Astrolabe. Atlas. 1833.   201

Duncker, Alexander.
  Grosser Atlas der Eisenbahnen und Schiffahrt von Europa. 24. Aufl.   1922.   7748
  —— 26. Aufl.   1925.   7749
  —— 36. Aufl.   [1936]   7750
  Grosser Atlas der Eisenbahnen und Schiffahrt von Mittle-Europa. 22. Aufl.   1920.   7747
  Grosser Atlas der Eisenbahnen von Mittel-Europa.   1909.   3972

Dunham, F. A.
  Atlas of the city of Plainfield ... N.J.   1894.   2194

Dunham, J. R.
  Atlas of Hamilton County, Nebr.   1888.   2112

Dunlop Rubber Company.
  Road maps of France, Belgium, Holland, Switzerland.   [1926]   8429
  Touring maps of the British Isles. 8th ed. [1931?]   8034

Duy, Albert William, 1892–
Atlas and directory of the town of Blooms-
burg ... Pa., 1769–1951. [1952]   16821

Earl's Street Guide.
Rural route [maps of Phoenix, Ariz.] 1956.   11269

Eastman, Harlan John, 1894– and Jackson, John Gordon.
Denver; complete map atlas of Metropolitan
region. [1947]   11682

Eaton, David Wolfe, 1862–
Historical atlas of Westmoreland County, Va.
1942.   17361

Ebel, Johann Gottfried, 1764–1830.
Atlas to Ebel's Traveller's guide through
Switzerland. [1818?]   9442

Ebeling, Philipp, and Gruber, Christian, 1858–1906.
Neuer Atlas für Handels– und kaufmännische
Fortbildungsschulen. 1907.   5431

Ebeling, Philipp, and others.
Wirtschaftsatlas. 6. Aufl. 1930.   5432

Eckert, John D.
Logansport, Ind. 1920.   12987

Eckert-Greifendorff, Max, 1868–1938.
Wirtschaftsatlas der deutschen Koloien.
[1912]   5241

Eckstein, John.
Picturesque views of the Diamond Rock.
1805.   3951

The Economist, London.
U. S. S. R. and eastern Europe. 1956.   9215

Ecuador. Dirección General de Obras Públicas.
Atlas geografico de la red de carreteras,
caminos y ferrocarilles de la República.
1947.   18358

Ecuador. Instituto Geográfico Militar.
Instituto Geográfico Militar: XXXIV aniver-
sario, 1928–1962. [1962]   18356

Ecuador. Legación. U.S.
Ecuador y sus limites meridionales. 1937.   18354

Eddy, Gerald A.
Farmers American Auto Club ... Pocketrip
map of California. [1954]   11348
—— 1955.   11349
San Francisco–Los Angeles–San Diego,
California; U.S. 101 souvenir road maps.
1953.   11346

Ediciones Ateneo.
Atlas geográfico de la República Mexicana.
[1966]   18109

Editions Blondel la Rougery.
See Blondel la Rougery, Éditions.

Éditions d'Utilité Publique.
Bruxelles voyages. 21. éd. [1951]   7975

Éditions Géographiques de France.
Atlas de l'industrie textile. [1948]   8414

Editorial Campano.
Campano atlas de Amercia. [1965]   10280

Editorial Escolar "Piedra Santa," Guatemala.
Datos geográficos de Guatemala. [1962?]   18132

Editorial Ftd.
Atlas universal y del Perú. [1967?]   18397

Editorial Luis Vives.
Atlas de España. [194–]   9334
Atlas universal y de España. [1950]   7397

Editorial Mapa.
Atlas de la República Argentina y sus caminos.
[1964]   18234

Editorial Patria.
Atlas geográfico de México. 1949.   18103

Editorial "Sag".
Guía automovilista de España. [1946]   9320

Editorial Seix Barral.
Atlas escolar de la República Dominicana.
[1956]   18170
Atlas geográfico de España, físico, político y
estadístico. 1950.   9339
—— 1953.   9341
—— 1957.   9344
España. [1945]   9336

Editrice "Il Porto."
Atlante cartografico descrittivo del porto di
Napoli. [1940]   9008
—— [1941]   9009

Editura de Stat pentru Literatură Ştiinţifică.
Atlas geografic. 1953.   7551

Edmands, Benjamin Franklin.
Boston school atlas. 5th ed. 1832.   6070

Edmonds, Sir James Edward, 1861–
Military operations, France and Belgium,
1914. 2v. 1922–[25]   5818
—— 1915. 2 v. [1927–28]   5819
—— 1916. 2 v. [1932–38]   5820
—— 1918. 2 v. [1935]   5821

Edmont, Edmond, 1849–1926.
See Gilliéron, Jules Louis, 1854–1926, and Edmont, Edmond, 1849–1926.

Educational Productions.
Empire information project. [1955]   7990

Edvi Illés, Aladár, 1858-   and Halász, Albert.
Economies of Hungary in maps. [1920]   8908
Hungary before and after the war in economic
Hungary before and after the war in economic-
statistical maps. [1926]   8909
Magyarország gazdasági térképekben.
2. böv. kiad. [1920]   8910
—— 3. böv. kiad. [1920]   8911
—— 6. átdolg. kiad. [1921]   8912
Ungarn vor und nach dem Krieg in wirt-
schaftsstatistischen Karten. [1926]   8913

Edwards, Bryan, 1743–1800.
History of the British West Indies. Maps and
plates. 1818.   2706
New atlas of the British West Indies. 1810.   2704
New atlas of the West India Islands. 1818.   2707

Edwards, D. C.
Atlas of the state of Illinois. 1879.   4555

Edwards, John P.
Atlas of Cloud County, Kans. 1885.   1716
Historical atlas of Sumner County, Kans.
[1883]   1741

Edwards, W. B.
Track chart of the Yukon River, Alaska.
1899.   11242

Edwards Brothers.
[Historical atlas of Sedgwick County,
Kans.] 1882.   4698
Historical plat book of Lyon County, Kans.
1879.   1726
Illustrated historical atlas of Andrew County,
Mo. 1877.   4828
Illustrated historical atlas of Boone County,
Mo. 1875.   15217
Illustrated historical atlas of Bourbon
County, Kans. 1878.   1714
Illustrated historical atlas of Caldwell
County, Mo. 1876.   4832
Illustrated historical atlas of Callaway
County, Mo. 1876.   4834
Illustrated historical atlas of Chariton
County, Mo. 1876.   4837
Illustrated historical atlas of Clark County,
Mo. 1878.   2076
Illustrated historical atlas of Clay County,
Mo. 1877.   4840
Illustrated historical atlas of Coffee County,
Kans. 1878.   1717
Illustrated historical atlas of Harrison
County, Kans. 1876.   4850
Illustrated historical atlas of Lawrence
County, Mo. 1879.   2081

Illustrated historical atlas of Lewis County,
Mo. 1878.   2083
Illustrated historical atlas of Livingston
County, Mo. 1878.   4858
Illustrated historical atlas of Lyon County,
Kans. 1878.   4686
Illustrated historical atlas of Miami County,
Kans. 1878.   1728
Illustrated historical atlas of Monroe County,
Mo. 1876.   4863
Illustrated historical atlas of Osage County,
Kans. 1879.   1731
Illustrated historical atlas of Putnam County,
Mo. 1877.   4868
Illustrated historical atlas of Ralls County,
Mo. 1878.   2090
Illustrated historical atlas of Ray County,
Mo. 1877.   4869
Illustrated historical atlas of Schuyler County,
Mo. 1878.   2094
Illustrated historical atlas of Shelby County,
Mo. 1878.   2097
Illustrated historical atlas of Sullivan County,
Mo. 1877.   4874

Eeckhaute, Jos. van.
Empire militaire ... de l'épopée napoléon-
ienne. 1952.   7707

Eekhoff, Wopke, 1809–1880.
Nieuwe atlas van de Provincie Friesland.
1849–59.   9100

Eggers, Hans Jürgen, 1906–
Römische Import im freien Germanien.
1951.   8520

Eggers, Willy, 1901–
Deutsches Land, deutsches Volk und die
Welt; ein Kartenwerk. 12. Aufl. 1937.   6909
Deutschland und die Welt. 10. Aulf. 1937.   6910
—— [1954]   7593
Grosser Schulatlas. 17. Aufl. 1941.   7050
Kleiner deutscher Volksschulatlas. 1938.   6945
Kleiner Weltatlas. [1949?]   7340
—— 2. Aufl. [1950]   7398
—— 3. Aufl. [1951]   7447
—— 4. Aufl. 1951.   7448
Länder der Erde. Atlas für die deutsche
Schule. [1950]   7399
—— 3. Aufl. 1952.   7504
—— 4. Aufl. 1953.   7552

Eggink, H., 1895–
Schoolatlas van Nederlands Nieuw-Guinea.
[1956]   10192
See also Bolkestein, G.W., and Eggink, H.,
1895–
—— Cohen, L., and Eggink, H., 1895–

Egypt. *Dept. of Surveys and Mines.*
Atlas of the normal 1:100,000 scale topographical series of Egypt. [1944]   10131

Egypt. *Maṣlaḥat al-Āthār.*
Carte de la nécropole memphite, Dahchour,
Sakkarah, Abou-sir. 1897.   10126

Egypt. *Minstry of Education.*
Atlas harat el'dunẙa. [1913]   6357
Atlas ibtidāii El'katr el'Musrī. [Elementary
atlas of Egypt] 1914.   10129

Egypt. *Public Works Dept.*
Meteorological atlas of Egypt. 1931.   10127

Egypt. *Survery of Egypt.*
Atlas of Egypt. 1928.   10130
Egypt. Aeronautical strip map. [1933]   10125
Guide plan of Cairo. [1928]   10134
Pocket atlas of Alexandria. 1st ed. 1935.   10133
Upper White Nile, Air Survey maps. [1948]   10103

Egypt Exploration Society.
Atlas of ancient Egypt. 1894.   3239

Ehringer, James Walter.
Plat book of Clark County, Ind. 1951.   12754

**[Eight military scenes in connection with one of the
many Indian wars]** [1837]   3685

**[Eight original water color sketches in Guadeloupe
...]** MS. [1820]   5128

Eikens, Owen.
Illinois waterways: Grafton, Ill. to Lake
Michigan. 1958.   12070
Mississippi River plat. 1958.   11141

Eisler, Max, 1881–
Historischer Atlas des Wiener Stadtbildes.
1919.   7926

Eitel, Edward E.
County atlas of California. [1894]   3704
County atlas of California and Nevada.
1909.   11353
County atlas of Oregon and Washington.
[1894]   2438, 2622

El Dorado, *Ark. City Planning Commission.*
Planning ordinances and maps for El
Dorado, Ark. [1957]   11305

Ellefsen, Ellef, *and* **Sollesnes, Karl Birger, 1899–**
Cappelens atlas. 1953.   7553
Kartbok over Norge. 1954.   9126
—— 1955.   9127

Elliot, William, *engraver.*
See Pownall, Thomas. Six remarkable views
... in North America. [1761]

Elliot, William Henry Harrison.
Official plat book [of] the city of East St.
Louis [Ill.] and environs. 1904.   2098, 12679

Elliott, Charles L., *and* **Flynn, Thomas.**
Atlas of the city of Newport, R.I. 1893.   2566

Ellis, G.
General atlas of the world. [1823?]   6051
New and correct atlas of England and Wales.
[1819]   8127

Ellis, John, *fl.* **1750–1796.**
English atlas. 1766.   8118
—— 1768.   8119

Elsevier, Uitgevers Maatschappij.
Atlas voor buitenlandse handel. 1950.   5433
Grote Elsevier atlas voor buitenlandse handel.
2 v. 1950.   7400
Kleine wereld atlas met encyclopaedische in-
formatie. 1950.   7401

Elton, Edward F.
Class-room atlas of physical, political, Biblical, and classical geography. 1908.   3368

Elwe, Jan Barend, *fl.* **1785–1809.**
Atlas. 1792.   674, 675
Volkomen reis-atlas van geheel Duitschland.
1791.   8683

Elwe en Langeveld.
Compleete zak-atlas van de zeventien Nederlandsche Provinciën. 1786.   9084

Emery, Arthur T., *and* **Emery, W. H.**
Charts and maps showing growth and distribution of United States manufactures.
1919.   10542

Emmons, Samuel Franklin, 1841–1911.
Geology and mining industry of Leadville,
Colo., with atlas. 1882.   1472

Encyclopaedia Britannica.
New volumes of the Encyclopaedia Britannica
... Maps. 1903.   1085
World atlas. [1942]   7093, 7094
—— [1943]   7134, 7135
—— [1944]   7175
—— [1945]   7206, 7207
—— [1946]   7228
—— [1947]   7261, 7262
—— [1949]   7341, 7342
—— [1951]   7449
—— [1952]   7505
—— [1954]   7594
—— [1955]   7615

Encyclopédie Polonaise.
Atlas de l'Encyclopédie Polonaise. 1919–20. 9161

Engelbrecht, Thiess Hinrich, 1853–1934.
Feldfrüchte des Deutschen Riechs. 1928.   8513
Feldfrüchte Indiens. Atlas. 1914.   9679
Landwirtschaftlicher Atlas des Russischen
Reiches in Europa und Asien. 1916.   9210

Engelhardt, Georg.
  Atlas zur Bürgerkunde. 1912.   4035a

Engineering News.
  Atlas of railway progress, 1888–1889. 1890. 10727

English atlas. 1680–83.   2831, 7785

English pilot.
  Part I. [Describing the sea coasts for the
    southern navigation.] 1715.   5179
  —— 1718.   2837
  —— 1747.   3496
  —— 1758.   2842
  —— 1764.   2843
  —— 1790.   2846
  —— 1792.   2847
  Part II. [Describing the sea coasts ... in the
    whole northern navigation ...] 1716. 2836
  —— 1723.   2838
  —— 1775.   2844
  Part III. [Describing the sea coasts ... in the
    whole Mediterranean Sea ...] 1736.   190, 2805
  —— 1786.   191
  Third book. [Describing the sea coasts ... in
    the oriental navigation ...] 1716.   4278
  —— 1748.   606
  Fourth book. [Describing the West-India
    navigation ...] 1689. *Facsim.* 1967. 10313
  —— 1706.   1155
  —— 1721.   10314
  —— 1737.   1157
  —— 1745.   3650
  —— 1749.   3651
  —— 1755.   3652
  —— 1758.   .   1158
  —— 1759.   10315
  —— 1760.   1160
  —— 1767.   1162, 1163
  —— 1773.   3653
  —— 1775.   1164
  —— 1778.   10318
  —— 1780.   1168
  —— 1783.   10324
  —— 1784.   1171
  —— 1789.   4460
  Part V. [Describing the sea coasts ... on the
    west-coast of Africa ...] 1751.   10094
  —— 1766.   3230
  —— 1780.   10095

Ennis, Arthur F.
  Big Fork River float trip map. [1962]   15170
  —— [1963]   15171

Ensign, D. W., and Company.
  Atlas of Kane County, Ill. 1892.   1540
  Plat book of Carroll County, Ill. 1893. 12108
  Plat book of Cass County, N.Dak. 1893.   2341
  Plat book of DeKalb County, Ill. 1892.   1527
  Plat book of Grand Forks, Walsh and Pem-
    bina Counties N.Dak. 1893.   2343

Enthoffer, Joseph, 1818–1901.
  See Bastert, A., *and* Enthoffer, Joseph, 1818–
    1901.

Erckert, Roderich von, 1821–1900.
  Wanderungen und Siedelungen der germani-
    schen Stämme in Mittel-Europa. 1901.   2786

Erdmann, William F.
  Ownership & road maps of Lincoln County,
    Oreg. 1964.   16701

Erickson, C. E., and Associates.
  Colorado River and Lake Meade. [1952]   11093
  Colorado River fishing–hunting atlas. [1951] 11092
  Fishing, boating atlas; San Francisco Bay.
    [1949]   11624
  Northern California sportsman's atlas.
    [1957]   11338
  Steelhead fishing atlas; northern Cal-
    ifornia coastal streams. [1949]   11339

Erickson, Clarence Elmer, 1908–
  High Sierra; hiking, camping fishing. [1955] 11632
  Northern California boating atlas. 1st ed.
    1963.   11336
  San Francisco Bay and Delta area. [1st ed.
    1952]   11625
  —— Rev. [2d] ed. [1955]   11626
  —— [1960]   11627
  Southern California coast. [1st ed. 1953] 11337

**Erödi, Béla, 1864–1936, Berecz, Antal, 1836–1905,
  and Brózik, Károly, 1849–1911.**
  Nagy magyar atlasz. 1906.   2786

Erskine, R.
  To the right honorable Sᵣ. Charles Wager ...
    these [Mediterranean] views, plans and re-
    marks are most humbly inscribed. [1727–
    1734] MS.   2804

Escudé y Bartolí, Manuel, 1856–1930.
  Atlas geográfico Ibero-Americano. [1900–
    1903]   5288

Espinosa y Tello, José, 1763–1815.
  Relacion del viage hecho por las goletas Sutil
    y Mexicana ... 1792. Atlas. 1802.   1221

Espinoza, Enrique, 1848–
  Atlas de Chile. [1897]   2758
  —— [1903]   18329

Essen, Léon van der, ca. 1883–1960, and others.
  Atlas de géographie historique de la Belgique.
    1919–32.   7947

Esso AG., *Hamburg*.
  Reise-Atlas für Kraftfahrer. [1956]   8664
  Reise-Atlas von Deutschland. [1955]   8657

Estévanez, Nicolas, 1838–1914.
    Atlas geográfico de América.   1885   10270
    —— [1896]   4458

Estonia. *Riigi Statistika Keskbüroo.*
    Eesti. Statistiline album. [1925]–28.   8361

Estrada, Angel, & Cia.
    Atlas general de la República Argentina. 9. ed.
    1910.   5136
    Atlas general de las dos Américas. 1907.   4465

Estudio técnico de las salinas del Perú. 1896.   18380

Etcheson, Warren Wade, 1920–
    Statistical atlas of Washington counties.
    1959.   17408

Ettling, Theodor, *b.* **1823.**
    Drawing-room atlas of Europe. 1855.   7794

Euler, Leonhard, 1707–1783.
    Atlas geographicus. 1753.   3500
    Geographischer Atlas. 1760.   625

Eureka, Montevideo.
    Guía de Montevideo y sus alrededores.
    [1958]   18404

Europäischer Fernsprechdienst.
    Atlas des Weltfernsprechnetzes. 6. Ausg.
    1938.   5799
    —— 7. Ausg. 1940.   5800

Evans, *Rev.* **John, 1767–1827.**
    New royal atlas. [1810]   717

Evans Brothers.
    Visual geography atlas. [1954]   7595

Evans Lembcke, Allan A.
    Guía general de las carreteras del Perú.
    [1936]   18383

Evans' Atlas, Australia and abroad. [1941]   5428

Evening Post Company.
    Atlas of American cities. [1910–11]   3674
    Louisville Evening Post's atlas of the world.
    1910–11.   3616

Evening Star, *Washington, D.C.*
    First six months of war (Sept. 1, 1939–March
    1, 1940). 1940.   5863
    Global map supplement. 1942.   5864
    War map supplement. 1939.   5865

Everts, Louis H., *b.* **1836.**
    Combination atlas map of Fairfield County,
    Ohio. 1875.   2375
    —— 1967.   16409
    Combination atlas map of Licking County,
    Ohio. 1875.   2394

    Combination atlas map of Medina County,
    Ohio. 1874.   16440
    Combination atlas map of Trumbull County,
    Ohio. 1874   16455
    New historical atlas of Butler County, Ohio.
    1875.   2357

Everts, L. H., and Company.
    Combination atlas map of Greene County,
    Ohio. 1874.   16414
    Combination atlas map of Portage County,
    Ohio. 1874.   16443
    Combination atlas map of Stark County,
    Ohio. 1875.   16451
    Combination atlas map of Tuscarawas
    County, Ohio. 1875.   16456
    [Illustrated historical atlas of Clark County,
    Ohio. 1875]   16388
    Illustrated historical atlas of Miami County,
    Ohio. 1875.   4986
    Official state atlas of Kansas. 1887.   1710

Everts and Kirk.
    Official state atlas of Nebraska. 1885.   2107

Everts and Richards.
    New topographical atlas of surveys, Bristol
    County, Mass. 1895.   1811
    New topographical atlas of surveys, Provi-
    dence County, R.I. 1895.   2563
    New topographical atlas of surveys, southern
    Rhode Island. 1895.   16950

Everts and Stewart.
    Combination atlas map of Dauphin County,
    Pa. 1875.   2473
    Combination atlas map of Jackson County,
    Mich. 1874.   1977
    Combination atlas map of Lenawee County,
    Mich. 1874.   1984
    Combination atlas map of Middlesex County,
    N.J. 1876.   2165
    Combination atlas map of St. Clair County,
    Mich. 1876.   3807
    Combination atlas map of Salem & Glouces-
    ter Counties, N.J. 1876.   2159, 2169
    Combination atlas map of Washtenaw
    County, Mich. 1874.   2000
    Combination atlas of Lancaster County, Pa.
    1875.   16789

Everts, Baskin and Stewart.
    Combination atlas map of McHenry County,
    Ill. 1872.   4577, 12364
    Combination atlas map of Ogle County, Ill.
    1872.   12432
    Combination atlas map of Rock County, Wis.
    1873.   2660, 17899
    Combination atlas map of Walworth County,
    Wis. 1873.   2665, 17948

Everts, Ensign and Everts.
    Combination atlas map of Broome County,
    N.Y. 1876.   15857

Combination atlas map of Cortland County, N.Y. 1876.   15875

Combination atlas map of Erie County, Pa. 1876.   16785

Combination atlas map of Genesee County, New York. 1876.   3839c

Combination atlas map of Yates County, N.Y. 1876.   4935

Everts, Stewart and Company.
Combination atlas map of Sandusky County, Ohio. 1874.   16447

Everts Publishing Company.
New century atlas of counties of the state of New York. 1911.   3839a
—— 1912.   3839b

Everyman's Atlas of ancient and classical geography. [1952]   5603

Ewald, Ludwig Wilhelm, 1813–1881.
Handatlas der allgemeinen Erdkunde. 1860.   6139

Ewing, Thomas.
New general atlas. 1828.   6060

Faber, Samuel, 1657–1716.
Atlas scholastichodoeporicvs. [171–?]   5963

Fachbuchverlag, *Leipzig*.
Weltspiegel. Taschenatlas. [1949]   7343

Faden, William, 1750–1836.
Atlas minimus universalis. 1798.   690
Atlas of battles of the American Revolution. [1845?]   1337
General atlas. [1797]   6010
—— [1799]   6013
—— 1821–[22]   6047
North American atlas. 1777.   1207, 1208
See also Petit neptune français.

Faehtz, Ernest F. M., *and* Pratt, Frederick W.
Real estate directory of the city of Washington, D. C. 1874.   1498, 3714
—— [1874]   3715

Fage, J. D.
Atlas of African history. [1958]   10089

Fairchild, John F.
Atlas of the city of Mount Vernon and the town of Pelham, N. Y. 1899.   2288, 2321
—— 1908.   2288a, 2321a

Fairfax County, *Va. Dept. of Assessments*.
Real property identification map of Fairfax County, Va. 1956–58.   17349
—— [1964]   17351

Falk Verlag.
Auto-Atlas der Bundesrepublik Deutschland. [15. Aufl. 1952]   8640

Auto-Atlas der Westzonen. [1949]   8622
Autostrassen-Atlas der Bundesrepublik Deutschland. [27. Aufl. 1955]   8658
Autostrassen-Atlas von Kopenhagen bis Mailand. [28. Aufl. 1956]   8665
Ford Auto-Atlas, Bundesrepublik Deutschland. [2. Aufl. 1953]   8647
Hamburg. [1955]   8860
Kleiner Führer durch Köln. [1950]   8857
Kleiner Welt-Atlas. [1949?]   7344
Patent-folded road atlas and New York World's Fair guide. [1964]   10947
Städteatlas Ruhrgebiet. [2. Aufl. 1955?]   8882

Fallex, Maurice, *i.e.*, Albert Maurice, 1861–1929.
Atlas de géographie économique. 1923.   5434
Novel atlas classique. 1921.   6439
See also Niox, Gustave Léon, 1849–1921, *and* Fallex, Maurice, *i.e.*, Albert Maurice, 1861–1929.

Fallex, Maurice, *and* Gibert, André.
Nouvel atlas classique. 1949.   7345

Far Eastern Geographical Establishment.
New atlas and commercial gazetteer of China. [1917]   5295
—— [1918]   9510
New atlas and commercial gazetteer of the Straits Settlements and Federated Malay States. 1917.   10055

Farm maps of Putnam County, Ohio. [19—]   16444

Farm Operators Rural Residence Map Company.
Adair County [Iowa] 1955.   13024
—— 1956.   13025
—— 1957.   13026
—— 1958.   13028
—— 1959.   13029
Adams County [Iowa] 1955.   13035
—— 1956.   13036
—— 1957.   13037
—— 1958.   13038
—— 1959.   13039
Allamakee County [Iowa] 1955.   13045
—— 1956.   13047
—— 1957.   13048
—— 1958.   13049
—— 1959.   13050
Appanoose County [Iowa] 1955.   13055
—— 1956.   13057
—— 1957.   13058
—— 1958.   13059
Audubon County [Iowa] 1955.   13068
—— 1956.   13069
—— 1957.   13070
—— 1958.   13071, 13072
—— 1959.   13073, 13074
Benton County [Iowa] 1955.   13079
—— 1956.   13081
—— 1957.   13082
—— 1958.   13083
Blackhawk County [Iowa] 1955.   13089

—— 1956.	13091
—— 1957.	13092
—— 1958.	13093
—— 1959.	13094
Boone County [Iowa] 1955.	13099
—— 1956.	13100
—— 1957.	13101
—— 1958.	13102
Bremer County [Iowa] 1955.	13108
—— 1956.	13110
—— 1957.	13111
—— 1958.	13112, 13113
—— 1959.	13114, 13115
Buchanan County [Iowa] 1955.	13121
—— 1956.	13123
—— 1957.	13124
—— 1958.	13125
—— 1959.	13126
Buena Vista County [Iowa] 1955.	13134
—— 1956.	13135
—— 1957.	13136
—— 1958.	13137
—— 1959.	13138
Butler County [Iowa] 1955.	13143
—— 1956.	13145
—— 1957.	13146
—— 1958.	13147
—— 1959.	13148
Calhoun County [Iowa] 1955.	13157
—— 1956.	13158
—— 1957.	13159
—— 1958.	13160
—— 1959.	13161
Carroll County [Iowa] 1955.	13169
—— 1956.	13171
—— 1957.	13172
—— 1958.	13173, 13174
—— 1959.	13175, 13176
Cass County [Iowa] 1955.	13184
—— 1956.	13185
—— 1957.	13186
—— 1958.	13187, 13188
—— 1959.	13189, 13190
Cedar County [Iowa] 1955.	13194
—— 1956.	13196
—— 1957.	13197
—— 1958.	13198, 13199
—— 1959.	13200, 13201
Cerro Gordo County [Iowa] 1955.	13206
—— 1956.	13208
—— 1957.	13209
—— 1958.	13210
—— 1959.	13211
Cherokee County [Iowa] 1955.	13220
—— 1956.	13221
—— 1957.	13222
—— 1958.	13223
—— 1959.	13224
Chickasaw County [Iowa] 1955.	13229
—— 1956.	13231
—— 1957.	13232
—— 1958.	13233
—— 1959.	13234
Clarke County [Iowa] 1955.	13239
—— 1956.	13240
—— 1957.	13241
—— 1959.	13242
Clay County [Iowa] 1955.	13249
—— 1956.	13250
—— 1957.	13251
—— 1958.	13252
—— 1959.	13253
Clayton County [Iowa] 1955.	13259
—— 1956.	13261
—— 1957.	13262
—— 1958.	13264
—— 1959.	13265
Clinton County [Iowa] 1955.	13272
—— 1956.	13274
—— 1957.	13275
—— 1958.	13276
—— 1959.	13277
Crawford County [Iowa] 1955.	13285
—— 1956.	13286
—— 1957.	13287
—— 1958.	13288, 13289
—— 1959.	13290, 13291
Dallas County [Iowa] 1955.	13298
—— 1956.	13299
—— 1957.	13300
—— 1958.	13301
—— 1959.	13302
Davis County [Iowa] 1955.	13306
—— 1956.	13308
—— 1957.	13309
—— 1959.	13310
Decatur County [Iowa] 1955.	13314
—— 1956.	13315
—— 1957.	13316
—— 1959.	13317
Delaware County [Iowa] 1955.	13324
—— 1956.	13327
—— 1957.	13328
—— 1958.	13329
—— 1959.	13330
Des Moines County [Iowa] 1955.	13334
—— 1956.	13336
—— 1957.	13337
—— 1958.	13338, 13339
—— 1959.	13340, 13341
Dickinson County [Iowa] 1955.	13347
—— 1956.	13348
—— 1957.	13349
—— 1958.	13350
—— 1959.	13351
Dubuque County [Iowa] 1955.	13356
—— 1956.	13358
—— 1957.	13359
—— 1958.	13360
—— 1959.	13361
East [and West] Pottawattamie County [Iowa] 1955.	13872
—— 1956.	13873
—— 1957.	13875
—— 1958.	13876
—— 1959.	13878
Emmet County [Iowa] 1955.	13367
—— 1956.	13368

——— 1957.	13370	
——— 1958.	13371	
——— 1959.	13372	
Fayette County [Iowa] 1955.	13380	
——— 1956.	13382	
——— 1957.	13383	
——— 1958.	13384	
——— 1959.	13385	
Floyd County [Iowa] 1955.	13391	
——— 1956.	13393	
——— 1957.	13394	
——— 1958.	13395	
——— 1959.	13396	
Franklin County [Iowa] 1955.	13400	
——— 1956.	13402	
——— 1957.	13403	
——— 1958.	13404	
——— 1959.	13405	
Fremont County [Iowa] 1955.	13412	
——— 1956.	13413	
——— 1957.	13414	
——— 1958.	13415	
——— 1959.	13416	
Greene County [Iowa] 1955.	13423	
——— 1956.	13424	
——— 1957.	13425	
——— 1958.	13426	
——— 1959.	13427, 13428	
Grundy County [Iowa] 1955.	13432	
——— 1956.	13434	
——— 1957.	13435	
——— 1958.	13436	
——— 1959.	13437	
Guthrie County [Iowa] 1955.	13443	
——— 1956.	13444	
——— 1957.	13445	
——— 1958.	13446	
——— 1959.	13447	
Hamilton County [Iowa] 1955.	13452	
——— 1956.	13453	
——— 1957.	13454	
——— 1958.	13455	
——— 1959.	13456	
Hancock County [Iowa] 1955.	13462	
——— 1956.	13463	
——— 1957.	13464	
——— 1958.	13465	
——— 1959.	13466	
Hardin County [Iowa] 1955.	13472	
——— 1956.	13474	
——— 1957.	13475	
——— 1958.	13476	
——— 1959.	13477	
Harrison County [Iowa] 1955.	13484	
——— 1956.	13485	
——— 1957.	13486	
——— 1958.	13487	
——— 1959.	13488	
Henry County [Iowa] 1955.	13493	
——— 1956.	13495	
——— 1957.	13496	
——— 1958.	13497, 13498	
——— 1959.	13499, 13500	
Howard County [Iowa] 1955.	13504	
——— 1956.	13506	
——— 1957.	13507	
——— 1958.	13508	
——— 1959.	13509	
Humboldt County [Iowa] 1955.	13514	
——— 1956.	13515	
——— 1957.	13516	
——— 1958.	13517	
——— 1959.	13518	
Ida County [Iowa] 1955.	13526	
——— 1956.	13527	
——— 1957.	13528	
——— 1958.	13529	
——— 1959.	13530	
Iowa County [Iowa] 1955.	13535	
——— 1956.	13537	
——— 1957.	13538	
——— 1958.	13539	
——— 1959.	13540	
Jackson County [Iowa] 1955.	13546	
——— 1956.	13548	
——— 1957.	13550	
——— 1958.	13551	
——— 1959.	13552	
Jasper County [Iowa] 1955.	13557	
——— 1956.	13559	
——— 1957.	13560	
——— 1958.	13561	
Jefferson County [Iowa] 1955.	13566	
——— 1956.	13568	
——— 1957.	13569	
——— 1958.	13570, 13571	
——— 1959.	13572, 13573	
Johnson County [Iowa] 1955.	13581	
——— 1956.	13583	
——— 1957.	13584	
——— 1958.	13585, 13586	
——— 1959.	13587, 13588	
Jones County [Iowa] 1955.	13595	
——— 1956.	13597	
——— 1957.	13598	
——— 1958.	13599	
——— 1959.	13600	
Keokuk County [Iowa] 1955.	13605	
——— 1956.	13607	
——— 1957.	13608	
——— 1958.	13609, 13610	
——— 1959.	13611	
Kossuth County [Iowa] 1955.	13618	
——— 1956.	13619	
——— 1957.	13620	
——— 1958.	13621	
——— 1959.	13622	
Lee County [Iowa] 1955.	13626	
——— 1956.	13628	
——— 1957.	13629	
——— 1958.	13630	
——— 1959.	13631	
Linn County [Iowa] 1955.	13636	
——— 1956.	13638	
——— 1957.	13639	
——— 1958.	13640	
——— 1959.	13641	
Louisa County [Iowa] 1955.	13645	

—— 1957.	13947	—— 1957.	14104
—— 1958.	13948	—— 1958.	14105
—— 1959.	13949	—— 1959.	14106
Story County [Iowa] 1955.	13955		
—— 1956.	13957	**Farmer, Arthur John, 1876–**	
—— 1957.	13958	Automobile road atlas of southern Michigan.	
—— 1958.	13959	1908.	14576
Tama County [Iowa] 1955.	13965	[Twenty-one plate series railroad and political	
—— 1956.	13967	atlas of Michigan. 1911]	4728
—— 1957.	13968	—— [1913]	4730
—— 1958.	13969	—— 1915.	4729
Taylor County [Iowa] 1955.	13977		
—— 1956.	13978	**Farmer, Silas, and Company.**	
—— 1957.	13979	*See* Farmer, Arthur John, 1876–	
—— 1958.	13980		
—— 1959.	13981	**Fatout, Hervey B.**	
Union County [Iowa] 1955.	13987	Atlas of Indianapolis and Marion Coutny,	
—— 1956.	13988	Ind. 1889.	1618, 1637
—— 1957.	13989		
—— 1958.	13990	**Fauvel, Albert Auguste, 1851–1909.**	
Van Buren County [Iowa] 1955.	13994	Ancient maps of Seychelles Archipelago.	
—— 1956.	13996	[1909]	10247
—— 1957.	13997		
—— 1958.	13998	**Fava, Francis R., and Company.**	
—— 1959.	13999	Subdivisions of the city of Washington and	
Wapello County [Iowa] 1955.	14006	the District of Columbia. 1890–[92]	11772
—— 1956.	14008		
—— 1957.	14009	**Favolius, Hugo, 1523–1585.**	
—— 1958.	14010, 14011	Theatri orbis terrarum. 1585.	391
—— 1959.	14012		
Warren County [Iowa] 1955.	14020	**Fay, Theodore Sedgwick, 1807–1898.**	
—— 1956.	14022	Atlas of universal geography. 1869.	6161
—— 1957.	14023	—— [1871]	6175
—— 1958.	14024	Great outline of geography ... Atlas. [1867]	
Washington County [Iowa] 1955.	14029		222, 282
—— 1956.	14031	—— [1867?]	3369
—— 1957.	14032	Views in New-York and its environs. 1831.	4941
—— 1958.	14033, 14034		
—— 1959.	14035, 14036	**Fayard de la Brugère, Jean Arthême, 1836–**	
Wayne County [Iowa] 1955.	14041	Atlas national ... de la France. [187–]	8466
—— 1956.	14042	Atlas universel. [1896]	3575
—— 1957.	14043		
—— 1958.	14044	**Fayard de la Brugère, Jean Arthême, 1836–**	
Webster County [Iowa] 1955.	14052	**and Baralle, Alphonse.**	
—— 1956.	14053	Atlas universel. 1877.	884
—— 1957.	14054		
—— 1958.	14055	**Feist, Erhard.**	
Winnebago County [Iowa] 1955.	14062	Heimatatlas Nürnberg-Fürth. [1954]	8873
—— 1956.	14063		
—— 1957.	14064	**Felix, Keith G.**	
—— 1958.	14065	Plat maps, Fulton County, Ind. 1953.	12791
—— 1959.	14066		
Winneshiek County [Iowa] 1955.	14072	**Fên yeh yü t'u. [Atlas of China and the Barbarian**	
—— 1956.	14074	**regions] MS. [16—]**	9541
—— 1957.	14075		
—— 1958.	14076	**Fêng-t'ien ch'üan shêng yü t'u. [Complete provincial**	
—— 1959.	14078	**atlas of Feng-t'ien (*i.e.* Liaoning)] [1911]**	9660
Woodbury County [Iowa] 1955.	14083		
—— 1956.	14084	**Fennema, Reinder, 1849–1897.**	
—— 1957.	14085	*See* Verbeek, Rogier Diederik Marius, *and*	
—— 1958.	14086	Fennema, Reinder, 1849–1897.	
—— 1959.	14087		
Wright County [Iowa] 1955.	14102		
—— 1956.	14103		

Finley, Charles M.
Map of Sioux City, Iowa. 1948.   14134

Fiol y Menendez.
Manual de planos ... de la ciudad de Buenos
Aires. [1955]   18243
—— [1957]   18246
Planos suburbanos. [Buenos Aires.   1957]   18256

Fire Underwriters Map Association.
Springfield, Ohio. [1889]   16558

Firestone de la Argentina, S.A.
Mapa Firestone; red caminera de la República
Argentina. [195–]   18211

Firestone road maps of America.   1946.   10867

First National Bank of Arizona.
Metro Tucson street atlas. [1963]   11277
—— [1967]   11278

Fischer, Heinrich, 1861–1924.
Einheitsatlas. 11. Aufl. 1931.   6740

**Fischer, Heinrich, 1861–1924, and Geistbeck,
Michael.**
Stufenatlas für höhere Lehranstalten. 3 v.
1927–29.   6665

Fischer, Hermann von, 1851–1920.
Atlas zur Geographie der Schwäbischen Mun-
dart. 1895.   3024, 3047

Fischer, Theobald, 1846–1910.
Raccolta di mappa-mondo, 1871–81.   249

Fischer, Wilhelm, and Streit, Friedrich Wilhelm, Jr.
Historischer und geographischer Atlas von
Europa. 1834–37.   2789

Fischera, Filadelfo.
Progretti di massima pel risanamento di
Catania ... [Atlante.   1887]   2789

Fisher, Marjory Ingram, 1922–
Location of streets & road of Duval County,
Fla. 1955.   11821

Fisher, Richard Swainson.
Chronological history of the Civil War in
America. 1863.   1350

Fisher, W. A., Company.
Superior—Quetico canoe maps, covering the
Superior National Forest in Minnesota.
1952.   14916

Fisk, George Victor, 1896–
Plat book of Vigo County [Ind.   1954]   12940

Fisquet, Honoré Jean Pierre, 1818–1883.
Grand atlas départemental de la France.
[1878]   3006

Five Star Oil Report.
Midland County [Tex.] oil (data ...) [1952]   17180

Flemmings Weltatlas.   1949.   7346

Flinders, Matthew, 1774–1814.
[Voyage to Terra Australis.   1814]   3251

Flores, San Roman y Cia.
Bolivia: Atlas escolar. [193–?]   18260

Florida. State Road Dept.
[Atlas of Florida.   1934–35]   11794

Florida Grower.
Atlas of Florida. [1914]   11796

Floyd, William H., Jr., and Company.
Atlas of the city of Saint Joseph ... Mo.
1884.   2104

Flynn, T.
See Lathrop, J. M., and Flynn, T.

Flynn, Thomas.
Atlas of the city of Manchester, N.H. 1886.   2140
—— 1896.   15660
See also Elliott, Charles L., and Flynn,
Thomas.

Flynn, Thomas, and others.
Atlas of the suburbs of Cleveland, Ohio.
1898.   2428

Folkers, Johann Ulrich, 1887–
24 Karten zur Rassen- und Raumgeschichte
des Deutschen Volkes. [1937]   8559

Foncin, Pierre François Charles, 1814–1916.
Géographie historique. 1888.   4134

Fonton, Feliks Petrovich, 1801–1862.
Russie dans l'Asie-Mineure. Atlas. 1840.
3102, 9230

Foote, Charles M., 1849–1899, and Brown, W. S.
Plat book of Brown County, Wis. 1889.   2636
Plat book of Dunn County, Wis. 1888.   2644
Plat book of Waupaca County, Wis. 1889.   2670

**Foote, Charles M., 1849–1899, and Henion, John
W., ca. 1832–1904.**
Plat book of Columbia County, Wis. 1890.   2639
Plat book of Dane County, Wis. 1890.   17704
Plat book of Dodge County, Wis. 1890.   2643
Plat book of Fond du Lac County, Wis.
1893.   2645
Plat book of Goodhue County, Minn. 1894.   2018
Plat book of Grant County, Wis. 1895.   17746
Plat book of Green County, Wis. 1891.   17753
Plat book of Lafayette County, Wis. 1895.   2651
Plat book of Manitowoc and Calumet Coun-
ties, Wis. 1893.   2637, 2652
Plat book of Morrison County, Minn. 1892.   15046

Plat book of Rock County, Wis. 1891.   2661
Plat book of Washington and Ozaukee Coun-
ties, Wis. 1892.   2654, 2667
Plat book of Waukesha County, Wis. 1891.   2669
Plat book of Winona County, Minn. 1894.   2047

Foote, Charles M., *and* Hood, Edwin C.
Plat book of Barron County, Wis. 1888.   2635
Plat book of Chisago County, Minn. 1888.   2013
Plat book of Isabella County, Mich. 1899.   4748
Plat book of Jefferson County, Wis. 1899.   2648
Plat book of Juneau County, Wis. 1898.   2649
Plat book of Keokuk County, Iowa. 1887.   4645
Plat book of Polk County, Wis. 1887.   2656
See also Warner, George E., *ca.* 1826–1917,
and Foote, Charles M.

Foote, Charles M., and Company.
Atlas of the city of Minneapolis, Minn.
1892.   4825
Plat book of Stearns County, Minn. 1896.   2042

Foote, Ernest B.
Plat book of Adams County, Wis. 1900.   17647
Plat book of Marquette County, Wis. 1900.   17837
Plat book of Sebastian County, Ark. 1903.   11302

Forman, Samuel David.
Tax & registers block, street, and avenue sectional maps of Queens, N.Y.C. [1946]   16125

Formby, John.
American Civil War. Maps. [1910]   10657

Forsyth, William.
Plats of the subdivision of the city of Washington, D.C. 1856.   1496
—— [1856]   3713

Fort Dearborn Publishing Company.
National standard family and business atlas.
[1896]   1007
—— [1899]   1034
—— [1901]   1066
—— [1902]   1077
New international office and family atlas.
1897.   6277

Fort Pierce, *Fla.*
Plat book, city of Fort Pierce, Fla. [1957]   11874

Foscue, Edwin Jay, 1889–
See Beaty, John Owen, 1890–   *and* Foscue,
Edwin Jay,   1899–

Foster, Eli Greenawalt.
Forty maps illustrating United States history.
1905.   1284
Historical outline maps and note book for
students in United States history. 1904.   1286
Historical outline maps for students of American history. 1942.   10601
Historical outline maps for students of mediaeval and modern history. [1907]   7734

Foster, Fred William, 1909–
School and library atlas of the world.   [1953]   7554

Foth and Porath.
Plat book of Brown County, Wis. 1967.   17673

Foundry.
Market atlas.   [1950]   10543

Four years of war … in maps.   [1944?]   5866

Foust and Jungblut.
Plat book of Price County, Wis. [1910]   3933

Fowler, L. D.
Official assessment map of Jersey City, N.J.
1894.   2183
Title and assessment map of that part of Jer-
sey City which constituted the city of
Bergen … 1870. [1883]   2173, 2182

Fox, Dixon Ryan, 1887–1945.
Harper's Atlas of American history.   [1920]   10602

Fox, Edward Whiting.
Atlas of American history. 1964.   10603
Atlas of European history. 1957.   7676

Fraccaro, Plinio, 1883–
See Baratta, Mario, 1868–1935, *and* Fraccaro,
Plinio,   1883–

Frahm, H. C.
Pocket plat-book of Ward County, N. Dak.
1913.   4978
—— 1914.   4979

France. *Armée. 2. Armée.*
Étude sur les Ardennes Belges. 1940.   7983

France. *Armée. Armée d'Orient, 1854–56. Artillerie.*
Guerre d'Orient. Siège de Sébastopol …
Atlas. 1859.   9231

France. *Armée. Service Géographique.*
Atlas archéologique de l'Algérie. 1911.   10105
Carte de l'Afrique. [1886–1900]   3235

France. *Comité d'Études.*
Enquête sur les richesses minérales du nord-
est de la France et des régions voisines.
Atlas. 1918.   8402

France. *Comité d'Études, 1917–1918.*
Travaux … Atlas. 1918–19.   7677

France. *Commission de l'Afrique du Nord.*
Atlas archéologique de la Tunisie. 1914–32.   10155

France. *Commission Scientifique du Nord.*
Voyages en Scandinavie, en Laponie, au
Spitzberg et aux Féröe. [1855?]   7829

France. *Dépôt de la Guerre.*
Atlas de l'aperçu historique ... d'Alger. 1830.   10107
Atlas de l'expédition de Chine en 1860. 1861–62.   3184
Atlas des campagnes de l'Empereur Napoléon en Allemagne et en France. 1844.   2966, 7708
Atlas historique et topographique de la Guerre d'Orient. 1858.   9232
Campagne de l'Empereur Napoleon III en Italie 1859. Atlas. [1863]   8956
Carte de la France. 1852.   5220

France. *Dépôt de la Marine.*
Pilote de l'Isle de Saint-Domingue. 1787– [88]   2716

France. *Dépôt des Cartes et Plans de la Marine.*
Atlas hydrographique de la Nouvelle Calédonie. [1859–62]   10194
Cartes des vents sur la côte est de l'Amérique du Sud. 1861.   18186
Neptune Americo-Septentrional. [1778–80]   1211
[Portulan général. Mer des Antilles et Golfe du Mexique. 1856?]   2711
Recherches hydrographiques sur le régime des côtes. 1878.   5218
Terre-Neuve. [1854–81]   10401

France. *Direction des Mines.*
Tourbières Françaises. Atlas. 1949.   8425

France. *Direction Générale des Contributions Directes.*
Nouvelle évaluation du revenu foncier des propriétés non bâties de la France. 1884.   8448

France. *Gouvernement Général de l'Afrique Occidentale Française. Service Géographique.*
See French West Africa. *Service Géographique.*

France. *Ministère de l'Education Nationale.*
Atlas archéologique de la Tunisie. Pt.1–15. 1892–1913.   3240, 4086, 5314
—— 2. sér. liv. 1– 1914.   5315
Atlas des Territoires Français d'outre-mer. [1912?]   8390

France. *Ministère de l'Instruction Publique et des Beaux-Arts.*
See France. *Ministère de l'Education Nationale.*

France. *Ministère de la Marine.*
Atlas des colonies françaises. 1866.   2950
Atlas des côtes méridionales de France. 1850.   3001
[Collection of charts by various hydrographers. 1792–1831]   2849
Pilote de l'Isle de Corse. 1831–[55]   5239
Pilote de l'Isle de Saint-Domingue. 1787– [88]   18174
Pilote des Iles Britanniques. [1757–1815]   8000
Pilote français. 1822–43.   2997

France. *Ministère des Colonies.*
Mission de Bonchamps. [1900]   3236

France. *Ministère des Finances.*
Atlas de statistique financière. 1889.   8397

France. *Ministère des Travaux Publics.*
Atlas des canaux de la France. 1879.   8383
Ports maritimes de la France. [1871–98]   2955, 8384
Routes nationales. Recensement de la circulation en 1882. Atlas. 1884.   8428

France. *Ministère des Travaux Publics. Direction des Cartes, Plans et Archives.*
Album de statistique graphique de 1883. 1884.   8450

France. *Préfecture de la Seine. Service de l'Assainissement.*
See Seine *(Dept.) Prefecture. Service de l'Assainissement.*

France. *Secrétariat Général à l'Aviation Civile et Commerciale.*
Atlas des aérodromes. 3 v. [194–]   5330

France. *Service des Topographies Souterraines.*
Bassin houiller de la Saare et de la Lorraine. 1932.   8780

France. *Service Géographique de l'Armée.*
See France. *Armée. Service Géographique.*

France. *Service Géographique des Colonies.*
See France. *Ministère des Colonies.*

France. *Service Hydrographique.*
Chine. Haut Yang-Tseu et Yalong ... Atlas. 1914.   5298

France. *Sous-Secrétariat d'État des Colonies. Service Géographique.*
Atlas des côtes du Congo Français. 1893.   10137

France. *Treaties, etc., 1895–1899. (Faure)*
Mémoire contenant l'exposé des droits de la France dans la question des frontières de la Guyane et du Brésil. [1899]   2764

Frank, Charles P.
Atlas of the city of Duluth, Minn. 1902.   2052

Franklin, Thomas, 1877– *and* **Griffiths, Evan Dalton.**
Atlas geographies. pt. 2, Junior geography. [1913]   4394a
—— [1914]   4192

Franklin Survey Company.
Atlas of Bloomfield, Belleville and Nutley, Essex County, N.J. 1932.   15695
Atlas of boroughs of Caldwell, North Caldwell ... Essex County, N.J. 1933.   15697

Atlas of East Orange, Orange, and West Orange, Essex County, N.J. 1932. 15696

Atlas of Essex County, N.J. [1954] 15701

Atlas of "Greater Northeast" Philadelphia, Pa. 1939. 16875

Atlas of Montclair, Glen Ridge, Cedar Grove and Verona, Essex County, N.J. 1933. 15698

Atlas of Montgomery County, Pa. 1935–38. 16796

Atlas of "North City" Philadelphia, Pa. 1936. 16874

Atlas of ... Philadelphia, Pa. 1953–55. 16882

Authentic street atlas of Philadelphia and suburbs. [1951] 16879

Farm atlas of Bucks County, Pa. 1948. 16772

One hundred per cent "intra city" business property atlas of Philadelphia, Pa. 1939. 16876

Original "han-dy size" property atlas, including Miami Beach ... [Fla. 1935] 11903

Plat book of Arlington County, Va. 1943. 17345

—— 1952. 17346

Plat book of Columbus, Ohio and vicinity. 1937. 16521

Plat book of Monmouth County, N.J. 1941. 15715

Plat book of Prince George's County, Md. 1940. 14362

Property atlas of Absecon Island, N.J. 1938. 15731

Property atlas of Arlington County, Va. 1935. 17343

Property atlas of Bergen County, N.J. 1936. 15683

Property atlas of Chester County, Pa. 1933–34. 16775

Property atlas of city of Lowell ... Mass. 1936. 14486

Property atlas of city of Wilmington ... Del. 1936. 11759

Property atlas of Delaware County, Pa. 1934. 16783

Property atlas of "lower" Fairfield County, Conn. 1938. 11698

Property atlas of Montgomery County, Pa. 1949. 16797

Property atlas of the Main Line, Pa. 1937. 16896

—— [1939] 16897

—— 1948–50. 16898

—— 1961. 16899

Property atlas of Upper Merion Township, Montgomery County, Pa. 1955. 16799

Real estate atlas of Upper Darby, Pa. and vicinity. 1942. 16784

Real estate plat-book of the city of Trenton and borough of Princeton ... N.J. 1930. 15801

Street & occupancy atlas of Philadelphia and suburbs. 1946. 16878

Fransche neptunus. 1693–1700. 517

Fraser, S. L.
Mercantine guide. 1886. 1276

Frazee, Alva T.
See Petrie, Thomas Edward, 1859–1932, *and* Frazee, Alva T.

Frazier Map Company.
Chicago neighborhood maps. [1950] 12655

Freducci, Conte di Ottomano, *fl.* 1497–1539.
Portolan atlas ... MCCCCCXXX 7:—Facsimile. 1915. 5171

Freeborn County, *Minn.*
Freeborn County, Minn. 1935. 14989

Freeman, Edward Augustus, 1823–1892.
Historical geography of Europe. 1882. 3967

Freissler, Max.
Nouvelle carte des chemins de fer de l'Europe centrale. [1923] 7751

French and Bryant.
Atlas of the town of Brookline, Mass. 1897. 4720

French West Africa. *Service Géographique.*
Atlas des cartes ... de l'A. O. F. 1922. 10138

Atlas des cartes ethnographiques et administratives des différentes colonies du Gouvernement Général. 1911. 5308

Atlas des cercles de l'A. O. F. 1924–26. 10139

Petit atlas ... de l'Afrique Occidentale Française. 3. éd. 1928. 10140

Frenzel, Konrad, 1902–
See Ambrosius, Ernst, 1866–1940, *and* Frenzel, Konrad, 1902–
See also Leers, Johann von, 1902– *and* Frenzel, Konrad, 1902–

Frey, Heinrich, 1878–1957.
Schöne Schweizerland. [1939] 9455

Freybe, Otto, 1865–1923.
Wetterkartenatlas. 2. Aufl. [1913?] 4156

Freycinet, Louis Claude Desaulses de, 1779–1842.
Voyage autour du monde ... Navigation et hydrographie. 1826. 4214

Voyage de découvertes aux terres Australes, exécuté ... sur les corvettes, Le Géographe, Le Naturaliste ... Atlas. 1807–16. 3249

—— 1812. 3250

Freye, Alexis Everett, 1859–1936.
Home and school atlas. 1896. 284

Freytag, Berndt und Artaria.
Atlas für Hauptschulen. [1951] 7450

Atlas für Mittelschulen. [1952] 7506

Auto-Atlas von Österreich. [1931] 7900

—— [1933] 7901

—— [1934] 7902

—— [1936] 7903

—— [1950] 7906

—— [1954] 7907

—— [1956] 7908

—— [1958] 7910

Buchplan von Wien. [1949] 7929

—— [1956]	7931
—— [1958]	7932
Donau: Passau-Linz-Wien. [1953]	7840
—— [1954]	7841
Wienerwald-Atlas. [1953]	7936

Freytag, G., und Berndt.
Atlas zum Zeitgeschehen. 1940.	7010
—— [2. Aufl.] 1940.	7011
Taschen–Atlas. 1938.	6946
Taschen–Weltatlas. [1950]	7402

Freytag, Gustav, 1852–1938.
Export-atlas. [1903]	72
Welt–Atlas. [1925]	6580
—— 1927.	6649
—— 1928.	6674
—— 1929.	6702
—— 1932.	6773

Fricx, Eugène Henri, d. 1733.
Table des cartes des Pays-Bas et des frontières de France. 1712.	4049, 7962

Friederichsen, L., & Co.
Völker-Verteilung in West-Russland. 2. Aufl. 1917.	9270

Friederichsen, Maximilian Hermann, 1874–
Methodischer Atlas zur Länderkunde von Europa. 1914–15.	5169

Friedrich, Ernst, 1867–1937.
Minerva Atlas. [1926]	6612
—— [1928]	6675

Friendly Map and Publishing Company.
Atlas and directory of Noble County, Ind. [1939]	12869

Friis, Jens Andreas, 1821–1896.
Ethnographisk kart over Finmarken. 1861.	3092

Frijlink, Hendrik, 1800–1886.
Kleine School-Atlas. 2. uitgave. 1847.	4193

Frobenius, Leo, 1873–1938, and Wilm, Ludwig, Ritter von.
Atlas Africanus. [1921–31]	10087

Frontière proposée et la réalité dans la Marche Julienne. 1946. | 8999 |

Fry, Varian.
Atlas comentado de la guerra. 1940.	5867
War atlas. [1940]	5868
—— [3d ed. 1942]	5869
—— [5th ed. 1943]	5870

Frye, Alexis Everett, 1859–1936.
Home and school atlas. 1895.	6272

Fu, I-li.
Fu-chien ch'üan shêng ti yü t'u shuo. [Provin-	

cial atlas of Fukien with explanations. 1901]	9632

Fu-chien shêng hai fang t'u. Atlas of the coast defenses of Fukien Province. MS. [17–] | 9631 |

Fuchs, Caspar Friedrich, 1803–1874.
See Danz, C. F., and Fuchs, Caspar Friedrich, 1803–1874.

Fuchs, Walter, 1902–
"Mongol atlas" of China, by Chu Ssu-pen, and the Kuang-yü-t'u ... about 1555. 1946.	9537

Fugmann, Erich Richard, and Pries, Hugo.
Flemmings Weltatlas. 1949.	7346

Fujita, Motoharu, 1879–
New atlas of Japan. 1943.	9816

Fukuoka Kanku Kishōdai.
Kyūshū kikō zuchō. [Climatic atlas of Kyushu. 1949]	10041

Fuller, John F.
See Roberts, William Jackson, and Fuller John F.

Fuller and Whitney.
Schedule of sales, Commonwealth Avenue [Boston] lands, 1880–81. With plan. 1881.	14417
—— 1882.	14419
Sectional plans of Commonwealth Avenue lands from Dartmouth Street to West Chester Park [Boston] 1882.	14420
Set of plans showing the Back Bay [Boston] 1814–1881. 1881.	14418

Fulmer, F. S.
See Beers, Frederick W., Fulmer, F.S., and others.

Fulneck Academy.
Moravian atlas. 1853.	180

Fulton, Henry.
Farm line map of the city of Brooklyn [N.Y.] 1874.	15939

Funk and Wagnalls Company.
Literary Digest atlas of the world. 1934.	6810
Literary Digest atlas of the world and gazetteer. 1926.	6613
—— 1927.	6650
—— 1931.	6741
—— [1933]	6793
Literary Digest 1931 atlas of the world. [1930]	6742
New comprehensive atlas of the world. 1911.	3617
—— 1916.	4426
1923 Atlas of the world and gazetteer. 1923.	6519

1924 Atlas of the world and gazetteer. 1924. 6550
1925 Atlas of the world and gazetteer. 1925. 6581
Standard atlas. [1896] 1008
—— 1903. 1086
—— 1905. 1100
Standard atlas and gazetteer of the world.
[1934] 6811
Standard Biblical atlas. 1908. 4079

Funke, Karl Philipp, 1752–1807.
See Vieth, Gerhard Ulrich Anton, 1763–1836,
  and Funke, Karl Philipp, 1752–1807.

Furlong, Lawrence, 1734–1806.
American coast pilot. 1809. 3676

Furnas, Boyd Edwin, 1848–1897.
Combined atlas-directory of Miami County,
  Ohio. 1883. 2400

Fuzambō, *Tokyo.*
Saishin Nihon chizu. [New atlas of Japan.
  1916] 9806

Gaebler, Eduard, 1842–1911.
Hand–Atlas über alle teile der Erde. [1923] 6520
Kleiner Hand–Atlas über alle Teile der Erde.
  1934. 6812
See also Diercke, Carl, 1842–1913, *and*
  Gaebler, Eduard, 1842–1911.

Gärtner, Karl.
Heimatatlas der Südwestmark Baden.
  [1934] 8714
—— 2. Aufl. [1937] 8715

Gage, William Leonard, 1832–1889.
Modern historical atlas. 1869. 106

Gail, Jean Baptiste, 1755–1829.
Atlas contenant ... les cartes relatives à la
  géographie d'Hérodote. [182–] 5606

Gakushū no Tomo Sha, *Tokyo.*
Skakaikayō Nihon hakuchizu. [Outline maps
  of Japan for social studies. 1950] 9798

Galletti, Johann Georg August, 1750–1828.
Allgemeine Weltkunde. [2. Ausg.] 1807–
  1810. 6025

**Gallois, Iucien Louis Joseph, 1857–1941, *and*
Chabert-Ostland, Clément Casimir de.**
Atlas général de l'Indochine Française.
  1909. 4073

**Gallouédec, Louis, *i.e.* Renato Louis Maria, 1864–
1937.**
See Schrader, Franz, 1844–1824, *and* Gallouédec, Louis, *i.e., Renato Louis Maria,
  1864–1937.

Gallup Map and Supply Company.
Atlas of Jackson County, Mo. 1931. 15231

Highway atlas. A map of every state in the
  United States. 1932. 10825
—— 1934. 10828
—— 1935. 10832
—— 1936. 10836
—— 1937. 10841
Highway atlas of the United States. 1928. 10799
—— 1929. 10806
Highway atlas of the United States and Canada. 1930. 10811
—— 1931. 10818

Gambino, Giuseppe, 1841–1913.
Atlante scolastico muto. 1888. 3343a
Nuovo atlante muto di geografia fisica.
  [1890] 3344

Gamerith, Hermann.
See Walleczek, Erich, *and* Gamerith, Hermann.

Gannett, Henry, 1846–1914.
See Hewes, Fletcher Willis, 1838–1910, *and*
  Gannett, Henry, 1846–1914.

Ganzer, Karl Richard, 1909–
Werden des Reiches. 1939. 8560

García Cubas, Antonio, 1832–1912.
Atlas geográfico, estadístico é histórico de la
  República Mexicana. 1858. 2683
Atlas geográfico y estadístico de los Estados
  Unidos Mexicanos. 1886. 2687
Atlas metódico para la enseñanza de la geo-
  grafía de la República Mexicana. 1874. 2684
Atlas Mexicano. 1884–86. 2685
Atlas pintoresco é histórico de los Estados
  Unidos Mexicanos. 1885. 2686

García O., Juan Alfredo.
See Castillo Cordero, Clemente, *and* García
  O., Juan Alfredo.

Garde, Vilhelm, 1859–1926.
Vindkort over den nordligste del af Atlanter-
  havet og Davis-Stráede. 1900. 10213

Gardette, Pierre, 1906–
Atlas linguistique et ethnographique du
  Lyonnais. 1950. 8420

Gardiner, Samuel Rawson, 1829–1902.
School atlas of English history. New ed. 1895.
  107, 2881
—— 1905. 8016
—— 1910. 4011
—— [New ed. rev. and enl. 1936] 8017

Garnerey, Hippolyte Jean Baptiste, 1787–
[Vues de la Havane et des environs. 1830?] 5127

Garnier, F. A., 1803–1863.
Atlas sphéroïdal. 1862. 836

Garnier, Francis, *i.e.,* **Marie Joseph François, 1839–1873.**
Voyage d'explorations en Indo-Chine. Atlas. 1873.   3206

Garnot, Eugène Germain.
Expédition française de Formose 1884–1885. Atlas. [1894]   9673

Garofalo, Franco, 1898–
Storia Navale. [Atlas] v. l. 1942.   5503

Garran, Andrew, 1825–1901.
Australasia illustrated. 1892.   5320
Picturesque atlas of Australasia. 1886.   5319

Garretson, Cox and Company.
Columbian atlas. 1891.   965
—— 1895.   999
—— 1896.   1009

Garris, Milton Berry.
Atlas of city of Coral Gables, Fla. 1947.   11862
Coral Gables, Biscayne Bay section [Fla.] 1947.   11863

Gary, Ind. Dept. of City Engineer.
Zone map of the city of Gary [Ind. 1942]   12969

Gaskell's New and complete family atlas of the world. [1887?]   6235
—— [1889]   6246

Gaspari, Adam Christian, 1752–1830.
Allgemeiner Hand-Atlas. [1804–11]   6023
—— [1821]   3544
Neuer methodischer Schul-Atlas. 1799.   5740a

Gásperi, Federico E. de.
Atlas general de la República del Paraguay. 1920.   18370
—— 2. ed. 1939.   18371

Gastaldo, Jacopo, 16th cent.
Carta dei paesi Danubiani e delle regioni contermini (1546) 1939.   7778

Gaston, Samuel N.
Campaign atlas for 1861. 1861.   1351

Gaultier, Aloïsius Édouard Camille, 1746?–1818.
Atlas de géographie. [1810?]   4127
Complete course of geography. 1792.   5741
—— 4th ed. 1800.   94

Gaustad, Edwin Scott.
Historical atlas of religion in America. [1962]   10531

Gay, Claude, 1800–1873.
Atlas de la historia fisica y politica de Chile. 1854.   18320

Gay, Leonard W.
New atlas of Dane County, Wis. 1899.   17705

Gayler, J. L, and others.
Sketch-map economic history of Britain. [1957]   8003

Gaylord, Cecil Roy, 1898–
Doge County, Minn., plat book & farm directory. 1951.   14975

Gazzettiere Americano. 1763.   1161

GEA, Instytut Kartograficzny, Warsaw.
Atlas pocztowo-komunikacyjny Rzpl. Polskiej. [1929]   9158

Gebbie Publishing Company.
Spofford's Cabinet cyclopaedia atlas. 1900.   1050

Gebhard, Hannes, 1864–1933.
Yhtieskuntatilastollinen kartasto Suomen maalaiskunnista v. 1901. Atlas de statistique sociale sur les communes rurales de Finlande en 1901. 1908.   8364

Gebhardt, Gerhard.
Wegweiser durch den Ruhrkohlenbezirk. 1951.   8880

Gedde, Christian, 1729–1798.
Stadskonduktøren i København. 1757. 1940.   8296

Geisler, Walter, 1891–
Oberschlesien-Atlas. 1938.   8814
Wirtschafts- und verkehrsgeographischer Atlas von Schlesien. 1932.   8807

Geistbeck, Alois, 1853–1925.
Seen der deutschen Alpen. 1885.   3023

Geistbeck, Michael, 1846–1918.
See Fischer, Heinrich, *and* Geistbeck, Michael, 1846–1918.

Gelder, Willem van.
Schoolatlas van Nederlandsch Oost-Indië. 1900.   3216
—— 11. druk. 1911.   9742
—— 15. druk. 1918.   9744

Gelder, Willem van, and Lekkerkerker, Cornelis, 1869–
Schoolatlas van Nederlandsch Oost-Indië. 16. druk. [1922]   9747
—— 19. druk. 1928.   9748
—— 22. druk. 1938.   9749

Gendron, Pedro.
Atlas ô compendio geographico del globo terrestre. 1756–58.   4291

General Cartography Company.
Greater Norfolk and Portsmouth map book.
1967.   17383
Metropolitan Washington map book.   1961.   11787
—— 1966.   11788

General collection of maps, charts, views, &c.
1824.   6053

General Drafting Company.
Atlas América Latina. [1919]   18046
Family travel atlas. 1965.   10956
—— 1967.   10973
Markets of the world. 1920.   5435
Markets of the world. United States &
Canada series. 1922.   10544
Pocket atlas of the United States. [1962] 10937

General Drafting Service.
Ownership plats of portions of Las Vegas
Valley ... Nev. 1963.   15651
—— 1964.   15652

General Map Company.
Altas and plat book, Muskegon County,
Mich. 1948.   14757
Atlas and plat book of Kenosha County, Wis.
1950.   17795
Atlas and plat book, Racine County, Wis.
1950.   17891
Atlas of La Salle County, Ill. 1952.   12337
Atlas of Richland County, Wis. 1951.   17896
Mason County [Mich.] land ownership direc-
tory, atlas and plat book. 1949.   14737
Oceana County, Mich., land ownership direc-
tory, atlas and plat book. 1950.   14779
Plat book, Alexander County, Ill. 1950. 12086
Plat book, Branch County, Mich. 1951.   14623
Plat book, Christian County, Ill. 1948. 12127
Plat book, Clayton County, Iowa. 1950. 13256
Plat book, Columbia County, Wis. 1947. 17696
Plat book, Delaware County, Iowa. 1948.
                                    13320, 13321
Plat book, Dodge County, Wis. 1950.   17718
Plat book, Dubuque County, Iowa. 1947. 13353
Plat book, Du Page County, Ill. 1947.   12201
Plat book, Hamilton County, Ill. 1951. 12256
Plat book, Henry County, Ill. 1950.   12272
Plat book, Howard County, Mo. 1952.   15229
Plat book, Ingham County, Mich. 1952.   14678
Plat book, Jackson County, Iowa. 1948. 13543
Plat book, Jefferson County, Wis. 1950. 17786
Plat book, Jersey County, Ill. 1950.   12293
Plat book, Johnson County, Ill. 1950.   12302
Plat book, Livingston County, Ill. 1952. 12350
Plat book, Logan County, Ill. 1951.   12356
Plat book, Marshall & Putnam Counties, Ill.
1951.   12395
Plat book, Monroe County, Ill. 1951.   12416
Plat book, Montgomery County, Ill. 1949. 12419
Plat book, Moultrie County, Ill. 1949. 12429
Plat book of Bureau County, Ill. 1948. 12101
Plat book, Perry County, Ill. 1952.   12450
Plat book, Pike County, Ill. 1950.   12458

Plat book, Pulaski County, Ill. 1950.   12465
Plat book, Racine County, Wis. 1950.   17892
Plat book, Randolph County, Ill. 1951. 12470
Plat book, Rock County, Wis. 1947.   17903
Plat book, St. Clair County, Ill. 1952. 12485
Plat book, Tazewell County, Ill. 1950. 12515
Plat book, Walworth County, Wis. 1948. 17952
Plat book, Washington County, Ill. 1952. 12539

Generalstabens Litografiska Anstalt.
Adresskartan över Stockholm. [1957]   9419
Bilkartan. [Sweden. 1947]   9373
Gotland. [1957]   9406
Karta över Gotland. [1951]   9405
Motormännens   vägkarta   över   Sverige.
[1949]   9378
Post– och järnvägskarta över Sverige. 1942. 9355
—— [1957]   9356
Stockholms kartan. [1954]   9415
Svenska orter; atlas över Sverige. [1932] 9401
Sverige i 32 kartblad. [1916]   9395
—— [1920]   9397
Sveriges städer. 1932.   9352
Taxikartan över Stockholm. 1944.   9409
—— [1952]   9413
Topografiska   kartor   öfver   Norbottniska
turistleder. 1896.   9407

Geneva *(Canton)*
Plan officiel de Genève et de ses environs.
1958.   9458

Geodéziai és Kartográfiai Intézet.
GKI Zseb–atlas. [1954]   7596

Geografiska Sällskapet i Finland.
Suomen kartasto. Atlas of Finland. [1925–
28]   8374

Geographia, ltd.
Atlas and guide to Liverpool. [1926]   8153
Atlas of London and outer suburbs. [1948] 8182
—— [1951]   8186
Authentic atlas and guide to London. [1922] 8169
—— [1939?]   8175
Greater London atlas. [1937]   8174
Road atlas and route guide [of the British
Isles. 195–]   8051
—— [1951]   8054
Road atlas of England and Wales. [1931] 8105
Vest pocket atlas of Central London. [1951] 8187

Geographia classica. 3d ed. 1721.   5607
—— 8th ed. 1747.   5608

Geographia Map Company.
Atlas of Greater Boston. 1963.   14440
—— 1965.   14441
Atlas of Hartford and vicinity. 1964.   11727
Atlas of the United States. 1936.   11066
—— 1943.   11068
—— 1948.   11075
—— 1962.   11086

Complete street atlas of Nassau County [N.Y. 1965]   15893

Ideal atlas of Cleveland [Ohio] and vicinity. 1963.   16514

New five borough atlas of New York City. 1965.   16108

Street atlas of Rochester [N.Y.] and vicinity. 1963.   16160

—— 1967.   16161

Geographic Institute.
Atlas of Muskingum County, Ohio. 1916.   4987

Geographical Publishing Company.
Commercial & library atlas of the world. [1941]   7051

—— [1944]   7176

—— [9th ed. 1946]   7229

—— [11th ed. 1947]   7263

Commercial atlas of the world. [1931]   6743

—— [1937]   6911

Handy reference atlas and gazetteer of the world. 1911.   3618

Imperial royal Canadian world atlas. [1935]   6838

[Maps of the United States. 1911]   4528

Modern world wide atlas. [1949]   7347

New international atlas of the world. [1922]   6483

Wings war atlas. [1942]   5871

Géographie universelle. Atlas-Migenn. 1882.   903

Geographisch–Kartographische Anstalt.
Weltmeere. [15 Aufl. des Seeatlas] 1954.   5689

Geographischer Verlag, *Leipzig.*
Kriegs-Atlas über sämtliche Kriegsschau-plätze. [1914]   7798

—— 1915.   7799

Geographisches Institut, *Weimar.*
Atlas minimus universalis. 2. éd. 1805.   6024

Topographisch-militairische Charte von Teutschland. [1807–13]   5244

Verkleinerter Hand-Atlas. [1806?]   3538

George, Clarence W., 1920–
Street finder ... Portsmouth and Norfolk County [Va.] west of the Elizabeth River. 1952.   17388

Gerards, W. J.
Teekenatlas van Nederl. Oost-Indië. 6. verb. druk. [191–]   9741

Gerland, Georg Karl Cornelius, 1833–1919.
Atlas der Völkerkunde. 1892.   5477a

Germany. *Amt des Siedlungsbeauftragten.*
Geschichte der Bevölkerungsentwicklung. [1935]   8587

Germany. *Beauftragter für den Vierjahresplan.*
Goerings's Atlas. [1946]   8551

Germany. *Deutsche Seewarte, Hamburg.*
See Hamburg. Deutsche Seewarte.

Germany. *Generalinspektor für des Deutsche Stras-senwesen.*
Strassenzustand von Deutschland. Atlas. 1937.   8614

Germany. *Heer. Generalstab.*
Atlas [von Weissrussland. 194–]   9291

Feldzug gegen Sowjet-Russland. [1942]   9239

Militärgeographische Angaben über England. 1940.   8140

—— London. 2. Aufl. 1941.   8177

Militärgeographische Angaben über Irland. 1940.   8234

Militärgeographische Einzelangaben über England. 1941–42.   8141

Ober-Italien: Strassenkarten und Stadtdurch-fahrtspläne. 1940.   8972

Schweiz: Strassenzustand. 1940.   9423

Stadtdurchfahrtspläne der Niederlande. 1939.   9032

Stadtdurchfahrtspläne Südwest-Frankreich. 1940.   8385

Germany. *Heer. Generalstab. Abteilung für Kriegs-Karten und Vermessungswesen.*
Iran. Flugplätze. [1941]   9762

Germany. *Heer. Inspektion des Erziehungs– und Bildungswesens.*
Kartenskizzen zum Weltkrieg. 1943.   5823

Germany. *Kolonialamt.*
Grosser deutscher Kolonial-Atlas. 1901–12.   3020, 4033, 5242

Grosser deutscher Kolonial-Atlas. Ergän-zungs-Lieferung. 1909–11.   4034

Germany. *Kriegsmarine. Oberkommando.*
Sowjetunion. Flottenstützpunkte und Häfen. 1941.   9265

Ubootshandbuch der Ostküste der Vereinigten Staaten. 1943.   10508

Ubootshandbuch der Ostüste Kanadas (Atlas) 1942.   10340

Germany. *Luftwaffe. Führungsstab.*
Südostküste England. [1940]   8084

Taschen–Welt–Atlas der Luftwaffe. 1942.   7095

Germany. *Publikationsstelle Berlin-Dahlem.*
Gemeindegrenzenkarte der Provinzen West-preussen und Posen. 1939.   8764, 8767

Kartenfolge zur Landes- und Wirtschafts-kunde der eingegliederten Deutschen Ostgebiete. 1940–41.   9129

Germany. *Publikationsstelle Stuttgart-Hamburg.*
Sieben Rassenkarten der Vereinigten Staaten, 1930. 1943.   10575

Germany. *Reichsamt für Landesaufnahme.*
 Atlas des Deutschen Reiches. [1922] 8692
 —— [1929–38] 8696

Germany. *Reichsluftfahrtsministerium.*
 Schüleratlas für den Gebrauch an den Schulen
  der Luftwaffe. 1943. 7136

Germany. *Reichsstelle für das Schul– und Unter-
richtsschrifttum.*
 Deutscher Schulatlas. 1942. 7096
 —— 1943. 7137
 Deutscher Schul Atlas: Heimatteil Gau
  Baden. 1942. 8716
 Heimatteil Gau Bayreuth. [1943] 8731
 Heimatteil Gau Berlin. [1943] 8840
 Heimatteil Gau Kurhessen. [1944] 8753
 Heimatteil Gau Ostpreussen. [1943] 8766
 Heimatteil Gau Südhannover-Braunsch-
  weig. [1943] 8702

Germany. *Reichsverkehrsministerium.*
 Schiffahrtkarte der Donau von Kelheim bis
  Pressburg. 1941. 7838

Germany. *Statistisches Reichsamt.*
 Bodenkultur des Deutschen Reichs. 1881. 8514
 Deutscher Landwirtschaftsatlas. 1934. 8515

Germany. *Wehrmacht. Oberkommando.*
 Wehrwirtschaft Frankreichs. [1939] 8398

Germany *(Democratic Republic, 1949–) Institut für Bodenkartierung.*
 Bodenkunde und Bodenkultur. 1951–56. 8673

Germany *(Democratic Republic, 1949–) Me-
teorologischer und Hydrologischer Dienst.*
 Klima-Atlas für das Gebiet der Deutschen
  Demokratischen Republik. 1953. 8530

Germany *(Federal Republic, 1949–) Deutsches
Hydrographisches Institut.*
 Atlas der Eisverhältnisse der Deutschen Bucht
  und westlichen Ostsee. 1956. 7866
 Atlas der Eisverhältnisse des Nordatlantischen
  Ozeans. 1950. 10230
 Atlas der Gezeitenströme für die Nordsee.
  1956. 7867
 Monatskarten für den Nordatlantischen
  Ozean. 1956. 10214

Germany *(Federal Republic, 1949–) Wetter-
dienst.*
 Klima-Atlas von Baden-Württemberg. 1953. 8713
 Klima-Atlas von Rheinland-Pfalz. 1957. 8769

Geschichtsverein für Kärnten.
 Kärntner Heimatatlas. 1951–56. 7912

Gesellschaft der Freunde des Vaterländischen
Schul– und Erziehungswesens. *Hamburg.*
 Atlas für Hamburger Schulen. 1912. 4194

—— 2 v. 1952–53. 7540
—— 3 v. 1955. 7616

Gesellschaft für Rheinische Geschichtskunde.
 Archaeologische Karte der Rheinprovinz.
  [1932] 8768
 [Geschichtlicher Atlas der Rheinprovinz]
  1894–1923. 4035, 8771
 Wald-, Kultur-, und Siedlungskarte der
  Rheinprovinz 1801–1820. 1930. 8772

Gherzi, Ernesto, 1886–
 Climatological atlas of East Asia. 1944. 9476

Ghisleri, Arcangelo, 1855–1938.
 Atlante d'Africa. 1909. 4083

Gibb Brothers and Moran.
 Gibb's Travelers' route and reference book of
  the United States and Canada. 1909. 3663

Gibelli, Giuseppe, 1831–1898, Brunamonti, G., *and*
Danesi, C.
 Desegni e descrittioni dell fortezze … e fan-
  teria dello Stato Ecclesiastico. [1888] 3056

Gibert, André.
 See Fallex, Maurice, *i.e.,* Albert Maurice,
  1861–1929, *and* Gibert, André.

Gibson, Arthur.
 Plat book of Cottonwood County, Minn.
  1896. 2014

Gibson, George E., *and* Gibson, William.
 Map of Omaha and South Omaha. [1887] 2129

Gibson, John, *fl.* 1750–1792.
 Atlas minimus. 1758. 621
 —— 1774. 3516
 —— 1779. 3518
 —— 1792. 6001
 —— New ed. 1792. 676
 —— 1798. 691
 New and accurate maps of the counties of
  England and Wales. [1758?] 2917

Gibson, William.
 See Gibson, George E., *and* Gibson, William.

Giffen, Guy J.
 Historic California in maps. 1938. 11330
 Maps showing old adobes and historic sites in
  San Diego … Monterey. [1936] 11331

Gilbert, Edmund William.
 How the map has changed, 1938–1940.
  [1941] 5872

Gilbert, Frank Theodore, *b.* 1846.
 Illustrated atlas and history of Yolo County,
  Cal. 1879. 4539

Gildemeister, Johann, 1753–1837, *and* Heineken, Christian Abraham, 1752–1818.
Gebiet der freien Hansestadt Bremen. 1928.   8850

Gill, Reginald.
Sphere atlas. 1900.   6294

Gill, Somers.
Muttall's Simplified atlas of the world. [1950?]   5436

Gilleland, J. C.
Ohio and Mississippi pilot. 1820.   1323

Gillen and Davy.
Atlas of Mitchell County, Kans. 1884.   1729
Atlas of Wabaunsee County, Kans. 1885.   14206

Gillespie's Guide; complete Los Angeles City and County. 1952.   11546
—— 1953.   11547

Gillespie's Guide for the automobile driver ... Los Angeles [Calif.] 1939.   11538
—— [1948]   11544

Gillespie's Guide; Los Angeles City and County. 1950.   11545
—— 1956.   11552

Gilliéron, Jules Louis, 1854–1926, *and* Edmont, Edmond, 1848–1926.
Atlas linguistique de la France. 1902–1908.   2960
—— 1902–1910.   4020
—— Corse. 1914–15.   5238

Ginn and Company.
Classical atlas. [1882]   5609
—— 1895.   5610

Girard, Barrère et Thomas.
France: Atlas administratif. [1945?]   8476

Girard et Barrère.
France ... Atlas administratif et départemental. [1937]   8474

Girault-Gilbert.
Carte routière de Belgique. [193–]   7960

Giuffra, Elzear Santiago, 1893–1939.
Atlas esquemático de ciencias geográficas. 6. ed. 1946.   7230
Atlas esquemático de geografía universal. 5. ed. 1936–37.   6900

Giustiniani, Francisco.
Atlas abreviado. 1739.   4285

Gläser, Carl.
Vollständiger Atlas. [1840]   6088

Glassman, Alfred.
Universal atlas of metropolitan Boston. 1963.   14439

Gleason Engineering Corporation.
Atlas, town of Wellesley [Mass.] 1935.   14538

Gleditsch, Kristen Gran, 1867–
Sør-Norge. 1936.   9118

Gley, Werner, 1902–
See Wolfram, Georg Karl, 1858–1940, *and* Gley, Werner, 1902–

Goad, Charles E.
Atlas of the city of Toronto. 1884.   4485
—— 2d ed. 1890.   4486

Godshall, Wilson Leon, 1895–   *and* Langer, William Leonard,   1896–
Map studies in European history and international relations. [1940]   7735

Goedecke, Otto.
Atlante Goedecke delle varietá di cotone degli Stati Uniti e del Messico. 1959.   10510
Carte Goedecke des variétés de coton des Étas-Unis et du Mexique. 1959.   10511
Cotton variety map of the United States and Mexico. 1951.   10512
—— 1952.   10513
—— 1953.   10514
—— 1954.   10515
—— 1955.   10516
—— 1956.   10517
—— 1958.   10518
—— 1959.   10519
—— 1960.   10520
—— 1961.   10521
—— 1962.   10522
—— 1963.   10523
—— 1964.   10524
—— 1965.   10525
Karte der verschiedenen Baumwollarten der Vereinigten Staaten von Amerika und Mexiko. 1959.   10526

Görög, Demeter, 1760–1833.
Magyar átlás. 1802–[1806]   8922
—— [2. kiad.] 1802–11 [*i.e.,* 1817]   8923
Magyar atlasz. 1848.   8925
—— 1860.   8926

Görög, László.
Magyarország mezőgazdasági földrajaza. 1954.   8907

Gösmann, Gottfried, *and* Lucas, Otto.
Planungsgrundlagen für den Landkreis Lippstadt (Westf.) 1953.   8826

Göttinger Arbeitskreis.
Staats- und Verwaltungsgrenzen in Ostmitteleuropa. 1954–55.   7628

Götz, Andreas, 1698–1780.
Brevis introdvctio ad geographiam antiqvam.
1729. 15

Gold Coast _(Colony) Survey Dept._
Atlas of the Gold Coast. [1927–28] 10142
—— 2d ed. 1935. 10143
—— 5th ed. 1949. 10145
Modified atlas of the Gold Coast. 1947. 10144

Golf Digest.
Rand McNally golf course guide. [1966] 10749
—— [1967] 10750

Gomes, Bernardino Antonio Barros, 1839–1910.
Cartas elementares de Portugal. 1878. 9193

Gómez, Hernán Félix, 1888–
Jurisdicciónes territoriales gráficos; Provincia
de Corrientes. 1936. 18242

Gómez de Arteche y Moro, José, 1821–1906.
Atlas de la guerra de la independencia.
[1869–1901] 3127

Gonzales, Alexandro.
Atlas maritimo del Reyno de el Perú, Chile,
costa Patagonica. MS. 1797. 2768

Gonzáles de la Rosa, Manuel Toribio.
Nuevo atlas geográfico universal. 1911. 3370
—— 15th ed. 1913. 4395

González R. Cosío, Enrique, 1909–
Geografía postal de España. Atlas. 1933. 9314

Goodall, George, 1895–1955.
Soviet Russia in maps. 1942. 9247
—— 1943. 9248
Soviet Union in maps. 1947. 9250
—— 1949. 9252
—— 1954. 9259
War in maps. [1941] 5873
World War in maps. 1942. 5874
World War in maps, third, fourth and fifth
years. 1944. 5875

Goode, Clement Tyson, 1883–   _and_ Shannon,
Edgar Finley,   1874–1938.
Atlas of English literature. 1925. 8021

Goode, John Paul, 1862–1932.
Base maps and graphs. [1926] 5742
Rand McNally Regional atlas. 1953. 7556
Rand McNally World atlas. [1935] 6839
School atlas. Advance pages. [1922] 6484
School atlas. [1923] 6521
—— [1925] 6582
4th ed. [1932] 6774
—— [4th ed. 1933] 6794
—— [7th ed. 1937] 6912
—— [7th ed. 1939] 6975
—— [7th ed. 1943] 7138
—— [7th ed. 1946] 7231

—— [7th ed. 1948] 7303
—— [8th ed. 1949] 7348
—— [8th ed. 1950] 7403
World atlas, physical, political, and economic.
9th ed. [1953] 7555

Goodell, Hubert E.
Atlas of Champaign County, Ill. 1951. 12121
Champaign County, Ill. 1952. 12122

Goodman, H. J.
Illustrated historical atlas of Ottawa County,
Ohio. 1900. 2406a

Goodrich, Charles Augustus, 1790–1862.
Atlas accompanying Rev. C. A. Goodrich's
Outlines of modern geography. [1826] 6055

Goodrich, Samuel Griswold, 1793–1860.
Atlas designed to illustrate the Malte-Brun
school geography. 1830. 285
—— 1838. 286
General atlas of the world. 1841. 6092
See also Bradford, Thomas Gamaliel, _and_
Goodrich, Samuel Griswold, 1793–1860.

Goodwin, I. B.
Plat book of Platte County, Nebr. 1914. 4900

Goor, D. Noothoven van.
Nieuwe school–atlas der geheele aarde. 9.
druk. [1875] 6190

Goos, Abraham, _ca._ 1590–1643.
Nieuw Nederlandtsch caertboeck. [1616] 9081

Goos, Hendrik, _b._ 1641.
See Jacobsz, Theunis, or Anthonie, _called_
Loots-man, Doncker, Hendrik, _and_ Goos,
Hendrik, _b._ 1641.

Goos, Pieter, 1616–1675.
Atlas de la mer. 1670. 3435
Grand & nouveau miroir. 1671. 483
Lichtende colomne, ofte Zee-spiegel. 1656–
[57] 3984
Lighting colomne. 1660–[61] 5164
Nieuwe groote zee-spiegel. 1676. 3440
Sea-atlas. 1670. 481a
Zee-atlas. 1666. 473, 474
—— 1669. 5690

Gorand's Street map of Chicago and suburbs.
1951. 12656

Gordon, Robert, _of Burma._
[Report on the Irrawaddy River. Atlas.
1879–80] 9502

Gordon, Thomas Francis, 1787–1860.
Gazetteer of the state of New York. 1836. 4921

Gorissen, Friedrich.
Stede-atlas van Nijmegen. 1956. 9101

Gorjan, August, 1837–   *and* **Luncan, I.**
Atlas-géografie. 1895.   1000
Atlas-géografie România. 1895.   3097

Gould, F. A.
See Lake, D. J., Sanford, George P., *and*
Gould, F. A.

Gould, Hueston T., *and others.*
Illustrated atlas of Ross County and Chil-
licothe, Ohio. 1875.   2413
See also Caldwell, Joseph A., *and* Gould,
Hueston T.

Gourné, Pierre Mathias, 1702–1770?
Atlas abrégé et portatif. 1763.   637

Goushá, H. M., Company.
American highway atlas. [1955]   10898
—— [1956]   10901
—— [1957]   10906
—— [1959]   10918
—— [1960]   10926
—— [1961]   10931
—— [1962]   10938
American road guide; United States, Canada,
and Mexico. 1959.   10919
Arizona points of interest and touring map.
[1952]   11249
—— [1953]   11250
California points of interest and touring map.
[1946]   11342
—— [1947]   11343
—— [1949]   11344
—— [1952]   11345
—— [1953]   11347
Conoco deluxe touraide. 1963.   10943
Conoco deluxe touraide travel guide. 1964.   10948
Conoco pocket touraide travel guide. [1965]   10957
Idaho points of interest and touring map.
[1952]   12001
—— [1953]   12002
Maine points of interest and touring map.
[1953]   14301
National road atlas, United States, Canada,
Mexico. [1957]   10907
—— Rev. ed. 1961.   10932
Nevada points of interest and touring map.
[1952]   15647
—— [1953]   15648
New Hampshire, Vermont points of interest
and touring map. [1953]   15657
New Jersey points of interest and touring
map. [1953]   15678
New redi-map road atlas. [1951]   10882
—— [1952]   10887
—— [1954]   10894
North American vacation guide and road
atlas. [1967]   10310
Official road map[s. 1942]   10858
Oregon points of interest and touring map.
[1952]   16644
—— [1953]   16645

Pennsylvania points of interest and touring
map. [1953]   16763
Redi-map road atlas. [1955]   10899
—— [1956]   10902
Richfield highway maps: Western States.
[1938]   10844
Shell complete road atlas of the Southeast.
1966.   10963
[Shell official road maps: United States and
Canada. 1938–41]   10849
[Shell road maps … United States and Can-
ada. 1954]   10895
Skelly highway atlas. [United States, Canada
and Mexico. 1959]   10920
Southern California street and recreation
guide. [1966]   11617
Trip plan, Allstate Motor Club. [1961]   10303
—— [1962]   10304
—— 1963.   10305
—— 1964.   10306
—— [1965]   10307
—— [1966]   10308
United States road atlas. [1959]   10921
—— [1960]   10927
—— [1962]   10939
Utah points of interest and touring map.
[1952]   17294
—— [1953]   17295
Vacation guide and atlas. [1965]   10958
Vacation guide and road atlas. [1957]   10908
—— [1958]   10913
—— [1966]   10964
Washington points of interest and touring
map. [1952]   17413
—— [1953]   17414
World's road atlas and vacation guide of North
America. [1966]   10309
—— [1967]   10311

**Gouvion Saint-Cyr, Laurent, *Marquis* de, 1764–
1830.**
Atlas des cartes et plans relatifs aux campagnes
du Maréchal Gouvion St. Cyr. 1828.   2967
Atlas des mémoires pour servir à l'histoire
militaire sous le Directoire, le Consulat et
l'Empire. 1831.   2968
Atlas des plans et cartes … du 7e corps de la
Grande Armée. [1821]   7709

Gover, Edward.
Atlas of universal historical geography. 1854.   108
Two shilling physical atlas. 1854.   223

Gräf, A.
See Kiepert, Heinrich, Gräf, Carl, Gräf, A.,
and Bruhn, Karl Christian, 1830–1881.

Gräf, Adolf.
Atlas des Himmels und der Erde. [1863–66]   6147

Gräf, Carl.
See Kiepert, Heinrich, Gräf, Carl, Gräf, A.,
and Bruhna, Karl Christian, 1830–1881.

Graf, Horace.
River maps of the Current & Jacks Fork [Mo. 1966]   15303

Gramatica, Aloisius.
Atlas geographiae Biblicae. Editio minor. 1921.   5348

Gramatica, Luigi.
Testo e atlante di geografia ecclesiastica. [1927]   5407

Grandidier, Alfred, 1836–1921.
Histoire de la géographie. 1885–92.   4085

Grandidier, Guillaume, 1873–1957.
Atlas des Colonies Françaises, protectorats et territoires sous mandat de la France. [1934]   8391

Granger, Ernest, 1876–
Atlas–guide géographique "Alpina" [1929]   6703

Grant, A. A.
Bankers' and brokers' railway system atlas. [1907]   1258
Standard indexed atlas. [1885]   4363

Graphic Design Services.
Ownership plat book, Boulder County, Colo. 1958.   11652

Graves and Hardy.
Eureka pocket atlas of the Red River valley. 1894.   2340

Graves and Steinbarger.
Atlas of surveys of the county of Lancaster ... Pa. 1899.   16790

Gray, Arthur, 1852–1940.
See Clark, John Willis, 1833–1910, *and* Gray, Arthur, 1852–1940

Gray, Henry, 1892–
Historical atlas of colonial North America. [1942]   10293

Gray, O. W., and Son.
Atlas of the world. Supplement. 1876.   875, 876
National atlas. 1875.   873, 1391
—— 1876.   878, 1394
—— 1877.   885, 1398
—— 1878.   6196, 11037
—— 1882.   904, 1412
—— 1886.   6229, 11048
New illustrated atlas of Dutchess County, N.Y. 1876.   2224
New topographical atlas of Essex County, N.Y. 1876.   2227

Gray, Ormando Willis.
Atlas of the United States. 1873.   1390
—— 1874.   4526

—— 1876.   877, 1393
—— 1878.   11036
Atlas of Windham and Tolland Counties, Conn. 1869.   4546, 4547
See also Martenet, Simon J., Walling, Henry Francis, *and* Gray, Ormando Willis.
See also Walling, Henry Francis 1825–1888, *and* Gray, Ormando Willis.

Great Britain.
Appendix No. III. Maps to accompany documents ... relating to ... boundary between British Guiana and Venezuela. [1896]   18410
Atlas to accompany the Case ... between Great Britain and the United States of Venezuela. 1898.   18411
North Atlantic Coast Fisheries Arbitration. Maps. 1909.   10286

Gt. Brit. *Admiralty.*
Manual of Alsace-Lorraine. Atlas. [1920]   8484

Gt. Brit. *Board of Trade.*
Geographical maps of the development areas. 1946.   8007

Gt. Brit. *British Information Services.*
Maps of Britain. [1943?]   8004
—— [1952?]   8005
—— 1956.   8006

Gt. Brit. *Colonial Office.*
Colonial Office list. Map supplement. 1948.   8001

Gt. Brit. *Foreign Office. Historical Section.*
Ethnographical maps of Central & South Eastern Europe. 1919.   7801
Maps of Austria-Hungary. 1919.   7939
Maps of Poland. 1919.   9160
Maps of the Balkan Peninsula. 1919.   7824

Gt. Brit. *Hydrographic Office.*
Atlas of tides and tidal streams, British Islands. 3d ed. 1943.   8068
—— 4th ed. 1946.   8069
Channel Islands and adjacent coasts of France. 1946.   7848
France, west coast; pocket tidal stream atlas. 1943.   8449
Meteorological charts for the world. [1928–29]   5392
Meteorological charts of the world. [1935]   5393
Monthly current charts for the Atlantic Ocean. [1897]   10226
Monthly current charts for the Indian Ocean. [1896]   10239
Monthly fishery charts for the British Islands. 1953.   8011
Pentland Firth and approaches to Kirkwall [Orkney Islands] Pocket tidal stream atlas. 1946.   8217
Pilot charts for the Atlantic Ocean. [1868]   10215
Quarterly current charts for the Pacific Ocean. [1897]   10249

Sea ice north of the U.S.S.R. 1958. 10208

Shetland Islands; pocket tidal stream atlas.
[1953] 8218

Solent and adjacent waters. 1946. 8199

Thames estuary, pocket tidal stream atlas.
1946. 8201

Tidal streams, Channel Islands. [1903] 7849

Tidal streams, coasts of Scotland. [1899] 8203

Wind charts for the coastal regions of South
America. [1902] 18187

Gt. Brit. *India Office.*
[Indian atlas. 1827–62] 5301
—— [1827–68] 9699

Gt. Brit. *Meteorological Office.*
Charts illustrating the weather of the North
Atlantic Ocean in the winter of 1898–9.
1901. 10216

Charts showing the surface temperature of the
Atlantic, Indian, and Pacific Oceans.
1884. 5394

Charts showing the surface temperature of the
South Atlantic Ocean. 1869. 10217

Climatological atlas of the British Isles.
1952. 7993

Currents on the main trade routes of the
North Atlantic. 1930. 10227

Meteorological charts for the ocean district
adjacent to the Cape of Good Hope. 1882. 10234

Monthly ice charts: Western North Atlantic.
1946. 10231

Monthly meteorological charts and ocean
current chart of the Greenland and Barents
Seas. [194–] 10207

Monthly meteorological charts of Baffin Bay
and Davis Strait. 1916–[17] 10206

Monthly meteorological charts of the Atlantic
Ocean. 1948. 10218

Monthly meteorological charts of the Indian
ocean. 1949. 10235

Quarterly surface current charts of the Atlantic
Ocean. 1945. 10228

Quarterly surface current charts of the western Northern Pacific Ocean. 2d ed. 1949. 10250

South Pacific Ocean currents. 1938. 10251

Gt. Brit. *Ministry of Information.*
M. O. I. map service. Book[s] 1–12. 1942–
[43] 5743

Outline maps ... Book[s] A–D. 1943. 5744

Small atlas of the war. 1918. 4223a

Gt. Brit. *Naval Intelligence Division.*
Manual of Belgium. 1918. 7944
—— 1922. 7945

Peoples of Austria-Hungary. I. Hungary.
Atlas. 1919. 8915

Gt. Brit. *Ordnance Survey.*
Atlas of England & Wales. 1922. 8136
Atlas of Scotland. 1924. 8213
[Maps of counties of England and Wales.
1805–20] 5208

Routes through towns ... of Great Britain.
[1935] 7992

Ten outline sketches of the island of Hong
Kong. [1846] 5297

Gt. Brit. *Ordnance Survey of Lreland.*
Maps of the escheated counties in Ireland,
1609. [1863] 8236

Gt. Brit. *Privy Council. Judicial committee.*
Atlas to accompany the case of the Colony of
Newfoundland in regard to the Labrador
boundary. [1926] 10397

Labrador boundary. Canadian atlas. [1926] 10399
—— Maps. [Prelim. ed. 1926] 10400
—— Maps to accompany the Memorandum ... on the use of the term coast in
cartography. 1926. 10398

Gt. Brit. *War Office.*
Plans &c. ... to accompany the Journal of the
Siege of Sebastopol. [1859] 9233

Gt. Brit. *War Office. General Staff. Geographical
Section.*
Belgium: Town plans. [1943] 7942
Denmark: Town plans. [1944] 8259
Germany: Town plans. [1944] 8528
Holland: Town plans. [1943] 9033
Throughway town plans of Austria. 1944. 7889
Throughway town plans of France. 1944. 8386
Throughway town plans of Italy north of
Rome. 1944. 8946

Great Britain *and* **Brazil.**
Atlas annexé au Congre-mémoire. [1903]
2722, 2724, 2742, 2743

Grebenau, Heinrich.
Theorie der Bewegung des Wassers in Flüssen
und Canälen. 1867. 11099

Greece. *Genikē Statistikē Hypēresia.*
Ἄτλας τῶν δήμων χαὶ χοινοτήτων τῆς
Ἑλλάδος ἐπὶ τῇ βάσει τῆς ςοιχητιχῆς
διαιρέσεως τῆς 31/12/1948 [Atlas des
municipalités et communes de la Grèce,
suivant la division administrative du 31/12/
1948. 1951] 8884

Greece. *Hypourgeion Anoikodomēseōs.*
Αἱ γυσίαι τῆς Ἑλλάδος στὸν δεύτερο
παγχόσμιο πόλεμο. [Les sacrifes de la
grèce à la seconde guerre mondiale. 1946] 8901

Greek War Relief Association.
Atlas of World II. 1st ed. 1943. 5876

Greeley and Carlson.
Atlas of Hyde Park, Ill. 1880. 1592

Greeley, Carlson and Company.
Atlas of the city of Chicago. 1884. 1582
Atlas of the town of Lake, Ill. 1883–92. 1594

Second atlas of the city of Chicago. 1891–
92.   1586, 12594

Green, Frank J., 1887–
Maps of property and intersection corners in
the city of Kearney, Nebr. 2d ed. [1961]   15636
Property and intersection corners of the city of
Kearney, Nebr. [1959]   15635

Green, Howard Whipple, 1893–
Census tract street index for Cuyahoga
County [Ohio] 5th ed. [1951]   16509
—— 6th ed. [1955]   16513

Greene, Francis Vinton, 1850–1921.
Russian army and its campaigns in Turkey in
1877–1878. Atlas. 1879.   9234

Greenleaf, Jeremiah, 1791–1864.
New universal atlas. 1842.   784

Greenleaf, Moses, 1777–1834.
Atlas accompanying Greenleaf's map and
statistical survey of Maine. [1829]   1772

Greensboro, *N.C. Planning Dept.*
Greensboro atlas. [1967]   16234

Greenwood, Arthur, 1880–
See Clay, *Sir* Henry, 1883–1954, *and* Greenwood, Arthur, 1880–

Greenwood and Company.
Atlas of the counties of England. 1834.   2925

Gregory, Henry Duval, 1819–1897.
Index to Mitchell's New school atlas. 1871.   287

Gregory, James Stothert, 1912–
See Horrabin, James Francis, 1884–   *and*
Gregory, James Stothert, 1912–

Grēgouras, K.
Hellas. Peloponnissos. [1936]   8904

Grenet, L'abbé —— 1750–
Atlas portatif. [1779–82?]   288
Atlas portatif [de la France] a l'usage des col-
leges. [1785]   8456
Compendio di geografia. 1794.   680

Grieg, John, *firm.*
Kart over Bergen. [1948]   9128

Griera y Gaja, Antonio, 1887–
Atlas lingüístic de Catalunya. 1923–26.   9313

Griffen, Joseph.
Atlas designed to illustrate "Elements of
modern geography," 1833.   289

Griffin, L. W.
See Lawrence, C. H., *and* Griffin, L. W.

Griffin, Paul Francis, *and* Young, Robert N., 1923–
Atlas of California. [1956]   11359

Griffin, William M.
See Meleney, Clarence Edmund, 1853–
and Griffin, William M.

Griffing, B. N.
Atlas of Darke County, Ohio. 1888.   2370
Atlas of Defiance County, Ohio. 1890.   2371
Atlas of Fulton County, Ohio. 1888.   2377
Atlas of Mercer County, Ohio. 1888.   2399
Atlas of Vanderburgh County, Ind. 1880.   1631
Atlas of Wood County, Ohio. 1886.   16466
Illustrated historical atlas of Knox County,
Ind. 1880.   12831
See also Lake, D. J., *and* Griffing, B. N.
See also Lathrop, J. M., *and* Griffing, B. N.

Griffing, Dixon and Company.
Atlas of Davies County, Ind. 1888.   1601

Griffing, Gordon and Company.
Atlas of Hancock County, Ind. 1887.   1608
Atlas of Jay County, Ind. 1887.   1614

Griffith, William, Jr.
Illustrated atlas of Gallia County, Ohio.
1874.   2378

Griffiths, Evan Dalton.
See Franklin, Thomas, 1877–   *and* Griffiths, Evan Dalton.

Grilo, Miguel.
Atlas geográfico de España. 2. ed. [1876]   9325

Grimoard, Philippe Henri, *comte* de, 1753–1815.
[Histoire des quatre dernières campagnes du
Maréchal de Turenne, en 1672–1675. Atlas.
1782]   3976

Grondona, Nicolas.
America del Sur, provincias Argentinas.
1875.   3956

Gros, C.
See Lavoisne, C. V. *and* Gros, C.

Grosmann, Charles W. F.
Donnelley's Sectional atlas of the city of Chicago. 1891.   1585

Gross, Alexander, 1879–1958.
Authentic atlas of the world. [1947]   7264
—— [1950]   7404
Daily Telegraph pocket atlas of the war.
[1917]   4224
Daily Telegraph victory atlas of the world.
[1920]   6410
—— [1921]   6440
Eleven war maps with … events World War II.
[1945]   5877

Geographers' atlas of Greater London.
[1948]   8183
—— [1956]   8193
"Geographia" Atlas of Greater New York.
1937.   16047
—— 1944.   16059
"Geographia" Atlas of the world. 1935.   6840
—— 1937.   6913
—— [1942]   7097
—— [1951]   7451
"Geographia" Far East atlas. [1945]   9495
Geographia Five borough atlas of New York
City. 1950.   16077
—— 1954.   16084
—— 1964.   16106
Geographia Ideal atlas of Essex County, N.J.
1948.   15700
"Geographia" Ideal atlas of the world.
[1944]   7177
Ideal atlas of Baltimore. [1946]   14384
Ideal atlas of Buffalo [N.Y.] and vicinity.
1952.   15956
Ideal atlas of Chicago and vicinity. 1952.   12657
Ideal atlas of Detroit and vicinity. 1954.   14861
Ideal atlas of Greater Boston. 1946.   14435
Ideal atlas of Nassau County [N.Y.] 1953.   15891
Ideal atlas of Philadelphia and vicinity.
1953.   16880
Ideal atlas of Pittsburgh and vicinity. 1955.   16913
Ideal atlas of Washington, D.C., and vicinity.
1953.   11784
Perma Handy world atlas. [1st ed. 1950]   7405
Universal atlas of the world. 1923.   6522

Gross, H., *and* Berson, Arthur, 1859–
Atlas graphischer Darstellung der Flugbahnen
... von 75 wissenschaftlichen Luftfahrten.
1900.   8521

Gross, Henry Emmett.
Map book, St. Louis and St. Louis County
[Mo.] 1956.   15288
—— [2d ed.] 1959.   15289
—— [3d ed.] 1961.   15291
—— [4th ed.] 1963.   15293
—— [5th ed.] 1964.   15295
—— [6th ed.] 1966.   15297

Grosse Berliner Strassenbahn.
Planheft enthaltend 10 Zeichnungen ... der
Grossen Berliner und Berlin-Charlotten-
burger Strassenbahn. [190–]   882

Grove, *Sir* George, 1820–1900.
See Smith, *Sir* William, 1813–1893, *and*
Grove, *Sir* George, 1820–1900.

Gruber, Christian, 1858–1906.
See Ebeling, Philipp, *and* Gruber, Christian,
1858–1906.

Grundeman, Reinhold, *i.e.*, Peter Reinhold, 1836–1924.
Allgemeiner Missions-Atlas. 1867–71.   5408
Neuer Missions-Atlas. 2. Aufl. 1903.   181

Grundy, George Beardoe, 1861–1948.
Murray's Small classical atlas. [1904]   3277, 5611
—— 2d ed. 1917.   5612

Gruner, Édouard, 1849–1932 or 33, *and* Bousquet, J. G.
Atlas général des houillières. 1909–11.   4106a

Guadet, Joseph, 1795–1881.
Atlas de l'histoire de France. 1833.   8407

Gualdi, Pedro.
[Views of the city of Mexico. 1850?]   5122

Guatemala.
Guatemala-Honduras Boundary Arbitration.
Supplement to the Cartographical atlas.
[1931]   18118

Guatemala. *Comisión de Limites.*
Cartografía de la América Central. 1929.   18119

Guatemala. *Dirección General de Cartografía.*
Atlas preliminar de Guatemala. 1964.   18133

Guatemala (City) Observatorio Meteorológico y Estacion Sismográfica.
Atlas climatológico de Guatemala. [1964]   18130

Guest Engineering Company.
Atlas of Jefferson County, Ark. 1921.   11297

Gueudeville, Nicholas, 1654?–1721 *or* 22.
Nouveau théâtre du monde. 1713.   558

Guí Pla, *General San Martin, Argentina.*
Capital Federal y Gran Buenos Aires, Re-
pública Argentina. 1955.   18244
—— 2. ed. 1956.   18245
—— 3. ed. 1957.   18247
—— 4. ed. 1958.   18249
—— 5. ed. 1959.   18251

Guía de planos, ciudad de Buenos Aires y suburbanos.
1957.   18248
—— 1959.   18250
—— 1961.   18252
—— 1964.   18253
—— 1965.   18254
—— 1967.   18255

Guía General, Caracas. [1963]   18435

Guía Rex de Ruas.
Planta portátil do estado de Guanabara.
[1965]   18305

Guicciardini, Lodovico, 1521–1589.
Descrittione ... di tvtti i paesi bassi. 1588.   5274

Guigoni, Maurizio.
Atlante geografico universale.   1875.   874

Guilbaudière, Jouhan de la.
See La Guilbaudière, Jouhan de.

Guillén y Tato, Julio Fernando, 1897–
Monumenta chartográphica indiana.   1942.   18189

Guilmin, L.
Plan de Paris par arrondissement. [191–?]   8496
—— [1924?]   8498
—— [1925?]   8499
—— [1927]   8500

Guizot, François Pierre Guillaume, 1787–1874.
Vie, correspondance et écrits de Washington.
Atlas.   1840.   1338

Gulf Refining Company.
Aviation atlas.   2d ed.   1931.   5331
—— [3d ed.]   1933.   5332
—— 4th ed.   1935.   5333

Gunn, Angus Macleod, 1920–
British Columbia landforms and settlement.
[1967]   10386

Gunter, Helen Rees Clifford, 1905–
Illustrated California history maps.   1953.   11332

Gupta, Hari Ram.
See Kohli, Sita Ram, and Gupta, Hari Ram.

Gurrey, Alfred R.
Honolulu.   [1906]   3263
Map of Honolulu.   1900.   3262

Guthe, Hermann, 1849–1936.
Bibelatlas.   1911.   4080
—— 2. Aufl.   1926.   5349

Guthrie, William, 1708–1770.
Atlas to Guthrie's System of geography.
[1795]   6006
—— 1808.   6026
Atlas universel.   1802.   698
General atlas.   1820.   738
General atlas for Carey's edition of Guthrie's
Geography improved.   1795.   6007

Gyldendals Verdensatlas. [1951]   7488

H & H Graphics.
Indexed street atlas of northern Virginia.
1966.   17341

Haack, Hermann, 1872–1966.
Justus Perthes' Kleinster Schulatlas.   1925.   6583
Oro–hydrotopischer Atlas.   [1925]   7545

Haack, Hermann, 1872–1966 and **Hertzberg, Heinrich, 1859–1931.**
Grosser historischer Wandatlas. [1912–
1916?]   4134a
See also Lüddecke, Richard, 1859–1898, and
Haack, Hermann, 1872–1966.
—— Schmidt, Max Georg, 1870–1956, and
Haack, Hermann, 1872–1966.

Haack, Hemann, Geographisch-Kartographische Anstalt.
Deutschland, Taschenatlas. 20., berichtigte
Aufl.   1955.   8709
—— 21., berichtigte Aufl.   1956.   8710
—— 22., berichtigte Aufl.   1958.   8711
Taschenatlas von Deutschland. 18., beri-
chtigte- und erweiterte Aufl.   1953.   8708

Habenicht, Hermann, 1844–1917.
See Sydow, Emil, i.e., Theodor Emil, 1812–
1873, and Habenicht, Hermann, 1844–
1917.

Hachette et Companie.
Champs de bataille. [1915]   5824
Plan de Paris et de sa proche banlieue. [1947]   8505
—— [2. éd. 1954]   8507

Hacke, William.
Description of the sea coasts, rivers & a. of
Monomotapa. MS. [1690?]   3162

Hader, Berta Hoerner, and **Hader, Elmer, 1889–**
Picture book of the states. 1st ed.   1932.   11063

Haeberlin, Carl, 1870–   and **Perlewitz, Paul Julius Georg, 1878–**
Klima-Atlas für die Meeresheilkunde an der
Deutschen Seeküste.   1932.   8531

Haefke, Fritz, 1896–
Atlas zur Erd– und Länderkunde.   1952.   7507
—— 1953.   7557

Haestrup, Jørgen.
See Strehle, Aksel, and Haestrup, Jørgen.

Hagelgans, Johann Georg, d. 1765.
Atlas historicus.   1751.   3308

Hagemann, Ernst, 1899–   and **Voigts, Heinrich, 1895–**
Bioklimatischer Atlas für Schleswig-Holstein.
1948.   8800

Hagerup, H.
Verdens atlas.   1935.   6841

Hagnauer, Robert.
See Riniker, H., Hagnauer, Robert, and Dickson, George K.

Hagstrom Company.

Atlas and official postal zone guide ... Philadelphia ... Camden, N.J. 1957.   16885

Atlas and official postal zone guide of the city of New York. 5th ed. 1947.   16067

—— 6th ed. 1949.   16075

—— 7th ed. 1953.   16082

—— 8th ed. 1957.   16093

—— 9th ed. 1961.   16099

Atlas of Bergen County, N.J. 1955.   15684

—— 1959.   15685

—— 3d ed. 1962.   15686

—— 4th ed. 1965.   15687

Atlas of Essex County, N.J. 1954.   15702

—— 1961.   15703

—— 1965.   15704

Atlas of Fairfield County, Conn. 1st ed. 1959.   11700

—— 2d ed. 1966.   11701

Atlas of Middlesex County, N.J. 1961.   15713

—— 2d ed. 1966.   15714

Atlas of Monmouth County, N.J. 1956.   15716

—— 2d ed. 1967.   15717

Atlas of Nassau County, Long Island, N.Y. 3d ed. 1962.   15892

—— 4th ed. 1965.   15894

—— 5th ed. 1967.   15895

Atlas of Ocean County, N.J. 1963.   15718

Atlas of Passaic County, N.J. 1955.   15719

—— 1963.   15720

Atlas of Queens and Nassau Counties ... N.Y. 1946.   16126

—— 1950.   16128

—— 1954.   16129

Atlas of Suffolk County, Long Island, N.Y. [1st ed.] 1961.   15909

—— 2d ed. 1964.   15910

Atlas of the city of New York, the five boroughs. 1941.   16054

—— 1943.   16057

—— 1944.   16060

—— 1945.   16062

Atlas of Union County, N.J. 1955.   15723

—— 1962.   15724

—— 1965.   15725

Atlas of Westchester County, N.Y. 1957.   15922

—— 2d ed. 1961.   15923

—— 3d ed. 1967.   15924

Loose leaf market atlas of the United States. 1935.   10545

—— 2d ed. 1946.   10546

Our fair city; a map guide to New York City. [1963]   16103

Pocket atlas and general information guide of ... New York. 1957.   16096

Pocket atlas of Huntington Township, Suffolk County, Long Island, N.Y. 1960.   15912

—— [2d ed.] 1964.   15913

—— [3d ed.] 1967.   15914

Pocket atlas of the city of New York. 1962.   16102

—— 1967.   16111

Street and road atlas of Suffolk County, Long Island, N.Y. 1952.   15908

Street, road and land ownership atlas of Suffolk County, Long Island, N.Y. 1941.   15906

—— 1944.   15907

Street, road and land ownership atlas of Westchester County, N.Y. 1947.   15920

—— 1953.   15921

Hague, Arnold, 1840–1917.

Atlas to accompany monograph XXXII on the geology of the Yellowstone National Park. 1904.   5115

Atlas to accompany the monograph on the geology of the Eureka District, Nevada. 1883.   2131

Hahn, Paul.

See Schüttau, Bruno, *and* Hahn, Paul.

Halász, Albert.

États d'Europe centrale. [1936]   7652

Neue Mitteleuropa in wirtschaftlichen Karten. 1928.   7653

New Central Europe in economical maps. 1928.   7654

See also Edvi Illés, Aladár, 1858–   *and* Halász, Albert.

Hales, John Groves, 1785–1832.

Plans and records of the streets, lanes, courts ... of Boston. 1894.   4718

Halfeld, Henrique Guilherme Fernando, 1797–1873.

Atlas e relatorio concernente a exploração do Rio de S. Francisco desde Cachoévia da Pirapóra ao Oceano Atlantico. 1860.   2745

Halfpenny, H. E.

Atlas of Kennebec County, Maine. 1879.   14312

See also Barthel, Otto, Halfpenny, H. E., Hasson, Thomas W., *and* Doyle, Joseph B.

Halfpenny, H. E., *and* Caldwell, John W.

Atlas of Oxford County, Me. 1880.   3763

Halkin, Joseph, 1870–1937.

Algemeene atlas. 1946.   7232

Atlas classique. 1923.   6523

—— 1934.   6813

—— [4. éd.] 1938.   6947

—— 1948.   7304

Hall, Basil, 1788–1844.

Forty etchings, from sketches made ... in North America, in 1827 and 1828. 1829.   4469

Hall, Sidney, *fl.* 1817–1860.

Black's General atlas. 1840.   777

—— 1841.   779

—— 1844.   793

—— 1851.   4328

—— 1852.   4330

—— 1854.   4334

New British atlas. 1836.   8130

New general atlas. 1830.   756
—— [1857]   821
Travelling county atlas [of England. 1846] 2928
See also Black, Adam, 1784–1874, *and* Black,
  Charles.

Hallwag, *firm.*
Deutschland Automobilführer. [1934?]   8608

Hamburg. *Deutsche Seewarte.*
Atlantischer Ozean. 1882.   184
Atlas der Bodenbeschaffenheit des Meeres.
  [1940–43]   5728
Atlas der Dichte des Meerwassers. [194–]   5729
Atlas der Eisverhältnisse im Deutschen und
  benachbarten Ost- und Nordseegebiet.
  1942.   7832
Atlas der Eisverhältnisse im Nordatlantischen
  Ozean. 1944.   10233
Atlas der Gezeiten und Gezeitenströme für
  das Gebiet der Nordsee und der Britischen
  Gewässer. 1905.   4166, 7868
—— 1925.   7869
Atlas der Meeresströmung in dem Indischen
  Ozean. 1913.   4165
Atlas der Stromversetzungen auf den wich-
  tigsten Dampferwegen im Indischen Ozean.
  1905.   4164, 10240
Atlas der Vereisungsverhältnisse Russlands
  und Finnlands. 1940.   9273
—— 1942.   9274
Atlas für Temperatur, Salzgehalt und Dichte
  der Nordsee und Ostsee. 1927.   7876
Eis um Island und Ost-Grönland. 1940.   8931
Indischer Ozean. 1891.   4163
Klimatologie des östlichen Teils des Mittelat-
  lantischen Ozeans. 1944–[47]   10219
Monatskarte für den Südatlantischen Ozean.
  [1928]   10221
Monatskarten der Eisverhältnisse im Nor-
  datlantischen Ozean. 1940.   10232
Monatskarten für den Nordatlantischen
  Ozean. 1940.   10220
Monatskarten für die Breiten 50° bis 70° Nord
  des Nordatlantischen Ozeans. 1940.   10222
Stiller Ozean. 1896.   206
Tidal-current atlas for the region of the North
  Sea. [1943]   7870

Hamburger Fremdenblatt.
Neue Reich. Ein Atlas des Deutschen Reiches.
  [1937]   8699

Hamburger Segel-Club.
Elbe von Cuxhaven bis Lauenburg. [1951]   7846
—— [1954]   7847
—— [1958]   8875

Hamilton, Theodore F.
See Jones, Charles Henry, 1837–1911, *and*
  Hamilton, Theodore F.

Hammond, C. S., and Company.
Advanced reference atlas. 1949.   7349, 7350

Air-line atlas of the world. [1928]   5334
Alaska-Yukon-Pacific atlas. 1909.   3673, 3699
Ambassador world atlas. [1954]   7598
American Exporter concise atlas of the world.
  1912.   4386a
American history atlas. [1948]   10604
—— 1949.   10605
—— 1951.   10606
—— 1953.   10607
—— 1957.   10608
—— 1959.   10609
—— 1961.   10610
—— 1963.   10611
—— 1965.   10612
American history wall atlas. [1952]   10613
Atlas of American history. [1963]   10614
Atlas of New York City. 1907.   2315
—— 1908.   2316a
—— 1910.   3849
—— [1915]   4948
Atlas of New York City and the metropolitan
  district. 1916.   16005
Atlas of the Bible lands. 1950.   5350
Atlas of the Dominion of Canada. 1946.   10372
Atlas of the Metropolitan district. 1915.   4949
Atlas świata; world atlas of today. [1944]   7178
Auto route distance atlas. 1924.   10781
Auto route distance atlas of Illinois, Indiana,
  Michigan ... 1925.   10785
Auto route distance atlas of New England.
  [1934]   10829
Auto route distance atlas of New England,
  New York, New Jersey ... [1930]   10812
—— 1931.   10819
Auto route distance atlas of New Jersey, New
  York and New England. 1924.   10782
Auto route distance atlas of New Jersey, New
  York, Pennsylvania ... 1924.   10783
Auto route distance atlas of Ohio, Michigan,
  Indiana ... 1925.   10786
Auto route distance atlas of Wisconsin,
  Illinois (northern), Minnesota. 1925.   10787
Brentano's Record atlas of the World War.
  1918.   4225
Business atlas of economic geography. 1919. 4124
Business survey atlas of the United States.
  1947.   11073
California atlas. 1967.   11367
Chalkboard wall atlas. 1953.   5746
City street map atlas and trip guide. [U.S.
  1951]   10489
Collegiate atlas. [1949]   7351
Commercial and library atlas of the world.
  1911.   3619
—— 1919.   4449a
Compact atlas of the world. 1912.   4387
—— 1915.   4417
—— [1917]   4437
Compact indexed atlas of the world. 1925.   6584
Comparative wall atlas. 1942.   7098
—— 1943.   7139
—— 1948.   7305
—— 1952.   7508
Comparative world atlas. [1947]   7265

New world atlas. 1936.	6874
—— 1939.	6977
—— 1941.	7053
—— 1947.	7268
New world atlas and gazetteer. [1954]	7599
New world loose leaf atlas. [1919]	6395
—— [1920–40]	6432
—— 1922–[31]	6512
—— 6th ed. [1927?–40]	6666
Our planet; the blue book of maps. 1935.	6842
Outlook readers' reference collection of war maps. 1918.	5826
Pastene war atlas. [1943]	5878
Peerless atlas of the world. 1922.	6486
Perpetual atlas of the world. 1937.	6915
Pictorial atlas. 1905.	1102
—— 1909.	3591
—— 1910.	3605
—— 1914.	4410
Pictorial atlas of the world. 1936.	6785
—— [1945]	7210
Pictorial ready reference atlas and gazetteer of the world. 1938.	6948
Pictorial world atlas. 1954.	7600
Pocket atlas of the United States. 1918.	4535
Pocket atlas of the world. 1910.	3606
Pocket atlas of the world and the United States. 1921.	6446
Popular atlas of the United States. [1958]	11079
—— [1960]	11081
Popular atlas of the world. 1911.	3620
—— 1916.	4427
—— 1934.	6817
Ready reference atlas. [1906]	1111
—— [1910]	3607
Ready reference atlas of the world. 1932.	6777
Ready reference historical atlas. [1921]	5516
—— [1940?]	5517
Record atlas of the World War. 1918.	4226
Reference atlas of the world. 1947.	7269
—— 1952.	7513
Replogle Comprehensive atlas of the world. [1953]	7564
—— [1954]	7601
Replogle World atlas. [1950]	7409
Road atlas and city street guide of the United States, Canada, Mexico. 1962.	10940
—— 1963.	10944
Road atlas of the United States, Canada, Mexico. 1964.	10949
—— 1965.	10959
—— 1966.	10965
Route maps, PAA: Pan American World Airways. [1952]	5335
Sales planning atlas of the United States and Canada. [1962]	10547
Sears Family world atlas. [1954]	7602
Self-revising world atlas and gazetteer. 1940.	7015
—— 1941.	7054
Standard atlas and gazetteer of the world. 1946.	7235
—— 1947.	7270
—— 1949.	7354

Standard atlas of the world. 1st ed. 1914.	4412
—— 1917.	4439
Standard world atlas. 1950.	7410
—— 1952.	7514
—— 1953.	7565
Superior atlas and gazetteer of the world. 1938.	6949
—— 1946.	7236
Superior atlas of the world. 1923.	6524
Telegram & Times concise atlas of the world. 1913.	4397
Times atlas and gazetteer of the world. [1927]	6654
—— [1933]	6796
Unabridged atlas and gazetteer of the world. [1924]	6551
United States Army and Navy pictorial. [1917]	4226a
Universal world atlas. 1942.	7101
—— 1944.	7182
—— 1947.	7271
—— 1949.	7355
—— 1952.	7515
—— 1953.	7566
War atlas. 1914.	4227
World atlas. 1933.	6797
—— War ed. [1944]	7186
—— Handy desk ed. [1948]	7306
—— Classics ed. 1951.	7456
—— 1952.	7516
—— [1952]	7517
—— 1953.	7567, 7568
World atlas and gazetteer. 1941.	7055
—— 1942.	7102
—— 1943.	7141, 7142, 7143, 7144
—— 1944.	7183, 7184, 7185
—— 1945.	7211
—— 1946.	7237
World atlas for students. [1955]	7619
World atlas of to-day. War ed. [1942]	7103
World history wall atlas. 1953.	5518
World wide atlas. War ed. [1942]	7104
—— [1954]	7603
World wide atlas and gazetteer. [1949]	7356

Hammond Incorporated.
Road atlas of the United States, Canada, Mexico. 1967.   10974

Hammond Publishing Company.
Plat book of Greene and Jersey Counties, Ill. 1893.   1534, 1538

Hammond's New historical atlas for students. 4th ed. [1920]   5537

Hammond's Sports atlas of America. 1956.   10299

Hancock, C. F.
See Weston, William J., and Hancock, C. F.

Hancock County, Ohio.
[Atlas of Hancock County, Ohio. 1945]   16416

Handtke, Friedrich H., 1815–1879.
Special-Karte der Europäischen Turkei.
[1876]   3159

Handy Map.
Dallas County [Tex.] census tract directory.
1961.   17158

Hannak, Emanuel, 1841–1899, *and* Umlauft, Friedrich, 1844–1923.
Historischer Schulatlas. 1908.   2789a

Hannig, Emil, 1872–1955, *and* Winkler, Hubert, 1875–1941.
Pflanzenareale. 5 v. 1926–40.   5380

Hannum, E. S.
Atlas of Fairfield County, Ohio. 1866.   4985

Hansa Welt-Atlas. [1935]   6843
—— [1936]   6876
—— 4. Aufl. 1943.   7145
—— 5. Aufl. 1949.   7357
—— 7. Aufl. 1952.   7518
—— 8. Aufl. 1954.   7604

Hansen, Hans Edvard, 1887–
Atlas over dele av det Antarktiske kystland.
1946.   10211

Hansen, Kenneth L., *and* O'Loughlin, Thomas John.
Plat book of Olmsted County [Minn. 1946]   15068

Hansteen, Christopher, 1784–1873.
Magnetischer Atlas. 1819.   224

Hantzsch, Viktor, *i.e.*, Karl Viktor Gustav, 1868–1910.
Ältesten gedruckten Karten der Sächsisch-Thüringischen Länder. [1905]   3042

Hardesty, H. H.
Illustrated historical atlas of Carroll County,
Ohio. 1874.   16386

Hardesty, Hiram H., 1834–1898.
Historical and geographical encyclopedia.
1883.   1287, 2350
—— 1884.   1288, 2351
Historical hand-atlas illustrated. 1882.   11040
—— 1883.   11041

Hardesty, L. Q.
Illustrated historical atlas of Ottawa County,
Ohio. 1874.   3877

Harding, Samuel Bannister, 1866–1927.
European history atlas. [1916–20]   7678

Harding, Samuel Bannister, 1866–1927, *and* Lingelbach, William Ezra, 1871–
Geography of the war. 1918.   5827

Hare, A. J.
Atlas of Wyandot Co., Ohio. 1879.   16468

Harford County, *Md. Planning and Zoning Commission.*
Photogrammetric map[s] of Harford County,
Md. 1967.   14351

Harmjanz, Heinrich, 1904–   *and* Röhr, Erich, 1905–1943.
Atlas der Deutschen Volkskunde. 1937–39.   8556

Harms, Heinrich, 1861–1933.
Atlas für Polizeischulen. [1930]   6724
Berlin und die Mark. [1924]   8830
Berliner Grundschulatlas. [1927]   8831
Berliner Volksschulatlas für die oberen Klassen. [1930]   6725
Grosser Schulatlas für Mittelschulen. [1926]   6617
Neuer Deutscher Geschichts- und Kulturatlas.
Ausg. A. [1934]   8561
—— Ausg. B. [1934]   8562
—— 2. neubearb. Aufl. 1937.   8563
—— 1943.   8564
—— Sonderausg. 1943.   8565
—— 1944.   8566
Schulatlas. [1927]   6655
Übungsatlas für Geschichte und Erdkunde.
[1934]   7736
Vaterländischer Reform-Schulatlas. [1911]   3371

Harms Heimatatlas für Nordrhein-Westfalen.
[1952]   8824

Harms Heimatatlas Hannover. [1956]   8862

Harms Heimatatlas Mannheim. [1958]   8866

Harms Heimatatlas Regensburg. [1958]   8874

Harms Hessen in Bild und Karte. [1955]   8752

Harms Nordrhein-Westfalen in Karte, Bild und Wort. [1956]   8825

Harms Rheinland-Pfalz. [1953]   8776
—— [1957]   8779

Harmsworth Atlas and gazetteer. [1908] 1132

Harmsworth's Atlas of the world and pictorial gazetteer. [1922]   6487

Harney and Tucker.
Illustrated atlas of Fond du Lac County, Wis.
1874.   17738

Harper's Atlas of American history. [1920]   10602

Harrap, George G., and Company.
General school atlas. [1932]   6778

Harrap's Modern school atlas. [1940]   7001

Harriman, George W. R.
Index geograph of the United States. 2d ed.
[1929]   11060
Selection of atlas unit geographs in the United
States. [1925]   11056
——— [1926]   11057

Harrisburg Title Company.
Atlas of the city of Harrisburg, Dauphin
County, Penn. 1901.   2512

Harrison, Ballard and Allen.
Property line map of the village of East Hamp-
ton ... N.Y. 1955.   15959

Harrison, John.
School atlas. 1791.   6000

Harrison, Richard Edes, 1901–
Atlas for the U.S. citizen. [1940]   7016
Look at the world. The Fortune atlas for
world strategy. 1944.   7187

Harrison, Robert H.
Atlas of Allen County, Ohio. 1880.   16378
Illustrated historical atlas of Scotland County,
Mo. 1876.   4873

Harrison, Robert H., *and others*.
Atlas of Hamilton County, Ohio. 1869.
                                                                   2381, 2422

Harrison and Warner.
Atlas of Benton County, Iowa. 1872.   1644
Atlas of Cedar County, Iowa. 1872.   1651
Atlas of Clinton County, Iowa. 1874   1655
Atlas of Columbia County, Wis. 1873.   2638
Atlas of Dane County, Wis. 1873.   2641
Atlas of Dodge County, Wis. 1873.   2642
Atlas of Dubuque County, Iowa. 1874.   1657
Atlas of Green County, Wis. 1873.   2647
Atlas of Hardin County, Iowa. 1875.   1667
Atlas of Iowa County, Iowa. 1874.   1673
Atlas of Keokuk County, Iowa. 1874.   1679
Atlas of Madison County, Iowa. 1875.   1682
Atlas of Marion County, Iowa. 1875.   1684
Atlas of Marshall County, Iowa. 1871.   1685
Atlas of Muscatine County, Iowa. 1874.   1688
Atlas of Tama County, Iowa. 1875.   1697
Atlas of Warren County, Iowa. 1872.   1702
Atlas of Washington County, Iowa. 1874.   1704
Atlas of Waukesha County, Iowa. 1873.   2668
Illustrated historical atlas of Adair County,
Mo. 1876.   1395, 2064, 2066

Harrison, Sutton and Hare.
Atlas of Marion County, Ohio. 1878.   2398
Atlas of Union County, Ohio. 1877.   4990

Harrow Atlas of modern geography. 1864.   6151

Harrower, Henry Draper.
See Mecutchen, Samuel, 1827–   *and*
Harrower, Henry Draper.

See also Swinton, William, 1833–1892, *and*
Harrower, Henry Draper.

Hart, Albert Bushnell, 1854–1943.
Epoch maps illustrating American history.
1891.   1188, 1289
——— 1893.   4466
——— 1899.   1189, 1290
——— 1904.   1190, 1291
——— 1910.   3662

Hart, Albert Bushnell, *and others*.
American history atlas. [1918]   10615
——— [1924]   10616
——— 3d rev. ed. [1930]   10617
——— [4th rev. ed. 1940]   10618
——— [5th rev. ed. 1942]   10619
——— [6th rev. ed. 1945]   10620
——— [7th rev. ed. 1947]   10621
——— [8th rev. ed. 1949]   10622
——— [9th rev. ed. 1953]   10623

Hart, Joseph C., *d.* 1855.
Modern atlas. 5th ed. 1828.   290
——— 7th ed. 1830.   291, 757

Hartford Electric Light Company.
Area map of the territory served by the Hartford Electric Light Company. 1955.   11703
——— 1957.   11704

Hartleben, Alois, 1859–
Atlas von Afrika. 1886.   10097
Erde in Karten und Bildern. 1889.   6245
Volks-Atlas. [1910?]   3608

Hartley, F. G.
Atlas of business district of Des Moines, Iowa.
1913.   4669

Hart's Maps of New York City. 1964.   16107

**Harvard University. *Graduate School of Public
Administration. Bureau for Research in Munici-
pal Government*.**
Metropolis in maps; graphic reference for the
Boston area. 1946.   14436

Hasius, Johann Matthias, 1684–1742.
Vorstellung der Grundrisse von den jenigen
weltberühmten Staedten. 1745.   5388

Haskell, W. W.
Atlas of Valley County, Nebr. 1904.   3829

Hassenstein, Bruno, 1839–1902.
Atlas von Japan. 1885–87.   3210

Hassinger, Hugo, 1877–1952.
Kunsthistorischer Atlas der K. K. Reichs-
haupt- und Residenzstadt Wien. 1916.   7927

Hasson, Thomas W.
See Barthel, Otto, Halfpenny, H. E., Hasson, Thomas W., and Doyle, Joseph B.

Hastain, E.
Township plats of the Creek nation. [1910]   3883
Township plats of the Seminole nation. 1913.   5006

Hatfield Mapping Service.
Pasadena [Calif.] area. [1954]   11568

Hatier, A.
Atlas d'actualité: où est-ce? [194–]   6995

Havenga, W. J.
Atlas van Nederlandsch Oost-Indië. 1885.   9738

Hawaii. *Highway Planning Section.*
General highway map, city & county of Honolulu. 1962.   11986, 11987

Hawes, *Mrs.* Harriet Ann Boyd, 1871–
Ready-guide: Boston, Cambridge, Brookline.
1936.   14431

Hawes, J. B.
[Maps showing the consular and diplomatic offices of the United States. 189–?]   4498

Hawkesworth, John, 1715?–1773.
Account of the voyages. Atlas. [1773]   642, 3241

Hayden, Ferdinand Vandiveer, 1829–1887.
Geological and geographical atlas of Colorado. 1877.   1473
—— 1881.   3707a

Hayes, Carlton Joseph Huntley, 1882–
Map supplement to ... Political and cultural history of modern Europe. [1944]   7679

Hayes, E. L.
Atlas of Grand Traverse County, Mich.
1881.   1969
Atlas of Isabella County, Mich. 1879.   1976
Atlas of Leelanau County, Mich. 1881.   1983
Atlas of Mecosta County, Mich. 1879.   1987
Atlas of Newaygo County, Mich. 1880.   1992
Atlas of Osceola County, Mich. 1878.   1995
Atlas of Sebastin County, Ark. [1887]   1455
Illustrated atlas of the upper Ohio River and Valley from Pittsburgh, Pa. to Cincinnati, Ohio. 1887.   2348, 2442

Haynes, M. B.
Atlas of Renville County, Minn. 1888.   2037

Hayward and Howard.
Atlas of the city of Brockton, Mass. 1898.   1866

Hazard, Harry W.
Atlas of Islamic history. 1951.   7624
—— 3d ed. 1954.   7625

He Mau palapala aina a me na niele e pili ana.
1840.   778, 3259
—— 1842.   4087

He Ninau no ka palapala honau. [1860?]   830, 3260

Headington, J. N.
See Starr, J. W., and Headington, J. N.

Health and Welfare Federation of Allegheny County.
Bureau of Social Research.
Population maps and analysis of Pittsburgh census tracts and adjacent areas. [1933]   16908

Hearne Brothers.
Official real estate atlas of the city of Detroit.
1929.   14856
—— [1950]   14860

Hearnshaw, Fossey John Cobb, 1869–
Macmillan's Historical atlas of modern Europe. 1920.   7680

Hearst Advertising Service.
Working sales control of the Baltimore mar-
ket. [1947]   14383
Working sales control of the Boston market area. [1947]   14437
Working sales control of the Detroit market. [1947]   14858
Working sales control of the New York mar-
ket. [1947]   16068
Working sales control of the northern Califor-
nia market area 1947.   11356
Working sales control of the Pittsburgh mar-
ket area. 1947.   16911
Working sales control of the southern Cali-
fornia market area. 1947.   11357

Hearst Magazines. *Marketing Division.*
Basis of sales quota making. [1935]   10548
—— [3d ed. 1938]   10549
58 individual state marketing maps. [1952]   10550

Heath, Willis Roberton, 1908– *and* Morris, Frank Lemerise, 1907–
Cruising charts ... of British Columbia waters.
1949.   10382
See also Morris, Frank Lemerise, 1907– and Heath, Willis Robertson, 1908–

Heather, William, *fl.* 1790–1812.
Marine atlas. [1804]   704
—— [1808?]   713
New Mediterranean harbour pilot. New ed.
1814.   193
New Mediterranean pilot. 1802.   192, 7864
[North Sea and Baltic pilot. 1807]   2850

Heck, Herbert Lothar, 1904–1968.
Grundwasseratlas von Schleswig-Holstein.
1948.   8803

Hedin, Sven Anders, 1865–1952.
Scientific results of a journey in Central Asia,
1899–1902. Maps. [1907]   9627
Southern Tibet. Maps. [1922]   9628

Heermans, Anna A.
Hieroglyphic geography of the United States.
1875.   1284

Heeroma, Klaas Hanzen, 1909–
Taalatlas van Oost-Nederland en aangren-
zende gebieden. [1957]   9048

Hefling Engineering Company.
City of Kingman ... Kans. [196–]   14217

Heineken, Christian Abraham, 1752–1818.
See Gildemeister, Johann, 1753–1837, *and*
Heineken, Christian Abraham, 1752–
1818.

Heinemeyer, W. F., *and* Romein, J. E.
Bezige Bij wereldatlas. [1951]   7457

Heise, Georg.
Atlas über Deutschlands Welthandel von
Heute. [1927]   5437
See also Schmidt, Walther, 1888–   *and*
Heise, Georg.

Helburn, Nicholas, *and others*.
Montana in maps. [1962]   15309

Hellert, J. J.
Nouvel atlas, physique, politique et historique
de l'Empire Ottoman. 1843.   3158

Hellmann, Gustav, 1854–1939.
Klima-Atlas von Deutschland. 1921.   8532

Helms, J. C.
Plat book of Hancock County [Ill.] by town-
ships. 1908.   1536

Helsingfors. *Stadsmätningsavdelningen*.
Helsinki, osoitekartta 1 : 10,000. [1958]   8379

Henion, John W., *ca*. 1832–1904.
See Foote, Charles M., 1849–1899, *and*
Henion, John W., *ca*. 1832–1904.

Hennessey and Company.
Rock County [Wis.] plat book. 1940.   17902

Hennessey and Deist.
Township atlas of Walworth County, Wis.
1936.   17950

Henning, Burt Lawton, 1878–
Atlas and history of Kendall County, Ill.
1941.   12315

Henry, F.
See Alm, B. C., *and* Henry, F.

Henry County, *Ohio*.
Henry County, Ohio. 1947.   16418

Hepburn, Andrew.
Complete guide of New York City. 1952.   16080

Herbert, Karl.
See Michel, Hans, 1887–   *and* Herbert
Karl.

Herbertson, Andrew John, 1865–1915.
See Bartholomew, John George, 1860–1920,
and Herbertson, Andrew John, 1865–1915.

Herbin de Halle, P. Etienne, 1772–
See Chanlaire, Pierre Grégoire, 1758–1817,
and Herbin de Halle, P. Etienne, 1772–

Herders Welt– und Wirtschaftsatlas. 1932.   6779

Hérisson, Eustache, 1759–
Atlas du Dictionnare de géographie uni-
verselle. 1806.   710

Hermelin, Samuel Gustav, *Friherre*, 1744–1820.
Geografiske kartor öfver Swerige. [1797–
1807]   9388
Special kartor och rigningar till beskrifning
öfver Sverige. 1806.   9353

Hernández Millares, Jorge.
Atlas del Nuevo Mundo. [1962]   10278

**Hernández Millares, Jorge, *and* Carrillo Escribano,
Alejandro.**
Atlas Porrúa de la República Mexicana.
1966.   18110

Hernández-Pacheco, Francisco.
Estudio la región volcánica central de España.
[1932]   9308

Herrera y Tordesillas, Antonio de, 1559–1625.
Descripcion de las Indias Ocidentales. 1601.   1141
—— 1726.   1156
Description des Indes Occidentales. 1622.   1144
Historia general de los hechos de los castel-
lanos en las islas i terra firme del Mar
Oceano. 1726-[27]   3649
Nievwe werelt, anders ghenaempt West-
Indien. 1622.   1145
Novi Orbis pars dvodecima. 1590–1624.   3646
Novvs orbis, sive descriptio Indiae Occiden-
talis. 1622.   1146

Herrmann, Albert, 1886–1945.
Ältesten Karten von Deutschland bis Gerhard
Mercator. 1940.   8600
Historical and commercial atlas of China.
1935.   9517

Hertzberg, Heinrich, 1859–1931.
See Haack, Hermann, 1872–1966, *and* Hertzberg, Heinrich, 1859–1931.

Hesse, Kurt, 1894–
Kartenwerk zu ... Über Schlachtfelder vorwärts! [1941]   5879

Hesse, Paul, 1893–
Landvolk und Landwirtschaft in den Gemeinden von Württemberg-Hohenzollern. 1939.   8827

Hesse. *Landesplanungsamt.*
Hessischen Gemeinden im Bevölkerungsausgleich. 1952.   8746

Hettema, Hette Hettes, 1868–
Grote historische schoolatlas. 16. herziene en verm. druk. 1947.   9041
H. B. S.-uitgaaf van den Historische Schoolatlas. 11. herziene en verm. druk. 1927.   9042
Historische schoolatlas. 2e verb. en verm. druk. 1899.   9043
See also Boer, Michiel George de, 1867–
and Hettema, Hette Hettes, 1868–

Heussi, Karl, 1877–1961, *and* Mulert, Hermann, *i.e.*, Christian Hermann, 1879–1950.
Atlas zur Kirchengeschichte. 1905.   82, 2784
—— 2. Aufl. 1919.   5409

Hevenor, Charles D., Company.
Handy book of county maps ... [New York State] 1919.   15848
Handy book of loose leaf county maps, Arkansas. [1941]   11291
Handy book of loose leaf county maps, California. [1941]   11355
Handy book of loose leaf county maps, Delaware. [1938]   11753
Handy book of loose leaf county maps, Florida. [1938]   11800
Handy book of loose leaf county maps, Georgia. [1944]   11935
Handy book of loose leaf county maps, Idaho. [1944]   12005
Handy book of loose leaf county maps, Illinois. [1934]   12072
Handy book of loose leaf county maps, Indiana. [1934]   12731
Handy book of loose leaf county maps, Iowa. [1935]   13016
Handy book of loose leaf county maps, Kansas. [1935]   14143
Handy book of loose leaf county maps, Kentucky. [1935]   14234
Handy book of loose leaf county maps, Maryland. [1938]   14335
Handy book of loose leaf county maps, Michigan. [1936]   14582
Handy book of loose leaf county maps, Minnesota. [1936]   14921
Handy book of loose leaf county maps, Missouri. [1937]   15208
Handy book of loose leaf county maps, Neraska. [1942]   15343

Handy book of loose leaf county maps, Nevada. [1946]   15649
Handy book of loose leaf county maps, New Jersey. 1921.   15680
Handy book of loose leaf county maps, New York State. 1919.   15849
Handy book of loose leaf county maps, North Carolina. [1939]   16209
Handy book of loose leaf county maps, North Dakota. [1939]   16253
Handy book of loose leaf county maps, Ohio. [1934]   16377
Handy book of loose leaf county maps, Oklahoma. [1942]   16592
Handy book of loose leaf county maps, Oregon. [1943]   16648
Handy book of loose leaf county maps, Pennsylvania. 1919.   16765
Handy book of loose leaf county maps, South Carolina. [1939]   16985
Handy book of loose leaf county maps, South Dakota. [1939]   17012
Handy book of loose leaf county maps, Utah. [1944]   17296
Handy book of loose leaf county maps, Virginia. [1938]   17336
Handy book of loose leaf county maps, Washington [1943]   17419
Handy book of loose leaf county maps, West Virginia. [1938]   17609
Handy book of loose leaf county maps, Wisconsin. [1937]   17644
Handy book of loose leaf state maps, Colorado. [1946]   11646
Loose leaf county maps, New England States. 1921.   11054

Hewes, Fletcher Willis, 1838–1910.
Citizen's atlas of American politics, 1789–1888. 1888.   1298
Citizen's atlas of American politics, 1789–1892. [1892]   1299

Hexamer, Ernest, *and* Locher, William.
Maps of the city of Philadelphia. 1859.   2518

Hexamer, Ernest, and Son.
Insurance maps of the city of Philadelphia. 1872–1911.   5026
—— 1887–91.   5028–5031
—— 1894–1914.   5033–5051
Maps of the city of Philadelphia. v. 5. 1859.   5025

Heylen, L.
See Libot, M., *and* Heylen, L.

Heyns, Peeter, 1537–1597.
Miroir dv monde. 1579.   385
—— 1583.   387

Hī Wā Map Company.
Strip maps of California, Oregon, Washington ... U.S. 101 [and] U.S. 99. [1948]   10873

Touring log and directory, Canada to Mexico; U.S. 101. [1947]   10870

Hialeah, *Fla.*
Official map of city of Hialeah ... Fla. [1958]   11877
—— [1962]   11879

Hickmann, Anton Leo, 1834–1906.
Atlas universel. [1924]   6552
Geographical-statistic universal pocket atlas.
[1907]   346
—— 2. ed. 1909.   4213
Geographisch-statistischer Taschen-Atlas von Österreich-Ungarn. [1910]   3994
Geographisch-statistischer Universal–Atlas.
[1925]   6585
—— [1927]   6656
—— [1929]   6704
—— [1931]   6748
Geographisch-statistischer Universal-Taschen-Atlas. 1900.   1051
—— [1904]   6313
—— [1909]   3592
—— [1910]   3609
—— [1915]   4419
Sprachen-Atlas ... Österreich-Ungarn.
[1918]   7937

Hicks-Judd Company.
Handy block book of San Francisco [Calif.]
1894.   11584
San Francisco block book. 1901.   1468
—— 1906.   1469
—— 1907.   1470

Higgins, Belden and Company.
Illustrated historical atlas of Elkhart County, Ind. 1874.   1604
Illustrated historical atlas of La Porte Co., Ind. 1874.   12841
Illustrated historical atlas of St. Joseph County, Ind. 1875.   4616

Highsmith, Richard Morgan, 1920–
Atlas of Oregon agriculture. [1958]   16637

Hildebrand, Curt.
Slagfält och bombmål. [1943]   5880

Hildebrand, Emil, *i.e.*, Henrik Robert Teodor Emil, 1848–1919, *and* Selander, Nils Johan Teodor, 1845–1922.
Atlas till allmänna och svenska historien.
[1883]   109, 2790, 3141
—— [1883–95]   5519

Hilgers, Alfons, 1910–
See Palm, Valentin, 1895– *and* Hilgers, Alfons, 1910–

Hillebrands, A. J.
Atlas van de Vereenigde Staten van Noord-Amerika. [1850?]   3693

Hills, John, *fl.* 1777–1817.
Collection of plan's [sic] ... in the province of New Jersey. MS. [1776–82]   1339, 2143

Himmelbaur, Wolfgang, 1886– *and* Hollinger, Bernhard.
Drogen–Weltkarte. 1927.   5719

Hinsdale, Wilbert B., 1851–1944.
Archaeological atlas of Michigan. 1931.   14553

Hinton, John Howard, 1791–1873.
[History and topography of the United States. Atlas. 1830–32]   11027

Hintze, Louis.
Atlas of Norman County, Minn. [1907]   2030

Hiroshima, *Japan. Kensetsukyoku.*
Gesui kankyo fusetsu genkyōzu. [Atlas of the present sewer pipe system. 1958]   9877

Hispanic Society of America.
Facsimiles of portolan charts [1466–1637]
1916.   4178, 4212

Historical Association, *London.*
Philips' Junior historical atlas. [1922]   5520

Historical Atlas Publishing Company.
Historical atlas of the County of Wellington, Ont. 1906.   10421

Historical Records Survey. *New York (City)*
Atlas of Congressional roll calls. 1943.   10709
Atlas of Congressional roll calls for the Continental Congresses, 1777–1781. 1943.   10710

Historisch-geographischer Atlas der Schweiz.
1870.   3154

Historische Kommission für die Provinz Brandenburg und die Reichshauptstadt Berlin.
Historischer Atlas der Provinz Brandenburg.
[1929–39]   8736

Historische Kommission für die Provinz Sachsen und für Anhalt.
Mitteldeutscher Heimatatlas. [1935–40]   8698

Historische Kommission für Schlesien.
Geschichtlicher Atlas von Schlesien. [1933]   8808

Historischer Atlas von Bayern ... Teil Altbayern.
1950–55.   8723
—— Teil Franken. 1951–56.   8724
—— Teil Schwaben. 1952.   8725

Hitchcock, Charles Henry, 1836–1919.
See Walling, Henry Francis, 1825–1888, *and* Hitchcock, Charles Henry.

Hitt, Willaim Mayo, 1888–
Better maps of all danger zones. 1950.   7411

Maps of Western States. [1941]	11325
Studebaker Radio listeners' atlas. 1943.	7146
"Up–to–the–minute" war atlas. 1943.	5881
War atlas and history of World War II. [1944]	5882

Hitt Map Company.

Better maps of the Pacific. 1944.	10191
Pocket invasion atlas. 1944.	7188

Hixson, W. W., and Company.

Anoka County, Minn. [193–?]	14924
Atlas of Illinois. [1934?]	12073
Atlas of Indiana. [1934?]	12732
Atlas of Minnesota. [193–?]	14920
Atlas of Montana. [193–?]	15314
Atlas of North Dakota. [1933?]	16252
Atlas of the State of West Virginia. [1936?]	17608
Atlas of Wisconsin. [1934?]	17643
Atlas of Wyoming. [1933?]	18035
Becker County, Minn. [193–?]	14926
Beltrami County, Minn. [193–?]	14929
Benton County, Minn. [193–?]	14932
Bigstone [sic] County, Minn. [193–?]	14934
Blue Earth County, Minn. [193–?]	14938
Boone County, Ill. [1921?]	12090
Brown County, Minn. [193–?]	14940
Carlton County, Minn. [193–?]	14943
Carver County, Minn. [193–?]	14946
Chippewa County, Minn. [193–?]	14948
Chisago County, Minn. [193–?]	14950
Clay County, Minn. [193–?]	14953
Clearwater County, Minn. [193–?]	14957
Cook County, Minn. [193–?]	14958
Cottonwood County, Minn. [193–?]	14961
Crow Wing County, Minn. [193–?]	14963
Dakota County, Minn. [193–?]	14967
Dodge County, Minn. [193–?]	14972
Douglas County, Minn. [193–?]	14977
Faribault County, Minn. [193–?]	14982
Fillmore County, Minn. [193–?]	14985
Freeborn County, Minn. [193–?]	14988
Goodhue County, Minn. [193–?]	14992
Grant County, Minn. [193–?]	14996
Houston County, Minn. [193–?]	14999
Hubbard County, Minn. [193–?]	15003
Isanti County, Minn. [193–?]	15004
Itasca County, Minn. [193–?]	15008
Jackson County, Minn. [193–?]	15011
Kanabec County, Minn. [193–?]	15014
Kandiyohi County, Minn. [193–?]	15016
Kittson County, Minn. [193–?]	15019
Lac Qui Parle County, Minn. [193–?]	15024
Manistee County, Mich. [193–?]	14731
Marshall County, Minn. [193–?]	15033
Martin County, Minn. [193–?]	15037
Meeker County, Minn. [193–?]	15041
Menard Co., Ill. [193–?]	12408
Millelacs [sic] County, Minn. [193–?]	15044
Morrison County, Minn. [193–?]	15048
Nobles County, Minn. [193–?]	15060
Norman County, Minn. [193–?]	15064
Olmsted County, Minn. [193–?]	15067
Pennington County, Minn. [193–?]	15072

Pine County, Minn. [193–?]	15075
Pipestone County, Minn. [193–?]	15076
Plat book of Adams County, Ill. [192–?]	12078
—— [193–?]	12079
Plat book of Adams County, Ind. [192–?]	12734
Plat book of Adams Co., Wis. [193–?]	17648
Plat book of Alcona Co. [Mich. 193–?]	14591
Plat book of Alexander Co., Ill. [193–?]	12085
Plat book of Alger County, Mich. [193–?]	14593
Plat book of Allegan Co., Mich. [193–?]	14595
Plat book of Allen County, Ind. [192–?]	12737
Plat book of Alpena County, Mich. [193–?]	14599
Plat book of Antrim Co., Mich. [193–?]	14601
Plat book of Arenac Co., Mich. [193–?]	14604
Plat book of Ashland County, Wis. [193–?]	17652
Plat book of Baraga County, Mich. [193–?]	14607
Plat book of Barron County, Wis. [193–?]	17656
Plat book of Barry Co. [Mich. 193–?]	14609
Plat book of Bartholomew County, Ind. [193–?]	12741
Plat book of Bay Co., Mich. [193–?]	14612
Plat book of Benton County Ind. [192–?]	12744
Plat book of Benzie Co. [Mich. 193–?]	14615
Plat book of Berrien County, Mich. [193–?]	14618
Plat book of Blackford County, Ind. [192–?]	12745
Plat book of Bond Co., Ill. [193–?]	12087
Plat book of Boone Co. [Ill. 193–?]	12092
Plat book of Boone County, Ind. [193–?]	12746
Plat book of Branch County, Mich. [193–?]	14622
Plat book of Brown Co., Ill. [193–?]	12096
Plat book of Brown County, Ind. [192–?]	12747
Plat book of Brown County, Wis. [193–?]	17667
Plat book of Buffalo County, Wis. [193–?]	17674
Plat book of Bureau County, Ill. [193–?]	12100
Plat book of Burnett County, Wis. [193–?]	17678
Plat book of Calhoun County, Ill. [193–?]	12105
Plat book of Calhoun Co., Mich. [193–?]	14627
Plat book of Calumet County, Wis. [193–?]	17684
Plat book of Carroll County, Ill. [193–?]	12109
Plat book of Carroll County, Ind. [1928?]	12749
Plat book of Cass Co., Ill. [193–?]	12115
Plat book of Cass County, Ind. [192–?]	12751
Plat book of Cass County, Mich. [193–?]	14631
Plat book of Champaign Co., Ill. [193–?]	12118
Plat book of Charlevoix Co, Mich. [193–?]	14633
Plat book of Cheboygan Co., Mich. [193–?]	14635
Plat book of Chippewa County, Mich. [193–?]	14637
Plat book of Chippewa County, Wis. [193–?]	17688
Plat book of Christian Co. [Ill. 193–?]	12126
Plat book of Clare Co. [Mich. 193–?]	14638
Plat book of Clark Co., Ill. [193–?]	12130
Plat book of Clark County, Ind. [192–?]	12753
Plat book of Clark County, Wis. [193–?]	17692
Plat book of Clay Co. [Ill. 193–?]	12134
Plat book of Clay County, Ind. [192–?]	12755
Plat book of Clinton Co. [Ill. 193–?]	12137
Plat book of Clinton County, Ind. [192–?]	12758
Plat book of Clinton Co., Mich. [193–?]	14639
Plat book of Coles Co., Ill. [193–?]	12140
Plat book of Columbia Co., Wis. [193–?]	17694
Plat book of Cook County, Ill. [193–?]	12143
—— [194–]	12147
Plat book of Crawford Co., Ill. [193–?]	12175

Plat book of La Porte County, Ind. [192–?] 12842
Plat book of La Salle County, Ill. [193–?] 12335
Plat book of Lawrence Co., Ill. [193–?] 12340
Plat book of Lawrence County, Ind. [192–?] 12845
Plat book of Leelanau County, Mich.
 [193–?] 14712
Plat book of Lenawee Co. [Mich. 193–?] 14716
Plat book of Lincoln County, Wis. [193–?] 17818
Plat book of Livingston Co., Ill. [193–?] 12349
Plat book of Livingston Co. [Mich. 193–?] 14721
Plat book of Logan Co., Ill. [193–?] 12355
Plat book of Luce Co., Mich. [193–?] 14723
Plat book of McDonough Co., Ill. [193–?] 12359
Plat book of McHenry Co., Ill. [193–?] 12366
Plat book of Mackinac County, Mich.
 [193–?] 14724
Plat book of McLean County, Ill. [193–?] 12371
Plat book of Macomb County, Mich.
 [193–?] 14727
Plat book of Macon County, Ill. [193–?] 12376
Plat book of Macoupin County, Ill [1931?] 12380
Plat book of Madison Co., Ill. [193–?] 12385
—— [194–] 12386
Plat book of Madison County, Ind. [192–?] 12847
Plat book of Manitowoc County, Wis.
 [193–?] 17822
Plat book of Marathon County, Wis.
 [193–?] 17827
Plat book of Marinette County, Wis.
 [193–?] 17831
Plat book of Marion Co., Ill. [193–?] 12389
Plat book of Marion County, Ind. [192–?] 12849
Plat book of Marquette County, Mich.
 [193–?] 14734
Plat book of Marquette Co., Wis. [193–?] 17839
Plat book of Marshall Co., Ill. [193–?] 12394
Plat book of Marshall County, Ind. [192–?] 12851
Plat book of Martin County, Ind. [192–?] 12855
Plat book of Mason Co., Mich. [193–?] 14736
Plat book of Massac Co., Ill. [193–?] 12403
Plat book of Mecosta Co., Mich. [193–?] 14740
Plat book of Menominee County, Mich.
 [193–?] 14742
Plat book of Mercer County, Ill. [193–?] 12410
Plat book of Miami County, Ind. [192–?] 12857
Plat book of Michigan. [194–?] 14583
Plat book of Midland County, Mich.
 [193–?] 14744
Plat book of Milwaukee County, Wis.
 [193–?] 17843
Plat book of Missaukee Co. [Mich. 193–?] 14746
Plat book of Monroe County, Ill. [193–?] 12415
Plat book of Monroe County, Ind. [192–?] 12858
Plat book of Monroe County, Mich. [193–?] 14747
Plat book of Monroe County, Wis. [193–?] 17846
Plat book of Montcalm Co. [Mich. 193–?] 14751
Plat book of Montgomery Co., Ill. [193–?] 12418
Plat book of Montgomery County, Ind.
 [192–?] 12862
Plat book of Montmorency Co., Mich.
 [193–?] 14754
Plat book of Morgan Co., Ill. [193–?] 12424
Plat book of Morgan County, Ind. [192–?] 12864
Plat book of Moultrie Co., Ill. [193–?] 12428

Plat book of Muskegon County, Mich.
 [193–?] 14756
Plat book of Newaygo Co. [Mich. 193–?] 14760
Plat book of Newton County, Ind. [192–?] 12866
Plat book of Noble County, Ind. [192–?] 12868
Plat book of Oakland Co., Mich. [193–?] 14765
Plat book of Oceana Co., Mich. [193–?] 14778
Plat book of Oconto County, Wis. [193–?] 17850
Plat book of Ogemaw County, Mich.
 [193–?] 14781
Plat book of Ogle Co. [Ill. 193–?] 12433
Plat book of Ohio County, Ind. [192–?] 12872
Plat book of Oneida County, Wis. [193–?] 17854
Plat book of Ontonagon Co., Mich. [193–?] 14783
Plat book of Orange County, Ind. [192–?] 12873
Plat book of Osceola Co., Mich. [193–?] 14784
Plat book of Oscoda Co., Mich. [193–?] 14788
Plat book of Otsego Co., Mich. [193–?] 14789
Plat book of Ottawa Co., Mich. [193–?] 14791
Plat book of Outagamie County, Wis.
 [193–?] 17858
Plat book of Owen County, Ind. [192–?] 12874
Plat book of Ozaukee Co., Wis. [193–?] 17863
Plat book of Parke County, Ind. [192–?] 12877
Plat book of Peoria County, Ill. [193–?] 12439
—— [194–?] 12440
Plat book of Pepin County, Wis. [193–?] 17867
Plat book of Perry County, Ill. [193–?] 12449
Plat book of Perry County, Ind. [192–?] 12881
Plat book of Piatt Co., Ill. [193–?] 12453
Plat book of Pierce County, Wis. [193–?] 17871
Plat book of Pike County, Ill. [193–?] 12457
Plat book of Pike County, Ind. [192–?] 12882
Plat book of Polk County, Wis. [193–?] 17876
Plat book of Pope Co., Ill. [193–?] 12461
Plat book of Portage County, Wis. [193–?] 17881
Plat book of Porter County, Ind. [192–?] 12884
Plat book of Posey County, Ind. [192–?] 12886
Plat book of Presque Isle Co. [Mich. 193–?] 14794
Plat book of Price County, Wis. [193–?] 17886
Plat book of Pulaski County, Ill. [193–?] 12464
Plat book of Pulaski County, Ind. [192–?] 12888
Plat book of Putnam Co., Ill. [193–?] 12466
Plat book of Putnam County, Ind. [192–?] 12893
Plat book of Racine Co., Wis. [193–?] 17890
Plat book of Randolph Co., Ill. [193–?] 12469
Plat book of Randolph County, Ind. [192–?] 12895
Plat book of Richland County, Ill. [193–?] 12472
Plat book of Richland County, Wis. [193–?] 17894
Plat book of Ripley County, Ind. [192–?] 12899
Plat book of Rock County, Wis. [193–?] 17900
Plat book of Roscommon Co., Mich.
 [193–?] 14797
Plat book of Rush County, Ind. [192–?] 12901
Plat book of Rusk County, Wis. [193–?] 17905
Plat book of Saginaw County, Mich.
 [193–?] 14798
Plat book of St. Clair County, Ill. [193–?] 12482
—— 1939. 12484
Plat book of St. Clair County, Mich. [193–?] 14801
Plat book of St. Croix County, Wis. [193–?] 17908
Plat book of St. Joseph County, Ind. [192–?] 12904
Plat book of St. Joseph Co. [Mich. 193–?] 14804
Plat book of Sangamon Co. [Ill. 193–?] 12491

Plat book of Sanilac Co., Mich. [193–?]	14809
Plat book of Sauk County, Wis. [193–?]	17915
Plat book of Sawyer County, Wis. [193–?]	17921
Plat book of Schoolcraft County, Mich. [193–?]	14812
Plat book of Schuyler County, Ill. [193–?]	12495
Plat book of Scott County, Ill. [193–?]	12499
Plat book of Scott County, Ind. [192–?]	12908
Plat book of Shawano County, Wis. [193–?]	17923
Plat book of Sheboygan County, Wis. [193–?]	17928
Plat book of Shelby County, Ill. [193–?]	12502
Plat book of Shelby County, Ind. [192–?]	12910
Plat book of Shiawassee Co., Mich. [193–?]	14815
Plat book of South Dakota. [1933?]	17011
Plat book of Spencer County, Ind. [192–?]	12913
Plat book of Stark Co., Ill. [193–?]	12507
Plat book of Stark County, Ind. [192–?]	12914
Plat book of Stephenson Co., Ill. [193–?]	12509
Plat book of Steuben County, Ind. [192–?]	12917
Plat book of Sullivan County, Ind. [192–?]	12923
—— [193–?]	12924
Plat book of Switzerland County, Ind. [192–?]	12926
Plat book of Taylor County, Wis. [193–?]	17933
Plat book of Tazewell Co., Ill. [193–?]	12514
Plat book of the State of Iowa. [1933?]	13015
Plat book of Tippecanoe County, Ind. [192–?]	12928
Plat book of Tipton County, Ind. [192–?]	12932
Plat book of Trempealeau County, Wis. [193–?]	17937
Plat book of Tuscola Co., Mich. [193–?]	14817
Plat book of Union Co., Ill. [193–?]	12520
Plat book of Union County, Ind. [192–?]	12934
Plat book of Van Buren Co. [Mich. 193–?]	14820
Plat book of Vanderburg County, Ind. [192–?]	12936
Plat book of Vermilion Co. [Ill. 193–?]	12524
Plat book of Vermilion County, Ind. [192–?]	12937
Plat book of Vernon County, Wis. [193–?]	17942
Plat book of Vigo County, Ind. [192–?]	12939
Plat book of Wabash Co., Ill. [193–?]	12530
Plat book of Wabash County, Ind. [192–?]	12941
Plat book of Walworth County, Wis. [193–?]	17949
Plat book of Warren Co., Ill. [193–?]	12534
Plat book of Warren County, Ind. [192–?]	12943
Plat book of Warrick County, Ind. [192–?]	12944
Plat book of Washburn Co., Wis. [193–?]	17958
Plat book of Washington Co., Ill. [193–?]	12537
—— [194–?]	12538
Plat book of Washington County, Ind. [192–?]	12945
Plat book of Washington County, Wis. [193–?]	17964
Plat book of Washtenaw County, Mich. [193–?]	14823
Plat book of Waukesha County, Wis. [193–?]	17970
Plat book of Waupaca County, Wis. [193–?]	17977
Plat book of Waushara County, Wis. [193–?]	17982
Plat book of Wayne Co., Ill. [193–?]	12542

Plat book of Wayne County, Ind. [192–?]	12946
Plat book of Wayne County, Mich. [193–?]	14831
Plat book of Wayne County, Nebr. [193–?]	15619
Plat book of Wayne County, Ohio. [1938]	16463
Plat book of Wells County, Ind. [192–?]	12947
Plat book of Wexford County, Mich. [193–?]	14838
Plat book of White Co., Ill. [193–?]	12546
—— [194–?]	12547
Plat book of White County, Ind. [192–?]	12949
Plat book of Whiteside Co., Ill. [193–?]	12550
Plat book of Whitley County, Ind. [192–?]	12950
Plat book of Will Co., Ill. [193–?]	12556
Plat book of Williamson Co., Ill. [193–?]	12566
Plat book of Winnebago County, Ill. [193–?]	12569
Plat book of Winnebago County, Wis. [193–?]	17986
Plat book of Wood County, Wis. [193–?]	17992
Plat book of Wyandot County, Ohio. [193–?]	16469
Polk County, Minn. [193–?]	15078
Pope County, Minn. [193–?]	15080
Publication of the Lincoln Highway. 1921.	10776
Ramsey County, Minn. [193–?]	15082
Red Lake County, Minn. [193–?]	15083
Redwood County, Minn. [193–?]	15086
Renville County, Minn. [193–?]	15089
Rock County, Minn. [193–?]	15093
Roseau County, Minn. [193–?]	15096
Scott County, Minn. [193–?]	15097
Sherburne County, Minn. [193–?]	15100
Sibley County, Minn. [193–?]	15102
Stevens County, Minn. [193–?]	15109
Swift County, Minn. [193–?]	15111
Todd County, Minn. [193–?]	15113
Township plats of Waupaca County, Wis. [1901?]	2671
Traverse County, Minn. [193–?]	15116
Wabasha County, Minn. [193–?]	15119
Wadena County, Minn. [193–?]	15122
Waseca County, Minn. [193–?]	15123
Watonwan County, Minn. [193–?]	15129
Winona County, Minn. [193–?]	15133
Wright County, Minn. [193–?]	15137
Yellow Medicine County, Minn [193–?]	15139

Hoang, Pierre, 1830–1909.
Exposé du commerce public du sel. [China]
1898.   9528

Hobson William Colling.
Fox-hunting atlas. [1848?]   2903

**Hochstetter, Ferdinand von, 1829–1884, *and*
Petermann, August Heinrich, 1822–1878.**
Geologisch-topographischer Atlas von Neu
Seeland. 1863.   3265

Hodder, Frank Heywood, 1860–1935.
Outline historical atlas of the United States.
[1921]   10624
Outline maps for an historical atlas of the
United States. 1901.   1292

——— 1903.	10625
——— Rev. ed. 1913.	4507

Hölzel, Eduard, 1844–
Physikalisch-statistischer Hand-Atlas von Oesttterreich-Ungarn. 1887. — 3991

Hölzel, Eduard, *firm.*
Autostraszenkarte von Österreich. [194–?] — 7904

Hörle, Emil.
Württembergischer Schulatlas. [1938] — 6950
——— [1941] — 7056

Hoffmeister, Johannes, 1894– *and* Schnell, Fritz, 1900–
Klima-Atlas von Niedersachsen. 1945. — 8790

Hogenberg, Franz, *d.* 1590?
See Braun, Georg, 1561–1618, *and* Hogenberg, Franz, *d.* 1590?

Hollar, Wenceslaus, 1607–1677.
Kingdome of England. [1644] — 2914

Hollinger, Bernhard.
See Himmelbaur, Wolfgang, 1886– *and* Hollinger, Bernhard.

Hollman, Frank, 1904– *and* Hollman, John, 1908–
Current & historical atlas, St. Clair County, Ill. 1936. — 12483

Holman, A. J., and Company.
New Biblical atlas. 1898. — 83
——— 1904. — 5351

Holmden's Register of Greater Johannesburg townships. [1951?] — 10168
——— [1954?] — 10169

Holmes, James Macdonald, 1896–
Atlas of population and production for New South Wales. 1932. — 10176
Regional atlas of Australia and the world. 1937. — 6916

Holt, Roy H.
Plat book, Jefferson County, Ill. 1951. — 12288

Holy Ghost Fathers.
Atlas missionnaire des Pères du Saint–Esprit. [1936] — 5410

Holy Land in ancient maps. [1956] — 9768

Homann, Johann Baptist, 1664–1724.
Atlas Germaniae specialis. 1753. — 3035
Atlas novus terrarum orbis imperia. [1702–50] — 539
——— 3 v. [1705–73] — 5959

Grosser Atlas uber [sic] die gantze Welt. 1716. — 5966
——— 1737. — 586
Kleiner Atlas scholasticus. [1732?] — 577
Neuer Atlas. 1707. — 5960
——— 1710–[31] — 556
——— 1712–[30] — 3474

Homann Erben.
Atlas compendiarivs. 1752–[55] — 3498
——— 1752–[65] — 3499
——— 1753–[57] — 3501
——— [1753–90] — 294
Atlas geographicvs. 1759–[81] — 622
——— 1759–[84] — 623, 624
Atlas mapparum geographicarum. [1728–93] — 3484
Atlas novus Reipublicae Helveticae. 1769. — 3151, 4066
Atlas Regni Bohemiae. 1776. — 2866
Atlas Silesiae. 1750–[1808] — 3046, 8809
Beqvemer Hand Atlas. 1754. — 615
——— 1754–[90] — 4289
Homannischer Atlas. 1747–[57] — 604
Kleiner Atlas. 1803. — 3987
Maior atlas scholasticvs. [1752–73] — 4195
Schul-Atlas. 1743. — 292, 3372
——— 1745–[46] — 293
Städt-Atlas. 1762. — 61, 3293

Homans, James Esward, 1865–
See Collier, P. F., and Son.

Homem de Mello, Francisco, 1859–
See Marcondes Homem de Mello, Francisco Ignacio, Barão Homem de Mello, 1837–1918, *and* Homem de Mello, Francisco, 1859–

Hondius, Henricus, 1587–1638.
Nouveau théâtre dv monde. 1639. — 452

Hondius, Henricus, *and* Jansson, Jan, *ca.* 1588–1664.
Nouveau théâtre dv monde. 1639–40. — 3422

Hondius, Jodocus, 1563–1612.
Nova et accvrata Italiae hodiernae descriptio. 1627. — 4041

Honduras.
Serie de mapas presentados por Honduras. [1932] — 18129

Honduras. *Dirección General de Estadistica y Censos.*
Principales poblaciones del país. [1963] — 18135

Hong Kong.
Road maps of Hong Kong. [1953] — 9677

Hood, Edwin C.
Plat book of Richland County, Wis. 1895. — 2659
Plat book of Vernon County, Wis. 1896. — 2664

See also Foote, Charles M., 1849–1899, *and* Hood, Edwin C.

Hooghe, Romein de, 1646?–1708.
Zee atlas tot het gebruik van de vlooten des
konings van Groot Britanje. 1694.   2835

Hooijer, G. B.
Atlas ... Krijgsgeschiedenis van Nederlandsch
Indië. [1895–97]   9735

Hooks, W. N. *and* Jones, C. G.
Ownership map of Jefferson County, Tex.
1930.   17175

Hoover, H. S.
Atlas of Bremer County, Iowa. 1875.   1646

Hoover Publications.
Camden County, N.J., suburban street maps.
[1966]   15689

**Hopkins, Albert Allis, 1869– *and* Read, New-
bury Frost.**
Dickens atlas, including twelve walks in London with Charles Dickens. 1923.   8155

Hopkins, Dorothy Elliott.
Standard atlas of the world for home, school
[and] office. 1949.   7358

Hopkins, Griffith Morgan.
Atlas of Baltimore County, Md. 1877.   1783
Atlas of Bryn Mawr [Pa.] and vicinity. 1881.
                                          2443, 2508
Atlas of Danbury Conn. 1880.   1486
Atlas of Delaware County, Pa. 1870.   2474
Atlas of fifteen miles around Baltimore, in-
cluding Anne Arundel County, Md. 1878.   1728
Atlas of fifteen miles around Baltimore, in-
cluding Howard County, Md. 1878.   1784, 1789
Atlas of fifteen miles around Washington,
including the counties of Fairfax and
Alexandria, Va. 1879.   1500, 2608, 2610
Atlas of fifteen miles around Washington,
including the county of Montgomery, Md.
1879.   1501, 1790, 2611
Atlas of fifteen miles around Washington, in-
cluding the county of Prince Georges, Md.
1878.   1499, 1791, 2607, 2609
Atlas of Marblehead, Mass. 1881.   1903
Atlas of Philadelphia and environs. 1877. 2524
Atlas of properties along the Philadelphia,
Wilmington and Baltimore Railroad and
the Philadelphia & Westchester Railroad.
1882.   2444, 2526
Atlas of properties near the North Pennsyl-
vania Rail road from Wayne Junc't. to
Penllyn Sta'n. [Pa.] 1883.   2445
Atlas of properties near the Philadelphia and
Trenton Railroad, New York div. Penna.
R. R. Frankfort to Trenton. 1885.
                         2148, 2446, 5010

Atlas of the cities of Pittsburgh & Allegheny
[Pa.] 1882.   2503
Atlas of the city and town of Bridgeport,
Conn. 1888.   1484
Atlas of the city of Allegheny [Pa.] 1890–91. 2505
Atlas of the city of Binghamton, N.Y. 1885.   2271
Atlas of the city Buffalo, N.Y. 1884.   2280
——— 1891.   2281
Atlas of the city of Cambridge, Mass. 1873.   1871
——— 1886.   1872
Atlas of the city of Chattanooga, Tenn.
1889.   2585
Atlas of the city of Gloucester and the town of
Rockport, Mass. 1884.   1885, 1934
Atlas of the city of Louisville, Ky. and en-
virons. 1884.   1770
Atlas of the city of Nashville, Tenn. 1889.   2587
Atlas of the city of New Haven, Conn. 1888.   1490
Atlas of the city of Newport, R. I. 1883.   2565
Atlas of the city of Newton ... Mass. 1874.   1914
Atlas of the city of Norfolk, Va. and vicinity,
including the city of Portsmouth. 1889.
                                     2617, 2619
Atlas of the city of Philadelphia. 1st, 26th, and
30th wards. 1885.   2529
——— 11th, 12th, & 14th wards. 1885.   2530
——— 15th ward. 1885.   2531
——— 21st & 28th wards. 1884.   2528
——— 22nd ward. 1885.   2532
——— 23rd ward. [1887]   2534
——— 25th ward. 1886.   2533
Atlas of the city of Pittsburgh. 1889–90.
                                     2542, 2543
Atlas of the city of Providence, R.I., and en-
virons. 1882.   2569
Atlas of the city of St. Louis, Mo. 1883.   2105
Atlas of the city of St. Paul, Minn. 1884.   2055
Atlas of the city of Somerville, Mass. 1884.   1938
Atlas of the city of Utica, N.Y. 1883.   2332
Atlas of the city of Waterbury, Conn. 1879.   1491
Atlas of the city of Worcester, Mass. 1886.   1959
Atlas of the county of Allegheny, Pa. 1876.   2459
Atlas of the environs of Kansas City ... Mo.
1886.   2099
Atlas of the environs of St. Paul, including the
whole of Ramsey County, Minn. 1886.
                                     2035, 2056
Atlas of (the late borough of) Germantown
... city of Philadelphia. 1871.   2520
Atlas of the town of Beverly, Mass. 1880.   1852
Atlas of the town of Brookline, Mass. 1874.   1869
——— 1884.   1870
Atlas of the town of East Orange, N.J. 1879.   2179
Atlas of the town of Nahant, Mass. 1880.   1911
Atlas of the town of Pawtucket, R.I. 1880.   2567
Atlas of the town of Swampscott, Mass.
1880.   1943
Atlas of the town of Woburn, Mass. 1875.   1956
Atlas of the vicinities of the cities of Niagara
Falls, North Tonawanda and Buffalo, N.Y.
1893.   2282, 2318, 2319
Atlas of the vicinity of the cities of Pittsburgh
and Allegheny, Pa. 1886.   2504, 2541
Atlas of West Philadelphia. 1872.   2521

City atlas of Albany, N.Y. 1876.	2266
City atlas of Alexandria, Va. 1877.	2615
City atlas of Atlanta, Ga. 1878.	1507
City atlas of Auburn, N.Y. 1882.	2268
City atlas of Baltimore, Md., and environs. 1876–77.	1796
City atlas of Boston, Mass. 1882.	1858
City atlas of Camden, N.J. 1877.	2174
City atlas of Cleveland, Ohio. 1881.	2424
City atlas of Covington, Ky. 1877.	1769
City atlas of Hartford, Conn. 1880.	1488
City atlas of Haverhill, Mass. 1881.	1890
City atlas of Lawerence, Mass. 1875.	1896
City atlas of Lowell, Mass. 1879.	14482
City atlas of Lynn, Mass. 1880.	1898
City atlas of Macon, Ga. 1878.	1509
City atlas of Mobile, Ala. 1878.	1451
City atlas of Newport, R.I. 1876.	2564
City atlas of Orange and township of West Orange, N.J. 1878.	2190
City atlas of Oswego, N.Y. 1880.	2320
City atlas of Philadelphia by wards. 1875–76.	2523
City atlas of Providence, R.I. by wards. 1875.	2568
City atlas of Rochester, N.Y. 1875.	2322
City atlas of Schenectady, N.Y. 1880.	2325
City atlas of Scranton, Pa. 1877.	2556
City atlas of Toledo, Ohio. 1881.	2436
City atlas of Troy, N.Y. 1881.	2331
City atlas of Wilmington, Del. 1876.	1493
City atlas, Philadelphia. 29th ward. 1882.	2527
Combined atlas of the state of New Jersey and the city of Newark. 1873.	2145, 2187
Combined atlas of the state of New Jersey and the County of Hudson. 1873.	2146, 2160
Complete set of surveys and plats of properties in the City of Kansas, Mo. [1886]	2100
—— [1887]	2101
Complete set of surveys and plats of properties in the city of Minneapolis, Minn. [1885]	2053
Complete set of surveys and plats of properties in the city of Omaha and environs, Nebr. 1887.	2130
Complete set of surveys and plats of properties in the city of Washington, District of Columbia. 1887	1503
Complete set of surveys and plats of properties in Wyandotte County and Kansas City, Kans. [1887]	1744, 1745
Complete set of surveys and plats of properties of Kansas City, Mo. [1891]	2102
Detailed estate and old farm line atlas of the city of Brooklyn [N.Y.] 1880.	2275
Real estate plat-book of Pittsburgh. 1898–1901.	16903
Real estate plat-book of the city of Pittsburgh [Pa] 1898–1901.	2547
Real estate plat-book of the eastern vicinity of Pittsburgh, Pa. 1895.	2544
Real estate plat-book of the northern vicinity of Pittsburgh, Pa. 1897.	2546
Real estate plat-book of the south-eastern vicinity of Pittsburgh, Pa. 1900.	2548

Real estate plat-book of the southern vicinity of Pittsburgh, Pa. 1896.	2545
Real estate plat-book of Washington, District of Columbia. 1892–96.	1504

Hopkins, G. M., Company.

Atlas of Greater Pittsburgh, Pa. 1910.	3894
Atlas of Hudson County, N.J. 1908–1909.	2162a, 2183a, 3833
—— 1919–23.	15710
—— 1934.	15711
Atlas of the city of Nashville, Tenn. 1908.	2589
Atlas of the city of Rochester, N.Y. 1910.	3853
Atlas of the city of Syracuse, N.Y. 1908.	2329a, 3854
Atlas of the city of Syracuse, N.Y., and suburbs. 1924.	16170
—— 1938.	16172
Atlas of the vicinity of Camden, N.J. 1907.	2177
Atlas of Westchester County, N.Y. 1929–31.	15918
Plat book including towns of Irondequoit and Brighton . . . N.Y. 1959.	15967
Plat book of Cuyahoga County, Ohio. 1914.	4984
—— 1920.	16396
—— 1927.	16397
—— 1941–42.	16399
—— 1950–57.	16400
Plat book of Ft. Lauderdale, Fla., and vicinity. 1953.	11871
Plat book of Greater Miami, Fla. and suburbs. 1925.	11892
—— 1936.	11897
Plat book of Jersey City . . . N.J. 1928.	15761
Plat book of lower Broward County, Fla. 1960.	11809
Plat book of Miami Beach to Golden Beach [Fla.] 1952.	11908
Plat book of Miami, Fla., and suburbs. 1947–57.	11900
—— 1965–67.	11902
Plat book of Monroe County, N.Y. 1924.	15883
Plat book of the city of Akron, Ohio and vicinity. 1915.	4992
—— 1921.	16473
Plat book of the city of Bridgeport, Conn. 1917.	11712
Plat book of the city of Chattanooga, Tenn., and vicinity. 1914.	5065
Plat book of the city of Cleveland, Ohio and suburbs. 1912.	3880, 4994
—— 1921–22.	16502
—— 1932–38.	16504
Plat book of the city of Providence, R.I. 1918.	5056
—— 1926.	16967
—— 1937.	16968
Plat book of the city of Rochester, N.Y. 1918.	4955
—— 1926.	16155
—— 1934–41.	16156
Plat book of the city of Saint Paul, Minn. 1916.	4827
—— 1928.	15164

Plat book of the city of Toledo, Ohio, and
  suburbs. 1913.   4997
Plat book of upper Broward County, Fla.
  1960.   11810
Plat book of western Broward County, Fla.
  1967.   11811
Real estate plat book of the city of Allegheny
  [Penna.] 1907.   2507
Real estate plat book of the city of Chat-
  tanooga [Tenn.] and vicinity. 1904.   2586
Real estate plat book of the city of Miami
  Beach, Fla. 1936.   11904
Real estate plat-book of the city of Pittsburgh.
  1903.   2550
——— 1904–1906.   2551, 3893
——— 1911.   3895
——— 1911–14.   16905
——— 1914–17.   5052
——— 1915–40.   16906
——— 1939.   16909
Real estate plat-book of the eastern vicinity of
  Pittsburgh, Pa. 1903.   2549
Real estate plat-book of the northern vicinity
  of Pittsburgh, Pa. 1906.   2553
Real estate plat-book of the southern vicinity
  of Pittsburgh, Pa. 1905.   2552

Hopkins, G. M., and Company.
Atlas of the city of Buffalo, Erie Co., N.Y.
  1872.   2279
Atlas of the city of Salem, Mass. 1874.   1935
Atlas of the city of Somerville, Mass. 1874.   1937
Atlas of the county of Fayette and the state of
  Pennsylvania. 1872.   2452, 2476
Atlas of the county of Montgomery and the
  state of Pennsylvania. 1871.   2451, 2487
Atlas of the county of Suffolk, Mass. 1873–
  75.   1825, 1857
Combination atlas of the county of Butler and
  the state of Pennsylvania. 1874.   2455, 2465
Combination atlas of the county of Mercer
  and the state of Pennsylvania. 1873.   2454, 2484

Hopkins, Henry Whitmer, 1838–1920.
Atlas of the county of Levis, Prov. Quebec.
  1879.   10432
Atlas of the town of Sorel and county of
  Richelieu, Province of Quebec. 1880.   10433
R al estate plat-book of the city of Allegheny
  ₍Penna.₎ 1901–1902.   2506

Hopley Printing Company.
Atlas [of] Crawford County [Ohio] 1912.   3873a

Hopple, William H.
County of Sandusky, Ohio. 1898.   16448

Horch, ———
Landstrassen Atlas. [192–?]   8601

Horn, Georg, 1620–1670.
Accuratissima orbis antiqui delineatio.
  1654.   16
Accuratissima orbis delineatio. 1660.   3278

——— 1684.   5613
——— 1740.   17
Compleat body of ancient geography. 3d ed.
  1741.   3279
Full and exact description of the earth, or
  Ancient geography. 1700.   5614

Horrabin, James Francis, 1884–1962.
Atlas de historia de Europa. [1. ed. 1941]   7681
Atlas de política mundial. [1935]   5659
——— 1937.   5660
Atlas-history of the second great war. 1940.   5883
——— 10 v. [1942–46]   5884
Atlas of Africa. 1960.   10101a
Atlas of current affairs. 1934.   5661
——— [1st American ed.] 1934.   5662
——— 2d ed. 1935.   5663
——— 3d ed. 1937.   5664
——— 4th ed. 1938.   5665
——— 5th ed. 1939.   5666
——— 6th ed. 1939.   5667
——— 1939.   5668
——— 7th ed. 1940.   5669
Atlas of empire. 1937.   5670, 6917
Atlas of European history. 1935.   7683
——— [1st American ed.] 1935.   7682
Atlas of post-war problems. [1943]   5671
Plebs atlas. 1926.   5438

**Horrabin, James Francis, and Gregory, James
Stothert, 1912–**
Atlas of the U.S.S.R. 1945.   9215a

Horsburgh, James, 1762–1836.
[Atlas of the East Indies and China Sea.
  1806–21]   3171
See also Steel, Penelope, *and* Horsburgh,
  James, 1762–1836.

**Horsetzky, Adolf von, *Edler von Hornthal*, 1847–
1929.**
33 Tafeln zur Kriegsgeschichtlichen Uebersicht
  der wichtigsten Feldzüge der letzten 100
  Jahre. 2. Aufl. 1889.   7728
38 Tafeln zur Kriegsgeschichtlichen Übersicht
  der wichtigsten Feldzüge in Europa seit ...
  1792. 6. neubearb. Aufl. 1905.   7729

Horwood, Richard, *ca.* 1758–1803.
Plan of the cities of London and Westminster.
  [1799]   8157

Hoshino, Shizue.
Saishin Gumma-ken bungun chizu. [New
  atlas of Gumma Prefecture, cities and coun-
  ties. 1948]   9851a

Hospital Council of Greater New York.
Sectional map of the city of New York.
  1945.   16063

Hotchkiss, David S.
Spanish missions of Texas from 1776. [1966]   17130

House, W. M.
North Dakota and Richland County chart.
1897. 4959

Household Goods Carriers' Bureau.
Mileage guide No. 8. 1966. 10980
Mileage guide No. 9. 1967. 10981

Housing Authority of the Birmingham (Ala.) District.
Real property inventory ... Birmingham.
[1939] 11214

Houston Geological Society.
Geologic strip maps: Highway 77, Texas—
Oklahoma State line to Dallas. 1952. 17128
—— U.S. Highway 80, Texas—New Mexico
State line to Van Horn. 1959. 17129

Houzé, Antoine Philippe.
Atlas histórico de España. 1841. 9309
Atlas historico de Francia. 1840. 8408
Atlas universel historique et géographique.
1848. 110
—— [1849] 111

Hovey, Arthur Miller, 1873–
Atlas of Lawrence County, Mo. 1900. 2082
Atlas of Mahaska County, Iowa. 1936. 13686

Hovey and Frame.
Atlas of Monroe County, Iowa. [1902] 1687
Atlas of Warren County, Iowa. 1902. 1703

Howat, W. A., and Son.
Farm ownership maps and plat book guide of
McDonough County, Ill. [192–] 12358

Howatt, Lester A.
Wabasha County [Minn.] farm identification
directory. 1965. 15120

Howden, J. A., and Odbert A.
Atlas of Warren County, Penn. 1878. 2498

Howe, Samuel Gridley, 1801–1876.
Atlas of the United States, printed for the use
of the blind. 1837. 10471

Howell, John Pryse, 1887–
Agricultural atlas of England and Wales.
[1925] 8081
Agricultural atlas of Wales. [1921] 8219

Howland, C. W.
See Sherman, W. A., and Howland, C. W.

Howland, Charles Roscoe, 1871–
Military history of the World War. 1923. 5828

Howland, H. G.
Atlas of Hardin Co., Ohio. 1879. 2382

Hsia lan chih chang. [Looking at distant places as if they were in the palm of your hand 1368–1644]
MS. 9534

Hsin-chiang ch'üan t'u. [Complete atlas of Sinkiang 18–?] 9624

Hsin-chiang shih yeh yen ch'an yu chêng tien hsien tao li t'u. [Distance atlas showing industries, salt products, post offices, and telegraph lines in Sinkiang 191–?] 9626

Hsin kuang yü ti hsüeh shê, *Hongkong*.
Chung-kuo ti li chiao k'o t'u (Ti hsing pan)
[Textbook—atlas of China (Topographic
edition) 2d ed.] 1955. 9609
Tsui hsin Chung-kuo fên shêng t'u. [New provincial atlas of China. Topographic ed.]
1956. 9612

Hsü, Lun, *chin shih*, 1524.
Chiu pien t'u lun. [Frontier defense atlas of
China. 1538] 9518
Chiu pien t'u shuo. Wei Huan hsü. [Frontier
defense atlas of China. Revised by Wei
Huan 1569] 9519

Hu, Lin-i, 1812–1861, and Kuan-wên.
Huang ch'ao Chung wai i t'ung yü t'u. [Atlas
of China and adjacent regions in the Ch'ing
period. 1863.] 9553a

Huai-tzŭ-t'ang, *pseud*.
Yü ti ch'üan t'u. [Complete atlas of China.
162–] 9544

Huang, P'êng-nien, 1823–1891.
Ch'i-fu yü ti ch'üan t'u. [Complete atlas of
Hopei. 1884] 9635

Hubault, Gustave, 1825–
Atlas de géographie. [1873?] 867

Huberts, Wilhelmus Jacobus Arnoldus de Witt, 1829–
Nieuwe geographische atlas. [1870] 857

Hudson, Geoffrey Francis, 1903– *and* Raj-chman, Marthe.
Atlas of Far Eastern politics. 1942. 9492
Explanatory atlas of the Far East. [2d ed.
1942] 9493

Hudson Map Company.
Street atlas of the Greater Twin City metropolitan area. [1st ed. 1965] 15157
—— [2d ed. 1967] 15158

Hudson Star-Observer, *Hudson, Wis*.
Plat book, St. Croix County, Wis. 1938. 17909

Huë, Jean François, 1751–1823.
See Miger, Pierre Auguste Marie, 1771–1837.

Hueber, Blasius, 1735–1814.
    See Anich, Peter, 1723–1766, *and* Hueber,
      Blasius, 1735–1814.

Huebinger, Melchior.
Atlas of Scott County, Iowa. 1894.	4658
Atlas of the State of Iowa. 1904.	1640
Atlas of the town of the city of Peoria and environs ... Ill. 1909.	3737
Automobile and good road atlas of Iowa. 1912.	3742a
Map of the city of Burlington, Iowa. 1910.	3755
Map of the city of Des Moines, Iowa. 1909.	3756
Pocket automobile guide for Iowa. 1913.	13004
—— [1914]	13005
—— 1915.	13006
—— 1917.	13007
—— 1918.	13008

Huebinger, M., and Company.
Plat book of Clinton County, Iowa. 1894.	13267

Huebinger Surveying and Map Publishing Company.
Atlas of Johnson County, Iowa. 1900.	13577
Atlas of Story County, Iowa. 1902.	1696
Standard historical atlas of Jasper County, Iowa. 1901.	1676

Hughes, William, 1817–1876.
Atlas of classical geography. New York ed. [1856]	19
—— Philadelphia ed. 1856.	18
—— 1856.	4093
—— 1867.	5615
—— 1870.	5616
Grammer school atlas of classical geography. 1882.	5617
Little corporal's pocket Scripture atlas. 1869.	5352
Philips' Handy classical atlas. [1900?]	3280
Philips' School atlas of classical geography. [1900?]	3373
Philips' Scripture atlas. 1869.	5353
Philips' Student's atlas. 1882.	6210
Popular atlas of comparative geography. 1876.	112

    See also Hall, Sidney, Hughes, William, *and others.*

Hulbert, Archer Butler, 1873–1933.
Crown collection of American maps. Series IV. [1925–28]	10764
—— Vol. 1. [1926]	10765
—— Series V. [1930]	10766
Crown collection of photographs of American maps. 1904–1908.	1191, 3664
—— Index. 1909.	3666
—— Series II. [1909–12]	3665
—— Series III. [1914–16]	4468
Deadwood trails in South Dakota. [1930]	10767

Hull, Edward, 1829–1917.
Monograph on the sub-oceanic physiography of the North Atlantic Ocean. 1912.	3341a

Humboldt, Friedrich Wilhelm Heinrich Alexander, *Freiherr* von, 1769–1859.
Atlas géographique et physique du Royaume de la Nouvelle-Espagne. 1811.	5118
—— 1812.	2682
Ensayo politico sobre el Reino de la Nouva España. 1941.	18086
Voyage de Humboldt et Bonpland. Atlas géographique et physique. 1805–34.	2726
Voyage de Humboldt et Bonpland. Première partie, relation historique. Atlas géographique et physique. 1814–[20]	5131

Humlum, Johannes, 1911–
Kulturgeografisk atlas. 1944.	5439
—— [2. udg.] 1947.	5440
Lille verdensatlas. 1950.	7412

Hungary. *Honvéd Térképészeti Intézet.*
Magyarország kistérképei. [1943]	8914

Hunnicutt and Associates.
City of St. Augustine, Fla., atlas. 1962.	11922, 11923

Hunt, F. W.
J. H. Colton's Historical atlas. 1860.	113

Hunt & Eaton.
Columbian atlas. [1893]	981

Hunter, C. M.
Atlas of boroughs & towns in Philadelphia, Bucks and Montgomery Counties. 1886.	16890
Atlas of the city of Williamsport, Pa. 1888.	2560

Hunter, H. W.
New atlas of Highland County, Ohio. 1916.	16419

Hunter, Robert, 1824–1897, *and* Morris, Charles.
Imperial dictionary and cyclopaedia. [Atlas] 1901.	6298

Hunter, *Sir* William Wilson, 1840–1900.
Atlas of India. 1894.	9700

Huntington, Nathaniel Gilbert, 1785–1848.
School atlas. 1833.	295
—— 4th ed. 1835.	6077

Huntington Township, *N.Y. Town Planning Board.*
Town of Huntington, Suffolk County, N.Y. [1956]	15911

Hu-pei, *China. Shan hou chü.*
Kuang-hsi Hu-pei yü ti t'u ssŭ chüan i pai ch'i shih san fu. [Atlas of Hu-pei in the Kuang-hsi period. 1901]	9642

Hu-Pei shêng ch'êng nei wai chieh tao tsung fên t'u. [Detailed atlas of streets ... of the Capital City of Hu-pei Province (Wuchang) 18–?]   9669

Hurd, Duane Hamilton, and Company.
Town and city atlas of the state of Connecticut.
1893. 1476
Town and city atlas of the state of New Hampshire. 1892. 2137

Hurd, Edgar Blake, 1899–
See Scudder, Henry Desborough, 1881–
and Hurd, Edgar Blake, 1899–

Hurd, Mark, Aerial Surveys.
Aerial photo maps of free public access to 52
lakes near the Twin City area. [1961] 14913

Hurlbert, Jesse Beaufort.
Physical atlas ... of Canada. 1880. 1234

Hurlbut, Jesse Lyman, 1843–1930.
Bible atlas. [1910] 5354
—— [1928] 5355
—— [1938] 5356
Manual of Biblical geography. [1884] 84

Husson, Pieter, 1678–1733.
Variae tabulae geographicae. [1709?] 5174

Hutchison and Nesbit.
Stephenson County, Ill., plat book. 1947. 12510
—— 1950. 12511
—— 1952. 12512

Huth, Carl Frederick, 1883–
See Breasted, James Henry, 1865–1935, *and*
Huth, Carl Frederick, 1883–

Hutt, *N. Z. (County) Council.*
Road and street maps of Paraparaumu.
1950. 10204

Hyde, E. Belcher, 1850?–1916.
Atlas of Nassau County, Long Island, N.Y.
1906. 2240
—— 1914. 4925
Atlas of Suffolk County, Long Island, N.Y.
1902–1909. 2255
Atlas of the rural county district north of New
York City embracing the entire Westchester
County, N.Y. 1908. 1477, 2264, 2317
Miniature atlas of Far Rockaway and Rock-
away Beach ... N.Y. 1912. 4939, 4956
Miniature atlas of the borough of Brooklyn.
1912. 4937
Miniature atlas of the borough of Manhattan.
1912. 4946
Miniature atlas of the borough of the Bronx.
1912. 4945

Hyde, Merritt B.
Atlas of a part of Suffolk County, Long Is-
land, N.Y. North side. 1917. 4932
—— South side. 1915–16. 4931

I-lu-chu-jên, *pseud.*
Hsiu chên Hsiang-kang Chiu-lung ti t'u. [Poc-

ket atlas of Hong Kong and Kowloon.
1940] 9675

Ice, John R., *and* Moore, Berlie.
Pictorial and official atlas of Vernon County,
Wis. 1931. 17943

Ice, R. P., and Company.
Plat book of Meade County, Kans. 1909. 3758

Idaho. *Bureau of Highways.*
[Highway atlas of Idaho. 1940] 12000

Idaho. *Dept. of Highways.*
Route of the Oregon Trail in Idaho. 1963. 12003

Idaho Title Company.
Map of Boise City and vicinity. [1949] 12062

Il'in, Aleksiei Afinogenovich, 1832–1889.
Опытъ статистическаго атласа. [Statistical
atlas of the Russian Empire.] 1874. 3114

Il'in, A., *firm.*
Жельаныя дороги Россіи. [Railroads of
Russia. 1916] 9241

Illinois. *Dept. of Revenue. Property Tax Division.*
Atlas of taxing units. 1946. 12074

Illinois. *Division of Waterways.*
Plan for flood control ... Salt Creek, Cook
and Du Page Counties. 1958. 12067

**Illinois. *Post-War Planning Commission. Commit-
tee on Resources.***
Illinois resources; an atlas. 1944. 12065

Illinois. *Rivers and Lakes Commission.*
Kaskaskia River Valley, Ill. 1910–11. 12722
Little Wabash and Skillet Fork River, Ill.
[1911] 12723
Report upon the prevention of overflow of the
Little Wabash and Skillet Fork Rivers.
1911. 12068

Illinois. *University. Dept. of Geography.*
Atlas of Illinois resources. [1958–63] 12066

Illinois Central Railroad Company.
Sectional maps, showing 2,500,000 acres farm
and wood lands, of the Illinois Central Rail
Road Company. [1856?] 12071

Imhof, Edouard, 1895–
Haus–Atlas. 1935. 6844
See also Becker, Fridolin, 1854–1922, *and*
Imhof, Eduard, 1895–
See also Kläui, Paul, 1908– *and* Imhof,
Eduard, 1895–

Imperial gazetteer of India ... Atlas. 1909. 9701
—— 1931. 9703

Joint maps of the international boundary between United States and Canada from Cape Muzon to Mt. St. Elias. [1952]   10486

Joint maps of the international boundary between United States and Canada from the Gulf of Georgia to the northwesternmost point of the Lake of the Woods. [1937]   10481

Joint maps of the international boundary between United States and Canada from the northwesternmost point of Lake of the Woods to Lake Superior. [1931]   10479

Joint maps of the international boundary between United States and Canada from the St. Lawrence River to the source of the St. Croix River. [1925]   10477

Joint maps of the international boundary between United States and Canada from the source of the St. Croix River to the Atlantic Ocean. [1934]   10480

International Boundary Commission (U.S. and Mexico) 1882.

Boundary between the United States and Mexico ... 1882. Revived ... 1889. [1898]   1262, 2680

Linea divisoria entre México y los Estados Unidos al oueste del Rio Grande. [1901]   1263, 2681

International Boundary Commission (U.S. and Mexico) 1893–

Proceedings of the International Boundary Commission, United States and Mexico. American section. [1913]   10487

Proceedings of the International (water) Boundary Commission, United States and Mexico. 1903.   4492

International Council for the Study of the Sea.

Atlas de température et salinité de l'eau de surface de la Mer du Nord. 1933.   7877

International Geological Congress. 11th, Stockholm, 1910.

Iron ore resources of the world. Atlas. [1910]   5479

International Geological Congress, 12th, Toronto, 1913.

Coal resources of the world. 1913.   4106b

International Joint Commission (U.S., and Canada) 1909–

Atlas to accompany Report ... re levels of Rainy Lake and other upper waters. 1930.   10478

Atlas to accompany Report to International Joint Commission relating to official reference re Lake of the Woods levels. 1915.   4487

Plates to accompany Report ... upon the improvement of the St. Lawrence River. [1922]   10334

International Magazine Company. *Marketing Division.*

Marketing atlas of the United States. [1931]   10552

Trading area system of sales control. [1929]   10551

International Railway Union.

Atlas complétant la carte des chemins de fer de l'Europe. 1932.   7752

International Road Federation.

Pan American Highway system. [1953]   10261

International standard atlas of the world. [1949]   7359

—— [1952]   7519

International standard encyclopedic world atlas and gazetteer. [1947]   7272

International Telecommunication Bureau, Bern.

Carte des stations côtières. 1935.   5850

—— 4e éd. 1938.   5806

—— 5. éd. 1948.   5807

—— 6. éd. 1952.   5808

International Telecommunication Union. *General Secretariat.*

Atlas des circuits internationaux d'Europe sous câble. 1953.   7774

International Telegraph Bureau, Bern.

Carte des stations radiotélégraphiques. 1929.   5803

—— 1932.   5804

Carte officielle des stations radiotélégraphiques. 1922–23.   5801

—— 1925–26.   5802

International Water Boundary Commission (U.S. and Canada) 1909–

See International Joint Commission (U.S. and Canada) 1909–

International Waterways Commission (U.S. and Canada)

International boundary between the United States and Dominion of Canada through the St. Lawrence River and Great Lakes. [1914]   10476

International's World reference atlas and gazetteer. [1942]   7105

Iowa. *Highway Commission.*

Complete State atlas of Iowa. 1938.   13010

—— 1939.   13011, 13012

—— 1941.   13013

General highway and transportation maps. [1952]   13014

[Official county road maps. 1933]   13009

[Topographic maps of seventy lakes. 1917]   13003

Iowa. *State Planning Board.*

Urban land use, Muscatine, Iowa. 1936.   14129

Iowa Publishing Company.
Atlas of Black Hawk County, Iowa. 1910.   3743
Atlas of Carroll County, Iowa. 1906.   1650
Atlas of Dubuque County, Iowa. 1906.   1659
Atlas of Grundy County, Iowa. 1911.   3747
Atlas of Linn County, Iowa. 1907.   1681
Atlas of Rock Island County, Ill. 1905.   1563
Atlas of Scott County, Iowa. 1905.   1694
Atlas of Washington County, Iowa. 1906.   1706

Ira, Rudolf, *and* **Klettner, Edgar.**
Atlas do Brasil. [1953]   18289
—— [1960]   18295

Iraq.
Maps of 'Iraq. 1929.   9764

Irby, William B.
Map of Mobile County [Ala. 1957]   11204

Irick, Simon Henry.
Clinton County, Ind., historical atlas.
[1966?]   12761

Irmédi–Molnár, László, 1895– *and* **Tolnay, Dezső.**
Ideiglenes földrajzi térképfüzet a közép–és
középfokú iskolák részére. [1946]   7238

Irving, Peyton.
See Newton, Lewis W., *and* Irving, Peyton.

Ishikawa, *Japan (Prefecture) Sōmubu. Kikaku Chōsashitsu.*
Ishikawa kensei zuhyō. [Graphic guide to
Ishikawa Prefecture. 1958]   9853

Ishirkov, Anastas, 1868– *and* **Zlatarski, V. N.**
Bulgaren in ihren historischen, ethnograph-
ischen und politischen Grenzen. 1917.   8237

Israel. *Defence Army.*
Atlas geografi-histori shel Erets-Yisrael.
[195–?]   9769

Israel. *Surveys Dept.*
Atlas Yisrael. [1956]   9771

Istanbul.
İstanbul şehri rehberi. 1934.   10080

Istituto Cartografico Italiano.
Guida toponomastica di Roma e suburbio.
[1951]   9016

Istituto Geografico Centrale.
Atlante di Milano. [1953]   9005
Atlante di Torino. [1952]   9019
Guida toponomastica di Milano. [1954]   9006
Guida toponomastica di Torino. [1952]   9020

Istituto Geografico De Agostini.
Atlante automobilistico tascabile. Europa
Centrale. [1928]   7760
—— Italia. [1926]   8968
Atlante della guerra mondiale. 1918.   4229, 5829
Alante della nostra guerra. 1916.   4228
Atlante geografico muto. [1911]   5747
Atlante geografico muto fisico–politico a
colori. v. 1. [1950]   5748
Atlante illustrato delle regioni d'Italia. [1932] 8987
Atlas de geografia moderna. [1952]   7520
Atlas der Kath. Weltmission. 2. Aufl. [1933] 5412
Calandario-atlante de Agostini. [1914]   4413
—— [1915]   4420
—— [1916]   4428
Europa etnico-linguistica. Atlante. 1916.   7659
Europe ethnique et linguistique. [1917]
5155, 5162a

Istituto Italiano d'Arti Grafiche.
Atlante filatelico. 3. ed. 1929.   5784
Atlante universale. 2v. 1927.   6657

Istituto Italo-Britannico.
See Istituto Geografico De Agostini.

Istituto Nazionale di Economia Agraria.
Carta dei tipi d'impressa nell'agricoltura italiana. 1958.   8936

Italatlas Touring.
Atlas. Guida atlante delle strade d'Italia.
[1956?]   8976

Italgeo.
Atlante turistico d'Italia. [1948]   8974

Italy. *Azienda di Stato per i Servizi Telefonici.*
Sintesi su alcuni servizi di telecomunicazioni.
[1953]   8980

Italy. *Commissione per Studiare e Proporre i Mezzi di Rendere le Piene del Tevere Innocue alla Città di Roma.*
Atti della Commissione . . . (Atlante) [1872] 9024

Italy. *Direzione Generale della Statistica.*
Carte topografiche, idrografiche e geologiche
annesse alle monografia statistica della città
di Roma. 1883.   3070

Italy. *Ente Nazionale per le Industrie Turistiche.*
Pianta di Roma. [1932]   9014

Italy. *Istituto Centrale di Statistica.*
Atlante dei comuni d'Italia. 1951.   8935
Atlante statistico italiano. 1929–33.   8964

Italy. *Istituto Geografico Militare.*
Atlante dei tipi geografico. 1922.   8962
—— 2a ed. 1948.   8963
Carta corografica del Regno d'Italia. [1922] 8984
—— [1925]   8986
Carta topografica . . . dell'Isola di Rodi. [1925] 8905

Carte del teatro di guerra Italo-Austriaco.
[1917]   8983

Italy. *Istituto Topografico Militare.*
Carte delle Province Napolitane.   [1874]   5264

Italy. *Magistrato alle Acque. Ufficio Idrografico.*
Atlante. [Venezia. 1934]   8997
[Carte delle provincie meridionali.   1876–84]   5262
Vedute delle coste d'Italia. 1884.   4040
—— 1897.   5255
Vedute di costa dell'Isola di Sardegna.   1882. 4044
—— 1882–86.   9022

Italy. *Ministero dei Lavori Pubblici.*
Album dei porti I, II e III classe.   [1873]   3057

Italy. *Ministero dell'Africa Italiana. Ufficio Studi e Propaganda.*
Atlante meteorologico della Libia.   1930.   10147

Italy. *Ministero della Guerra.*
Genio nella campagna d'Ancona e della bassa Italia. Atlante. [1864]   5256

Italy. *Ministero della Marina.*
Portolano della Liguria. 1855.   3066, 5263
Portolano della Sardegna. [1842]   3071

Italy. *Servizio Idrografico. Sezione di Napoli.*
Carta delle irrigazioni nella Campania. 1941.   8992

Italy. *Servizio Idrografico. Sezione di Palermo.*
Carta delle irrigazioni Siciliane. 1940.   9023

Italy. *Ufficio Tecnico del Corpo di Stato Maggiore.*
Quadro d'Unione della carta della Sicilia.
1872.   5265

Ivanhoe, L. F.
Alaska geology maps. [1959]   11231

Ivison, Blakeman, Taylor and Company.
Descriptive atlas of the United States. 1884.   11042
Handy atlas of the world. 1884.   4360
—— [1884]   917
Standard classic atlas. [1885]   20

Jaberg, Karl, 1887–1958, and Jud, Jakob, 1882–
Sprach- und Sachatlas Italiens und der Süd-schweiz. 1928–40.   8961

Jackson, John Gordon.
See Eastman, Harlan John, 1894–   *and* Jackson, John Gordon.

Jackson, W. M.
Atlas manual del mundo Jackson. 1952.   7521
Gran atlas universal Jackson. [1948]   7307

Jackson County, *Missouri. Highway Dept.*
Road district maps. [1949]   15233

Jackson Map Company.
Twentieth century plat book of Grayson County, Tex. 1908.   3922, 3582

Jacobs, J. L., and Company.
Unit value land maps for assessment districts in Jackson County, Mo. 1940.   15232

Jacobsen, Birger.
Kartskitser for geografiundervisningen.
[1904]   5749
Landomrids for karttegningen i middelskolen.
[1904]   5750

Jacobsz, Theunis, *or* Anthonie, *called* Loots-man, 1607 or 8–1650.
Fifth part of the New great sea-mirrour.
1717.   3648
Grand & nouveau miroir ou Flambeau de la mer. 1680.   7726
Lighting colom of the Midland-Sea. 1692.   194
Lightningh columne. 1692.   510, 2834
Nieuw groot straets-boeck, inhoudende d'Middellantse Zee. 1648.   3341
Nieuwe groote geoctroyeerde verbeterde en vermeerderde Loots-man zee-spiegel.
1707.   3467

Jacobsz, Theunis, *or* Anthonie, *called* Loots-man, Doncker, Hendrik, 1626–1699, and Goos, Hendrik.
Lightning colume. 1689–[92]   504, 2832

Jacquemart, Alfred, *i.e.*, Eugène Alfred, 1836–
See Mager, Henri, 1859–   *and* Jacque-mart, Alfred, *i.e.*, Eugene Alfred, 1836–

Jäger, Johann Wilhelm Abraham, 1718–1790.
Grand atlas d'Allemagne. 1789.   8682

Jaeger, Julius, 1848–
Atlas van het Koningrijk der Nederlanden.
[1883]   3085

Jaeggli, Alfredo L., *and* Bordón, F. Arturo.
Cartografía explicada de la Guerra contra la Triple Alianza. [1961]   18369

Jaillot, Alexis Hubert, *ca.* 1632–1712.
Atlas françois. 1695.   520
—— 1695–[96]   519
—— 2 v. 1695–[97]   5953
—— 2 v. 1695–1701 [*i.e.*, 1702]   5954
—— 1700–[24]   534

James, George Wharton, 1858–1923, and others.
Atlas of the world. [1922]   6488
New pictorial atlas of the world. [1919]   6396
—— [1920]   6414
—— [1924]   6553
—— [1925]   6586

Jancsó, Benedek, 1854–1930.
   Quelques réflexions critiques sur ... "La Terre
   Roumaine à travers les âges." 1920.   9205

Janiszewski, Michał.
   Geograficzny atlas Polski. 1952.   9177
   ——   1954.   9180
   ——   1955.   9181
   ——   1956.   9182
   ——   1957.   9183

Janson, William.
   Atlas of Richland County, Mont. 1917.   4876
   Atlas of Roosevelt and Sheridan Counties,
   Mont. 1919.   15318
   [McKenzie County, N.Dak. In township
   form. 1916]   4969

Jansson, Jan, 1588–1664.
   Atlantis majoris. Editio secunda. v. 5. 1657.   465
   Atlas contractus. 2 v. 1666.   475
   Atlas minor. 1651.   3426
   [Atlas of the world. 1663]   5946
   Guerre d'Italie. 1702.   3060
   Illustriorum Hispaniae urbium tabulae.
   [1652?]   3294
   Illvstriorvm principumque urbium septen-
   trionalium Europae tabulae. [1657?]   5153
   Nieuwen atlantis aenhang. v. 3. 1644.   4258
   Nieuwen atlas, ofte Werelt beschryvinge. 3 v.
   1642–44.   5937
   ——   5 v. 1652–53.   3427
   ——   6 v. 1657–[87]   5945
   Novus atlas. v. 4. 1646.   2894
   ——   4 v. 1646–49.   459
   ——   v. 1–2, 5–6. 1657–58.   5944
   Nuevo atlas. 4v. 1653.   463
   Tooneel der vermaarste koop-steden en han-
   del-plaatsen van de geheele wereld. 2 v.
   1682.   5389
   See also Hondius, Henricus, 1587–1638, *and*
   Jansson, Jan, 1588–1664.

Jantzen, Walther, 1904–
   Indien und der Indische Ozean. [1943]   9704
   Vereinigte Staaten von Amerika. [1941]   10711
   Verrat an Europa. [1943]   7684

Japan.
   Political maps of China. [1931?]   9520

Japan. *Autonomy Agency.*
   See Japan. *Jichichō.*

Japan. *Bureau of Education.*
   [Census atlas of Japan. 1902]   3207

Japan. *Daiichi Fukuinshō. Shiryōka.*
   Zenkoku shuyō toshi sensai gaikyō zu. [Gen-
   eral maps showing war damage in the principal cities. 1945]   9777

Japan. *Hydrographic Dept.*
   See Japan. *Suirobu.*

Japan. *Jichichō.*
   Shūgiin giin senkyoku gazu. [Atlas of election
   districts for members of the House of Re-
   presentatives. 1956]   9773

Japan. *Ministry of Agriculture and Forestry. Agricultural Administration Bureau.*
   See Japan. *Nōrinshō. Nōgyō Kairyōkyoku.*

Japan. *Ministry of Education.*
   See Japan. *Mombushō.*

Japan. *Mombushō.*
   Jinjō shōgaku chirisho fuzu. [Atlas appendix
   to the textbook of geography for primary
   schools. 1938]   9814
   Kyōiku tōkeihyō zu. [Statistical atlas of edu-
   cation] 1903.   9791

Japan. *Nōrinshō. Nōgyō Kairyōkyoku.*
   Fushoku ganryō o arawasu zu. [Humus distribution map] 1952.   9776
   Keisōdo bumpu zu. [Light soil distribution
   map] 1953.   9802

Japan. *Suirobu.*
   Gyogu teichi kasho ichiran zu. [Synoptic atlas
   of fishing gear locations. 1940]   9795
   Nihon kinkai kairyū zu. [Charts of ocean currents in seas adjacent to Japan. 1935]   9792
   Nihon kinkai kishōzu. [Meteorological charts
   of seas adjacent to Japan. 1913]   9785
   ——   [1935]   9786
   Shina hōmen no jōsō fūzu. Shōwa 15-nen 3-
   gatsu. [Upper strata wind direction charts
   for Chinese regions. March 1940. 1940]   9507

Japan. *Teishinshō.*
   Kaisei yūbin senro zu. [Revised atlas of post
   routes. 1909]   9799
   ——   [1930]   9800

Japan. *Un'yushō. Kankōkyoku.*
   Nihon kankō chizu. [Tourist atlas of Japan.
   1948]   9819
   ——   [Rev. ed. 1950]   9825

Jażdżewski, Konrad.
   Atlas to the prehistory of the Slavs. 1949.   7660

Jefferson County, *Wis.*
   Atlas and plat book of Jefferson County, Wis.
   [1941]   17785

Jefferys, Thomas, 1695–1771.
   American atlas. 1775.   1165
   Atlas des Indes Occidentales. French ed.
   1777.   3943
   Complete pilot for the West Indies. [1794–
   95]   3944
   ——   1801.   18157

Description of the maritime parts of France.
1761. 8424
—— 2d ed. 1774. 4021
Description of the Spanish islands and settlements on the coast of the West Indies.
1762. 3941
General topography of North America and
the West Indies. 1768. 1196, 2697
Laurie & Whittle's Complete pilot for the
West Indies. [1794]–1805. 3945
Neptune occidental. A small pilot for the
West-Indies. 1778. 18155
West-India atlas. 1775. 2699
—— 1780–[81] 18156
—— 1783–[87] 2701
—— 1794. 2702
—— 1794–[96] 2703
—— 1807. 3947
—— 1818. 2708
West India Islands. 1775–[78] 3942
—— New ed. 1795. 5126
—— 1796–[97] 3946
—— 1810. 2705

**Jefferys, Thomas, _and_ Kitchin, Thomas, 1718–
1784.**
Small English atlas. [1806?] 8123

Jefferys, Thomas, _and others_.
American atlas. 1776. 1166
—— 1778. 3659a
—— 1782. 1169

Jefford, Edward.
See Bartholomew, John George, 1860–1920,
and Jefford, Edward.

Jeheber, J. H.
Atlas de poche universel. [1910?] 4381
—— [1920] 6415

Jenks, William, 1778–1866.
Explanatory Bible atlas. 1847. 84a
—— 4th ed. 1849. 85

Jenner, Thomas, _fl._ 1631–1656.
New booke of mapps exactly describing
Evrope. [1645?] 3983

Jensen, Jaan, 1904–
Eesti ajaloo atlas. 1933. 8362

Jeppesen and Company.
Air maps of United Air Lines, main line airway. [1949] 10467
—— [1951] 10468
Your air maps of United Air Lines, main line
airway. [1954] 10469

Jesus, Domingo D. de.
Map directory, suburbs of Manila. [1955] 10070

Jewett, Clarence Frederick, 1852–1909.
See Walker, G. Hiram, _and_ Jewett, Clarence
Frederick, 1852–1909.

Jimbunsha.
New style saishin Nihon bunken chizu. [New
prefectural atlas of Japan. 195–] 9822
Nihon bunken chizu chimei sōran narabini
kōkyō shisetsu benran. [Prefectural atlas of
Japan with gazetteer and handbook of public institutions. 1959 ed. 1958] 9844
—— [1960 ed. 1959] 9846
Nihon toshi chizu zenshū. [Atlas of all cities
in Japan] [1957–59] 9778
Saikin chōsa Tōkyō-to kubun jitsuyō hakuchizu. [Ward atlas of Tokyo in monochrome
maps based on the latest surveys. 1954] 9979
Saikin chōsa zenkoku kembetsu jitsuyō hakuchizu. [Prefectural atlas in monochrome
maps based on the latest surveys. 1954] 9832
Tōkyō-to kubetsu chizu taikan. [Tokyo ward
atlas. 1955] 9982
—— [1956] 9984
—— [1958] 9988
—— 1959. 9996

Joanne, Adolphe Laurent, 1813–1881.
Atlas de la défense nationale cartes des dix-
sept départements envahis ou menacés par
l'ennemi. 1870. 2969
Atlas de la France. 1873. 3005
Géographie, histoire, statistique et archéologie
... de la France. 1882. 3004

**Jode, Gerard de, 1515–1591, _and_ Jode, Cornelis de,
1568–1600.**
Specvlvm orbis terrae. [1593–1613] 398, 399
Specvlvm orbis terrarvm. [1578] 383

Joerns Brothers.
Illustrated historical atlas of Sheboygan
County, Wis. 1902. 2663

Johnson, Albert G.
East Side Oil Field, San Joaquin Valley,
Bakersfield and vicinity. 1928. 11631

Johnson, Alvin Jewett, 1827–1884.
New illustrated ... family atlas. 1860. 6140
—— 1862. 837, 4343
—— 1863. 840
—— 1864. 843
—— 1865. 4345
—— 1866. 4346
—— 1868. 4349
—— 1870. 858
—— 1883. 913
New illustrated family atlas of the world.
1869. 6162
—— 1885. 6224

Johnson, A. J., and Company.
New general cyclopaedia and ... hand-atlas. 1885. 926
New illustrated family atlas. 1884. 918

Johnson, Berkley E.
Atlas of St. Louis County ... Mo. 1893. 15246

Johnson, Fred F.
Graphic street guide of Greater Akron [Ohio. 1961] 16478
Graphic street guide of Greater Battle Creek [Mich. 1958] 14843
Graphic street guide of Greater Canton and Massillon [Ohio. 1965] 16483
Graphic street guide of Greater Cincinnati [Ohio. 1963] 16494
—— [1964] 16495
Graphic street guide of Greater Columbus [Ohio. 1961] 16524
—— [1963] 16525
—— [1964] 16526
Graphic street guide of Greater Dayton [Ohio. 1956] 16533
—— [1957] 16536
—— [1960] 16537
—— [1961] 16538
Graphic street guide of Greater Grand Rapids ... [Mich. 1957] 14876
Graphic street guide of Greater Kalamazoo [Mich, 1958] 14885
Graphic street guide of Greater Muskegon ... [Mich. 1960] 14894
Graphic street guide of Greater Pontiac ... [Mich. 1958] 14897
Graphic street guide of Greater Saginaw ... [Mich. 1958] 14903
Graphic street guide of Greater Toledo [Ohio. 1961] 16570
—— [1964] 16571
Graphic street guide of Greater Youngstown [Ohio. 1960] 16577
—— [1964] 16578
Suburban Detroit—North; graphic street guide. [1961] 14864

Johnson, Fred F., Company.
Graphic street guide of Greater Dayton [Ohio. 1964] 16539
—— [1965] 16540
Graphic street guide of Greater Flint ... [Mich. 1960] 14869
—— [1963] 14870
Graphic street guide of Greater Fort Wayne [Ind.] 1966. 12966
Graphic street guide of Greater Grand Rapids ... [Mich. 1960] 14877
—— [1961] 14878
—— [1965] 14880
Graphic street guide of Greater Kalamazoo [Mich. 1964] 14887
Graphic street guide of Greater Louisville [Ky.] 1966. 14256

Graphic street guide of Greater Pontiac ... [Mich. 1961] 14898
—— [1965] 14899
Indianapolis—Marion County [Ind. 1966] 12984

Johnson, Humphrey Cyril, 1905–
Gem hunters atlas, California-Nevada. 1959. 11329
Gem hunters atlas; Southwest. 1958. 10582
Western gem hunters atlas. 1962. 10583
—— 1964. 10584

Johnson, Joe C., Map Company.
Plat book of Fayette County, Iowa. 1947. 13377
Plat book of Humboldt County, Iowa. 1941. 13510
Plat book of Winneshiek County, Iowa. 1940. 14068
—— 1948. 14069
Plat book of Wright County, Iowa. 1943. 14098

Johnson, Oney A.
South Lake Tahoe book of maps. [1964] 11633
Sunland real estate [Calif.] 1967. 11493

Johnson, Robert Neil.
California-Nevada ghost town atlas. 1967. 11333

Johnson, Stanley Currie, 1878–
News readers' war atlas. [1942] 7106
Penguin political atlas. [1940] 5672

Johnson, William, 1571–1638.
See Blaeu, Willem Janszoon.

Johnson, William Evans, 1892–
Earth; an elementary treatment of the earth's surface. 1938. 6951

Johnston, Alexander Keith, 1804–1871.
Atlas to Alison's History of Europe. 1848. 7685
—— 1850. 7686
Half-crown atlas of British history. [1871] 5192
Half-crown atlas of physical geography. [1870] 230
Handy royal atlas of modern geography. 1868. 853
—— 1913. 6358
—— 1921. 6447
—— 1924. 6554
—— 1927. 6658
—— 1943. 7147
Index geographicus. [1864] 842
National atlas. 1844. 4323
—— 1846. 4325
—— [1849] 6108
—— 1850. 799
—— [1854] 4335
—— 1855. 6117
Physical atlas. 1848. 4172a
—— Blackwood ed. 1848. 4173
—— 1849. 225, 226
Physical atlas of natural phenomena. 1850. 227
—— New ed. 1856. 229
Royal atlas of modern geography. 1861. 835

Portable atlas ... of Waterloo and Ligny.
1851. 7722
Traité des grandes opérations militaires ... de
la Revolution. Atlas. [1811–16] 7700
[Traité des grandes opérations militaires ... de
Frédéric le Grand. Atlas. 4. éd. 1851] 7701
Treatise on grand military operations. Atlas.
1865. 7702

Jonasson, Olof Georg, 1894– *and others*.
Agricultural atlas of Sweden. 1938. 9349
Jordbruksatlas över Sverige. 1937. 9350
—— 2. uppl. 1952. 9351

Jondet, Gaston.
Atlas historique ... d'Alexandrie. [1921] 10132

Jones, A. W.
Popular atlas. [1892] 972

Jones, C. G.
See Hooks, W. N., *and* Jones, C. G.

Jones, Charles Henry, 1837–1911, *and* Hamilton, Theodore F.
Historical atlas of the world illustrated.
1875. 4136
—— 1876. 115
Peoples' pictorial atlas. 1873. 869

Jones, Clarence Fielden, 1893–
Manual to accompany American history and
its geographic conditions. [1933] 10626

Jones, David Tracy, 1900–
Lake Bonneville maps. 1940. 17309

Jones, G. H., and Company.
Atlas of Philadelphia. 1874–75. 2522

Jones, James Idwal, 1900–
Atlas of Wales. [1957] 8222

Jones, Laurence G.
Ogle County [Ill.] farm atlas & business guide.
1942. 12434

Jones, T. W.
See Moore, S. S., *and* Jones, T. W.

Jones, Theodore Francis, 1885–
Land ownership in Brookline [Mass.] from the
first settlement. 1923. 14449

Jones Parra, Juan.
Atlas de bolsillo de Venezuela. 5. ed. 1951. 18426
—— 6. ed. 1952. 18427
—— 8. ed. 1954. 18428
—— 9. ed. 1957. 18430
Pocket atlas of Venezuela. 1st English ed.
1957. 18431

Jong, Dirk de, *fl.* 1779–1805.
Atlas van alle de zee havens der Bataafsche
Republiek. 1802. 4047

Jongh, G. J. J. de.
Route–atlas van de Rotterdamsche Lloyd.
2e druk. 1925. 5691

Jongh, J. W. de.
Toelichting bij de Twaalf historische wand-
kaarten der vaderlandsche geschiedenis.
1909. 9044

Jonghe, Clemendt de, 1624–1677.
Tabula atlantis. [1675?] 3437

Joppen, Charles, 1878–
Historical atlas of India. 1907. 3199
—— 1910. 4071
—— 1914. 5299

Jordan, Emil Leopold, 1900–
Hammond's Sports atlas of America. 1956. 10299

Jordan, Hans.
Heimat-Atlas Regierungsbezirk Oberbayern.
[1951] 8730

Jouanny, L. A.
Atlas del Perú. 1867. 2770

Joüon, René.
Géographie de la Chine. [3e éd.] 1932. 9563

Jourdan, Emilio Carlos, 1835–
Atlas historico de guerra do Paraguay.
1871. 2766

Journal de Genève.
Atlas du Congrès. 1919. 7802

Journal of Commerce and Commercial Bulletin.
Atlas of the electric light and power properties
of the public utility companies in the United
States. 1936. 10573

Jud, Jakob, 1882–
See Jaberg, Karl, 1877– *and* Jud, Jakob,
1882–

Juehne, Charles.
West end district of the city of St. Louis.
1899. 15273

Jürgens, Oskar, *d.* 1923.
Spanische Städte. 1926. 9304

Juko Shiga.
[Atlas of Japan. 1902] 3208

Julien, Roch Joseph, *fl.* 1750–1780.
Atlas géographique et militaire de la France.
1751. 2972
Atlas topographique et militaire qui comprend

le Royaume de Bohême . . . et du théatre de
la guerre présenté en Allemagne. 1758.   3029
— Nouv. éd. 1760.   8578
Nouveau théâtre de guerre ou atlas topo-
graphique et militaire qui comprend le
Royaume de Bohême. 1758.   3030
Théâtre du monde. 1768.   641

Junié, Jean, 1756–
See Rittmann,——*and* Junié, Jean, 1756–

Jurczyński, Juljusz.
See Romer, Eugeniusz, 1871–1954, *and*
Jurczyński, Juljusz.

Jurva, Risto, 1888–
Atlas der Eisverhältnisse des Baltischen
Meeres. 1937.   7831

Justus Perthes' Alldeutscher Atlas. 3. Aufl. 1905.   8690

Justus Perthes Atlas antiquus. [192–?]   5619

Justus Perthes Atlas portatil de España y Portugal.
2. ed. 1936.   9331
— 3. ed. 1938.   9333

Justus Perthes Atlas portatil de Espanha e Portugal.
2. ed. 1936.   9332

Justus Perthes' Kleinster Schulatlas. 1925.   6583

Justus Perthes' Staatsbürger-Atlas. 2. Aufl.
1896.   8688
— 4. Aufl. 1904.   8689

Juta's Large print atlas for South Africa. 17th ed.
1949.   7365

**Juta's Modern teaching atlas for South African
schools.** 2d ed. [1948]   7309

Jūtaku Chizu Kyōkai.
Takaishi-chō annaizu. [Takaishi real estate
maps. 1957]   9964

Jūtaku Kyōkai.
Aichi-ken Narumi-chō zenjūtaku annai zuchō.
[Real estate atlas of Narumi, Aichi Prefec-
ture. New ed. 1957]   9932
Aichi-ken Nishibiwajima-chō zenjūtaku annai
zuchō. [Real estate atlas of Nishibiwajima,
Aichi Prefecture. New ed. 1957]   9935
Gifu-shi zenshōkō jūtaku annai zuchō. [Gifu
real estate atlas. New ed. 1958]   9867
Ichinomiya-shi zenjūtaku annai zuchō. [Ichi-
nomiya real estate atlas. New ed. 1958]   9879
Ikeda-shi zenjūtaku annai zuchō. [Real estate
atlas of Ikeda. New ed. 1957]   9881
Itami-shi zenjūtaku annai zuchō. [Real estate
atlas of Itami. New ed. 1957]   9883
Kariya-shi zenjūtaku annai zuchō. [Real estate
atlas of Kariya. New ed. 1957]   9890

Kasugai-shi zenjūtaku shōkō annai zuchō.
[Kasugai real estate atlas. New ed. 1958]   9892
Kawanishi-shi zenjūtaku annai zuchō. [Real
estate atlas of Kawanishi. New ed. 1957]   9896
Kōbe-shi zenjūtaku annai zuchō. [Real estate
atlas of Kobe. New ed. 1957]   9902
Minoo-shi zenjūtaku annai zuchō. [Real estate
atlas of Minoo. New ed. 1957]   9915
Moriyama-shi zenjūtaku annai zuchō. [Real
estate atlas of Moriyama. New ed. 1957]   9919
Ōtsu-shi shigai jūtaku annai zuchō. [Real
estate atlas of Otsu. New ed. 1957]   9951
Seto-shi zenjūtaku annai zuchō. [Real estate
atlas of Seto. New ed. 1957]   9957
Suita-shi zenjūtaku annai zuchō. [Real estate
atlas of Suita. New ed. 1957]   9961
Takarazuka-shi zenjūtaku annai zuchō. [Real
estate atlas of Takarazuka. New ed. 1957]   9966
Tōkyo-tō shimbu zenjūtaku annai zuchō.
[Real estate atlas of the heart of Tokyo.
1956]   9985
Tōkyō-to zenjūtaku annai zuchō. [Real estate
atlas of Metropolitan Tokyo. 1957]   9987
— [1958–59]   9994, 9995
Toyohashi-shi zenjūtaku annai zuchō. [Toyo-
hashi real estate atlas. New ed. 1958]   10004
Toyonaka-shi zenjūtaku annai zuchō. [Real
estate atlas of Toyonaka. 1957]   10006
Tsushima-shi zenjūtaku annai zuchō. [Real
estate atlas of Tsushima. 1957]   10011
Yokkaichi-shi shigai jūtaku annai zuchō.
[Real estate atlas of Yokkaichi. 1957]   10020

Jūtaku Kyōkai. *Kyōto Shisho.*
Kyōto-shi zenjūtaku annai zuchō. [Real estate
atlas of Kyoto. New ed. 1956–57]   9909

Jūtaku Kyōkai. *Nagoya Eigyōsho.*
Nagoya-shi zenjūtaku annai zuchō. [Atlas of
all dwelling houses in Nagoya. 1955]   9925
— 1957.   9928
Nagoya-shi zenjūtaku shōkō annai zuchō.
[Atlas of all dwelling houses and commercial building in Nagoya] 1958–59.   9930

Jūtaku Kyōkai. *Ōsaka Eigyōsho.*
Daitō-shi jūtaku annaizu. [Daito real estate
atlas. 1957?]   9863
Hirakata-shi zenjūtaku annai zuchō. [Hirakata
real estate atlas. 1957?]   9873, 9874
Kawachi-shi zenjūtaku annai zuchō. [Kawachi
real estate atlas. 1957?]   9894
Matsubara-shi zenjūtaku annai zuchō. [Mat-
subara real estate atlas. 1957?]   9912
Moriguchi-shi (Niwakubo) oyobi Kadoma-
chō zenjūtaku annai zuchō. [Moriguchi
(formerly Niwakubo) and Kadoma real
estate atlas. 1957?]   9918
Mukō-machi, Kuze-mura zenjūtaku annai
zuchō. [Muko and Kuze real estate atlas.
1958?]   9920
Nagaoka-chō, Oyamazaki-machi zenjūtaku
annai zuchō. [Nagaoka and Oyamazaki
real estate atlas. 1958?]   9923

Neyagawa-shi zenjūtaku annai zuchō.
[Neyagawa real estate atlas. 1957?]   9933
Ōsaka-shi zenjūtaku annai zuchō. [Real estate
atlas of Osaka. New ed. 1956]   9944
—— [New rev. ed. 1957]   9947
Ōsaka-shi zenshōkō jūtaku annai zuchō.
[Real estate atlas of Osaka. 1958–59]   9950
Uji-shi zenjūtaku annai zuchō. [Uji real estate
atlas. 1957]   10013
Yao-shi zenjūtaku annai zuchō. [Yao real
estate atlas. 1957?]   10018

Jūtaku Kyōkai. *Tōkyō Shisho.*
Tōkyō-to zenjūtaku annai zuchō. [Real estate
atlas of Metropolitan Tokyo. New ed.
1958]   9989

Jūtaku Shōsai Annaizu Kankōkai.
Beppu-shi jūtaku annaizu. [Atlas of dwelling
houses in Beppu. 1956]   9862
Hiroshima-shi jūtaku annaizu. Hiroshima
[real estate atlas. 1956]   9876
Kokura-shi jūtaku annaizu. [Atlas of dwelling
houses in Kokura. 1956]   9904
Kumamoto-shi jūtaku annaizu. [Atlas of
dwelling houses in Kumamoto. 2d rev. ed.
1957]   9906
Moji-shi jūtaku annaizu. [Atlas of dwelling
houses in Moji. Rev. ed. 1956]   9917
Ōita-shi jūtaku annaizu. [Atlas of dwelling
houses in Oita. 1956]   9939
Wakamatsu-, Tobata-shi jūtaku annaizu.
[Atlas of dwelling houses in Wakamatsu
and Tobata. 2d rev. ed. 1957]   10014
Yahata-shi jūtaku annaizu. [Atlas of dwelling
houses in Yahata. 2d rev. ed. 1957]   10016

Jūtakuzu Kankō Kyōkai.
Matsue-shi jūtaku annaizu (Furue o fukuma).
[Matsue (including Furue) real estate atlas.
1958]   9913
Wakayama-shi jūtaku annaizu. [Wakayama
real estate atlas. 1958]   10015

Jutikkala, Eino Kaarlo Ilmari, 1907–
Suomen historian kartasto. Atlas of Finnish
history. 1949.   8368

Kaarre, Reuben.
Alcona County [Mich.] plat book. 1967.   14592

Kagawa-ken Nōgyō Shikenjō, *Takamatsu, Japan.*
Nōgyō zusetsu. Agricurtural [sic] atlas of
Kagawa-ken. 1956.   9854

Kaisarov, Vladimir Dmitrievich, 1878–
Элементарный уиебный атлас для школ
первой ступени. [Elementary teaching
atlas for primary schools.] 2d ed. 1924.   6555a

Kallbrunner, Josef, 1881–
Österreichs Weg durch die Deutsche Geschichte, 799–1938. [1938]   8567

Kaltenborn, Hans von, 1878–
World wide war atlas. [1943]   7148

Kameníček, František, 1856–1930.
See Balcar, Antonín, 1847–1888, *and* Kameníček, František, 1856–1930.

Kampen, Albert van, 1842–1891.
Justus Perthes' Atlas antiquus. [1915?]   4094
—— [192–?]   5619
Orbis terrarum antiquus. 1884.   23
—— 2. ed. [1888]   5620

Kandul, Stanley.
Atlas map guide of Chicago. 1916.   4599

**Kandul's Tillotson pocket map and street guide of
Chicago and suburbs.** 1919.   12615
—— 1921.   12618
—— 1922.   12621
—— 1923.   12623
—— 1924.   12627
—— 1925.   12629
—— 1926.   12632
—— 1929.   12641

Kansas. *Industrial Development Commission.*
Kansas atlas. 1952.   14136
Kansas industrial resources; basic location
data. [1956]   14137

Kansas. *State Highway Commission.*
Highway & transportation map[s. 1942]   14142

Kansas. *State Highway Dept.*
24 hour annual average traffic flow map[s.
1936]   14141

Kansas Farmer Company.
Plat book, directory and survey of Shawnee
County, Kansas. 1913.   4699

Kapelusz y Cía.
América y mi patria. [1947]   18051
Atlas América Central y Antillas. [194–?]   18122
Atlas América y mi patria. [194–?]   18049
Atlas continente americano. [1941]   10272
Atlas elemental. [1941?]   18223
Atlas general y de Asia y Africa. [1946]   7239
Atlas Humboldt: América del Norte, del Sur,
Central y Antillana. 2. ed. [1945]   10275
—— [10. ed. 1959]   10277
—— [10. ed. 1964]   10279
Atlas Mercator. [1941]   7057
Atlas, mi provincia y mi patria. [194–]   18221
Atlas mundi. 3. ed. [1946]   7240
Atlas orbe. [194–]   6996
Atlas Reclus, Europa y Oceanía. [1940]   7808
—— [1946]   7810
Mí patria; mapas físico y político. [194–]   18050
Mi patria [Venezuela. 1946]   18424

Karl, *Archduke of Austria,* **1771–1847.**
[Principes de la stratégie, développés par la

relation de la campagne de 1796 en Allemagne. 1818]   7714

Karn, Edwin D.
See Sale, Randall D., *and* Karn, Edwin D.

Karpinski, Louis Charles, 1878–1956.
Historical atlas of the Great Lakes and Michigan. 1931.   10332

Kartográfiai Vállalat.
Magyarországi autóutak térképe. [1955]   8919
—— [2. jav. kiad.] 1956.   8920

Kartographisches Institut und Verlag Hans König.
CALTEX Städte– und Reiseatlas der Bundesrepublik Deutschland. [1. Aufl. 1958]   8529

Kator över Stockholm. 18. årg. 1946–47.   9410
—— 19. årg. 1948–49.   9411
—— 20. årg. 1950–51.   9412
—— 21. årg. 1952–53.   9414
—— 22. årg. 1954–55.   9417
—— 23. årg. 1956–57.   9418

**Karty kontsessionnykh ob'ektov SSSR. [Maps of
(foreign) concessions in the USSR.]** 1926.   9216

Kauffman, William J., *and* Kauffman, Orrin F.
Atlas of Stark County, Ohio. 1896.   2416

Kaufmann, Charles D.
Street atlas of Philadelphia. 1895.   2538

Kaupert, Johann August, 1822–1899.
See Curtius, Ernst, 1814–1896, *and* Kaupert,
Johann August, 1822–1899.

Kaushal, Biba Singh.
Coloured states atlas of India. 1958.   9707

Kausler, Franz Georg Friedrich von, 1794–1848.
Atlas des plus memorables batailles. 1831–
[37]   349

Kawada, S.
See Shigeno, Y., *and* Kawada, S.

Kay, Russell.
Atlas of Florida. [1926]   11799

Keere, Pieter van den, 1583–1646.
Germanie Inférievre. 1621.   4048
Germanie Inferior. 1622.   3075

Keil, Wilhelm, *b.* 1838.
Berliner Elementar–Atlas. [1884]   6218

Keil, Wilhelm, *and* Riecke, Friedrich.
Deutscher Schul–Atlas. 50. Aufl. 1903.   6308
—— 55. Aufl. [1920]   6416

Keizai Chizu Sha, *Yokohama*.
Kawasaki-shi meisai chizu. [Detailed atlas of
Kawasaki. 1958]   9897
Yokohama-shi keizai chizu. [Economic maps
of Yokohama. 1956–59]   10024

Keller, Christoph, 1638–1707.
Geographia antiqua. 1774.   24
—— New ed. 1799.   25
See also Cellarius, Christoph, 1638–1707.

Keller and Fuller.
Illustrated atlas of Posey County, Ind. 1900.   1622

Kellogg, W. K., Foundation.
Allegan County [Mich.] 1942.   14596
Calhoun County [Mich.] Basic county map.
1942.   14628
Eaton County [Mich.] Basic county map.
1942.   14648

Kelly, Cassius W., and others.
Atlas of New Haven, Conn. 1911.   3710

Kelly, Jerome Aemilian, 1910–
See Seraphin, Eugene William, 1898–
and Kelly, Jerome Aemilian, 1910–

Kemp, George Samuel Foster, 1878–
Atlas for China. [1934]   6818

Kemper, Walter Z.
Maps of Iberia Parish, La. 1921.   14273

Kendall, George Wilkins, 1809–1867.
War between the United States and Mexico
illustrated. 1851.   3686

Kenna, Thomas J.
Land map of the county of Kings, state of
New York. 1894.   2234

**Kentucky. *Agricultural and Industrial Development
Board.***
Economic atlas of Kentucky. 1952.   14229

Kentucky. *Dept. of Commerce.*
Kentucky's Ohio River industrial sites.
[1962]   14230

Kentucky. *Dept. of Highways.*
General highway county maps of Kentucky.
1950.   14231

Kentucky. *Dept, of Highways. Division of Planning.*
General highway county maps of Kentucky.
[1965]   14232
—— [1967]   14233

Kenya Colony and Protectorate. *Survey of Kenya.*
Atlas of Kenya. 1st ed. 1959.   10145a

Kenyon Company.
Atlas and plat book of Allen County, Kans. 1921. — 14145
Atlas and plat book of Barton County, Kans. 1916. — 4670
Atlas and plat book of Calhoun County, Iowa. 1920. — 13150
Atlas and plat book of Carroll County, Ind. 1919. — 12748
Atlas and plat book of Ford County, Kans. 1916. — 4678
Atlas and plat book of Hamilton County, Ind. 1922. — 12804
Atlas and plat book of Jones County, Iowa. [1921] — 13590
Atlas and plat book of Labette County, Kans. 1916. — 4684
Atlas and plat book of Lapeer County, Mich. 1921. — 14709
Atlas and plat book of Lenawee County, Mich. 1921. — 14715
Atlas and plat book of Mahaska County, Iowa. 1920. — 13685
Atlas and plat book of Merrick County, Nebr. 1921. — 15509
Atlas and plat book of Ripley County and part of Franklin County, Ind. 1921. — 12900
Atlas and plat book of Seward County, Nebr. 1921. — 15588
Atlas and plat book of Shawnee County, Kans. 1921. — 14202
Atlas and plat book of Sherman County, Nebr. 1920. — 15594
Atlas and plat book of Woodford County, Ill. 1920. — 12576
Atlas of Fulton County, Ill. 1916. — 12243
Atlas of Stearns County, Minn. 1912. 3816a, 15105
Atlas of the World War. [1918] — 4230
"Following the boys thru France." 1919. — 5830
Revised atlas of the world. [1921] — 5831
Revised atlas of the world and history of the World War. 1919. — 4230a

Kepulauan di seluruh Indonesia. [1952] — 9754

Kerhallet, Charles Marie Philippe de, 1809–1863.
Manuel de la navigation à la côte occidentale d'Afrique. 1852. — 3234
Manuel de la navigation dans la Mer des Antilles et dans le Golfe du Mexique. Vues de côtes. 1854. — 2710

Kermack, William Ramsay, 1886–
W. & A. K. Johnston's Commercial & economic atlas of the world. [1926] — 5442

Kern Trading and Oil Company.
Topographic atlas of the Sunset-Midland oil field, California. 1916. — 4542

Kerr, Donald Gordon Grady, 1913–
Historical atlas of Canada. [1960] — 10346
—— 2d ed. [1966] — 10347

Kessel, M. S. van.
Atlas van Suriname. 7. druk. [1960?] — 18398

Kessler, Otto.
"Adler"—Kriegskarten–Sammlung. [1914] — 5832

Keulen, Gerard van, *d.* 1726.
Groote nieuwe vermeerderde zee-atlas. [1720] — 5693

Keulen, Joannes van, 1654–1711.
Grand nouvel atlas de la mer. 169[6] — 3333
Great and newly enlarged sea atlas. 3 v. 1682–[86] — 5692
Groote nieuwe vermeerderde zee-atlas. 1695. — 3453
—— 1734. — 584
[Lichtende zeefakkel. 1681–96] — 3444
See also Marre, Jan de, 1696–1763, *and* Keulen, Joannes van.

Keussen, Hermann, 1862–1943.
Topographie der Stadt Köln im Mittelalter. 1910. — 8856

Key Maps.
Houston [Tex.] Key map. 1958. — 17261
—— 1959. — 17263
Official Houston [Tex.] Key map. 1960. — 17264
—— 1961. — 17265
—— 5th ed. [1962] — 17266
—— 6th ed. 1963. — 17267
—— 7th new ed. 1964. — 17269

Keyser, Erich, 1893–
Atlas der Ost- und Westpreussischen Landesgeschichte. 1936. — 8760

Khanzadian, Zadig, 1886–
Atlas de géographie économique de la Grèce. [19—] — 8897
Atlas de géographie économique de la Palestine. [1932] — 9766
Atlas de géographie économique de Syrie et du Liban. 1926. — 10073
Atlas de géographie economique de Turquie. 1924. — 10077

Kieffer, John Elmer, 1910–
Manual of political geography. 1951. — 5751
Studies in political geography. 2d ed. 1952. — 5752

Kiepert, Heinrich, 1818–1899.
Atlas antiquus. 6. Aufl. [1876] — 4095
—— 10th ed. 1891. — 5621
—— [12. Aufl. 1899] — 26, 5622
—— [12. Aufl. 1902] — 5623
—— 12 ed. impr. 1903. — 4096
—— [1908] — 5624
Cartes des nouvelles frontières entre la Serbie, la Roumanie, la Bulgarie, la Roumélie orientale et les provinces immédiates de la Turquie. 1881. — 5185
Compendiöser allgemeiner Atlas. 11 verb. Aufl. 1855. — 815

—— 1773.		3514
—— 1777.		4296
—— 1780.		653
—— 1782.		3521
—— 1782–[87]		3522
—— 1790.		4300
—— [1794]		6004
—— 1795.		3529
—— 1796.		6008
—— 1797.		687
—— 1801.		3533
—— 1804.		4305a
—— 1808.		6027
—— 1810–[16]		6029
Geographia Scotiȃe. 1756.		8204

[Miniature atlas of Scotland from the latest surveys. 1770?] 5215
New universal atlas. [1789]–96. 685

—— 1795.		682
—— 2d ed. 1798.		6012
—— 3d ed. 1799.		3531
—— 4th ed. 1800.		6015
—— 5th ed. 1801.		3534
—— 6th ed. 1802.		699
—— 7th ed. 1805.		709

See also Bowen, Emanuel, Kitchin, Thomas, *and others.*
—— Jefferys, Thomas, 1695?–1771, *and* Kitchin, Thomas, 1718–1784.

Kizaki, Jun'ichi.
Kembetsu shin Nihon chizu. [Prefectural atlas of new Japan. Rev. ed. 1948] 9820

Klaar, Adalbert.
Siedlungsformenkarte der Reichsgaue Wien, Kärnten ... 1942. 7897

Kläui, Paul, 1908– *and* Imhof, Eduard, 1895–
Atlas zur Geschichte des Kantons Zürich. [1951] 9457

Klett, Ernst.
Geographischer Weltatlas. 1953. 7570

Klettner, Edgar.
See Ira, Rudolf, *and* Klettner, Edgar.

Klinckowström, Axel Leonhard, *Friherre,* 1775–1837.
Atlas ... om de Förente Staterne. [1824] 1375

Klinge, Frank H. M.
Atlas of Montgomery County ... Md. 1931. 14355

—— 1941.		14356
—— 1948–49.		14357
—— 1959.		14358

Atlas of the Reading main line ... Montgomery Co. Penna. 1927. 16795
Atlas of the 35th ward, Philadelphia. 1927. 16870

Klint, Gustaf, 1771–1840.
Sveriges sjö atlas. [1832–45] 2854

Klokk, Knut.
Cappelens Atlas [for folkeskolen] 1951. 7459

Knapp, Charles, 1855–1921.
See Michel, Gaston, 1882–1940, *and* Knapp, Charles, 1855–1921.

Knapton, John, *d.* 1770, *and* Knapton, Paul, *d.* 1755.
Geographia classica. 8th ed. 1747. 29

Knaurs Welt–Atlas. [1928] 6677

—— 1936.		6877
—— 1938.		6952
—— 1939.		6978
—— 1951–52.		7460

Knight, Thomas Harold.
See Benians, Ernest Alfred, 1880–

Knoch, Karl, 1883–
[Niederschlag und Temperatur in Europa. 1956] 7647

Knoch, Karl, *and* Schulze, Alfred, 1912–
Niederschlag, Temperatur und Schwüle in Afrika. [1956] 10085

Knoxville, *Tenn. Office of the City Engineer.*
Official ward map of Knoxville, Tenn. [1947] 17101

Kobe, *Japan. Kensetsukyoku.*
Kōbe toshi keikaku zu. [City planning maps of Kobe] 1953. 9899

Kōbe Chigaku Kyōkai.
Zensangyō jūtaku annai zuchō. [Atlas of all commercial and industrial buildings and dwelling houses. 1956–57] 9901

Kōbe Tosho Kabushiki Kaisha, *Kobe.*
Chōmei, banchi iri, kubun Kōbe chizu. [Ward atlas of Kobe, street names and house numbers. 1958?] 9903

Koch, Christophe Guillaume, 1737–1813.
Maps and tables of chronology and genealogy. 1831. 2791

Koch, Lauge, 1892–1964.
Map of north Greenland. [1932] 10209

Koch, Wilhelm, 1823–1902.
Verkehrs-Atlas von Europa. 1906. 2783

Koch, Wilhelm, *and* Opitz, Carl Albert, 1847–1924.
Eisenbahn- und Verkehrs-Atlas von Europa. 11. Aufl. 1920. 7753
—— 12. Aufl. 1925. 7754
Eisenbahn- und Verkehrsatlas von Russland. [1900] 3115
—— 3. verb. Aufl. 1912. 5278

Koch and Shigley.
Atlas and directory of Buckeye Lake. 1911. 3869

Kochersperger, H. L., *and* Kochersperger, D. H.
People's illustrated and descriptive family
atlas. 1884. 919
—— [1886] 930

Kodama, Toshio.
Ōsaka chizeki chizu. [Cadastral atlas of Osaka.
1956–60] 9946

Köhler, Johann David, 1684–1755.
Atlas manualis. [1724?] 567, 568, 569
Bequemer Schul- und Reisen-Atlas. [1734?] 582
[Descriptio orbis antiqvi. 1720?] 30, 31

Köhlin, Harald.
See Bagrow, Leo, 1888–1957, *and* Köhlin,
Harald.

Köllner, August, 1812–1906.
Views of cities ... in the United States and
Canada. [1848–51] 1267

Koeman, Cornelis, 1918–
Tabvlae geographicae qvibvs Colonia Bonae
spei antiqva depingitvr ... Eighteenth-
century cartography of Cape Colony.
1952. 10167

Kogutowicz, Károly, 1886–1947.
Ethnographical map of Hungary. 1919. 8916
Hongrie. Cartes et notions géographiques,
historiques, ethnographiques. [1920] 8927

Kogutowicz, Manó, 1851–1908.
Teljes földrajzi és történelmi atlasza. 5. kiad.
1911. 6344

Kohl, Johann Georg, 1808–1878.
Die beiden ältesten General-Karten von
Amerika. 1860. 1135

Kohli, Sita Ram, *and* Gupta, Hari Ram.
Students' historical atlas of India. 1945. 9693

Kokusai Chigaku Kyōkai.
Hokkaidō shichōbetsu chizuchō. [Atlas of
Hokkaido by administrative districts.
1955] 10031
Saishin Hokkaidō shichōbetsu chizu. [Atlas of
Hokkaido by administrative districts.
1959] 10033

Kokusai Gakujtsu Hyōronsha.
Saikin chōsa Dai Nihon chimei Jiten narabini
kōtsū chizu taikan. [Gazetteer and comprehensive communications atlas of Japan
based on the latest surveys. 1933] 9811

Kolter, Fred E.
Real estate plat book of Adams County, Ind.
1950. 12735

Kompas.
Zakkompas van Nederland voor toerisme.
[1956?] 9074

Konferenz der Kantonalen Erziehungsdirektoren.
Atlante svizzero per le scuole medie. 9. ed.
1948. 7310
Atlas für schweizerische Mittelschulen. 2.
Aufl. 1911. 4209, 6345
—— 3. Aufl. 1915. 6377
Schweizerischer Mittelschul–Atlas. 7. Aufl.
1936. 6878
—— 9. Aufl. [1948] 7311

Kongelig Dansk Automobil Klub.
Automobilkort over Danmark. [1919] 8267
Byplaner og fortegnelse over hoteller, garager
og benzindepoter. 1925. 8260

Kongelig Norsk Automobilklub.
Kartbok for Norge. 1. utg. 1948. 9113
—— 2. utg. 1954. 9114

Koninklijke Nederlandsche Toeristenbond.
Atlas van Nederland. [1908] 9087
Vijftig plattegronden ... voor Nederland.
1917. 9034

Koops, Matthias.
Map of the River Rhine. 1797. 7879

Kopp, Jul.
Taschen-Weltatlas. [1908?] 1128

Korabinsky, Johann Matthias, 1740–1811.
Atlas Regni Hungariae portatilis. [1817] 8924

Korbe, Carl.
See Weber, Richard, *and* Korbe, Carl.

Korbel, Stanisław, *and* Sawicki, Ludomir.
Atlas geograficzny. 1922–25. 6511a

Korean Affairs Institute.
Map of Korea. 1945. 10048

Koren, Kristian Brinck, 1863–
Karter og topografiske tegninger vedkom-
mende Trondhjem og Trøndelagen. 1899. 5275

Korherr, Richard.
Volk und Raum; Atlaswerk. 1938. 8588

Kornrumpf, Martin.
Bayern Atlas. [1949] 8721

Kōseisha, Osaka.
Dōmyōji-chō zenjūtaku annai zuchō. [Dom-
yoji real estate atlas. 1958] 9864
Hikisho-chō zenjūtaku annai zuchō. [Hikisho
real estate atlas. 1958] 9871
Izumi-shi. [Izumi real estate atlas] 1957. 9884
Izumisano-shi zensangyō jūtaku annai zuchō.
[Izumi-sano real estate atlas. 1957–59] 9885

Kaizuka-shi zenjūtaku annai zuchō. [Kaizuka
real estate atlas. 1958]   9887

Kishiwada-shi jūtaku annai zuchō. [Kishiwada
real estate atlas. 1957–58]   9898

Minami-ōsaka-chō zenjūtaku annai zuchō.
[Minami-ōsaka real estate atlas. 1958]   9869

Sen'i seihin kouri bumpu zu. [Atlas showing
distribution of retail stores] 1957.   9948

Shinoda-mura [oyobi Yasaka-chō] Semboku-
gun. [Shinoda and Yasaka real estate atlas.
1958]   9960

Tadaoka-chō zenjūtaku annai zuchō. [Ta-
daoka real estate atlas. 1958]   9963

Takaishi-chō. [Takaishi real estate atlas.
1958]   9965

Tomioka-chō. [Tomioka real estate atlas.
1958]   10000

Tondabayashi-shi zenjūtaku annai zuchō.
[Tondabayashi real estate atlas] 1958.   10001

Yao-shi chisekizu. [Yao cadastral maps.
1957]   10019

Zensangyō jūtaku annai zuchō; Takasago-shi.
[Real estate atlas of Takasago. New ed.]
1958.   9967

Koselleck, A.
2000 Jahre Europäischer Geschichte. 1957.   7687

Kosminskiĭ, Evgeniĭ Alekseevich, 1886–
Атлас истории средних веков. [Historical
atlas of the Middle Ages.] 1951.   5655
—— 1953.   5656

Kotzebue, Otto von, 1787–1846.
Атласъ къ путешествию лейтенанта Коцебу.
[Atlas to the voyage of Lieutenant Kotze-
bue.] [1823]   5812

Kozenn, Blasius, 1821–1871.
Atlas. 50. Aufl. 1929.   6705
—— 71.–74. Aufl. [1945]   7212
Atlas geograficzny dla szkół średnich. Wyd.
6. 1926.   6618
Geographischer Atlas. [190–]   6291
Geographischer Atlas für Mittelschulen.
43. Aufl. [1926]   6619
Geographischer Schul–Atlas. 32. Aufl.
1888.   6241
Österreichischer Mittelschulatlas. 75. Aufl.
1951.   7461
—— 76. Aufl.   7522

Kozierowski, Stanisław, 1884–1949.
Atlas nazw geograficzynch słowiańszczyzny
zachodniej. 1935–37.   7806
—— [Wyd. 2] 1945.   7809

Krafft, A. J. C., and others.
Werkschrift voor middelbare scholen. 6.
druk. v. 3–4. [1949]   5753

Kraks Legat.
Kort over København og omegn. [1937]   8298
—— [1944]   8299

—— [1945]   8300
—— [1947]   8301
—— [1948]   8302
—— [1949]   8303
—— [1950]   8306
—— [1951]   8308
—— [1952]   8310
—— [1953]   8311
—— [1955]   8314
—— [1956]   8316
—— [1957]   8318
—— [1958]   8319

Krallert, Wilfried, 1912–
Volkstumskarte der Slowakei. 1941.   8252
Volkstumskarte von Jugoslawien. 1941.   9461
Volkstumskarte von Rumänien. [194–]   9197
Volkstumskarte von Ungarn. 1941.   8917

**Krasil'nikov, Andrei Dmitrïevich, 1704–1760, and
Rychkov, Petr Ivanovich, 1712–1777.**
Оренбургская губернія [Province of Oren-
burg.] 1880.   3122

Kraskov, S. F.
Река Конда от устья р. Ах (Евра) до
впадения В р. Иртыш. [River Konda from
the mouth of the Akh (Evra) to its conflu-
ence with the Irtysch River] 1929.   9301

Krause, Bruno.
Dresdener Heimats-Atlas. 2. verb. Aufl.
1897.   8858.

Krause, F. L., and others.
Atlas of the city of Cleveland, Ohio. 1898.   2429

Krauss, Paul, 1861– and Uetrecht, Erich, 1879–
Meyers Deutscher Städteatlas. 1913.   5240

Krauss and Smith.
Atlas and directory of Indian Lake [Ohio]
1911.   3870

Krebs, Norbert, 1876–1947.
Atlas des Deutschen Lebensraumes in Mitteleuropa. [1937–42]   7807

Kremling, Ernst, 1901–
Grosser IRO Weltatlas. [1950]   7413
—— 3. Aufl. [1951]   7462
—— 3. Aufl. [1952]   7523
IRO Atlas für Kraftfahrer. [3. Aufl.
1950]   8627
IRO Autoatlas. [11. Aufl. 1953]   8648
—— [12. Aufl. 1954]   8650
—— [13. Aufl. 1955]   8659
IRO Autoatlas Italien. [1955]   8975
IRO Autoatlas Österreich. [1956]   7909
IRO Bildatlas der Welt. 1. Aufl. [1953]   7571
—— 2. Aufl. [1954]   7605
IRO Deutschland Spezialatlas. [1950]   8703
IRO-Kraftfahrer-Atlas Deutschland. [1932]   8605

IRO Strassen-Taschenatlas. [1951]   8633
——— 2. Aufl. [1954?]   8651
IRO Verkehrsatlas für Strasse, Eisenbahn und
    Büro; Deutschland. [1953]   8674

Kretschmer, Konrad, 1864–1945.
Die Entdeckung Amerika's in ihrer Bedeutung
    für die Geschichte des Weltbildes. 1892.   1136

Krieger, Ernst.
Stadtplan-Buch von Leipzig. [1952]   8865

Kriegsverlag Aktiengesellschaft. *Berlin.*
Taschen-Atlas. [191–]   7796
Taschen-Atlas der Kriegsschauplätze. 5.
    Aufl. [1916?]   5833, 7800

Krische, Paul, 1878–
Landwirtschaftliche Karten. 1933.   5325
Mensch und Scholle; Kartenwerk zur Geschi-
    chte und Geographie des Kulturbodens.
    1936.   5326

Krogsgaard, Anders Meinert Rindom, 1869–
See Christensen, Carl Christian, 1860–1935,
    and Krogsgaard, Anders Meinert Rindom,
    1869–

Kroll Map Company.
Atlas of Bellingham, Wash. 1929.   17550
Atlas of Bremerton, Wash. 1940.   17551
Atlas of Clark County [Wash.] 1928.   17435
Atlas of Cowlitz County [Wash.] 1927.   17443
Atlas of Edmonds—Lynnwood [Wash.
    1949]   17552
Atlas of Island County [Wash.] 1927.   17457
Atlas of Kennewick [Wash.] and vicinity.
    [1962]   17558
[Atlas of King County, Wash. 1912]   3925a
——— [1926]   17465
——— [1958]   17469
Atlas of Kitsap County [Wash.] 1926.   17473
——— [1953]   17476
Atlas of Pasco [Wash.] and vicinity. [1962]   17559
Atlas of Richland [Wash.] and vicinity.
    [1962]   17560
Atlas of Seattle [Wash. 1927]   17565
——— [1932]   17566
——— [1939]   17567
——— [1950]   17570
——— [1966]   17572
Atlas of Skamania County [Wash.] 1928.   17513
Atlas of the city of Everrett [Wash.] and vi-
    cinity. [1949]   17555
Atlas of the city of Yakima [Wash.] and vicin-
    ity. [1948]   17587
Atlas of Wenatchee [Wash.] East Wenatchee,
    and vicinity. [1955]   17585
Atlas of Yakima County [Wash. 1931]   17544
City of Everett [Wash.] and vicinity. [1957]   17556
Main thoroughfare map [Puget Sound area.
    1965]   17424
Ownership atlas of central Seattle. 1917.   5078
Quadrangles; new district street maps ...

Metropolitan Seattle and Everett [Wash.
    1960]   17571

Kromayer, Johannes, 1859–1934, *and* **Veith, Georg.**
Schlachten–Atlas zur antiken Kriegsge-
    schichte. 1922–[29]   5627

Krüger, Karl, 1897–
Weltatlas der Erdölindustrie. [1941]   5770
——— 2. Aufl. [1941]   5771
——— 3. Aufl. [1942]   5772

Kruse, Karsten Christian, 1753–1827.
Atlas zur Übersicht der Geschichte aller Euro-
    päischen Länder und Staaten. [1822?]   2792
Tabellen und Charten zur allgemeinen Ge-
    schichte der drey letzten Jahrhunderte.
    1821.   2793

Kruzenshtern, Ivan Fedorovich, 1770–1846.
Атласъ къ путешествію вокругъ света кап-
    итана Крузенштерна. [Atlas to Captain
    Kruzenshtern's Voyage around the world.]
    1813.   5813
Атласъ южнаго мора. [Atlas de l'Océan
    Pacifique.] 1826–27.   3242
——— 1827–[38]   200

Kuan-wên.
See Hu, Lin-i, 1812–1861, *and* Kuan-wên.

Kuang-hsi yü ti ch'üan t'u. [Complete atlas of
    Kwangsi. 1898]   9652

Kuang hua yü ti hsüeh shê.
Chung-hua jên min kung ho kuo hsin ti t'u.
    [New atlas of the People's Republic of
    China] 1950.   9592
——— 1951.   9596a
Hsin Chung-kuo fên shêng ti t'u. [New pro-
    vincial atlas of China] 1950.   9593

Kuang-tung t'u. [Atlas of Kwangtung. 1866]   9655

Kubiĭovych, Volodymyr, 1900–
Atlas der Ukraine und benachbarten Gebiete.
    1943.   9290

Kuchař, Karel, 1906–
See Šalamon, Bedřich, 1880–   *and* Kuchař,
    Karel, 1906–

Kühn, Ernst.
Historische Entwickelung des Deutschen und
    Deutsch-Oesterreichischen   Eisenbahn-
    Netzes. 1882.   8595

Kühn, Franz Hermann, 1876–
Terra (politico) Atlas general. [193–?]   6718

Kümmerly und Frey.
All about Switzerland. Kleines Schweizer
    Brevier. [1957?]   9440

Lake, Griffing and Stevenson.
Atlas of Wicomico, Somerset & Worcester
Counties, Md. 1877.   1792, 1794, 1795
Illustrated atlas of Carroll County, Md.
1877.   1786
Illustrated atlas of Talbot & Dorchester
Counties, Md. 1877.   1787, 1793
Illustrated atlas of Washington County, Md.   14372
Illustrated historical atlas of Clinton County,
Ohio. 1876.   2362

Lalande, Joseph Jérome Le Français de, 1732–1807.
Voyage en Italie. [Atlas] 1786.   4042

Lamarche, Charles François de, 1740–1817.
See Delamarche, Charles François,

Lanagan, J.
See Beers, Daniel G., and Lanagan, J.

Lanciani, Rodolfo Amadeo, 1847–1929.
Forma vrbis Romae. [1901]   3068

Land Title Guaranty Company.
[Sioux Falls, S. Dak; maps and index. 1955] 17066

Land Use Surveys Company.
New Los Angeles City property zoning maps
of San Fernando Valley. 1946.   11619
Property zoning atlas of San Fernando Valley.
1948.   11620

Landesplanung für den Engeren Mitteldeutschen Industriebezirk. *Merseburg.*
Landesplanung im engeren Mitteldeutschen
Industriebezirk. 1932.   8552

Landkartenverlag, *Berlin.*
Buchplan Berlin. [1957]   8849
Wasserwanderbuch der Märkischen Gewässer.
[1955]   8738
—— 2. verb. Aufl. [1958]   8739

Landsberg, Helmut, 1906– *and* Biel, E. R.
Preliminary climatic atlas of the world.
[1942]   5394a

Landsberger, P.
Taschenatlas Berlin. [1956?]   8848

Lane, Michael.
See Cook, James, Lane, Michael, and others.

Lange, Friedrich, 1885–
Landwirtschaftlich statistischer Atlas. 1917.   5443
Volksdeutsche Kartenskizzen. 4. neubearb.
Aufl. [1937]   7661

Lange, Henry, *i.e.*, Karl Julius Henry, 1821–1893.
Atlas von Nord-Amerika. 1854.   1230
Atlas von Sachsen. 1860.   3045
Bibelatlas. 1860.   5358
Brockhaus' Reise-Atlas. 1857.   8685

Geographischer Handatlas über alle Theile
der Erde. 1866.   6156
Kartenwerk zu Dr. Karl Andree's Nord-
Amerika. 1854.   1231
Neuer Volksschul-Atlas. 48. Aufl. 1876.   6194
Volksschul-Atlas. 26. Aufl. [1892]   3573
See also Liechtenstern, Theodor, Freiherr
von, b. 1799, and Lange, Henry, i.e. Karl
Julius Henry, 1821–1893.

Lange, Henry, *and* Diercke, Carl, 1842–1913.
Schulatlas. [1932]   6781

Langenes, Barent.
Caert-thresoor. 1599.   410
Hand-boeck. 1609.   424
Thrésor de chartes. [1602]   415
—— [1610?]   428

Langer, William Leonard, 1896–
See Godshall, Wilson Leon, 1895– and
Langer, William Leonard, 1896–

Langeren, Jacob van.
Direction for the English traviller. 1643.   5203a

Langhans, Paul Max Harry, 1867–1952.
Deutscher Kolonial-Atlas. 1897.   5243
Handelsschul–Atlas. 4. Aufl. [1909]   5444
Justus Perthes' Alldeutscher Atlas. 3. Aufl.
1905.   8690
Justus Perthes' Deutscher Marine-Atlas. 2.
Aufl. 1898.   173, 3025
Justus Perthes' Staatsbürger-Atlas. 2. Aufl.
1896.   8688
—— 4. Aufl. 1904.   8689

Langlois, Hyacinthe.
Atlas portatif et itinéraire de l'Europe. 1817.   2809
Grand atlas français départemental. 1856.   4028

Langwith Publishing Company.
Folding road map atlas of the United States
and Canada. [1928]   10800
Road map atlas of the United States &
Canada. 1929.   10807
—— 1930.   10813

Lapérouse, Jean François de Galaup, *Comte* de, 1741–1788.
Voyage de La Pérouse. Atlas. 1797.   688
Voyage round the world. Atlas. 1798.   693

Lapie, Alexandre Émile, fils, *and* Lapie, Pierre, 1779–1850.
Atlas universel. 1829–[33]   754, 765
—— 1829–[42]   123
—— 1841–[42]   123a, 787

Lapie, Pierre, 1779–1850.
Atlas classique et universel. 1812.   6032
—— 3 ed. 1824.   744
See also Lapie, Alexandre Émile, fils, and
Lapie, Pierre, 1779–1850.

Laplace, Cyrille Pierre Théodore, 1793–1875.
Voyage autour du monde. Atlas hydrogra-
phique. 1833–39.   202, 3174

Laporte, Joseph de, 1713–1779.
Atlas moderne portatif. 1781.   654
Atlas ... pour l'intelligence du voyageur
françois. 1787.   662

Larmat, Louis, 1890–
Atlas de la France vinicole. 1941–47.   8415
—— 1944.   8416
—— 1949.   8417

La Rougery, Édouard Blondel.
See Blondel la Rougery, Édouard.

Larousse, Librairie.
Atlas de poche. [1949]   7361
Atlas de poche du théâtre de la guerre. 2.
éd. [1916]   4231, 5184, 5834
Atlas de poche Larousse. [1940]   7019
Atlas départemental Larousse. [1913–19]   8468
—— [1914]   5230
Atlas international Larousse. [1950]   7414
—— [1951]   7463
Atlas Larousse illustré. [1899]   1035
—— [190–]   6292
Cartes Larousse.—[Atlas de la guerre. 1915–
19]   5835
Geógraphie de la guerre. [1917]   5836
Paris-atlas. [1900]   8495

Larrance, Isaac.
Post Office chart, and maps of ten states.
1866.   11030

Larsen, Walt, Enterprises.
Plat-atlas of Atchison County, Mo. 1950.   15213
Plat-atlas of Douglas County, Nebr. 1950.   15428

Larson's Inc.
Metro Dade County [Fla.] street map guide.
1962.   11818
—— 1966.   11819
Official ... Map of Metropolitan Miami [Fla.
1957]   11901

La Salle Extension University.
Atlas of railway traffic maps. [1913]   10728
—— [1914]   10729
—— 1919.   10730
—— 1920.   10731
Atlas of traffic maps. 1924.   10732
—— 1925.   10733
—— 1930.   10734
New loose-leaf atlas of traffic maps. 1936.   10735
—— 1938.   10736
—— 1947.   10737
—— 1950.   10738

Las Cases, Emmanuel, *i.e.,* **Marie Joseph Auguste
Emmanuel Dieudonné,** *Comte* **de, 1766–1842.**
Atlante storico. 1813–[14]   3540

—— 1826.   126
—— Veneta ed. 1826–[40]   127
Atlas historico. 1826.   3312
Atlas historique. [1803]   124
—— 1806.   5525
—— [1807]   125
—— [1829]   3313
—— Ed. populaire [1835]   128
—— 1853.   129
Historisch-genealogisch-geographischer Atlas.
[1831]   3550
—— [1835]   5526
Le Sage's [pseud.] Historical ... atlas. 2d ed.
1818.   130
Mappe geografiche storiche. [1835?]   3314

Lasor a Varea, Alphonsus, *pseud.*
See Savonarola, Raffaelo, 1680–1748.

Lat, Jan de, *fl.* **1734–1750.**
Atlas portatif. 1747.   4287

Latham, E. B., *and* **Baylor, H. B.**
Atlas of Atlanta, Ga. 1893.   1508

Lathrop, J. M.
Atlas of the city of Trenton and borough of
Princeton, Mercer County, N.J. 1905.
2195, 2199

Lathrop, J. M., *and* **Dayton, A. W.**
Atlas of Frederick County, Va. 1885.   2612

Lathrop, J. M., *and* **Flynn, T.**
Atlas of the Oranges ... N.J. 1911.   3837

Lathrop, J. M. *and* **Griffing, B. N.**
Atlas of Shenandoah and Page Counties, Va.
1885.   17360

Lathrop, J. M., *and* **Kiser, Ellis.**
Atlas of Atlantic City ... N.J. 1908.   2172a

Lathrop, J. M., *and* **Penny, H. C.**
Atlas of Belmont County, Ohio. 1888.   16383
Atlas of Highland County, Ohio. 1887.   2385

Lathrop, J. M., and Company.
Plat book of Monroe County, N.Y. [1902]   2238

Lathrop, J. M., *and others.*
Atlas of ... city of Newark, N.J. 1911–12.   3836
Atlas of Marion and Monongalia Cos., W.Va.
1886.   17612
Atlas of Orange County, N.Y. 1903.   2245
Atlas of the city of Erie, Pa. 1900.   2510

Latour, Arsène Lacarrière, *d.* **1839.**
Atlas to the historical memoir of the war in
West Florida and Louisiana. 1816.   1345

Lattré, Jean.
Atlas topographique des environs de Paris.
[1762?]   3013

Petit atlas moderne. 1783.   5994
—— 1793.   6002
—— [1821?]   741

Latvia. *Šoseju un Zemes Celu Departaments.*
Latvijas ceļu karte. 1940.   9027

Latvijas Automobiļu un Aero Klubs.
Latvijas auto ceļu karte. 1930.   9026

Latvijas-Lietavas Robežkomisija.
Latvijas-Lietavas robežas karte. [1927]   9025

Launay, Adrien Charles, 1853–1927.
Atlas des missions de la Société des Missions-
Étrangères. 1890.   9478

**Laurie, Robert, *ca.* 1755–1836, *and* Whittle, James,
ca. 1757–1818.**
African pilot. 1801.   3232
—— 1804.   10096
—— [1816]   3233
Complete East-India pilot. 1800.   3170
—— 1803.   700
—— 1804.   9488
—— 1806.   3172
—— Improved ed. 1810.   5292
Country trade East-India pilot. 1799.   4069
—— New ed. 1803.   5291
East-Indian pilot, or Oriental navigator.
[1795]   9487
New and elegant general atlas. 1804.   6022
New and elegant imperial sheet atlas. 1796.   6009
—— 1798.   4302
—— 1800.   6016
—— 1808.   716
—— 1813–[14]   720
New juvenile atlas. 1814.   4307

La Valette, John de.
See De La Valette, John.

Lavallée Théophile Sébastien, 1806–1866.
Atlas de géographie militaire. 1859.   177, 2973
—— 1902.   2973a

Lavoisne, C. V.
Complete genealogical, historical ... atlas.
1st American ed. 1820.   5527
—— 2d American ed. 1820.   131
—— 3d American ed. 1821.   132
—— 4th ed. 1830.   5528

Lavoisne, C. V. *and* Gros, C.
New genealogical, historical ... atlas. 1807.   3315

Lawler, Finn.
Plat book of Wisconsin lake region. 1908.   2632

Lawrence, C. H., *and* Griffin, L. W.
Atlas of Lorain County, Ohio. 1912.   16430

Lawson's Atlases and Plat Books.
Grant County, Ind., plat book. 1955.   12798

Plat book, Christian County, Ill. 1953.   12128
Plat book, Delaware County, Iowa. 1954–
[55]   13325
Plat book, Eaton County, Mich. 1953.   14649
Plat book, Jackson County, Iowa. 1956.   13549
Plat book, Livingston County, Ill. 1952.   12351
Plat book, Mason County, Ludington, Mich.
1953.   14738
Plat book, Montgomery County, Ill. 1957. 12421
Plat book, Moultrie County, Ill. 1953.   12430
Plat book, Tazewell County, Ill. 1955.   12517

Lazius, Wolfgang, 1514–1565.
Karten der Österreichischen Lande und des
Königreichs Ungarn aus den Jahren 1545–
1563. 1906.   3992

Lea, Isaac, 1792–1886.
See Garey, Henry Charles, 1793–1879, *and*
Lea, Isaac, 1792–1886.

Lea, Philip, 1656–1700.
[Collection of maps. 1699?]   4271
Hydrographia universalis. [1700?]   527, 5694

Leach, Harvey W.
Atlas of the city of Oshkosh, Wis. 1895.   2678

League of American Wheelmen.
Hand-book and road-book of New York.
1887.   15840

League of American Wheelmen. *Connecticut Division.*
Cyclist's road-book of Connecticut. 1888.   11692
Road book of the Connecticut Division.
1897.   11693

League of American Wheelmen. *Illinois Division.*
Official cyclist's road book of Illinois. 1892.   12069

League of American Wheelmen. *Indiana Division.*
Official L. A. W. road book of Indiana. 1896.   12727

**League of American Wheelmen. *New Jersey
Division.***
Cyclists' road book of New Jersey. 1890.   15674
—— [2d ed.] 1893.   15675

**League of American Wheelmen. *New York State
Division.***
Fifty miles around Brooklyn. 1896.   15841
Fifty miles around New York. 1896.   15842

League of American Wheelmen. *Ohio Division.*
Road book of the Ohio Division. 1897.   16368

**League of American Wheelmen. *Pennsylvania
Division.***
Road book of Pennsylvania. Eastern section.
1900.   16761
—— Western section. 1898.   16760

League of Nations.
Question de la frontière entre la Turquie et
l'Irak. [1925]   10076

Lean, Wilfrid Scarnell.
Drug atlas for students of pharmacy and
medicine. 1937.   5720

Leard, John, *and others.*
[Charts and plans of Jamaica] 1793.   5129

Leavenworth, A.
See Beers, Frederick W., Leavenworth, A.,
Warner, George E., *and others.*

Lebègue, J., et Companie.
Nouvel atlas de Belgique. [1901]   7965
—— 1921.   7966
—— 1933.   7968
Nouvel atlas et géographie de Belgique.
1923.   7967

Le Boucher, Odet Julien, 1744–1826.
Atlas pour servir à l'intelligence . . . de la guerre
de l'independances des États-Unis. [1830]   1340

Le Clerc, Jean, d. 1621.
Theatre geographiqve dv Royavme de France.
1632–[33]   8452

Le Clerc, Jean, 1657–1736.
Atlas antiquus. [1705]   3283, 5628

Lecomte, Ferdinand, 1826–1899.
Atlas et légendes pour l'intelligence de . . . le
Général jomini. 1861.   7715
—— 3. éd. 1888.   7716

Leconte, André.
Guide indicateur des rues de Paris. [1936]   8502
—— [1946]   8504

Lecuna, Vicente, 1870–1954.
Atlas de los Estados Unidos de Venezuela.
1916–21.   18422
Atlas de Venezuela. 1916.   5151

Lee, C. Y.
See T'an, Hsi-ch'ou, *and* Lee, C. Y.

Lee, R. H.
Farm atlas of Carroll County, Ohio. 1915.   4983

Leer, Genrikh Antonovich, 1829–1904.
Карты къ стратегіи. [Strategical maps.]
1885–87.   2821

Leers, Johann von, 1902– *and* **Frenzel, Konrad,
1902–**
Atlas zur Deutschen Geschichte der Jahre
1914 bis 1933. 1934.   8569
—— 3. verb. Aufl. 1936.   8570

Leete, Charles Henry, 1857–1936.
See Chisholm, George Goudie, 1850–1930,
and Leete, Charles Henry, 1857–1936.

Lefèvre, Isadore A.
Atlas of Manhattan Island, N.Y. 1894–98.
                                                                                                                    2311, 15994
Atlas of Staten Island, Richmond County,
N.Y. 1894.   2205
Index to atlas of Manhattan Island, N.Y.
1895–97.   2312, 2313, 15993

Legendre, Pierre.
See Malleterre, Gabriel, *i.e.*, Pierre Marie
Gabriel, 1858–   *and* Legendre, Pierre.

Le Grand,——
See Ancelín,——*and* Le Grand,——

Legrand, Augustin.
Exposition geógraphique. 1839.   6084

**Lehmann, Richard, 1845–1942, and Petzold,
Wilhelm, 1848–1897.**
Atlas für Mittel- und Oberklassen höherer
Lehranstalten. 1897.   6278
—— 3. Aufl. 1904.   297

**Lehmann, Richard, 1845–1942 and Scobel, Albert,
i.e., Carl Paul Albert, 1851–1912.**
Atlas für höhere Lehranstalten. 1903.   74, 298

Lehrmittel–Verlag, *Offenburg, Ger.*
Geographischer Weltatlas. [1949]   7362

Leibathēnos, Athanasios N.
See Mariolopoulos, Élias G., 1900–   *and*
Leibathēnos, Athanasios N.

Leidel, Edward F.
See Poetsch, Charles J., *and* Leidel, Edward F.

Leinweber, Walter.
Wortgeographie der Kreise Frankenberg,
Kirchhain, Marburg. 1936.   8582

Leiviskä, Livari Gabriel, 1876–
Uusi kartasto. [1949]   7363

Lekkerkerker, Cornelis, 1869–
Atlas Indonesia. [195–]   9752
—— [1957?]   9755
Atlas van Indonesië. [195–]   9753
See also Gelder, Willem van, *and* Lekkerker-
ker, Cornelis, 1869–

Lelewel, Joachim, 1786–1861.
Atlas do dziejów polskich. 1830.   9144
Atlas do J. Lelewela. 1818.   133
Géographie du moyen âge. Atlas. 1850.   252
Histoire de Pologne . . . Atlas. 1844.   9145

Le Mars Sentinel.
Atlas and farm directory ... of Plymouth County, Iowa. 1914. 4653

Le Masson du Parc,——
[Collection of maps. 1637–1717] 560, 5934
Vües, plans et perspectiues de diuers lieux et places considérables. [1713] 2781, 7642

Lemau de la Jaisse, Pierre.
Plans des principales places de guerre et villes maritimes frontières du Royaume de France. 1736. 2974

Lendl, Egon, 1906–
Salzburg-Atlas. [1955] 7914

Lengacher, Clarence W., 1903–
Atlas and plat book of Green County, Wis. [1945] 17756

Lenglet Dufresnoy, Nicolas, 1674–1755.
Kurzverfassete Kinder Geographie. 5. Aufl. 1764. 4197

Leningrad. Geografo-ékonomicheskiĭ Nauchno-issledovatel'skiĭ Institut.
Атлас Ленинградской области и Карельской АССР. [Atlas of the Leningrad Oblast and Karelian ASSR] 1934. 9284
Петербург—Ленинград; историко-географический атлас. [St. Petersburg—Leningrad; historical, geographical atlas] 1957. 9292

Lenormant, François, *i.e.* Charles François, 1837–1883.
Atlas d'histoire ancienne de l'Orient. [1868] 31a

Leonard-Stuart, Charles, 1868–
Standard atlas and chronological history of the world. 1912. 3637

Leonhardt, Karl.
Atlas zur Weltgeschichte. 1951. 5529

Leoni, Leonida.
Testo-atlante delle ferrovie e tramvie italiane. 1913. 8965

Leopold's Wereldatlas. 1939. 6971

Leopolds Wereldatlas. [1947?] 7257

Le Rouge, Georges Louis, *d.* 1778.
Atlas Amériquain Septentrional. 1778–[92] 1212
Atlas général. [1741–62] 5975
Atlas nouveau portatif. [1748] 607
—— [1748?] 3497
—— [1756] 5983
—— [1756]–59. 618
—— 1767–[73] 3510

[Collection of maps of all parts of the world. 1740–47] 4286
—— [1741–48] 5974
Pilote Américain Septentrional. 1778. 1210
—— 1778–79. 10319
Recueil des fortifications, forts et ports de mer de France. [1760?] 2975
Recueil des plans de l'Amérique Septentrionale. 1755. 1185
Recueil des villes, ports d'Angleterre. 1759. 3997

Le Roux, Pierre.
Atlas linguistique de la Basse-Bretagne. 1924–37. 8421

Leroy, Charles.
See Drioux, Claude Joseph, 1820–1898, *and* Leroy, Charles.

Le Sage, A., *pseud.*
See Las Cases, Emmanual, *i.e.*, Mario Joseph Auguste Emmanuel Dieudonné, *Comte* de, 1766–1842.

Leslie-Judge Company.
New world atlas. 1920. 6417

Lesnoe Obshchestvo, *Leningrad.*
Лѣсохозяйственный статистическій атласъ Европейской Россіи. [Atlas statistique et forestière de la Russie d'Europe] 1873. 9271

Leth, Hendrik de, *de jonge, fl.* 1742–1762.
Nieuwe geographische en historische atlas van ... Nederlandsche Provintien. [1740] 3080

Letoschek, Emil.
Geographischer Repetitions- und Zeichen-Atlas. I. Europa. 1888. 2801

Letronne, Antoine Jean, 1787–1848.
Atlas de géographie ancienne. 1827. 5629

Letts, Son and Company.
Popular atlas. 1881–83. 900
Popular county atlas. 1884. 2929

Leutemann, Heinrich, *i.e.*, Gottlob Heinrich, 1824–1905.
Illustrirter Handatlas. 1863. 841

Levanto, Francesco Maria.
Prima parte dello specchio del mare ... del Mediterraneo. 1664. 2803, 7858

Levasseur, Émile, *i.e.*, Pierre Émile, 1828–1911.
Atlas de géographie économique. [1904] 75

Levasseur, Victor.
Atlas national illustré des 86 départements ... de la France. 1847. 3000
—— 1849–[51] 8464
—— 1854. 8465
—— 1856. 3003

Leverich, Jess.
Maps and descriptions of rural routes served
by the Olympia, Wash., Post Office. 1948. 17411

Lewis, *Sir* Clinton Gresham, 1885– *and* **Camp-
bell, James Donald, 1884–**
American Oxford atlas. 1951. 7464
Canadian Oxford atlas. 1951. 7465
Oxford atlas. 1951. 7466

Lewis, George Gregory.
See Birkett, Walter Snowden, *and* Lewis,
George Gregory.

**Lewis, Meriwether, 1774–1809, *and* Clark, William,
1770–1838.**
Atlas accompanying the original journals
of the Lewis and Clark expedition, 1804–
1806. 1905. 4499

Lewis, Samuel, 1754–1822.
See Arrowsmith, Aaron, 1750–1823, *and*
Lewis, Samuel.

Lewis, Samuel, *d.* 1865.
Atlas comprising the counties of Ireland.
1837. 8233
Atlas to the topographical dictionaries of
England and Wales. 1844. 2927
Topographical dictionary of Scotland . . . Map.
1846. 8211

Leynadier, Camille, *d.* 1862.
Nouveau plan de Paris illustré. 1855. 5234

Li, Chao-lo, 1769–1841.
Huang ch'ao i t'ung yü ti ch'üan t'u. [Com-
prehensive atlas of the Ch'ing dynasty.
1842] 9552

Li, Ju-ch'un, *chin shih* 1637.
Ti t'u tsung yao. [Essential atlas of China.
1645] 9545

Li, Min-fei.
Ma-lai-ya lien ho pang fên chou t'u. [Maps of
the States of the Federation of Malaya.
1st ed.] 1958. 10056
Tung-nan Ya ti t'u chi. [Southeast Asia in maps.
2d. rev. ed.] 1958. 9496
Tung nan Ya tsui hsin ta ti t'u chi. [Southeast
Asia in maps. 1955] 9479

**Li tai ti li chih chang t'u. [Historical atlas of China.
ca. 1550]** 9533

**Li tai yen ko t'u. [Historical atlas of China. 1739 or
1740]** 9521

Liais, Emmanuel, 1826–1900.
Hydrographie du haut San-Francisco et du
Rio das Velhas. 1865. 2746

Liang, Ch'i-shan.
Chung-kuo ti li hsin t'u chi. [New geographical
atlas of China] 1956. 9613

Liaskoronskii, Vasilii Grigor'evich, 1859–1928.
Иностранные картыи атласы XVI и XVII вв.,
относящіеся южной Россіи—Foreign
maps and atlases of the XVI and XVII centuries, pertaining to southern Russia.
1898. 4057a

Libot, M.
Oefenatlas. Belgisch Congo. [1940] 10111

Libot, M., *and* Heylen, L.
Oefenatlas . . . Azië en Africa. [1939] 9480

Librairie Générale de l'Enseignement Libre.
Atlas de l'Indo-Chine Française. [1922] 9731

Licent, Émile.
Hoang Ho, Pai Ho, Loan Ho, Leao Ho.
Itinéraires suivis dans le bassin du Golfe du
Pei Tcheuly 1914–1923. [1924] 9561
——— (1923–1933) [1935–36] 9571

**Liechtenstern, Theodor, *Freiherr* von, *b.* 1799, *and*
Lange, Henry, *i.e.*, Karl Julius Henry, 1821–1893.**
Schul-Atlas. pt. 2–3. 1855–57. 6122
——— 21. Aufl. 1872. 6181
Schul-Atlas zum Unterricht in der Erdkunde.
50. Aufl. 1880. 4198

Liga Československých Motoristů.
Československo, průvodce pro automobilisty.
[1933?] 8242

Lighter, J. W.
Plat book of Pocahontas County, Iowa.
1897. 1691

L'Illustration.
Atlas colonial Français. 1929. 8392
Atlas de l'Afrique du Nord. 1939. 10100
Atlas de la France et de ses colonies. 1934. 8473

Lima, Afonso Guerreiro.
Atlas escolar. pt. 3. 6. ed. [1946] 7242

Lindsay, Lloyd E.
Oil development maps. Townships of Caddo
County, Okla. [1931] 16595
Oil development maps. Townships of Grady
County, Okla. [1931] 16603

Lingelbach, William Ezra, 1871–
See Harding, Samuel Bannister, 1866–1927,
and Lingelbach, William Ezra, 1871–

Linn County, *Iowa. Engineering Dept.*
Atlas of Linn County, Iowa. [1944] 13632

Lipp, Franz.
Art und Brauch im Land ob der Enns. [1952] 7920

Lippincott, J. B., and Company.
Handy atlas. 1877.   4355
Popular family atlas. 1886.   931

Lippold, R. Max, Verlag.
See Verlag der Literaturwerke "Minerva" R.
Max Lippold.

L'Isle, Guillaume de, 1675–1726.
See Delisle, Guillaume, 1675–1726.

List, Paul, Atlantik-Verlag.
See Atlantik-Verlag Paul List.

List's Taschenatlas der Welt. [1953]   7544

Literary Digest.
Literary Digest European war maps. [1914]   4232
—— [1916]   4233

Literary Digest atlas of the world. 1926.   6613
—— 1927.   6650
—— 1931.   6741
—— [1933]   6793
—— 1934.   6810

Literary Digest 1931 atlas of the world. [1930]   6742

Litografia Nacional Franco.
Atlas (mapa provincial) del Ecuador. [1940?] 18361

Lithoprint Map Company.
Farm plat book of Marshall County [Ind.]
1949.   12853

Liu, Hsün *fl.* **1866.**
Ho-nan shêng t'u. [Atlas of Honan Province.
1870]   9633

Lizars, Daniel, *d.* 1812.
Edinburgh geographical and historical atlas.
[1831?]   761

Lizars, William Home, 1788–1859.
Edinburgh geographical atlas. [1842?]   782

Lloyd, H. H., and Company.
Handy atlas. 1872.   864
Mammoth map of the United States. 1878.   11038

Lloyd's.
Book of port plans. 1930.   7643
Maritime atlas. [1st ed. 1951]   5695
—— [2d ed. 1953]   5696

Lo, K'ai-fu.
Climatic atlas of China proper. 1944.   9508

Lobaugh, Doris.
See Bowen, Emily, *and* Lobaugh, Doris.

Lobeck, Armin Kohl, 1886–1958.
Atlas of American geology. 1932.   10585
Historical geology of the United States. [1947] 10586

Lobeck, Tobias.
Atlas geographicus portatilis [!] [1762?]   631, 632
Kurzgefasste Geographie. [1762?]   630

Locchi, Domenico.
Nuovissimo atlante geografico. [1943]   7149

Locher, William.
See Hexamer, Ernest, *and* Locher, William.

Lockwood, Anthony, *d.* 1855.
Brief description of Nova Scotia. 1818.   1252

Lodge, B., and Company.
Ward maps of Albany, N.Y. 1916.   4936

Lönborg, Sven Erik, 1871–1959.
Swedish maps. First series. [1907]   9357

Löw, Conrad.
Königen Buch oder Register darin fein orden-
lich erzehlt werden. 1598.   7783

Löwenberg, Julius, 1800–1893.
Historisch-geographischer Atlas. 1839.   134

Logan, Leonard Marion, 1891–
Oklahoma history map book. [1916]   4999

Logan Map Company.
Atlas of Texas county ownership maps.
[1930]   17140

Lo-Kāt-It.
[Dallas, Tex.] 1958.   17226
Houston [Tex.] 1958.   17262

**London. *County Council. Valuation, Estates and
Housing Dept.***
Municipal map of London. 1913.   8162

Lone Star Gas Company.
Transmission pipeline system map book.
1963.   17135

Long Island Title Guarantee Company.
War atlas. 1898.   3688a

Longini, Arthur.
Economic atlas of the Pittsburgh—Youngs-
town economic area. 1960.   16914

Longnon, Auguste Honoré, 1844–1911.
Atlas historique de la France. 1885–89.   2957
Texte explicatif des planches. 1885–89.   2957a

Longwell, Alden R.
See Searcy, Nelson Donald, 1933–   *and*
Longwell, Alden R:

Lonsdale, Richard E.
Atlas of North Carolina. 1967.   16213

Loon, Joannes van, *ca.* **1611–1686.**
Klaer lichtende noort-star ofte Zee atlas.
1661.   470
—— 1666.   476
—— 1668.   3433

Loon, Joannes van, *and* **Voogt, Claes Jansz,** *d.* **1696.**
Nieuwe groote lichtende zee-fackel. 1699–
[1702]   4272

Loots, Johannes, 1665–1726.
[Atlas. 1705?]   3464

Loots-man, Jacques, *and* **Loots-man, Caspar Anthoine.**
See Jacobsz, Theunis.

López, Elpidio.
Atlas escolar. 1945.   7216

López, Felicisimo.
Atlas geográfico del Ecuador. 1907.   2763

López de Vargas Machuca, Tomás, 1731–1802.
Atlas elemental moderno. 1792.   677
Atlas geográfico de España. 1804.   9322
—— 1810–[18]   4053, 4065
—— 2. ed. 1830–[35]   5277, 5286
Atlas geographico de la America Septentrional
y Meridional. 1758.   1159
Atlas geographico del Reyno de España.
[1757]   3132
—— 1757.   4064

López Rosado, Diego G.
Atlas histórico geográfico de Mexico. 1940. 18066
Historia de México. [1959]   18067

Lorain County, *Ohio.*
Official tax maps of Lorain County, Ohio.
1963.   16432

Lord, Clifford Lee, 1912–   *and* **Lord, Elizabeth Sniffen Hubbard, 1912–**
Historical atlas of the United States. [1944] 10627
—— Rev. ed. [1953]   10628

Lord, Harry Dyson, 1897–
Indexed street atlas of Bristol County, Mass.
[1944]   14404
Indexed street atlas of eastern Middlesex
County [Mass. 1950]   14409
Indexed street atlas of Essex County [Mass.
1949]   14406
—— [1955]   14407
Indexed street atlas of northern Worcester
County [Mass. 1944]   14410
Indexed street atlas of the metropolitan Boston
area. [1943]   14432
Indexed street atlas of Worcester [Mass.] and
vicinity. [1944]   14545
—— [1950]   14546

Lord, Harry D., and Son.
Indexed street atlas of the Greater Springfield
[Mass.] area. [1962]   14531
Indexed street atlas of the metropolitan Boston
area. [1954]   14438

Lord, John King, 1848–1926.
Atlas of the geography and history of the
ancient world. [1902]   32

Loreck, Carl, *and* **Winter, Albert.**
Schul-Atlas für höhere Lehranstalten. 2.
Aufl. 1913.   4199

Lorenzen, Vilhelm Birkedal, 1877–
Haandtegnede kort over København 1660–
1757. 1942.   8295

Lorenzo, A. M.
Atlas of India. [2d ed.   1944]   9705

Loriente Cancio, V.
See Dantín Cereceda, Juan, 1881–1943, *and*
Loriente Cancio, V.

Lorimer, Frank, 1894–
[Population of the Soviet Union ... Maps.
1946]   9240

Lorini P., Ernesto.
See Dunn Lahore, Jorge, *and* Lorini P.,
Ernesto.

Lorrain, A.
France et ses colonies.   [1836]   4026

Los Angeles. Chamber of Commerce. *Research Dept.*
Los Angeles marketing atlas.   [1954]   11551

Los Angeles Saturday Post.
Unrivalled atlas. 1901.   1067a

Lothian, John, *fl.* **1825–1846.**
Bible atlas. 1832.   3302a, 5359
Historical atlas of Scotland. 1829.   5213

Lotter, Tobias Conradus, 1717–1777, *and others.*
Atlas géographique. 1778.   3517
Atlas minor. [1744?]   3491, 3492, 3493
Atlas novus. [1772?]   3513

Lotz, Heinrich, 1873–1943.
See Sprigade, Paul, 1863–1928, *and* Lotz,
Heinrich, 1873–1943.

Loua, Toussaint, 1824–1907.
Atlas statistique de la population de Paris.
1873.   8494

Louisiana. *Dept. of Education.*
Thirty maps showing the public school situa-
tion. [1915]   4707

Louisiana. *Dept. of Highways.*
Louisiana. [General highway maps of the
parishes. 1955]   14269
Traffic survey of New Orleans metropolitan
area. [1945?]   14288

Louisiana. *Dept. of Public Works.*
State of Louisiana. 1944.   14270

Louisiana. *Dept. of Public Works. Aeronautics
Division.*
Louisiana air facilities. [1947]   14265

Louisiana. *Division of Employment Security.*
Economic maps of Louisiana. [1966]   14266
Economic observations in Louisiana. 1967.   14267

Louisville Evening Post's Atlas of the world. 1910–
11.   6341

Louisville Title Company.
New map of Louisville and Jefferson County,
Ky. 1913.   4705, 4706

Loureiro, Adolpho Ferreira, 1836–1911.
Estudos sobre alguns portos commerciaes de
Europa, Asia, Africa e Oceania. Atlas.
1886.   4106
Portos maritimos de Portugal . . . Atlas. 1904–
1909.   9187

Louvre–atlas. [187–]   6168

Louw, Pieter Johan Frederik, 1856–1924.
Java-Oorlog van 1825–30. [1894–1908]   4077

Low Bridge and Viaduct Map Company.
Low bridges and viaducts having vertical
clearances of 13 ft. or less. [1953]   10488

Lowry, Joseph Wilson, 1803–1879.
Table atlas. [1852]   806
Universal atlas. 1853.   6115

Lowry, Robert Lee, 1900–
Surface water resources of Texas. 1958.   17139

Lozier, Lemuel.
Assessment map of Hackensack, N.J. 1911.   15754

Lubin, Augustin, 1624–1695.
Orbis Avgvstianvs. 1659.   466

Lubrecht, Charles.
Pictorial and comprehensive atlas. 1885.   927

Lucas, *Sir* **Charles Prestwood, 1853–1931.**
Our empire atlas. 1897.   2900

Lucas, Fielding, 1781–1854.
General atlas. 1823.   742
New and elegant general atlas. [1816?]   3542
New general atlas of the West India Islands.
[1824?]   2709

Lucas, Otto.
Planungsgrundlagen für den Landkreis Borken
(Westf.) 1950   8821
Planungsgrundlagen für den Landkreis Olpe
(Westf.) 1952.   8823
See also Gösmann, Gottfried, *and* Lucas, Otto.

Lucas County, *Ohio. County Auditor.*
Lucas County, Ohio; unit value land maps.
1937.   16436

Luchtvaartterreinen Nederland. [194–]   9029

Lüddecke, Richard, 1859–1898.
Atlas escolar Portuguez. 2 ed. 1902.   6304

Lüddecke, Richard, *and* **Haack, Hermann, 1872–
1966.**
Deutscher Schulatlas. 3. Aufl. 1901.   299
—— 7. Aufl. 1914.   4200
—— 12. Aufl. 1926.   6620

Lüdtke, Gerhard, 1875– *and* **Mackensen, Lutz,
1901–**
Deutscher Kulturatlas. 1928–38.   8571

Lüssenhop, Friedrich.
Heimatatlas Bremerhaven. [1955]   8854

Lütke, Fedor Petrovich, *Graf,* **1797–1882.**
Атласъ къ путешествію вокругъ свѣта
шлюпа Сенявина ... [Atlas du voyage
autour du monde.] 1835.   203, 773

Luetzelburg, Philipp *Freiherr* **von, 1880–**
Mappas botanicos do nordéste do Brasil.
[1922]   18271

Luffman, John, *fl.* **1776–1820.**
Geographical & topographical atlas. 1815–
16.   725
[Geographical principles. Maps. 1803]   4461
Select plans of the principal cities . . . &c. in the
world. 1801–[1802]   62
—— 1801–[1803]   63

Luginbühl, G.
Routes d'Europe. [1930]   7763

Lukas, Filip, 1871–1958 *and* **Peršić, Nikola.**
Minervin svjetski atlas. [1938]   6954

Luncan, I.
See Gorgan, August, 1837–   *and* Luncan,
I.

Lundqvist, Magnus.
Bergvalls nya skolatlas. [1952]   7524
See also Anrick, Carl Julius, 1895–   *and*
Lundqvist, Magnus.

Lundqvist, Magnus, *and* **Moberg, Oskar.**
Skåne. 1926.   9408

Lunet de Lajonquière, Etienne Edmond, 1861–
Atlas archéologique de l'Indo-Chine.   1901.   9728

Luth, Rudolf zu der, 1880–1961.
Wehrwissenschaftlicher Atlas.   [1933]   5723
—— 3. Ausg.   1936.   5724
—— 5. Ausg.   1938.   5725
—— 6. Ausg.   1939.   5726
—— 7. Ausg.   1940.   5727

Luyts, Jan, 1655–1721.
Introductio   ad   geographiam   novam   et
veterem.   1692.   511

Lyde, Lionel William, 1863–1947.
Home-work atlas of maps.   1910.   3374

Lyman, Azel Storrs, 1815–
Historical chart.   1874.   135

Lyman, Dean Belden, 1896–
Atlas of Old New Haven.   1929.   11737

Lyon County Reporter, *Rock Rapids, Ia.*
Land ownership atlas of Lyon County [Iowa]
1946.   13661

Lysons, Fred H., *and* Sallee, J. S.
Map-guide, Seattle to Dawson, over the Chil-
koot … and down the Yukon.   1897.   10440

McAlpine, W. S., Map Company.
Atlas of city of Pontiac, Mich.   1926.   14896
Atlas of Oakland County, Mich.   1930.
                                         14766, 14767
—— 1947.   14769
Bloomfield   Township   [Oakland   County,
Mich.] details.   1928.   14773
—— 1960.   14774
Official map of southeastern Oakland County,
Mich.   1926.   14764
Royal   Oak   Township   [Oakland   County,
Mich.] details.   1928.   14775
—— 1960.   14776
Southfield township, now city of Southfield
… Mich.   1960.   14904
State of Michigan and counties.   [1934]   14579
Troy Township, now city of Troy … Mich.
1960.   14905
Troy Township, [Oakland County, Mich.] de-
tails.   1928.   14777
Wayne County farm atlas, Mich.   1942.   14832
White Star map of Michigan and counties.
[1933]   14578

McCleneghan, Thomas J.
See Baker,   Simon,   *and*   McCleneghan,
Thomas J.

McClure, Edmund, *d.* 1922.
Historical church atlas.   1897.   86

McComiskey, Alexander H.
Maps of parish of Orleans [La.]   1904.   3760

McConnell, Wallace Robert, 1881–1960.
See Philip, George, 1870–1937, *and* McConnell, Wallace Robert, 1881–1960.

MacCoun, Townsend, 1845–1932.
Bible atlas.   1912.   5360
Early New York.   [1909]   3839
Historical geography of the United States.
1889.   1293
—— 1890.   1294
—— Rev. ed.   1892.   10629
—— [1901]   1295
—— New and rev. ed.   [1911]   10630

McCown, Chester Charlton, 1877–
See May, Herbert Gordon, 1904–   *and*
McCown, Chester Charlton,   1877–

McCracken, Charles Chester, 1882–
Local school district boundaries within the
county school districts of … Ohio.   1926.   16372
—— 1929.   16373

McCulloch, John Ramsey, 1789–1864.
Dictionary … of commerce … Atlas.   1859.   76

McDavid, Raven Ioor.
See Kurath, Hans, 1891–   *and* McDavid,
Raven Ioor.

Macdonald, D.
Illustrated atlas of the Dominion of Canada.
1881.   4482

McDougall's Educational Company.
Contour atlas of the British Isles.   [1919?]   5189
Pictorial atlas.   [1951]   7467
School atlas.   South African ed.   [195–?]   7378

McDowell, Robert M.
Maps illustrating Gen'l Sherman's "March to
the Sea."   MS.   [1864–65]   10658

MacFadden, Clifford Herbert, 1908–
Atlas of world review.   [1940]   7020
Primary productions of the world.   1937.   5445

MacFadden, Clifford Herbert, *and others.*
Atlas of world affairs.   [1946]   7243

McFadden, Joseph Guy, 1898–
Jasper County [Iowa] atlas.   [1938]   13553

**McGill University, *Montreal. Arctic Meteorology
Research Group.***
Atlas of surface temperature frequencies for
North America and Greenland.   1961.   10283

McGlumphy, William Harvey Sheridan.
Atlas of Caldwell County, Mo.   1907.   3818
Atlas of Cameron and Shoal Township, Clin-
ton County,   Mo.   1921.   15250

Machát, František, 1876–1935.
Atlas Republiky Československé.   1921.   8245

Machuca Martínez, Marcelino.
Mapas históricos del Paraguay Gigante.
[1951]   18368

McKamy Realty Company.
Plat book of Crawford County, Ill.   1947.   12176

McKay, L. F.
"Why Texas is first."   [1922]   17119

Mackensen, Lutz, 1901–
See Lüdtke, Gerhard, 1875–   *and* Mackensen, Lutz,   1901–

McKenzie, Murdoch, *the elder*, d. 1797.
Aanwyzing voor de zeelieden, door de Orcadi-
sche Eylanden.   [1753]   2943

Mackey, Dick.
Plat book of Clark County, Kans.   1909.   3757

McKinley Publishing Company.
Historical notebook for ancient history.
[1915]   4097
Historical notebook for European history.
[1915]   7738
Map notebook for United States history.
[1933]   10631
Outline atlases … Ancient history. 2d rev.
ed. [1915]   4098
Outline atlases … European history. [1915] 5158
Outline atlases for history classes. 6 v.
1922.   5754
Outline notebook for ancient history. [1922] 5755
Outline notebook for early European history.
1922.   7739
Outline notebook for English history. Rev.
ed. 1922.   8023
Outline notebook for European history. Rev.
ed. 1922.   7740
Outline notebook for later European history.
1922.   7741
Outline notebook for United States history.
Rev. ed.   1922.   10632

McKnight and McKnight Publishing Company.
Samples of outline maps.   [193–]   5756

McLagan, Paul R., *and* McLagan, Wayne.
Dakota County plat book, Minnesota.
1964.   14969

McLean, Robert.
New atlas of Australia.   [1886]   3253

Maclot, Jean Charles, 1728–1805.
Atlas général méthodique et élémentaire.
1770.   645
—— 1786.   658

Macmillan and Company.
Caribbean atlas.   1953.   18160
Historical atlas of the British Empire.   1925. 7986
Student's atlas of Indian history.   [192–]   9694

Macmillan's Atlas for South-East Asia.   1st ed.
1953.   7573

Macmillan's English-Sinhalese wall atlas of Ceylon.
[1927]   9504

Macmillan's Historical atlas of modern Europe.
1920.   7680

McMurray, S. M., Engineering Company.
Plat book of Nashville, Tenn.   [1930]   17112

Macpherson, D., *and* Macpherson, Alexander.
[Atlas of ancient geography.   1806]   4099, 4100

McReynolds, Edwin C.
See Morris, John Wesley, *and* McReynolds,
Edwin C.

Macullar, Parker and Company.
Atlas sample book.   [1879]   1404

Madagascar. *Service Météorologique*.
Atlas climatologique de Madagascar.   [1948] 10148

Maddox, Charles J.
See Deets, Edward Henderson, 1888–1958,
and Maddox, Charles J.

**Madhya Bharat, *India. Central Economic and Sta-
tistical Organization*.**
Madhya Bharat in maps.   1951.   9721

**Madhya Pradesh, *India. Directorate of Economics
and Statistics*.**
Economic & statistical atlas of Madhya
Pradesh.   1958.   9722

Madison Daily Democrat.
Atlas of Dane County [Wis.]   1904.   17706

Madison Heights, *Mich*.
Book of maps of Madison Heights.   1957.   14890

**Madras (*State*) *Director of Information and Pub-
licity*.**
Madras in maps & pictures.   1952.   9723
—— 2d ed.   1955.   9724

Madrolle, Claudius, 1870–
Itinéraires dans l'ouest de la Chine, 1895.
1900.   9554

Maebashi, Sokkōjo.
Gumma-ken kikōzu, 50-nempō. [Climatic
atlas of Gumma Prefecture, covering the
50-year period 1897–1946.   1950]   9852

Maelen, Philippe Marie Guillaume van der, 1795–1869.
See Vandermaelen, Philippe Marie Guillaume.

Maestre, M. Rivera.
Atlas Guatemalteco.   1832.   3939

Magellan Map Company.
Atlas of California.   [1961]   11350
California travel-guide.   [1962]   11351

Mager, Henri, 1859–
Atlas colonial.   [1885]   68, 2951
Atlas complet de géographie en relief.
[189–?]   3354

Mager, Henri, *and* Jacquemart, Alfred, *i.e.*, Eugène Alfred, 1836–
Atlas colonial.   1890.   2952

Maggiolo, Vesconte de, *d.* 1551, *supposed author.*
Atlas of portolan charts.   1911.   3357

Magin Atlas Company.
Atlas of the city of Dayton, Ohio.   1956.   16534
Central business section map of the city of
Dayton, Ohio.   1956.   16535

Magini, Giovanni Antonio, 1555–1617.
Italia.   1620.   3061

Maguire, Charles A., and Associates.
Master highway plan for the Fall River—New
Bedford—Taunton Metropolitan area.
1956.   14396

Magyar Földrajzi Társaság, *Budapest. Balaton-Bizottsága.*
Resultate der wissenschaftlichen Erforschung
des Balatonsees.   1903.   8930

Mahr, Johann Georg, 1800–1864.
Atlas der Alpenländer.   1858–75.   3989

Maine. *Fishery Research and Management Division.*
Maine lakes; a sportsman's inventory.   1953–
64.   14295

Maine. *State Highway Commission.*
General highway atlas, Maine.   [1964]   14304
Maine general highway atlas.   1946.   14300
—— [1959]   14302
—— [1961]   14303
Maine general highway maps.   [1941]   14296
—— [1943]   14298
—— [1944]   14299
Maine traffic flow maps.   [1941]   14297

Maine. *State Planning Board.*
List of State Planning Board maps showing
existing conditions in Maine.   1935.   14294

Mainichi Shimbun Sha.
Dai Kinki meikan chizu. [Atlas of the Greater
Kinki area]   1958.   9949

Mainstreet Publications.
Highway 66, the mainstreet of America.
1947.   10871

Maire, N. M.
Plan de la ville de Paris.   [1803]   8493

Mairs Geographischer Verlag.
Shell-Atlas. Karten von Deutschland. 20.
Aufl.   [1957]   8669
Shell-Autoatlas ... Deutschland. 2. Aufl.
[1950]   8628
—— 5. Aufl.   [1951]   8635
—— 7. Aufl.   [1952]   8641
—— 10. Aufl.   [1952]   8642
—— 11. Aufl.   [1952]   8643
—— 12. Aufl.   [1954]   8652
—— 14. Aufl.   [1954]   8653
—— 15. Aufl.   [1955]   8660
Shell-Autoatlas ... Germany.   [1951]   8634
—— [1954]   8654
—— [1956]   8666

Maksimov, I. V.
Атлас приливо-отливных и постоянных
течений в проливе Карские Ворота. [Atlas
of the constant and tidal-currents in the
Kara Strait]   1937.   9264

Malaya *(Federation) Survey Dept.*
Street directory and guide to Kuala Lumpur.
[1st ed.   1957]   10057

Malaya Publishing House.
Malayan atlas.   [1936]   6880

Malham, John, 1747–1821.
Naval atlas.   2d American ed.   1804.   5697

Mallat de Bassilan, Jean Baptiste, 1808–1863.
Lee Philippines ... Atlas.   [1846]   3223

Mallet, Alain Manesson, 1630–1706?
Beschreibung des gantzen Welt-Kreises.
1719.   4280
Description de l'univers.   1683.   3447

Malleterre, Gabriel, *i.e.*, Pierre Marie Gabriel, 1858–   *and* Legendre, Pierre.
Livre-atlas des colonies françaises.   [1900]   2953

Malone, F. J. J.
Plat book: City of Kenai, Alaska.   1964.   11238

Malte-Brun, Conrad, *originally* Malthe Conrad Bruun, 1775–1826.
Atlas complet du précis de la géographie uni-
verselle.   1812.   4306
—— 1837.   6079
New general atlas.   1837.   775

Universal geography. 1827–29.   751
—— 1832.   763
See also Mentelle, Edme, 1730–1815, *and*
Malte-Brun, Conrad.

Manatee County, Fla. Board of Commissioners.
Manatee County, Fla. 1961.   11833

Manchester, Ernest A.
Collins' Clear school atlas. [1921]   6449
Thacker's Indian clear school atlas. [1929?] 6490

Manen, Léopold, *i.e.*, Eugène Marie, Léopold, 1829–1897.
Atlas de la Basse Cochinchine. [1863]   3205

Manesson Mallet, Alain, 1630–1706?
See Mallet, Alain, Manesson.

Manila. *Observatorio.*
Atlas de Filipinas. 1900.   3225
Islas Filipinas. MS. [1900]   3224

Manitoba and Ontario Boundary Commission.
Report of the Commissioners ... Atlas.
1925.   10390

Manitoba-Saskatchewan Boundary Commission.
Report of the Commission ... Atlas. 1965.   10391

Mantey, Fritz von.
Kartenbild der Grenzschlachten im Westen
im August 1914. 1926.   5837
Kartenbild des Herbstfeldzuges 1914 im Osten.
1931.   5838
Kartenbild des Marnefeldzuges und der
Marneschlacht ... 1914. 1927.   8413
Kartenbild des Sommerfeldzuges 1914 im
Osten. 1930.   5839

Mantnieks, P., Cartografisch Instituut.
See Cartografisch Instituut P. Mantnieks,
Brussels.

Mantnieks, Pēteris.
See Ošiņš, Aleksandrs, *and* Mantnieks, Pēteris.

Manufacture Française des Pneumatiques Michelin.
See Michelin et Cie.

Manuila, Sabin, 1894–
Atlas etnografic al României, 1930. [1943]   9198
Ethnographic atlas of Rumania, 1930. 1943. 9199

Map and Print Service.
Coast-Columbia atlas. [1961]   16653

Map Corporation of America.
Mapco Street map guide of Los Angeles
County, Calif. 1960.   11414

Map of 1250 lots & gores, situated on Nostrand, Marcy, Tompkins ... Streets ... Brooklyn [N.Y. 1872]   15938

Map Office Pty.
Holmden's Register of Greater Johannesburg
townships. [1951?]   10168
—— [1954?]   10169

Map Service.
Street guide of Jacksonville, Fla. [1962]   11889

Mapa general de las almas. 1845.   5305

Mapping Unlimited.
Navigation charts of the Antrim County
Chain-o'-Lakes, Mich. 1967.   14602

[Maps of the world] [1787?]   4299

Maps or plans ... of the city of New York. 1895.   3847

Mapsco.
Routing and delivery system, combined with
city of Dallas [Tex.] maps and guide to
streets. 1952.   17217
—— 1954.   17220
—— 1955.   17221
—— 1956.   17222
—— 1957.   17224
—— 1960.   17227
Routing and delivery system, combined with
city of Houston maps and guide to streets.
1954.   17258
—— 1955.   17259

Marathon Atlas Publishers.
Atlas and plat book of farms & land ownership directory, Monroe County, Wis.
[1953]   17848
Atlas and plat book of farms & land owner-
ship directory, Ozaukee County, Wis.
[1954]   17865
Atlas and plat book of farms & land owner-
ship directory, Schoolcraft County, Mich.
[1958]   14813
Atlas and plat book of farms & land owner-
ship directory, Taylor County, Wis.
[1953]   17935
Atlas and plat book of farms & lands, owner-
ship directory, Brown County, Wis. [1958] 17671
Atlas and plat book of farms & lands, ownership directory, Outagamie County, Wis.
[1957]   17860

Marathon Map Publishers.
Farms & land ownership atlas and plat book
of Shawano County, Wis. [1953]   17926

Marathon Map Service.
Atlas and plat book of farms & lands, ownership directory, Washington County, Wis.
[1958]   17968
Farm & land ownership plat book of Sheboy-
gan County, Wis. [1950]   17930
Farm & land ownership plat book of Waukesha County, Wis. [1949]   17971
Farms & land ownership directory, atlas, and

plat book of Washington County, Wis
[1953]   17967
Ownership plat book of Adams County, Wis.
[1947]   17649
Ownership plat book of La Crosse County,
Wis. [1948]   17803
Ownership plat book of Mackinac County,
Mich. [1948]   14725
Ownership plat book of Portage County, Wis
[1949]   17882
Ownership plat book of Wood County, Wis.
[1950]   17993
Plat book of Marathon County, Wis. [1948]   17829
Plat book of Oconto County, Wis. [1947]   17852

Marcel, Gabriel Alexandre, 1843–1909.
Choix de cartes et mappemondes des xive et
xve siècles. 1896.   254
Recueil de portulans. [1886]   3358
Recueil de voyages et de documents pour
servir à l'histoire de la géographie. 1894.   1138
Reproductions de cartes & de globes relatifs à
la découverte de l'Amérique du xvie au
xviiie siècle. 1894.   1138

March, Sterling.
See Roterus, Victor, *and* March, Sterling.

March of man. [1935]   5530

Marcondes Homem de Mello, Francisco Ignacio,
Barão Homem de Mello, **1837–1918,** *and* **Homem
de Mello, Francisco, 1859–**
Atlas do Brazil. 1909.   3959, 18287
Geographia-atlas do Brazil. l. ed. 1912.   5142

Marden Maps.
[City maps, Boulder, Colo. 1952]   11671
Ownership plat book of Boulder County,
Colo. 1953.   11651

Mardešić, Petar, 1900–
Geografski atlas. 1951.   7468
—— 2. izd. 1951.   7469

Marescalchi, Arturo, 1869– *and* **Vistintin,
Luigi, 1892–1958.**
Atlante agricolo dell'Italia fascista. [1935]   8937

Marga, Anatole Alexandre, 1843–
Géographie militaire. Atlas. 1884–85.   2822

Marinelli, Olinto, 1874–1926.
Atlante dell'Italia e delle sue colonie. [1924]   8985
Atlante scolastico di geografia moderna.
1911–12.   4201
—— [1929]   6706
Piccolo atlante Marinelli. 1924.   6556

Marinković, Vladimir, 1885–
Географски атлас за гимназије и друге
школе. [Geographical atlas for high
schools and secondary schools.] [193–]   6718a

Mariolopoulos, Ēlias G., 1900– *and* **Leibathēnos, Athanasios N.**
Atlas climatique de la Grèce. 1935.   8885

Marks, A. F.
Атласъ. [Large general table atlas.] 1904–
1905.   1095
Ъольшой всемірный настольный атласъ
Маркса. [Large reference atlas of the
world.] 1910.   6336

Markwart, Leo Louis.
See Thibedeau, Joseph Edwin, *and* Markwart,
Leo Louis.

Marmocchi, Francesco Celestino, 1805–1858.
Globo atlante di carte geografiche compilate.
1858.   828
Nuovo atlante cosmografico. 1878.   887

**Maroc; atlas historique, géographique et économi-
que.** 1935.   10149

Marre, Jan de, 1696–1763, *and* **Keulen, Joannes
van.** *d.* **1755.**
Nieuwe groote lichtende zee fakkel. 1753.   3164

Marshall, John, 1755–1835.
Atlas to Marshall's Life of Washington.
[1832]   1342
—— [1833]   10652
—— [1850]   4520
Life of George Washington. Maps. 1807.   1341
Vie de George Washington: Collection de
planches. 1807.   3684

Marsigli, Luigi Ferdinando, *conte*, **1658–1730.**
Hongrie et le Danube. 1741.   2867

Martenet, Simon J., 1832–1892.
Map of Maryland. Atlas ed. [1866]   1779

Martenet, Simon J., Walling, Henry Francis, *and*
Gray, Ormando Willis.
New topographical atlas of . . . Maryland and
the District of Columbia. 1873.   1497, 1780

Martín, Alberto.
Atlas geográfico de España. [192–]   9327
—— 6. ed. 1953.   9342

Martin, Jean, 1889–
Atlas rex. [1951]   7470

Martin, Lawrence, 1880–1955.
Constitution sesquicentennial atlas. [1944]   10759
George Washington atlas. 1932.   10653
—— 1932 [i.e. 1933]   10654
Maps showing territorial changes since the
World War. [1924]   6557

Martín, Pedro.
Atlas del Uruguay. [1957?]   18400

Martin, Robert Montgomery, 1803?–1868.
Illustrated atlas. [1857]   822
Tallis's Illustrated atlas. 1851.   804

Martin de Moussy, Jean Antoine Victor, 1810–1869.
Description géographique et statistique de la
     Confédération Argentine. 1873.   2731

Martín Medrano, Ramiro.
Novísimo atlas de geografía postal universal.
     4. ed. 1931.   6749

Martines, Joan, *16th cent.*
Portolan atlas. 1582. Facsim. 1915.   4179

Martinez, Benigno T.
Cartografía histórica de la República Argentina. 1893.   2734

Martínez de la Torre, Fausto, *and* Asensio, José, *b.* 1759.
Plano de la villa y corte de Madrid. 1800.   3140

Martini, Martino, 1614–1661.
Novus atlas Sinensis. [1655]   3186, 3187, 3188
—— French ed. [1655]   5294

Maryland. *Dept. of Chesapeake Bay Affairs.*
Guide for cruising Maryland waters; complete
     marine atlas of tidal waters. 3d ed. 1965.   14334

Maryland. *Dept. of Economic Development.*
Maryland economic atlas. [1st ed. 1967]   14329

Maryland. *Dept. of Tidewater Fisheries.*
Guide for cruising Maryland waters; a marine
     atlas. [1961]   14332
—— [2d ed. 1963]   14333

Maryland. *Geological Survey.*
Physical atlas of Maryland, Allegany County.
     1900.   1781

Maryland. *Shell Fish Commission.*
Charts of Maryland oyster survey. 1906–12.
     [1913]   4708

Maryland. *State Dept. of Assessments and Taxation. Map Division.*
Property maps of Allegany County. 1967.   14337
Property maps of Anne Arundel County.
     1967.   14338
Property maps of Anne Arundel County, city
     of Annapolis. 1967.   14376
Property maps of Baltimore County. 1967.   14339
Property maps of Calvert County. 1967.   14340
Property maps of Caroline County. 1967.   14342
Property maps of Carroll County. 1967.   14343
Property maps of Cecil County. 1967.   14344
Property maps of Charles County. 1967.   14345
Property maps of Dorchester County. 1967.   14347
Property maps of Dorchester County, city of
     Cambridge. 1967.   14386

Property maps of Frederick County. 1967.   14349
Property maps of Garrett County. 1967.   14350
Property maps of Harford County. 1967.   14352
Property maps of Howard County. 1967.   14353
Property maps of Kent County. 1967.   14354
Property maps of Montgomery County.
     [1967]   14361
Property maps of Prince Georges County.
     1967.   14363
Property maps of Queen Annes County.
     1967.   14366
Property maps of St. Marys County. 1967.   14367
Property maps of Somerset County. 1967.   14369
Property maps of Talbot County. 1967.   14370
Property maps of Washington County.
     1967.   14373
Property maps of Wicomico County. 1967.   14374
Property maps of Worcester County. 1967.   14375

Maryland. *State Planning Commission.*
Maryland airport directory. [1950]   14326

Maryland. *State Roads Commission.*
Detail sheets and maps showing locations of
     road construction and reconstruction.
     1952.   14331

Massachusetts. *Dept. of Commerce. Division of Planning.*
Areas for regional planning in Massachusetts.
     1960.   14394

Massachusetts. *Dept. of Public Works.*
General highway maps of the counties in Massachusetts. [1940]   14395
—— [1966]   14397

Massachusetts. *Harbor and Land Commission.*
Atlas of the boundaries of the cities of Cambridge, Somerville, Waltham. 1903.   1836
Atlas of the boundaries of the cities of
     Chicopee and Springfield. 1912.   3771a
Atlas of the boundaries of the cities of Fall
     River, New Bedford. 1904.   1839
Atlas of the boundaries of the cities of Gloucester and Newburyport. 1905.   1842
Atlas of the boundaries of the cities of Haverhill, Lawrence. 1906.   1843
Atlas of the boundaries of the cities of North
     Adams and Pittsfield. 1913.   4713
Atlas of the boundaries of the city of Boston.
     1902.   1831
Atlas of the boundaries of the city of Fitchburg. 1909.   3771
Atlas of the boundaries of the city of Holyoke.
     1914.   4714
Atlas of the boundaries of the city of Lowell.
     1907.   1845
Atlas of the boundaries of the city of Lynn.
     1902.   1833
Atlas of the boundaries of the city of Marlborough. 1908.   1846
Atlas of the boundaries of the city of Newton.
     1904.   1840

Atlas of the boundaries of the city of Quincy. 1903.   1837

Atlas of the boundaries of the city of Salem. 1902.   1835

Atlas of the boundaries of the city of Worcester. 1908.   3770

Atlas of the boundaries of the towns of Arlington. 1901.   1828

Atlas of the boundaries of the towns of Acton, Bedford. 1904.   1838

Atlas of the boundaries of the towns of Alford, Becket. 1915.   4712

Atlas of the boundaries of the towns of Amherst, Enfield. 1912.   4715

Atlas of the boundaries of the towns of Ashland, Framingham. 1905.   1841

Atlas of the boundaries of the towns of Barnstable, Brewster. 1907.   1844

Atlas of the boundaries of the towns of Carver and Wareham. 1902.   1832

Atlas of the boundaries of the towns of Cohasset, Weymouth. 1901.   1829

Atlas of the boundaries of the towns of Marshfield, Pembroke. 1902.   1834

Massachusetts. *Topographical Survey Commission.*
Atlas of Massachusetts. 1890.   1801

Atlas of the boundaries of ... Abington. 1898.   1848

Atlas of the boundaries of ... Attleborough. 1900.   1851

Atlas of the boundaries of ... Beverly. 1898.   1854

Atlas of the boundaries of ... Bourne. 1899.   1862

Atlas of the boundaries of ... Bridgewater. 1899.   1864

Atlas of the boundaries of ... Brockton. 1898.   1867

Atlas of the boundaries of ... Chelsea. 1898.   1873

Atlas of the boundaries of ... Duxbury. 1899.   1876

Atlas of the boundaries of ... East Bridgewater. 1898.   1877

Atlas of the boundaries of ... Easton. 1899.   1879

Atlas of the boundaries of ... Everett. 1898.   1881

Atlas of the boundaries of ... Halifax. 1899.   1887

Atlas of the boundaries of ... Hanover. 1898.   1888

Atlas of the boundaries of ... Hanson. 1898   1889

Atlas of the boundaries of ... Kingston. 1899.   1894

Atlas of the boundaries of ... Lakeville. 1889.   1895

Atlas of the boundaries of ... Malden. 1898.   1901

Atlas of the boundaries of ... Mansfield. 1899.   1902

Atlas of the boundaries of ... Marion. 1899.   1904

Atlas of the boundaries of ... Mattapoisett. 1899.   1905

Atlas of the boundaries of ... Medford. 1898.   1906

Atlas of the boundaries of ... Melrose. 1898.   1907

Atlas of the boundaries of ... Middleborough. 1899.   1909

Atlas of the boundaries of ... North Attleborough. 1900.   1919

Atlas of the boundaries of ... Norton. 1900.   1921

Atlas of the boundaries of ... Norwell. 1899.   1922

Atlas of the boundaries of ... Plymouth. 1899.   1924

Atlas of the boundaries of ... Plympton. 1899.   1925

Atlas of the boundaries of ... Raynham. 1900.   1927

Atlas of the boundaries of ... Rehoboth. 1900.   1928

Atlas of the boundaries of ... Revere. 1898.   1929

Atlas of the boundaries of ... Rochester. 1899.   1931

Atlas of the boundaries of ... Rockland. 1898.   1933

Atlas of the boundaries of ... Seekonk. 1900.   1936

Atlas of the boundaries of ... Springfield. 1900.   1941

Atlas of the boundaries of ... Stoneham. 1899.   1942

Atlas of the boundaries of ... Taunton. 1900.   1945

Atlas of the boundaries of ... West Bridgewater. 1898.   1946

Atlas of the boundaries of ... Whitman. 1898.   1950

Atlas of the boundaries of ... Winchester. 1899.   1953

Atlas of the boundaries of ... Winthrop. 1898.   1954

Atlas of the boundaries of ... Woburn. 1899.   1957

Massachusetts Geodetic Survey.
[Massachusetts city and town map series. 1936–38]   14400
—— 1938–39.   14401
—— 1940.   14402

Mast, Crowell and Kirkpatrick.
New home atlas. 1899.   1036
New peerless atlas. 1897.   1017
—— 1898.   1022
New people's atlas. 1898.   1023
Peerless atlas. 1889.   951
People's atlas. [1894]   987
Popular atlas. [1892]   973
See also Crowell and Kirkpatrick Company.

Matal, Jean, 1520?–1597.
Insvlarivm orbis aliqvot insvlarvm. 1601.   3326

Mathews and Leigh.
Scripture atlas. 1812.   87

Mathews, Edward Bennett, 1869–1944, *and* **Nelson, Wilbur Armistead, 1889–**
Report on the location of the boundary line along the Potomac River between Virginia and Maryland. 1928   14327
Report on the marking of the boundary line

along the Potomac River in accordance
with the Award of 1877. 1930. 14328

Mathijsse, S. J.
Blinde kaarten van de landen van Europa. 5e
druk. [194–] 7742
Blinde provinciekaarten van Nederland. 5e
druk. [194–] 9050

Matson, Nehemiah, 1816–1883.
Map of Bureau County, Ill. 1867. 1519

Matthews, J. N., Company.
War atlas of Europe. [1914] 4234

Matthews, John, R. N.
Twenty-one plans ... of different actions in
the West Indies. 1784. 2700

Matthews, William B.
Macmillan marine atlas: Long Island Sound
& South Shore [N.Y. 1967] 16196

Matthews-Northrop Company.
Adequate travel-atlas of the United States.
[1893] 1435
Complete handy atlas of the world. [1898] 1024
—— 1899. 6284
Handy atlas of the world. 1916. 4429
Sweet home atlas of the world. 1899. 6285
Up-to-date handy atlas. [1898–99] 1030
See also Clement, J. W., Company. *Matthews–
Northrup Division.*

Matthews-Northrup Atlas of the world at war.
[1942] 7086

Matthews–Northrup New international atlas. [1st
ed. 1937] 6905
—— 1938. 6941

Matthews–Northrup New world atlas. [1948] 7296

Matz, Rudolf.
Agraratlas über das Gebiet der Deutschen
Demokratischen Republik. [1. Aufl.]
1956. 8516

Mau palapala aina a me na niele no ka hoikehonua.
1840. 6089

Maull, Otto, 1887–1957.
See Behrmann, Walter, 1882–1955, *and*
Maull, Otto, 1887–1957.

Maurette, Fernand, 1878–1937.
Atlas de la paix, 1914–1919. 1919. 5840
Atlas pratique. 1929. 6707
Petit atlas de la guerre et de la paix. 1918. 4235

Mauritius. *Archives Branch.*
Atlas souvenir de l'Abbé de La Caille. 1953. 10246

Maury, Matthew Fontaine, 1806–1873.
Wind and current charts. Gales in the Atlantic.
1857. 10223

Maverick, Peter, 1780–1831.
[General atlas. 1816] 728

**Mawson, Christopher Orlando Sylvester, 1870–
1938.**
Geographical manual and new atlas. 1917. 4440
—— 1918. 4447a

Maximinus *a Guchen, Father,* d. 1655.
Chorographica descriptio provinciarvm, et
conventvvm Fratrvm Minorvm S. Francisci
Capvcinorvm. 1649. 7650

May, B., and Company.
Album pintoresco de la Isla de Cuba. [1860?] 3948

May, Herbert Gordon, 1904– *and* **McCown,
Chester Charlton, 1877–**
Remapping of the Bible world. [1949] 5361

Mayo, Robert, 1784–1864.
Atlas of ten select maps of ancient geography.
1814. 4101
—— 1815. 4102
[Atlas to accompany ... ancient geography.
1813] 33

Mayr, Johann Georg, 1800–1864.
Atlas der Alpenländer. 1858-[62] 7795

Meacham, J. H., and Compay.
Illustrated historical atlas of the counties of
Frontenac, Lennox, and Addington, Ont.
1878. 3671a
Illustrated historical atlas of the province of
Prince Edward Island. 1880. 10426

Mechow, Alexander von.
Karte der Kuango-Expedition. [1884] 10102

Mecutchen, Samuel, 1827– **and Harrower,
Henry Draper.**
Pocket atlas. [1887] 941

Meer, Frederik van der, 1904–
Atlas de la civilisation occidentale. 1952. 5531
Atlas van de westerse beschaving. 1951. 5532

Meertens, Pieter Jacobus, 1899–
See Blancquaert, Edgard, 1894– *and*
Meertens, Pieter Jacobus, 1899–

Mees, Gregorius, 1802–1883.
Historische atlas van Noord-Nederland.
1865. 3073

Méhner, Vilmos.
Általános iskolai atlasz. [1886] 6230

Meier, Paul Jonas, 1857–1946.
Niedersächsischer Stäteatlas. 1926–33.   8789

Meissas, Achille, 1799–1874, *and* Michelot, Auguste Charles Jean, 1792–1866.
Petit atlas universel de géographie ancienne, du moyen âge et moderne. 1855.   5533

Meissner, Daniel, *d.* 1684.
Thesavrvs philo-politicvs. 1625–27   64

Meitzen, August, 1822–1910.
Boden und die landwirtschaftlichen Verhältnisse des Preussische Staates. [1868–71]   8758

Mejer, Johannes, 1606–1674.
Johannes Mejers Kort over det Danske Rige. [1638–72] 1942.   8271

Mekeel, Charles Haviland, 1863–1921.
Stamp collector's maps of the world. 1895.   345

Mela, Pomponius, *fl.* A.D. 50.
Pomponii Melae De situ orbis. 1739.   3284

Melantrich, *firm.*
Atlas SSSR. 1951.   9255
Fysikální mapy světadílů, svět. [1949]   5779a
Kapesní atlas. [3. vydáni] 1948.   7312
Pocket atlas. [1948]   7313
Praha. 2. doplněné vyd. 1948.   8253
Svet v kapse. [1. vyd. 1948]   7314

Meleny, Clarence Edmund, 1853   *and* Griffin, William M.
Primary geography of the state of New Jersey. 1884.   2147

Melish, John, 1771–1822.
Military and topographical atlas of the United States. 1813.   1346
—— 1815.   1347

Mellottée, Paul.
Atlas de route Mellottée. [France. 1950]   8439

Melvill van Carnbée, Pieter, *Baron*, 1816–1856, *and* Versteeg, Willem Frederick, 1824–1913.
Algemeene atlas van Nederlandsch Indië. [1875]   3214

Mendel, P. J.
Album voor de aardrijkskunde. 1841.   4050a

Mendes de Almeida, Candido, 1818–1881.
Atlas do Imperio do Brazil. 1868.   2749

Mendioroz, Luciano.
Atlas de Centro-America. [1912]   5123
—— [1912?]   18120

Menéndez Pidal, Gonzalo.
Atlas historico español. 1941.   9310

Menke, Heinrich Theodor, 1819–1892.
Orbis antiqui descriptio. Editio secunda. 1854.   34

Mentelle, Edme, 1730–1815.
Atlas de la Monarchie Prussienne. 1788.   4037
Atlas de tableaux. 2. éd. 1804–[1805]   706

Mentelle, Edme, *and* Chanlaire, Pierre Grégoire, 1758–1817.
Atlas universel. [1797–1801]   6011
—— [1807?]   712
—— 1807.   3539

Mentelle, Edme, *and* Malte-Brun, Conrad, *originally* Malthe Conrad Bruun, 1775–1826.
Géographie mathématique, physique, et politique. 1804.   705

Mentzer, Thure Alexander von, 1807–1892.
Atlas öfver Sveriges län. [1869]   9390

Mercator, Gerardus, 1512–1594.
Atlas minor. Latin ed. [1607]   423
—— French ed. [1608]   4253
—— German ed. [1609]   425
—— Latin ed. 1610.   429
—— French ed. [1613]   3415
—— Latin ed. 1621.   435
—— —— 1628.   437
—— Dutch ed. 1630.   439, 5929, 5930
—— French ed. 1630.   3419
—— German ed. 1631.   5932
—— Latin ed. 1634.   446
—— German ed. 1648.   5940
—— —— 1651.   461, 5943
Atlas, or A Geographicke description. English ed. [1636]   449
Atlas, ou Méditations cosmographiqves. French ed. 1609.   426
Atlas sive cosmographicae meditationes de fabrica mvndi. Latin ed. 1595.   3400, 5918
—— —— [1595]   5919
—— —— 1602.   5920
—— —— 1611.   3412
—— —— 1613.   3416
Drei Karten … Europa—Britische Inseln—Weltkarte. 1891.   253
Galliae tabule geographicae. [1585]   7779
—— [1606?]   3982
Gerardi Mercatoris atlas. Latin ed. 1607.   422
—— French ed. [1619]   5926
—— Latin ed. 1619.   434
—— —— 1623.   5927
—— Editio decima. French ed. 1628.   438
—— —— Latin ed. 1630.   441
—— French ed. 1630.   440
—— Latin ed. 1632.   443
—— French ed. 1636.   450
Gerardi Mercatoris et I. Hondii Atlas. German ed. 1633.   444
—— Ed. nouvelle. French ed. 1633.   445
Gerardi Mercatoris et I. Hondii Atlas novus. Latin ed. 1638.   5935

Germaniae tabulę geographicae. [1585] 8678

Historia mvndi. English ed. 1637. 451, 4255

Italiãe, Sclavoniãe, et Graeciãe tabule geographice. [1589] 5175

Mercator, Gerardus, *and* Hondius, Jodocus, 1563–1612.

Atlas ofte afbeeldinghe vande gantsche weerldt. Dutch ed. [1634] 447

Merian, Matthäus, 1593–1650.

See Zeiller, Marin, 1589–1661.

Merrill, Arthur A., 1906–

Roads and lanes of Chappaqua [N.Y.] 1962. 15957

Merz, Alfred, 1880–1925.

Атлас течений в проливах Ъосфор и Дарданеллы. [Atlas of currents in the straits of the Bosporus and Dardanelles] 1941. 10082

Hydrographische Untersuchungen in Bosporus und Dardanellen. [1928] 10081

Mesnard, H. W., *and* Perrin, William N.

Atlas of Huron County, Ohio. 1891. 2387

Messer, Malcolm.

Agricultural atlas of England and Wales. 2d ed. [1932] 8082

Metelka, Jindřich, 1854–1921.

Ottův zeměpisný atlas. 1924. 6558

Methodist Episcopal Church. *General Conference*.

Atlas of the Methodist Episcopal Church. [1925] 10532

Metropolitan Engineering Corporation.

Twin city metro maps, Minneapolis—St. Paul. 1964. 15156

Metropolitan Surveys, *Los Angeles*.

Industrial survey of the city of Los Angeles [Calif. 1935] 11535

Saunders Geographic atlas of the San Fernando Valley, city of Los Angeles, Calif. [1967] 11622

Metsker, Charles Frederick, 1881–

Atlas of Ada County, Idaho. 1938. 12006

Atlas of Adams County, Idaho. 1940. 12009

Atlas of Adams County, Wash. [1934] 17425

Atlas of Asotin County, Wash. [1933] 17427

Atlas of Baker County, Oreg. 1933. 16654

Atlas of Bannock County, Idaho. 1940. 12010

Atlas of Bear Lake County, Idaho. 1940. 12011

Atlas of Benewah County, Idaho. 1938. 12012

Atlas of Benton County, Oreg. 1929. 16655

—— 1938. 16656

Atlas of Benton County, Wash. 1934. 17428

Atlas of Bingham County, Idaho. 1940. 12014

Atlas of Blaine County, Idaho. 1939. 12015

Atlas of Boise County, Idaho. 1940. 12016

Atlas of Bonner County, Idaho. 1939. 12017

Atlas of Bonneville County, Idaho. 1940. 12019

Atlas of Boundary County, Idaho. 1939. 12020

Atlas of Butte County, Idaho. 1940. 12021

Atlas of California. [1937–38] 11354

—— [1953] 11358

Atlas of Camas County, Idaho. 1939. 12022

Atlas of Canyon County, Idaho. 1939. 12023

Atlas of Caribou County, Idaho. 1940. 12025

Atlas of Cassia County, Idaho. 1939. 12026

Atlas of Chelan Co., Wash. [1931] 17430

Atlas of Clackamas County, Oreg. [1928] 16658

—— 1937. 16659

Atlas of Clallam County, Wash. 1925. 17432

—— 1935. 17433

—— [1955] 17434

Atlas of Clark County, Idaho. 1940. 12027

Atlas of Clark County, Wash. 1929. 17436

—— 1937. 17437

Atlas of Clatsop County, Oreg. [1930] 16662

—— 1956. 16663

Atlas of Clearwater County, Idaho. 1940. 12028

Atlas of Columbia County, Oreg. [1928] 16664

—— 1956. 16665

Atlas of Columbia Co., Wash. [1933] 17441

Atlas of county maps, State of Idaho. [1939–40] 12004

Atlas of Cowlitz County, Wash. 1925. 17442

—— 1936. 17444

—— 1956. 17445

Atlas of Crook County, Oreg. 1935. 16668

—— 1938. 16669

—— 1954. 16670

Atlas of Curry Co., Oreg. [1932] 16672

—— 1936. 16673

—— 1955. 16674

Atlas of Custer County, Idaho. 1940. 12029

Atlas of Del Norte County, Calif. 1949. 11384

Atlas of Deshutes County, Oreg. 1935. 16675

Atlas of Douglas Co., Oreg. 1932. 16677

—— 1954. 16679

Atlas of Douglas Co., Wash. [1932] 17446

Atlas of Elmore County, Idaho. 1940. 12030

Atlas of Ferry County, Wash. 1934. 17447

Atlas of Franklin County, Idaho. 1940. 12031

Atlas of Franklin County, Wash. 1934. 17448

Atlas of Fremont County, Idaho. 1940. 12032

Atlas of Garfield County, Wash. 1933. 17450

Atlas of Gem County, Idaho. 1939. 12033

Atlas of Gilliam County, Oreg. 1934. 16681

Atlas of Gooding County, Idaho. 1939. 12035

Atlas of Grant Co., Oreg. 1935. 16682

Atlas of Grant County, Wash. 1933. 17451

Atlas of Grays Harbor County, Wash. 1927. 17453

—— 1935. 17454

—— 1952. 17455

Atlas of Harney County, Oreg. 1935. 16683

—— 1955. 16684

Atlas of Hood Riv. Co., Oreg. [1931] 16685

Atlas of Humboldt County, Calif. 1949. 11387

Atlas of Idaho County, Idaho. 1939. 12036

Atlas of Island County, Wash. [1933] 17458

—— 1937. 17459

—— [1949] 17460

Atlas of Jackson Co., Oreg. [1932]	16686	Atlas of Skagit County, Wash. 1925.	17509
—— 1955.	16687	—— 1935.	17510
Atlas of Jefferson County, Idaho. 1940.	12037	Atlas of Skamania Co., Wash. [1932]	17514
Atlas of Jefferson County, Oreg. 1935.	16688	—— 1956.	17515
Atlas of Jefferson County, Wash. 1925–[26]	17463	Atlas of Snohomish County, Wash. 1927.	17516
—— 1936.	17464	—— 1936.	17517
Atlas of Jerome County, Idaho. 1939.	12038	Atlas of Spokane Co., Wash. [1930]	17521
Atlas of Josephine Co., Oreg. [1932]	16689	—— [1957]	17522
—— 1955.	16690	Atlas of Stevens Co., Wash. [1933]	17524
Atlas of King County, Wash. 1926.	17466	—— 1937.	17525
—— 1936.	17467	—— 1956.	17526
Atlas of Kitsap County, Wash. 1926.	17474	Atlas of Teton County, Idaho. 1940.	12057
—— 1936.	17475	Atlas of the Pacific Northwest. [1935]	17418
—— 1955.	17477	Atlas of Thurston County, Wash. 1925–[27]	17528
Atlas of Kittitas County, Wash. 1934.	17478	—— 1937.	17529
—— 1956.	17479	—— 1948.	17530
Atlas of Klamath County, Oreg. 1936.	16691	Atlas of Trinity County, Calif. 1955.	11496
Atlas of Klickitat County, Wash. 1934.	17480	Atlas of Twin Falls County, Idaho. 1939.	12058
Atlas of Kootenai County, Idaho. 1939.	12039	Atlas of Umatilla County, Oreg. [1932]	16718
Atlas of Lake County, Oreg. 1936.	16693	Atlas of Union Co., Oreg. 1935.	16719
Atlas of Lane County, Oreg. [1931]	16695	Atlas of Valley County, Idaho. 1940.	12059
—— 1954.	16697	Atlas of Wahkiakum County, Wash. 1926.	17533
Atlas of Latah County, Idaho. 1938.	12042	—— 1935.	17534
Atlas of Lemhi County, Idaho. 1940.	12044	Atlas of Walla Walla Co., Wash. [1931]	17535
Atlas of Lewis County, Idaho. 1939.	12045	Atlas of Wallowa County, Oreg. 1935.	16720
Atlas of Lewis County, Wash. 1937.	17481	Atlas of Wasco Co., Oreg. 1933.	16721
—— 1948.	17482	Atlas of Washington County, Idaho. 1939.	12060
Atlas of Lincoln County, Idaho. 1939.	12046	Atlas of Washington Co., Oreg. [1928]	16722
Atlas of Lincoln Co., Oreg. [1930]	16698	—— 1937.	16723
—— 1937.	16699	Atlas of Washington [State. 1952]	17421
—— 1956.	16700	Atlas of Whatcom County, Wash. 1925.	17538
Atlas of Lincoln County, Wash. 1934.	17484	—— 1936.	17539
Atlas of Linn County, Oreg. [1930]	16702	Atlas of Wheeler County, Oreg. 1935.	16726
Atlas of Madison County, Idaho. 1940.	12047	Atlas of Whitman County, Wash. 1934.	17542
Atlas of Malheur Co., Oreg. 1935.	16704	—— [1957]	17543
Atlas of Mason County, Wash. 1925.	17486	Atlas of Yakima County, Wash. 1934.	17545
—— 1935.	17487	—— 1938.	17546
—— [1955]	17488	Atlas of Yamhill County, Oreg. [1928]	16727
Atlas of Mendocino County, Calif. 1954.	11426	Complete atlas of Tacoma, Wash. [1926–	
Atlas of Minidoka County, Idaho. 1939.	12048	30]	17580
Atlas of Morrow County, Oreg. 1935.	16708	Coos Co. atlas, State of Oregon. 1929.	16666
Atlas of Multnomah County, Oreg. 1927.	16709	Marion Co. atlas, Oreg. 1929.	16707
—— 1936.	16710	State of Oregon atlas. [1931]	16646
Atlas of Nez Perce Co., Idaho. 1938.	12049	—— [1933]	16647
Atlas of Okanogan County, Wash. 1934.	17490	State of Washington atlas. [1932]	17417
Atlas of Oneida County, Idaho. 1940.	12051	Tillamook Co. atlas, Oreg. 1930.	16715
Atlas of Oregon. [1952]	16652	—— 1957.	16716
Atlas of Owyhee County, Idaho. 1940.	12052		
Atlas of Pacific County, Wash. 1927.	17492	**Metsker Maps.**	
—— 1936.	17493	Atlas of Adams County, Wash. [1963]	17426
Atlas of Payette County, Idaho. 1939.	12053	Atlas of Benewah County, Idaho. [1960]	12013
Atlas of Pend Oreille Co., Wash. [1933]	17494	Atlas of Benton Co., Oreg. 1962.	16657
—— [1957]	17495	Atlas of Benton County, Wash. [1960]	17429
Atlas of Pierce County, Wash. 1924–[26]	17497	Atlas of Bonner County, Idaho. [1960]	12018
—— 1930.	17499	Atlas of Chelan County, Wash. [1959]	17431
—— 1936.	17500	Atlas of Clackamas Co., Oreg. 1966.	16661
—— 1951.	17501	Atlas of Clark County, Wash. [1961]	17440
Atlas of Polk County, Oreg. 1929.	16711	Atlas of Coos County, Oreg. 1958.	16667
Atlas of Power County, Idaho. 1940.	12054	Atlas of Douglas County, Oreg. 1967.	16680
Atlas of San Juan County, Wash. [1933]	17505	Atlas of Franklin County, Wash. 1963.	17449
—— [1949]	17506	Atlas of Grant County, Wash. 1961.	17452
Atlas of Sherman County, Oreg. 1934.	16713	Atlas of Grays Harbor County, Wash. 1962.	17456
Atlas of Shoshone County, Idaho. 1939.	12055	Atlas of Island County, Wash. [1960]	17462
Atlas of Siskiyou County, Calif. 1957.	11487	Atlas of Klamath County, Oreg. 1961.	16692

Atlas of Kootenai County, Idaho. [1959]	12040	—— [1930]	18093
Atlas of Lake County, Oreg. 1958.	16694	—— [1933]	18094
Atlas of Lassen County, Calif. [1958]	11391	—— 1943.	18100
Atlas of Latah County, Idaho. [1960]	12043	Atlas geográfico de los Estados Unidos Mexi-	
Atlas of Lewis County, Wash. [1962]	17483	canos. [1936]	18095
Atlas of Lincoln County, Wash. [1960]	17485	—— [1939]	18096
Atlas of Linn County, Oreg. 1967.	16703	—— [1941]	18098
Atlas of Modoc County, Calif. [1958]	11428	—— [1942]	18099
Atlas of Nez Perce County, Idaho. [1960]	12050	—— [1946]	18101
Atlas of Okanogan Co., Wash. [1959]	17491	—— [1947]	18102
Atlas of Pierce County, Wash. 1965.	17502		
Atlas of Polk Co., Oreg. 1962.	16712		

Atlas of San Juan County, Wash. [1961] 17507
Atlas of Shasta County, Calif. [1959] 11486
Atlas of Shoshone County, Idaho. [1965] 12056
Atlas of Skagit County, Wash. [1959] 17511
Atlas of Snohomish Co., Wash. [1960] 17519
Atlas of State of California. [1963] 11363
Atlas of Stevens County, Wash. [1963] 17527
Atlas of Thurston Co., Wash. [1962] 17532
Atlas of Walla Walla Co., Wash. [1961] 17536
Atlas of Washington County, Oreg. [1964] 16725
Atlas of Whatcom County [Wash. 1960] 17540
Atlas of Yakima County, Wash. [1959] 17547

Meunier, Jean Marie, 1862–1929.
Atlas linguistique et tableaux des pronoms
personnels du Nivernais. [1912] 8422

Mexico. *Comisión del Papaloapan.*
Atlas climatológico e hidrológico de … Papaloapan. 1956–[58] 18058, 18117

Mexico. *Comisión Federal de Electricidad.*
Sistemas electricos de servicio público.
1951. 18063

Mexico. *Comisión Geográfico-Exploradora.*
Carta general del estado de S. Luis Potosí.
[1894] 18111
—— 1904. 2689
Carta geográfica general … Atlas topográfico
de los alrededores de Puebla. l. ed. [1879–
83] 5121

Mexico. *Comisión Lerma-Chapala-Santiago.*
Atlas general de la cuenca [Lerma-Santiago.
1961] 18115

Mexico. *Comité Coordinador del Levantamiento de
la Carta Geográfica.*
Hojas correspondientes al centro, sur y sureste
de la República. 1956. 18105

Mexico. *Departamento de Asuntos Indígenas.*
Mapas lingüísticos de la República Mexicana.
1944. 18072

Mexico. *Dirección de Geografía, Meteorología e
Hidrología.*
Atlas geográfico de la República Mexicana.
[1921] 18089
—— [1922] 18091
—— [1923] 18092

Mexico. *Dirección General de Correos. Sección de
Transportes.*
Cartas postales de los Estados Unidos Mexi-
canos. 1908. 18073

Mexico. *Dirección General de Marina, Puertos y̓
Faros.*
Atlas del estado de la iluminación y
balizamiento de las costas del Golfo de
Mexico. 1923. 18071

Mexico. *Dirección Nacional de Estadística.*
México en cifras. (Atlas estadístico) [1934] 18062

Mexico. *Instituto Nacional de Antropología é
Historia.*
Atlas arqueológico [sic] de la República Mexi-
cana. 1939. 18057

Mexico. *Ministerio de Comunicaciones y Obras
Públicas.*
Atlas de la República Mexicana con los
caminos. 1952. 18075

Mexico. *Ministerio de Fomento.*
Memoria presentada al congreso de la Unión
… Atlas. 1887. 2688

Mexico. *Secretaría de Comunicaciones y Obras
Públicas.*
Atlas de la Memoria de labores … 1955–
1956. [1957] 18083
Atlas; resumen de los avances logrados en el
sexenio 1953–1958. [1959] 18084

Mexico. *Secretaría de Comunicaciones y Transportes. Departamento de Planeación.*
Cartas e información sobre vías generales de
comunicación. 1964. 18085

Mexico. *Secretaría de Recursos Hidráulicos.*
Carta de aprovechamiento de aguas y suelos.
1958. 18070

Mexico. *Servicio Meteorológico.*
Atlas climatológico de la República Mexi-
cana. [1926?] 18059
Atlas climatológico de México. [1939] 18060
Atlas termopluviometrico de la Republica
Mexicana. 1924. 18061

159

Michigan. *State Highway Dept.*
Michigan county atlas of general highway
maps. [1940] 14580

Michigan. *State Highway Dept. Road Division.*
Trunkline atlas; road and bridge types.
1954. 14581

Michigan. *Stream Control Commission.*
Coastline pollution surveys of Michigan.
[1933] 14555

Michigan Manufacturers' Association.
Roadmaps for politics. [1954] 14552

Michotte, Paul, 1876–1940.
Atlas classique de géographie. 1911. 6346

Mickleburgh, *Rev.* **James,** *of Ashill.*
Index to the principal places in the world.
1844. 794a

Midcontinent Map Company.
Tulsa County [Okla.] atlas. 1967. 16620

Middendorff, Alexander Theodor von, 1815–1894.
Karten-Atlas zu Dr. A. v. Middendorff's
Reise in den äussersten Norden und Osten
Sibiriens. 1859. 3125

Middle-West Publishing Co.
20th century atlas of Du Page County, Ill.
1904. 1529
20th century atlas of Kane County, Ill. 1904. 1541

Midgley, Cyril, 1897–
Picture atlas of the world we live in. [1935] 6851
Wheaton's Modern teaching atlas. 1936. 6883
See also Johnston, William Deas, *and* Midgley,
Cyril, 1897–
—— Parry, Roy Edgardo, *and* Midgley,
Cyril, 1897–

Midland Atlas Company.
Atlas, Big Stone County, Minn. 1966. 14936
Atlas, Burleigh County, N.Dak. 1966. 16270
Atlas, Davison & Hanson Counties [S.Dak.
1965] 17029
Atlas, Grand Forks County, N.Dak. 1967. 16285
Atlas, Kandiyohi County, Minn. 1967. 15018
Atlas, Lac Qui Parle, Minn. 1967. 15025
Atlas, Lyon County, Minn. 1967. 15030
Atlas of Aurora County, S.Dak. [1965] 17013
Atlas of Grant County, S.Dak. 1966. 17032
Atlas of Haakon County, S.Dak. [1965] 17034
Atlas, Pepin County, Wis. 1966. 17870
Atlas, Perkins County, S.Dak. 1965. 17052
Atlas, Redwood County, Minn. 1967. 15087
Atlas, Renville County, Minn. 1967. 15091
Atlas, Sibley County, Minn. 1966. 15104
Atlas, Stevens County, Minn. [1967] 15110
Atlas, Watonwan County, Minn. 1966. 15131

Midland Map Company.
Atlas of Appanoose County, Iowa. 1915. 4622
Atlas of Greene County, Iowa. 1909. 4638
Atlas of Mahaska County, Iowa. 1913. 4649
Atlas of Sac Sounty, Iowa. 1912. 4657
Atlas of Warren County, Iowa. 1915. 4663

Midwest Drafting Service.
Township maps of Du Page County, Ill.
1956. 12206
—— 1959. 12208
—— 1960. 12211
—— 1961. 12212
—— 1962. 12214
—— 1963. 12215
—— 1964. 12216
—— 1965. 12218
—— 1967. 12221

Mid-West Map Company.
Highway and radio atlas, United States,
Canada. [1938] 10845
Sears Cross country highway atlas of the
United States. 1935. 10833

Mid-West Map Publishers.
Plat book, Adair County, Iowa. 1951. 13021
Plat book, Audubon County, Iowa. 1951. 13065
Plat book, Calhoun County, Iowa. 1951. 13154
Plat book, Cass County, Iowa. 1950. 13180
Plat book, Cherokee County, Iowa. [1952] 13217
Plat book, Hancock County, Ohio. 1952. 16417
Plat book, Iowa County, Iowa. 1952. 13533
Plat book, Jones County, Iowa. [1951] 13592
Plat book, Madison County, Iowa. [1951] 13677
Plat book, Monroe County, Iowa. 1952. 13761
Plat book, Winnebago County, Iowa. 1952. 14059

Mid-West Publishers.
Plat book, Hancock County, Iowa. 1952. 13459

Midwest Publishing Company.
Huntington County, Ind., farm plat book and
directory. [1964] 12820
Sandusky County, Ohio, farm plat book and
directory. [1964] 16449

Migeon, J.
Géographie universelle. [1873] 6184
—— [1882] 6211

Miger, Pierre Auguste Marie, 1771–1837.
Ports de France, peints par Joseph Vernet et
Hüe. 1812. 5219

Might Directories.
Metro square map system [Toronto. 13th ed.]
1967. 10425

Migne, Jacques Paul, 1800–1875.
Atlas géographique et iconographique du
Cours complet d'Ecriture Sainte. 1864. 5362

Miguel, Gregorio.
Estudio sobre las Islas Carolinas. [1887] 3258

Mihăilescu, Vintilă.
Carte ethnique de la Roumanie ... 1930.
[193–] 9200

Mikieshin, Konstantin Osipovich, d. 1868.
Geographical atlas. 1864. 3560

Mikov, Vasil, *and* Ormandzhiev, Ivan.
Исторически атласъ на срѣдновѣковна
България. [Historical atlas of medieval
Bulgaria] 1943. 8238

Milan. *Istituto Geographico Militare.*
See Austria. *Militärgeographisches Institut.*

Milbert, Jacques Gérard, 1766–1840.
Itinéraire pittoresque du Fleuve Hudson.
[1828–29] 4957

Miles and Company.
Illustrated historical atlas of the county of
York ... Ont. 1878. 1253
New topographical atlas of the Province of
Ontario, Canada. 1879. 10410

Miller, D. L.
Atlas of Chemung County, N.Y. 1904. 4923, 4938
Atlas of the city of Fitchburg ... Mass.
1895. 1883
Atlas of the city of Northampton and town of
Easthampton ... Mass. 1895. 1878, 1918
Atlas of the city of Pittsfield ... Mass. 1893. 1923
Atlas of the city of Schenectady, N.Y. 1905.
2327, 2328
Atlas of the city of Utica, N.Y. 1896. 2333
Atlas of the town and city of New Britain ...
Conn. 1902. 1489
Atlas of the town of Leominster ... Mass.
1895. 1897
Atlas of the towns of Harrison and Kearny
and the borough of East Newark ... N.J.
1903. 2178, 2181, 2184
Atlas of the towns of North Adams, Adams,
Williamstown, and Cheshire ... Mass.
1894. 1808, 1849, 1874, 1916, 1951

Miller, David E.
Utah history atlas. 1964. 17293

Miller, David William, 1929–   *and others*.
Water atlas of the United States. [1962] 10998
—— [2d ed. 1963] 10999

Miller, Eugene Willard, 1915–
Economic atlas of Pennsylvania. 1964. 16747

Miller, Herman P., 1863–
Outline maps of ... Pennsylvania. 1906. 16759
Outline maps of the counties of Allegheny,
Berks, Bucks, Cambria, Dauphin, Fayette
... Pa. 1901. 2458

Miller, James Matin, 1859–1939.
Twentieth century atlas. [1899] 1037
—— [1903] 6309
—— [1909] 3593
World up-to-date. [1899] 1038

Miller, Konrad, 1844–1933.
Mappae Arabicae. 6v. 1926–31. 5788
Mappaemundi: Die ältesten Weltkarten.
1895–98. 255

Miller, William A.
City of Plainfield, N.J. 1888. 15791
Insurance map of the city of Elizabeth [N.J.]
1874. 15745
Insurance map of the city of Paterson [N.J.]
1874. 15782
Insurance map of the city of Plainfield [N.J.]
1874. 15790
Insurance map of the city of Rahway [N.J.]
1873. 15794
Insurance map of the town of Union [N.J.]
1872. 15806
Insurance map of the town of West Hoboken
[N.J.] 1873. 15808

Miller, William S., *and others*.
Farm line and borough atlas of Delaware Co.
Penna. 1892. 16780

**Miller & Lord's Indexed street atlas of the metro-
politan Boston area. [1943]** 14432

Millett, John David, 1912–
Atlas of higher education in the United States.
1952. 10527

Milling, Martin Alexander.
Plat book, Madison County, Ind. 1954. 12848

**Mills, John Saxon, d. 1929, *and* Chrussachi,
Matthew George.**
Question de Thrace. 1919. 7817
Question of Thrace. 1919. 7816

Mills, Robert, 1781–1855.
Atlas of the state of South Carolina. [1825] 2570
—— *Facsim.* 1938. 16983
—— *Facsim.* 1965. 16984

Mills, William Corless, 1860–1928.
Archeological atlas of Ohio. 1914. 16362

Milner, Thomas, d. 1882.
See Petermann, August Heinrich, *and* Milner,
Thomas.

Milwaukee. *Tax Dept.*
Tentative land value maps of the city of Milwaukee. [1931] 18010
—— [1932] 18011
—— [1935] 18012

Milwaukee Journal.
Milwaukee Journal book of war maps.
[1942]   5886

Milwaukee Sentinel.
Practical road atlas of Wisconsin.   [1928]   17635

Minas Geraes, *Brazil. Serviço de Estatistica Geral.*
Album chorographico municipal do estado de
Minas Geraes.   1927.   18307
Atlas chorographico municipal   1926–27.   18306

"Minerva" Verlag der Literaturwerke.
See Verlag der Literaturwerke "Minerva" R.
Max Lippold.

Miniscalchi-Erizzo, Francesco, *conte,* 1811–1875.
Scoperte artiche atlante.   [1855]   3641

Minneapolis Journal.
Buying power; a study of the automobile
market . . . of Minneapolis.   1923.   15152

Minneapolis Real Estate Board.
Atlas of Minneapolis . . . Minn.   1903.   15150

Minneapolis Tribune.
Unrivaled atlas.   1899.   1039

Minnesota. *Dept. of Civil Defense.*
Survival plan map book.   [1957?]   14914

Minnesota. *Dept. of Highways.*
1941 traffic map . . . Counties of Minnesota.
[1942]   14918
Sectional maps showing counties, by town-
ship.   [1936]   14917

Minnesota. *State Drainage Commission.*
Atlas to accompany Report of water resources
investigation of Minnesota.   [1910–12]   14919

Missalowa, Gryzelda, *and* Schoenbrenner, Janina.
Historia Polski. Mapy.   1951.   9146

**Mississippi. *Highway Dept. Traffic and Planning
Division.***
Mississippi county traffic maps.   [1963]   15173
—— [1964]   15174

Missouri. *Geological Survey.*
Atlas accompanying reports of Missouri
Geological Survey.   1874.   15205
Geologic and topographic atlas.   1899.   15206
Report on the iron ores and coal fields. Atlas.
1873.   2059

Missouri. *State Highway Commission.*
Atlas of county maps.   [1938]   15207

Missouri Publishing Company.
Plat book of Barton County, Mo.   1903.   2069

Mitchell, Samuel Augustus, 1792–1868.
Ancient atlas.   [1844]   35
—— 1847.   5630
—— 1851.   5631
—— 1854.   5632
—— 1859.   36
—— 1860.   5633
—— 1863.   5634
—— 1864.   5635
—— 1874.   5636
—— 1880.   5637
Atlas of outline maps.   1839.   300
Maps of New Jersey, Pennsylvania, Maryland
& Delaware.   1846.   3692
New American atlas.   1831.   11026
New atlas of America.   1874.   1183
New atlas of North and South America.
1851.   1179
New general atlas.   1860.   831
—— 1862.   3558
—— 1863.   6145
—— 1864.   6150
—— 1865.   846
—— 1866.   848
—— 1867.   850
—— 1868.   3563
—— 1869.   6164
—— 1870.   859
—— 1873.   870
—— 1874.   6187
—— 1875.   6191
—— 1876.   880
—— 1878.   888
—— 1879.   890
—— 1880.   892
—— 1881.   895
—— 1882.   906
—— 1884.   920
—— [1887]   6234
—— 1893.   983
New reference atlas.   1865.   847
New school atlas.   1865.   301
—— 1867.   6160
—— 1869.   6165
—— 1871.   302
—— 1872.   6182
—— 1875.   6192
—— New and rev. ed.   1886.   4203
New universal atlas.   1846.   6103
—— 1847.   6104
—— 1848.   6106
—— 1849.   797
—— 1850.   800
—— 1851.   805
—— 1852.   807
—— 1853.   809
—— 1854   813, 814
—— 1855   6118
—— 1856.   4336
—— 1857.   823
—— 1858.   4340
—— 1859.   6135
School atlas.   [1839]   6085
—— [1842]   6094a

Montana. *State Engineer.*
 Water resources survey, Big Horn County,
 Mont. 1947.   15315

Montana. *State Highway Commission.*
 General highway and transportation maps.
 [1942]   15311
 Montana county maps. [1965]   15312
 —— [1967]   15313

Montgomery, Bernard Law Montgomery, *1st viscount,* **1887–**
 De la Normandie à la Baltique. Cartes.
 1948.   5890

Montieth, James, 1831–1890.
 Boys' and girls' atlas. [1884]   921
 Maps for Barnes' Complete Geography.
 1885.   11045
 School and family atlas of the world. [1890]   303

Montilla y Benítez, Rafael.
 Atlas geográfico de España. l. ed. [1941]   9335

Mooij, Jakob, 1868–
 Atlas der Protestantsche Kerk in Nederlandsch Oost-Indië. 1925.   9734

Moor, A. de.
 Nieuwe wereld atlas. [1921]   6450
 Nieuwste uitgebreide wereld atlas. [194–]   6997

Moore, Berlie.
 See Ice, John R., *and* Moore, Berlie.

Moore, *Sir* **Jonas, 1617–1679.**
 New geography. 1681.   3443

Moore, S. S., *and* **Jones, T. W.**
 Traveller's directory. 1802.   1327
 —— 1804.   1328

Moore, William L.
 Plat book, Jefferson County, Ill. 1961.   12290

Morales, P.
 Atlas geográfico del Ecuador. 1942.   18362

Morales y Eloy, Juan.
 Ecuador, atlas histórico-geográfico. 1942.   18357
 Pequeño atlas geográfico del Ecuador.
 [1938]   18360

Morden, Robert, *d.* **1703.**
 Atlas terrestris. [1700]   5957
 Geography rectified. 1680.   4265
 —— 2d ed. 1688.   498
 —— 3d ed. 1693.   4268
 —— 1700.   3454

Morgan, F. B.
 See Nash, G. V., *and* Morgan, F. B.

Mori, Alberto.
 See Mori, Assunto, 1872– *and* Mori,
 Alberto.

Mori, Assunto, 1872–
 Atlante di geografia fisica, politica et economica. [1918]   6383
 Piccolo atlante di geografia fisica, politica,
 economica. 1928.   6679

Mori, Assunto, 1872– *and* **Mori, Alberto.**
 Atlante di geografia politica economica.
 [1936]   5446

Mori, Giuseppe, 1911–
 "Itinera," atlante storico commentato.
 [1942]   5535
 "Itinera," atlante storico: evo antico. [1949]   5641
 Via maestra, atlante storico. 1951.   5536

Morin, P. L.
 [Plans, cartes, vues et dessins relatifs a l'histoire de la Nouvelle France. 1853]   10353

Morley, Harvey W., 1876–
 Atlas of Steuben County, Ind. 1912.   3739a
 Atlas section [of] the 1954 history of Steuben
 County, Ind. 1954.   12919
 1955 history of Steuben County, Ind. 1956.   12921

Morris, Charles.
 See Hunter, Robert, 1824–1897, *and* Morris,
 Charles.

Morris, Frank Lemerise, 1907– *and others.*
 Marine atlas. [1959]   10287

Morris, Frank Lemerise, *and* **Heath, Willis Robertson, 1908–**
 Magnetic courses, distances ... Puget Sound
 and adjacent waters. 1948.   17590
 See also Heath, Willis Robertson, 1908–
 and Morris, Frank Lemerise, 1907–

Morris, John Wesley.
 See Rutherford, James C., *and* Morris, John
 Wesley.

Morris, John Wesley, *and* **McReynolds, Edwin C.**
 Historical atlas of Oklahoma. [1965]   16588

Morris, Lewis, 1701–1765.
 Plans of harbours ... in St. George's Channel.
 1748.   3999
 Plans of the principal harbours ... in St.
 George's and the Bristol Channels. 1801.   2889

Morris Motor, *Cowley, Eng.*
 Along the roads of Britain. [1948]   8047

Morrison, Olin Dee, 1892–
 Canada and the Provinces; new historical
 atlas. v. 2. 1958.   10348

Indiana, "Hoosier State"; new historical atlas
1958. 12725
Ohio in maps and charts. 1956. 16367

Morrow, F. E.
Plat book of Iowa County, Wis. 1895. 17764

Morrow, Franklin H.
Land ownership plat book of Craighead
County, Ark. 1965. 11294
Land ownership plat book of Jackson County,
Ark. 1945. 11296
Land ownership platbook of Lawrence
County, Ark. 1958. 11298

Morrow, Oliver.
Atlas and directory of Paulding County,
Ohio. [1906] 2407

**Morrow, Oliver, *and* Bashore, Frederick William.
1831–1902.**
Historical atlas of Paulding County, Ohio.
[1967?] 16441

Morse, Charles Walker, 1823–1887.
Diamond atlas. 1857. 824
General atlas. 1856. 817

Morse, E. D.
See Covington, C. C., *and* Morse, E. D.

Morse, Jedidiah, 1761–1826.
American geography. 1794. 1361

**Morse, Jedidiah, 1761–1826 *and* Morse, Sidney
Edwards, 1794–1871.**
Modern atlas. 1822. 304
—— 1828. 305
New universal atlas. 1822. 306

Morse, Sidney Edwards, 1794–1871.
Atlas of the United States. 1823. 11025
Cerographic Bible atlas. 1844. 3221
—— 1845. 3222
—— 1860. 5363
New universal atlas. 1825. 746
See also Brigham, John C., *and* Morse, Sidney
Edwards.
—— Morse, Jedidiah, *and* Morse, Sidney
Edwards.

**Morse, Sidney Edwards, *and* Breese, Samuel, 1802–
1873.**
Cerographic atlas of the United States. 1842. 1383
North American atlas. 1842–[45] 1228

Morse, Sidney Edwards, and Company.
Cerographic missionary atlas. [1848] 182

Morse-Warren Engineering Company.
Plat book of Macoupin County, Ill. 1911. 4579

Mortgage Conference of New York.
Population survey No. 3–B, Brooklyn [N.Y.]
1945. 15948
Queens population survey No. 4–A. 1942. 16123

Mortier, Cornelis, 1699–1783.
See Cóvens, Johannes, 1697–1774, *and*
Mortier, Cornelis, 1699–1783.

Mortier, David, 1673–*ca.* 1728.
Nouveau théâtre de la Grande Bretagne.
1715–28. 4002

Mortier, Pieter, *d.* 1711.
Atlas nouveau des cartes géographiques
choisies. 1703. 2823
Forces de l'Europe, Asie, Afrique et Amérique.
[1702?] 537, 2781a

**Moscow. Nauchno-issledovatel'skiĭ Institut Ėkono-
miki Moskovskoĭ Oblasti.**
Атлас Московской области. [Atlas of the
Moscow Oblast] 1933–[34] 9286

Moscow Publishing Company.
Atlas of Latah County, Idaho. 1937. 12041

Moskvin, M. M.
See Bogdanov, A. A., *and* Moskvin, M. M.

Motormännens Riksförbund.
Vägvisare: Kartor och ortsbeskrivningar över
Sverige. 1957. 9386

Moule, Thomas, 1784–1851.
English counties delineated. 1838. 2926

Mount, Richard, *d.* 1722, *and* Page, Thomas.
Atlas maritimus novus. 1702. 3334

Mountain States Map Company.
See Smith Map Company.

**Mowrer, Edgar Ansel, 1892– *and* Rajchman,
Marthe.**
Global war. 1942. 5891
—— [1943] 5892

Mudie, Robert, 1777–1842.
Gilbert's Modern atlas. [1841?] 780

Mück, Ida.
Preussen-Atlas. 1915. 8761

Mueller, August H.
Atlas of Absecon Island, N.J. 1984.
4915, 4916, 4917, 4919, 4920
Atlas of Delaware County [Pa.] 1909–13.
3888, 5016
Atlas of Lower Merion, Montgomery Co.,
including part of Delaware Co. [Pa.] 1896. 2514
Atlas of part of Morris County, N.J. 1910. 3834
Atlas of properties on main line Pennsylvania

Railroad from Devon to Downington and West Chester [Pa.] 1912.   3887a

Atlas of properties on main line Pennsylvania Railroad from Overbrook to Paoli [Pa.] 1908.   2450

—— 1913.   5011

—— 1920.   16893

Atlas of properties on the Reading Railway embracing Cheltenham, Abington, Springfield [Pa.] 1909.   3890, 3891, 3897

Atlas of the city of Erie, Pa. 1917.   5021

Atlas of the city Paterson, N.J. 1915.   4918

Atlas of the city of Yonkers, N.Y. 1907. 2337

Atlas of the North Penn section of Montgomery County, Pa. 1916.   5018

Mueller, A. H., and Company.

Atlas of Cheltenham, Abington, and Springfield townships and vicinity, Montgomery Co., Pa. 1897.   2490, 2501, 2509, 2557

Atlas of Essex County, N.J. [1901]–1906. 2157

Atlas of properties on line of Pennsylvania R.R. from Rosemont to Westchester [Pa.] 1897.   2449, 2555, 2558

Atlas of surveys of Mahoning County, Ohio. 1899–1900.   2397

Müller, Johann Christoph, 1673–1721.

Schweizerischer Atlas. [1712?]   3150

Müller, Johann Ulrich.

Kurtz-bündige Abbild- und Vorstellung der gantzen Welt. 1692.   512

Müller, Maximilian.

See Schenk, Alois, *and* Müller, Maximilian.

Mueller and Coe.

Atlas of Sedgwick County, Kans. 1931. 14200

Muir, Ramsay, *i.e.*, John Ramsay Bryce, 1872–1941.

Hammond's New historical atlas for students. 2d ed. [1914?]   4138

—— 4th ed. [1920]   5537

Historical atlas. 8th ed. [1952]   5538

New school atlas of modern history. 1911. 3316

—— 7th ed. 1921.   5673

—— 9th ed. 1926.   5674

Philips' Atlas of ancient and classical history. 1938.   5642

Philips' Atlas of ancient, mediaeval and modern history. 1938.   5539

Philips' New historical atlas for students. 1911.   5540

—— 5th ed. 1923.   5541

Philips New school atlas of universal history. 11th ed. 1929.   5542

—— 12th ed. 1935.   5543

Putnam's Historical atlas, mediaeval and modern. 6th ed. 1927.   5544

Muirhead, James Herbert Hawksworth, 1860–1954.

Atlas of Congressional districts, 79th Congress. 1945.   10441

City of New York, political divisions. [1936] 16046

State and city of New York political divisions. [1945]   15825

Mulert, Hermann, *i.e.*, Christian Hermann, 1879–1950.

See Heussi, Karl, 1877–1961, *and* Mulert, Hermann, *i.e.*, Christian Hermann, 1879–1950.

Munger, William P.

Historical atlas of New York State. [1941] 15851

Municipal Plat Map Service.

Plat map of the city of Davenport, Iowa. [1948?]   14117

Munn, A. M.

Atlas of Otoe County, Nebr. 1902.   2122

Muris, Oswald, 1884–1964, *and* Wand, Otto, 1879–1949.

Grosse Weltatlas der Deutschen Buch-Gemeinschaft. [1929]   6708

Henius Weltatlas. 1929.   6709

Welt–Atlas. 1936.   6884

Murray, Allan.

British Isles. [1958]   8008

Murray, Paul R.

Atlas of Morgan County, Ohio. 1902.   3876

Murray-Aaron, Eugene, 1852–1941.

Home and library map-atlas of the United States. 1914.   4532

Murray's Small classical atlas. [1904]   5611

—— 2d ed. 1917.   5612

Muskingum Climatic Research Center, *New Philadelphia, O.*

Hourly precipitation on the upper Ohio and Susquehanna drainage basins. [1939–41] 10501

Precipitation on the Muskingum River watershed, Ohio. [1939–42]   16584

Mutual Broadcasting System.

Standard broadcast allocation maps. 1946. 10720

—— [1948]   10721

—— [1954]   10722

Mysore. *Dept. of Statistics.*

Mysore State in maps. 1958.   9725

Naake-Nakęski, Kazimierz.

Mapa królestwa Polskiego. [1920?]   9154

Naeff, M. A.

Property atlas of Montgomery County, Pa. 1893.   2489

Nagano-ken Chizu Kenkyūjo, *Nagano, Japan.*
Nagano-ken chizu taikei. [General atlas of
Nagano Prefecture. 1954] 9856

Nágera, Juan José.
Atlas de la República Argentina. 1926. 18216

Nagoya Jūtaku Kyōkai.
Nagoya-shi zenjūtaku annaizu. [Real estate
map of Nagoya. 1957?] 9929

Nanke, Czesław, 1883- *and others.*
Mały atlas historyczny. 1950. 7688
—— 1951. 7689
—— 1955. 7690

Napier, *Sir* **William Francis Patrick, 1785–1860.**
[History of the war in the Peninsula and in the
south of France. Maps. 1842] 7717

Napoléon I, *Emperor of the French,* **1769–1821.**
Guerre d'Orient. Atlas. 1847. 2976, 4084

Napoléon III, *Emperor of the French,* **1808–1873.**
Histoire de Jules César. Atlas. 1865–66. 3285

Nascimento, Augusto do.
Atlas de geografia. 3. ed. 1946. 7244

Nash, G. V.
Illustrated historical atlas of Manitowoc
County, Wis. 1878. 3932

Nash, G. V., and Morgan, F. B.
Atlas of Pierce County, Wis. 1877–78. 2655

Nassau County, *N.Y.*
Land map of the county of Nassau ... N.Y.
1938. 15889

Natanson-Leski, Jan.
Atlas historyczny szkolny. 1931. 9147
Atlas szkolny do dziejów áredniowiecza.
1928. 5657

National atlas of the United States. [1955–63] 11078

National Broadcasting Company.
NBC affiliated station maps. 1939. 10723

National Bus Traffic Association.
Atlas of motor bus routes. [1949] 10876
—— 1956. 10903
—— 1966. 10966

National Cash Register Company.
Money of the world. [1935?] 6852

National Geographic Society.
National Geographic atlas of the fifty United
States. [1960] 11082

National Map Company.
New standard atlas of the United States.
1916. 4533, 4533a
—— 1917. 4534
New standard atlas of the world. 1916. 4430
Official paved road and commercial survey of
the United States. [1927] 11059
—— [1929] 11061
—— [1930] 11062
—— 1931. 10820

National Outdoor Advertising Bureau.
Buyer's guide to poster advertising. 1959. 10553

National Petroleum Bibliography.
Geological maps: Oklahoma oil & gas. 1961. 16587
Geological maps—Panhandle oil & gas.
1965. 17134

National Publishing Company.
Imperial atlas of Gratiot County, Mich.
1901. 1971
Tourists' standard road book and directory of
New York State. 1897. 15843

National Publishing Company, *Philadelphia.*
Bible atlas. [1944] 5364

National Research Council, Canada. *Division of*
Building Research.
Climatological atlas of Canada. 1953. 10339

National Roads and Motorists' Association.
Touring grounds around Sydney. [8th ed.
195–] 10177
—— [14th ed. 1956] 10178

National Safety Council.
Road atlas, travel safety guide. [1964] 10950
Travel safety guide and road atlas. [1967] 10975

National Society for Promoting the Education of the
Poor.
Maps illustrative of the physical, political, and
historical geography of the British Empire.
[1851] 7987

National Survey Company.
Eastern ski atlas. 1964. 10751
—— [2d ed.] 1965. 10752
—— 1966. 10753
Jenney road atlas ... New England and vicinity. [1952] 10888
—— [1958] 10914
—— [1960] 10928
—— [1961] 10932a
—— [1964] 10951
Official map of Maine. [1934] 14308
Official maps of New England. [1920] 10774
—— [1921] 10777
Official maps of New York. [1921] 15850
Official National Survey maps. [1925] 10788
—— 1927. 10794
—— 1928. 10801

Official National Survey maps ... New England. [1936]   10837

Road atlas, New England and vicinity. [1940]   10853

—— [1942]   10859

—— [1948]   10874

Nationalsozialistische Deutsche Arbeiter-Partei. *Reichsjugendführung. Amt für Weltanschauliche Schulung.*

Kampf um das Reich. 1940.   8572

Nationalsozialistische Gemeinschaft "Kraft durch Freude." *Amt "Reisen, Wandern, Urlaub."*

Taschen atlas. [194–]   8701

Nationalsozialistisches Fliegerkorps.

Dem Reichsminister Dr. Inf. Ohnesorge ... zum 70. Geburtstage. MS. 1942.   8518

Navarro, Tomás.

Español en Puerto Rico. 1948.   18177

Naymiller, Filippo, *and* **Allodi, Pietro,** *fl.* **1859–1878.**

Atlante di geografia universale. [1867]   851

Neal, M. Prouse.

Township map, Oswego County, N.Y. 1928.   15900

Nebraska. *State Engineer.*

Nebraska county maps showing State and federal highway system. 1934.   15341

Nebraska. *Survival Project.*

Operational survival plan, State of Nebraska. [1958]   15340

Nebraska. University. *Conservation and Survey Division.*

Ground water atlas of Nebraska. 1966.   15342

Nebraska Farmer.

What makes Nebraska tick—agriculturally. [1951?]   15338

Nederlandsch Aardrijkskundig Genootschap, Amsterdam.

Atlas van Indië. [194–]   9751

Atlas van tropisch Nederland. 1938.   9750

Nederlandsch Onderwijzers-Genootschap.

Atlas van het Koningrijk der Nederlanden. 2. druk. [1855]   9086

Nederlandsche Rijnvaartvereeniging.

Rhine and connecting waterways. [1950]   7883

Neeper, Alexander M.

Maps and descriptions of the election districts in the cities of Pittsburgh and Allegheny. 1886.   16901

Nejdl, B., *and* **Palášek, J.**

Přehledná Silniční mapa. [1947]   8243

Nellans, George.

Atlas of Decatur County, Kans. 1949.   14157

Nelson, E. A.

Atlas of Traverse County, Minn. 1902.   15115

Nelson, Helge, *and* **Rydefält, Elvi.**

Vem är orienterad på kartan? [1947]   7274

Nelson, John L.

Mitchell [S.Dak.] Gas Co. system of mains, street lamps [etc.] 1905.   17064

Township map and manual of Davison County, S.Dak. [1915]   5060

Nelson, Thomas, 1822–1892, *and* **Davies, Thomas.**

New atlas of the world. 1859.   6136

Nelson, Thomas, and Sons.

Map book of the world-wide war. [1915?]   4236

Universal hand-atlas [1925]   6587

Nelson, Thomas O., Company.

Aerial-photographic atlas of Freeborn County, Minn. 1965.   14990

Aerial-photographic atlas of Meeker County, Minn. 1965.   15043

Aerial-photographic atlas of Morrison County, Minn. 1965.   15049

Aerial-photographic atlas of Ransom County, N.Dak. 1965.   16314

Aerial-photographic atlas of Renville County, N.Dak. 1965.   16316

Aerial-photographic atlas of Steele County, N.Dak. 1965.   16331

Atlas of Barnes County, N.Dak. 1958.   16256

—— 1963.   16257

Atlas of Becker County, Minn. 1964.   14928

Atlas of Benson County, N.Dak. 1959.   16259

—— 1964.   16260

Atlas of Benton County, Minn. 1961.   14933

Atlas of Big Stone County, Minn. 1960.   14935

Atlas of Blue Earth County, Minn. 1962.   14939

Atlas of Bottineau County, N.Dak. 1959.   16264

—— 1964.   16265

Atlas of Brookings County, S.Dak. 1963.   17019

Atlas of Brown County, Minn. 1964.   14941

Atlas of Brown County, S.Dak. 1960.   17020

Atlas of Buchanan County, Iowa. 1966.   13127

Atlas of Burke County, N.Dak. 1963.   16267

Atlas of Cass County, N.Dak. 1957.   16271

—— 1966.   16272

Atlas of Cavalier County, N.Dak. 1958.   16274

—— 1964.   16275

Atlas of Chippewa County, Minn. 1964.   14949

Atlas of Chisago County, Minn. 1961.   14951

Atlas of Clark County, S.Dak. 1959.   17021

Atlas of Clay County, Minn. 1964.   14956

Atlas of Codington County, S.Dak. 1959.   17025

Atlas of Cottonwood County, Minn. 1961.   14962

Atlas of Deuel County, S.Dak. 1957.   17030

Atlas of Dickey County, N.Dak. 1958.	16276	Atlas of Pembina County, N.Dak. 1958.	16304
—— 1964.	16277	—— 1963.	16305
Atlas of Dickinson County, Iowa. 1962.	13352	Atlas of Pierce County, N.Dak. 1960.	16306
Atlas of Douglas County, Minn. 1958.	14978	—— 1965.	16307
—— 1966.	14980	Atlas of Pierce County, Wis. 1959.	17874
Atlas of Dunn County, Wis. 1959.	17729	Atlas of Pipestone County, Minn. 1961.	15077
Atlas of Emmet County, Iowa. 1962.	13373	Atlas of Polk County, Minn. 1964.	15079
Atlas of Emmons County, N.Dak. 1962.	16279	Atlas of Polk County, Wis. 1959.	17879
Atlas of Faribault County, Minn. 1962.	14983	Atlas of Pope County, Minn. 1963.	15081
Atlas of Fayette County, Iowa. 1966.	13387	Atlas of Ramsey County, N.Dak 1959.	16311
Atlas of Fillmore County, Minn. 1966	14987	Atlas of Ransom County, N.Dak. 1960.	16313
Atlas of Floyd County, Iowa. 1960.	13397	Atlas of Renville County, Minn. 1962.	15090
Atlas of Goodhue County, Minn. 1958.	14993	Atlas of Rice County, Minn. 1964.	15092
—— 1965.	14994	Atlas of Richland County, N.Dak. 1960.	16317
Atlas of Grand Forks County, N.Dak. 1957.	16283	—— 1965.	16318
—— 1963.	16284	Atlas of Roberts County, S.Dak. 1961.	17053
Atlas of Grant County, Minn. 1964.	14997	—— 1966.	17054
Atlas of Grant County, N.Dak. 1964.	16286	Atlas of Rock County, Minn. 1961.	15095
Atlas of Griggs County, N.Dak. 1959.	16287	Atlas of Rolette County, N.Dak. 1959.	16321
—— 1964.	16288	—— 1964.	16322
Atlas of Hamlin County, S.Dak. 1957.	17035	Atlas of St. Croix County, Wis. 1959.	17911
Atlas of Hettinger County, N.Dak. 1963.	16289	—— 1967.	17913
Atlas of Houston County, Minn. 1958.	15000	Atlas of Sargent County, N.Dak. 1958.	16324
—— 1965.	15001	—— 1963.	16325
Atlas of Hutchinson County, S.Dak. 1961.	17037	Atlas of Sibley County, Minn. 1958.	15103
Atlas of Isanti County, Minn. 1962.	15006	Atlas of Spink County, S.Dak. 1961.	17056
Atlas of Jackson County, Minn. 1961.	15013	Atlas of Stark County, N.Dak. 1963.	16328
Atlas of Kanabec County, Minn. 1961–[62]	15015	Atlas of State of North Dakota. 1961.	16254
Atlas of Kandiyohi County, Minn. 1961.	15017	Atlas of State of Wisconsin. 1959.	17645
Atlas of Kingsbury County, S.Dak. 1957.	17039	Atlas of Stearns County, Minn. 1963.	15106
—— 1966.	17040	Atlas of Steele County, N.Dak. 1960.	16330
Atlas of La Moure County, N.Dak. 1958.	16290	Atlas of Stutsman County, N.Dak. 1958.	16333
—— 1963.	16291	Atlas of Swift County, Minn. 1961.	15112
Atlas of Lake County, S.Dak. 1957.	17041	Atlas of the State of Iowa. 1956.	13017
Atlas of Le Sueur County, Minn. 1963.	15026	Atlas of the State of Minnesota. 1954.	14922
Atlas of Lincoln County, Minn. 1965.	15028	—— 1962.	14923
Atlas of Lincoln County, S.Dak. 1962.	17043	Atlas of Towner County, N.Dak. 1959.	16337
Atlas of Logan County, N.Dak. 1964.	16292	—— 1964.	16338
Atlas of Lyon County, Iowa. 1962.	13672	Atlas of Traverse County, Minn. 1960.	15117
Atlas of Lyon County, Minn. 1961.	15029	—— 1965.	15118
Atlas of McCook County, S.Dak. 1961.	17044	Atlas of Turner County, S.Dak. 1958.	17059
Atlas of McIntosh County, N.Dak. 1964.	16294	—— 1966.	17060
Atlas of McLeod County, Minn. 1963.	15031	Atlas of Walsh County, N.Dak. 1957.	16341
Atlas of Martin County, Minn. 1961.	15039	Atlas of Waseca County, Minn. 1957.	15125
Atlas of Meeker County, Minn. 1959.	15042	—— 1964.	15126
Atlas of Mille Lacs County, Minn. 1962.	15045	Atlas of Watonwan County, Minn. 1959.	15130
Atlas of Miner County, S.Dak. 1961.	17046	Atlas of Wells County, N.Dak. 1960.	16345
Atlas of Minnehaha County, S.Dak. 1966.	17049	—— 1965.	16346
Atlas of Mitchell County, Iowa. 1960.	13743	Atlas of Wilkin County, Minn. 1964.	15132
Atlas of Moody County, S.Dak. 1957.	17050	Atlas of Williams County, N.Dak. 1965.	16349
—— 1965.	17051	Atlas of Winona County, Minn. 1957.	15134
Atlas of Mountrail County, N.Dak. 1966.	16299	—— 1966.	15136
Atlas of Mower County, Minn. 1966.	15052	Atlas of Worth County, Iowa. 1960.	14096
Atlas of Murray County, Minn. 1961.	15055	Atlas of Wright County, Minn. 1964.	15138
Atlas of Nelson County, N.Dak. 1963.	16302	Atlas of Yellow Medicine County, Minn. 1964.	15140
Atlas of Nicollet County, Minn. 1962.	15058		
Atlas of Nobles County, Minn. 1961.	15061		
—— 1966.	15062	**Nelson, Wilbur Armistead, 1889–**	
Atlas of Norman County, Minn. 1958.	15065	*See* Mathews, Edward Bennett, 1869–1944	
Atlas of Oliver County, N.Dak. 1964.	16303	*and* Nelson, Wilbur Armistead, 1889–	
Atlas of Osceola County, Iowa. 1962.	13810		
Atlas of Otter Tail County, Minn. 1960.	15071	**Neptune François.** 1693–1700.	517
		—— [1792–1803]	2848

Neptunia *(Buenos Aires)*
  Guía náutica Neptunia del Rio de La Plata.
  [1949]   18197

Netherlands *(Kingdom, 1815–   ) Bijhoudings-*
dienst der Rijksdriehoeksmeting.
  Atlas der Rijksdriehoeksmeting met de topo-
  grafische kaart. [1935]   9039

Netherlands *(Kingdom, 1815–   ) Bureau voor de*
Wegen- en Verkeersstatistiek.
  Atlas van de rijkswegen, 1946. [1947]   9063
  —— 1949. [1950]   9068
  —— 1954. [3. uitg. 1954]   9073

Netherlands *(Kingdom, 1815–   ) Centraal*
Bureau voor de Statistiek.
  Landbouwatlas van Nederland. [1939]   9028

Netherlands *(Kingdom, 1815–   ) Commissie van*
den geschiedkundigen atlas van Nederland.
  De Bourgondische tijd. [Text] 1915   5270
  Geschiedkundige   atlas   van   Nederland.
  [1911]–1916.   4046, 5271
  Holland, Zeeland en Westfriesland in 1300.
  [Text] 1916.   5272
  Rechterlijke indeeling na 1795. [Text] 1915. 5273

Netherlands *(Kingdom, 1815–   )Departement*
van Marine.
  Meteorologie Nederlands Nieuw Guinea.
  1959.   10193
  Stroom-atlas, monden van de Eems. 1944.   9075
  Stroom-atlas, monden van de Wester- en
  Ooster-Schelde. 1944.   9076
  Stroomatlas voor de Nederlandse kust.
  1951.   9077
  Stroom-atlas, zeegat aan de Hoek van Hol-
  land en de Maas. 1944.   9078

Netherlands *(Kingdom, 1815–   ) Dienst der*
Zuiderzeewerken.
  Verspreiding van verzorgende diensten en in-
  stellingen in Nederland. [1953]   9046

Netherlands *(Kingdom, 1815–   ) Meteorologisch*
Instituut.
  Monatskarten der Meeresströmungen im
  Indischen Ozean. [193–?]   10241
  Oceanographische   en   meteorologische
  waarnemingen in de Chineesche Zeeën.
  1935–36.   9497
  Oceanographische   en   meteorologische
  waarnemingen in den Atlantischen Oceaan.
  [1919–31]   10224
  Oceanographische   en   meteorologische
  waarnemingen in den Indischen Oceaan.
  [1908]   10237
  —— [1911–15]   10238
  Rode Zee en Golf van Aden. [1949]   9499
  Temperatuur van het zeewater … van den
  Noorder Atlantischen Oceaan. 1872.   10225
  Zeegebieden rond Australië. [1949]   10248

Netherlands *(Kingdom, 1815–   ) Rijksdienst*
voor het Nationale Plan.
  Benelux, gemeentenatlas. [1952]   7826
  [Cartogrammenatlas. 1946?–48?]   9038

Netherlands. *Council of Voorn.*
  Voorne caart-boek van alle de dorpen, en
  polders gelegen inden lande van oost ende
  west Voorne. 1701.   3089

Netherlands. *Topographische Inrichting.*
  Atlas van het Koninkrijk der Nederlanden.
  1900.   3086

Neto, Martinho Prado.
  Os valores dos terrenos na cidade de São
  Paulo. 1957.   18318

Neubauer, Friedrich, 1861–
  Geschichts-Atlas   insbesondere   zu   den
  Lehrbüchern der Geschichte. 13. Aufl.
  1914.   5159

Neussel, Otto.
  See Vilanova y Piera, J. Atlas geográfico universal. 1877.

Nevada. *Dept. of Economic Development.*
  Basic data on industrial Nevada. 1956.   15650

Nevada Evening Journal, *Nevada, Iowa.*
  Plat book, Story County, Iowa. [1944]   13950

New Brunswick. *Dept. of Lands and Mines.*
  New Brunswick. [1967]   10395

New Hampshire. *Geological Survey.*
  Geology of New Hampshire. Atlas. 1874–
  78.   2135

New Jersey. *Dept. of Conservation and Develop-*
ment.
  [Topographic atlas of New Jersey. 1917]   15679

New Jersey. *Geological Survey.*
  Atlas of New Jersey. [1889]   2149

New Jersey. *State Highway Dept.*
  General highway maps of New Jersey.
  [1947]   15677

New Mexico. *State Engineer.*
  Maps of the San Juan River Hydrographic
  Survey. [1938]   15822

New Mexico. *State Highway Dept.*
  Cities, towns, villages in New Mexico.
  [1953]   15811

New Rochelle, N.Y. *Assessors.*
  City of New Rochelle, N.Y. 1907.   2289

New South Wales.
 Historical records of New South Wales. Atlas.
 1893.   3254

New York *(City) Board of Education.*
 Maps showing territory covered by the local
 school board districts and location of the
 public schools of the city of New York.
 [1910]   3850

New York *(City) Board of Estimate and Apportion-*
ment.
 Area district map. [1924] 16015
 —— [1927]   16025
 —— [1937]   16048
 Desk map of the city of New York. [1937] 16049
 Height district map. [1924] 16016
 —— [1927]   16026
 —— [1937]   16050
 Map of the city of New York. [1914] 16003
 —— [1924]   16017
 Sectional aerial map of the city of New York.
 [1924]   16018
 Use district map. [1924] 16019
 —— [1927]   16027
 —— [1937]   16051

New York *(City) Board of Taxes and Assessments.*
 Land map of the city of New York. 1890. 2307

New York *(City) City Planning Commission.*
 Sectional map of the city of New York.
 [1942]   16055
 —— [1945]   16064, 16065
 —— [1947]   16069
 —— [1951]   16079
 —— [1955]   16090
 —— [1957]   16094
 —— [1963]   16104
 Zoning maps. [1961] 16100

New York *(City) Commissioner of Street Improve-*
ments.
 Maps . . . showing location, width, grades, and
 class of streets, roads . . . 23rd and 24th
 wards of the city of New York. 1895. 3847

New York *(City) Dept. of City Planning.*
 Area zoning map of the city of New York.
 [1947]   16070
 —— [1954]   16085
 Height zoning map of the city of New York.
 [1947]   16071
 —— [1954]   16086
 Sectional map of the city of New York.
 [1940]   16053
 Use zoning map of the city of New York.
 [1947]   16072
 —— [1954]   16087

New York *(City) Dept. of Street Cleaning.*
 Borough of Brooklyn [N.Y.] 1905. 15943
 —— 1909.   15944
 Borough of the Bronx. 1903. 16114

New York *(City) Dept. of Taxes and Assessments.*
 Land map of the county of Bronx. 1918. 4954
 Land map of the county of New York.
 [1917]   4926
 Tentative land value maps of the city of New
 York. 1916–17.   4952
 See also New York *(City) Tax Dept.*

New York *(City) Tax Dept.*
 Land value maps. [1909] 15999
 Tentative land value maps of the city of New
 York. 1912.   16000
 —— 1915.   16004
 —— 1916.   16006
 —— 1917.   16008
 —— 1918.   16009
 —— 1921.   16011
 —— 1922.   16012
 —— 1923.   16014
 —— 1924.   16020
 —— 1925.   16022
 —— 1926.   16023
 —— 1927.   16028
 —— 1928.   16029
 —— 1929.   16033
 —— 1930.   16035
 —— 1931.   16036
 —— 1932.   16037
 —— 1933.   16039
 —— 1934.   16042
 —— [1935]   16044
 —— 1939.   16052

New York *(County) Board of Supervisors.*
 Maps of Senate and Assembly Districts in the
 county of New York. 1866. 15986

New York *(State) Niagara Frontier Planning*
Board.
 Atlas, Erie County [N.Y. 1939] 15877
 Atlas, Niagara County [N.Y. 1938] 15896

New York *(State) University. Regents' Inquiry into*
the Character and Cost of Public Education.
 School district atlas of the State of New York.
 [1937]   15846

New York Evening Journal.
 Working sales manual of the New York market. [1928]   16030

New Zealand. *Atlas Committee.*
 Descriptive atlas of New Zealand. 1959. 10202a

New Zealand. *Census and Statistics Dept.*
 Maps of urban areas. 1952. 10195

Newnes, George.
 Comprehensive war atlas. [1939] 5893
 Handy pocket atlas of the world and gazet-
 teer. [1925]   6588
 Modern pictorial atlas. [1939] 6979
 Motorists' touring guide of the British Isles.
 [1928?]   8032

Motorists touring maps and gazetteer ... of
the British Isles. [1931]   8035
—— [1935]   8037
—— [1950]   8053
New motoring atlas of Great Britain and
Ireland. [1935]   8038

Newnes' Modern world atlas. [1933]   6791

Newsweek.
Global war, 1939–1943. [1944?]   5894
Global war atlas. 1944.   5895

Newton, Joseph H., 1836–1922.
See Caldwell, Joseph A.

Newton, Lewis W., *and* Irving, Peyton.
Victory historical map and outline book.
[1921]   10633
—— [1922]   10634

Nichols, Beach.
Atlas of Armstrong County, Pa. 1876.   16770
Atlas of Blair and Huntingdon Counties, Pa.
1873.   2462, 2477
Atlas of Chenango County, N.Y. 1875.   15874
Atlas of Lycoming County, Pa. 1873.   2483
Atlas of Ontario County, N.Y. 1874.   4928
Atlas of Perry, Juniata, and Mifflin Counties,
Pa. 1877.   2479, 2485, 2493
Atlas of Schuyler County, N.Y. 1874.   15903
Atlas of York Co., Pa. 1876.   2500
See also Beers, Frederick W., *and* Nichols,
Beach.

Nichols, Beach, *and others.*
Atlas of Herkimer County, N.Y. 1868.   2230
Atlas of Montgomery and Fulton Counties,
N.Y. 1868.   2228, 2239

Nichols, Francis, *fl.* 1809.
New atlas. 1811.   3375

Nicolay, Charles Grenfell.
See Ansted, David Thomas, 1814–1800, *and*
Nicolay, Charles Grenfell.

Nicolet, Hercule.
Atlas de physique. 1855.   233

Nicolosi, Giovanni Battista, 1610–1670.
Dell'Hercole e studio geografico. 1660.   467
Hercvles, Sicvlvs sive stvdivm geographicvm.
1670–71.   482

Nicolson, William, 1655–1727.
Description of part of the Empire of Germany.
1681.   3032
Description of the remaining part of the Em-
pire of Germany. 1683.   2864, 3034

Niedermayer, Oskar von, 1885–*ca.* 1945.
Wehrgeographischer Atlas der Union der
Sozialistischen Sowjetrepubliken. 1941.   9217

Wehrgeographischer Atlas von Frankreich.
1939.   8399
Wehrgeographischer Atlas von Grossbritan-
nien. 1940.   8009
—— 2. ergänzte Aufl. 1941.   8010

Niel, Adolphe, 1802–1869.
Siège de Sébastopol. Atlas. 1858.   3103

Nielsen, Axel, 1897–
Geografisk tegne– og arbejdsbog. 7. opl.
v. 2. 1951.   5757

Nielsen, Niels, 1893–
Atlas over Danmark. 1949.   8286

Niemcowna, Stanisław.
See Romer, Eugeniusz, 1871–1954, *and*
Niemeowna, Stanisław.

Niermeyer, Jan Frederik, 1866–1923.
See Bos, Pieter Roelof, 1847–1902, *and*
Niermeyer, Jan Frederik, 1866–1923.

Niessen, Josef, 1864–1942.
Geschichtlicher Handatlas der Deutschen
Länder am Rhein. [1950]   8773

Nietmann, Wilhelm.
Eisenbahn-Atlas   für   Deutsches   Reich,
Luxemburg,   Schweiz,   Oesterreichisch-
Ungarische Monarchie und angrenzende
Gebiete. 1902.   2797, 3147
Grosser Atlas der Eisenbahnen von Mittel-
Europa. ll. Aufl. 1892–93.   7755

Nihill, J. J.
See Dunne, Thomas Joseph, *and* Nihill, J. J.

Nihon Chihō Gyōsei Kenkyūkai.
Zenkoku shi-chō-son benran fu bunken chizu.
[Manual of cities, towns, and villages, to-
gether with a prefectural atlas. Rev. ed.
1950]   9779

Nihon Chizu Gakkai.
Suchūdentsu Nihon chizuchō. [Students' atlas
of Japan. 1948]   9821

Nihon Chizu Kabushiki Kaisha, *Tokyo.*
Kantō-Chihō poketto rekuriēshon chizuchō.
[Pocket recreation atlas for the Kanto Dis-
trict. 1958]   10035
—— [1959]   10036
Sutandādo Tōkyō-to kubun chizuchō. [Stan-
dard Tokyo atlas. 1953–58]   9978
Sutandādo Yokohama-shi kubun chizu.
[Standard ward atlas of Yokohama. 1956]   10023
—— [1957]   10025
Zenkoku shi-chō-son haichi bungō benran.
[Consolidation manual of cities, towns, and
villages throughout Japan. 1955]   9780

Nitz, E.
Militärgeographische Beschreibung von Rumänien. 1919. — 9209

Noack, Arthur, 1881–1943.
Assessment map of city of Garfield ... N.J. 1930. — 15753
Assessment map of Saddle River Township, Bergen County, N.J. 1930. — 15688
Assessment map of the borough of East Paterson ... N.J. 1930. — 15743
Sewer assessment map of the borough of East Paterson ... N.J. 1930. — 15744

Noble, Claude Emerson.
Plat book of Gibson County, Ind. [1950] — 12795

Nørlund, Niels Erik, 1885–
Danmarks kortlægning, en historisk fremstilling. 1942. — 8264
—— 2. udg. 1943. — 8265
Færøernes kortlægning. 1944. — 8360
Islands kortlægning, en historisk fremstilling. 1944. — 8932

Nolin, Jean Baptiste 1648–1708.
Nouvelle edition du Théâtre de la guerre en Italie. [1702–17] — 8981
—— 1718. — 5258
Théâtre du monde. 170 [0?–44] — 5958

Nolin, Jean Baptiste, 1686–1762.
Atlas général à l'usage des collèges et maisons d'éducation. 1783. — 4297

Noll, E. P., and Company.
Property atlas of St. Joseph County, Mich. 1893. — 1997

Nolli, Giovanni Battista, ca. 1692–1756.
Nuova pianta di Roma. 1748. — 9012

Nordenskiöld, Nils Adolf Erik, _Freiherre_, 1832–1901.
Bidrag till Nordens äldsta kartografi. [1892] — 256, 3091
Facsimile atlas. 1889. — 257
Periplus. 1897. — 258

Nordisk världsatlas. 1926. — 6622

Nordiska Turisttrafikkommittén.
Atlas över Norden. [1932] — 7830

Norges Automobil-Forbund.
Bilkart Norges-fylker. [1932] — 9109
—— [1935] — 9110

Norie, John William, 1772–1843.
Complete East India pilot. 1816. — 3173

Noriega, Eduardo.
Atlas miniatura de la República Mexicana. 1899. — 3938

Norman, John, 1748–1817.
American pilot. 1792. — 4474a
—— 1794. — 4475

Norman, William.
American pilot. 1798. — 1217
—— 1803. — 4477

Normanns Historiske Atlas. [1947] — 5677

Norris, John, 1660?–1749.
Compleat sett of new charts, containing the North-Sea, Cattegatt, and Baltick. 1723. — 2839

Norris, Robert, _d._ 1791, _and others_.
African pilot. [1794]–1804. — 4082

North American Boundary Commission, 1872–1876.
Joint maps of the northern boundary of the United States from the Lake of the Woods to the ... Rocky Mountains. [1878] — 10475

North American pilot.
—— 2 v. 1777. — 1209
—— First part. 1784–[88] — 10325
—— —— New ed. 1799. — 4476
—— —— —— 1806. — 1236
—— —— —— 1809–[1810] — 10328
—— Second part. 1776. — 10316
—— —— New ed. 1795. — 3668
—— —— —— 1800. — 1220
—— —— —— 1807. — 10327

North Carolina. _Mental Health Planning Staff_.
Baseline maps for mental health planning in North Carolina. 1965. — 16208
Problems and resources; a map supplement. [1964] — 16201

North Carolina. _State Council of Civil Defense_.
Operational survival plan. [1958] — 16202, 16203

North Carolina. _State Highway and Public Works Commission_.
State, county and municipal highway systems. [1953] — 16205

North Carolina. _State Highway Commission_.
Municipal, State, primary and interstate highway systems. [1962] — 16207
State primary and secondary highway-road systems. [1957] — 16206

North Dakota. _State Highway Dept_.
General highway and transportation map[s. 1942] — 16250

North Dakota. _State Tourist Bureau_.
Visit North Dakota. [1963?] — 16249

North Rhine-Westphalia. _Landesplanungsbehörde_.
Nordrhein-Westfalen-Atlas. [1949–60] — 8818
Verwaltungsatlas Nordrhein-Westfalen. 1951–53. — 8822

Northern Trust Company Bank.
    Complete atlas. 1904.   1091

Northern Virginia Regional Planning and Economic Development Commission.
    Northern Virginia region: Land use & useful-
    ness. [1959]   17320
    —— Parks, recreation & open space. 1960. 17322

Northwest Airlines.
    Northwest passage, coast-to-coast! Air map.
    [1945]   10470

Northwest Mapping Service.
    New Alaska Highway packet. [1954]   10302

Northwest Publishing Company.
    Plat book of Anderson County, Kans. 1901. 1712
    Plat book of Appanoose County, Iowa.
    1896.   1643
    Plat book of Audrain County, Mo. 1898.   2068
    Plat book of Barton County, Kans. 1902.   1713
    Plat book of Bates County, Mo. 1895.   2070
    Plat book of Benton County, Minn. 1903. 14931
    Plat book of Boone County, Iowa. 1896.   1645
    Plat book of Boone County, Mo. 1898.   2071
    Plat book of Boone County, Nebr. 1899.   2109
    Plat book of Brown County, Kans. 1904.   1715
    Plat book of Carver County, Minn. 1898. 14945
    Plat book of Cass County, Mo. 1895.   2074
    Plat book of Chariton County, Mo. 1897.   2075
    Plat book of Chippewa County, Minn.
    1900.   2012
    Plat book of Coffey County, Kans. 1901.   1718
    Plat book of Dallas County, Iowa. 1901.   1656
    Plat book of Darke County, Ohio. 1910. 16403
    Plat book of De Kalb County, Mo. 1897.   2077
    Plat book of Des Moines County, Iowa.
    1897.   4634
    Plat book of Dodge County, Wis. 1910. 17714
    Plat book of Dubuque County, Iowa. 1892. 1658
    Plat book of Franklin County, Kans. 1903. 1720
    Plat book of Fremont County, Iowa. 1891. 1664
    Plat book of Greene County, Iowa. 1896. 1665
    Plat book of Greenwood County, Kans.
    1903.   1721
    Plat book of Hamilton County, Iowa. 1896. 1666
    Plat book of Henry County, Mo. 1895.   2078
    Plat book of Howard County, Nebr. 1900. 2114
    Plat book of Humboldt County, Iowa. 1896. 1672
    Plat book of Jackson Co., Iowa. 1893.   1675
    Plat book of Jackson County, Kans. 1903. 1722
    Plat book of Jasper County, Mo. 1895.   2079
    Plat book of Jefferson County, Nebr. 1900. 2115
    Plat book of Jo Davies County, Ill. 1893.   1539
    Plat book of Jones County, Iowa. 1893.   1678
    Plat book of Kandiyohi County, Minn. 1886. 2023
    Plat book of Kingman County, Kans. 1903. 1723
    Plat book of Lafayette County, Mo. 1897. 2080
    Plat book of Le Sueur County, Minn. 1898. 2024
    Plat book of Lincoln County, Kans. 1901. 1725
    Plat book of Lincoln County, Minn. 1898. 15027
    Plat book of Lyon County, Minn. 1902.   2025
    Plat book of McLean County, Ill. 1895.   1547

Plat book of McPherson County, Kans.
    1903.   1727
Plat book of Madison County, Iowa. 1901. 1683
Plat book of Madison County, Nebr. 1899. 2118
Plat book of Marathon County, Wis. 1901. 2653
Plat book of Merrick County, Nebr. 1899. 2119
Plat book of Nance County, Nebr. 1899.   2120
Plat book of Nicollet County, Minn. 1899. 2029
Plat book of Nodaway County, Mo. 1893. 2086
Plat book of Norton County, Kans. 1900. 1730
Plat book of Nuckolls County, Kans. 1900. 1730
Plat book of Nuckolls County, Nebr. 1900. 2121
Plat book of Osborne County, Kans. 1900. 1732
Plat book of Ottawa County, Kans. 1902. 14192
Plat book of Page County, Iowa. 1902.   1689
Plat book of Pettis County, Mo. 1896.   2087
Plat book of Platte County, Nebr. 1899.   2123
Plat book of Polk County, Minn. 1902.   2034
Plat book of Portage County, Wis. 1895.   2657
Plat book of Reno County, Kans. 1902.   1733
Plat book of Renville County, Minn. 1900. 2038
Plat book of Rice County, Kans. 1902.   1735
Plat book of Rice County, Minn. 1900.   2039
Plat book of Rock Island County, Ill. 1894. 12476
Plat book of Rush County, Kans. 1901.   1736
Plat book of Russell County, Kans. 1901. 1737
Plat book of St. Louis County, Mo. 1909.   3821
Plat book of Saline County, Kans. 1903.   1738
Plat book of Saline County, Mo. 1896.   2093
Plat book of Saline County, Nebr. 1900. 2124
Plat book of Schuyler County, Mo. 1898. 2095
Plat book of Scotland County, Mo. 1898. 2096
Plat book of Sherburne County, Minn. 1903. 2041
Plat book of Stanton County, Nebr. 1899. 2125
Plat book of Stephenson County, Ill. 1894. 1570
Plat book of Tama County, Iowa. 1892.   1698
Plat book of Taylor County, Iowa. 1894. 1699
Plat book of Thayer County, Nebr. 1900. 2126
Plat book of Union County, Iowa. 1894.   1700
Plat book of Van Buren County, Iowa.
    1897.   1701
Plat book of Walworth County, Wis. 1891. 2666
Plat book of Washington County, Iowa.
    1894.   1705
Plat book of Wayne County, Nebr. 1898. 2127
Plat book of Webster County, Nebr. 1900. 2128
Plat book of Wilkin County, Minn. 1903. 2045
Plat book of Wright County, Minn. 1901. 2049
Plat book of Yellow Medicine County, Minn.
    1900.   2050

Northwest Regional Council.
Economic atlas of the Pacific Northwest.
    [1942]   10554
    —— 2d ed. 1942.   10555

Norway. *Geografiske Oppmaaling*.
Norge. 1948.   9123

Norway. *Meteorologiske Institutt*.
Storm-atlas. 1870.   7648

Norway. *Poststyret*.
Postkart over Norge. [1952]   9107

Norway. *Statistisk Sentralbyrå.*
Bosettingskart over Norge. 1955. 9106

Norway.*Vegdirektoratet.*
Kart over riks- og fylkesveger i Norge. 1942. 9112

Nouvel atlas des enfans. Nouvelle éd. 1776. 307

Nova, *firm.*
Nieuwe toeristen kaart van Belgie en Gr. Hert. Luxemburg. [192–?] 7958

Nova Scotia. *Dept. of Mines.*
Map of the Province of Nova Scotia. 1954. 10405

Novak, Joseph J.
New map of Johnson County, Iowa. [1889] 13576

Novák, Vladimír J.
Sovětský svaz v mapách. [Vyd. l. 1948] 9251

Novi Sad, Yugoslavia. Zavod za poljoprivredna istrazivanja.
Pedološka karta Vojvodine. Soil map of Voyvodina. 1958. 9472

Nuttall's Simplified atlas of the world. [1950?] 5436

Nystrom, A. J., and Company.
New reference atlas. [1926] 6623

O shêng chou hsien i ch'uan ch'üan t'u. [Atlas of chou, hsien and post routes of Hu-peh. 18—] 9641

Oakland, *Calif. City Planning Commission.*
1936 real property survey. [1937] 11562

Oakland County, *Mich. Treasurer's Office.*
Township sectional maps, Oakland County, Mich. [1937] 14768

Oberhummer, Eugen, 1859–1944.
Konstantinopel unter Sultan Suleiman dem Grossen. 1902. 10079

Oberschlesischer Berg- und Hüttenmännischer Verein.
Denkschrift. [1921?] 8811

Oberthur, *firm.*
Atlas des départements Français. [1927?] 8395
—— [1954] 8482
—— [1958] 8483

Obiols, Alfredo, *and* **Perdomo, Rodolfo.**
Atlas de información básica ... de la República Dominicana. 1966. 18172

O'Brien, Boyd K.
Lo-Kãt-It street guide with maps: Fort Worth [Tex. 1958] 17239

Occidental Publishing Company.
Plat book of Clinton County, Ill. 1892. 1524
Plat book of Marion County, Ill. 1892. 1552

Ockerson, John Augustus, 1849– *and* **Stewart, Charles West, 1859–**
Mississippi River from St. Louis to the sea. 1892. 1324

Ocylok, Georg, und Compagnie.
Atlas von Westeuropa. [1948] 7811
Autostrassen-Atlas von Deutschland. 1948. 8621

Odbert, A.
See Howden, J. A., *and* Odbert A.

Odhams Press.
New atlas of the world. [1950] 7415
New illustrated atlas. [1945] 7217

Oestergaard, Paul.
See Columbus Verlag, Paul Oestergaard KG.

Österreichischer Kajak-Verband.
Österreichischer Faltbootführer auf der Donau. [1928] 7898

Office de Propagande Philatélique, *Paris.*
Atlas de l'Empire Colonial Français. [193–] 8393

Official Farm Plat Book and Directory.
Official county plat book and farmers' directory of Martin County, Minn. 1962. 15040

Ogée, Jean, 1728–1789.
Atlas itineraire de Bretagne. 1769. 8486

Ogilby, John, 1600–1676.
Britannia. 1675. 2907
—— 1698. 8090
Britannia depicta. 1720. 5203
—— 4th ed. 1724. 8091
—— —— 1730. 8092
—— —— 1731. 8093
—— —— 1736. 2908
—— —— 1751. 2909
—— —— 1753. 8094
—— 1764. 2910
Itineraire de toutes les routes de l'Angleterre. 1766. 8096
Roads out of London ... 1675. 1911. 8156
Roads through England delineated. 1762. 8095

Ogle, George A., and Company.
Atlas of Adair County, Mo. 1919. 15209
Laporte County, Ind. 1921. 12843
Plat book of Champaign County, Ill. 1893. 1521
Plat book of Clark County, Ill. 1892. 1522
Plat book of La Porte County, Ind. 1892. 1616
Plat book of Logan County, Ill. 1893. 12354
Plat book of McHenry County, Ill. 1892. 1545
Plat book of Ogle County, Ill. 1893. 1557
Plat book of Shelby County, Ill. 1895. 1567
Plat book of Warren County, Ill. 1893. 1575

Plat book of Whiteside County, Ill. 1893.	1577
Plat book of Will County, Ill. 1893.	1578
Standard atlas of Adair County, Mo. 1898.	2067
Standard atlas of Adams County, Ill. 1901.	1515
Standard atlas of Adams County, N.Dak. 1917.	4960
Standard atlas of Adams County, Wash. 1912.	3925
Standard atlas of Adams County, Wis. 1919.	5080
Standard atlas of Allegan County, Mich. 1913.	4732
Standard atlas of Allen County, Ind. 1898.	4606
Standard atlas of Antelope County, Nebr. 1904.	2108
Standard atlas of Antrim County, Mich. 1910.	3801
Standard atlas of Arenac County, Mich. 1906.	4733
Standard atlas of Asotin County, Wash. 1914.	5072
Standard atlas of Audrain County, Mo. 1918.	4829
Standard atlas of Barber County, Kans. 1923.	14148
Standard atlas of Barry County, Mich. 1895.	1963
—— 1913.	4734
Standard atlas of Barry County, Mo. 1909.	4830
Standard atlas of Beadle County, S.Dak. 1913.	5057
Standard atlas of Becker County, Minn. 1911.	3810
Standard atlas of Benson County, N.Dak. 1910.	3856
Standard atlas of Benton County, Ind. 1909.	4607
Standard atlas of Benzie County, Mich. 1915.	4735
Standard atlas of Blue Earth County, Minn. 1914.	4776
Standard atlas of Bon Homme County, S.Dak. 1912.	5058
Standard atlas of Bond County, Ill. 1900.	4557
Standard atlas of Boone County, Ill. 1923.	12091
Standard atlas of Boone County, Mo. 1917.	4831
Standard atlas of Bottineau County, N.Dak. 1910.	3857
Standard atlas of Bourbon County, Kans. 1920.	14149
Standard atlas of Bowman County, N.Dak. 1917.	4961
Standard atlas of Box Butte County, Nebr. 1913.	4877
Standard atlas of Boyd County, Nebr. 1904.	15353
Standard atlas of Branch County, Mich. 1915.	4736
Standard atlas of Bremer County, Iowa. 1917.	4625
Standard atlas of Brown County, Ill. 1903.	1518
Standard atlas of Brown County, Kans. 1919.	14150
Standard atlas of Brown County, Nebr. 1912.	3824
Standard atlas of Brown County, S.Dak. 1911.	3898

Standard atlas of Brule County, S.Dak. 1911.	3899
Standard atlas of Burke County, N.Dak. 1914.	4962
Standard atlas of Burleigh County, N.Dak. 1912.	16268
Standard atlas of Burnett County, Wis. 1915.	5083
Standard atlas of Butler County, Kans. 1905.	4671
Standard atlas of Caldwell County, Mo. 1917.	4833
Standard atlas of Calhoun County, Iowa. 1911.	3744
Standard atlas of Calhoun County, Mich. 1916.	4737
Standard atlas of Callaway County, Mo. 1919.	4835
Standard atlas of Calumet County, Wis. 1920.	17683
Standard atlas of Campbell County, S.Dak. 1911.	3900
Standard atlas of Canyon County, Idaho. 1915.	4553
Standard atlas of Carroll County, Ill. 1908.	4558
Standard atlas of Carroll County, Mo. 1896.	2073
—— 1914.	4836
Standard atlas of Cass County, Ill. 1899.	12114
Standard atlas of Cass County, Mich. 1896.	1967
—— 1914.	4738
Standard atlas of Cavalier County, N.Dak. 1912.	3857a
Standard atlas of Cedar County, Nebr. 1917.	4880
Standard atlas of Champaign County, Ill. 1913.	4559
Standard atlas of Charles Mix County, S.Dak. 1912.	5059
Standard atlas of Chase County, Nebr. 1908.	15381
Standard atlas of Chautauqua County, Kans. 1921.	14154
Standard atlas of Cherry County, Nebr. 1919.	15382
Standard atlas of Cheyenne County, Nebr. 1913.	4881
Standard atlas of Chippewa County, Wis. 1920.	17687
Standard atlas of Christian County, Ill. 1911.	3719
Standard atlas of Clark County, Ill. 1916.	4560
Standard atlas of Clark County, Mo. 1915.	4839
Standard atlas of Clark County, S.Dak. 1911.	3901
Standard atlas of Clark County, Wis. 1906.	5084
Standard atlas of Clay County, Kans. 1900.	14155
—— 1918.	4672
Standard atlas of Clay County, Mo. 1914.	4841
Standard atlas of Clay County, S.Dak. 1912.	3901a
Standard atlas of Clayton County, Iowa. 1902.	1654
Standard atlas of Clinton County, Ill. 1913.	4561
Standard atlas of Clinton County, Mich. 1915.	4740

Standard atlas of Hand County, S.Dak. 1910.	3906
Standard atlas of Hanson County, S.Dak. 1910.	3907
Standard atlas of Harlan County, Nebr. 1921.	15469
Standard atlas of Harper County, Kans. 1919.	4680
Standard atlas of Harrison County, Iowa. 1902.	1669
Standard atlas of Harrison County, Mo. 1917.	4851
Standard atlas of Harvey County, Kans. 1918.	4681
Standard atlas of Hendricks County, Ind. 1904.	1611
Standard atlas of Henry County, Ill. 1911.	3721
Standard atlas of Henry County, Iowa. 1917.	4642
Standard atlas of Hettinger County, N.Dak. 1917.	4966
Standard atlas of Hillsdale County, Mich. 1916.	4744
Standard atlas of Hitchcock County, Nebr. 1906.	15471
Standard atlas of Holt County, Mo. 1918.	4852
Standard atlas of Holt County, Nebr. 1904.	2113
Standard atlas of Houston County, Minn. 1896.	2022
Standard atlas of Howard County, Nebr. 1917.	4889
Standard atlas of Hughes County, S.Dak. 1916.	5062
Standard atlas of Hutchinson County, S.Dak. 1910.	3908
Standard atlas of Hyde County, S.Dak. 1911.	3909
Standard atlas of Ionia County, Mich. 1906.	4747
Standard atlas of Iowa County, Wis. 1915.	5089
Standard atlas of Iroquois County, Ill. 1904.	4572
—— 1921.	12275
Standard atlas of Jackson County, Kans. 1921.	14173
Standard atlas of Jackson County, Mich. 1911.	3804
Standard atlas of Jackson County, Minn. 1914.	4789
Standard atlas of Jasper County, Ind. 1909.	4610
Standard atlas of Jefferson County, Kans. 1916.	4682
Standard atlas of Jefferson County, Nebr. 1917.	4890
Standard atlas of Jefferson County, Wis. 1919.	5091
Standard atlas of Jersey County, Ill. 1916.	4573
Standard atlas of Jo Daviess County, Ill. 1913.	4574
Standard atlas of Johnson County, Kans. 1922.	14175
Standard atlas of Johnson County, Nebr. 1900.	2116
—— 1918.	4891
Standard atlas of Jones County, Iowa. 1915.	4644
Standard atlas of Kalamazoo County, Mich. 1910.	3805

Standard atlas of Kay County, Okla. 1910.	3884
Standard atlas of Keith County, Nebr. 1913.	4892
Standard atlas of Kendall County, Ill. 1922.	12313
Standard atlas of Kent County, Mich. 1907.	14700
Standard atlas of Kewaunee County, Wis. 1912.	3931a
Standard atlas of Keya Paha County, Nebr. 1912.	3827
Standard atlas of Kidder County, N.Dak. 1912.	3858a
Standard atlas of Kingfisher County, Okla. 1906.	5003
Standard atlas of Kingman County, Kans. 1921.	14178
Standard atlas of Kiowa County, Kans. 1922.	14179
Standard atlas of Kit Carson County, Colo. 1922.	11658
Standard atlas of Kittson County, Minn. 1912.	4792
Standard atlas of Klickitat County, Wash. 1913.	5077
Standard atlas of Knox County, Ill. 1903.	1543
Standard atlas of Knox County, Mo. 1898.	15235
—— 1916.	4854
Standard atlas of Kosciusko County, Ind. 1914.	4611
Standard atlas of La Moure County, N.Dak. 1913.	4967
Standard atlas of La Salle County, Ill. 1906.	12334
Standard atlas of Labette County, Kans. 1906.	4683
Standard atlas of Lafayette County, Wis. 1916.	5094
Standard atlas of Lake County, Ill. 1907.	4575
Standard atlas of Lake County, S.Dak. 1911.	3910
Standard atlas of Lane County, Kans. 1920.	14180
Standard atlas of Langlade County, Wis. 1913.	5095
Standard atlas of Latah County, Idaho. 1914.	4554
Standard atlas of Leavenworth County, Kans. 1903.	1724
Standard atlas of Lee County, Ill. 1921.	12343
Standard atlas of Lee County, Iowa. 1916.	4647
Standard atlas of Lenawee County, Mich. 1916.	4751
Standard atlas of Lewis County, Mo. 1916.	4856
Standard atlas of Lincoln County, Kans. 1918.	4685
Standard atlas of Lincoln County, Mo. 1899.	2085
Standard atlas of Lincoln County, Nebr. 1907.	15502
Standard atlas of Lincoln County, S.Dak. 1910.	3911
Standard atlas of Lincoln County, Wash. 1911.	3926
Standard atlas of Lincoln County, Wis. 1914.	5096
Standard atlas of Livingston County, Ill. 1911.	3723
Standard atlas of Livingston County, Mich. 1915.	4752

Standard atlas of Livingston County, Mo. 1917.	4859
Standard atlas of Logan County, Colo. 1917.	4544
Standard atlas of Logan County, Ill. 1910.	3724
Standard atlas of Logan County, N.Dak. 1916.	4968
Standard atlas of Louisa County, Iowa. 1917.	4648
Standard atlas of Lyman County, S.Dak. 1911.	3912
Standard atlas of Lyon County, Kans. 1918.	4687
Standard atlas of McCook County, S.Dak. 1911.	3913
Standard atlas of McDonald County, Mo. 1909.	4860
Standard atlas of McDonough County, Ill. 1913.	4576
Standard atlas of McHenry County, Ill. 1908.	12365
Standard atlas of McHenry County, N.Dak. 1910.	3859
Standard atlas of McIntosh County, N.Dak. 1911.	3860
Standard atlas of McLean County, Ill. 1914.	4578
Standard atlas of McLean County, N.Dak. 1914.	4970
Standard atlas of McLeod County, Minn. 1898.	2026
Standard atlas of Macomb County, Mich. 1916.	4753
Standard atlas of Macon County, Mo. 1918.	4861
Standard atlas of McPherson County, Kans. 1921.	14182
Standard atlas of McPherson County, S.Dak. 1911.	3914
Standard atlas of Madison County, Nebr. 1918.	4893
Standard atlas of Manitowoc County, Wis. 1921.	17821
Standard atlas of Marinette County, Wis. 1912.	3932a
Standard atlas of Marion County, Ill. 1915.	4580
Standard atlas of Marion County, Kans. 1921.	14183
Standard atlas of Marion County, Mo. 1913.	4862
Standard atlas of Marquette County, Wis. 1919.	17838
Standard atlas of Marshall and Putnam Counties, Ill. 1911	3725, 3727
Standard atlas of Marshall County, Ind. 1922.	12852
Standard atlas of Martin County, Minn. 1911.	3812
Standard atlas of Mason County, Mich. 1904.	4754
Standard atlas of Menard County, Ill. 1920.	12407
Standard atlas of Menominee County, Mich. 1912.	3805a
Standard atlas of Mercer County, N.Dak. 1918.	4971
Standard atlas of Merrick County, Nebr. 1917.	4894
Standard atlas of Midland County, Mich. 1914.	4757

Standard atlas of Minnehaha County, S.Dak. 1903.	3915
Standard atlas of Missaukee County, Mich. 1906.	4758
Standard atlas of Mitchell County, Kans. 1917.	4688
Standard atlas of Moniteau County, Mo. 1920.	15238
Standard atlas of Monroe County, Iowa. 1919.	13757
Standard atlas of Monroe County, Mich. 1896.	1989
Standard atlas of Monroe County, Mo. 1917.	4864
Standard atlas of Monroe County, Wis. 1897.	17845
—— 1915.	5097
Standard atlas of Montcalm County, Mich. 1921.	14750
Standard atlas of Montgomery County, Ill. 1912.	4583
Standard atlas of Montgomery County, Ind. 1917.	4612
Standard atlas of Montgomery County, Mo. 1918.	4865
Standard atlas of Morgan County, Colo. 1913.	4545
Standard atlas of Morrill County, Nebr. 1913.	4895
Standard atlas of Morton County, N.Dak. 1917.	4972
Standard atlas of Moultrie County, Ill. 1913.	4584
Standard atlas of Mountrail County, N.Dak. 1917.	4973
Standard atlas of Mower County, Minn. 1896.	2028
Standard atlas of Murray County, Minn. 1908.	15053
Standard atlas of Muskegon County, Mich. 1909.	1991
Standard atlas of Nance County, Nebr. 1920.	15518
Standard atlas of Nemaha County, Nebr. 1913.	4896
Standard atlas of Neosho County, Kans. 1906.	4689
Standard atlas of Newaygo County, Mich. 1900.	1993
—— 1922.	14759
Standard atlas of Newton County, Ind. 1916.	4613
Standard atlas of Noble County, Okla. 1912.	5004
Standard atlas of Nobles County, Minn. 1914.	4802
Standard atlas of Norton County, Kans. 1917.	4690
Standard atlas of Nuckolls County, Nebr. 1917.	4897
Standard atlas of Oakland County, Mich. 1908.	14763
Standard atlas of O'Brien County, Iowa. 1911.	3751
Standard atlas of Oceana County, Mich. 1913.	4760

Standard atlas of Sheridan County, Kans.
1906–1907.   4700
Standard atlas of Sheridan County, Nebr.
1914.   4906
Standard atlas of Sheridan County, N.Dak.
1914.   4976
Standard atlas of Sherman County, Oreg.
1913.   5008
Standard atlas of Shiawassee County, Mich.
1915.   4766
Standard atlas of Sioux County, Nebr.
1916.   4907
Standard atlas of Smith County, Kans.
1917.   4701
Standard atlas of Spink County, S.Dak.
1909.   17055
Standard atlas of Spokane County, Wash.
1912.   3927
Standard atlas of Stafford County, Kans.
1904.   4702
Standard atlas of Stanton County, Nebr.
1919.   4908
Standard atlas of Stark County, N.Dak.
1914.   4977
Standard atlas of Steele County, N.Dak.
1911.   3865
Standard atlas of Stephenson County, Ill.
1913.   4591
Standard atlas of Stutsman County, N.Dak.
1911.   3866
Standard atlas of Sully County, S.Dak.
1916.   5063
Standard atlas of Sumner County, Kans.
1902.   1742
—— 1918.   4703
Standard atlas of Taylor County, Wis.   1913.   5105
Standard atlas of Tazewell County, Ill.
1910.   3728
Standard atlas of Thayer County, Nebr.
1916.   4909
Standard atlas of Tripp County, S.Dak.
1915.   5064
Standard atlas of Turner County, S.Dak.
1911.   3918
Standard atlas of Umatilla County, Oreg.
1914.   5009
Standard atlas of Union County, Ill.   1908.   4592
Standard atlas of Union County, Iowa.
1916.   4661
Standard atlas of Union County, S.Dak.
1910.   3919
Standard atlas of Van Buren County, Iowa.
1918.   4662
Standard atlas of Van Buren County, Mich.
1912.   3808a
Standard atlas of Vermilion County, Ill.
1915.   4593
Standard atlas of Wabasha County, Minn.
1896.   2043
Standard atlas of Wabaunsee County, Kans.
1902.   1743
—— 1919.   4704
Standard atlas of Walla Walla County, Wash.
1909.   3928

Standard atlas of Walworth County, S.Dak.
1911.   3920
Standard atlas of Wapello County, Iowa.
1922.   14002
Standard atlas of Ward County, N.Dak.
1915.   4980
Standard atlas of Warren County, Ill.   1912.   3728a
Standard atlas of Waseca County, Minn.
1896.   2044
Standard atlas of Washburn County, Wis.
1915.   5108
Standard atlas of Washtenaw County, Mich.
1915.   4767
Standard atlas of Waukesha County, Wis.
1914.   5109
Standard atlas of Waupaca County, Wis.
1923.   17976
Standard atlas of Wayne County, Ill.   1910.   3729
Standard atlas of Wayne County, Nebr.
1918.   4911
Standard atlas of Webster County, Iowa.
1909.   14045
Standard atlas of Wells County, N.Dak.
1911.   3868
Standard atlas of Wheeler County, Nebr.
1917.   4912
Standard atlas of White County, Ind.   1896.   1636
Standard atlas of Whiteside County, Ill.
1912.   3730
Standard atlas of Whitley County, Ind.
1916.   4618
Standard atlas of Wichita County, Kans.
1920.   14208
Standard atlas of Will County, Ill.   1909–
1910.   3731
Standard atlas of Williams County, N.Dak.
1914.   4981
Standard atlas of Williams County, Ohio.
1918.   4991
Standard atlas of Williamson County, Ill.
1908.   4594
Standard atlas of Wilson County, Kans.
1910.   3759
Standard atlas of Winnebago County, Ill.
1905.   4595
Standard atlas of Woodford County, Ill.
1912.   3732
Standard atlas of Woods County, Okla.
1906.   5007
Standard atlas of Wright County, Iowa.
1912.   4668
Standard atlas of Yankton County, S.Dak.
1910.   3921
Standard atlas of York County, Nebr.   1911.   3830
Standard atlas of Yuma County, Colo.
1922.   11670
Standard county atlas [of Red Lake County,
Minn.]   1911.   3816

Oglesby, Milton Landis.
Oglesby-Burke atlas of the city of Salt Lake.
[1909]   17305

Ohio. *Anthony-Wayne Parkway Board.*
War of 1812 in the Northwest. [1961?]   10655

Ohio. *Dept. of Highways.*
Report of the Columbus—Franklin County
traffic survey. [1950]   16523

Ohio. *Division of Water.*
Hydrologic atlas of average annual precipitation ... in Ohio. 1962.   16375

Ohio. *Geological Survey.*
Geological atlas of the State of Ohio. 1879.   16366
Report of the Geological Survey of Ohio ...
Atlas. 1873–78.   2349

Ohio. *Highway Dept.*
General highway map[s. 1948]   16371
Highway map of Ohio. June 1910.   3871
—— 1919.   4981a
Highway maps of the counties of Ohio.
1910.   3872

Ohio. *Secretary of State.*
Maps of Ohio, showing Congressional, senatorial and judicial districts. 1945.   16354
—— 1955.   16355
—— 1957.   16356
—— 1959.   16357
—— 1961.   16358
—— 1962.   16359
—— 1963.   16360
—— 1965.   16361

Ohio Bell Telephone Company.
Ohio telephone exchange boundaries. 1955.   16374

Okayama, *Japan (Prefecture)*
Nōgyō zusetsu. [Agricultural atlas of Okayama Prefecture] 1954.   9858
Sakumotsu ritchi kubun zu. [Agronomical
atlas of Okayama Prefecture] 1957.   9859

Oklahoma. *Dept. of Highways.*
[Highway atlas of Oklahoma. 1939]   16591

Oklahoma. *Geological Survey.*
Oil and gas in Oklahoma. 1928–30.   16590

Oklahoma. *State Planning Board.*
Compendium of maps and charts pertaining
to state planning. [1936]   16586

Olcott, George C.
Land value maps of Chicago. 1910.   3735
Land value maps of Chicago and suburbs.
1914.   12612

Oliveira, Francisco.
See Silva, Francisco, *and* Oliveira, Francisco.

Oliver and Boyd.
Travelling map of Scotland. [1830?]   8207

Olivier, Jean.
Livre de plusieurs plans des ports & rades de la
Mer Méditerranée. [1796?] MS.   2807

Ollacarizqueta, ——
Frentes de la Revolucion Española. [193–]   9328

Olney, Jesse, 1798–1872.
Atlas ... to accompany the Practical system of
geography. 1860.   6142
New and improved school atlas. 1829.   308
—— 1830.   6065, 6066
—— 1837.   6080
School atlas. [1844–47]   309

O'Louglin, Thomas John.
See Hansen, Kenneth L., *and* O'Loughlin,
Thomas John.

Olson, Marian K.
Clark County [Wash.] rural route maps.
1948.   17438

Onondaga County, N.Y. *Dept. of Planning.*
Tax map, town of De Witt ... N.Y. 1966.   15958
Tax map, village of East Syracuse ... N.Y.
1965.   15960
Tax map, village of Fayetteville ... N.Y.
1967.   15963
Tax map, village of Manlius ... N.Y. 1967.   15978
Tax map, village of Minoa, town of Manlius,
N.Y. 1967.   15979

Ontario. *Dept. of Lands and Forests.*
Ontario forest atlas. [1949]   10408
Ontario forest atlas for schools. [1943]   10409
Ontario resources atlas. 1958.   10406
—— 4th ed. 1963.   10407

Opitz, Carl Albert, 1847–1924.
Reise-Atlas für den Auto- und Eisenbahn-
Verkehr von Deutschland, Österreich. 2.
Aufl. [1934]   7776
Taschen–Weltatlas. [1943?]   7150
Verkehrs-Taschen-Atlas von Deutschland.
[1922]   8597
—— 25. Aufl. [1930]   8596
—— 25. Aufl. [1931]   8598
See also Koch, Wilhelm, 1823–1902, *and*
Opitz, Carl Albert, 1847–1924.

Orbis, *firm.*
Československo v mapách. [1954]   8250
Politicko-hospodářský atlas světa. [1952–
54]   5447

Oregon. *State Highway Dept.*
Plan and profile of proposed State highway,
Federal aid project, Idaho—Oregon—
Nevada highway. 1933–34.   16642
Traffic station maps. 1938.   16643

Oregon. State University, *Corvallis.*
Atlas of the Pacific Northwest. [1953]   10703

Palairet, Jean, 1697–1774.
Atlas méthodique. 1755.   3502
Bowles's Universal atlas. [1775–80]   5988

Palairet, Jean, and others.
Bowles's Universal atlas. [1794–98]   681
[Collection of maps. 1755–71]   4290

Palášek, J.
See Nejdl, B., and Palášek, J.

Palestine. Dept. of Lands and Surveys.
Maps of Palestine. 1947.   9770

Palm, Valentin, 1895–   **and Hilgers, Alfons, 1910–**
Atlas für die Schulen in Rheinland-Pfalz.
[1954]   8777

Palmer, Hermann.
Bahn-Atlas. [1949]   8599

Palmer, Loomis T., b. 1844.
Gaskell's New and complete family atlas of
the world. 1886.   932
—— [1887?]   6235
—— [1889]   6246
Standard atlas and gazetteer of the world.
1888.   6242
—— 1889.   6247
—— 1890.   6254
—— [1892]   6261
Unique album atlas. 1894.   988

Palmer, Richard.
Bible atlas. 1836.   5365
—— 1847.   5366

Palmer, Sir Thomas, and Covert, Walter.
Survey of the coast of Sussex, made in 1587.
1870.   2891

Pan American Institute of Geography and History.
Cartografía histórica de Venezuela, 1635–
1946. 1946.   18418

Pan American Institute of Geography and History. Commission on Cartography.
Atlas de América. 1955.   10276

Pan American Union. Dept. of Economic Affairs.
Argentina: Indice anotado de los trabajos
aerofotográficos y los mapas topográficos.
[1965]   18235
Bolivia: Indice anotado de los trabajos aerofotográficos y los mapas topográficos.
[1964]   18266
Brasil: Indice anotados dos trabalhos aerofotográficos e dos mapas topográficos.
[1965]   18296
Chile: Indice anotado de los trabajos aerofotográficos y los mapas topográficos. [1964]   18338
Colombia: Indice anotado de los recubri-
mientos aerofotográficos y los mapas topográficos. 1963.   18347
Colombia: Indice anotado de los trabajos
aerofotográficos y los mapas topográficos.
[1966]   18350
Costa Rica: Indice anotado de los trabajos
aerofotográficos y los mapas topográficos.
[1965]   18127
Ecuador: Indice anotado de los trabajos
aerofotográficos y los mapas topográficos.
[1964]   18364
El Salvador: Indice anotado de los trabajos
aerofotográficos y los mapas topográficos.
[1965]   18153
Guatemala: Indice anotado de los trabajos
aerofotográficos y los mapas topográficos.
[1965]   18134
Haiti: Index annoté des travaux de photo-
graphie aérienne et des cartes topogra-
phiques. [1964]   18173
Honduras: Indice anotado de los trabajos
aerofotográficos y los mapas topográficos.
[1965]   18136
Indice anotado de los trabajos aerofotográficos y los mapas topográficos y de recursos naturales ... de la América Latina.
[1967?]   18056
Mexico: Indice anotado de los trabajos aerofotográficos y los mapas topográficos.
[1965]   18107
Nicaragua: Indice anotado de los trabajos
aerofotográficos y los mapas topográficos.
[1965]   18140
Panama: Indice anotado de los trabajos aerofotográficos y los mapas topográficos.
[1965]   18147
Paraguay: Indice anotado de los trabajos
aerofotográficos y los mapas topográficos.
[1964]   18375
Peru: Indice anotado de los trabajos aerofotográficos y los mapas topográficos. [1964]   18395
Republica Dominicana: Indice anotado de los
trabajos aerofotográficos y los mapas topográficos. [1964]   18171
Uruguay: Indice anotado de los trabajos
aerofotográficos y los mapas topográficos.
[1964]   18401
Venezuela: Indice anotado de los trabajos
aerofotográficos y los mapas topográficos.
[1964]   18432

Panair do Brasil.
Artérias do Brasil. [1946]   18269
—— [195–?]   18270

Panama. Comisión del Atlas de Panamá.
Atlas de Panamá. 1965.   18146

Panorama (Mexico)
Planos de caminos para automóviles. [1928]   18074

**Państwowe Przedsiębiorstwo Wydawnictw Karto-
graficznych, Warsaw**
Atlas samochodowy Polski. [1958]   9157

Papadakis, Juan.
Mapa ecológico de la Republica Argentina.
1951.   18198

Papen, Augustus, d. 1858.
Topographischer Atlas des Königreichs
Hannover und Herzogthums Braunschweig.
1832–47.   3039

Papinot, Edmond, 1860–
Dictionnaire d'histoire et de géographie du
Japon. Cartes géographiques. [1910]   9805

Paraguay. *Dirección de Hidrografía y Navegación.*
Atlas del derrotero paraguayo, Rio Paraguay.
1950.   18377

Paraná, *Brazil (State) Departamento de Geografia,*
Terras e Colonização. Divisão de Geografia.
Coleção de mapas municipais do estado do
Paraná. 1953.   18309

Paravia, G. B., & C.
Pianta della città di Torino. [1928]   9017
—— [194–]   9018

Paris, Louis Philippe Albert d'Orléans, *Comte* **de,**
1838–1894.
[Histoire de la guerre civile en Amérique] Atlas.
[1874–90]   1352

Paris. *Bibliothèque Nationale.*
Choix de documents géographiques. 1883.   259

Paris. *Conseil Municipal.*
Histoire générale de Paris. Atlas des anciens
plans de Paris. 1880.   3011

Pairs. *Diocèse.*
Atlas de la censive de l'archevêché dans Paris.
1906.   3017

Paris. *Observatoire.*
Atlas météorologique. 1875.   8388

Paris. *Peace Conference, 1919. Hungary.*
Magyar béketárgyalások. 1920.   8928

Parker, Ben, Inc.
Plats of Lincoln [Nebr.] and environs. 1948. 15640

Parker, R. G.
Road and sectional map of Tippecanoe
County, Ind. 1913.   4617

Parkinson, T. W. F.
Atlas of practical geography. [1914?]   4169

Parrish, John Maxey.
Popular road book of Great Britain. [1945]   8044
—— [1948]   8048
Wonder atlas. [1941]   7060

Parry, Roy Edgardo.
Macmillan's Atlas for South–East Asia. 1st
ed. 1953.   7573

Parry, Roy Edgardo, *and* **Midgley, Cyril, 1897–**
Wheaton's Modern atlas of Africa. [1937]   10099

Pasquier, Jacques Jean, 1718–1785, *and* **Denis,**
Louis, 1725–1795.
Plan topographique et raisonné de Paris.
1758.   3012

Passonneau, Joseph R., *and* **Wurman, Richard Saul,**
1935–
Urban atlas: 20 American cities. 1966.   10498

Paterson, Daniel, 1739–1825.
British itinerary. 1785.   8029

Patterson, Timothy Joseph.
Farm plat book, Harrison County, Ind.
[1961]   12810
—— 1965.   12811
Plat book, Daviess County, Ind. [1951]   12764
Plat book, Dubois County, Ind. [1950]   12774
—— [1958]   12775
Plat book, Martin County, Ind. [1959]   12856

Patteson, *Rev.* **Edward,** *of Richmond, Surrey.*
General and classical atlas. 1804–[1806]   707

Pattison, William David, 1921–
Plat book of Pulaski County, Ind. 1947.   12889
—— 1953.   12890
—— 1960.   12891

Patton, Alfred B., Inc.
Atlas of Bucks County [Pa.] 1st ed. 1967.   16773

Paul, Hosea.
Atlas of Wabash County, Ind. 1875.   1633

Paullin, Charles Oscar, 1868 or 9–1944.
Atlas of the historical geography of the United
States. 1932.   10635

Pauwels, Geraldo José.
Atlas geográfico Melhoramentos. 8. ed.
1950.   7416

Pavie, Auguste Jean Marie, 1847–1925.
Mission Pavie. Indo-Chine. Atlas. 1903.   4072

Pavlishchev, Nikolaï Ivanovich, 1802–1879.
Историческій атласъ Россіи. [Historical
atlas of Russia] 1845.   9222
Историческій атласъ Россіи. [Military historical atlas of Russia.] 1845.   3099
—— 1873.   3100

Pawlowski, Stanisław, 1882–1939.
See Romer, Eugeniusz, 1871–1954, *and* Pawlowski, Stanisław, 1882–1939.

Pennsylvania. *Geological Survey.*
See Pennsylvania. *Topographic and Geologic Survey.*

Pennsylvania. *Geological Survey, 2d.*
Grand atlas. 1884–85.   2440

Pennsylvania. *Indian Forts Commission.*
Report of the Commission. 1896.   2439

Pennsylvania. *Topographic and Geologic Survey.*
Geological hand atlas of ... Pennsylvania. 1885.   16757
Oil and gas field atlas of the Bradford quadrangle, Pa. 1951.   16749
Oil and gas field atlas of the Butler quadrangle, Pa. 1955.   16750
Oil and gas field atlas of the Smethport quadrangle, Pa. 1951.   16751
Oil and gas field farm line maps of the Franklin and Oil City quadrangles, Pa. 1945.   16752
Oil and gas field property line maps of the Hilliards quadrangle, Pa. 1946.   16753
Oil and gas field property line maps of the Titusville quadrangle, Pa. 1946.   16754
Oil-bearing sands in southwestern Pennsylvania. 1944.   16755
Preliminary report on a regional stratigraphic study of Devonian rocks of Pennsylvania. 1957.   16756

Pennsylvania Indemnity Corporation.
Auto trails atlas. [1930]   10814
—— [1931]   10821

Pennsylvania Railroad Company.
Ticket agents atlas. 1905.   1305

Penny, H. C.
See Lathrop, J. M., *and* Penny, H. C.

Peoples' Popular atlas of the world. [1903]   6311

People's Publishing Company.
Illustrated & descriptive family atlas of the world. 1884.   6220
—— [7th ed. 1886]   6231
—— [10th ed. 1887]   6236
—— [14th ed. 1889]   6248

Pequeño atlas; el Istmo Centroamericano ... y el Salvador. [1929]   18121

Pequeño atlas escolar. 1967.   18299

Peralta, Manuel Maria de, 1844–1930.
Límites de Costa-Rica y Colombia. Atlas. 1890.   2691, 2759

Percy, Willard H.
Highlands county [Fla.] atlas. 1946.   11826

Perdomo, Rodolfo.
See Obiols, Alfredo, *and* Perdomo, Rodolfo.

Perez Garcia, Jacinto.
See Torres Gómez, Juan, *and* Perez Garcia, Jacinto.

Perfect Survey Engineering Company.
Macomb County [Mich.] atlas. 1959.   14728
—— 1961.   14729
North Oakland County [Mich.] atlas. [1964]   14771
South Oakland County [Mich.] atlas. 1960.   14770
Washtenaw County [Mich.] atlas. [1966]   14826
—— [1967]   14827
West Wayne County [Mich.] atlas. 1960.   14833
—— [1967]   14835

Perkins Printing and Stationery Company.
Plat book of Dodge County, Nebr. [1924?]   15420

Perlewitz, Paul Julius Georg, 1878–
See Haeberlin, Carl, 1870–   *and* Perlewitz, Paul Julius Georg, 1878–

Perly, Allan Morris.
Bluemap atlas of Greater Toronto. [1953]   10423
—— Executive ed. 1961.   10424
Detail atlas, Province of Ontario. [1957]   10413

Perrin, William N.
See Mesnard, H. W., *and* Perrin, William N.

Perris, William.
Maps of the city of New York. 1859–62.   15985

Perris and Browne.
Insurance maps of the city of New York. 1867–69.   15987
—— 1870–82.   15988
—— 1879–89.   15990
Insurance maps of the city of Newark [N.J.] 1874.   15766

Perrot, Aristide Michel, 1793–1879.
Atlas géographique, statistique et progressif des departemens de la France. [1845?]   8463

Perrot, Aristide Michel, *and* Aragon, Anne Alexandrine, *b.* 1798.
Atlas de 59 cartes. 1843.   790a

Perrot d'Ablancourt, Nicolas, 1606–1664.
Vervolg van de neptunus. 1700.   3229

Peršić, Nikola.
See Lukas, Filip, 1871–   *and* Peršić, Nikola.

Perthes, Justus, 1749–1816.
Atlas antiquus. 6. Aufl. 1898.   50
Atlas portátil. 8. ed. 1914.   4414
—— 13. éd. 1926.   6625
Atlas portatil de España y Portugal. 2. ed. 1936.   9331
—— 3. ed. 1938.   9333
Atlas portatil de Espanha e Portugal. 2. ed. 1936.   9332

Petri, Eduard IUl'evich, and Shokal'skii, IUlii Mikhailovich, 1856–1940.
Географический атлас. [Geographical atlas.] [1926]   6626a

Petrie, Thomas Edward, 1859–1932, and Frazee, Alva T.
Sectional map showing all additions to the city of Marion, Ind. 1932.   12988

Petrocaltex.
Italia, carta stradale. [1957]   8978

Petty, Sir William, 1623–1687.
Geographicall description of ye Kingdom of Ireland. [1689]   2938
Hiberniæ delineatio. [1730]   8228

Petzold, Wilhelm, 1848–1897.
See Lehmann, Richard, 1845–1942, and Petzold, Wilhelm, 1848–1897.

Peucker, Karl, 1859–1940.
Atlas für commercielle Lehranstalten. 1893.   6267
Atlas für Handelsschulen. 3. Ausg. [1913?]   6261
——— 8. Aufl. 1929.   6710

Peuser, Jacobo.
Atlas geográfico de la República Argentina. [1945]   18225

Pferdmenges, Hans.
Deutschlands Leben. 1930.   8574

Pfohl, Ernst, 1874–
Průmyslový atlas Československé Republiky. [1921]   8240
Rohstoof– und Kolonial-Atlas. [1938]   5451
Wirtschafts-Atlas des Tschecho-Slowakischen Staates. [1920]   8241

Pfrommer, Fritz.
Afrika-Atlas. [194–]   10101

Pfuhl, Th.
Post-Taschen-Atlas von Deutschland. 13. Aufl. 1920.   8589

Pharus Verlag.
Pharus-Atlas deutscher Städte. 1904.   4032

Phelps' Hundred cities and large towns of America. 1853.   3675

Philadelphia. City Planning Commission.
Comprehensive plan: The physical development plan for the city of Philadelphia. 1960.   16888
Land use in Philadelphia, 1944–1954. [1956]   16884
Population and housing, Philadelphia 1950. 1954.   16883

Philadelphia. City Plans Division.
Philadelphia street map. 1964.   16889

Philadelphia Electric Company.
Aerial photography and line maps, suburban divisions. 1953.   16881

Philadelphia Public Ledger's Unrivaled atlas of the world. 1899.   1041, 6287

Philadelphia Real Estate Directory.
Suburban Philadelphia atlas directory of Delaware County [Pa.] 1926.   16782
Suburban Philadelphia atlas directory of main line. 1926.   16895

Philip, George, 1823–1902.
Comprehensive atlas of physical, political, and classical geography. 1898.   3576

Philip, George, 1870–1937.
Atlas of the British Empire. 1924.   7988
British Empire universities up–to–date atlas–guide. [1925]   6590
Cartocraft geography school atlas. 1947.   7275
Cassell's New atlas. [1921]   6452
——— 6th ed. [1932]   6784
Centenary handy general atlas of the world. 4th ed. 1934.   6820
Elementary atlas of comparative geography. [1914]   4204
Elementary school atlas of comparative geography. [1913]   6362
Handy administrative atlas of England & Wales. [1928]   8138
Handy administrative atlas of Scotland. [1911]   8212
Handy general atlas of the world. 4th ed. [1939]   6981
International atlas. 1931.   6751
——— 1936.   6886
——— 3d ed. 1937.   6919
——— 1940.   7021
——— Interim ed. [1940]   7022
——— 5th ed. 1945.   7218
——— 5th ed. [1945]   7219
Mercantine marine atlas. 2d ed. 1905.   175
——— 1909.   3335
——— 4th ed. [1913]   4147
——— 5th ed. 1915.   4149
Modern school atlas. 41st ed. 1950.   7417
——— 42d ed. 1951.   7471
Modern school atlas of comparative geography. 1911.   3376
——— 1913.   4205
——— 16th ed. 1924.   6561
Modern school commercial atlas. 1923.   5452
New handy general atlas & gazetteer. 2d ed. 1921.   6453
——— 3d ed. 1926.   6627
——— 3d ed. 1930.   6728
New mercantile marine atlas. 6th ed. 1916.   4148
New modern school atlas of comparative geography. 1936.   6887
Pictorial atlas of the world. [1934]   6821
Primary atlas of the British Empire. [1909?]   4009
Record atlas. 1917.   4236a

Post, L. D.
Maps of States locating paper and pulp mills in the United States. [1939]   10706

Poståpnernes Landsforbund.
Post-, vei- og fylkeskarter. [1950]   9108

Potel, Felice.
Atlante universale. 1850.   802

Potocki, Jan, hrabia, 1761–1815.
Археологическій атласъ—Atlas archéologique de la Russie européenne. 1823.   3113

Potter, J. E., and Company.
Potter-Bradley atlas. 1894.   989

Potter, Paraclete.
[Atlas of the world. 1820]   4313

Potts, Frances E., *and others.*
Texas in maps. 1966.   17125

Poussielgue Frères.
Atlas de géographie moderne. [187–]   6169

Poussin, Guillaume Tell, 1794–1876.
Travaux d'amélorations intérieures, projetées ou exécutés par le gouvernement général des États-Unis, de 1824–1831. 1834.   1265

Pownall, Thomas, 1722–1805.
Six remarkable views in the provinces of New-York, New-Jersey, and Pennsylvania, in North America. [1761]   4472

Pozo Cano, Raúl del.
Cartografia del Chaco paraguayo. [1935]   18376

Prague. Státní zeměměřický a kartografický ústav.
Malý politický atlas světa. 1953.   7578

Prague. Universität. *Geographisches Institut.*
Atlas der Sudetenländer. 1929–31.   8246

Pramberger, Emil.
Atlas zum Studium der Militär-Geographie von Mittel-Europa. [1907]   2824

Pranzl, Sepp.
See Walleczek, Erich, *and* Pranzl, Sepp.

Pratt, Frederick W.
See Faehtz, Ernest F. M., *and* Pratt, Frederick W.

Pratt's Road atlas of England and Wales. 1905.   8103
—— 1929.   8104

Pressberger, Murray Ira.
13 rural routes of Phoenix, Ariz. 1945.   11267

Price, Earl M., and Company.
Map book showing ownership of farm lands in Kern County, Calif. 1954.   11389
—— 1959.   11390

Price, Francis A.
Atlas of suburban layouts in and near Wilmington, Del. 1912.   3710a, 11757
Atlas of Wilmington, Del. 1914.   4548

Price, T. T.
See Rose, T. F., Woolman, Harry C., *and* Price, T. T.

Price, Theodore Hazeltine, 1861–
Atlas of the cotton-producing states. 1902.   4497

Prichard, James Cowles, 1786–1848.
Six ethnographical maps. [1843]   92
—— 2d ed. 1851.   93

Pries, Hugo.
See Fugmann, Erich Richard, *and* Pries, Hugo.

Primax.
Mapas rodoviários do Brasil. [1956?]   18285

Princeton University. *Library.*
New Jersey road maps of the 18th cent. 1964.   15673

Prindle, A. B.
See Beers, Frederick W., Prindle, A. B., *and others.*

Prine, John B.
Complete indexed street guide showing all of Duval County and Jacksonville, Fla. [1956]   11888
Street guide of Atlanta, Ga. [1962]   11963

Prins, Anthonij Winkler, 1817–1908.
Winkler Prins Atlas. 1950.   7422

Prior, Vilhelm.
Lomme-atlas over Danmark. 10. udg. 1918.   8275

Prljević, Dragutin.
Историски атлас за националну историју. [Historical atlas of national history] 1953.   9463
—— 1956.   9464

Progressive Farmer.
National farm market coverage. 1951.   10447

Prony, Gaspard Clair François Marie Riche, *Baron* de, 1755–1839.
Atlas des Marais Pontins. 1823.   5267

Prop, G.
Atlas van Europa en de werelddelen. 35. druk. 1948.   7317
—— Beknopte uitgave. 3. druk. 1949.   7366
—— 45. druk. 1955.   7620

Atlas van Nederland, de West en Indonesië.
53. druk. 1951. 9095
—— 2. druk. 1953. 9096
—— 58. druk. 1955. 9098
Atlas van Nederland en de Indiën. 7. druk.
[1927] 9090
—— 23. druk. 1935. 9091
—— 46. druk. [1949] 9093
—— 50. druk. [1949?] 9094
Begin–atlas van Europa (en de werelddelen).
[1947] 7276
Begin–atlas van Nederland. 23. druk.
1953. 9097
Tekenatlas van Europa en de werelddelen.
[194–] 5758

Prudent, Ferdinand Pierre Vincent, 1835–1915.
See Schrader, Franz, 1844–1924, Prudent,
Ferdinand Pierre Vincent, 1835–1915, *and*
Anthoine, Edouard, 1847–1919.

Prussia. *Armee. Grosser Generalstab.*
Deutsch-Französischer Krieg, 1870–1871.
[1874–81] 2979

Prussia. *Kriegsgeschichtliche Abtheilung.*
Campaign in Germany of 1866. [1907] 3031

**Prussia. *Ministerium für Handel, Gewerbe und
Öffentliche Arbeiten.***
See-Atlas. 1841. 5254

Prussia. *Statistisches Landesamt.*
Sprachenatlas der Grenzgebiete des Deutschen
Reiches. 1929. 8584
Statistischer Atlas für den Preussischen Staat.
1905. 8759

Prussia. *Wasser-Ausschuss.*
Memel-, Pregel- und Weichselstrom. 1899. 7885
Oderstrom, sein Stromgebiet und seine wich-
tigsten Nebenflüsse. 1896. 7878
Weser und Ems. 1901. 8883

Ptolemaeus, Claudius, *d.* A.D. 147?
Geographia. *Greek.* Mt. Athos. 12th cent.
Repr. Paris, 1867. 350
—— *Greek.* Vatican. 12th cent. Repr.
Leiden, 1932. 5909
—— *Arabic.* Aya Sofia, Constantinople.
14th cent. Repr. [1928?] 5910
—— *Latin and English.* Ebnerianus. 1460.
Repr. New York, 1932. 5911
—— *Latin.* Vicenciae. 1475. 351
—— *Latin.* Bologna. 1477. Repr. Jen-
kintown, 1941. 5912
—— *Italian.* Firenze. 1478? 352
—— *Latin.* Rome. 1478. 5913
—— *Latin.* Ulmae. 1482. 353
—— *Latin.* Ulmae. 1486. 354
—— *Latin.* Romae. 1490. 355
—— *Latin.* Romae. 1507. 356
—— *Latin.* Romae. 1508. 357
—— *Latin.* Venetiis. 1511. 358

—— *Latin.* Argentinae. 1513. 359
—— *Latin.* Nuremberg. 1514. 4252
—— *Latin.* Argentorati. 1520. 360
—— *Latin.* Argentorati. 1522. 361
—— *Latin.* Argentorati. 1525. 362
—— *Greek.* Basileae. 1533. 363
—— *Latin.* Lugduni. 1535. 364
—— *Latin.* Basileae. 1540. 365, 3388
—— *Latin.* Lugduni-Viennae. 1541. 366
—— *Latin.* Basileae. 1542. 367
—— *Latin.* Basileae. 1545. 368
—— *Italian.* Venetia. 1548. 369
—— *Latin.* Basileae. 1552. 370
—— *Italian.* Venetia. 1561. 371, 5915
—— *Latin.* Venetiis. 1562. 372
—— *Italian.* Venetia. 1564. 373
—— *Italian.* Venetia. 1574. 380, 381
—— *Latin.* Coloniae Agrippinae. 1578. 384
—— *Latin.* Coloniae Agrippinae. 1584. 390
—— *Latin.* Venetiis. 1596. 403
—— *Latin.* Coloniae Agrippinae. 1597. 404
—— *Italian.* Venetia. 1598. 405
—— *Italian.* Venetia. 1599. 409
—— *Greek and Latin.* Francofurti. 1605. 421
—— *Latin.* Coloniae Agrippinae. 1608. 5921
—— *Latin.* Arnhemi. 1617. 432
—— *Greek and Latin.* Lvgdvni Batavorvm.
1618. 433
—— *Greek and Latin.* Amstelodami. 1618. 3418
—— *Italian.* Padova. 1621. 436
—— *Latin.* Franequerāe; Trajecti ad
Rhenum. 1695. 518, 5952
—— *Latin.* Trajecti ad Rhenum; Frane-
querae. 1698. 526
—— *Latin.* Trajecti ad Rhenum. 1704. 3463
—— *Latin.* Amstelodami. 1730. 575
—— *Greek and Latin.* Essendiae. 1838–45. 776

Publicaciones Educativas Ariel.
Atlas del Ecuador. [1965?] 18366

Publishers Moderna.
Peoria County [Ill.] farmer's platbook and directory. [1958] 12444

**Pudelko, Alfred, 1899–   and Ziegfeld, Arnold
Hillen, 1894–**
Kleiner Deutscher Geschichtsatlas. 2. verb.
und erweiterte Aufl. 1938. 8575

Puerto Rico. *Planning Board.*
Mapa de zonificación de Rio Piedras. [1949] 18179
Mapa de zonificación de San Juan. 1949. 18180
Mapa de zonificación del caserio Puerto
Nuevo de Rio Piedras. 1949. 18178
Plan regional area metropolitana de San Juan.
[1956] 18181

**Puerto Rico. *Urban Renewal and Housing Adminis-
tration.***
Old San Juan and Puerta de Tierra. [1964] 18182

Puffer, Lorenz.
Puffer-Erben Geographischer Atlas für alle

Arten von Mittelschulen und Handelslehr-
anstalten. 4. Aufl. 1931. 6752

Pulaski Co., *Ark. County Planning Board.*
Atlas of Pulaski County, Ark. 1950. 11300

Pullé, Francesco Lorenzo, *Conte*, 1850–1934.
Italia, genti e favelle (disegno antropologico-
linguistico) Atlante. 1927. 8954

**Purdue University, *Lafayette, Ind. Engineering Ex-
periment Station. Joint Highway Research Project.***
Atlas of county drainage maps: Indiana.
1959. 12726

Putnam, G. P., Sons.
Handy map book. [1922] 6499
Handy volume atlas of the world. [1921] 6458
Motor road and mileage atlas [of the United
States. 1925] 10789

Putnam's Economic atlas. 1925. 5456
—— 1926. 5457
—— [1928] 5458

Putnam's Historical atlas, mediaeval and modern.
6th ed. 1927. 5544

Putzger, Friedrich Wilhelm, *b.* 1849.
Historički školski atlas. 1904. 5545
Historischer Schul-Atlas. 1878. 5546
—— 17. Aufl. 1891. 138
—— 19. Aufl. 1893. 5547
—— 26. Aufl. 1902. 5548
—— American ed. [1903] 140
—— 28. Aufl. 1904. 5549
—— 30. Aufl. 1906. 139
—— 34. Aufl. 1910. 3317
—— 36. Aufl. 1913. 5550
—— 41. Aufl. 1918. 5551
—— 42. Aufl. 1920. 5552
—— 44. Aufl. 1923. 5552a
—— 49. Aufl. 1929. 5553
—— 50. Aufl. 1931. 5554
—— 54. Aufl. 1937. 5556
—— 57. Aufl. 1939. 5557
—— 59. Aufl. 1942. 5558
—— 60. Aufl. 1942. 5559
—— 63. Aufl. [1954] 5561
—— 64. Aufl. [1954] 5561a
—— Kleine Ausg. 6. Aufl. 1931. 5555
—— Kleine Ausg. 11. Aufl. 1942. 5560
See also Andree, Richard, *and* Putzger, Friedrich Wilhelm.

Quad, Matthias, 1557–1613.
Evropae totivs orbis terrarvm. 1592. 7780
—— 1592–[93] 5176, 7781
—— 1594. 2828, 7782
Fascicvlvs geographicvs. 1608. 4253a
Geographisch Handtbuch. 1600. 411

Quax, *firm.*
Atlas für Luftfahrer. 1. Aufl. [1957] 8519

**Quebec (City) Université Laval. *Institut d'Histoire
et de Géographie.***
Collection de cartes ... de l'histoire de l'Amérique et du Canada. 1948. 10300

Quebec *(Province) Economic Research Bureau.*
Atlas du Québec; l'agriculture. [1965] 10428

Queens County, *N.Y.*
Land map of the county of Queens, city and
State of New York. [1915] 4930, 16120

Queensland. *Geological Survey.*
Geological and topographical atlas of the
Gympie goldfield. 1910–11. 5323

Queensland. *Registrar-general's Office.*
Queensland. 1891. 3256

Question Italo-Yougoslave. [1919] 7818

Quin, Edward, 1794–1828.
Historical atlas. 1836. 4139
—— New ed. 1846. 141
—— —— [1856] 5562

**Quinette de Rochemont, Émile Théodore, *Baron*,
1838–1908, *and* Vétillart, Henri, 1848–**
Ports maritimes de l'Amérique du Nord sur
l'Atlantique. 1904. 4503

Quintana, Sebastian Acosta.
Planos de comunicaciones de las provincias de
la Isla de Cuba. 1884. 2713

**Raccolta di le piv illvstri et famose citta di tvtto il
mondo.** [1579] 5390

Radcliffe, William H.
Sight-seeing map of the Hudson River.
1946. 16194

**Radefeld, Carl Christian Franz, 1788–1874, *and*
Renner, L.**
Atlas zum Handgebrauche für die gesammte
Erdbeschreibung. [1841] 781

Radford, Albert E.
Atlas of the vascular flora of the Carolinas.
1965. 16198

Radó, Alexander.
Atlas für Politik, Wirtschaft, Arbeiterbewe-
gung. v. 1. [1930] 5462
Atlas of to-day and to-morrow. 1938. 6957

Radovanović, Mihaile S.
Велики атлас. [Great atlas.] 1924. 6562a

Räddningskåren.
Karta, hjälpstations-förteckning, turist-information. [Sweden. 1956]   9385

Ragozin, Viktor Ivanovich, 1833–1901.
Волга. [Volga.] [1880–81]   4058

Rainfall of Jamacia. 1963.   18175

Raisz, Erwin Josephus, 1893–1968.
Atlas of Florida. 1964.   11802
Atlas of global geography. [1944]   7191

Rajchman, Marthe.
Europe; an atlas of human geography. 1944.   7655
New atlas of China. [1941]   9578
See also Hudson, Geoffrey Francis, 1903–
and Rajchman, Marthe.
—— Mowrer, Edgar Ansel, 1892– *and*
Rajchman Marthe.

Ramsey, George D.
Atlas of Texas history. [1914]   5066
—— [1918?]   5067
—— [1925]   17131

Rand, McNally and Company.
Amoco streamlined strip map from Maine to Florida. [1939]   10850
Atlas and globe revision supplement. 1951.   7474
Atlas [of] Canada. [1962]   10379
Atlas of Chicago. 1922.   12620
Atlas of China. 1900.   9555
Atlas of foreign countries (A companion volume to the Commercial atlas of America) 1st ed. 1913.   4398
Atlas of Mexico. 1916.   5120
Atlas of reconstruction for schools. [1921]   6459
Atlas of the city of Chicago. 1916. [1915]   4600
Atlas of the European conflict. 1914.   4238
Atlas of the Mexican conflict. 1913.   5119
Atlas of the United States. [1935]   11064
Atlas of the world. 1911.   3624, 6347
—— 1920.   6422
—— 1922.   6500
—— 1923.   6527
—— 1936.   6889
Atlas of the world and Europe made over. 1919.   6398
Atlas of the World War. 1917.   4239
—— 1918.   4240, 5842
Atlas of the zonal system of bituminous coal distribution. [1918]   4494
Auto road atlas of the United States. 1926.   10791
—— 1929.   10808
—— 1930.   10815
—— 1931.   10822
Auto road atlas of the United States and eastern Canada. 1928.   10802
Battle fields of today. [1616]   4240a
—— [1917]   5843
Best atlas of America, with foreign supplement. 1918.   6384

Black and white mileage atlas of the United States, Canada and Mexico. [1922]   10746
Book of the United States; an illustrated atlas of today's world. [1963]   11087
Business atlas. 1876–77.   1397
—— 1877.   1399
—— 1878.   1401
—— 1878–79.   1402
—— 1880.   1406
Cadillac La Salle touring and service atlas. [2d ed. 1927?]   10795
Challenge Pocket atlas of the world. [1945?]   7220
Chevrolet's family travel guide. [1967]   10976
City rating guide. [1964]   10557
Classroom atlas. 1950.   7423
Columbian atlas. [1925]   6591
Commercial atlas of America. 1911.   3642
—— 1912.   3643
—— 3d ed. 1913.   4451
—— 4th ed. 1914.   4452
—— 5th ed. 1915.   4453
—— 47th ed. 1916.   4454
—— 48th ed. 1917.   4455
—— 49th ed. 1918.   4456, 4496
—— Special ed. with foreign supplement. 1918.   4109
—— 51st ed. 1920.   6423
—— 52d ed. 1921.   6460
—— 53d ed. 1922.   6501
—— 54th ed. 1923.   6528
—— 55th ed. 1924.   6563
—— 56th ed. 1925.   6592
—— 57th ed. [1926]   6631
Commercial atlas. 58th ed. [1927]   6659
—— 59th ed. [1928]   6683
—— 60th ed. [1929]   6712
—— 61st ed. [1930]   6729
—— 62d ed. [1931]   6753
—— 63d ed. [1932]   6786
—— 64th ed. [1933]   6802
—— 65th ed. [1934]   6823
—— 66th ed. [1935]   6854
Commercial atlas and marketing guide. 67th ed. [1936]   6890
—— 68th ed. [1937]   6921
—— 69th ed. [1938]   6958
—— 70th ed. [1939]   6982
—— 71st ed. [1940]   7029
—— 72d ed. [1941]   7063
—— 73d ed. [1942]   7109
—— 74th ed. [1943]   7154
—— 75th ed. [1944]   7192
—— 76th ed. [1945]   7221
—— 77th ed. [1946]   7247
—— 78th ed. [1947]   7277
—— 79th ed. 1948.   7318
—— 80th ed. 1949.   7367
—— 81st ed. [1950]   7424
—— 82d ed. [1951]   7475
—— 83d ed. [1952]   7530
—— 84th ed. [1953]   7579
—— 85th ed. [1954]   7608
—— 86th ed. [1955]   7621

Commercial atlas of foreign countries. 2d ed. 1921.	6461
Competitive route maps. [188–?]	10739
Complete atlas of the world. 1912.	3638
—— 1917.	4441
—— [1920]	6424
—— [1922]	6502
Complete radio atlas of the United States. 1922.	10724
—— 1925.	10725
Comprehensive atlas of the new Europe. [1919]	4240b
Concise atlas of the world. 1930.	6730
Concise atlas of the World War. 1917.	4241
Concise peace atlas. 1919.	4242
Cosmo relief series maps. 1952.	7531
Cosmo series maps. 1949.	7368
Cosmopolitan world atlas. [1949]	7369
—— [2d ed. 1951]	7476
—— [2d ed. 1953]	7580
—— [1955]	7621a
Current events world atlas. 1943.	7155
—— 1944.	7193
—— [1946]	7248
—— 1952.	7532
Cyclopedic atlas. 1900.	1055
Desk atlas of the world. [1921]	6462
Dollar atlas of the world. 1911.	3631
—— 1916.	4431
—— 1917.	4443
Enlarged business atlas. 1889.	952, 1429
—— 1890.	959, 1430
—— 1891.	6257
—— 1892.	974, 1432
—— 1893.	984, 1436
—— 1894.	990, 1438
—— 1895.	1001, 1442
—— 1896.	1011, 1443
—— 1897.	1019, 1445
—— 1899.	1042
—— 1900.	1056
—— 1901.	1068
—— 1903.	1088
—— 1904.	1092
—— 1905.	1105
—— [1906]	1112
—— 1907.	1125
—— 1908.	1132a, 1448
—— 1909.	3595
—— 1910.	3610
Everybody's new census atlas. 1901.	1069
Excelsior atlas of the world. 1917.	4442
Expansion atlas. 1899.	4377
Family atlas of the United States. 1892.	1431
Fast find street and highway map of Chicago and vicinity. [1960]	12663
Fast find street map of Philadelphia. 1959.	16887
15¢ pocket atlas of the world. 1902.	6305
—— 1911.	3625
Firestone road maps of America. 1946.	10867
Firestone world atlas. 1942.	7110
—— 1944.	7194
Foreign trade atlas. Detailed maps of Central and South America. [1920]	18047

Gem atlas of the world. [1921]	6463
General atlas of the world. 1887.	942
—— 1905.	1104
—— [1921]	6464
Global war atlas. [1943]	7156
Graphic representation of the battle fields of today. [1915]	4243
Guide to Chicago. [1964]	12667
Handy atlas of the world. 1920.	6425
—— 1921.	6465
Handy railroad maps of the United States. 1937.	10740
—— 1942.	10741
—— [1944]	10742
—— 1948.	10743
—— [1952]	10744
—— 1965.	10745
Historical development atlas of U.S.A. 1650–1926. 1926.	10636
History of the Spanish-American War. 1898.	1358
Household atlas. 1898.	1025
Ideal atlas of the world. 1915.	4422
—— 1921.	6466
—— [1922]	6503
Illustrated atlas. [1937]	6922
—— [1938]	6959
Illustrated road guide. 1956.	10904
Improved indexed business atlas. 8th and 9th eds. 1881.	896, 897
—— 11th ed. 1883.	914
—— 13th ed. 1884.	922
—— 1885.	928, 1422
—— 1886.	933, 1423
—— 1887.	943, 1424
—— 1888.	945, 1427
Indexed atlas of the Dominion of Canada. [1905]	1248
Indexed atlas of the world. 1881.	898
—— 3d, 6th, and 7th eds. 1882.	908, 3568, 6212
—— 8th ed. 1883.	6215
—— 1884.	4361
—— 1892.	975
—— 1894.	991, 992, 993, 1439, 6270
—— 1895.	4527
—— [1898]	1026, 1446
—— v. 1. [1899]	6286
—— [1902]	1079, 1447
—— [Rev. ed.] 1903.	4378
—— 2v. 1904.	6314
—— 2v. [1905]	1106, 6318
—— 1907.	1126
—— 2v. 1908.	6329
International atlas of the world. 1915.	4423
—— 1916.	6378
—— 1921.	6467
—— [1923]	6529
—— 1926.	6632
Interstate road atlas. [1967]	10977
Landowner's directory of northeast Illinois. [1914]	4556
Library atlas. [1894]	994, 995
—— 1895.	1002
—— [1912]	3637b
Library atlas of the world. v. 2. [1913]	6363

Michigan fishing and hunting guide. [1941]	14570	
Michigan road atlas. [1944]	14571	
—— [1950]	14573	
Mileage guide No. 1. 1936.	10982	
Mileage guide No. 2. 1936.	10983	
Model atlas. 1889.	953	
Motoroad atlas of the United States. [1930]	10816	
Neuer familien Atlas. 1891.	966	
New atlas of the state of Minnesota [and the world] 1907.	1124, 2010	
New census atlas of the world. 1911.	3628	
New dollar atlas of the United States and Dominion of Canada. 1884.	1416	
New family atlas. 1888.	946, 946a	
—— [1891]	967	
—— 1912.	3639	
—— 1916.	4432	
—— 1917.	4444	
New family atlas of Canada and the world. 1913. [1912]	4399	
New family atlas of the world. 1913.	6364	
New general atlas. [1895]	1003	
New handy atlas of the United States and Dominion of Canada. 1884.	11043	
New handy atlas ... of the United States and the Dominion of Canada. 1892.	1433	
—— 1893.	985	
New handy atlas of the world. [1908]	3584	
—— [1911]	3626	
—— [1917]	6379	
New handy census gazetteer and atlas. [1894]	996	
New handy family atlas of the United States and Canada. 1885.	11046	
New ideal state and county survey and atlas containing a ... map of Connecticut. 1911.	3709	
New ideal state and county survey and atlas containing a ... map of Illinois. 1911.	3718	
New ideal state and county survey and atlas containing a ... map of Indiana. 1908.	1132b, 1600	
—— 1909.	3596	
New ideal state and county survey and atlas containing a ... map of Ohio. 1909.	3873	
New imperial atlas of the world. 1903.	6310	
—— 1904.	6315	
—— 1905.	1107	
—— 1911.	3629	
—— 1914.	6370	
—— 1917.	4445	
New indexed atlas of the Northwest. [1880]	1407	
New indexed atlas of the world. 1886.	934	
—— 1887.	6237	
—— 1894.	1440	
New indexed business atlas and shippers' guide. 1881.	1408, 1409, 1410	
—— 1883.	1413	
—— 1884.	1417, 1418, 11044	
New international indexed atlas. 1898.	1027	
New pictorial atlas of the world. [1896]	1010	
New pocket atlas ... of all states and territories in the United States. 1892.	1434	
—— 1893.	1437	

New popular atlas of the world. 1896.	1012	
—— 1897.	6279	
New reference atlas of the world and the war. [1918]	4449	
New standard atlas of the world. [1890]	960	
—— [1892]	976, 977	
—— 1897.	4375	
—— [1899]	1043	
—— [1901]	6301	
On the battle lines. [1915]	4244, 5183	
Peace conference world atlas. [1947]	5897	
Philadelphia Public Ledger's Unrivaled atlas of the world. 1899.	6287	
Philco Radio atlas of the world, 1934–1935. [1934]	5809	
—— [1935]	5810	
Pioneer atlas of the American West. [1956]	11035	
Pocket atlas of the world. 1886.	935	
—— [1900]	1057	
—— 1902.	6306	
—— 1911.	3627	
—— 1915.	4424	
—— 1917.	4446	
Pocket atlas of Canada. [1922]	10369	
Pocket atlas of the world. [1921]	6468	
—— [1924]	6564	
—— [1939]	6983	
—— [1944]	7195	
Pocket world atlas. [1951]	7477	
Political atlas. 1908.	10712	
—— 1920.	10713	
—— 1928.	10714	
—— 1932.	10715	
—— 1936.	10716	
Popular world atlas. 1942.	7111	
—— 1943.	7157	
Premier atlas of the world. [1923]	6530	
—— 1924.	6565	
—— [1925]	6593	
Readers world atlas. [1951]	7478	
Ready–reference atlas of the world. [1934]	6824	
—— [1935]	6855	
—— [1936]	6891	
—— [1937]	6923	
—— [1938]	6960	
—— [1939]	6984	
—— [1941]	7064	
—— [1942]	7112	
Reliable world atlas. [1941]	7065	
—— 1942.	7113	
Road atlas and guide to places of interest of the United States and eastern Canada. 1932.	10826	
Road atlas and radio guide of the United States. 1950.	10880	
—— 1951.	10883	
—— 1952.	10889	
—— 1957.	10909	
—— 1958.	10915	
Road atlas and travel guide. [1961]	10933	
—— [1962]	10941	
—— [1963]	10945	
—— [1964]	10952	
—— [1966]	10967	

Road atlas of the United States and eastern Canada. 1933.	10827
—— 1934.	10830
Road atlas of the United States, Canada and Mexico. 1935.	10834
—— 1936.	10838
—— 1937.	10842
—— 1938.	10846
—— 1939.	10851
—— 1940.	10854
—— 1941.	10856
—— 1942.	10860
—— 1944.	10864
—— 1945.	10866
—— 1946.	10868
—— 1947.	10872
—— 1948.	10875
—— 1949.	10877
—— 1951.	10884
Road atlas of U.S., Mexico, and S. Canada. 1954.	10896
Road atlas, United States, Canada, Mexico. 1952.	10890
—— 1953.	10892
—— 1954.	10897
—— 1955.	10900
—— 1956.	10905
—— 1957.	10910
—— 1958.	10916
—— 1959.	10922
—— 1960.	10929
—— 1961.	10934
—— 1962.	10942
—— 1963.	10946
—— 1964.	10953
—— 1965.	10960
—— 1966.	10968
—— 1967.	10978
Russo-Japanese war atlas. 1904.	9236
Sales control atlas of the United States. 1959.	11080
Special auto road atlas of the United States and eastern Canada. [1928]	10803
—— 1930.	10817
—— 1931.	10823
Stamp collector's atlas and dictionary. [1933]	5785
Standard atlas of the world. [1888]	6243
—— [1938]	6961
—— [1939]	6985
—— [1941]	7066
—— [1943]	7158
—— [1948]	7319
Standard highway mileage guide. [1934]	10984
—— [1941]	10985
—— 1949.	10986
—— 1955.	10987
—— 1961.	10988
—— 1966.	10989
Standard war atlas. [1898]	3689
Standard world atlas. [1951]	7479
Texaco international road atlas. 1959.	10923
—— 1961.	10935

Texaco road maps. 1938.	10847
—— 1942.	10861
Texaco touring atlas: United States, Canada, Mexico. [1965]	10962
—— [1966]	10969
—— [1967]	10979
Texaco touring maps. [1946]	10869
—— [1952]	10891
This is my country. [1944]	11069
Toronto Mail and empire atlas of Canada. [1904]	1247
Travelog. 1951.	10885, 10886
—— 1953.	10893
Twentieth century atlas. 1896.	1013
Unabridged world atlas. [1937]	6924
Universal atlas. 1892.	978
—— 1893.	986
—— 1895.	1004, 1005
—— 1896.	1014
—— [1899]	1044
—— 1901.	1067
—— 1916.	4433
Unrivaled atlas of the world. 1910.	6337
—— 1911.	3630
—— 1912.	6352
Vacation atlas and guide: Canada, United States, Mexico. [1965]	10961
Victory world atlas. 1943.	7159
War atlas. 1898.	4521, 10689
War map of Europe. 1914.	4245
World atlas. [1933]	6803
—— [1937]	6925, 6929
—— [1939]	6986
—— [1941]	7067
—— [1943]	7160
—— [1948]	7320
—— 1950.	7425
—— Commonwealth ed. [1927]	6660
—— [1928]	6684
—— European War. [1939]	6987
—— Ideal ed. [1937]	6926
—— International ed. [1927]	6661
—— —— [1929]	6713
—— —— [1930]	6731
—— —— [1931]	6754
—— —— [1935]	6856
—— —— [1936]	6892
—— —— [1937]	6927
—— —— [1939]	6988
—— —— [1941]	7068
—— —— [1943]	7161
—— —— [1944]	7196
—— —— [1946]	7249
—— —— [1947]	7278
—— Pictorial ed. [1934]	6825
—— —— [1935]	6857
—— Pocket ed. [1927]	6662
—— Premier ed. [1927]	6663
—— —— [1929]	6714
—— —— [1931]	6755
—— —— [1932]	6787
—— —— [1935]	6858
—— —— [1936]	6893
—— —— [1937]	6928

—— —— [1938]	6962
—— —— [1940]	7030
—— —— [1941]	7069
—— —— [1942]	7114
—— —— [1943]	7162
—— —— [1944]	7197
—— —— [1946]	7250
—— —— [1947]	7279
—— —— [1948]	7321
—— —— [1949]	7370
—— Readers ed. [1930]	6732
—— —— 1931.	6756
—— —— [1936]	6894
—— —— [1941]	7070
—— —— [1943]	7163
—— —— [1944]	7198
—— —— [1945]	7222
—— Travel ed. [1931]	6757
—— —— [1936]	6895
World atlas and international gazetteer. [1935]	6859
—— [1936]	6896
World today and yesterday. [1919]	6399
World's resources and where to find them. 1921.	5463

Rand McNally Golf course guide. [1966]   10749
—— [1967]   10750

Rand McNally Regional atlas. 1953.   7556

Rand McNally World atlas. [1935]   6839

Radall, G. A., and Company.
  Illustrated historical atlas of Sheboygan County, Wis. 1875.   3935

Randall, Philip S., and Reilly, R. R.
  Atlas of Morrison County, Minn. [1920]   15047

Randall and Denne.
  Index atlas of Kern County, Cal. [1901]   1461

Randle, Charles, 1749–1833.
  83 drawings. MS. [1810]   4477a, 5208a

Rapin-Thoyras, Paul de, 1661–1725.
  [Atlas to accompany Rapin's History of England. 1784–89]   5206
  [Maps and plans from The History of England. 1744–47]   8019

Rascher, Charles.
  Atlas of Lake View Twp., Cook Co., Ill. 1887.   12169
  Atlas of the north half of Hyde Park [Ill.] 1890.   12167
  Map of Chicago suburbs. 1885.   12591

Rascher Insurance Map Publishing Company.
  Atlas of Bay City, Mich. 1891.   14844
  Atlas of Chicago. 1886–93.   12592
  —— 1891.   1587
  Atlas of Duluth, Minn. 1892.   15142

Atlas of Kansas City, Kans. 1893.	14212
Atlas of Minneapolis and suburbs, Minn. 1892.	15148
Atlas of Muskegon, Mich. 1891.	14892
Atlas of northwestern elevators; is Minnesota ... Wisconsin. 1891.	14907
Atlas of St. Paul, Minn. 1891	15160
Atlas of Superior, Wis. [1892]	18026
Atlas of the Chicago packing houses and Union Stock Yards. 1891.	12593
Atlas of the town of Lake [Ill.] 1891.	12168
Atlas of West Bay City, Mich. 1891.	14845
Block book of Chicago business district. 1893.	12596
Block book of Kansas City, Mo. 1891.	15253

Raseri, Enrico.
  Atlante di demografia e geografia medica d'Italia. 1906.   3058

Raspe, Gabriel Nicolaus, 1712–1785.
  Schauplatz des gegenwaertigen Kriegs. [1757–64]   2825

Ratelband, Johannes, 1715–1791.
  Kleyne en beknopte atlas, of Tooneel des oorlogs in Europa. 1735.   2840

Ratisbonna, Leandro.
  See Serra, Adalberto B., *and* Ratisbonna, Leandro.

Ratthey, Wilhelm.
  Heimatatlas für Berlin und die Kurmark. 1. Aufl. 1937.   8837
  Heimatatlas für Berlin und die Mark Brandenburg. 12. Aufl. 1940.   8839

Raup, Henry A., 1933–
  See Bier, James Allen, 1927–   *and* Raup, Henry A., 1933–

Rausch, B., firm.
  München in der Tasche. [1946]   8867
  —— [1949]   8868
  —— [1952]   8869
  —— [1956]   8870

Ravenstein, August, i.e., Friedrich August, 1809–1901.
  Plastischer Schul-Atlas. 3. Aufl. 1854.   4183

Ravenstein, Ernest George, 1834–1913.
  New census physical ... atlas of the world. [1911]   3632
  Philips' Handy–volume atlas of the world. 1905.   6319
  —— 1908.   3585
  —— 12th ed. 1918.   6385
  —— 14th ed. 1923.   6531
  —— 15th ed. 1925.   6594
  Philip's Systematic atlas. [1912]   6353

Ravenstein, Ludwig, 1838–1915.
[Atlas des Deutschen Reiches. 1884]   8686

Ravenstein Geographische Verlagsanstalt und Druckerei.
Dunlop Atlas von Deutschland. [1933] 8606, 8607
Jugendherbergs-Taschenatlas der Bundesrepublik. [1953]   8677
Leuna Zapfstellen-Atlas. [1938]   8618
Strassen Atlas Bundesrepublik Deutschland.
[1955]   8661
—— [1957?]   8670

Rayback, Robert J.
Richards Atlas of New York State. [1959]   15852
—— 1965.   15854
Student guide for the Richards Atlas of New
York State. [1962]   15853

Raynal, Guillaume Thomas François, 1713–1796.
Atlas de toutes les parties connues du globe
terrestre. [1780]   5992
—— [1783–84]   5995
Atlas portatif. 1773.   5987

Rea, Clarendon Rudolph, 1913–
Plat maps of Carroll County, Mo. 1940.   15219

Read, Newbury Frost.
See Hopkins, Albert Allis, 1869–   *and*
Read, Newbury Frost.

Real, Baldomero.
Mapa general de las almas que administran
los pp. Augustinos calzados en estas Islas
Filipinas. 1845.   5305

Real Automóvil Club de España.
Mapa de carreteras ... de España. [1914?]   9319

Real Estate Index Company.
Atlas and ownership index ... Minneapolis.
1913–16.   4826

Real Estate Map Publishing Company.
Atlas of township of Cicero, Cook County,
Ill. 1913.   4602
Atlas of township of Proviso, Cook County,
Ill. 1914.   4603
Atlas of the township of Jefferson, Ill. 1908.   1593
Official atlas of the township of Lake View,
Rogers Park & Westridge and part of West
Town, Chicago. 1909.   3733

Real Property Inventory of Metropolitan Cleveland.
Planes of living in Cuyahoga County [Ohio.
1941]   16398

Realty Map and Ownership Service Company.
New Los Angeles [Calif.] plat book. 1947–
53.   11543
—— 1953.   11548

Reclus, Onésime, 1837–1916.
Atlas de la plus grande France. [1913]   5229
—— [1920]   8470
Atlas pittoresque de la France. [1910–12]   5228
Nouvel atlas départemental de la France.
[1927]   8471

Record and Indianola Tribune.
Atlas of Warren County, Iowa. 1951.   14017

Record and Tribune Company.
Farm atlas of Warren County, Iowa. 1940.   14015

Rectigraph Abstract and Title Company.
Atlas and industrial geography of Summit
County, Ohio. 1910.   3878

Redd, T. Crawford, and brother.
Sectional map of that portion of Henrico
County, Va., adjacent to the city of Rich-
mond. 1901.   2613

Redman, Charles C.
Map of the city of Kennett, Mo. 1956.   15260
Plat book, Dunklin County, Mo. 1956.   15227

Reed, Alexander Wyclif.
Atlas of New Zealand. [1952]   10202
See also Reed, Alfred Hamish, 1875–   *and*
Reed, Alexander Wyclif.

Reed, Alfred Hamish, 1875–   and Reed, Alexander Wyclif.
New world atlas. 3d ed. [1948]   7322
—— 5th ed. 1951.   7480

Reed, Carroll E., and Seifert, Lester W.
Linguistic atlas of Pennsylvania German.
1954.   16758

Reed, Hugh T.
Pocket atlas. 1889.   954

Rees, Abraham, 1743–1825, and others.
Cyclopaedia; or Universal dictionary of arts,
sciences ... Ancient and modern atlas.
[1806]   711
—— 1820.   4312a

Rees, William, 1887–
Historical atlas of Wales. [2d ed.] 1951.   8220

Refsdal, Ivar, 1866–
Norge i vestelommeformat. 4. utg. 1949.   9124
Skole–atlas. 15. utg. 1945.   7223
—— 16. utg. 1947.   7280
Skolekart over Norge. [13. utg. 1928]   9116
—— 16. omarbeidede utg. 1937.   9119
—— 18. utg. 1942.   9120
—— 19.–21. utg. 1947.   9121
—— 22. oppl. 1950.   9125

Regal Cartographers.
Santa Clara County [Calif.] "Locaide".
[1949]   11477

Regal Map Company.
Santa Clara County [Calif.] LoCaide. 1963.   11483
Santa Clara County [Calif.] street locater.
1967.   11485

Regensburg. *Wasser- und Schiffahrtsdirektion.*
Schiffahrtskarte der Donau. [1952–56]   7839

Reich, Emil, 1854–1910.
Atlas antiquus. 1908.   2794a
New students' atlas of English history. 1903.   2884

Das Reich; Deutsche Wochenzeitung.
100 Karten. [1943]   5898
—— [1944]   5899

Reichard, Christian Gottlieb, 1758–1837.
Orbis terrarum antiquus. 1824.   3286
—— 6th ed. [1861]   51
Orbis terrarum veteribus cognitus. 1833.   5646

Reichard, Heinrich August Ottokar, 1752–1828.
Atlas portatif et itinéraire de l'Europe. 1818–
[21]   2810

Reichel, Friedrich Carl Helmut.
Westermanns Deutscher Reichs-Atlas.
[1935]   8697

Reichel, Levin Theodore, 1812–1878.
Missions-Atlas der Brüder-Ünität. 1860.   3338

Reichsarbeitsgemeinschaft für Raumforschung.
Atlas Bayerische Ostmark. 1939.   8722
Thüringen-Atlas. [1939–40]   8816

Reichsforschungsrat. *Fach: Raumforschung.*
Donau-Karpatenraum. [1943]   7842

Reichskolonialbund.
Deutscher Kolonial-Atlas. 21. Ausg.
1939.   8547
—— 22. Ausg. 1941.   8548
Kolonialer Taschenatlas. [1938]   8546

Reicke, Erich, 1884–
See Diercke, Paul, 1874–1937, *and* Reicke,
Erich, 1884–

Reid, Alexander, 1802–1860.
Introductory atlas of modern geography.
1837.   6081

Reilly, Franz Johann Joseph von, 1760–1820.
Atlas universae. 1799   2851
Atlass von Deutschland. 1803.   8684
Grosser deutscher Atlas. [1796]   686
Schauplatz der fünf Theile der Welt. v.1, v.2,
pt.2–3. 1789–[91]   2845, 5997

Reilly, R. R.
See Randall, Philip S., *and* Reilly, R. R.

Reimer and Olcott.
Insurance map of the city of Orange, N. J.
1875.   15774

Reina, Vincenzo, 1862–1919.
Media pars vrbis. [Roma] 1911.   9013

Reinbek, Ger. Bundesanstalt für Forst– und Holzwirtschaft.
Weltforstatlas. 1951–53.   5478

Reinoso, José.
Atlas geográfico universal. 5. ed. 1951.   7481

Reitzenstein, Heinrich Hans Wilhelm, *Freiherr* **von.**
Atlas zur Expedition der Franzosen und Eng-
länder gegen ... Antwerpen. 1833.   7972

Reizinger, Nándor.
Budapest album térképe. [1948]   8929

Reliable Directory Service.
Plat book of Cerro Gordo County, Iowa.
1937.   13203

Remarkable maps of the xvth, xvith, & xviith **centuries. 1894–99.**   260

Remezov, Semen Ul'îanovich, *ca.,* **1662–1715.**
Atlas of Siberia. 1958.   9300
Чертежная книга Сибири ... [Book of maps
of Siberia.] 1701 ... 1882.   4080a

Remondini, Giuseppe.
Atlas géographique. 1801.   3377

Renard, Louis.
Atlas de la navigation. 1715.   559
—— 1739.   592
Atlas van zeevaert en koophandel door de
geheele weereldt. 1745.   601

Renard, Rudolf.
Harms Rheinland-Pfalz. [1953]   8776
—— [1957]   8779

Renié, Jack Joseph.
Atlas of greater southern California counties
and cities. [1962]   11362
—— [1963]   11364
New Renié atlas of Los Angeles City and
County [Calif. 1942]   11392, 11393
—— [1943]   11394
New Renié pocket atlas of Los Angeles ...
City and County [Calif. 3d ed. rev. 1945]   11396
—— [5th ed. 1947]   11399
New Renié pocket atlas of Orange County
and cities [Calif. 1943]   11429
New Renié pocket atlas of Riverside and San
Bernardino Counties [Calif. 1947]   11446

Pocket atlas ... San Diego, Calif., City [and]
County, [1948]   11457

Renié Map Service.
New map atlas. Index to the city of Los Angeles
[Calif. 1936]   11536

Rennard, T. A.
See Dale, W., *and* Rennard, T. A.

Rennell, James, 1742–1830.
Bengal atlas. 1780.   3201
—— 1781.   9710
Recueil de cartes géographiques, pour la
description de l'Indostan. 1800.   9697

Renner. L.
See Radefeld, Carl Christian Franz, 1788–
1874, *and* Renner, L.

Replogle Comprehensive atlas of the world. [1953]   7564
—— [1954]   7601

Replogle Globes.
Illustrated atlas. [1937]   6930

Replogle World atlas. [1950]   7409

Republican Publishing Company.
Butler County [Ohio] atlas and pictorial re-
view. 1914.   4982

Rerick Brothers.
County of Butler, Ohio. 1895.   16384
County of Clark, Ohio. 1894.   2359
County of Henry, Ind. [1893]   1612
County of Miami, Ohio. 1894.   2401
County of Richland, Ohio. 1896.   2412
County of Seneca, Ohio. 1896.   2414
County of Vigo, Ind.; an imperial atlas.
1895.   12938
County of Wayne, Ind.; an imperial atlas.
1893.   3742

Restrepo, José Manuel, 1780–1864.
Historia de la revolución de la República de
Colombia. Atlas. 1827.   2760

Retail Credit Company, *Atlanta*.
Atlas of North America. [1934]   10290

Revise-O-Map, *Austin, Tex*.
Revise-O-Map of South Texas. [1961]   17120

Reynolds, Francis Joseph, 1867–1937.
After-war atlas and gazetteer of the world.
[1919]   4450a
—— [1920]   6426
Comprehensive atlas and gazetteer of the
world. 1921.   6469
—— 1922.   6504
—— [1923]   6532
—— [1925]   6595
—— [1926]   6633

Reynolds, James.
Travelling atlas of England. [1848]   8132

Reynolds & Proctor.
Illustrated atlas of Sonoma County, Cal.
[1898]   1466

Rhode, C. E.
Historischer Schul-Atlas. 8. Aufl. 1871.   4140
—— 11. Aufl. [187–?]   4141

Rhodes, Edwin S.
First centennial history and atlas of
Tuscarawas County, Ohio. 1908.   2418

Rhodes, Glenn, *and* Rhodes, Dale.
Camping maps, Canada. 1961.   10352
Camping maps, U.S.A. [1957]   10754
—— [1961]   10755
—— [1963]   10756
Camping maps, U.S.A. and Canada. [1964]   10757
Private campgrounds. 1964.   10758

Ribeiro, Guaracy.
Geografia e atlas do Brasil. [1966]   18298

Ribeiro Campos, Carlos Augusto.
Atlas estatístico do Brasil. 1941.   18279

Riccardi, Mario.
See Riccardi, Riccardo, 1897–   *and* Riccardi, Mario.

Riccardi, Riccardo, 1897–
See Dardano, Achille, 1870–1938, *and* Riccardi, Riccardo, 1897–

Riccardi, Riccardo, *and* Riccardi, Mario.
Atlantino I. G. E. I. [1953]   7581

Ricci, Matteo, 1552–1610.
Mappamondo cinese ... (3. ed. Pechino, 1602)
1938.   5790

Rice, G. Jay.
See Wright, George Burdick, 1832–1882, *and*
Rice, G. Jay.

Richard, F. J., and Company.
Quarter section atlas: Fargo, N.Dak. 1959.   16352

Richards, Horace Gardiner, 1906–
Book of maps of Cape May, 1610–1878.
1954.   15691

Richards, Lucius J.
Atlas of Dorchester, West Roxbury, and
Brighton, city of Boston. 1899.   1861

Richards, L. J., and Company.
Atlas of the city of Newport and towns of
Middletown and Portsmouth, R.I. 1907.   16957
Atlas of the city of Wheeling, W.Va. 1889.   2629
Atlas of the city of Worcester, Mass. 1896.   4727

Atlas of the town of Brookline, Mass. 1893.   3775
Memorial atlas of Ireland. 1901.   2940
New topographical atlas of the county of
  Hampden, Mass. 1894.   1816
New topographical atlas of the county of
  Worcester, Mass. 1898.   1827

Richards Atlas of New York State. [1959]   15852
—— 1965.   15854

Richards Map Company.
Atlas of the city of Hartford, Conn. 1896.   11720
—— 1909.   11722
Atlas of the city of Lawrence . . . Mass. 1926.   14480
Atlas of the city of Lowell, Mass. 1896.   14484
Atlas of the city of Springfield, Mass. 1899.   14526
—— 1910.   14527
Standard atlas of the city of Portland . . .
  Maine. 1914.   14323
Standard atlas of the city of Worcester, Mass.
  1922.   14542

Richardson, A. T.
Bacon's Biblical atlas. 1926.   5367

Richmond. *Civil War Centennial Committee.*
Troop movements at the Battle of Cold Harbor, 1864. [1964]   10686

Richter, Eduard, 1847–1905.
See Penck, Albrecht, *i.e.,* Friedrich Karl
Albrecht, 1858–1945, *and* Richter, Eduard,
1847–1905.

Richthofen, Ferdinand Paul Wilhelm, *Freiherr* **von,
1833–1905.**
Atlas von China. 1885.   3191
—— [1912]   4070a

Ricker, Mayme Alma, 1896–
Instructor hectograph book of maps. [1946]   10294

Riecke, Friedrich.
See Keil, Wilhelm, *and* Riecke, Friedrich.

Riedl, Adrian von, 1746–1809.
Reise Atlas von Bajern. 1796–[1806]   8728

Riemeck, Renate.
Kleiner Geschichtsatlas. [1950]   5563

Riess, Richard von, 1823–1898.
Atlas scripturae sacrae. 1906.   3303
Bibel-Atlas. 2. Aufl. 1887.   88
—— 3. Aufl. 1895.   5368

Rimli, Eugen Theodor.
Neuer Welt–Atlas. [1949]   7371

Rinaudo, Costanzo, 1847–1937.
Atlante storico per le scuole secondarie.
  [1911]   4142
Variazioni politiche e territoriali dell'Europa.
  [1914]   7693

Rinehart, Ira.
Structure maps of Texas oil fields. 1954.   17132

Ringborg, Axel.
Atlas of Clearwater County, Minn. 1912.   3810a

Ringgold, Cadwalader, 1802–1867.
Series of charts, with sailing direction, embracing surveys of the Farallones, entrance
  to the Bay of San Francisco. 1851.   11623

Riniker, H., Hagnauer, Robert, *and* **Dickson,
George K.**
New atlas of Madison County, Ill. 1892.   1551

Rio, Manuel E., 1872– *and* **Achával, Luis, 1870–**
Geografía de la provincia de Córdoba.
  1905.   2737, 5137

Rios Valdivia, Alejandro, 1901–
Atlas universal. 1. ed. 1949.   7372
—— 2. ed. 1952.   7533
Cuaderno de mapas. v.2–3. [1941–43]   5759
—— v.3. [1942]   5760

Ristow, Walter William, 1908–
World is yours; an atlas of global relations.
  [1944]   7199

Rittmann, André, *and* **Junié, Jean, b. 1756.**
Atlas des plans de la censive de l'Archevêché
  dans Paris . . . 1786. [Reprint] 1906.   4031

Riu Batista, Agustín.
Esquemas cronológicos . . . de la historia de
  España. [2. ed.] 1946.   9311

Rivera Cambas, Manuel, *i.e.,* **Ignacio Manuel, 1840–
1917.**
Atlas y catecismo de geografía y estadística de
  la República Mexicana. 1874.   3937

Rizzi-Zannoni, Giovanni Antonio, 1736–1814.
[Atlante geografico del Regno di Napoli.
  1788–1804]   8995
Atlas géographique et militaire, ou Théatre de
  la guerre presente en Allemagne. [1761]   7704
[Atlas historique de la France ancienne et
  moderne. 1764]   8409
Carte de la Pologne. 1772.   9159

Robbins Studio.
New sportsman's maps of Cape Cod lakes &
  ponds. [1936]   14403

Robert de Vaugondy, Didier, 1726–1786.
Atlas d'étude. 1797–[98]   3530
[Carte coloriée du Royaume de France.
  1778]   2994
Novissimo atlante geografico. 1819–[20]   737
[Recueil de 10 cartes . . . traitant particulière-
  ment de l'Amérique du Nord. 1779]   1195
See also Robert de Vaugondy, Gilles, 1688–

1766, *and* Robert de Vaugondy Didier, 1726–1786.

Robert de Vaugondy, Gilles, 1688–1766.
Atlas portatif. 1748–[49]   608
—— [Supplement] 1748–[49]   5981
Nouvel atlas portatif. 1762.   5984
—— 1778.   649
—— 1784.   4298
—— [1794–1806]   3528
Tablettes parisiennes. 1760.   5232

Robert de Vaugondy, Gilles, *and* Robert de Vaugondy, Didier, 1723–1786.
[Atlas universel. 1749–92]   5982
—— 1757–[58]   619
—— 1757–[86]   4292
—— [1783–99]   3524, 5996
—— [1793?]   678

Roberts, William Jackson, *and* Fuller, John F.
Atlas of Whitman County, Wash. 1895.   2625

Robertson, *Sir* Charles Grant, 1869–1948, *and* Bartholomew, John George, 1860–1920.
Historical and modern atlas of the British Empire. 1905.   2885
Historical atlas of modern Europe from 1789 to 1914. 1915.   5161
—— 2d ed. 1914.   7694

Robertson, Edward, 1879–
Bible atlas. New ed. [1915?]   4119

Robertson, W. Bruce.
Jackson County, Minn. 1923.   15010

Robijn, Jacobus, *b.* 1649.
Zee, zea-atlas-aquatique, del mare. 1683.   493

Robinson, Earl J., and Company.
Illustrated review showing commercial ... development of the state of Iowa. [1915]   4620

Robinson, Edward Kilburn, 1883–
See Bishop, Mildred Catherine, 1886– *and* Robinson, Edward Kilburn.
See also Willard, R. C., *and* Robinson, Edward Kilburn.

Robinson, Elisha.
Atlas of Essex County, N.J. 1890.   2155
Atlas of Jefferson County, N.Y. 1888.   2232
Atlas of Kings County, N.Y. 1890.   2233
Atlas of Morris County, N.J. 1887.   2168
Atlas of Norfolk County, Mass. 1888.   1822
Atlas of the borough of Richmond, city of New York. 1898.   16131
Atlas of the city of Chicago, Ill. 1886.   1583
Atlas of the city of Rochester, Monroe County, N.Y. 1888.   2323
Atlas of the Oranges, Essex County, N.J. 1904.   2180, 2191, 2196, 2200
Atlas of the 29th, 30th, 31st and 32nd wards

... borough of Brooklyn, city of New York. 1898.   2278
Certified copies of important maps appertaining to the 23rd and 24th wards, city of New York. 1888–90.   2035
Certified copies of important maps of wards 8, 17, 18, 21, 22, 23, 24, and 25, city of Brooklyn. 1889.   2277

Robinson, Elisha, *and* Pidgeon, Roger H.
Atlas of the borough of Richmond, city of New York. 1907.   2316
Atlas of the city of Brooklyn, N.Y. 1886.   2276
Atlas of the city of Cincinnati, Ohio. 1883–84.   2423
Atlas of the city of Detroit and suburbs ... Mich. 1885.   2003
Atlas of the city of Mansfield, Ohio. 1882.   2433
Atlas of the city of New Orleans, La. 1883.   1771
Atlas of the city of New York. 1883–87.   2302
—— 1884.   2303
—— 1885.   2304
—— 1890–93. 3d ed.   2308
Atlas of the city of Paterson, N.J. 1884.   2193
Atlas of the city of Springfield, Ohio. 1882.   2435
Real estate atlas of the city of New York. 1889–90.   2306

Robinson, Elisha, *and* Tenney, Lucius E.
Atlas of the city of Newark, N.J. 1901.   2189

Robinson, Elisha, and Company.
Certified copies of maps of the annexed district ... city of New York. 1897.   2314

Robinson, Elisha, *and others*.
Atlas of Irvington, south Orange, Maplewood and Millburn, Essex County, N.J. 1928.   15694
Atlas of the city of Denver, Colo. 1887.   1475
Atlas of the city of Newark, N.J. 1926–27.   15769
Atlas of the city of Passaic and Acquackanonk Township, Passaic County, N.J. 1901.   2192
Atlas of the city of Summit, N.J. 1900.   2107

Robinson, H. E. C.
Complete street directory, city & suburbs of Melbourne. [195–]   10185
Official Brisadex street directory of Greater Brisbane. [194–]   10183
Street directory of Sydney & suburbs. [1957]   10186

Robinson, H. E. C., pty.
Modern school atlas of the world. [1940]   7031
—— [195–?]   7379

Robiquet, Aimé.
Atlas hydrographique. [1844–51]   795
—— 1882.   909

Rochambeau, Jean Baptiste Donatien de Vimeur, *Comte* de, 1725–1807.
Amérique campagne, 1782. MS. [1782]   1335

Rochester Bureau of Municipal Research.
    Map section; a real property inventory of
      Rochester, N.Y. [1940]   16157

Rockford Map Publishers.
    Atlas & plat book, Clinton County, Mich.
      1964.   14640
    Atlas & plat book, Emmet County, Mich.
      1967.   14653
    Atlas & plat book, Hillsdale County, Mich.
      1964.   14670
    Atlas & plat book, Iron County, Mich.
      1964.   14688
    Atlas & plat book, Iron County, Wis. 1965.   17776
    Atlas & plat book, Marquette County, Wis.
      1965.   17841
    Atlas & plat book, Midland County, Mich.
      1966.   14745
    Atlas & plat book, Oceana County, Mich.
      [1965]   14780
    Atlas & plat book, Ogemaw County, Mich.
      1965.   14782
    Atlas & plat book, Pike County, Ill. 1966.   12460
    Atlas & plat book, Polk County, Wis. 1966.   17880
    Atlas & plat book, Richland County, Ill.
      1966.   12475
    Atlas of Butler County, Ohio. 1958.   16385
    Atlas of Green Lake County, Wis. 1951.   17761
    Biennial atlas & plat book, Carroll County,
      Ill. 1967.   12113
    Biennial atlas & plat book, Green County,
      Wis. 1967.   17758
    Biennial atlas & plat book, Macoupin County,
      Ill. 1967.   12383
    Biennial farm atlas & residents directory,
      Dakota County, Minn. 1967.   14971
    Biennial farm atlas & residents directory,
      Manitowoc County, Wis. 1967.   17825
    Biennial farm atlas & residents directory, Por-
      tage County, Wis. 1967.   17884
    Biennial farm atlas & residents directory, Scott
      County, Minn. 1967.   15099
    Biennial farm atlas & residents directory,
      Waukesha County, Wis. 1967.   17975
    Biennial farmers atlas & residents directory,
      Fayette County, Ind. 1967.   12782
    Biennial farmers atlas & residents directory,
      Kendall County, Ill. 1967.   12320
    Biennial farmers atlas & residents directory,
      Randolph County, Ind. 1967.   12897
    Biennial farmers atlas & residents directory,
      Whiteside County, Ill. 1967.   12554
    County atlas & plat book, Isabella County,
      Mich. 1964.   14690
    De Kalb County [Ill.] farm atlas and business
      guide. [1947]   12184
    Enjoy Illinois: State atlas. [1965]   12075
    ——— [1966]   12076
    Explore Indiana: State atlas and sportsman's
      guide. [1966]   12733
    Farm plat book, Allegan County, Mich.
      [1954]   14597
    Farm plat book and business guide, Berrien
      County, Mich. [1954]   14619

    Farm plat book and business guide, Bond
      County, Ill. [1949]   12088
    Farm plat book and business guide, Boone
      County, Ill. [1946]   12093
    Farm plat book and business guide, Calhoun
      County, Ill. 1948.   12106
    Farm plat book and business guide, Calhoun
      County, Mich. [1954]   14629
    Farm plat book and business guide, Carroll
      County, Ill. [1951]   12110
    Farm plat book and business guide, Cham-
      paign County, Ill. [1950]   12120
    Farm plat book and business guide, Chippewa
      County, Wis. [1954]   17690
    Farm plat book and business guide, Clark
      County, Ill. [1951]   12131
    Farm plat book and business guide, Clinton
      County, Ill. [1950]   12138
    Farm plat book and business guide, Clinton
      County, Ind. [1953]   12759
    Farm plat book and business guide, Coles
      County, Ill. [1952]   12141
    Farm plat book and business guide, Columbia
      County, Wis. [1953]   17697
    Farm plat book and business guide, Crawford
      County, Ill. [1954]   12177
    Farm plat book and business guide, Cumber-
      land County, Ill. [1951]   12180
    Farm plat book and business guide, De Witt
      County, Ill. [1948]   12187
    ——— [1952]   12188
    Farm plat book and business guide, Douglas
      County, Ill. [1950]   12193
    Farm plat book and business guide, Du Page
      County, Ill. [1951]   12202
    Farm plat book and business guide, Eau Claire
      County, Wis. [1955]   17733
    Farm plat book and business guide, Edgar
      County, Ill. [1948]   12224
    Farm plat book and business guide, Edwards
      County, Ill. [1951]   12229
    Farm plat book and business guide, Effingham
      County, Ill. [1949]   12231
    Farm plat book and business guide, Elkhart
      County, Ind. [1951]   12777
    Farm plat book and business guide, Ford
      County, Ill. [1948]   12237
    Farm plat book and business guide, Fulton
      County, Ill. [1951]   12245
    Farm plat book and business guide, Grant
      County, Wis. [1948]   17749
    Farm plat book and business guide, Grundy
      County, Ill. [1950]   12252
    ——— [1955]   12253
    Farm plat book and business guide, Henderson
      County, Ill. [1950]   12268
    Farm plat book and business guide, Hillsdale
      County, Mich. [1954]   14669
    Farm plat book and business guide, Iowa
      County, Wis. [1952]   17767
    Farm plat book and business guide, Jackson
      County, Mich. [1953]   14693
    Farm plat book and business guide, Jackson
      County, Wis. [1953]   17779

Farm plat book and business guide, Jasper County, Ill. [1951]   12284

Farm plat book and business guide, Jo Daviess County, Ill. [1947]   12297

Farm plat book and business guide, Juneau County, Wis. [1952]   17791

Farm plat book and business guide, Kalamazoo County, Mich. [1954]   14696

Farm plat book and business guide, Kane County, Ill. [1950]   12304

Farm plat book and business guide, Kankakee County, Ill. [1951]   12310

Farm plat book and business guide, Kendall County, Ill. [1947]   12316

—— [1951]   12317

—— [1955]   12318

Farm plat book and business guide, Knox County, Ill. [1953]   12324

Farm plat book and business guide, Kosciusko County, Ind. [1952]   12836

Farm plat book and business guide, La Crosse County, Wis. [1954]   17804

Farm plat book and business guide, Lagrange County, Ind. [1952]   12838

Farm plat book and business guide, La Porte County, Ind. [1951]   12844

Farm plat book and business guide, La Salle County, Ill. [1950]   12336

Farm plat book and business guide, Lawrence County, Ill. [1951]   12341

Farm plat book and business guide, Lenawee County, Mich. [1953]   14717

Farm plat book and business guide, McDonough County, Ill. [1954]   12362

Farm plat book and business guide, McHenry County, Ill. [1951]   12367

Farm plat book and business guide, McLean County, Ill. [1947]   12373

—— [1951]   12374

Farm plat book and business guide, Macon County, Ill. [1951]   12377

—— [1955]   12378

Farm plat book and business guide, Macoupin County, Ill. [1950]   12381

Farm plat book and business guide, Madison County, Ill. [1950]   12387

Farm plat book and business guide, Manitowoc County, Wis. [1952]   17823

Farm plat book and business guide, Marion County, Ill. [1948]   12390

—— [1953]   12391

Farm plat book and business guide, Mason County, Ill. [1948]   12400

—— [1953]   12401

Farm plat book and business guide, Massac County, Ill. [1953]   12404

Farm plat book and business guide, Milwaukee County, Wis. [1954]   17844

Farm plat book and business guide, Monroe County, Mich. [1955]   14748

Farm plat book and business guide, Montgomery County, Ill. [1953]   12420

Farm plat book and business guide, Morgan County, Ill. [1951]   12425

Farm plat book and business guide, Newton County, Ind. [1951]   12867

Farm plat book and business guide, Oconee County, S.C. [1953]   16993

Farm plat book and business guide, Ogle County, Ill. [1953]   12435

Farm plat book and business guide, Parke County, Ind. [1953]   12878

Farm plat book and business guide, Peoria County, Ill. [1953]   12441

Farm plat book and business guide, Piatt County, Ill. [1949]   12454

Farm plat book and business guide, Pope-Hardin Counties, Ill. [1955]   12462

Farm plat book and business guide, Rock County, Wis. [1951]   17904

Farm plat book and business guide, Rock Island County, Ill. [1950]   12478

Farm plat book and business guide, Rockingham County, N.C. [1952–53]   16218

Farm plat book and business guide, Saginaw County, Mich. [1955]   14799

Farm plat book and business guide, Saline County, Ill. [1952]   12489

Farm plat book and business guide, Sauk County, Wis. [1947]   17917

—— [1953]   17918

Farm plat book and business guide, Schuyler County, Ill. [1950]   12496

Farm plat book and business guide, Scott County, Ill. [1947]   12500

Farm plat book and business guide, Shelby County, Ill. [1950]   12503

Farm plat book and business guide, Steuben County, Ind. [1954]   12920

Farm plat book and business guide, Union County, Ill. [1951]   12521

Farm plat book and business guide, Vermilion County, Ill. [1948]   12525

—— [1953]   12526

Farm plat book and business guide, Wabash County, Ill. [1951]   12531

Farm plat book and business guide, Walworth County, Wis. [1950]   17953

Farm plat book and business guide, Wayne County, Ill. [1954]   12543

Farm plat book and business guide, White County, Ill. [1954]   12548

Farm plat book and business guide, Will County, Ill. [1948]   12557

—— [1953]   12558

Farm plat book and business guide, Winnebago County, Wis. [1951]   17988

Farm plat book and business guide, Woodford County, Ill. [1949]   12577

—— [1954]   12579

Farm plat book, Barry County, Mich. [1955]   14610

Farm plat book, Bay County, Mich. [1955]   14613

Farm plat book, Bayfield County, Wis. [1954]   17663

Farm plat book, Bureau County, Ill. [1952]   12102

Farm plat book, Clark County, Ill. [1955]   12132

Farm plat book, Du Page County, Ill. 1955.   12205

Farm plat book, Edgar County, Ill. [1955] 12225
Farm plat book, Emmet County, Mich. [1955] 14652
Farm plat book ... Fond du Lac County, Wis. [1963] 17741
Farm plat book, Gratiot County, Mich. [1955] 14665
Farm plat book, Green Lake County, Wis. [1951] 17762
Farm plat book, Hancock County, Ill. [1955] 12262
Farm plat book, Huron County, Mich. [1954] 14674
Farm plat book, Ionia County, Mich. [1955] 14682
Farm plat book, Iron County, Wis. [1953] 17775
Farm plat book, Iroquois County, Ill. [1955] 12278
Farm plat book, Isabella County, Mich. [1955] 14691
Farm plat book, Jo Daviess County, Ill. [1954] 12299
Farm plat book, Kent County, Mich. [1955] 14702
Farm plat book, Lee County, Ill. [1955] 12347
Farm plat book, Manistee County, Mich. [1954] 14732
Farm plat book, Marquette County, Wis. [1952] 17840
Farm plat book, Mercer County, Ill. [1953] 12412
Farm plat book, Newaygo County, Mich. [1955] 14761
Farm plat book, Noble County, Ind. [1951] 12870
Farm plat book, Ottawa County, Mich. [1955] 14792
Farm plat book, Piatt County, Ill. [1954] 12455
Farm plat book, Pierce County, Wis. [1955] 17873
Farm plat book, St. Joseph County, Mich. [1955] 14806
Farm plat book, Trempealeau County, Wis. [1954] 17939
Farm plat book, Vernon County, Wis. [1955] 17945
Farm plat book, Walworth County, Wis. [1956] 17954
Farm plat book, Washtenaw County, Mich. 1964. 14825
Farm plat book, Waupaca County, Wis. [1953] 17980
Farm plat book, Waushara County, Wis. [1948] 17984
—— [1956] 17985
Farm plat book, Wexford County, Mich. [1956] 14839
Farm plat book, Whiteside County, Ill. [1954] 12552
Farm plat book, with index to owners, Antrim County, Mich. [1967] 14603
Farm plat book, with index to owners, Charlevoix County, Mich. [1967] 14634
Farm plat book, with index to owners, Gratiot County, Mich. [1963] 14666
Farm plat book, with index to owners, Green Lake County, Wis. [1963] 17763
Farm plat book, with index to owners, Knox County, Ill. [1963] 12326
Farm plat book, with index to owners, Marion County, Ill. 1959. 12392

Farm plat book, with index to owners, Price County, Wis. [1963] 17888
Farm plat book, with index to owners, Richland County, Ill. [1963–64] 12474
Farm plat book, with index to owners, Scott County, Ill. 1967. 12501
Farm plat book, with index to owners, Wapello County, Iowa. [1963] 14013
Farm plat book, with index to owners, Washington County, Wis. 1966. 17969
Farm plat book, with index to owners, Winona County, Minn. [1963] 15135
Farmers atlas & resident directory, Adams County, Ill. 1967. 12084
Farmers atlas & resident directory, Boone County, Ill. 1967. 12095
Farmers atlas & resident directory, Dubuque County, Iowa. 1967. 13362
Farmers atlas & resident directory, Faribault County, Minn. 1967. 14984
Farmers atlas & resident directory, Juneau County, Wis. 1967. 17793
Farmers atlas & resident directory, Linn County, Iowa. 1967. 13642
Farmers atlas & resident directory, Morgan County, Ill. 1967. 12427
Farmers atlas & resident directory, Tazewell County, Ill. 1967. 12519
Farmers atlas & residents directory, Sauk County, Wis. 1967. 17920
Fayette County [Ill.] farm plat book. 1964. 12234
Lake County [Ill.] atlas and plat book. [1967] 12333
Land plat book, with index to land owners, Alpena County, Mich. 1967. 14600
Land plat book, with index to land owners, Gogebic County, Mich. 1965. 14660
Menominee County [Mich.] plat book & atlas. [1967] 14743
Michigan State atlas. [1966] 14590
North part, Cook County [Ill.] atlas and plat book. [1967] 12165
Official farm plat book, Montgomery County, Ind. [1963] 12863
Plat book and directory, Allegany County, N.Y. 1964. 15856
Plat book Ashland County, Wis. [1946] 17654
Plat book, Boone County, Ill. [1952–53] 12094
Plat book, Brown County, Ill. [1952] 12097
Plat book, Brown County, Wis. [1953] 17670
Plat book, Burnett County, Wis. [1948] 17680
—— [1952] 17681
Plat book, Clay County, Ill. [1953] 12135
Plat book, Crawford County, Wis. [194–] 17701
Plat book, Dane County, Wis. [1947] 17710
Plat book, Defiance County, Ohio. [1948] 16405
Plat book, Door County, Wis. [1946] 17723
Plat book, Grand Traverse County, Mich. 1964. 14662
Plat book, Iroquois County, Ill. [1950] 12277
Plat book, Jackson County, Wis. [1946] 17778
Plat book, Jefferson County, Wis. [194–] 17784
Plat book, Knox County, Ind. [1953] 12833
Plat book, La Crosse County, Wis. [194–] 17801
Plat book, Lafayette County, Wis. [1947] 17809

Plat book, Leelanau County, Mich. [1967]	14713
Plat book, Marinette County, Wis. [1947]	17833
—— [1954]	17834
Plat book, Oconto County, Wis. 1967.	17853
Plat book of Dodge County, Wis. [1947]	17717
Plat book of Montmorency County, Mich. 1967.	14755
Plat book, Ottawa County, Mich. 1965.	14793
Plat book, Richland County, Ill. [1948]	12473
Plat book, Shawano County, Wis. [194–]	17924
Plat book, Somerset County, Pa. 1964.	16801
Plat book, Washburn County, Wis. [1946]	17960
—— [1952]	17961
Plat book, Washington County, Wis. [194–]	17966
Plat book, Winnebago County, Ill. [1946]	12570
—— [1949]	12572
Plat book, Winnebago County, Wis. [194–]	17987
Plat book, with index to owners, Bayfield County, Wis. [1963]	17665
—— [1967]	17666
Plat book, with index to owners, Chippewa County, Wis. 1966.	17691
Plat book, with index to owners, Crawford County, Mich. 1965.	14643
Plat book, with index to owners, Lincoln County, Wis. [1963]	17819
—— [1966]	17820
Plat book, with index to owners, Marinette County, Wis. [1963]	17835
—— [1967]	17836
Plat book, with index to owners, Marquette County, Mich. [1967]	14735
Plat book, with index to owners, Oneida County, Wis. [1963]	17856
Plat book, with index to owners, Presque Isle County, Mich. [1963]	14795
Plat book, with index to owners, Rusk County, Wis. [1964]	17907
Three year atlas & plat book, Hancock County, Ill. 1963.	12263
Three year atlas & plat book, McHenry County, Ill. 1963.	12369
Three year atlas & plat book, Rush County, Ind. [1963]	12902
Three year atlas & plat book, Tippecanoe County, Ind. [1963]	12930
Three year atlas & plat book, Will County, Ill. 1963.	12563
Three year atlas & plat book, Winnebago County, Wis. 1963.	17989
Tri-annual atlas & plat book, Adams County, Ill. 1964.	12083
Tri-annual atlas & plat book, Adams County, Ind. 1966.	12736
Tri-annual atlas & plat book, Adams County, Wis. 1964.	17650
Tri-annual atlas & plat book, Allegan County, Mich. 1966.	14598
Tri-annual atlas & plat book, Allen County, Ind. 1965.	12740
Tri-annual atlas & plat book, Anoka County, Minn. 1965.	14925
Tri-annual atlas & plat book, Ashland County, Wis. 1965.	17655

Tri-annual atlas & plat book, Baraga County, Mich. 1964.	14608
Tri-annual atlas & plat book, Barron County, Wis. 1964.	17660
Tri-annual atlas & plat book, Barry County, Mich. 1966.	14611
Tri-annual atlas & plat book, Bartholomew County, Ind. 1964.	12742
Tri-annual atlas & plat book, Bay County, Mich. 1965.	14614
Tri-annual atlas & plat book, Berrien County, Mich. 1964.	14620
Tri-annual atlas & plat book, Bond County, Ill. 1966.	12089
Tri-annual atlas & plat book, Brown County, Ill. 1965.	12099
Tri-annual atlas & plat book, Brown County, Wis. 1966.	17672
Tri-annual atlas & plat book, Buffalo County, Wis. 1964.	17677
Tri-annual atlas & plat book, Bureau County, Ill. 1965.	12104
Tri-annual atlas & plat book, Burnett County, Wis. 1965.	17682
Tri-annual atlas & plat book, Calhoun County, Ill. 1965.	12107
Tri-annual atlas & plat book, Calhoun County, Mich. 1965.	14630
Tri-annual atlas & plat book, Calumet County, Wis. 1965.	17686
Tri-annual atlas & plat book, Carroll County, Ill. 1964.	12112
Tri-annual atlas & plat book, Cass County, Ill. 1964.	12116
Tri-annual atlas & plat book, Cass County, Mich. 1967.	14632
Tri-annual atlas & plat book, Champaign County, Ill. 1964.	12123
—— 1966.	12124
Tri-annual atlas & plat book, Chisago County, Minn. 1965.	14952
Tri-annual atlas & plat book, Christian County, Ill. 1965.	12129
Tri-annual atlas & plat book, Clark County, Ill. 1966.	12133
Tri-annual atlas & plat book, Clark County, Wis. 1964.	17693
Tri-annual atlas & plat book, Clay County, Ind. 1966.	12756
Tri-annual atlas & plat book, Clinton County & the Carlyle Reservoir area, Ill. 1965.	12139
Tri-annual atlas & plat book, Clinton County, Ind. 1965.	12760
Tri-annual atlas & plat book, Coles County, Ill. 1965.	12142
Tri-annual atlas & plat book, Columbia County, Wis. 1965.	17698
Tri-annual atlas & plat book, Crawford County, Ill. 1966.	12178
Tri-annual atlas & plat book, Crow Wing County, Minn. 1966.	14965
Tri-annual atlas & plat book, Cumberland County, Ill. 1966.	12181

Tri-annual atlas & plat book, Dakota County, Minn. 1964.   14970

Tri-annual atlas & plat book, Dane County, Wis. 1964.   17711

Tri-annual atlas & plat book, Daviess County, Ind. 1965.   12765

Tri-annual atlas & plat book, Decatur County, Ind. 1966.   12768

Tri-annual atlas & plat book, De Kalb County, Ill. 1966.   12186

Tri-annual atlas & plat book, De Kalb County, Ind. 1965.   12770

Tri-annual atlas & plat book, Delaware County, Ohio. 1965.   16408

Tri-annual atlas & plat book, De Witt County, Ill. 1965.   12189

Tri-annual atlas & plat book, Dickinson County, Mich. 1966.   14646

Tri-annual atlas & plat book, Douglas County, Ill. 1966.   12194

Tri-annual atlas & plat book, Douglas County, Minn. 1965.   14979

Tri-annual atlas & plat book, Dunn County, Wis. 1967.   17730

Tri-annual atlas & plat book, Du Page County, Ill. 1964.   12217

Tri-annual atlas & plat book, Eaton County, Mich. 1966.   14650

Tri-annual atlas & plat book, Eau Claire County, Wis. 1964.   17734

Tri-annual atlas & plat book, Edgar County, Ill. 1964.   12226

Tri-annual atlas & plat book, Effingham County, Ill. [1966]   12232

Tri-annual atlas & plat book, Elkhart County, Ind. 1965.   12778

Tri-annual atlas & plat book, Fayette County, Ind. 1964.   12781

Tri-annual atlas & plat book, Fond du Lac County, Wis. 1966.   17743

Tri-annual atlas & plat book, Ford County, Ill. 1964.   12238

—— 1966.   12239

Tri-annual atlas & plat book, Forest County, Wis. 1966.   17745

Tri-annual atlas & plat book, Franklin County, Ill. 1964.   12241

Tri-annual atlas & plat book, Franklin County, Ind. 1966.   12789

Tri-annual atlas & plat book, Freeborn County, Minn. 1966.   14991

Tri-annual atlas & plat book, Fulton County, Ill. 1964.   12247

Tri-annual atlas & plat book, Genesee County, Mich. 1966.   14656

Tri-annual atlas & plat book, Gladwin County, Mich. 1965.   14658

Tri-annual atlas & plat book, Goodhue County, Minn. 1966.   14995

Tri-annual atlas & plat book, Gratiot County, Mich. 1967.   14667

Tri-annual atlas & plat book, Green County, Wis. 1964.   17757

Tri-annual atlas & plat book, Greene County, Ind. 1964.   12802

Tri-annual atlas & plat book, Hamilton County, Ill. 1965.   12257

Tri-annual atlas & plat book, Hamilton County, Ind. 1964.   12805

Tri-annual atlas & plat book, Hancock County, Ill. 1966.   12264

Tri-annual atlas & plat book, Hancock County, Ind. 1966.   12808

Tri-annual atlas & plat book, Henderson County, Ill. 1966.   12270

Tri-annual atlas & plat book, Hendricks County, Ind. 1965.   12814

Tri-annual atlas & plat book, Henry County, Ill. 1965.   12274

Tri-annual atlas & plat book, Henry County, Ind. 1966.   12816

Tri-annual atlas & plat book, Houghton County, Mich. 1964   14672

Tri-annual atlas & plat book, Houston County, Minn. 1966.   15002

Tri-annual atlas & plat book, Howard County, Ind. 1964.   12818

Tri-annual atlas & plat book, Huron County, Mich. 1965.   14676

Tri-annual atlas & plat book, Ingham County, Mich. [1963]   14679

Tri-annual atlas & plat book, Ionia County, Mich. 1967.   14683

Tri-annual atlas & plat book, Iowa County, Wis. 1965.   17769

Tri-annual atlas & plat book, Iroquois County, Ill. 1964.   12279

—— 1967.   12280

Tri-annual atlas & plat book, Isanti County, Minn. 1965.   15007

Tri-annual atlas & plat book, Jackson County, Ill. 1964.   12282

Tri-annual atlas & plat book, Jackson County, Ind. 1964.   12822

Tri-annual atlas & plat book, Jackson County, Mich. [1965]   14694

Tri-annual atlas & plat book, Jackson County, Wis. 1964.   17780

Tri-annual atlas & plat book, Jasper County, Ill. 1964.   12285

Tri-annual atlas & plat book, Jefferson County, Ill. 1966.   12291

Tri-annual atlas & plat book, Jefferson County, Wis. 1966.   17788

Tri-annual atlas & plat book, Jersey County, Ill. 1965.   12295

Tri-annual atlas & plat book, Jo Daviess County, Ill. 1966.   12300

Tri-annual atlas & plat book, Johnson County, Ind. 1966.   12830

Tri-annual atlas & plat book, Juneau County, Wis. 1964.   17792

Tri-annual atlas & plat book, Kalamazoo County, Mich. 1954.   14697

—— 1966.   14698

Tri-annual atlas & plat book, Kane County, Ill. 1964.   12307

Tri-annual atlas & plat book, Kankakee County, Ill. 1964.	12311
Tri-annual atlas & plat book, Kendall County, Ill. 1964.	12319
Tri-annual atlas & plat book, Kenosha County, Wis. 1966.	17796
Tri-annual atlas & plat book, Kent County, Mich. 1966.	14704
Tri-annual atlas & plat book, Knox County, Ill. 1966.	12327
Tri-annual atlas & plat book, Knox County, Ind. 1965.	12834
Tri-annual atlas & plat book, Knox County, Ohio. 1964.	16424
Tri-annual atlas & plat book, Lafayette County, Wis. 1965.	17811
Tri-annual atlas & plat book, Lagrange County, Ind. 1964.	12839
Tri-annual atlas & plat book, Lake County [Ill. 1965]	12331
Tri-annual atlas & plat book, Lapeer County, Mich. 1964.	14711
Tri-annual atlas & plat book, La Salle County, Ill. 1964.	12338
Tri-annual atlas & plat book, Lawrence County, Ill. 1965.	12342
Tri-annual atlas & plat book, Lawrence County, Ind. 1966.	12846
Tri-annual atlas & plat book, Lee County, Ill. 1965.	12348
Tri-annual atlas & plat book, Lenawee County, Mich. 1964.	14719
Tri-annual atlas & plat book, Licking County, Ohio. 1965.	16427
Tri-annual atlas & plat book, Livingston County, Ill. 1964.	12352
Tri-annual atlas & plat book, Livingston County, Mich. 1965.	14722
Tri-annual atlas & plat book, Logan County, Ill. 1965.	12357
Tri-annual atlas & plat book, McDonough County, Ill. 1966.	12363
Tri-annual atlas & plat book, McHenry County, Ill. 1966.	12370
Tri-annual atlas & plat book, Mackinac County, Mich. 1965.	14726
Tri-annual atlas & plat book, McLean County, Ill. 1966.	12375
Tri-annual atlas & plat book, Macomb County, Mich. 1966.	14730
Tri-annual atlas & plat book, Macon County, Ill. 1964.	12379
Tri-annual atlas & plat book, Macoupin County, Ill. 1963–[64]	12382
Tri-annual atlas & plat book, Madison County, Ill. 1966.	12388
Tri-annual atlas & plat book, Manistee County, Mich. 1966.	14733
Tri-annual atlas & plat book, Manitowoc County, Wis. 1964.	17824
Tri-annual atlas & plat book, Marathon County, Wis. 1965.	17830
Tri-annual atlas & plat book, Marion County, Ill. 1967.	12393
Tri-annual atlas & plat book, Marion County, Ohio. 1965.	16439
Tri-annual atlas & plat book, Marshall County, Ind. 1964.	12854
Tri-annual atlas & plat book, Marshall, Putnam, Stark Counties, Ill. 1965.	12398
Tri-annual atlas & plat book, Mason County, Ill. 1965.	12402
Tri-annual atlas & plat book, Mason County, Mich. 1966.	14739
Tri-annual atlas & plat book, Massac County, Ill 1966.	12405
Tri-annual atlas & plat book, Mecosta County, Mich. 1966.	14741
Tri-annual atlas & plat book, Menard County, Ill. 1966.	12409
Tri-annual atlas & plat book, Mercer County, Ill. 1966.	12414
Tri-annual atlas & plat book, Monroe County, Ill. 1965.	12417
Tri-annual atlas & plat book, Monroe County, Wis. 1965.	17849
Tri-annual atlas & plat book, Montcalm County, Mich. 1965.	14753
Tri-annual atlas & plat book, Montgomery County, Ill. 1963.	12422
—— 1966.	12423
Tri-annual atlas & plat book, Morgan County, Ill. 1964.	12426
Tri-annual atlas & plat book, Morgan County, Ind. 1966.	12865
Tri-annual atlas & plat book, Morrison County, Minn. 1965.	15050
Tri-annual atlas & plat book, Moultrie County, Ill. 1965.	12431
Tri-annual atlas & plat book, Mower County, Minn. 1965.	15051
Tri-annual atlas & plat book, Muskegon County, Mich. 1966.	14758
Tri-annual atlas & plat book, Newaygo County, Mich. 1965.	14762
Tri-annual atlas & plat book, Noble County, Ind. 1964.	12871
Tri-annual atlas & plat book, north part, Cook County [Ill. 1965]	12162
Tri-annual atlas & plat book, Oakland County, Mich. [1964]	14772
Tri-annual atlas & plat book, Ogle County, Ill. 1965.	12437
Tri-annual atlas & plat book, Olmsted County, Minn. 1965.	15069
Tri-annual atlas & plat book, Oneida County, Wis. 1966.	17857
Tri-annual atlas & plat book, Osceola County, Mich. 1963.	14786
—— 1967.	14787
Tri-annual atlas & plat book, Otsego County, Mich. 1965.	14790
Tri-annual atlas & plat book, Outagamie County, Wis. 1963.	17861
Tri-annual atlas & plat book, Ozaukee County, Wis. 1966.	17866
Tri-annual atlas & plat book, Parke County, Ind. 1965.	12879

Tri-annual atlas & plat book, Peoria County, Ill. 1965. 12446

Tri-annual atlas & plat book, Perry County, Ill. 1966. 12451

Tri-annual atlas & plat book, Pierce County, Wis. 1965. 17875

Tri-annual atlas & plat book, Pike County, Ind. 1964. 12883

Tri-annual atlas & plat book, Pike County, Mo. 1966. 15243

Tri-annual atlas & plat book, Pope County, Ill. 1966. 12463

Tri-annual atlas & plat book, Portage County, Wis. 1965. 17883

Tri-annual atlas & plat book, Posey County, Ind. 1964. 12887

Tri-annual atlas & plat book, Racine County, Wis. 1965. 17893

Tri-annual atlas & plat book, Randolph County, Ill. 1965. 12471

Tri-annual atlas & plat book, Richland County, Ohio. 1966. 16445

Tri-annual atlas & plat book, Rock Island County, Ill. 1965. 12480

Tri-annual atlas & plat book, Rush County, Ind. 1966. 12903

Tri-annual atlas & plat book, St. Clair County, Ill. 1965. 12487

Tri-annual atlas & plat book, St. Croix County, Wis. 1965. 17912

Tri-annual atlas & plat book, St. Joseph County, Ind. 1963. 12906

—— 1966. 12907

Tri-annual atlas & plat book, St. Joseph County, Mich. 1965. 14807

Tri-annual atlas & plat book, Sangamon County, Ill. 1965. 12493

Tri-annual atlas & plat book, Sanilac County, Mich. 1964. 14811

Tri-annual atlas & plat book, Sauk County, Wis. 1964. 17919

Tri-annual atlas & plat book, Schoolcraft County, Mich. [1964] 14814

Tri-annual atlas & plat book, Shawano County, Wis. 1966. 17927

Tri-annual atlas & plat book, Sheboygan County, Wis. 1964. 17931

Tri-annual atlas & plat book, Shelby County, Ill. 1964 12505

Tri-annual atlas & plat book, Shelby County, Ind. 1966. 12911

Tri-annual atlas & plat book, Shiawassee County, Mich. 1965. 14816

Tri-annual atlas & plat book, Stearns County, Minn. 1966. 15107

Tri-annual atlas & plat book, Stephenson County, Ill. 1966. 12513

Tri-annual atlas & plat book, Steuben County, Ind. 1966. 12922

Tri-annual atlas & plat book, Sullivan County, Ind. 1964. 12925

Tri-annual atlas & plat book, Tazewell County, Ill. 1964. 12518

Tri-annual atlas & plat book, Tippecanoe County, Ind. 1966. 12931

Tri-annual atlas & plat book, Todd County, Minn. 1966. 15114

Tri-annual atlas & plat book, Union County, Ill. 1964. 12522

Tri-annual atlas & plat book, Union County, Ind. 1966. 12935

Tri-annual atlas & plat book, Van Buren County, Mich. 1963. 14821

—— [1966] 14822

Tri-annual atlas & plat book, Van Wert County, Ohio. 1966. 16457

Tri-annual atlas & plat book, Vermilion County, Ill. 1963. 12528

—— 1966. 12529

Tri-annual atlas & plat book, Vernon County, Wis. 1965. 17946

Tri-annual atlas & plat book, Vilas County, Wis. 1965. 17947

Tri-annual atlas & plat book, Wabash County, Ill. 1966. 12533

Tri-annual atlas & plat book, Walworth County, Wis. 1964. 17955

—— 1966. 17957

Tri-annual atlas & plat book, Warren County, Ill. 1966. 12536

Tri-annual atlas & plat book, Warren County, Mo. 1964. 15249

Tri-annual atlas & plat book, Washburn County, Wis. 1963. 17962

—— 1966. 17963

Tri-annual atlas & plat book, Washington County, Ill. 1964. 12540

Tri-annual atlas & plat book, Washington County, Minn. 1966. 15128

Tri-annual atlas & plat book, Waukesha County, Wis. 1964. 17974

Tri-annual atlas & plat book, Waupaca County, Wis. 1965. 17981

Tri-annual atlas & plat book, Wayne County, Ill. 1966. 12545

Tri-annual atlas & plat book, Wells County, Ind. 1967. 12948

Tri-annual atlas & plat book, White County, Ill. [1965] 12549

Tri-annual atlas & plat book, Whiteside County, Ill. 1965. 12553

Tri-annual atlas & plat book, Will County, Ill. 1966. 12564

Tri-annual atlas & plat book, Williamson County, Ill. 1964. 12568

Tri-annual atlas & plat book, Winnebago County, Ill. 1964. 12574

Tri-annual atlas & plat book, Winnebago County, Wis. 1966. 17990

Tri-annual atlas & plat book, Wood County, Wis. 1964. 17994

Tri-annual atlas & plat book, Woodford County, Ill. 1964. 12580

Tri-annual atlas & plat book, Wyoming County, N.Y. 1966. 15926

Tri-annual plat book with index to owners, Saginaw County, Mich. 1966. 14800

Triennial atlas & plat book, Adams County, Wis. 1967.	17651
Triennial atlas & plat book, Arenac County, Mich. 1967.	14605
Triennial atlas & plat book, Bartholomew County, Ind. 1967.	12743
Triennial atlas & plat book, Branch County, Mich. 1967.	14625
Triennial atlas & plat book, Carlton County, Minn. 1967.	14944
Triennial atlas & plat book, Cheboygan County, Mich. 1967.	14636
Triennial atlas & plat book, Dane County, Wis. 1967.	17713
Triennial atlas & plat book, De Witt County, Ill. 1967.	12190
Triennial atlas & plat book, Douglas County, Wis. 1967.	17726
Triennial atlas & plat book, Edgar County, Ill. 1967.	12227
Triennial atlas & plat book, Fayette County, Pa. 1967.	16787
Triennial atlas & plat book, Fountain County, Ind. 1957.	12785
Triennial atlas & plat book, Genesee County, N.Y. 1967.	15880
Triennial atlas & plat book, Grant County, Wis. 1967.	17752
Triennial atlas & plat book, Grundy County, Ill. 1967.	12254
Triennial atlas & plat book, Hamilton County, Ind. 1967.	12806
Triennial atlas & plat book, Hardin County, Ill. 1967.	12266
Triennial atlas & plat book, Iosco County, Mich. 1967.	14686
Triennial atlas & plat book, Jasper County, Ill. 1967.	12286
Triennial atlas & plat book, Kankakee County, Ill. [1967]	12312
Triennial atlas & plat book, Langlade County, Wis. 1967.	17817
Triennial atlas & plat book, Lenawee County, Mich. 1967.	14720
Triennial atlas & plat book, Monroe County, Ind. 1967.	12860
Triennial atlas & plat book, Monroe County, Mich. 1967.	14749
Triennial atlas & plat book, Olmsted County, Minn. 1967.	15070
Triennial atlas & plat book, Orleans County, N.Y. 1967.	15899
Triennial atlas & plat book, Outagamie County, Wis. 1967.	17862
Triennial atlas & plat book, Owen County, Ind. 1967.	12876
Triennial atlas & plat book, Piatt County, Ill. 1967.	12456
Triennial atlas & plat book, Presque Isle County, Mich. 1967.	14796
Triennial atlas & plat book, Putnam County, Ind. 1967.	12894
Triennial atlas & plat book, Schuyler County, Ill. 1967.	12498

Triennial atlas & plat book, Shelby County, Ill. 1967.	12506
Triennial atlas & plat book, Susquehanna County, Pa. 1967.	16802
Triennial atlas & plat book, Taylor County, Wis. 1967.	17936
Triennial atlas & plat book, Tipton County, Ind. 1967.	12933
Triennial atlas & plat book, Trempealeau County, Wis. 1967.	17941
Triennial atlas & plat book, Washington County, Ill. 1967.	12541
Triennial atlas & plat book, Woodford County, Ill. 1967.	12581
Triennial farm atlas & residents directory, Carver County, Minn. 1967.	14947
Triennial farm atlas & residents directory, Eau Claire County, Wis. 1967.	17735
Triennial farm atlas & residents directory, Ingham County, Mich. 1967.	14680
Triennial farm atlas & residents directory, Jackson County, Ind. 1967.	12823
Triennial farm atlas & residents directory, Jay—Blackford Counties, Ind. 1967.	12826
Triennial farm atlas & residents directory, Kane County, Ill. 1967.	12308
Triennial farm atlas & residents directory, Kewaunee County, Wis. 1967.	17799
Triennial farm atlas & residents directory, La Salle County, Ill. 1967.	12339
Triennial farm atlas & residents directory, Peoria County, Ill. 1967.	12447
Triennial farm atlas & residents directory, Sheboygan County, Wis. 1967.	17932
Triennial farmers atlas & residents directory, Barron County, Wis. 1967.	17661
Triennial farmers atlas & residents directory, Clay County, Ill. 1967.	12136
Triennial farmers atlas & residents directory, Clinton County, Mich. 1967.	14641
Triennial farmers atlas & residents directory, Fulton County, Ill. 1967.	12248
Triennial farmers atlas & residents directory, Washtenaw County, Mich. 1967.	14828
Triennial farmers atlas & residents directory, Winnebago County, Ill. 1967.	12575
Waukesha County [Wis.] farms directory and plat book. 1950.	17972
Wonderful Wisconsin State atlas. [1966]	17646

Rockwood, C. H.
Atlas of Cheshire County, N.H. 1877.	2138

Rocque, Jean, *d.* 1762.
Irish surveys. [1760–1821]	8229
Set of plans and forts in America. 1763.	1186
Small British atlas. 1753.	8117
—— 1764.	5205
Topographical survey of the County of Berks [England] 1761.	8142

Rocque, Jean, *and* Bellin, Jacques Nicolas, 1703–1772.
Recueil de villes, ports d'Angleterre. 1766.	2878

Geograficzno-statystyczny atlas Polski. 1916.   9134
—— Wyd. 2. 1921.   9135
Kraje i morza pozaeuropejskie; atlas geogra-
ficzny. [1935]   6860
Mały atlas geograficzny. 1928.   6685
—— Wyd. 11. 1931.   6758
—— Wyd. 14. 1947.   7281
—— Wyd. 15. 1951.   7482
—— [Wyd. 15] 1952.   7534
Polityczny atlas kieszonkowy. Wyd. 2.
[1937]   6931
Polska; atlas geograficzny. [1935]   9171
—— Wyd. 2. [1937]   9173
Polski atlas kongresowy. 1921.   9150
Powszechny atlas geograficzny. 3v. 1925–
27.   6602
—— 1928.   6686
—— 1928 [i.e. 1931]   6759
—— Wyd. 2. 1934.   6826

**Romer, Eugeniusz, and Danysz-Fleszarowa,
Regina.**
Atlas krajoznawczy województwa warszaws-
kiego. 1923.   9162

Romer, Eugeniusz, and Jurczyński, Juljusz.
Atlas krajoznawczy województwa łódzkiego.
1923.   9163

Romer, Eugeniusz, and Niemcowna, Stanisław.
Atlas krajoznawczy dla szkół województwa
krakowskiego, kieleckiego i śląskiego.
1925.   9167

**Romer, Eugeniusz, and Pawlowski, Stanisław,
1882–1939.**
Atlas krajoznawczy dla szkół województwa
poznańskiego i pomorskiego. 1924.   9165

**Romer, Eugeniusz, and Szumański, Teofil,
1875–1944.**
Atlas krajoznawczy dla szkół województwa
lwowskiego, stanisławowskiego i tarnopolskiego. 1924.   9166
Atlas krajoznawczy województwa lwowskiego, stanisławowskiego i tarnopolskiego.
1931.   9170

**Romer, Eugeniusz, and Wąsowicz, Józef, 1900–
1964.**
Atlas Polski współczesnej. Wyd. 4. 1948.   9174
—— Wyd. 5. 1950.   9175
—— Wyd. 5. 1951.   9176
—— Wyd. 5. 1952.   9178

Romero, Emilio, 1899–
Nuevo atlas geográfico del Perú. [1940]   18389

Rónai, András, 1906–
Atlas of Central Europe. 1945   7656

Roolvink, Roelof.
Historical atlas of the Muslim peoples. 1957.   7626

Rooney, W. T., and Schleis, A. M.
Atlas of Kewaunee County, Wis. 1895.   5093

Ropes, John Codman, 1836–1899.
Atlas of the campaign of Waterloo. 1893.   2873
—— 1894.   7723

Rosaccio, Giuseppe, ca. 1530-ca. 1620.
Il mondo. 1595.   3401
Mondo elementare, et celeste. 1604.   3408
Teatro del cielo e della terra. 1599.   3403
—— 1615.   3417
—— 1642.   3423
Teatro del mondo. 1688.   3451
—— 1724.   3482

Rose, Harry B.
Ready reference book of the Chicago zoning
ordinance and maps. 1926.   12631

Rose, T. F., Woolman, Harry C., and Price, T. T.
Historical and biographical atlas of the New
Jersey coast. 1878.   2141

**Rosenberg, Hugo, 1895–   and Schenk, Eric,
1906–**
Harms Heimatatlas für Nordrhein-Westfalen.
[1952]   8824

Rosendal, Gustav.
Sønderjylland. [1919]   8290

Rossi, Giovanni Giacomo de, 17th cent.
Mercvrio geografico. [1685?]   497
—— [1692–94]   515
—— [1692–1714]   516

Rossi, Luigi, 1764–1824.
Nuovo atlante di geografia universale. 1820–
[21].   739

Rossi, Nelson.
Atlas prévio dos Falares Baianos. 1963.   18303

Rossiter, Edgar A.
Atlas of the city of De Land ... Fla. 1950.   11869
Elk Grove atlas, Cook County, Ill. 1946.   12166
Northfield atlas, Cook County, Ill. 1948.   12170
Schaumburg atlas, Cook County, Ill. 1947.   12172
Wheeling, Cook County, Ill. 1945.   12173

Roterus, Victor, and March, Sterling.
Economic development atlas. [1950]   10558

Roth, Magnus, 1828–1895.
Atlas för skolan. [1874]   6188
Atlas nr. I för allmänna läroverken. 28.
uppl. [1950]   7427
Geografisk atlas för allmänna läroverken. 14.
14. uppl.   6596
—— 16. uppl. [1931]   6760
Geografisk atlas för folkskolor. [1884]   3378
Tolf kartor ur Geografisk atlas. [1882]   6213

Rural Atlas Company.
Williams County, Ohio keyed farm plat book. 1965. 16465

Rushing Printing Company.
Shreveport-Bossier City atlas and street guide. 1967. 14291

Rusk County Abstract Co.
Plat book of Rusk County, Wis. 1915. 5102

Russell, J. C.
General atlas. [183–] 6063

Russell, John, b. 1745.
American atlas. 1795. 1363

Russell, Robert E. Lee.
Battle of Spottsylvania Courthouse, May 8–21, 1864. [1933] 10659
Battle of the Wilderness, May 5, 6, and 7, 1864. [1935] 10660
Fifteen pen and ink maps of the Battle of Chancellorsville. 1931. 10661
Fifteen pen and ink maps of the Battle of the Wilderness. 1931 10662
North Anna and movement from Spottsylvania, May 21–26, 1864. [1931–33] 10663
—— [1933–35] 10664
Retreat from Petersburg, April 2–9, 1865. 1934. 10665
Second Manassas campaign, Aug. 17–Sept. 1, 1862. 1943. 10667
—— (Aug. 28–Sept. 1, 1862) 1943. 10666
Thirty pen and ink maps of the Maryland campaign, 1862. 1932. 10668

Russia. *Departament Sel' Skogo Khoziaistva.*
Хоаяйственно-статистическік атлас. [Atlas économique et statistique de la Russie.] 1857. 3112

Russia. *Gidrograficheskii Departament.*
Атласъ устьн рѣки Амура. [Atlas of the mouth of the Amoor River.] 1864. 3227
Атласъ рѣки Невы. [Atlas of the River Neva.] 1863. 5283

Russia. *Glavnoe Gidrograficheskoe Upravlenie.*
Атласъ рѣки Енисея. [Atlas of the Yenisei River.] 1900. 3228

Russia. *Glavnoe Upravlenie Zemleustroistva i Zemledieliia. Pereselencheskoe Upravlenie.*
Азіатская Россія ... [Asiatic Russia.] 1914. 5306

Russia. *Gornvi Departament.*
Россійской атлась. [Atlas of Russia.] 1792. 3110

Russia. *Kommissiĩa Dlĩa Razbora Drevnikh Aktov. Kief.*
Карты Россіи. [Facsimile maps of Russia.] 1899–1906. 3107

Russia. *Kommissiĩa po Opisaniĩu Russko-Iaponskoĩ Voĩny 1904 i 1905 Godov.*
Русско-японская война 1904–1905 г. г. [Russo-Japanese War 1904–1905] 1910. 9237

Russia. *Komissiĩa po Ustroĩstyu Kommercheskikh Portov.*
Атласъ русскихъ коммерческихъ портовъ. [Atlas des ports de commerce de la Russie] 1892–93. 9266

Russia. *Mezhevoi Korpus Voennago Viedomstva.*
Атласъ Тверской губерніи. [Topographical survey atlas of the Tver Province.] 1853. 3126

Russia. *Ministerstvo Morskoe.*
Атласъ Чернаго моря. [Atlas of the Black Sea.] 1841. 3118
Атласъ Каспійскаго моря. [Atlas of the Caspian Sea.] 1826. 3181
Атласа Бѣлаго моря и Норвежскаго берега. [Atlas of the White Sea and Norwegian coast] 1839–52 9299

Russia. *Ministerstvo Vnutrennikh Del.*
Атласъ народонаселенія Западно-русскаго края по исповданіямъ. [Atlas of the peoples of the West Russian region by religions] 1864. 9278

Russia. *Otdiel Statistiki i Kartografii Ministerstva Putei Soobscheniia.*
Статистическій атласъ путей сообщенія Русскй. [Statistical atlas of the commerce and traffic of Russia.] 1902. 3101

Russia (1923– U.S.S.R.) Armiia. General'nyi shtab. Voenno-topograficheskoe unravlenie.
Атлас командира РККА. [Red army commanding officer's atlas.] 1938. 6963

Russia (1923– U.S.S.R.) Glavnoe Energeticheskoe Upravlenie
Атлас энергетических ресурсов СССР. [Atlas of the power resources of the USSR. 1934] 9218

Russia (1923– U.S.S.R.) Glavnoe Geodezicheskoe Upravlenie
Атлас промышленности С.С.С.Р. [Atlas of the industries of the USSR] 1929–31. 9219

Russia (1923– U.S.S.R.) Glavnoe Upravlenie Geodezii i Kartografii.
Атлас истории СССР. [Historical atlas of USSR] 1948. 9223
—— 1949–52. 9224
—— 1950. 9225
—— 1951. 9226
—— 1953. 9227
—— 1954. 9228
—— 1955. 9229
Атлас мира. [Atlas of the world.] 1954. 7608a

St. Louis. *City Plan Commission.*
Height, area and use districts and restrictions.
[1918]   15278

St. Louis Atlas Publishing Company.
Illustrated atlas map of Cooper County, Mo.
1877.   15225

St. Louis Plat and Record Co.
Atlas of St. Louis County [Mo.]   1909.   3822
Atlas of the city of St. Louis.   1905.   2106

St. Petersburg. *Gornoe Uchilishche.*
See Leningrad. *Gornvi Institut.*

**Šalamon, Bedřich, 1880–   *and* Kuchař, Karel,
1906–**
Školní zeměpisný atlas. 1. vyd. 1950.   7428
—— [2. vyd.] 1952   7535
Soubor map; ze školního zeměpisného atlasu
Brunclíkova – Machátova. [1948]   7325

Sale, Randall D., *and* **Karn, Edwin D.**
American expansion; a book of maps. 1962. 10637

Salem, *Oreg. Office of the City Engineer.*
Map of city of Salem, Oreg., and vicinity.
[1953]   16746

Salinas Bellver, Salvador, 1868–
Atlas de geografía universal. 21. ed. 1946. 7251
—— 22. ed. 1947.   7283
—— 27. ed. 1951.   7484
—— 29. ed. 1954.   7610

Sallee, J. S.
See Lysons, Fred H., *and* Sallee, J. S.

Salter, Herbert Edward, 1863–1951.
Map of mediaeval Oxford. 1934.   8197

Salvador. *Dirección General de Estadística y
Censos.*
Atlas censal de El Salvador. [1955]   18152
Croquis de areas urbanas municipales de la
República de El Salvador. 1960.   18151

Salvat y Ca.
Atlas geográfico Salvat. 2. ed. 1928.   6688

**Sammlung Deutscher, italienischer und magyarischer
Karten (1857–1930) 1940.**   9204

Samorządowy Instytut Wydawniczy, *Warsaw.*
Polski atlas turystyki samochodowej. 1938. 9156

Sampaio, Theodoro Fernandes, 1855–
Atlas dos Estados Unidos do Brazil. 1911.   5141
Exploração dos rios Itapetininga e Parana-
panema. 1889.   2747

Sampedro V., Francisco.
Atlas geográfico escolar del Ecuador
"SAM". 1963–64.   18365

Atlas histórico-geográfico del Ecuador.
1960.   18363

San Fernando Valley Board of Realtors.
San Fernando Valley realtor [district maps.
1957]   11621

San Francisco, *Board of Election Commissioners.*
Election precincts: 19th–[26th] assembly
district[s]. City and County of San
Francisco. 1947.   11593

San Francisco, *Ordinances,* etc.
City and county of San Francisco. [1935]   11590

San Jose, *Calif.*
Topographic survey of Evergreen area for city
of San Jose [Calif.] 1962.   11603

Sanborn, D. A.
Insurance map of Boston. 1867.   14416

Sanborn, Paul H.
Plat of Iron County, Wis. 1904.   17771

Sanborn Map Company.
Akron ... Ohio. 1892.   16470
Andrews ... Tex. 1954.   17192
Atlanta, Ga. 1886.   11953
—— 1892.   11954
Atlantic City, N.J. 1886.   15726
Atlas of Arlington, Mass. 1923.   14411
Atlas of Newport, Jamestown, Middletown
& Portsmouth, R.I. 1921.   16958
Atlas of Summit, N.J. 1922.   15797
Atlas of the city of Cincinnati, Ohio. 1922. 16488
Atlas of the city of Hartford ... Conn.
1917.   11723
—— 1920–21.   11724
Atlas of the Oranges, including Maplewood,
N.J. 1924.   15777
Atlas of West Hartford, Conn. 1923.   11749
Augusta ... Ga. 1890.   11966
—— 1904.   11967
Boston, Mass. 1885–88.   14422
Bridgeport, Conn. 1889.   11709
Brockton ... Mass. 1893.   14442
Butte City, Mont. 1891.   15324
Camden ... N.J. 1891.   15735
Charleston, S.C. 1888.   16997
Chattanooga ... Tenn. 1889.   17089
Chelsea, Mass. 1894.   14457
Chicago. 1894–97.   12598
Chicago packing houses, Union Stock
Yards. 1901.   12603
Covington, Ky. 1886.   14244
—— 1894.   14245
Dallas, Tex. 1888.   17208
—— 1892.   17209
Denver, Colo. 1887.   11676
Des Moines, Iowa. 1891.   14120
Duluth, Minn. 1888.   15141
Elizabeth & Elizabethport, N.J. 1889.   15746
Erie, Pa. 1888.   16829

Evanston, Ill. 1899.	12683
Fall River ... Mass. 1893.	14463
Ft. Wayne ... Ind. 1890.	12958
Fresno, Calif. 1888.	11519
Galveston, Tex. 1889.	17240
Grand Rapids, Mich. 1888.	14871
Harrisburg, Pa. 1890.	16834
Hartford, Conn. 1885.	11719
Harvard University, including miscellaneous property. 1940.	14455
Helena, Mont. 1892.	15331
Hialeah ... Fla. 1958.	11878
Insurance maps of Abilene, Tex. 1929.	17188
—— 1954.	17189
Insurance maps of Akron, Ohio. 1904.	16471
—— 1916.	16472
—— 1930–[41]	16474
Insurance maps of Alameda, Calif. 1897.	11505
—— 1897–1949.	11506
Insurance maps of Albany, N.Y. 1892.	15927
—— 1908–1909.	15928
—— 1934–35.	15929
Insurance maps of Albuquerque, N.Mex. 1942.	15817
—— 1957–58.	15819
Insurance maps of Alexandria ... La. 1928.	14276
—— 1954.	14277
Insurance maps of Alexandria. Va. 1941.	17363
Insurance maps of Alhambra, Calif. 1925–31.	11507
Insurance maps of Allegheny, Pa. 1893.	16807
—— 1906.	16808
Insurance maps of Allentown ... Pa. 1897.	16809
—— 1911.	16810
—— 1932.	16811
—— 1958.	16812
Insurance maps of Alton, Ill. 1926.	12582
Insurance maps of Altoona, Pa. 1894.	16813
—— 1909.	16814
—— 1932–33.	16815
Insurance maps of Amarillo, Tex. 1921.	17190
—— 1955.	17191
Insurance maps of Amsterdam ... N.Y. 1926.	15931
Insurance maps of Anaconda ... Mont. 1903.	15321
Insurance maps of Anderson, Ind. 1900.	12951
—— 1954.	12952
Insurance maps of Anniston, Ala. 1925.	11207
Insurance maps of Appleton ... Wis. 1924.	17995
Insurance maps of Arlington, Mass. 1927.	14412
Insurance maps of Arlington County, Va. 1936.	17344
Insurance maps of Asheville ... N.C. 1925.	16222
—— 1957.	16223
Insurance maps of Astoria ... Oreg. 1908.	16728
—— 1956.	16729
Insurance maps of Atlanta, Ga. 1899.	11955
—— 1911–25.	11956
—— 1931–32.	11958
Insurance maps of Atlantic City, N.J. 1896–97.	15727
—— 1906–1907.	15728

—— 1921.	15729
—— 1952–53.	15732
Insurance maps of Auburn and Lewiston, Maine. 1922.	14315
Insurance maps of Auburn, Maine. 1957.	14316
Insurance maps of Auburn, N.Y. 1904.	15932
—— 1956.	15933
Insurance maps of Augusta, Ga. 1923.	11968
—— 1954.	11969
Insurance maps of Aurora, Ill. 1907.	12583
—— 1958.	12584
Insurance maps of Austin, Tex. 1900.	17193
—— 1935.	17194
Insurance maps of Baker, Oreg. 1923.	16730
—— 1959.	16731
Insurance maps of Bakersfield, Calif. 1912.	11508
Insurance maps of Baltimore, Md. 1890.	14377
—— 1901–1902.	14379
—— 1914–15.	14380
—— 1928–36.	14382
—— 1952–54.	14385
Insurance maps of Bangor, Maine. 1955.	14318
Insurance maps of Baton Rouge, La. 1923.	14278
—— 1923–[47]	14279
Insurance maps of Battle Creek, Mich. 1919–20.	14842
Insurance maps of Bay City, Mich. 1912.	14846
Insurance maps of Beaumont, Tex. 1911.	17196
—— 1929–41.	17197
—— 1955.	17198
Insurance maps of Beaver Falls ... Pa. 1931.	16817
Insurance maps of Belleville, Ill. 1917.	12585
Insurance maps of Belleville, N.J. 1938.	15733
Insurance maps of Bellingham ... Wash. 1904.	17548
—— 1913.	17549
Insurance maps of Berkeley ... Calif. 1911.	11509
—— 1929.	11511
Insurance maps of Bethlehem, Pa. 1904.	16818
—— 1953.	16820
Insurance maps of Beverly ... Mass. 1907.	14413
—— 1958.	14414
Insurance maps of Billings, Mont. 1923.	15322
—— 1958.	15323
Insurance maps of Biloxi ... Miss. 1952.	15198
Insurance maps of Binghamton ... N.Y. 1898.	15934
—— 1918.	15935
—— 1952.	15936
Insurance maps of Birmingham, Ala. 1891.	11210
—— 1902.	11211
—— 1911.	11212
—— 1928–30.	11213
Insurance maps of Bloomfield, N.J. 1938.	15734
Insurance maps of Bloomington, Ill. 1907.	12587
—— 1953.	12588
Insurance maps of Boise, Idaho. 1912.	12061
—— 1957.	12063
Insurance maps of Boston, Mass. 1895–1900.	14427
—— 1908–38.	14430
Insurance maps of Braddock ... Pa. 1926.	16822
Insurance maps of Bridgeport, Conn. 1898.	11710
—— 1913.	11711
—— 1939.	11713

—— 1955–56.	16532
Insurance maps of Daytona ... Fla. 1924.	11865
Insurance maps of Daytona Beach, Fla. 1955.	11866
Insurance maps of Dearborn, Mich. 1930.	14848
Insurance maps of Decatur, Ala. 1927–52.	11216
—— 1927–53.	11217
Insurance maps of Decatur, Ill. 1915–16.	12673
—— 1915–[46]	12674
Insurance maps of Delaware County ... Pa. 1919–25.	16781
Insurance maps of Denver, Colo. 1890–93.	11677
—— 1903–1904.	11678
—— 1929–30.	11679
Insurance maps of Des Moines, Iowa. 1901.	14121
—— 1920.	14122
—— 1957.	14125
Insurance maps of Des Plaines, Ill. 1956.	12675
Insurance maps of Detroit, Mich. 1884–89.	14849
—— 1897.	14850
—— 1910–50.	14851
Insurance maps of Dubuque ... Iowa. 1891.	14126
—— 1909.	14127
Insurance maps of Duluth, Minn. 1909.	15143
—— 1955.	15145
Insurance maps of Durham, N.C. 1913.	16230
—— 1937.	16231
Insurance maps of East Chicago, Ind. 1930.	12953
Insurance maps of East Orange, N.J. 1911.	15741
—— 1958.	15742
Insurance maps of East Peoria, Ill. 1957.	12676
Insurance maps of East Providence, R.I. 1956.	16955
Insurance maps of East St. Louis, Ill. 1905.	12680
—— 1955.	12681
Insurance maps of Easton ... Pa. 1927.	16826
—— 1958.	16828
Insurance maps of Eau Claire, Wis. 1897–98.	17996
—— 1931.	17997
Insurance maps of El Dorado, Ark. 1929–53.	11304
Insurance maps of El Paso, Tex. 1908.	17229
—— 1927–49.	17230
—— 1954.	17232
Insurance maps of Elgin, Ill. 1913.	12682
Insurance maps of Elizabeth ... N.J. 1903.	15747
—— 1922–23.	15748
—— 1951.	15750
—— 1958.	15751
Insurance maps of Elizabeth City County ... Va. 1926.	17348
Insurance maps of Elkhart, Ind. 1927.	12954
Insurance maps of Elmira ... N.Y. 1903.	15961
—— 1931.	15962
Insurance maps of Erie ... Pa. 1900.	16830
—— 1921.	16831
—— 1951.	16833
Insurance maps of Essex County, N.J. 1906–1907.	15693
—— 1934.	15699
Insurance maps of Eugene, Oreg. 1925.	16732
Insurance maps of Eureka, Calif. 1920.	11517
—— 1957.	11518

Insurance maps of Evanston, Ill. 1920.	12684
—— 1946.	12685
Insurance maps of Evansville, Ind. 1884.	12955
—— 1895.	12956
—— 1910.	12957
Insurance maps of Everett ... Mass. 1910.	14461
—— 1955.	14462
Insurance maps of Everett, Wash, 1902.	17553
—— 1914.	17554
—— 1957.	17557
Insurance maps of Fall River ... Mass. 1905.	14464
—— 1933.	14465
Insurance maps of Fargo, N.Dak. 1929.	16350
—— 1958.	16351
Insurance maps of Fitchburg, Mass. 1902.	14467
—— 1936.	14468
Insurance maps of Flint, Mich. 1914.	14865
—— 1928.	14866
Insurance maps of Florence ... S.C. 1952.	17005
Insurance maps of Fond du Lac ... Wis. 1927.	17998
Insurance maps of Fort Myers, Fla. 1956.	11873
Insurance maps of Ft. Smith, Ark. 1908.	11306
Insurance maps of Fort Wayne ... Ind. 1902.	12959
—— 1918–19.	12960
Insurance maps of Fort Worth, Tex. 1898.	17233
—— 1910–11.	17234
—— 1926–27.	17236
Insurance maps of Fresno, Calif. 1898.	11520
—— 1906.	11521
—— 1918–19.	11522
—— 1918–48.	11523
Insurance maps of Gadsden, Ala. 1943–44.	11218
Insurance maps of Galesburg ... Ill. 1934.	12686
Insurance maps of Galveston, Tex. 1899.	17241
—— 1912.	17242
—— 1912–48.	17243
Insurance maps of Garfield, N.J. 1917.	15752
Insurance maps of Gary, Ind. 1915.	12967
—— 1945–46.	12971
Insurance maps of Glendale, Calif. 1925.	11524
Insurance maps of Glens Falls, N.Y. 1911.	15964
Insurance maps of Gloucester, Mass. 1917.	14469
Insurance maps of Grand Rapids, Mich. 1895.	14872
—— 1912–31.	14873
—— 1953.	14875
Insurance maps of Granite City, Ill. 1907.	12688
Insurance maps of Grays Harbor District, Wash, 1928.	17589
Insurance maps of Great Falls, Mont. 1900.	15328
—— 1929.	15329
—— 1957.	15330
Insurance maps of Green Bay ... Wis. 1907.	17999
—— 1936–37.	18000
Insurance maps of Greensboro ... N.C. 1925.	16232
Insurance maps of Greenville, S.C. 1920–28.	17006
Insurance maps of Greenville, Tex. 1923.	17244
Insurance maps of Greenwich, Conn. 1920.	11718
Insurance maps of Greggton ... Tex. 1955.	17245

Insurance maps of Hackensack. N.J.   1926.   15755
Insurance maps of Hagerstown ... Md.
1926.   14389
Insurance maps of Hamilton, Ohio.   1899.   16541
—— 1927.   16542
Insurance maps of Hammond, Ind.   1898.   12972
—— 1915.   12973
—— 1930.   12975
Insurance maps of Hampton ... Va.   1926.   17371
—— 1956.   17372
Insurance maps of Harrisburg, Pa.   1905.   16835
—— 1929.   16836
—— 1956.   16837
Insurance maps of Harrison, East Newark
and Kearny ... N.J.   1907.   15757
Insurance maps of Hartford, Conn.   1900.   11721
—— 1922–23.   11725
Insurance maps of Haverhill ... Mass.   1893.   14470
—— 1907.   14471
—— 1954.   14472
Insurance maps of Hazleton ... Pa.   1909.   16838
—— 1909–[46]   16839
—— 1955.   16840
Insurance maps of Helena ... Mont.   1930.   15332
—— 1958.   15333
Insurance maps of High Point ... N.C.   1924.   16235
—— 1956.   16236
Insurance maps of Holyoke ... Mass.   1895.   14473
—— 1915.   14474
—— 1956.   14475
Insurance maps of Homestead, Pa.   1926.   16841
Insurance maps of Honolulu.   1914.   11988
—— 1927.   11989
—— 1951.   11991
—— 1953–56.   11992
Insurance maps of Hot Springs, Ark.   1925.   11307
Insurance maps of Houston ... Tex.   1896–
97.   17246
—— 1907.   17247
—— 1924–50.   17249
Insurance maps of Hudson County, N.J.
1891–1900.   15708
—— 1906–12.   15709
—— 1936–38.   15712
Insurance maps of Huntington ... W.Va.
1909.   17621
—— 1931.   17622
—— 1954.   17623
Insurance maps of Hutchinson, Kans.   1942.   14210
Insurance maps of Indianapolis, Ind.   1887.   12976
—— 1898.   12977
—— 1914–15.   12978
—— 1956.   12982
Insurance maps of Inwood ... N.Y.   1909.   15965
—— 1940.   15966
Insurance maps of Jackson, Mich.   1907.   14881
—— 1930.   14882
Insurance maps of Jackson ... Miss.   1925.   15199
—— 1925–48.   15200
Insurance maps of Jacksonville, Fla.   1897.   11880
—— 1903.   11881
—— 1913.   11882
—— 1924–49.   11883

Insurance maps of Jamestown, N.Y.   1902.   15968
—— 1930.   15969
Insurance maps of Jeffersonville ... Ind.
1953.   12985
Insurance maps of Johnstown, Pa.   1894.   16842
—— 1913.   16843
—— 1954.   16844
Insurance maps of Joliet, Ill.   1898.   12689
—— 1924.   12690
Insurance maps of Joplin Mo.   1906.   15251
—— 1954.   15252
Insurance maps of Kalamazoo, Mich.   1908.   14883
—— 1932.   14884
—— 1958.   14886
Insurance maps of Kankakee ... Ill.   1954.   12691
Insurance maps of Kansas City, Kans.   1889.   14211
—— 1907–1908.   14213
—— 1931–32.   14214
Insurance maps of Kansas City, Mo.   1895–
96.   15254
—— 1909–17.   15255
—— 1930–40.   15257
Insurance maps of Kenosha, Wis.   1918.   18001
Insurance maps of Kewanee, Ill.   1928.   12692
Insurance maps of Kingston, N.Y.   1899.   15971
—— 1957.   15972
Insurance maps of Klamath Falls ... Oreg.
1931.   16733
Insurance maps of Knoxville, Tenn.   1903.   17097
—— 1917–24.   17098
Insurance maps of La Crosse, Wis.   1906.   18003
—— 1954.   18004
Insurance maps of La Fayette, Ind.   1915.   12986
Insurance maps of Lancaster, Pa.   1897.   16846
—— 1912.   16847
Insurance maps of Lansing, Mich.   1913–26.   14888
—— 1953.   14889
Insurance maps of Larchmont ... N.Y.
1919.   15973
Insurance maps of Lawrence and Methuen,
Mass.   1895.   14477
Insurance maps of Lawrence, Mass.   1911.   14478
—— 1911–50.   14479
—— 1957.   14481
Insurance maps of Leadville, Colo.   1895.   11684
Insurance maps of Levittown ... N.Y.   1953.   15974
Insurance maps of Lewiston, Maine.   1957.   14319
Insurance maps of Lexington ... Ky.   1907.   14248
—— 1934.   14249
—— 1958.   14250
Insurance maps of Lima, Ohio.   1911.   16543
—— 1957.   16544
Insurance maps of Lincoln ... Nebr.   1891.   15637
—— 1903.   15638
—— 1928.   15639
Insurance maps of Little Rock ... Ark.   1897.   11310
—— 1913.   11311
—— 1939.   11313
Insurance maps of Long Beach, Calif.   1914–
50.   11526
Insurance maps of Long Beach ... N.Y.
1922.   15975
—— 1955.   15976

Insurance maps of New Rochelle ... N.Y. 1911.	15983
—— 1931.	15984
Insurance maps of Newark, N.J. 1892.	15767
—— 1908–1909.	15768
—— 1926–31.	15770
Insurance maps [of] Newark, Ohio. 1920–21.	16551
Insurance maps of Newburgh, N.Y. 1913.	16137
—— 1957.	16138
Insurance maps of Newport, Ky. 1910.	14258
—— 1953.	14259
Insurance maps of Newport, R.I. 1903.	16956
—— 1953.	16959
Insurance maps of Newport News ... Va. 1926.	17375
—— 1955.	17376
Insurance maps of Newton, Mass. 1910.	14506
—— 1931.	14508
—— 1961.	14509
Insurance maps of Niagara Falls, N.Y. 1897.	16139
—— 1914–15.	16140
—— 1955.	16141
Insurance maps of Norfolk, Va. 1898.	17378
—— 1910–21.	17379
—— 1928.	17380
Insurance maps of Norristown, Pa. 1942.	16853
Insurance maps of North Plainfield, N.J. 1956.	15772
Insurance maps of North Providence ... R.I. 1956.	16960
Insurance maps of Norwalk, Conn. 1922.	11741
—— 1958.	11742
Insurance maps of Norwich, Gonn. 1926.	11743
Insurance maps of Nutley-Glen Ridge, N.J. 1938.	15773
Insurance maps of Oak Park ... Ill. 1908.	12697
—— 1908–48.	12698
Insurance maps of Oakland, Calif. 1889.	11557
—— 1902–1903.	11558
—— 1911–12.	11559
—— 1925–29.	11561
—— 1952–53.	11564
Insurance maps of Ogden, Utah. 1906.	17301
—— 1949–50.	17302
Insurance maps of Oil City, Pa. 1913.	16854
Insurance maps of Oklahoma City, Okla. 1906.	16624
—— 1922.	16625
—— 1932–49.	16626
—— 1955.	16629
Insurance maps of Omaha, Nebr. 1890.	15642
—— 1901–19.	15643
—— 1934–35.	15644
Insurance maps of Orange and West Orange, N.J. 1912.	15776
—— 1939.	15778
Insurance maps of Orlando, Fla. 1925.	11912
—— 1956.	11913
Insurance maps of Oshkosh, Wis. 1903.	18016
—— 1957.	18017
Insurance maps of Oswego, N.Y. 1924.	16143

Insurance maps of Owensboro, Ky. 1910.	14260
—— 1957.	14261
Insurance maps of Paducah, Ky. 1906.	14262
Insurance maps of Palm Beach and West Palm Beach, Fla. 1924.	11917
—— 1953.	11918
Insurance maps of Parkersburg, W.Va. 1926.	17624
Insurance maps of Pasadena ... Calif. 1903.	11565
—— 1910.	11566
—— 1930–31.	11567
Insurance maps of Passaic ... N.J. 1910.	15780
—— 1935.	15781
Insurance maps of Paterson, N.J. 1887.	15783
—— 1899.	15784
—— 1915.	15785
—— 1951.	15787
Insurance maps of Pawtucket ... R.I. 1902.	16962
—— 1923–24.	16963
Insurance maps of Pawtuxet Valley and Warwick, R.I. 1922.	16973
—— 1922–46.	16974
Insurance maps of Peekskill ... N.Y. 1923.	16144
—— 1958.	16145
Insurance maps of Pensacola, Fla. 1907.	11919
Insurance maps of Peoria, Ill. 1891.	12699
—— 1902.	12700
—— 1927–28.	12702
—— 1957.	12704
Insurance maps of Perth Amboy, N.J. 1914.	15788
—— 1955.	15789
Insurance maps of Petersburg, Va. 1915.	17384
—— 1957.	17385
Insurance maps of Philadelphia, Pa. 1916–29.	16869
Insurance maps of Phoenix, Ariz. 1915.	11265
—— 1915–47.	11268
—— 1958.	11270
Insurance maps of Pine Bluff, Ark. 1920.	11317
Insurance maps of Pittsburg [sic] Pa. 1893.	16902
—— 1905–1906.	16904
Insurance maps of Pittsburgh, Pa. 1924–27.	16907
Insurance maps of Pittsfield ... Mass. 1905.	14510
—— 1905–[38]	14511
—— 1956.	14512
Insurance maps of Pittston, Pa. 1910.	16915
—— 1957.	16916
Insurance maps of Plainfield, N.J. 1956.	15793
Insurance maps of Pontiac ... Mich. 1924.	14895
Insurance maps of Port Arthur, Tex. 1930.	17273
—— 1956.	17274
Insurance maps of Port Chester ... N.Y. 1934.	16147
Insurance maps of Port Huron, Mich. 1911.	14900
Insurance maps of Portland, Maine. 1896.	14321
—— 1909.	14322
—— 1954.	14324
Insurance maps of Portland, Oreg. 1889.	16736
—— 1901.	16737
—— 1908–1909.	16739
—— 1924–28.	16740
Insurance maps of Portsmouth, N.H. 1920.	15666
—— 1957.	15667

—— 1925.	16926	
—— 1956.	16928	
Insurance maps of Scranton suburban towns, Pa. 1956.	16929	
Insurance maps of Seattle, Wash. 1904–1905.	17563	
—— 1916–50.	17564	
Insurance maps of Sharon ... Pa. 1926.	16930	
—— 1958.	16931	
Insurance maps of Shawnee, Okla. 1928.	16631	
Insurance maps of Sheboygan ... Wis. 1903.	18023	
—— 1955.	18024	
Insurance maps of Shreveport ... La. 1909.	14289	
—— 1935–36.	14290	
Insurance maps of Sioux City, Iowa. 1902.	14131	
—— 1924.	14133	
Insurance maps of Sioux Falls, S.Dak. 1924.	17065	
Insurance maps of Somerville, Mass. 1900.	14521	
—— 1933–34.	14522	
Insurance maps of South Bend, Ind. 1899.	12996	
—— 1917.	12997	
Insurance maps of South Bethlehem, Pa. 1912.	16819	
Insurance maps of South Orange Village ... N.J. 1912.	15796	
Insurance maps of South Portland, Maine. 1954.	14325	
Insurance maps of South Richmond ... Va. 1952.	17396	
Insurance maps of Spartanburg, S.C. 1923.	17007	
—— 1953.	17008	
Insurance maps of Spokane, Wash. 1891.	17573	
—— 1902.	17574	
—— 1910.	17575	
—— 1953.	17576	
Insurance maps of Springfield, Ill. 1896.	12716	
—— 1917.	12717	
—— 1953.	12718	
Insurance maps of Springfield, Mass. 1896.	14525	
—— 1911.	14528	
—— 1931–32.	14529	
Insurance maps of Springfield, Mo. 1910.	15300	
—— 1933.	15301	
—— 1957.	15302	
Insurance maps of Springfield, Ohio. 1910.	16560	
—— 1928.	16561	
—— 1955.	16562	
Insurance maps of Stamford, Conn. 1929–30.	11744	
Insurance maps of Stockton, Calif. 1895.	11614	
—— 1917.	11615	
Insurance maps of Suffolk ... Va. 1926.	17401	
Insurance maps of Superior, Wis. 1914.	18027	
—— 1956.	18028	
Insurance maps of Syracuse, N.Y. 1892.	16168	
—— 1910–28.	16169	
—— 1953–54.	16174	
Insurance maps of Tacoma, Wash. 1896.	17578	
—— 1912.	17579	
Insurance maps of Tampa ... Fla. 1903.	11928	
—— 1915–22.	11929	
—— 1931.	11930	
Insurance maps of Taunton, Mass. 1898.	14533	
—— 1937.	14534	

Insurance maps of Terre Haute ... Ind. 1896.	12999	
—— 1911.	13000	
—— 1955–[56]	13001	
Insurance maps of Texarkana, Ark. 1953.	11318	
Insurance maps of Texarkana, Tex. and Ark. 1924.	17281	
—— 1953.	17282	
Insurance maps of the borough of Brooklyn ... N.Y. 1904–1908.	15942	
—— 1915–33.	15945	
—— 1935–51.	15946	
Insurance maps of the borough of Queens, city of New York. 1898–1903.	16118	
—— 1911–17.	16119	
—— 1925–43.	16121	
—— 1948–49.	16127	
Insurance maps of the borough of Richmond, city of New York. 1898.	16132	
—— 1910.	16133	
—— 1917.	16134	
—— 1937–38.	16135	
Insurance maps of the city of Bangor, Maine. 1914.	14317	
Insurance maps of the city of New Brunswick, N.J. 1912.	15765	
Insurance maps of the city of New York. 1890–1901.	15992	
—— 1902–19.	15997	
—— 1912–47.	16001	
Insurance maps of the city of Plainfield ... N.J. 1910.	15792	
Insurance maps of the New Jersey coast. 1890.	15668	
—— 1905–1909.	15669	
—— 1930.	15670	
Insurance maps of the Oranges, including Irvington and Milburn, N.J. 1895.	15775	
Insurance maps of the Palisades of lower Bergen County, N.J. 1911.	15681	
—— 1930.	15682a	
Insurance maps of the town of Pelham ... N.Y. 1932–33.	16146	
Insurance maps of Toledo, Ohio. 1888.	16563	
—— 1904–21.	16566	
—— 1931–44.	16568	
Insurance maps of Tonawanda, N.Y. 1893.	16175	
—— 1910.	16176	
Insurance maps of Topeka, Kans. 1896.	14218	
—— 1913.	14219	
—— 1954–55.	14220	
Insurance maps of town of Greenburgh, N.Y. 1924.	15925	
Insurance maps of Trenton ... N.J. 1890.	15798	
—— 1908.	15799	
—— 1927.	15800	
—— 1955.	15803	
Insurance maps of Troy ... N.Y. 1903–1904.	16178	
—— 1955.	16179	
Insurance maps of Tucson, Ariz. 1919.	11274	
—— 1919–48.	11275	
Insurance maps of Tulsa, Okla. 1915.	16632	
—— 1923–39.	16634	

Insurance maps of Tuscaloosa, Ala. 1923.	11227	Insurance maps of Winona, Minn. 1894.	15168
Insurance maps of Tyler, Tex. 1938.	17283	—— 1917.	15169
Insurance maps of Union Township, N.J. 1951.	15804	Insurance maps of Winston-Salem, N.C. 1917–28.	16243
—— 1958.	15805	—— 1958.	16245
Insurance maps of Utica, N.Y. 1888–89.	16180	Insurance maps of Winthrop, Mass. 1954.	14539
—— 1899.	16181	Insurance maps of Woonsocket, R.I. 1911.	16977
—— 1925.	16182	—— 1955.	16978
—— 1952.	16184	Insurance maps of Worcester, Mass. 1892.	14540
Insurance maps of Vancouver, Wash. 1928.	17582	—— 1910.	14541
Insurance maps of Ventnor City, N.J. 1953.	15807	—— 1936–37.	14543
Insurance maps of Waco ... Tex. 1899.	17284	Insurance maps of Yakima, Wash. 1920.	17586
—— 1926.	17285	—— 1952.	17588
—— 1952.	17286	Insurance maps of Yonkers ... N.Y. 1898.	16190
Insurance maps of Walla Walla ... Wash. 1905.	17583	—— 1917.	16191
—— 1955.	17584	—— 1957–58.	16193
Insurance maps of Waltham, Mass. 1918.	14535	Insurance maps of York, Pa. 1894.	16940
Insurance maps of Warren, Ohio. 1922.	16572	—— 1908.	16941
Insurance maps of Warwick, R.I. 1958.	16975	—— 1933.	16942
Insurance maps of Warwick, Va. 1955.	17402	Insurance maps of Youngstown, Ohio. 1896.	16573
Insurance maps of Washington, D.C. 1888.	11771	—— 1907.	16574
—— 1903–16.	11773	—— 1928.	16575
—— 1927–28.	11777	Insurance maps of Zanesville, Ohio. 1895–96.	16579
Insurance maps of Washington suburban ... Maryland. 1939–50.	11789	—— 1919.	16580
Insurance maps of Waterbury ... Conn. 1901.	11746	—— 1955.	16581
—— 1921–22.	11747	Kansas City, Kans. 1957.	14216
—— 1956.	11748	Kingston including Rondout, N.Y. 1887.	15970
Insurance maps of Waterloo, Iowa. 1918.	14135	Knoxville ... Tenn. 1890.	17096
Insurance maps of Watertown, Mass. 1928.	14537	La Crosse ... Wis. 1891.	18002
Insurance maps of Watertown, N.Y. 1909.	16185	Lowell, Mass. 1892.	14483
—— 1958.	16186	Lynn, Mass. 1887.	14490
Insurance maps of Waukegan, Ill. 1929.	12719	Map of New York City, south of Bleecker St., showing dry goods district. 1913.	16002
Insurance maps of Wausau, Wis. 1923.	18029	Minneapolis, Minn. 1885–89.	15147
—— 1954.	18030	Mobile, Ala. 1885.	11219
Insurance maps of West Orange, N.J. 1939.	15810	Mulberry ... Fla. 1955.	11911
Insurance maps of West Palm Beach, Fla. 1953.	11932	New Bedford ... Mass. 1893.	14501
Insurance maps of Wheeling, W.Va. 1890.	17625	New Orleans, La. 1885–93.	14282
—— 1902.	17626	Newburgh ... N.Y. 1890.	16136
—— 1921–22.	17627	Newport, Ky. 1886.	14257
—— 1953.	17628	Norfolk ... Va. 1887.	17377
Insurance maps of whiskey surveys, Pennsylvania, Maryland, Kentucky, Indiana, and Illinois. 1936.	10530	Ogden, Utah. 1890.	17300
		Omaha, Nebr. 1887.	15641
Insurance maps of White Plains, N.Y. 1911.	16187	Oshkosh ... Wis. 1890.	18015
—— 1930.	16188	Paramus ... N.J. 1956.	15779
Insurance maps of Wichita, Kans. 1903.	14223	Pawtucket and Central Falls, R.I. 1890.	16961
—— 1914.	14224	Pier map of New York harbor. 1922.	16013
—— 1935.	14225	—— 1928.	16031
Insurance maps of Wichita Falls, Tex. 1925.	17288	Pittsburgh, Pa. 1884.	16900
—— 1954.	17289	Portland, Maine. 1886.	14320
Insurance maps of Wilkes-Barre, Pa. 1910.	16934	Quincy, Ill. 1888.	12705
—— 1955.	16936	Racine ... Wis. 1894.	18018
Insurance maps of Williamsport and environs, Pa. 1912.	16938	Reading, Pa. 1887.	16919
—— 1958.	16939	Richmond and Manchester, Va. 1886.	17389
Insurance maps of Wilmington, Del. 1901.	11756	St. Joseph, Mo. 1888.	15262
—— 1927.	11758	St. Paul, Minn. 1885–88.	15159
Insurance maps of Wilmington, N.C. 1915.	16240	Salem ... Mass. 1890.	14518
—— 1955.	16241	Salt Lake City, Utah. 1889.	17303
Insurance maps of Wilson ... N.C. 1930.	16242	San Diego, Calif. 1888.	11578
		San Francisco, Calif. 1899–1900.	11585
		Sandusky, Ohio. 1893.	16554
		Scranton, Pa. 1888.	16923

Seattle, Wash. Ter. 1888.	17561
—— 1893.	17562
Sheboygan ... Wis. 1891.	18022
Shopping center diagrams, Houston—metro area ... Tex. 1955.	17260
Sioux City, Iowa. 1890.	14130
Springfield, Mass. 1886.	14524
Springfield, Ohio. 1894–95.	16559
Staten Island, N.Y. 1885.	16130
Sugar mill and cannery map of the Territory of Hawaii. 1919.	11985
Surveys of the distilleries and warehouses of Kentucky and Tennessee. 1910.	14228
Surveys of the whiskey warehouses of Illinois, Ohio and Indiana. 1894.	10528
Surveys of the whiskey warehouses of Kentucky and Tennessee. 1894.	14227
Surveys of the whiskey warehouses of Pennsylvania, West Virginia, Maryland, New Jersey and New York. 1894.	10529
Tacoma, Wash. Ter. 1888.	17577
Tax map, township of Upper, Cape May County, N.J. 1959.	15692
Toledo, Ohio. 1895.	16564
Troy, N.Y. 1885.	16177
Victoria, British Columbia. 1885.	10388
Warehouse map showing the detached plans of listed public storage warehouses. 1919–21.	16010
Wilkes Barre, Pa. 1891.	16933
Williamsport, Pa. 1891.	16937
Wilmington, Del. 1884.	11755
Yonkers, N.Y. 1886.	16189

Sanborn-Perris Map Company.
See Sanborn Map Company.

Sánchez, Alexandro.

Mapa general de les almas que administran los pp. Augustinos calzados en estas Islas Filipinas. 1845.	5305

Sanctis, Gabriello de.

Atlante corografico del regno delle due Sicilie. 1843.	4043

Sandby, Paul, 1725–1809.
See Pownall, Thomas.

Sanders, John L.

Maps of North Carolina congressional districts, 1789–1960. 1961.	16197

Sanderson, Peter, 1925–

Primary school atlas for Nandi and the Rift Valley Province [Kenya] 1955.	10146

Sandler, Christian, 1859–1912.

Reformation der Kartographie um 1700. Atlas. 1905.	261

Sanford, George P.
See Beers, F.W., *& others.*

See also Lake, D. J., Sanford, George P., *and* Gould, F. A.

Sanford & Everts.

Atlas of Strafford County, N.H. 1871.	2139

Sanford, Everts & Co.

Atlas and history of Androscoggin County, Me. 1873.	3761
Atlas of York Co., Me. 1872.	3766

Sanford Evans Services.

Maritimes and Newfoundland population maps. [1963]	10351

Sangamon County Abstract Co.

Plat book of Sangamon County, Ill. 1914.	4588

Sanson, Nicolas, *d'Abbeville*, 1600–1667.

Afriqve en plvsievrs cartes novvelles. 1656.	5310
—— [1667?]	10093
Amérique en plusieurs cartes. 1657.	1151
Amérique en plusieurs cartes nouvelles. 1662.	1152
—— [1667?]	1153
Asie en plusieurs cartes novvelles. 1652–[53]	4068
Atlas nouveau. 1689–[90]	503
—— 1692–96.	514, 3452
—— 1696.	524
Cartes générales de tovtes les parties dv monde. 1658.	4260
—— 1667.	5947
Cartes particulières de la France. 1676.	4017
Pays Bas Catholiqves. [1655–57]	7961

Sanson, Nicolas, *d'Abbeville*, Sanson, Guillaume, *d.* 1730, *and* Sanson, N., *fils.*

Cartes générales de la géographie. 1675.	486
Cartes générales de tovtes les parties dv monde. 1670.	3436
[Géographie universelle. 1675?]	484, 4264

Sanson, Nicolas, *d'Abbeville*, *and* Sanson, Nicolas, *fils*, 1626–1648.

Description de tout l'univers. 1700.	528
Europe [l'Asie, l'Afrique, l'Amérique] en plusieurs cartes. 1683.	494
Geographische en historische beschryvingh der vier bekende wereldsdeelen. 1683.	495

Santa Barbara County, *Calif. Assessor*.

Santa Barbara County, Calif. Assessor's maps. 1927.	11474

Santa Catharina, *Brazil (State) Departamento Estadual de Geografia e Cartografia*.

Pequeno atlas de Santa Catarina. 1955–[56]	18311
—— 1958.	18312

Santa Cruz, Alonso de, *d.* 1567.

Islario general de todas las islas del mundo. Atlas. [ca. 1560] Facsim. 1920.	5681
Karten von Amerika in dem Isolario general. 1908.	10263

Santa Rosa, Calif. Firemen's Association.
Santa Rosa [Calif.] street guide. 1965.   11613

Santarem, Manuel Francisco de Barros e Sousa, de Mesquita de Macedo Leitão e Carvalhosa, *2d visconde de*, 1791–1856.
Essai sur l'histoire de la cosmographie et de la cartographie pendant le moyen-âge. Atlas. 1849–52.   262

Santini, P.
Atlas portatif d'Italie. 1783.   3059
Atlas universel. 1776–[84]   647

São Paulo, Brazil. *Bolsa de Mercadorias*.
Mapas economicos do Estado de São Paulo. [1939?]   18314

São Paulo, Brazil. *Museu Paulista*.
Collectanea de mappas da cartographia Paulista antiga. 1922.   18313

Saratoga County, *N.Y.*
Saratoga Co., N.Y. [1944]   15902

Sardinia. *Corpo Reale dello Stato Maggiore*.
Carta topografica degli stati in terraferma di S.M. il Re di Sardegna. [1854–75]   5261

Sargent, Charles Sprague, 1841–1927.
Report on the forests of North America. Atlas. 1884.   1278
Sixteen maps accompanying report on forest trees of North America. [1884]   1187

Sargent, Winslow B.
Property map, city of Daytona Beach [Fla.] 1964.   11867

Saskatchewan-Alberta Boundary Commission.
[Collection consisting of Report ... blueprint map, and transmittal letter. 1939]   10436

Sauer, William C.
Detailed official atlas of Wayne County, Mich. [1905]   2002
General official atlas of Wayne County, Mich. [1893]   14830

Sauer Brothers.
Detailed official atlas of Wayne County, Mich. 1915.   4768

Saunders, Howard Raymond.
Atlas of Los Angeles County [Calif.] 1953.   11405
Atlas of the Los Angeles and Orange County metropolitan area. 1961.   11554
Atlas of the Los Angeles metropolitan area. 1959.   11411

Saunders, Howard Raymond, *and* Saunders Randall N.
Mapfax of Los Angeles County [Calif.] 1943.   11395

Saunders, Trelawney William, 1821–1910.
Atlas of twelve maps of India. 1889.   5300

Sauvage, Maxime Joseph Marie, 1869–
Guerre Sino-Japonaise. 1897.   3185

Savage, Robert Ferguson.
Atlas of commercial geography. 1905.   7

Savonarola, Raffaelo, 1680–1748.
Universus terrarum orbis. 1713.   3475

Sawicki, Ludomir, 1884–1929.
Atlas jezior Tatrzańskich; mapy. 1929.   9152

Saxony. *Militair Plankammer*.
Topographischer Atlas des Königreichs Sachsen. [1836–50]   8784
—— [1912] Repr.   8785

Saxony (Province) *Elbstrombauverwaltung in Magdeburg*.
Elbstrom. 1898.   7845

Saxony, Lower. *Amt für Landesplanung und Statistik*.
Wasserwirtschafts-Atlas von Niedersachsen. 1950.   8793

Saxton, Christopher, *b*. 1542?
[Atlas of England and Wales. 1579]   8107, 8108, 8109
—— 1574–79. 1936.   8110
Maps of England and Wales. 1574–79.   2913
[Shires of England and Wales. 1690]   8114

Sayer, Robert, 1725–1794.
Atlas Britannique. 1766.   4013
English atlas. 1787.   2922
[General atlas containing 41 colored maps of all countries of the world. 1757–94]   4293

Sayer, Robert, *and* Bennett, John, *d*. 1787.
American military pocket atlas. [1776]   1206, 1343
East-India pilot, or Oriental navigator. [1782]   9486

Scalé, Bernard, *fl*. 1760–1787.
Hibernian atlas. 1776.   8230
—— 1788.   8232

Scarborough Company.
Complete road atlas, Massachusetts and Rhode Island. 1905.   1799, 2562

Scarborough Motor Guide Company.
All-in-one interstate and city traffic maps. [1936]   10839
All-in-one interstate travel and city motorlogue. [1935]   10835
"All-in-one" interstate travel and city traffic maps. [1934]   10831
Green book; hotel, trailer, camp ... road guide. [1937]   10843

Scarlett & Scarlett.
Atlas of the city of Newark, N.J. 1889.   2188
Fire map of Essex County, N.J. 1891.   2156
Fire map of Mercer County, N.J. 1890.
                                          2164, 2198
Fire map of Harrison and Kearney ... N.J.
  1889.   15756
Fire map of the coast resorts of New Jersey.
  1890.   2142

Scarlett & Van Wagoner.
Fire map of Albany, N.Y. 1892.   2267

Scarzello, O.
Album di esercitazioni cartografiche. 2v.
  [1942]   5765

Schake, William, Company.
Ward directory of the city of Cleveland.
  [1894]   2426

Schall, Éditions.
Images du monde; atlas illustré. 1942.   7092

Schaper, William August, 1869–
Apportionment of representation in South
  Carolina from 1670–1860. MS. [1900?]   16981

Schapker, Bernard L.
See Applebaum, William, 1906–   *and*
  Schapker, Bernard L.

Scheda, Joseph von, 1815–1888, *and* Steinhauser,
Anton, 1802–1890.
Hand-Atlas. [1879]   6201

Schem, Alexander Jacob, 1826–1881.
See Cleveland, John Fitch, 1819–1876, *and*
  Schem, Alexander Jacob.

Schendel, H. W.
City plat maps of Sparta, Wis. 1963.   18025

Schenk, Alois, *and* Müller, Maximilian.
Österreichischer Sägewerksatlas. [1951]   7896

Schenk, Eric, 1906–
See Rosenberg, Hugo, 1895–   *and* Schenk,
  Eric.

Schenk, Pieter, 1660–1718 or 1719.
Atlas contractus. [1705?]   3465
—— [1709?]   551
Hecatompolis. 1702.   66, 3297
Schouwburg van den oorlog. 1707–[14]   3978
Theatre de Mars. 1706.   2826
See also Valck, Gerard, 1626–1720, *and*
  Schenk, Pieter.

Schenk, Pieter, *ca.* 1698–1775.
Afbeeldinge van eenhondert der voornaamste
  en sterkste steeden in Europa. 1752.   67
Atlas Saxonicus novus. 1752–[59]   3043

Flambeau de la guerre allumée au Rhin.
  1735.   4036
Neuer Sächischer atlas. 1752–[58]   3044
—— 1760.   8782

Scherer, Heinrich, 1628–1704.
Atlas Marianus. 1702.   538a, 3457
Critica quadripartita. 1710.   3471
Geographia artificialis. 1703.   3458
Geographia hierarchica. 1703.   3459
Geographia naturalis. 1703.   3460
Geographia politica. 1703.   3461
Tabellae geographicae. 1703.   3462

Scheuerlein, H.,
See Bauer, Karl, *and* Scheuerlein, H.

Schib, Karl, 1898–
See Ammann, Hektor, 1894–   *and* Schib,
  Karl.

Schiedt, Jacob E.
Atlas of the city of Philadelphia. 1892.   2537

Schier, Wilhelm Franz, 1880–
Atlas zur allgemeinen und Österreichischen
  Geschichte. 2. Aufl. [1935]   5569

Schierer, E.
Documents pour l'étude ... de Strasbourg et
  environs. [1949]   8509

Schirmer, Fritz.
Kriegsgeschichtlicher Atlas zum Studium der
  Feldzüge der neuesten Zeit. 2. Aufl. 1912.   4157

Schlee, Paul, 1868–
See Debes, Ernst, 1840–1923, *and* Schlee, Paul.

Schleis, A. M.
See Rooney, W. T., *and* Schleis, A. M.

Schleswig-Holstein *(State) Landesplanungsamt*.
Landesplanung in Schleswig-Holstein. 1949.   8801
—— 2. erweiterte Aufl. 1951.   8802

Schlieben, Wilhelm Ernst August von, 1781–1839.
Atlas von Amerika. 1830.   1178
Atlas von Europa nebst den Kolonien. 1825–
  30.   2853, 7792
[Lehrgebäude der Geographie mit histori-
  schen, statistischen und geschichtlichen
  Andeutungen. 1828–30]   3547

Schlieffen, Alfred, *Graf* von, 1833–1913.
Cannae. [1913]   7730
—— [1931]   7731

Schlüter, Otto, 1872–1959, *and* August, Oskar,
1911–
Atlas des Saale- und mittleren Elbegebietes.
  2., völlig neubearb. Aufl. [1959]   8712

Schmidt, Ludwig, 1862–1944.
See Hantzsch, Viktor, 1868–1910, *and*
Schmidt, Ludwig.

Schmidt, Max Georg, 1870–1956.
See Debes, Ernst, 1840–1923, *and* Schmidt,
Max Georg, 1870–1956.

**Schmidt, Max Georg, *and* Haack, Hermann, 1872–
1966.**
Geopolitischer Typen–Atlas. 1929.   5676

Schmidt, Rudolf.
Volksschul-Atlas. 110. Aufl. 1910.   6338
—— 181.–184. Aufl. 1931.   6761

Schmidt, Walther, 1888–   *and* Heise, Georg.
Welthandels–Atlas. [1927]   5464

Schmidt, Wilhelm, 1843–
See Schubert, F. W., *and* Schmidt, Wilhelm.

Schmitz, Leonhard, 1807–1890.
Student's atlas of classical geography. [188–]   5647
See also Bryce, James, 1806–1877, Collier,
William Francis, *and* Schmitz, Leonhard,
1807–1890.
—— Collier, William Francis, *and* Schmitz,
Leonhard.

Schmoll, H. Dieter.
Atlas + Führer Italien. [1957]   8979

Schneider, Adam Gottlieb, *and* Weigel, J. A. G.
[Atlas der Geographie von der bekannten
ganzen Welt. 1794–1805]   3527

Schneider, Antoine Virgile, *Baron, d.* 1847.
Nouvel atlas pour servir a l'Histoire des Iles
Ioniennes. 1823.   8903

Schneider, Arthur, 1876–
Das alte Rom. 1896.   3069

Schneider, Oskar, 1841–1903.
Typen-Atlas. 2. Aufl. 1881.   5477b
Typen-Atlas. Naturwissenschaftlich-geo-
graphischer Bilder-Atlas. [1909]   3379

Schneider, Ronald M.
Atlas of Latin American affairs. [1965]   18053
—— [1966]   18055

Schnelle, Fritz, 1900–
See Hoffmeister, Johannes, 1894–   *and*
Schnelle Fritz.

Schnitzius, Joseph E., 1868–
Maps of Andrew County, Mo. [1935]   15211

Schnitzler, Johann Heinrich, 1802–1871.
See Baquol, Jacques, 1813–1856, *and*
Schnitzler, Johann Heinrich.

Schoenbrenner, Janina.
See Missalowa, Gryzelda, *and* Schoenbrenner,
Janina.

**Schotanus à Sterringa, Bernardus, *and* Alting, Menso,
1637–1713.**
Uitbeelding der heerlijkheit Friesland zoo in't
algemeen, als in haare xxx bijzondere
grietenijen. 1718.   3088

Schou, Axel, 1902–
Politikens lommeatlas. 1954.   7611
Politikens verdensatlas. 1952.   7536

Schouw, Joakim Frederik, 1789–1852.
Pflanzengeographischer Atlas. 1823.   5382

Schrader, Erich.
Landschaften Niedersachsens. 1954.   8797
—— [2. Aufl.] 1957.   8799

**Schrader, Franz, *i.e.*, Jean Daniel François, 1844–
1924.**
Atlas de géographie historique. 1896.   144
—— 1907.   145
—— 1911.   5570
Atlas de poche. [1912?]   4390
See *also* Vivien de Saint-Martin, Louis, 1802–
1897, *and* Schrader, Franz.

**Schrader, Franz, *and* Gallouedec, Louis,
1864–1937.**
Atlas clásico de geografía moderna. 1908.   4207
Atlas classique de géographie ancienne et
moderne. 4. éd. 1914.   4208
—— 5. éd. 1918.   6388
—— 1922.   6505
—— [1926]   6634
—— [1929]   5571
—— [1938]   6964
—— [1948]   7326
Atlas classique de la France. [1946]   8477
France; atlas. 1918.   8469

**Schrader, Franz, Prudent, Ferdinand Pierre Vincent,
1835–1915, *and* Anthoine, Édouard, 1847–1919.**
Atlas de géographie moderne. 1889.   6250
—— 1890.   6255
—— 1891.   968
—— 1898.   1028
—— 1899.   6282
—— 1904.   6316
—— 1907.   1126a
—— 1913.   4400
—— 1914.   6371

Schräembl, Franz Anton, 1751–1803.
Allgemeiner grosser Atlass. [1786]–1800.   694

Schreiber, Johann Georg, 1676–1745.
Atlas selectus. [1749?]   609, 610, 611
—— [1800?]   6017

Schreuder, J.
Repetitie-atlas van Nederland en Oost- en West-Indië. [8e geheel herziene druk. 1947]   9051

Schropp, Simon.
Operationen zur Wiedergewinnung der alten Reichsstadt Metz. 1872.   8411

Schubert, F. W., _and_ Schmidt, Wilhelm, 1843–
Historisch-geographischer Schul-Atlas. [1909]   3319

Schuchert, Charles, 1858–1942.
Atlas of paleographic maps of North America. [1955]   10292

Schüttau, Bruno, _and_ Hahn, Paul.
Lüneburger Heimatatlas. 1950.   8744

Schuiling, Roelof, 1854–1936.
Atlas voor de lagere school. 3. druk. [1924]   6567
See also Beekman, Anton Albert, 1854–1947, _and_ Schuiling, Roelof.

Schultz, J. H., Forlag.
Kort over Danmarks købstæder. 1956.   8261

Schultze, Walther, 1862–1939.
Deutschlands Binnenhandel mit Vieh. 1900.   3022

Schulze, Alfred, 1912–
See Knoch, Karl, 1883–   _and_ Schulze, Alfred.

Schwabe, Ernst, 1858–
2000 Jahre Deutscher Geschichte. Atlas. 1916.   8576

Schwalm, Hans.
See Volz, Wilhelm Theodor August Hermann, 1870–1958, _and_ Schwalm, Hans.

Schwann, L.
See Bludau, Alois, 1861–1913.

Schweigger, Erwin.
Atlas de la Corriente Costanera Peruana. 1951.   18379

Schweizerische Zentrale für Verkehrsförderung, Zürich.
Schweiz. Taschenatlas für den Turisten. [193–]   9453
Suisse. Atlas de poche à l'usage des touristes. [1924]   9452

Sciuto-Patti, Carmelo.
Carta geologica della città di Catania. [1874?]   8993

Scobel, Albert, _i.e._, Carl Paul Albert, 1851–1912.
Handels-Atlas zur Verkehrs- und Wirtschafts-Geographie. 1902.   78

Velhagen & Klasings Kleiner Handatlas. 1912.   3640
Velhagen & Klasings Neuer Volks– und Familienatlas. 1901.   6302
See also Lehmann, Richard, 1845–1942, _and_ Scobel, Albert.

Scofield, Horace G.
Atlas of the city of Bridgeport, Conn. 1876.   1483

Scofield, Horace G., _and_ Bogart, James P.
Official land map of the town of Bridgeport, Conn. 1880.   11708

Scott, Adam.
Republica de Chile. Puerto de Valparaiso. 1910.   5147

Scott, James D.
Atlas of the 24th & 27th wards, West Philadelphia. 1878.   2525
Combination atlas map of Bucks County, Pa. 1876.   2464
Combination atlas map of Burlington County, N.J. 1876.   2153
Combination atlas map of Montgomery County, Pa. 1877.   2488
—— [1959]   16793

Scott, Joseph.
Atlas of the United States, 1795–1800. [1960]   11021
—— 1796.   4521a

Scott, Marlin Elmer, 1908–   _and_ Walker, Edwin Lesley, 1911–
Property map of Geary County, Kans. 1938.   14168

Scott–Ruud, Gunnar, 1897–
See Sømme, Axel Christian Zetlitz, 1899– _and_ Scott-Rudd, Gunnar.

Scoville, C. H.
Plat book of Douglas and Sarpy Counties, Nebr. 1889.   15425

Scribner's, Charles, sons.
Scribner-Black atlas. 1890.   961

Scudder, Henry Desborough, 1881–   _and_ Hurd, Edgar Blake, 1899–
Graphic summary of agriculture and land use in Oregon. [1935]   16638

Seaman, J. W.
Map of city of Long Branch, N.J. 1906.   2185

Seaman, James V.
New general atlas. 1820.   6045

Searcy, Nelson Donald, 1933–   _and_ Longwell, Alden R.
Nebraska atlas. [1964]   15339

Sears, J. H.
Historical atlas of Kearney County, Nebr. 1894.   2117

Sears Cross country highway atlas of the United States. 1935.   10833

Sears Family world atlas. [1954]   7602

Security-First National Bank of Los Angeles.
Freeway map, showing Harbor, Hollywood ... Golden State Freeways. [1956]   11553
Map of Orange County [Calif. 1957]   11435
—— [1967]   11445

Security Surveying Company.
Plat book, map plates of Dakota County, Minn. 1928.   14966

Seghers, W.
Schippers-atlas voor de binnenscheepvaart. [193–]   7644

Seghers Plans en Kaarten.
Nieuw stadsplan van Antwerpen. [1. uitg. 194–]   7973
—— 2. verb. uitg. [1948?]   7974

Ségur, Louis Philippe, *Comte* de, **1753–1830.**
Atlas pour l'histoire universelle. 1822.   146
—— 1840.   4143
Atlas pour servir à l'histoire ancienne, Romaine et du Bas-Empire. 1827.   3287

Séguy, Jean.
Atlas linguistique et ethnographique de la Gascogne. 1954.   8423

Seibel, George Leonard, 1889–
Lakeland area maps ... New Jersey. [1965]   15671
—— 1967.   15672

Seifert, Lester W.
See Reed, Carroll E., *and* Seifert, Lester W.

Seine (Dept.) Direction Générale des Travaux de Paris.
Atlas administratif des 20 arrondissements de la ville de Paris. 1868.   5235
Atlas municipal des vingts arrondissements de la ville de Paris. 1878.   5236

Seine (Dept.) Prefecture. Service de l'Assainissement.
Atlas administratif des égouts de la ville de Paris. [1896]   3016

Seive, Fleury Marius, 1896– *and* **Cholley, André, 1886–**
Atlas photographique du Rhône. 1931.   8510

Seix Barral, Editorial.
See Editorial Seix Barral.

Selander, Nils Johan Teodor, 1845–1922.
Karta öfver Sverige. 1881–83.   9391
See also Hildebrand, Emil, *i.e.* Henrik Robert Teodor Emil, 1848–1919, *and* Selander, Nils Johan Teodor.

Selen, Hâmit Sadi, *and* **Unat, Faik Resit, 1899–**
Coğrafya iş atlası. 1940–44.   5766

Self, Huber.
Atlas of Kansas. [1961]   14138

Selleck Abstract Company.
Township plats of Box Butte Co. [Nebr.] 1951.   15352

Seller, John, *fl.* **1667–1697.**
Atlas maritimus. [Copy A. 1670?]   4150
—— [Copy B. 1670?]   4151
—— [1671?]   4152
—— [1672?]   4153
—— 1675.   487, 4154
Atlas minimus. [1679]   490
Atlas terrestris. [1700?]   529
Coasting pilot. [1672]   2915, 3077
English pilot. First book. 1671.   3985
—— —— 1690.   2833
Hydrografia universalis. [1690?]   505
New systeme of geography. [1685]   3450
—— 1690.   4267

Sellman, Roger Raymond.
Outline atlas of Eastern history. [1954]   9485

Selves, Henri.
Atlas géographique. 1822–[29]   6049

Selvey, Leland I., 1895–
Plat book of Barton County, Mo. 1929.   15216

Sendai Shimpō Sha.
Sendai-shi seimitsu annai chishi. [Detailed atlas of Sendai. 1958]   9956

Senex, John, *d.* **1740.**
Itinéraire de toutes les routes de l'Angleterre. 1766.   2911
Modern geography. [1708–25]   550
New general atlas. 1721.   563

Senninger, Earl J.
Atlas of Michigan. [1963]   14559
—— 2d ed. [1964]   14560

Sepp, Jan Christiaan, 1739–1811.
Nieuwe geographische Nederlandsche reise- en zak-atlas. 1773.   3081

Seraphin, Eugene William, 1898– *and* **Kelly, Jerome Aemilian, 1910–**
Maps of the land of Christ. 1938.   5369
—— [1947]   5370

Serial Map Service.
    Serial maps. 9v. 1939–48.   6993

Serra, Adalberto B.
    Atlas de meteorologia, 1873–1909. 1948.   5395
    Atlas de meteorologia relativo ao periodo de
      1910–1934. 1946.   5396

Serra, Adalberto B., and Ratisbonna, Leandro.
    As ondas de frio da bacia Amazônica. 1941.   18276

Serryn, Pierre.
    Nouvel atlas général. [1954]   7612

Servoss, R. D.
    Sectional road map of Long Island. 1899.   16195

Sesti, Giovanni Battista.
    Piante delle città . . . in qvesto Stato di Milano.
      1707.   8947
    ——— [1718]   8948

Seutter, Matthaeus, 1678–1756.
    Atlas geographicus. 1725.   5968
    Atlas minor prǣcipua orbis terrarum imperia.
      [1744?]   3494, 5976
    Atlas novus indicibus instructus. 1730.   5969
    Atlas novus sive Tabulǣ geographicǣ totius
      orbis. [1740?]   593
    ——— [1741?]   5973
    ——— 2 v. [1745?]   5977
    Grosser Atlas. [1734?]   583

Seward, Walter H.
    Tax map of Landis Township, Cumberland
      Co., N.J. 1919.   4915a

Seyfert, Bernhard.
    Kleiner Geschichts-Atlas. 20. Aufl. 1930.   7695

Sha, Hsüeh-chüng.
    Chung-kuo ti li t'u chi. [Geographical atlas of
      China. 1953]   9600

Shanghai Meteorological Society.
    Atlas of the mean isobars and mean directions
      of the wind in the Far East. 1900–1901.   9477

Shannon, Edgar Finley, 1874–1938.
    See Goode, Clement Tyson, 1883–   and
    Shannon Edgar Finley.

Sharman, J.
    [Collection of maps. 1800?]   4304

Sharp, Charles Edward, 1897–
    Magicarpet maps, presenting world bee lines.
      1944.   5336
    Round the world maps. 1943.   5337
    ——— St. Louis series. 1944.   5338

Sharp, John, 1777–1860.
    Corresponding atlas. 1849.   4327
    Student's atlas. 1850.   803

Shaw, J.
    Picturesque views of American scenery.
      1820.   4518

Sheahan, James Washington, 1824–1883.
    Universal historical atlas. 1873.   147

Shearer, W. H., Publishing Co.
    Atlas of the Goldfield, Tonopah, and Bullfrog
      mining districts of Nevada. 1905.   2133

Shelbyville Democrat.
    Plat book of Shelby County, Ill. [194–?]   12504

Sheldrake, T. Swinborne.
    See Philip, George, 1870–1937, and Sheldrake,
      T. Swinborne.

Shell Caribbean Petroleum Company.
    Carreteras de Venezuela. [1951]   18419

Shell Company of New Zealand.
    Road maps, New Zealand. [194–]   10197
    ——— [1953?]   10200
    ——— [1956?]   10201
    Road maps, North Island, New Zealand.
      [193–]   10196

Shell Company of Singapore.
    Road map of Malaya. [1951]   10054

Shell Company of South Africa.
    Road map of southern Africa. 1953.   10166
    Road map of the Union of South Africa.
      [1931]   10163

Shell-Mex.
    Motorists' guide to London. [1951]   8189

Shelton, William Arthur, 1878–
    Atlas of railway traffic maps. [1913]   4510
    ——— [1914]   4511

Shên, Ting-chih, fl. 1638, and Wu, Kuo-fu, fl. 1638.
    Chin ku yü ti t'u. [Modern and ancient atlas of
      China. 1643]   9523

Shepherd, William Robert, 1871–1934.
    Atlas of medieval and modern history. 1932.   5572
    Historical atlas. 1911.   3320
    ——— 2d ed. 1921.   5573
    ——— 3d ed. 1923.   5574
    ——— 4th ed. 1924.   5575
    ——— 7th ed. 1929.   5576

Sherman, W. A.
    Atlas of Norfolk County, Mass. 1876.   1821
    Atlas of Penobscot County, Me. 1875.   1776

Sherman, W. A., and Howland, C. W.
    Atlas of Abington and Rockland, Mass.
      1874.   1847, 1932

Shewey, Arista C.
New, handy reference atlas. [1894]   997
Spanish American War atlas. [1898?]   10690

Shi-Chō-Son Jichi Kenkyūkai.
Zenkoku chō-son gappei genkyō su, Shōwa
33-nen 2-gatsu 1-tachi genzai. [Atlas of
towns and villages consolidated as of Feb-
ruary 1, 1958. 1958]   9774

Shiga, Jūkō, 1863–1927.
Hompō chizu. [Atlas of our country. Japan.
3d rev. ed. 1906]   9804

Shigeno, Y., _and_ Kawada, S.
[Shina kyō-eki en-kaku dzu. 1896]   3183

Shih chieh ch'u pan shê, _Hongkong._
Chung-kuo fên shêng t'u. [New provincial atlas
of China]   1957.   9614

Shih chieh yü ti hsüeh shê, _Shanghai._
Hsin Chung-kuo fên shêng t'u. [New pocket
provincial atlas of China. 1st rev. ed.]
1953.   9601
—— [7th rev. ed.]   1953.   9603
—— [21st rev. ed.]   1953.   9604

Shilling, Henry.
Foot steps of the Master.   1948.   5371

Shillington, T.
See Wallace, J. B., _and_ Shillington, T.

Shinshindō, _Osaka._
Kōbe-shi kubun chizu, banchi iri. [Kobe ward
atlas, with house numbers, newest ed.
1956]   9900
Osaka-shi kubun shōsaizu. [Detailed atlas of
Osaka City divided into wards]   1954.   9943

Shockley Engineering Company.
Atlas of Clay County, Mo. 1959.   15224
Atlas of Johnson County, Kans. 1940.   14176

Shokal'skiǐ, IUliǐ Mikhaǐlovich, 1856–1940.
Географический атлас. [Geographical atlas.]
1928.   6688a
See also Petri, Eduard IUlévich, 1854–1899,
and Shokal'skiǐ, IUliǐ Mikhailovich.

Shoshone Irrigation Company.
Homes in the Big Horn basin [Wyo. 1896]   18036

Showalter, Noah Daniel, 1886–
Atlas of Rockingham County, Va.   1939.   17359
Plat book of Cass County, Mo.   1926.   15220
Plat book of Pettis County, Mo.   1929.   15242
Plat book of Vernon County, Mo.   1928.   15247

Shutts, M. Russell.
Atlas of Hammond ... Ind.   1925.   12974

Sibel Publishing Company.
Street atlas and buyer's guide for central
Oklahoma. [1967]   16630

Sibert, J. L.
Plus petit atlas du monde. [1940]   7033
—— [1947]   7248
—— 755e ed. [1948]   7327
—— 990e ed. [1951]   7485

Siborne, William, 1797–1849.
[History of the war in France and Belgium, in
1815. Atlas. 1844]   7724
—— [1848]   2980

Sîdî 'Alî îbn Ḥusain, _Kâtib i Rûmî._
Topographischen Capitel des Indischen See-
spiegels Moḥiṭ ... [1554]   1897.   10242

Sidwell, Joe H.
Street numbered village maps of Du Page
County [Ill. 1933]   12198

Sidwell Studio.
Aer-o-plat atlas of Allen County, Ind.
1959–66.   12739
[Aer-o-plat atlas of Kane County, Ill. 1952–
60]   12305
—— 1961–67.   12306
Aer-o-plat atlas of Lake County, Ill. 1956–
66.   12332
Aer-o-plat atlas of Mahoning County, Ohio.
1955–65.   16438
Aer-o-plat atlas of Peoria County, Ill. 1964–
67.   12445
Aer-o-plat atlas of Polk County, Iowa.
1953–66.   13858
Aer-o-plat atlas of Summit County, Ohio.
1964–66.   16454
Aer-o-plat atlas of Will County, Ill. 1962–
66.   12562
Aer-o-plat of Du Page County, Ill. 1940.   12200
—— [1951]   12203
—— 1954.   12204
—— 1956.   12207
—— 1959.   12209
Aer-o-plat of Lake County, Ill. 1960.   12330
Aer-o-plat of Summit County, Ohio. 1942–
61.   16453
[Allen County, Ind.] 1955–56.   12738
Atlas of Champaign County, Ill. 1967.   12125
Atlas of Clark County, Ohio. [1953–61]   16389
—— 1963–67.   16391
Atlas of Des Moines and environs. [1930–46]   14123
Atlas of Kent County, Mich. 1960–67.   14703
Atlas of ... Lake County, Ill. [1948–64]   12329
[Atlas of McHenry County, Ill. [1951–65]   12368
Atlas of Mahoning County, Ohio. 1938.   16437
Atlas of Peoria County, Ill. 1955–61.   12443
[Atlas of Sangamon County, Ill.] 1955–67.   12492
Atlas of Stark County, Ohio. 2d. ed. [1950]–
65.   16452
Atlas of the city of Grand Rapids, Mich.
1961.   14879

Chicago suburban maps. [1939] 12647
—— [1957] 12660
Chicagoland village maps. 1961. 12666
—— [1965] 12668
Dade County, Fla. 1959. 11817
Du Page County, Ill. 1936. 12199
Election district maps of Du Page County
[Ill.] 1959. 12210
—— 1961. 12213
[Flint, Mich, and environs atlas] 1955–67. 14868
Maps of election districts of Du Page County,
Ill. 1965. 12219
Official atlas of city of Chicago. 1958. 12662
Official atlas of Cook County, Ill. 1958–59. 12154
Official atlas of Rogers Park Twp. [Ill. 1957] 12171
Official tax maps of Clark County, Ohio.
1964. 16392
Official tax maps of St. Clair County, Ill.
1965. 12488
Official tax maps of Will County, Ill. 1966–
67. 12565
Posting pages in Lorain Co., Ohio atlas.
1966. 16433
St. Joseph County, Ind., atlas. 1955–67. 12905
Sectional aerials of Milton Twp., Du Page
Co., Ill. 1962. 12222
Tax maps of Du Page County, Ill. 1966. 12220
Twp. maps of Will County, Ill., excluding
Joliet Twp. 1962. 12560
[Vermilion County, Ill., atlas] 1955–67. 12527
[Will County, Ill., atlas] 1957–61. 12559
Zoning map of Bensenville, Ill. 1960. 12586

Siebold, Philipp Franz von, 1796–1866.
Atlas von Land- und See-Karten vom Japanischen Reiche. 1851. 3209, 4075

Siedlungsverband Ruhrkohlenbezirk.
Gesamtverkehrsplanung für den Ruhrkohlenbezirk. [1953] 8881

Sieglin, Wilhelm, 1855–1935.
Schulatlas zur Geschichte des Altertums. 5.
Aufl. [1921] 5648
—— 6. Aufl. [193–?] 5649

Sierra Leone. *Survey and Lands Dept.*
Atlas of Sierra Leone. 1953. 10151

Siethoff, J. J. ten.
See Stemfoort, J. W., *and* Siethoff, J. J. ten.

Sieurin, E.
See Dubois, Edmond Marcel, 1856–1916, *and*
Sieurin, E.

Sievers, E.
Kriegs–Atlas. 1915. 5844

Sigmund, William F.
Ever-changing Europe. [1940] 7696

Sigourney Review.
Atlas of Keokuk County, Iowa. [1912?] 13601

Silishchenskiĭ, M. I.
Географический атлас. [Geographical atlas.]
1929. 6714a

Sill, Tucker & Co.
Ashtabula County [Ohio] Atlas. 1905. 2354

Silva, Francisco, *and* Oliveira, Francisco.
Atlas geográfico histórico. [1939] 6990

Silva, J. R.
Atlas do mundo comerical e politico. [195–] 7380

Silvestre, Israël, 1621–1691.
Recueil des vues de villes. 1751. 3963

Simon, Hilda.
Hart's Maps of New York City. 1964. 16107

Simpson, George Wilfrid.
Ukraine. A series of maps ... indicating the
historic and contemporary geographical
position of the Ukrainian people. 1941. 9288

Simpson, William, 1823–1899.
Seat of the war in the East. 1855–56. 5279

Sims, Edgar Barr, 1882–
Maps showing development of West Virginia
counties, 1738–1954. [1954] 17595

Simukov, A. D.
Географический атлас Монгольской
Народной Республики. [Geographical
atlas of the Mongolian People's Republic]
1934. 9623

Sindik, Ilija.
Старе карте југословенских земаља. [Cartes
anciennes des pays Yougoslaves] 1931. 7820

Singapore.
Master plan for Singapore. 1958. 10071

Sipman, Friedrich.
Ergänzungsheft für Haus- und Schulatlanten.
1907. 1126b

Skelton, Gordon Vernon, 1867–1939.
Atlas map of Washington County, Ark.
[1894] 1456

Skinner, Andrew.
See Taylor, George, *fl.* 1778, *and* Skinner,
Andrew.

Skok, Petar, 1881–
Slavenstvo i Romanstvo na jadranskim
otocima. 1950. 9462

Slanar, Hans, 1890–1955.
Atlas für Hauptschulen, Mittelschulen und
verwandte Lehranstalten. 1928. 6689

Sleeswijk, J. A.
Atlas van Nederland voor wandelaars.
[1917]   9053
—— [193–]   9057
Zak-atlas van Nederland. [192–]   9055

Sliva, Edmund M.
Directomap road map series [Washington]
1963.   17416

Sloss, Laurence Louis, 1913–   *and others.*
Lithofacies maps. An atlas of the United States
and southern Canada. [1960]   10587

Slum Clearance Committee of New York.
Maps and charts. [1934]   16043

Smedley, J. Melton.
Land atlas, Brevard County, Fla. 1963.
11805, 11806
Land atlas, Collier County, Fla. [1957]   11813
Land atlas, Lee County, Fla. [1958]   11830
Land atlas, Marion County, Fla. [1957]   11834
Land atlas, Nassau County [Fla. 1959]   11836
Land atlas of Brevard County [Fla. 1959]   11804
Land atlas, Pasco County, Fla. [1957]   11845
Land atlas, Polk County [Fla. 1958]   11850
Land atlas, St. Johns County, Fla. [1957] 11852
Land atlas, Volusia County, Fla. [1957]   11858
—— 1962.   11859
Land ownership atlas, Lee County, Fla.
[1957]   11829
Land ownership atlas, Manatee County, Fla.
[1957]   11831
Land ownership atlas of Citrus County, Fla.
[1957]   11812
Land ownership atlas of Columbia County,
Fla. [1965]   11814
Land ownership atlas of Escambia County,
Fla. [1957]   11822
Land ownership atlas of Hamilton County,
Fla. [1965]   11825
Land ownership atlas of Orange County, Fla.
[1955–58]   11838
Land ownership atlas, Osceola County, Fla.
[1957]   11842
Land ownership atlas, Putnam County [Fla.
1957]   11851
Subdivision atlas of Brevard County [Fla.
1958]   11803
Subdivision atlas of Orange County [Fla.
1962]   11840
Subdivision atlas of Orlando—Winter Park
[Fla. 1958]   11914
Street maps of Orlando area [Fla.] 1965.   11915

Smedley, Samuel Lightfoot, 1832–1894.
Atlas of the city of Philadelphia. [1862]   2519

Smiley, Thomas Tucker, *d.* 1879.
Improved atlas. 1824.   313
New atlas. 7th ed. [1830]   314
—— 14th ed. [1832]   315

—— [22nd ed. 1834]   316
—— [1838]   317

Smith, A. C.
See Bennett, L. G., *and* Smith, A. C.

Smith, Beatrice Young.
Arizona. 1962.   11245

Smith, Benjamin Eli, 1857–1913.
Century atlas of the world. [1897]   1020
—— [1889]   1045
—— [1901]   1070
—— [1902]   1080
—— [1903]   3577
—— [1904]   1093
—— [1906]   1112a
—— [1911]   3633
—— [1914]   6372

Smith, Benjamin H.
Atlas of Delaware County, Pa. 1880.   5015

Smith, Catharine.
Our United States. [1951]   10559

Smith, Charles.
Classical atlas. 1835.   5650
New English atlas. 1804.   5200
New general atlas. 1808.   6028
—— 1813.   6034
—— 1816.   729
—— 1818–[20]   6042
—— 1826.   6056
—— 1830.   6067
—— 1836.   6078
New pocket companion to the roads of England & Wales. 1827.   8102

Smith, Elvino V., 1870–1932.
Atlas of the 1st and 39th wards of the city of
Philadelphia. 1904.   16861
Atlas of the 2nd, 3rd, 4th & 30th wards of the
city of Philadelphia. 1905.   16862
Atlas of the 5th, 7th & 8th wards of the city of
Philadelphia. 1908.   16865
Atlas of the 5th to 10th wards of the city of
Philadelphia. 1927.   16871
Atlas of the 24th & 34th wards of the city of
Philadelphia. 1905.   16863
Atlas of 24th, 34th & 44th wards of the city of
Philadelphia. 1911.   3892
Atlas of the 25th & 45th wards of the city of
Philadelphia. [1910]   16867
Atlas of the 40th ward of the city of Philadel-
phia. 1910–[17]   16868
Atlas of the 48 wards of the city of Philadel-
phia. 1932.   16872

Smith, Everett G.
Marketing maps of the United States. [1942] 10560

Smith, *Sir* George Adam, 1856–1942.
Atlas of the historical geography of the Holy
Land. 1915.   5302
Historical atlas of the Holy Land. 2d ed.
1936.   5372

Smith, J. Mott.
Geography of the Hawaiian Islands. [1889]   3261

Smith, John L., 1846–1921.
Atlas of properties along the Philadelphia,
Wilmington and Baltimore R.R. 1889.   2448
Atlas of the 22nd [and] 42nd wards of the city
of Philadelphia. 1906.   16864
Atlas of the 23rd, 35th & 41st wards of the city
of Philadelphia. 1910.   16866

Smith, John Peter.
Genealogists' atlas of Lancashire. 1930.   8143

Smith, Lloyd Edwin, 1902–
Key to the universe. [1941]   7072
Monarch atlas of the world. [1936]   6897
New census atlas of the world. [1931]   6762
—— [1942]   7115
New international atlas of the world. [1931]   6763
—— [1934]   6827
—— [1935]   6862
—— [1938]   6965
—— [1940]   7034
—— [1941]   7073
—— [1942]   7116
—— [1944]   7200
—— [1945]   7224
New pictorial atlas. [1931]   6764
—— [1941]   7074
New world wonder atlas. [1941]   7075

Smith, Lucien Herbert.
Historical and chronological atlas of the
United States. 1881.   1296

Smith, Roswell Chamberlain, 1797–1875.
Atlas. 1835.   318
—— [1839]   319
Atlas designed to accompany the Geography.
Improved ed. 1839.   320
—— [1839–44]   6087
—— —— 1850.   321
Atlas of modern and ancient geography.
1853.   322
—— 1854.   3380
—— 1866.   4347
—— 1868.   323

Smith, Wilbur, and Associates.
Albuquerque transportation study. 1965.   15820

Smith, William, 1769–1839.
Delineation of the strata of England and
Wales, with part of Scotland. 1815.   3998

**Smith, *Sir* William, 1813–1893, *and* Grove, *Sir*
George, 1820–1900.**
Ancient atlas. 1874.   52

Smith, William S. R.
Maps of the world for coloring and stamps.
[1953]   5767

Smith and Finley.
Map of Sioux City, Iowa. 1911.   14132

Smith Map Company.
Adams County, Colo. 1937.   11647
—— 1948.   11648
Arapahoe County, Colo. [1937]   11649
—— 1949.   11650
Atlas of Cheyenne County, Colo. [1935]   11654
Atlas of Kiowa County, Colo. [1937]   11657
Atlas of Kit Carson County, Colo. [1935]   11659
Atlas of Morgan County, Colo. [1936]   11662
Atlas of Prowers County, Colo. [1936]   11665
Atlas of Washington County, Colo. [1936]   11669
Kit Carson County, Colo. 1943.   11660
Lincoln County, Colo. [1937]   11661
Phillips County, Colo. [1937]   11664
Sedgwick County, Colo. [1937]   11668

Smulders, J., and Company.
Zak-atlas van Nederland. 1938.   9061

Smyth, Hervey.
[View of the most remarkable places in the
Gulf and River of St. Lawrence. 1760]   4480

Snyder, Van Vechten & Company.
Historical atlas of Wisconsin. 1878.   2634

Soares, João.
Atlas histórico–geográfico. 2. ed. [1934]   6828

Sobel, Nathan.
Planning study of Brooklyn Heights, Brooklyn, N.Y. [1963]   15949

Šobić, Dobrosav Ž.
Школски атлас. [School atlas.] 1951.   7485a

Sobotha, E., *and others*.
Harms Hessen in Bild und Karte. [1955]   8752

Sobrequés, S.
See Vicens Vives, Jaime, *and* Sobrequés, S.

Sociedad Geográfica de Lima.
Atlas del Peru. [1921]   18386

Sociedade Nacional de Agricultura.
[Atlas do Brazil. 1908]   18268

Société Anonyme des Automobiles Peugeot.
Atlas routier Peugeot; carte de la France.
[1948]   8435
—— [1954]   8443

Société de Géographie de Finlande.
See Sällskapet för Finlands Geografi.

Society for Promoting Christian Knowledge, *London*.
Handy atlas of the counties of England. [1885?]   8134

Society for the Diffusion of Useful Knowledge.
Cyclopaedian, or Atlas of general maps. 1870.   6173
Family atlas. 1863.   3559
General atlas. [1853]   811
Harrow atlas of modern geography. 1864.   6151
Maps of the society. 2 v. 1844.   794, 6100
—— 1846–51.   4326
—— 2 v. 1849.   6109
Series of maps. [1829–35]   753
—— [1829–37]   6062

Society for the Propagation of the Faith.
Little atlas of Catholic missions. [1926]   5414

Society for the Propagation of the Gospel in Foreign Parts. *London*.
Colonial church atlas. 1842.   4159

Society of the Divine Word.
Atlas Societatis Verbi Divini. 1952.   5415

Soderberg, Melvin Palmer.
Atlas of Kittson County, Minn. 1952.   15020

Söderlund, Alfred, 1884–
Svensk skolatlas. 3 v. [1924–25]   6572

Soeiro, Augusto Cesar Gomes.
See Vilamariz, Carlos da Conceiçao Aquino, *and* Soeiro, Augusto Cesar Gomes.

Sømme, Axel Christian Zetlitz, 1899–
See Ouren, Tore Hans Petter, 1918–   *and* Sømme, Axel Christian Zetlitz,   1899–
See also Sund, Tore, 1914–1965, *and* Sømme, Axel Christian Zetlitz,   1899–

Sømme, Axel Christian Zetlits, *and* Scott–Ruud, Gunnar, 1897–
Atlas for folkeskolen. 1946.   7252

Sørensen, Jens, 1646–1723.
Danske søkort. 1916.   8266

Sohr, Kral.
Vollständiger Hand–Atlas. [1842–44]   6097
—— 5te. Aufl. 1859.   6137
Vollständiger Universal–Handatlas. 5te. Aufl. 1865.   6154

Sokolov, Sergeï Nikolaevich.
Малый географический атлас. [Small geographical atlas.] 1930.   6732a

Sola Ricardo, Irma de.
Contribución al estudio de los planos de Caracas. [1967]   18434

Sollesnes, Karl Birger, 1899–
See Ellefsen, Ellef, *and* Sollesnes, Karl Birger, 1899–

Sorensen, Franklin L.
Faribault County [Minn.] plat book and livestock breeders' guide. [1920]   14981
Kossuth County [Iowa] plat book and livestock breeders' guide. [1920]   13613
Martin County [Minn.] plat book and livestock breeders' guide. [1920]   15036

Sorenson, Frank England, 1903–
See Carls, Norman, *and* Sorenson, Frank Englan, 1903–

Soulier, E., *and* Andriveau-Goujon, J.
Atlas élémentaire. [1838]   324

Soult, Nicolas Jean de Dieu, *Duc de Dalmatie*, 1769–1851.
Mémoires du Maréchal-Général Soult. Atlas. [1854]   2981

Sousa, Ahmed.
Atlas of Iraq. 1st ed. 1953.   9765

South Africa [*Weekly journal*]
South Africa atlas of the Rand. 1903.   3238

South Australia. *Survey Dept*.
Plan of the southern portion of the province of South Australia. 1873.   3257

South Carolina. *Civil Defense Agency*.
Operational survival plan: Maps. 1959.   16980

South Carolina. *State Highway Dept*.
[Highway atlas of South Carolina. 1940]   16982

South Dakota. *State Highway Commission*.
General highway map[s. 1945]   17009
—— [1951]   17010

South Island Motor Union, *Christchurch, N.Z.*
A. A. road maps, South Island of New Zealand. [194–]   10198
—— [195–]   10199

Southam Printing Company.
Southam easy-fold maps of Montreal. 1st ed. 1960.   10434

Southampton Record Society.
Maps and plans of old Southampton. [1907]   2937

Southern California Edison Company.
Industrial map of central and southern California. [1957]   11327

Southern Mapping and Engineering Company.
  City of Cairo, Ga. [1957]   11970

Southern Publishing Company.
  Victory historical map and outline book. English history. [1924]   8024

Sozialistische Einheitspartei Deutschlands.
  Leipzig, gestern, heute, morgen. [1946]   8864

Spafar'ev, Leontii Vasil'evich, 1765–1847.
  Атлас Финскаго эалива. [Atlas of the Gulf of Finland] 1817.   8380
  —— 1821.   3120

Spain.
  [Atlas of the Philippine Islands. 1897]   5303

Spain. *Comision Especial Encargada de Proponer el Plan General de Ferro-Carriles.*
  Memoria presentada al gobierno por la Comision ... Cartas. 1867.   9318

Spain. *Consejo Superior de Misiones.*
  Atlas–guía de las misiones españolas. v. 1. 1947.   5416

Spain. *Dirección de Hidrografia.*
  Atlas maritimo español. 1789–[1814]   4155
  [Atlas of Mediterranean countries. 1810?]   4162
  Portulano de la América Setentrional. 1809.   1223
  —— [1818]   1224
  —— 1825.   1226
  [Portulano de los Estados Unidos de América. 1809?]   4522

Spain. *Dirección General de Aeronáutica.*
  Atlas de aeródromos, España. [2. ed. 1936?]   9302

Spain. *Dirección General de Aeronáutica Civil.*
  Atlas de los aeródromos de España. 1. ed. 193–]   9303

Spain. *Dirección General de Marruecos y Colonias.*
  Atlas histórico y geográfico de Africa Española. 1955.   10091

Spain. *Ejército. Cuerpo de Estado Mayor.*
  Atlas topográfico de la narración militar de la Guerre Carlista de 1869 á 1876. [1890?]   5284

Spain. *Ejército. Servicio Geográfico.*
  Cartografia de ultramar. 1949–57.   10258

Spain. *Instituto de Estudios de Administración Local. Seminario de Urbansimo.*
  Palanos de ciudades iberoamericanas y filipinas existentes en el Archivo de Indias. 1951.   18040

Spain. *Instituto Hidrográfico de la Marina.*
  Carta del Rio Guadalquivir. 1949.   9348

Spamer, Otto.
  Grosser Hand-Atlas. [1900]   1058
  —— 2. Aful. [1902]   6307

Specialty Surveys of Greensboro, *Greensboro, N.C.*
  Commercial and industrial property survey of Greensboro, N.C. 1960.   16233

Speed, John, 1552?–1629.
  Atlas of Tudor England and Wales. 1627. [1951]   8113
  England. 1611. [1953–54]   8111
  England, Wales, Scotland and Ireland described. 1627.   4000, 8073
  —— 1676.   3441
  English county maps. 1614. [1957]   8112
  Prospect of the most famovs parts of the vvorld. 1627.   5928
  —— 1631.   442
  —— 1646.   3425
  —— 1675.   3438
  Theatre of the empire of Great-Britain. 1676.   488, 5949
  Theatrum Imperii Magnáẽ Britanniáẽ. 1616.   8072

Speer, John L.
  Ottawa County, Okla. Ownership-map. [1927]   16612

Speer, Joseph Smith, d. 1781.
  West-India pilot. 1766.   2696
  —— 1771.   2698

Spencer, Harold A.
  Ownership service. Kansas City, Mo. 1915.   4875

Spielmann and Brush.
  Certified copies of original maps of Hudson County, N.J. 1882.   2162
  Certified copies of original maps of property in New York City. 1881.   2301
  Insurance map of the city of Hoboken, N.J. 1873.   15759
  Insurance map of West Hoboken and the town of Union ... N.J. 1874.   15809
  Insurance maps of Jersey City, N.J. [1873]   15760
  Sanitary & topographical map of Hudson County, N.J. 1880.   2161

Spirit Lake Beacon, *Spirit Lake, Ia.*
  Atlas of the Iowa great lakes. 1941.   13342

Spitzer, Frédéric, 1815–1890, *and* **Wiener, Charles, 1851–1913.**
  Portulan de Charles Quint. 1875.   263

Sprigade, Paul, 1863–1928, *and* **Lotz, Heinrich, 1873–1943.**
  Karte des Sperrgebiets in Deutsch-Südwestafrika. [1913]   5313

Sprigade, Paul, *and* **Moisel, Max, 1869–1920.**
  Grosser Deutscher Kolonialatlas. 1901-[14]   8549

Spruner von Merz, Karl, 1803–1892.
Atlas antiquus. 1850. 3321
—— Ed. 2a. 1855. 5651, 5652
Atlas zur Geschichte von Bayern. 1838. 5252
Hand-Atlas zur Geschichte Asiens, Afrika's,
Amerika's und Australiens. 2. Aufl. 1855. 3322
Historic geographical atlas. 1853. 3323
Historisch-geographischer   Hand-Atlas.
1846–51. 150
—— 2. Aufl. 1854–55. 151
Historisch-geographischer Hand-Atlas zur
Geschichte der Staaten Europa's. 1846. 2795
Historisch-geographischer   Schul-Atlas.
1856. 152
—— 7. Aufl. 1873. 5577
Historisch-geographischer Schul-Atlas von
Deutschland. 1858. 3027, 8577
Spruner-Menke Atlas antiquus. 1865. 3288
Spruner-Menke Hand-Atlas. 3. Aufl. 1880. 148
Spruner-Sieglin Hand-Atlas. 1893. 149

**Spruner von Merz, Karl, *and* Bretschneider, Carl
Anton, 1808–1878.**
Historischer Wandatlas. [1908] 3969

Spurr, Josiah Edward, 1870–1950.
Atlas to accompany Monograph xxxi on the
geology of the Aspen District, Colo. 1898. 1474

Srinivas Kini, K., *and* Bhavani Shanker Rao, U.
Oxford pictorial atlas of Indian history. 2d
ed. rev. 1935. 9695

Sroczyński, Jósef Nowina.
Atlas do dziejów Polski. [1900?] 9151

Stackhouse, Thomas, 1706–1784.
Universal atlas. 4th ed. 1790. 672

Stacy Map Publishers.
Atlas & street guide, metropolitan Denver.
[1943] 11680
Atlas & street guide of Los Angeles and Beverly
Hills . . . [Calif. 1936] 11537
Farm plat book, Henry County, Iowa. [1941] 13489
Farm plat book of Mercer County, Ill. [194–] 12411

Stadly, George W., and Company.
Atlas of the city of Medford . . . Mass. 1898. 14497
Atlas of the town of Hyde Park . . . Mass.
1899. 14476
Atlas of the town of Swampscott . . . Mass.
1897. 14532

**Stamp, Elsa Clara Rea, *and* Stamp, Laurence
Dudley, 1898–1966.**
First atlas. [1935] 6863
Practical atlas of modern geography. 3d ed.
1931. 6765

Stamp, Laurence Dudley, 1898–1966.
Agricultural atlas of Ireland. 1931. 8225
See also Stamp, Elsa Clara Rea, *and* Stamp,
Laurence Dudley, 1899–1966.

Standard Atlas Company.
Atlas of Grant County, Wis. 1966. 17751
Atlas of Iowa County, Wis. 1967. 17770
Atlas of Lafayette County, Wis. 1965. 17812
Atlas of Richland County, Wis. 1965. 17898
Atlas of Trempealeau County, Wis. 1964. 17940

Standard Map Company.
Atlas and farm directory of Isabella County,
Mich. 1915. 4749
Atlas and farm directory of Mason County,
Mich. 1915. 4755
Atlas and farm directory of Mercer &
Henderson Counties, Ill. 1914. 4570, 4581
Atlas of Wexford County, Mich. 1914.
4769, 14837

Standard Publishing Company.
Standard atlas. 1888. 947

Stanford, Edward, 1827–1904.
London atlas of universal geography. 1887. 944
—— 2d issue. 1896. 6276
—— —— Rev. and enl. 1898. 1029
—— 3d ed. rev. and enl. 1904. 1094
—— [1926] 6635
Parliamentary county atlas and handbook of
England and Wales. 1885. 8135

Stanford, Edward, 1856–1917.
Atlas of the Chinese Empire. [1908] 3195
Complete atlas of China. [1917] 5296
Indexed atlas of the county of London.
1911. 4015
—— 2d ed. 1920. 8166

Stanford, Edward, *ltd.*
Atlas of the World War. [1917?] 4246, 5845
Peace Conference atlas. [1919] 4245a

Standford, William.
Map and its story: A physical atlas. [1915?] 4175

**Stanford's Geological atlas of Great Britain and
Ireland.** 4th ed. [1925] 8014

Stanger, Roy Armour, 1902–
Atlas of McLean County [Ill.] 1935. 12372

Stanojević, Stanoje, 1874–1937.
Historički atlas za opću i narodnu historiju.
1925. 5577a

Starkweather, George A.
Sunday School geography. 1872. 89

Starling, Thomas.
Geographical annual, or Family cabinet atlas.
1832. 6071
—— 1833. 4319

Starr, Edward A.
Texas motor freight map & index. 1944. 17138

Stieler, Adolf, 1775–1836.

Atlante scolastico. 1855.	325
Atlas of modern geography. 9th ed. [1908]	3597
—— 9th ed. 1909.	6333
—— 9th ed. 1913.	6365
—— 10th ed. 2 v. 1925.	6597
—— 10th ed. 2 v. 1926–29.	6639
—— 10th ed. 1934–40.	6830
—— 10th ed., 1936. [1944]	6901
—— 10th ed. 2 v. [1938]	6966
Atlas von Deutschland. [1853]	2855
Grand atlas de géographie moderne. 10e éd. 1934–40.	6831
Grande atlante geografico. 9. ed. 1914.	6373
Hand-Atlas. [1816–50]	6039
—— [1834]	6075
—— [1853]	4333
—— 6. Aufl. [1855]	6120
—— [1856]	819
—— [1861]	6143
—— [1865]	3561
—— [1868]	4351
—— [10. Aufl. 1868]	4350
—— [1869]	6166
—— [10. Aufl. [1869]	6167
—— [1871–75]	4352
—— Specialkarte von Australien. 1875.	5322
—— [1876]	881
—— [1877]	3566
—— [17th ed. 1879–82]	4356
—— [1882]	910
—— [1885]	6226
—— [1887]	6238
—— [1891]	6258
—— [1893]	6268
—— [1896]	1015
—— [1899]	6289
—— 1905.	1071, 1108
—— 9. Aufl. 7. Abdr. 1910.	6339
—— 9. Aufl. 10. Abdr. 1918.	6389
—— 9. Aufl. 10. Abdr. 1922.	6506
—— 10. Aufl. 1925.	6598, 6600
—— 10. Aufl. 1928–30.	6696
—— 10. Aufl. 1933–35 [i.e., 37]	6807
Kleiner Atlas der deutschen Bundesstaaten. 1852.	3028
Schul-Atlas. 21. Aufl. 1841.	3381
—— 23. Aufl. 1843.	6098
—— 35. Aufl. 1855.	6121
—— 36. Aufl. 1856.	326
—— 37. Aufl. 1857.	6130
—— 74. Aufl. 1895.	6273
—— 89. Aufl. 1910.	3382

Stieler, Adolf, and Berghaus, Hermann, 1828–1890.

Atlante scolastico per la geografia politica e fisica. 1897.	6280

Stiffler, Andrew Jackson.

Standard atlas of Holmes County, Ohio. 1907.	16421

Stimson and Bracey.

Ownership maps of Harris County [Tex. 1927]	17171

Stinson, A. R.

Plat book of Cass County, Mo. 1912.	3818a
Plat book of Johnson County, Mo. 1914.	4853

Stock and Dairy Farmer.

Plat book, Carlton County [Minn. 1929]	14942

Stockdale, John, 1749?–1814.

See Cary, John, ca. 1754–1835, and Stockdale, John, 1749?–1814.

Stockholm. *Stadsingenjörskontoret.*

Officiella Stockholmskartan. [1954]	9416

Stoffel, Eugène Georges Henri Céleste, *Baron*, 1823–1907.

Histoire de Jules César, guerre civile. 1887.	5653

Stone, C. K.

New topographical atlas of Oswego County, N.Y. 1867.	2246

Stone and Stewart.

New topographical atlas of Erie County, N.Y. 1866.	2225
New topographical atlas of Tompkins County, N.Y. 1866.	2258
New topographical atlas of Washington County, N.Y. 1866.	15916

Storie, Raymond Earl, 1894–

See Weir, Walter Wallace, 1882– and Storie, Raymond Earl.

Stout, Neil J.

Atlas of forestry in New York. [1958?]	15838

Strabo, *ca.* 64 B.C.–*ca.* A.D. 19.

Strabonis nobilissimi et doctissimi philosophi ac geographi rerum geographicarum commentary libris XVII. 1571.	3390

Stranahan, H. B., and Company.

Atlas of Geauga County, Ohio. 1900.	16412
Atlas of Lake County, Ohio. 1898.	16425
Atlas of Portage County, Ohio. 1900.	2409
Maps of Cuyahoga County outside of Cleveland. 1903.	2369
Official atlas of Cleveland, Ohio. [1894]	2427

Strauss, Felix A.

Atlas of Boston & vicinity, 1874–1875. 1874.	1856

Strehle, Aksel, and Haestrup, Jørgen.

Normanns Historiske Atlas. [1947]	5677

Streit, Friedrich Wilhelm. *d.* 1839.

Topographisch-militairischer Atlas von dem Koenigreiche Sachsen. 1812.	8783

Streit, Friedrich Wilhelm, Jr.
See Fischer, Wilhelm, and Streit, Friedrich
Wilhelm, Jr.

Streit, Karl, 1874–1935.
Atlas hierarchicus. 1913. 4120
—— Ed. 2. 1929. 5417
Catholic world atlas. [2d ed.] 1929. 5418
Katholischer Missionsatlas. 1906. 183

Stridbeck, Johann, 1665–1714.
Galliæ sive Franciæ geographica descriptio.
[ca. 1700] 8454
Grafschafft Namur. [1700?] 7971

Strong, Arthur Lombard, 1883–
[Business district of Phoenix, Ariz. 1935] 11266

Stuart, J. H., and Company.
Atlas of the State of Maine. [1890] 1774
—— [1892–93] 14306
—— [1894–95] 14307
—— 11th ed. 1901. 3760a

Stuart, Leonard, i.e., Charles Leonard, 1868–
Standard atlas and chronological history of
the world. 1912. 6354

Stucchi, Stanislao.
Grande atlante universale. 1826. 748

Student Volunteer Movement for Foreign Missions.
World atlas of Christian missions. 1911. 4160

**Stülpnagel, Johann Friedrich von, 1786–1865, and
Bär, Joseph Christoph, 1789–1848.**
Eisenbahn-Atlas von Deutschland, Belgien,
Elsass, und dem nördlichsten Theile von
Italien. 1856. 2798

**Stuers, François Vincent Henri Antoine, ridder de,
1792–1881.**
Mémoires sur la guerre de l'Île de Java de 1825
à 1830. [Atlas] 1833. 4078

Stumpf, Johannes, 1500–1576.
Landkarten des Johann Stumpf 1538–1547.
1942. 9441

Sturdevant, John, 1870–
Atlas of city of Wilkes-Barre, Pa. [1933] 16935
Atlas of the borough of Kingston ... Pa.
1936. 16845

Sturdevant, William Henry.
Atlas of the city of Wilkes-Barre, Pa. 1894. 2559

Stuttgart. Wasser- und Schiffahrtsdirektion.
Neckar, Schiffahrtskarte. [1954–57] 8879

Styria.
Atlas der Steiermark. [1953–54] 7916

**Styria. Landeskammer für Land- und Forstwirt-
schaft.**
Steirischer Land- und Forstwirtschafts-Atlas.
[1954] 7917
Steirischer Waldatlas. [1950] 7915

Styx, Kurt.
See Walleczek, Erich, and Styx, Kurt.

Su, Chia-jung.
Chung-kuo ti li yen ko t'u. [Atlas of the
boundaries of China throughout the dynas-
ties. 3d rev. ed. 1930] 9523a
—— [4th rev. ed. 1936] 9523b

Su, Chia-jung, 1899–
Chung hua shêng shih ti fang hsin t'u. [New
city and provincial atlas of China. 1939] 9576

Su, Fêng-wên, fl. 1866.
Kuang-hsi ch'üan shêng ti yü t'u shuo. [Com-
plete atlas and description of Kwangsi
Province. 1866] 9651

Su Sung Ch'ang Chên T'ai wu li fang yü t'u. [Atlas
of Soochow, Sungkiang ... 186–] 9646

Suchet, Louis Gabriel, Duc d'Albufera, 1770–1826.
Mémoires ... sur ses campagnes en Espagne.
Atlas. 1828. 3129, 7718

**Sudan. Ministry of Irrigation and Hydro-Electric
Power.**
Sudan irrigation. 1957. 10152

Süreyya, Abdülkadir.
Lise ve ortaokullara mükemmel atlas.
[1924?] 6568

Sulte, Benjamin, 1841–1923.
Album de l'histoire des Trois-Rivières.
1881. 1255

Summer Residents Association.
Atlas of Bar Harbor and vicinity, Maine.
1904. 1777

Summers, George W.
[Plat book of Richmond County, Ga. 1929] 11947

**Sund, Tore, 1914–1965, and Sømme, Axel Christian
Zetlitz, 1899–**
Norway in maps. [1947] 9122

Sundial Map Company.
Metro Phoenix street atlas. 1960. 11271
—— [1961] 11272
—— [1967] 11273

Suomen Matkailijayhdistys.
Suomi kartasto. Kartbok över Finland.
[1918] 8371

—— 21. Aufl. 1941.	7076	
—— 21. Aufl. 1942.	7118	
—— 22. Aufl. 1943.	7164	
—— 23. Aufl. 1944.	7201	

Szkolny atlas historyczny. 1926–32.   7697

Szumański, Teofil, 1875–1944.
See Romer, Eugeniusz, 1871–1954, *and*
Szumański, Teofil, 1875–1944.

Ta Ch'ing fên shêng t'u. [Provincial atlas of China
in the Ch'ing period. 17—]   9546

Ta chung shu chü, *Hongkong.*
Tsui hsin Chung-kuo fên shêng ti t'u. [New
provincial atlas of China] 1955.   9610
—— 1958.   9619
—— [Topographic ed.] 1958.   9620
—— [1959]   9621
Tsui hsin Chung-kuo ti li chiao hsüeh t'u ts'ê.
[New atlas of China] 1957.   9615
Tsui hsin Chung-kuo ti t'u ts'ê. [New atlas of
China] 1957.   9616

Ta chung shu tien, *Dairen.*
Chung-kuo fên shêng t'u. [Provincial atlas of
China. 1948]   9585a

Ta chung ti hsüeh shê, *Shanghai.*
Hsin Chung-kuo fên shêng t'u. [New provincial atlas of China. 1st rev. ed.] 1953.   9511
—— [3d rev. ed.] 1953.   9512

Tackabury, Mead, and Moffett.
Combination atlas map of Summit County,
Ohio. 1874.   4989

Tackabury's Atlas of the Dominion of Canada.
1875.   10357

Taehan Sŏrim, *Seoul.*
Hoejung Hanguk chŏngmilto. [Detailed pocket atlas of Korean provinces. 1953]   10049

Tänzler, Karl. 1858–1944.
See Ambrosius, Ernst, 1866–1940, *and*
Tänzler, Karl, 1858–1944.

Tafel, Albert, 1877–1935.
Reise in China und Tibet, 1905–1908. 1912.   9558

**T'ai-wan shêng hsien shih hsing chêng ch'ü yü t'u
pien tsuan wei yüan hui,** *T'ai-pei.*
T'ai-wan shêng hsien shih hsing chêng ch'ü yü
t'u. [Hsien and city administrative atlas of
T'ai-wan Province. 1955]   9674

T'ai-wan ta hsüeh.
Chien ming Chung-kuo yen ko ti t'u. [Simpli-
fied historical atlas of China. 1952]   9524

Taintor Brothers and Merrill.
American household and commercial atlas.
1874.   872

Taitbout de Marigny, E.
Atlas de la Mer Noire et de la Mer d'Azov.
1850.   3117, 7836
Plans de golfes, baies, ports et rades de la Mer
Noire et de la Mer d'Azov. 1830.   3116, 7835

Takaoka, Masaji.
Saishin chōsa chōkai banchi iri Dai Tōkyō
kubun chizu. [Greater Tokyo ward atlas
with street numbers and boundary lines
based on the latest surveys. 1934]   9970

Talbot, A. M. and Talbot, William John.
Atlas of South Africa. [1947?]   10160

Talbot, William John.
See Talbot, A. M., *and* Talbot, William John.

Tamayo, Jorge L., 1912–
Atlasgeográfico general de México. 1949.   18104
—— 2. ed. 1962.   18106

T'an, Hsi-ch'ou, and Lee, C. Y.
Atlas for the geology of Szechuan Province
and eastern Sikang. 1935.   9664

Tanganyika. *Dept. of Lands and Survey.*
Atlas of Tanganyika, East Africa. 3d ed.
1956.   10154a
Guide map of Dar es Salaam. 1957.   10154b

Tanganyika Territory. *Dept. of Lands and Mines.*
Survey Division.
Atlas of the Tanganyika Territory. 1942.   10153
—— 2d ed. 1948.   10154

Tanner, Henry Schenck, 1786–1858.
Atlas classica. [1840]   3289
Atlas of the United States. 1835.   1380
New American atlas. [1818]–23.   4462
—— 1819–21.   4463
—— 1823.   1374, 4523a
—— 1825.   3669
—— 1825–[33]   1376
—— 1839.   1382
New general atlas. 1828.   6061
New pocket atlas of the United States. 1828.   4524
New universal atlas. [1833–34]   4320
—— 1836.   774
—— 1839.   6086
—— 1842–[43]   788
—— 1843.   6099
—— 1844.   4324
—— 1846.   3553

Tardieu, Ambroise, 1788–1841.
Atlas de geografia universal. 1878.   6197
Atlas universel. 1842.   785, 786
—— 1861.   6144

Taride, *firm.*
Plan-guide de Paris. [1949] 8506

Tasmania. *Dept. of Lands and Surveys.*
Hobart and suburbs aerial survey maps.
[1954] 10184

Tasmania. *Directorate of Industrial Development.*
Regional planning atlas; economic resources
of Tasmania. 3d ed. [1954] 10181

Tasmania. *State Economic Planning Authority.*
Regional planning; economic resources of
Tasmania. 1945. 10179
Regional planning atlas; economic resources
of Tasmania. [2d ed.] 1947. 10180

Tassin, Nicolas, *d.* **1660.**
Cartes generales des provinces de France et
d'Espagne. 1633. 8453
Cartes generalles des royaumes & prouinces
de la Haulte et Basse Alemaigne. 1633. 8679
Description de tovs les cantons, villes, bovrgs,
villages et avtres particularitez dv pays des
Svisses. 1635. 3145
Plans et profils de tovtes les principales villes
et lieux considérables de France. 1634. 2948
—— 1636. 2949
—— 1638. 5216

Tassin, Nicolas, *and others.*
Cartes générales de tovtes les prouinces de
France. [1640–43] 453, 4023

Tastu, Joseph, 1787–1849.
See Buchon, Jean Alexandre C., 1789–1846,
and Tastu, Joseph, 1787–1849.

Tata Iron and Steel Company.
Economic guide to India. [1956] 9688

Tate, John C., *and* **Tate, Frank C.**
Atlas of Des Moines. 1899. 1709

Taunt, Henry William.
New map of the River Thames. 1873. 8200

Tauril-Pneumatik R. T.
Osztrák-Magyar Monarchia automobil-
térképe. [191–] 7938

Tavernier, Melchior, 1594–1665.
Carte d'Alemagne. 1635. 5249
Théâtre géographiqve dv royavme de France.
1638. 5222

Taylor, Frank Hamilton, 1846–
Automobile road book of New Jersey. [1901] 15676

Taylor, Frank J., 1894–
Our U.S.A., a gay geography. 1935. 11065

Taylor, George, *fl.* **1778,** *and* **Skinner, Andrew.**
Maps of the roads of Ireland. 1778. 8226
—— 2d ed. 1783. 8227

Taylor, Thomas, *fl.* **1670–1730.**
England exactly described. [1715] 2912
Gentlemans pocket companion. 1722. 5173

Taylor, Thomas Griffith, 1880–1963.
Atlas of contour and rainfall maps of Aus-
tralia. 1918. 10171
Atlas of environment and race. [1933] 5477c
Atlas of the provinces of Canada. [1948] 10374
Atlas of topographic control in Europe.
1940. 7745

Taylor, W. R.
Synthetical atlas of Europe. 1900. 2856
Synthetical atlas [of the British Isles] 1901–
1902. 2901

Teben'kov, Mikhail Dmitrievich, 1820–1872.
Атласъ съеверо западныхъ береговъ
Америки. [Atlas of the northwestern coast
of America.] 1852. 1229

Technical Publications, inc., *Kansas City, Mo.*
ABOS Marine Division.
Lake maps; a guide to water fun ... in mid-
America. [1965] 14140

Teesdale, Henry, and Company.
Improved edition of the new British atlas.
[1835] 2898
New general atlas. 1848. 796

Teeuw, A.
Atlas dialek pulau Lombok. 1951. 9760
Dialect-atlas van Lombok. 1951. 9761

Tegengren, Felix Reinhold.
Iron ores and iron industry of China. Atlas.
1921–23. 9515

Teikoku Shi-Chō-Son Chizu Kankō Kyōkai, *Tokyo.*
Aichi-ken Chita-gun Toyohama-chō tochi
hōten. [Cadastral atlas of Toyohama,
Chita-gun, Aichi Prefecture. 1959] 10003
Kanagawa-ken Ashigarakami-gun Ōi-machi
tochi hōten. [Cadastral atlas of Oi,
Ashigarakami-gun, Kanagawa Prefecture.
1959] 9938
Kanagawa-ken Hiratsuka-shi, Asahi, Kaname
chiku tochi hōten. [Cadastral atlas of Asahi
and Kaname areas of Hiratsuka, Kanagawa
Prefecture. 1959] 9875

Teikoku Shoin, *Tokyo.*
Kihan Nihon dai chizu. [Standard atlas of
Japan. 1957] 9840
Saishin Nihon shi seizu. [New detailed histori-
cal atlas of Japan. 1954] 9796

Teixeira, João, *fl.* **1602–1648.**
Taboas geraes de toda a navegaçaõ. 1630.   5931

Teixeira, Pedro, 1575–1640.
Topographia de la villa de Madrid ... 1656.
1943.   9346

Teleki, Pál, *Gróf,* **1879–1941.**
Atlas zur Geschichte der Kartographie der
Japanischen Inseln. 1909.   4074
Some economic maps. 1930.   5467

Telford, Thomas, 1757–1834.
Atlas to the life of Thomas Telford. 1838.   8077
Charts and plans ... relative to the communication between England and Ireland.
[1809]   8076

Tellier, L.
Atlas historique du Nouveau Testament.
[1945]   5373

Tennessee. *Dept. of Highways. Research and Plan-*
ning Division.
Tennessee county traffic maps showing 1965
average daily traffic. [1966?]   17068

Tennessee. *Division of Water Resources.*
Tennessee hydrologic atlas. 1963–65.   17069

Tennessee Electric Power Company.
Distribution record map of Chattanooga.
1931.   17093

Tennessee Valley Authority. *Land Planning and*
Housing Division.
Atlas of the Tennessee Valley region. 1936.   11179
Cartographic summary of United States census
data, 1930. 1936.   11180
—— 1935. 1937.   11181

Tennessee Valley Authority. *Maps and Surveys*
Branch.
Navigation charts, Tennessee River Reser-
voirs. [1957]   11183

Tenney, Lucius E.
See Robinson, Elisha, *and* Tenney, Lucius E.

Teodorescu, C.
Atlas geografic. [1924]   6569

Terminal Engineering Corporation.
Proposed harbor and industrial terminal for
Greater Miami District. [1930]   11896

Ternay, Charles Gabriel d'Arsac, *Marquis* **de, 1771–**
1813.
Atlas du Traité de tactique. [1832]   7732

Terrell, John J.
Mileage table number ... wholly within the
State of Texas. 1965.   17137
Texas highway distance atlas. 1965.   17136

Tesnière, Lucien, 1893–
Atlas linguistique pour servir à l'étude du duel
en Slovène. 1925.   9467

Tessin, Louise Dorothea, 1894–
Picture maps of South American countries.
1942.   18190

Texas. University. *Bureau of Business Research.*
Industrial atlas of Texas. 1964.   17126
—— 1965.   17127

Texas Bond Reporter.
Texas county and road district atlas. 1936.   17143

Texas Eastern Transmission Corporation. *Little Big*
Inch Division.
Products system maps. [1957]   10708

Thacker's Indian clear school atlas. [1922?]   6490

Thailand. *General Staff.*
[phënthi nëv khét khën ra:hv́ang phra:rax
anachăk pra:thes Sayam kăb pra:thes rax
Frängses-Indochin matra.—Map defining
the boundaries between the Kingdom of
Siam and the country of French Indo-
China. 1909?]   10075

Thalheimer, Mary Elsie.
Eclectic historical atlas. [1874]   153, 154
—— [1885]   155

Thauren, Johannes, 1892–
Atlas der katholischen Missionsgeschichte.
1932.   5419

Therbu, L.
[Les plans de la Guerre de Sept Ans. 1789–
91]   3979

Thesaurus geographicus. 1695.   4269

Thibedeau, Joseph Edwin, *and* **Markwart, Leo Louis.**
Sportsman maps of the UP [*i.e.,* Upper Peninsula, Mich. 1952]   14574

Thiele, R. A.
IRO–Taschenatlas. [1943]   7165

Thiers, Adolphe, *i.e.,* **Marie Joseph Louis Adolphe,**
1797–1877.
Atlas de l'Histoire du Consulat et de l'Empire.
1859.   2982, 7719
—— 1875.   7720

Thomas, A., and Company.
National road atlas of Great Britain. [1954]   8060

Thomas, Frederic Venard, 1912–
1936 directory, atlas, plat book, Hancock
County [Ill. 1936]   12260

Thomas, Lewis Francis, 1887–1950.
Trading areas and geographic regions: Atlas
of the United States. 1948.   10563

**Thomas, Lewis Francis, *and* Crisler, Robert Morris,
1921–**
Manual of the economic geography of the
United States. [1953]   10564

Thomas Brothers.
Alameda County [Calif.] popular street atlas.
1963.   11372
—— 1965.   11373
—— 1967.   11376
Alameda County [Calif.] street guide. 1951.   11368
—— [1965]   11374
Block book of Berkeley [Calif.] 1924.   11510
Block book of El Cerrito [Calif.] 1926.   11516
Block book of Oakland [Calif. 1922–24]   11560
Block book of Santa Barbara [Calif.] 1927.   11607
Complete commercial street atlas of Los
Angeles County [Calif.] 1957.   11409
Contra Costa County [Calif.] popular street
atlas. 1965.   11382
—— 1967.   11383
East Bay area street guide. 1945.   11326
Golden Gate popular street atlas. 1961.   11628
—— 1965.   11629
—— 1967.   11630
King County [Wash.] popular street atlas.
1966.   17471
Los Angeles County [Calif.] popular street
atlas. 1963.   11417
—— 1964.   11419
—— 1965.   11421
—— 1966.   11422
Los Angeles County [Calif.] street guide.
[1963]   11418
Marin County [Calif.] street guide. 1965.   11425
Orange County [Calif.] popular street atlas.
1963.   11439
—— 1964.   11440
—— 1965.   11441
—— 1966.   11443
Pierce County [Wash.] popular street atlas.
1966.   17504
Popular atlas, Alameda County [Calif.]
1953.   11369
—— 1957.   11370
—— 1961.   11371
Popular atlas, Contra Costa County [Calif.]
1953.   11378
—— 1956.   11380
—— 1960.   11381
Popular atlas, King County [Wash.] 1954.   17468
Popular atlas, Los Angeles County [Calif.]
1946.   11397
—— 1949.   11400
—— 1950.   11401
—— 1951.   11402
—— 1952.   11404
—— 1953.   11406
—— 1954.   11407
—— 1956.   11408

—— 1957.   11410
—— 1959.   11412
—— 1960.   11415
—— 1961.   11416
Popular atlas, Marin County [Calif.] 1953.   11424
Popular atlas of Snohomish County [Wash.]
1956.   17518
Popular atlas, Orange County [Calif.] 1951.   11430
—— 1952.   11431
—— 1953.   11432
—— 1955.   11433
—— 1956.   11434
—— 1959.   11436
—— 1960.   11437
Popular atlas, Sacramento County [Calif.]
1960.   11450
Popular atlas, San Diego County [Calif.]
1951.   11459
—— 1954.   11460
—— 1956.   11461
—— 1960.   11462
Popular atlas, San Francisco. 1953.   11595
Popular atlas, San Mateo County [Calif.]
1953.   11471
Popular atlas, Santa Clara County [Calif.]
1952.   11479
—— 1955.   11481
Popular atlas, Sonoma County [Calif.] 1953.   11488
—— 1957.   11489
—— 1961.   11490
Popular street atlas, Orange County [Calif.]
1961.   11438
Popular street atlas, San Diego County, Calif.
1961.   11463
Property zone atlas, Los Angeles County
[Calif.] 1946.   11398
Riverside County [Calif.] popular street atlas.
1964.   11447
—— 1965.   11448
—— 1967.   11449
Sacramento County [Calif.] popular street
atlas. 1963.   11451
—— 1965.   11452
—— 1967.   11453
San Bernardino County [Calif.] popular street
atlas. 1964.   11454
—— 1965.   11455
—— 1967.   11456
San Diego County [Calif.] popular street atlas.
1964.   11464
—— 1965.   11465
—— 1966.   11466
—— 1967.   11467
San Francisco County auto street guide.
1961.   11596
San Francisco street atlas. [1952]   11594
San Francisco street guide. [1965]   11598
San Mateo County [Calif.] auto street guide.
1961.   11472
San Mateo County [Calif.] street guide. 1949.   11470
Santa Clara County [Calif.] auto street guide.
1961.   11482

Santa Clara County [Calif.] street guide.
1950. 11478
—— 1952. 11480
Snohomish County [Wash.] popular street
atlas. 1966. 17520
Sonoma County [Calif.] popular street atlas.
1964. 11491
—— 1965. 11492
Street guide, Los Angeles County [Calif.]
1951. 11403
Street guide of Greater Los Angeles [Calif.]
1947. 11542
Street guide of Los Angeles [Calif.] 1945. 11541
Street guide, San Diego County [Calif.] 1951. 11458
Ventura County [Calif.] popular street atlas.
1965. 11501
—— 2d ed. 1966. 11502

Thompson, Arthur Beeby.
Oil–field atlas. 1952. 5773

Thompson, George Alexander.
See Arrowsmith, Aaron, 1750–1823. Atlas to
Thompson's Alcedo. 1816–[17]

Thompson, K. R., Company.
Atlas of Clay County, Minn. 1957. 14955
Atlas of Dodge County, Minn. 1956. 14976
Atlas of Glenn County, Calif. 1962. 11385
Atlas of Kittson County, Minn. 1959. 15021
—— 1966. 15022
Atlas of Marshall County, Minn. 1956. 15034
—— 1964. 15035
Atlas of Pennington County and Red Lake
County, Minn. 1957. 15074
Atlas of Red Lake County and Pennington
County, Minn. 1957. 15084
Atlas of Winneshiek County, Iowa. 1958. 14077

Thompson, Thomas H.
Offical historical atlas of Tulare County
[Calif.] 1892. 11497

Thompson, Thomas H., and Company.
Historical atlas of Sonoma County, Cal.
1877. 1465

Thompson, Thomas S.
Coast pilot for the Upper Lakes. 1861. 1297

Thompson and Everts.
Combination atlas map of Henry County,
Iowa. 1870. 1670
Combination atlas map of Johnson County,
Iowa. 1870. 1677
Combination atlas map of Kane County, Ill.
1872. 3722
Combination atlas map of Stephenson
County, Ill. 1871. 1569

Thompson and Thomas.
Peoples' popular atlas of the world. [1903] 6311

Thompson and West.
Historical atlas map of Santa Clara County,
Cal. 1876. 1464
Official and historical atlas map of Alameda
County, Cal. 1878. 1460

Thompson Brothers and Burr.
Combination atlas map of Du Page County,
Ill. 1874. 12195
Combination atlas map of Will County, Ill.
1873. 12555

Thomson, John.
New general atlas. 1817. 731
—— 1821. 3545
—— 1827. 750

Thomson, John, and Company.
Atlas of Scotland. 1832. 8208

Thorne, Alexander Thomson Crago, 1887–
Atlas of Tulsa, Okla. 1937–61. 16635
Plat book, city of Tulsa [Okla.] and vicinity.
1920. 16633

Thornthwaite, Charles Warren, 1899–1963.
Atlas of climatic types in the United States,
1900–1939. 1941. 10502

Thornton, John.
Atlas maritimus. [1700?] 3455

Thorpe, Percy Henry.
Austin Road atlas of Great Britain. [1955] 8061
—— 3d ed. [1956] 8063
—— 4th ed. [1957] 8065
"Geographia" A l atlas of Glasgow. [1954] 8216
"Geographia" A l atlas of Leeds. [1954] 8152
"Geographia All in one" map guide, festival
London. [1951] 8190

Ti t'u ch'u pan shê.
Chung-hua jên min kung ho kuo fên shêng
ching t'u. [Detailed provincial atlas of the
People's Republic of China. Popular ed.]
1955. 9611
Chung-hua jên min kung ho kuo ti t'u chi.
[Atlas of the People's Republic of China
(Premier edition)] 1957. 9617
Chung-kuo fên shêng ti t'u. [Provincial atlas
of China. 195–] 9588
—— [De luxe ed. 195–] 9589
—— [Pocket ed. 1953?] 9605
—— [De luxe ed. 1957?] 9618
Chung-kuo ti li chiao hsüeh t'u; ch'u chung
shih yung. [Texbook—atlas of China for
junior high schools] 1953. 9513

Tideman, Philip L., 1926–
See Brown, Robert Harold, 1921–   *and*
Tideman, Philip L.,   1926–

Tidens världsatlas. [1952] 7537
—— 31:a–35:a tusendet. [1953] 7582

T'ien hsia tsung yü t'u. [World atlas. 16—]   9542

Tiessen, Ernst, 1871–1949.
Deutscher Wirtschaftsatlas. [1929–30]   8553
Seehafenverkehr und Binnenschiffahrt im
Deutschen Reich 1913 und 1922. 1925.   8554

Tillman and Fuller Publishing Company.
Illustrated plat book of Vanderburgh and
Warrick Counties, Ind. [1899?]   1632, 1635

Tillotson, Miles Davis, 1839–
Kandul's Tillotson pocket map and street
guide of Chicago and suburbs. 1919.   12615
—— 1921.   12618
—— 1922.   12621
—— 1923.   12623
—— 1924.   12627
—— 1925.   12629
—— 1926.   12632
—— 1929.   12641
Pocket atlas and guide of Chicago. 1893.   1589
Pocket map and street guide of Chicago and
Evanston [Ill.] 1895.   12599
Pocket map & street guide of Chicago and
suburbs. 1900.   12602
—— 1903.   12606
—— 1904–[1905]   12608
—— 1909.   3734
—— 1910.   3736
—— 1913.   4597
—— 1914.   12613

Time, the Weekly News–Magazine.
Atlas of the war. [1940]   5901
World and America; atlas of history maps.
[1944]   5578

The Times, _London._
Times Atlas. 1895.   4373
—— 1897.   6281
—— 1900.   1059
Times Atlas of the world. v. 3. 1955.   7622
Times Survey atlas of the world. 1920–[22]   6430
—— 1922.   6507
Time War atlas. [1914–15]   4247
—— Supplement to the Times War atlas.
[1915]   4248

Times Atlas and gazetteer of the world. [1933] 6796

Times Handy atlas. [1935]   6833

Tindal, Nicolas, 1687–1714.
Maps and plans of Tindal's continuation of
Rapin's History of England. [1785–89?]   2886

Ting, Ch'a-an.
Hsin Chung-hua chung têng pên kuo ti t'u.
Ch'u pan. [New atlas of China for high
schools. 1st ed. 1930]   9562

Ting, Jih-ch'ang.
See Tsêng, Kuo-fan, 1811–1872, _and_ Ting,
Jih-ch'ang.

Ting, Wên-chiang, 1887–1936.
Chung-hua min kuo hsin ti t'u. [New atlas of
the Republic of China. 1934]   9569
Chung-kuo fên shêng hsin t'u. [New provincial
atlas of China. 1st ed. 1933]   9564
—— [2d ed. 1934]   9570
—— [4th ed. 1939]   9577
—— [5th rev. ed. 1948]   9586, 9587

Tippets-Abbett-McCarthy-Stratton.
Comprehensive arterial highway plan, Cuyahoga County, Ohio. 1955.   16401

Tirion, Isaak, _d._ 1769?
Atlas van Zeeland. 1760.   3090
Nieuwe en beknopte hand-atlas. [1730–69]   4282
—— 1744–[69]   600
Nieuwe en keurige reis-atlas door de XVII
Nederlanden. 1793.   3083

Tissandier, Th. L. Leon de.
Additions to ... Atlas of the city of Rockford
and vicinity ... Ill. [1930]   12714
Atlas of the city of Rockford and vicinity ...
Ill. 1917.   12713

Tissot, Charles Joseph, 1828–1884.
Atlas de la province romaine d'Afrique.
1891.   10156

Title Abstract Company.
Map of Missoula, Mont. [1951]   15336

Title Atlas Company.
Atlas of Allamakee County, Iowa. 1964.   13051
Atlas of Benton County, Iowa. 1967.   13084
Atlas of Bremer County, Iowa. 1965.   13116
Atlas of Brown County, Kans. 1964.   14153
Atlas of Chickasaw County, Iowa. 1967.   13235
Atlas of Clayton County, Iowa. 1964.   13266
Atlas of Custer County, Nebr. 1964.   15400
Atlas of Dubuque County, Iowa. 1967.   13363
Atlas of Frontier County, Nebr. 1964.   15441
Atlas of Furnas County, Nebr. 1964.   15443
Atlas of Gosper County, Nebr. 1964.   15455
Atlas of Hancock County, Iowa. 1967.   13468
Atlas of Marshall County, Iowa. 1967.   13720
Atlas of Muscatine County, Iowa. 1967.   13788
Atlas of Nemaha County, Kans. 1964.   14191
Atlas of Scott County, Iowa. 1966.   13924
Atlas of Valley County, Nebr. 1964.   15612

Titus, C. O.
Altas of St. Joseph County, Mich. 1872.   3808

Tōa Kenkyūjo, _Tokyo._
Nampō chiiki shigen tōkei chizu. [Statistical
atlas of natural resources in regions south
of Japan. 1942]   9481

Tōbunsha, *Tokyo.*
Poketto bunken chizuchō. [Pocket prefectural
atlas. 1957] 9841
—— [1959] 9848
Sentoraru Tōkyō-to kubun chizu. [Ward atlas
of Central Tokyo. 1958] 9990

Todleben, Eduard Ivanovich, *Graf,* **1818–1884.**
Atlas der Karten und Plaene zu der Beschrei-
bung der Vertheidigung von Sebastopol.
1864. 3105
Atlas der Plane und Zeichnungen zu der
Beschreibung der Vertheidigung von
Sebastopol. 1864. 3106
Défense de Sébastopol. 1863. 3104

Toeppen, Max Polluz, 1822–1893.
Atlas zur Historisch-comparativen Geographie von Preussen. 1858. 3040

Tofiño de San Miguel, Vicente, 1732–1795.
[Atlas hidrografico de las costas de España en
el Mediterraneo. 1788] 5285, 9305
Atlas maritimo de España. 1789. 9306
—— 1789–[1803] 3133, 9307

Tokushu Chizu Kyōkai, *Osaka.*
Ayabe-shi. [Ayabe real estate atlas. 1959] 9861
Fukuchiyama-shi. [Fukuchiyama real estate
atlas. 1959] 9866
Gobō-shi sangyō jūtaku annaizu. [Gobo real
estate atlas. New ed. 1958?] 9868
Hashimoto-shi. [Hashimoto real estate atlas]
1958. 9870
Higashi-[Nishi-] Maizuru. [Maizuru real estate
atlas. 1958] 9911
Hikone-shi. [Hikone real estate atlas. 1958] 9872
Ise-shi jūtaku annai zuchō. [Ise real estate
atlas. 1958?] 9882
Kainan-shi zensangyō jūtaku annai zuchō.
[Kainan real estate atlas. 1958] 9886
Katsuyama-shi, Fukui-ken, zensangyō jūtaku
annai zuchō. [Katsuyama, Fukui Prefecture,
real estate atlas. New ed. 1959] 9893
Kei-Han-Shin jūtaku annaizu, Takatsuki-shi.
[Kyoto-Osaka-Kobe real estate atlas, Taka-
tsuki City. 1957?] 9968
Komatsu-shi zensangyō jūtaku annai zuchō.
[Komatsu real estate atlas. 1958] 9905
Kuwana-shi. [Kuwana real estate atlas.
1958] 9908
Matsuzaka-shi jūtaku annai zuchō. [Matsu-
zaka real estate atlas] 1958. 9914
Nabari-shi sangyō jūtaku annai zuchō. [Nabari
real estate atlas. 1958] 9921
Nagahama-shi. [Nagahama real estate atlas.
1959] 9922
Nagaoka-shi. [Nagaoka real estate atlas.
1959] 9924
Obama-shi. [Obama real estate atlas. 1959] 9937
Omihachiman-shi. [Omihachiman real estate
atlas. New ed. 1959] 9941
Ōno-shi, Fukui-ken, zensangyō jūtaku annai

zuchō. [Ono, Fukui Prefecture, real estate
atlas. New ed. 1959] 9942
Sabae-shi, Fukui-ken, zensangyō jūtaku annai
zuchō. [Sabae, Fukui Prefecture, real estate
atlas. New ed. 1959] 9952
Sakai-shi zensangyō jūtaku annai zuchō.
[Sakai real estate atlas. 1958] 9955
Shingū-shi sangyō jūtaku annai zuchō. [Shingu
real estate atlas] 1958. 9959
Sumoto-shi. [Sumoto real estate atlas. 1959] 9962
Tanabe-shi sangyō jūtaku annaizu. [Tanabe
real estate atlas. New ed. 1957?] 9969
Toyook-shi [Toyooka real estate atlas.
1959] 10007
Tsu-shi jūtaku annai zuchō. [Tsu real estate
atlas. 1958?] 10008
Tsuruga-shi. [Tsuruga real estate atlas. 1959] 10010
Ueno-shi jūtaku annai zuchō. [Ueno real estate
atlas. 1958?] 10012
Yokkaichi-shi sangyō jūtaku annai zuchō.
[Yokkaichi real estate atlas. 1958] 10021

**Tokyo. Central Meteorological Observatory of
Japan.**
Climatic atlas of Japan. 1943. 9788
Climatographic atlas of Japan. [1948] 9789
—— 1948–49. 9790

Tōkyō Chikeisha.
Konsaisu Dai Tōkyō chizu. [Concise map of
Greater Tokyo. 1935] 9971

Tōkyō Chizu Kabushiki Kaisha.
Yokohama-shi kubun chizu. [Yokohama ward
atlas. 1954] 10022

Tōkyō Chizu Shuppan Kabushiki Kaisha.
Kyapitaru, ōgata, Tōkyō-to saishin kubun
chizuchō. [Large size, new ward atlas of
Metropolitan Tokyo. 1958?] 9991
—— [1959] 9998
Kyapitaru Tōkyō-to kubun chizuchō. [Ward
atlas of Metropolitan Tokyo] 1956. 9986
—— [1959] 9999
Poketto-gata Tōkyō-to kubun chizu, 23-ku.
[Pocket ward atlas of Metropolitan Tokyo,
23 wards. 195–] 9974
Shichō kannaibetsu Hokkaidō chizuchō. [Pre-
fectural atlas of Hokkaido. 1958] 10032

Tokyo Geographical Society.
Geological atlas of eastern Asia. 1929. 9482

Toledo Metropolitan Housing Authority.
Real property survey, Toledo, Ohio. [1939] 16569

Tolnay, Dezsö.
See Irmédi-Molnár, László, 1895– *and*
Tolnay, Dezsö.

Toławiński, Konstanty, 1877–
Nowy atlas geologiczny Borysławia. 1930. 9140

Tongg Publishing Company.
Honolulu map, including rural Oahu.   [1961]   11997
—— [1965]   11999

[Tongguk chido. Atlas of Korea] [MS. 184–]   10045

Tongguk p'alto taech'ongdo. [Eight provinces of
Korea. 1568–1619]   10044

Tonnema en Compagnie.
Nederland; King atlas voor school en toerisme.
[2. druk. 1936]   9060

Tornau, Nikolaï Nikolaevich, Baron, 1848–
Учебный историческій атласъ. [Historical
school atlas.] 1893.   3324

Torres Gómez, Juan, *and* Perez Garcia, Jacinto.
Atlas de geografia postal de España. 1933.   9315

Tōsei Shuppan Kabushiki Kaisha.
Dai Nihon bunken chizu narabini chimei
sōran. [Prefectural atlas of Japan with gazetteer. 1953]   9831
—— [1955]   9837
—— [1956]   9838
—— [1957]   9842
—— [1959]   9849

Tosević, Dimitrije J.
World crisis in maps. [1949]   5678
—— [1954]   5679

Touring Club Argentino.
Atlas de las carreteras de la República Argentina. 1927.   18209

Touring Club do Brasil.
Rio de Janeiro. [1948?]   18317

Touring Club Italiano.
Atlante automobilistico d'Italia. 1935–36.   8971
Atlante d'Italia as 500.000. 1939.   8988
Atlante internazionale. [2. ed.] 1928.   6691
—— [3. ed.] 1929.   6715
—— 4. ed. 1933.   6805
—— 5. ed. 1936.   6898
—— 5. ed. 1. ristampa. 1938.   6967
—— 5. ed. 2. ristampa. 1938.   6968
—— 1951.   7486
Atlante stradale d'Italia. [1920–25]   8967
Bonniers Stora världsatlas. [1951]   7487
Centottantacinqve piante schematiche di città
ad vso dell'avtomobilista. 1936.   8949
Gyldendals Verdensatlas. [1951]   7488
Piante di attraversamento di 170 città. 1956.   8950

Touring Club Suisse.
Europa touring. 4.éd. [1929]   7761
—— 8.éd. [1930]   7764
—— [10.éd. 1932]   7765
—— [1934]   7766
—— [1936]   7767

—— [1939]   7768
—— [1940]   7769

Tōwa Shōkai, *Osaka*.
Fujiidera-machi zenjūtaku annai zuchō.
[Fujiidera real estate atlas. 1958]   9865
Kashihara-shi. [Kashihara real estate atlas.
1958]   9891
Kawachinagano-shi zenjūtaku annai zuchō.
[Kawachinagano real estate atlas. 1958]   9895

Toyokawa Shiyakusho.
Toyokawa toshi keikaku zu. [City plan of
Toyokawa. 1958]   10005

Träger, Richard.
Charlottenburger Grundschulatlas. [1927]   8855

Traffic Safety League.
Maps of suburban and rural additions, Fort
Wayne, Ind. [1959]   12963
—— Rev. ed. 1960.   12964
—— Rev. ed. [1965]   12965

Transportkroniek.
Nijverheids- en handels-atlas der Belgische
waterwegen. 1951.   7949

Transvaal Automobile Club.
Road maps for the Transvaal, etc. 1917.   10162

Trausel, W.
Kronlandsatlas für Böhmen. 1913.   8251

Travieso, Carlos, 1865–
Montevideo en la época colonial. 1937.   18402

Treat Brothers.
Pocket atlas of Lenawee County [Mich.]
1906.   1985

Tregear, Thomas R., *and* Berry, Leonard, 1930–
Development of Hong Kong and Kowloon as
told in maps. [1st ed.] 1959.   9678

Trietsch, Davis, 1870–
Palaestina Wirtschaftsatlas. 1925.   9767

Trinidad. *Registrar-General's Dept.*
Colony of Trinidad and Tobago census album.
1948.   18184

Trinidad and Tobago. *Central Statistical Office.*
Population census, 1960 … Maps showing
enumeration districts. 1964.   18185

Trinity House, *London*.
Maps and particulars of the lighthouse districts … [British Isles] 1902.   8085
—— 1913.   8086

Trolley Press.
Travelers atlas-guide to New England. 1910.   3696
—— 1911.   3698

—— 1912.	11051
—— 1913.	4530
—— 1914.	11053

Trondhjems historiske forening.
See Koren. Kristian Brinch, 1863–

Troutman, Arthur.
Oil & gas fields of the Rio Grande Valley in District 4 of South Texas. [1956] 17291

Trudel, Marcel.
Atlas historique du Canada Français. 1961. 10354

Trzaska, Evert, i Michalski.
Atlas kieszonkowy. Wyd 2. 1951. 7489

Ts'ao, Kuang-ch'üan, *fl.* **1900.**
Ch'i-hsien yü ti t'u shou. [Atlas of Ch'i-hsien. 1901] 9666

Tscheu Publishing Company.
Trading area rural route maps, Malheur County, Oreg. [1958] 16705

Tsêng, Kuo-fan, 1811–1872.
Chiang-hsi ch'üan shêng yü t'u. [Complete provincial atlas of Kiangsi. 1868] 9644

Tsëng, Kuo-fan, *and* **Ting, Jih-ch'ang.**
Chiang-su ch'üan shêng yü t'u. [Complete atlas of Kiangsu Province. 1868] 9647

T'sersteuens,——
Cartes descriptions générales et particulières. MS. [1726] 570

Tso, Chün-hêng.
Kuang yü t'u. [Enlarged terrestrial atlas of China. 1368–1644] MS. 9535

Tso, Hsüeh-lü.
See F'êng, Ch'ing-wei, *and* Tso, Hsüeh-lü.

Tsou, Hsing-chü.
Ch'un ch'iu Chan-kuo ti t'u. [Atlas of the Ch'un Ch'iu period and of the Warring States. 1912] 9525

T͡Sviich, Iovan.
See Cvijić, Jovan, 1865–1927.

T͡Sylov, Nikolaĭ Ivanovich, 1801–1879.
Атласъ Города Царскаго Села. [Atlas of the city of Tsarskoe Selo. 1857–58] 9295
Атласъ тринадцати частей С. Петербурга. [Atlas of the thirteen sections of St. Petersburg] 1849. 9293

T'u, Ssŭ-ts'ung.
Chung-hua tsui hsin hsing shih t'u. [New topographical atlas of China. 1938] 9575
—— [1941] 9579

Tucker, Sara Julia Jones, 1907–
Indian villages of the Illinois country ... Atlas. 1942. 10301

Türke, Juan.
Atlas de Chile. 1895. 2757

Tung, Fan-li, *fl.* **1832.**
Huang ch'ing ti li t'u. [Geographical atlas of China in the Ch'ing period. 1856] 9553

T'ung, Shih-hêng.
Chung-kuo hsing shih i lan t'u, fu shuo. [Political atlas of China, with appendixes. 1933] 9565
Hsiu chên Chung-hua hsin yü t'u. [New pocket atlas of China. 1st ed. 1916] 9560
—— [11th ed. 1926] 9561a

Tung fang hsüeh hui.
Hsin-chiang ch'üan shêng yü ti t'u. [Provincial atlas of hsin-chiang. 1909] 9625

Tunis en poche. [194–] 10159

Tunisie; atlas historique, géographique, économique.
1936. 10158

Tunison, Henry Cuthbert, 1855–
Atlas. 1901. 1072

Tunnicliff, William, *fl.* **1787–1791.**
Topographical survey of the counties of Hants, Wilts, Dorset, Somerset, Devon, and Cornwall. 1791. 2923

Tupper, Edward James.
Plat book of Knox County, Ill. 1948. 12323

Turčín, Rudolf.
Příruční atlas SSSR. [Vyd. 1] 1951. 9257

Turco Greco, Carlos A.
Cátalogo cartográfico de la República Argentina. [1967] 18236

Turist, *Belgrad.*
Spisak ulica i plan Beograda. [1952] 9473

Turist, *Fiume.*
Plan grada Rijeke sa popisom ulica i trgova. [1952] 9474

Turkey. *Millî Eğitim Bakanlığı.*
İlkokul coğrafya atlası. 5. basılış. 1942. 7119
—— 5. basılş. 1945. 7225
—— 7. basılş. 1947. 7286
—— 8. basılş. [1948?] 7328
—— 9. basılş. [1949?] 7376
Orta atlas. 1. basılış. 1947. 7287

Turner, Charles Heber.
Dollar atlas. [1890] 962
—— Peerless atlas. [1889] 955
Twentieth century peerless atlas. [1903] 1089

Turner, Harry, and Associates.
Distorted beef maps. 1963.   10448
Distorted maps. [10-year average production
of wheat, corn, rye, and sorghum, and
population in the U.S.] 1958.   10449
—— [Maps show new tractors on farms,
crop land harvested, number of farms 180
acres or more in 1965] 1965.   10450

Turney, Omar A.
Salt River valley. 1908.   3702

Tuttle, Frank W., *and* Pike, Daniel W.
Atlas of Kansas City and vicinity. 1908.   2103

Tuttle and Pike.
Atlas of Chariton County, Mo. 1915.   4838
Atlas of Lafayette County, Mo. [1914]   4855
Atlas of Linn County, Mo. 1915.   4857

Tuttle-Ayers-Woodward Company.
Atlas of Kansas City, Mo., and environs.
1925.   15256

Tyson, J. Washington.
Atlas of ancient and modern history. 1845.   156

Tyszkiewicz, Michel, 1858–
Cartes de l'Ukraine. 1919.   9289

Uetrecht, Erich, 1879–
See Krauss, Paul, 1861–   *and* Uetrecht,
Erich, 1879–

Uhl, John B.
Official atlas of Lucas County, Ohio. 1900.   2396

Uhlik, Josip J.
Atlas Federativne Narodne Republike
Jugoslavije. 1952.   9471

Ullitz, Hugo, *and others.*
Atlas of Suffolk County, Long Island, N.Y.
1902–1909.   2255, 3842

Ullstein, *firm.*
Europa Atlas. [1955]   7814
Kriegs–Atlas. [1916]   5846
—— [1918]   5847
Unser Europa. [1954]   7812
Weltatlas. [1923]   6534

Umlauft, Friedrich, 1844–1923.
See Hannak, Emanuel, 1841–1899, *and*
Umlauft, Friedrich, 1844–1923.

Umpqua Enterprises.
Boating & fishing maps [of Oregon. 1961]   16641

Unat, Faik Resit, 1899–
See Selen, Hâmit Sadi, *and* Unat, Faik Resit,
1899–

Union Automobile Club.
Touring atlas of the United States. [1927]   10796

Union Douanière Européenne.
Atlas économique de l'Europe. [1929]   7657

Union Postale Universelle. *Bureau International.*
Carte des lignes postales aériennes. 1929–
40.   5786
Conférence Aéropostale Européenne. Cartes-
annexes. 1933.   7746

Union Publishing Company.
Plat book of Bremer County, Iowa. 1894.   1647
Plat book of Butler County, Iowa. 1895.   1649
Plat book of Fayette County, Iowa. 1896.   1662
Plat book of Floyd County, Iowa. 1895.   1663
Plat book of Freeborn County, Minn. 1895.   2017

United Nations.
Census of traffic on main international traffic
arteries (1955) 1958.   7777

United Nations Command.
Armistice agreement. Maps. [Korea. 1953]   10050

**United Nations Conference on Food and Agriculture,
*Hot Springs, Va., 1943.***
Reference maps and charts. 1943.   5327

**United Nations Interregional Seminar on the Appli-
cation of Cartography for Economic Development, *Helsingør, Denmark.***
Informe sobre el estado de los trabajos carto-
gráficos en Colombia. 1965.   18349

U.S. *Adjutant General's Office.*
Atlas of ports, cities, and localities of the island
of Cuba. 1898.   2714

U.S. *Aeronautical Chart and Information Service.*
Pilot's handbook: Caribbean. [1946]   18159
Pilot's handbook: Europe. [1946]   7630
Pilot's handbook: North Atlantic. [1946]   10212

U.S. *Agricultural Conservation Program Service.*
Agricultural conservation program maps,
1955. 1957.   10451

U.S. *Alaska Railroad Commission.*
Railway routes in Alaska. 1913.   11234

U.S. *Antietam Battlefield Board.*
Atlas of the battlefield of Antietam. 1908.   10685

**U.S. *Army. American Expeditionary Force, 1917–
1918.***
Operations of American divisions in France.
1919.   8412

U.S. *Army. Caribbean Command.*
City plan, Panama City, Rep. of Panama.
[1954]   18150

U.S. *Army. Corps of Engineers.*

Alabama River, Alabama; navigation charts. 1958.	11228
Allegheny River navigation charts. [1960]	16943
Apalachicola, Chattahoochee and Flint Rivers. 1959.	11933
Atlas containing maps of Chicago River, Ill., and its branches. [1900]	1510, 4604, 12720
Atlas illustrating report ... of Board on examination and survey of Mississippi River. [1909]	3683
Baltimore District project maps. [1959]–60.	14330
Chicago harbor and adjacent waterways. 1913.	12669
Cumberland River, Cheatham Reservoir. 1954.	17115
—— Old Hickory Reservoir. [1954]	17116
Cumberland River survey for navigation. [1935]	11096
Detroit, Mich. District project maps. [1961]	14562
—— [1963]	14563
—— [1964]	14564
—— [1965]	14565
Encroachments and obstructions in the Chicago River and on the Chicago Lake front. 1918.	12721
Greenup locks and dam pool, Ohio River, topographic and property survey. 1959.	11165
Gulf Intracoastal Waterway, section from New Orleans, La. to Apalachee Bay, Fla. 1945.	11001
Hiwassee River, navigation charts. [1955]	17117
Intracoastal Waterway. 1948.	11002
—— 1951 [*i.e.*, 52]	11003
—— 1961.	11004
Intracoastal Waterway: Section from Sabine River to Brownsville, Tex. 1948.	11005
Kentucky River navigation charts. [1947]	14263
Map of a reconnaissance of the Mississippi River, from Cairo, Ill. to New Orleans, La. [1878?]	11100
Map of the Arkansas River, from Little Rock, Ark. to the mouth. 1886.	11089
Map of the Arkansas River, from Wichita, Kans to Fort Gibson, Ind'n Ter. 1889.	11090
Map of the Mississippi River from the Falls of St. Anthony to the junction of the Illinois River. 1887–88.	11103
Map of the Missouri River. [1882?]	11148
Map of the Ohio River. [1881]	11160
Map of the public lands under ferderal jurisdiction in the District of Columbia. [1916]	4551
Map of the White River from Forsyth, Mo. to the mouth. 1888.	11184
Map of the White River from its mouth to Bedford, Ind. [1878]	13002
Map of the Yellowstone River. [1878]	11187
Maps and diagrams ... along the Wisconsin River and Fox Rivers. [1876]	18032
Maps of Big Sunflower River in Mississippi. 1947.	15202
Maps of Red River from Fulton, Ark. to Mississippi River. 1947.	11175
Maps of Red River, from Index, Ark.-Tex. to Mississippi River. 1958.	11176

Maps of the Mississippi River, Angola, La. to the Head of Passes. [1938]	11112
Maps of the Mississippi River, Vicksburg, Miss. to Angola, La. [1940]	11116
Maps of the Yazoo, Tallahatchie and Coldwater Rivers in Mississippi. 1946.	15203
Middle Tennessee and Chattanooga campaigns ... 1863. [1891]	10671
Military maps. [1865–79]	10672
Military maps illustrating the operations of the armies of the Potomac & James, May 4, 1864 to April 9, 1865. [1869]	10673
Military maps of the United States. [1862–83]	10674
Military maps of the War of the Rebellion. [1865–79]	10675
Mississippi River levee and river charts, 1937, Cairo, Ill. to Rosedale, Miss. [1939]	11114
Mississippi River: Wisconsin River to Clarksville, Mo. [1943]	11121
Missouri River, mouth to Rulo, [Nebr. 1947]	11152
Missouri River, Yankton to Fort Buford. [1892–1933]	11149
Muskingum River, Ohio. 1934.	16582
Navigation charts, Cumberland River. [1947?]	11097
Navigation charts, Kanawha River, W.Va. 1938.	17629
—— [1963]	17630
Navigation charts, middle and upper Mississippi River. 1946.	11125
Navigation charts, Missouri River, Blair, Nebr. to mouth. [1959]	11153
Navigation charts of Tombigbee, Warrior and Black Warrior canalized system. [1954]	11229, 17118
Navigation charts, Ohio River, Huntington District. [1944–56]	11163
—— [1951–56]	11164
—— 1963.	11166
Navigation charts, Ohio River, Louisville District. [1943–51]	11161
Navigation charts, Ohio River, Pittsburgh District. [1944–47]	11162
Navigation charts, Snake River. 1960.	11178
Navigation charts, Tennessee River, Nashville District. [1946]	11182
Navigation maps of Gulf Intracoastal Waterway, New Orleans, La. to Apalachee Bay, Fla. 1948.	11006
—— 1956.	11007
Navigation maps of Gulf Intracoastal Waterway, Port Arthur to Brownsville, Tex. [1955]	11008
New York District project maps, flood control. [1955–56]	15830
—— [1959]	15831
—— [1961]	15832
—— [1964]	15833
New York District project maps, river and harbor. [1959]	15834, 15839
—— [1961]	15835
—— [1964]	15836

265

—— [1956]	15827
—— [1960]	15828
New York State barge canal system. [1964]	15829
South shore of Lake Erie. [1965]	16363
—— [2d ed.] 1966.	16364
West end of Lake Erie. [1963]	14556
—— [2d] ed. [1965]	14557

U.S. *Military Academy, West Point. Dept. of Military Art and Engineering.*

Atlas to accompany Steele's American campaigns. 1956.	10680
Civil War atlas to accompany Steele's American campaigns. [194–?]	10681
West Point atlas of American wars. [1959]	10639
West Point atlas of the Civil War. [1962]	10682

U.S. *Mississippi River Commission.*

Flood control and navigation maps of the Mississippi River, Cairo, Ill. to the Gulf of Mexico, La. 18th ed. [1950]	11130
—— 19th ed. [1951]	11131
—— 20th ed. [1952]	11133
—— 21st ed. [1953]	11135
—— 22nd ed. [1954]	11137
—— 23rd ed. [1955]	11138
—— 24th ed. [1956]	11139
—— 25th ed. [1957]	11140
—— 26th ed. [1958]	11142
—— 27th ed. [1959]	11143
—— 28th ed. [1960]	11144
—— 29th ed. [1961]	11145
—— 30th ed. [1962]	11146
Map of the lower Mississippi River. [1897]	11104
—— [1916]	11106
Map of the upper Mississippi River. [1915]	11105
—— [1928]	11107
Maps of Arkansas River in Arkansas. [1950]	11091
Maps of Ouachita and Black River, Arkansas and Louisiana. 1949.	11173
Maps of the Mississippi River, Cairo, Ill. to the Gulf of Mexico, La. [1934]	11108
—— 3d ed. [1935]	11109
—— 4th ed., rev. [1936]	11110
—— 5th ed., rev. [1937]	11111
—— 6th ed., rev. [1938]	11113
—— 7th ed., rev. [1939]	11115
—— 8th ed., rev. [1940]	11117
—— 9th ed., rev. [1941]	11119
—— 10th ed. [1942]	11120
—— 11th ed. [1943]	11122
—— 12th ed. [1944]	11123
—— 13th ed. 1945.	11124
—— 14th ed. 1946.	11126
—— 15th ed. 1947.	11127
—— 16th ed. 1948.	11128
—— 17th ed. 1949.	11129
Maps of the St. Francis River. [1946]	11177
Maps of the White River, Batesville, Ark. to the Mississippi River. 1946.	11186
Mississippi River hydrographic survey, 1937, Rosedale to Vicksburg, Miss. [1940]	11118
Mississippi River hydrographic survey, 1948–	

1949, mouth of Ark. River to Vicksburg, Miss. [1951]	11132
Mississippi River hydrographic survey, 1948–51 ... Vicksburg, Miss. to Angola, La. [1952]	11134
Mississippi River hydrographic survey, 1949–1952, Angola, La. to Head of Passes, La. [1953]	11136
Mississippi River hydrographic survey, 1961–1963, Cairo, Ill. to mouth of White River, Ark. 1964.	11147
Navigation maps of Intracoastal Waterway, Port Arthur, Tex. to New Orleans, La. [1942]	11009
—— 2d ed. [1944]	11010
—— 3d ed. [1946]	11011
—— 4th ed. [1948]	11012
—— 5th ed. [1951]	11013
—— 6th ed. 1954.	11014
—— 7th ed. 1956.	11015
—— 8th ed. 1958.	11016
—— 9th ed. 1960.	11017
—— 10th ed. 1962.	11018
—— 11th ed. 1964.	11019
—— 12th ed. 1966.	11020
Preliminary map of the lower Mississippi River. [1885]	11101
Survey of Mississippi River. 1885–92.	11102

U.S. *Missouri River Commission.*

Map of the Missouri River, from its mouth to Three Forks, Mont. [1895]	11150

U.S. *National Capital Planning Commission.*

Redevelopment plan, southwest redevelopment project. [1952]	11783

U.S. *National Recovery Administration.*

Geographic and population differentials in minimum wages. [1935]	10567
Study of natural areas of trade in the United States. [1935]	10568

U.S. *National Resources Planning Board.*

Altas ... to accompany the report of the Pecos River Joint Investigation. [1942]	11174

U.S. *Naval Oceanographic Office.*

Environmental atlas of the Tongue of the Ocean, Bahamas. 1967.	18162

See also U.S. *Hydrographic Office.*

U.S. *Office of Administrator, Bonneville Project.*

See U.S. *Bonneville Power Administration.*

U.S. *Office of Farm Management.*

Atlas of American agriculture. 1918.	4491

U.S. *Office of Foreign Agricultural Relations.*

Agricultural geography of Europe and the Near East. 1948.	7629

U.S. *Office of Naval Operations.*

U.S. life lines. [1948]	5469

U.S. *Production and Marketing Administration.*
Agricultural conservation program maps, 1946. 1948.   10466

U.S. *Public Health Service.*
[State maps locating hospitals. 1943?]   10700

U.S. *Selective Service System.*
Atlas of Selective Service local and appeal boards. 1946.   10445

U.S. *Soil Conservation Service.*
Lake Meade. [1935?]   11281
New York erosion and land-use conditions, Schuyler County [N.Y. 1940?]   15904
Soil survey, Acadia Parish, La. 1962.   14271
Soil survey, Adair County, Ky. 1964.   14235
Soil survey, Adair County, Okla. 1965.   16593
Soil survey, Adams County, Iowa. 1963.   13041
Soil survey, Adams County, Pa. 1967.   16768
Soil survey, Alamance County, N.C. 1960.   16214
Soil survey, Alameda area, Calif 1966.   11375
Soil survey, Allen County, Ohio. 1965.   16379
Soil survey, Amador area, Calif. 1965.   11377
Soil survey, and vegetation, northeastern Kodiak Island area, Alaska. 1960.   11241
Soil survey, area de Valle de Lajas ... Puerto Rico. 1965.   18183
Soil survey, Arenac County, Mich. 1967.   14606
Soil survey, Armstrong County, Tex. 1965.   17146
Soil survey, Aroostook County, Maine, northeastern part. 1964.   14309
—— Southern part. 1964.   14310
Soil survey, Bailey County, Tex. 1963.   17147
Soil survey, Baldwin County, Ala. 1964.   11193
Soil survey, Bamberg County, S.C. 1966.   16986
Soil survey, Bath County, Ky. 1963.   14236
Soil survey, Beaver County, Okla. 1962.   16594
Soil survey, Beaver Creek Area, Ariz. 1967.   11279
Soil survey, Berkeley County, W.Va. 1966.   17610
Soil survey, Beryl-Enterprise area, Utah. 1960.   17298
Soil survey, Bexar County, Tex. 1966.   17148
Soil survey, Bitterroot Valley area, Mont. 1959.   15337
Soil survey, Blount County, Tenn. 1959.   17070
Soil survey, Bluewater area, N.Mex. 1958.   15816
Soil survey, Bolivar County, Miss. 1958.   15175
Soil survey, Boone County, Mo. 1962.   15218
Soil survey, Bossier Parish, La. 1962.   14272
Soil survey, Bradley County, Ark. 1961.   11292
Soil survey, Bradley County, Tenn. 1958.   17071
Soil survey, Brazos County, Tex. 1958.   17150
Soil survey, Bremer County, Iowa. 1967.   13117
Soil survey, Brookings County, S.Dak. 1959.   17018
Soil survey, Brown County, Kans. 1960.   14152
Soil survey, Buffalo County, Wis. 1962.   17676
Soil survey, Caldwell County, Ky. 1966.   14237
Soil survey, Calhoun County, Ala. 1961.   11194
Soil survey, Calhoun County, Miss. 1965.   15176
Soil survey, Calhoun County, S.C. 1963.   16987
Soil survey, Camden County, N.J. 1966.   15690
Soil survey, Carbon County, Pa. 1962.   16774

Soil survey, Caroline County, Md. 1964.   14341
Soil survey, Carroll County, Ind. 1958.   12750
Soil survey, Carson County, Tex. 1962.   17151
Soil survey, Chambers County, Ala. 1959.   11195
Soil survey, Cherokee County, S.C. 1962.   16988
Soil survey, Cherokee County, Tex. 1959.   17153
Soil survey, Chicot County, Ark. 1967.   11293
Soil survey, Childress County, Tex. 1963.   17154
Soil survey, Cimarron County, Okla. 1960.   16596
Soil survey, Claiborne County, Miss. 1963.   15177
Soil survey, Clarion County, Pa. 1958.   16777
Soil survey, Clark County, Ky. 1964.   14238
Soil survey, Clark County, Ohio. 1958   16390
Soil survey, Clarke County, Miss. 1965.   15178
Soil survey, Clinton County, Ohio. 1962.   16393
Soil survey, Clinton County, Pa. 1966.   16778
Soil survey, Coahoma County, Miss. 1959.   15179
Soil survey, Cochran County, Tex. 1964.   17155
Soil survey, Codington County, S.Dak. 1966.   17026
Soil survey, Coffee County, Tenn. 1959.   17072
Soil survey, Columbia County, Pa. 1967.   16779
Soil survey, Comanche County, Okla. 1967.   16597
Soil survey, Cortland County, N.Y. 1961.   15876
Soil survey, Cotton County, Okla. 1963.   16598
Soil survey, Covington County, Miss. 1965.   15180
Soil survey, Crawford County, Wis. 1961.   17703
Soil survey, Creek County, Okla. 1959.   16599
Soil survey, Crosby County, Tex. 1966.   17156
Soil survey, Crow Wing County, Minn. 1965.   14964
Soil survey, Cullman County, Ala. 1962.   11196
Soil survey, Curry County, N.Mex. 1958.   15812
Soil survey, Dakota County, Minn. 1960.   14968
Soil survey, Dale County, Ala. 1960.   11197
Soil survey, Darlington County, S.C. 1960.   16989
Soil survey, Daviess County, Mo. 1964.   15226
Soil survey, Dawson County, Tex. 1960.   17162
Soil survey, De Kalb County, Ala. 1958.   11198
Soil survey, Delta-Montrose area, Colo. 1967.   11688
Soil survey, Deshutes area, Oreg. 1958.   16676
Soil survey, De Soto County, Miss. 1959.   15181
Soil survey, Deuel County, Nebr. 1965.   15413
Soil survey, Dewey County, Okla. 1963.   16600
Soil survey, Dodge County, Minn. 1961.   14974
Soil survey, Dorchester County, Md. 1963.   14346
Soil survey, Douglas County, Ga. 1961.   11937
Soil survey, Dundy County, Nebr. 1963.   15433
Soil survey, Duplin County, N.C. 1959.   16215
Soil survey, Dyer County, Tenn. 1965.   17073
Soil survey, Eastern Stanislaus area, Calif. 1964.   11494
Soil survey, Elbert County, Colo. 1966.   11656
Soil survey, Elliott County, Ky. 1965.   14239
Soil survey, Ellis County, Okla. 1966.   16601
Soil survey, Ellis County, Tex. 1964.   17163
Soil survey, Erie County, Pa. 1960.   16786
Soil survey, Escambia County, Fla. 1960.   11823
Soil survey, Fairbanks area, Alaska. 1963.   11239
Soil survey, Fairfax County, Va. 1963.   17350
Soil survey, Fairfield County, Ohio. 1960.   16410
Soil survey, Fayette and Union Counties, Ind. 1960.   12780

Soil survey, Fayette County, Ala. 1965. 11199
Soil survey, Fayette County, Tenn. 1964. 17074
Soil survey, Fillmore County, Minn. 1958. 14986
Soil survey, Finney County, Kans. 1965. 14165
Soil survey, Fisher County, Tex. 1966. 17164
Soil survey, Foard County, Tex. 1964. 17165
Soil survey, Ford County, Kans. 1965. 14166
Soil survey, Forsyth County, Ga. 1960. 11938
Soil survey, Fort Bend County, Tex. 1960. 17166
Soil survey, Fountain County, Ind. 1966. 12786
Soil survey, Franklin County, Ala. 1965. 11200
Soil survey, Franklin County, Mass. 1967. 14408
Soil survey, Franklin County, N.Y. 1958. 15879
Soil survey, Franklin County, Tenn. 1958. 17075
Soil survey, Fraser Alpine area, Colo. 1962. 11644
Soil survey, Frederick County, Md. 1960. 14348
[Soil survey] Fulton County, Ga. 1958. 11939
Soil survey, Fulton County, Ky. 1964. 14241
Soil survey, Gadsden County, Fla. 1961. 11824
Soil survey, Gage County, Nebr. 1964. 15450
Soil survey, Gaines County, Tex. 1965. 17167
Soil survey, Garfield County, Okla. 1967. 16602
Soil survey, Geary County, Kans. 1960. 14169
Soil survey, Gem County area, Idaho. 1965. 12034
Soil survey, Gloucester County, N.J. 1962. 15705
Soil survey, Gordon County, Ga. 1965. 11940
Soil survey, Grand Isle County, Vt. 1959. 17312
Soil survey, Grand Traverse County, Mich.
 1966. 14663
Soil survey, Grant County, Wis. 1961. 17750
Soil survey, Gray County, Tex. 1966. 17168
Soil survey, Greeley County, Kas. 1961. 14170
Soil survey, Greene County, Tenn. 1958. 17076
Soil survey, Greer County, Okla. 1967. 16604
Soil survey, Grenada County, Miss. 1967. 15182
Soil survey, Gwinnett County, Ga. 1967. 11941
Soil survey, Habersham County, Ga. 1963. 11942
Soil survey, Hall County, Nebr. 1962. 15462
Soil survey, Hall County, Tex. 1967. 17169
Soil survey, Hamilton County, Kans. 1961. 14172
Soil survey, Hansford County, Tex. 1960. 17170
Soil survey, Hardin County, Tenn. 1963. 17077
Soil survey, Harper County, Okla. 1960. 16605
Soil survey, Hart County, Ga. 1963. 11943
Soil survey, Hartford County, Conn. 1962. 11705
Soil survey, Haskell County, Tex. 1961. 17173
Soil survey, Henderson County, Ky. 1967. 14242
Soil survey, Henderson County, Tenn. 1960. 17078
Soil survey, Hillsborough County, Fla.
 1958. 11828
Soil survey, Hockley County, Tex. 1965. 17174
Soil survey, Holbrook-Show Low area, Ariz.
 1964. 11260
Soil survey, Hooker County, Nebr. 1964. 15472
Soil survey, Houston and Peach Counties, Ga.
 1967. 11944
Soil survey, Houston County, Tenn. 1958. 17079
Soil survey, Humboldt County, Iowa. 1961. 13519
Soil survey, Humphreys County, Miss. 1959. 15183
Soil survey, Ionia County, Mich. 1967. 14684
Soil survey, Iowa County, Iowa. 1967. 13542
Soil survey, Iowa County, Wis. 1962. 17768
Soil survey, Iredell County, N.C. 1964. 16216
Soil survey, Isanti County, Minn. 1958. 15005

Soil survey, Island County, Wash. 1958. 17461
Soil survey, Issaquena County, Miss. 1961. 15184
Soil survey, Jackson and Mason Counties,
 W.Va. 1961. 17611
Soil survey, Jackson County, Miss. 1964. 15185
Soil survey, Jackson County,Okla. 1961. 16606
Soil survey, Jefferson County, Iowa. 1960. 13574
Soil survey, Jefferson County, Ky. 1966. 14243
Soil survey, Jefferson County, Pa. 1964. 16788
Soil survey, Jefferson County, Tex. 1965. 17176
Soil survey, Judith Basin area, Mont. 1967. 15317
Soil survey, Kay County, Okla. 1967. 16608
Soil survey, Kearny County, Kans. 1963. 14177
Soil survey, Kenai-Kasilof area, Alaska.
 1962. 11240
Soil survey, Kimball County, Nebr. 1962. 15491
Soil survey, Kingfisher County, Okla. 1962. 16609
Soil survey, La Crosse County, Wis. 1960. 17805
Soil survey, Lafayette County, Wis. 1966. 17813
Soil survey, Lamb County, Tex. 1962. 17177
Soil survey, Lancaster County, Pa. 1959. 16791
Soil survey, Las Vegas and Eldorado Valleys
 area, Nev. 1967. 15653
Soil survey, Lawrence County, Ala. 1959. 11201
Soil survey, Lawrence County, Tenn. 1959. 17080
Soil survey, Lee County, S.C. 1963. 16990
Soil survey, Leflore County, Miss. 1959. 15186
Soil survey, Lehigh County, Pa. 1963. 16792
Soil survey, Lenawee County, Mich. 1961. 14718
Soil survey, Lewis County, N.Y. 1960. 15882
Soil survey, Lincoln County, Miss. 1963. 15187
Soil survey, Logan County, Kans. 1964. 14181
Soil survey, Logan County, Okla. 1960. 16610
Soil survey, Loudon County, Tenn. 1961. 17081
Soil survey, Loudoun County, Va. 1960. 17352
Soil survey, Love County, Okla. 1966. 16611
Soil survey, Lovelock area, Nev. 1965. 15654
Soil survey, Lucas County, Iowa. 1960. 13660
Soil survey, Lynn County, Tex. 1959. 17178
Soil survey, McIntosh County, Ga. 1961. 11945
Soil survey, McMinn County, Tenn. 1957. 17082
Soil survey, Madera area, Calif. 1962. 11423
Soil survey, Madison County, Ala. 1958. 11202
Soil survey ... Manatee County, Fla. 1958. 11832
Soil survey, Marion county, Tenn. 1958. 17083
Soil survey, Marlboro County, S.C. 1965. 16991
Soil survey, Marshall County, Ala. 1959. 11203
Soil survey, Marshall County, W.Va. 1960. 17613
Soil survey, Mason County, Wash. 1960. 17489
Soil survey, Mathews County, Va. 1962. 17353
Soil survey, Maury County, Tenn. 1959. 17084
Soil survey, Menard County, Tex. 1967. 17179
Soil survey, Merced area. Calif. 1962. 11427
Soil survey, Meriwether County, Ga. 1965. 11946
Soil survey, Merrimack County, N.H. 1965. 15658
Soil survey, Minnehaha County, S.Dak.
 1964. 17048
Soil survey, Moniteau County, Mo. 1964. 15239
Soil survey, Monona County, Iowa. 1959. 13755
Soil survey, Monroe County, Miss. 1966. 15188
Soil survey, Monroe County, W.Va. 1965. 17614
Soil survey, Montcalm County, Mich. 1960. 14752
Soil survey, Montgomery County, Ala. 1960. 11205
Soil survey, Montgomery County, Md. 1961. 14359

Soil survey, Montgomery County, Pa. 1967. 16798
Soil survey, Morton county, Kans. 1963. 14187
Soil survey, Nance County, Nebr. 1960. 15520
Soil survey, Newberry County, S.C. 1960. 16992
Soil survey, Newton County, Miss. 1960. 15189
Soil survey, Nicollet County, Minn. 1958. 15057
Soil survey, Norfolk County, Va. 1959. 17354
Soil survey, Northumberland and Lancaster Counties, Va. 1963. 17355
Soil survey, Nottoway County, Va. 1960. 17356
Soil survey, Nueces County, Tex. 1965. 17181
Soil survey, Oconee County, S.C. 1963. 16994
Soil survey, Ontario and Yates Counties, N.Y. 1958. 15897
Soil survey, Orange County, Fla. 1960. 11839
Soil survey, Ottawa County, Okla. 1964. 16613
Soil survey, Owen County, Ind. 1964. 12875
Soil survey, Panola County, Miss. 1963. 15190
Soil survey, Parke County, Ind. 1967. 12880
Soil survey, Pasquotank County, N.C. 1957. 16217
Soil survey, Paulding County, Ohio. 1960. 16442
Soil survey, Pawnee County, Okla. 1959. 16614
Soil survey, Penobscot County, Maine. 1963. 14313
Soil survey, Pepin County, Wis. 1964. 17869
Soil survey, Polk County, Iowa. 1960. 13864
Soil survey, Portales area, N.Mex. 1959. 15814
Soil survey, Potter County, Pa. 1958. 16800
Soil survey, Preston County, W.Va. 1959. 17615
Soil survey, Prince Edward County, Va. 1958. 17357
Soil survey, Prince Georges County, Md. 1967. 14364
Soil survey, Prinesville area, Oreg. 1966. 16671
Soil survey, Prowers County, Colo. 1966. 11666
Soil survey, Putnam County, Tenn. 1963. 17085
Soil survey, Queen Annes County, Md. 1966. 14365
Soil survey, Quitman County, Miss. 1958. 15191
Soil survey, Randolph County, Ala. 1967. 11206
Soil survey, Rappahannock County, Va. 1961. 17358
Soil survey, reconnaissance, Bayfield County, Wis. 1961. 17664
Soil survey, Red Willow County, Nebr. 1967. 15563
Soil survey, Reno County, Kans. 1966. 14195
Soil survey, Republic County, Kans. 1967. 14196
Soil survey, Richland County, Wis. 1959. 17897
Soil survey, Rockingham County, N.H. 1959. 15659
Soil survey, Roger Mills County, Okla. 1963. 16616
Soil survey, Rogers County, Okla. 1966. 16617
Soil survey, Roosevelt County, N.Mex. 1967. 15815
Soil survey, Roosevelt-Duchesne area, Utah. 1959. 17297
Soil survey, Ross County, Ohio. 1967. 16446
Soil survey, St. Francis County, Ark. 1966. 11301
Soil survey, St. Mary Parish, La. 1959. 14274
Soil survey, Saline County, Kans. 1959. 14198
Soil survey, Saluda County, S.C. 1962. 16995
Soil survey, San Juan area, Utah. 1962. 17299
Soil survey, San Juan County, Wash. 1962. 17508
Soil survey, San Mateo area, Calif. 1961. 11473
Soil survey, Sanilac County, Mich. 1961. 14810

Soil survey, Sarasota County, Fla. 1959. 11855
Soil survey, Sargent County, N.Dak. 1964. 16326
Soil survey, Saunders County, Nebr. 1965. 15584
Soil survey, Scotland County, N.C. 1967. 16219
Soil survey, Scott County, Ind. 1962. 12909
Soil survey, Scott County, Kans. 1965. 14199
Soil survey, Scott County, Minn. 1959. 15098
Soil survey, Seminole County, Fla. 1966. 11856
Soil survey, Seward County, Kans. 1965. 14201
Soil survey, Sharkey County, Miss. 1962. 15192
Soil survey, Shelby County, Iowa. 1961. 13938
Soil survey, Sherman County, Oreg. 1964. 16714
Soil survey, Skagit County, Wash. 1960. 17512
Soil survey, Somerset County, Md. 1966. 14368
Soil survey, southwest Quay area, N.Mex. 1960. 15813
Soil survey, Spalding County, Ga. 1964. 11948
Soil survey, Stanton County, Kans. 1961. 14203
Soil survey, Stephens County, Okla. 1964. 16618
Soil survey, Stevens County, Kans. 1961. 14204
Soil survey, Sunflower County, Miss. 1959. 15193
Soil survey, Suwannee County, Fla. 1965. 11857
Soil survey, Tate County, Miss. 1967. 15194
Soil survey, Tehama County, Calif. 1967. 11495
Soil survey, Terrebonne Parish, La. 1960. 14275
Soil survey, Terry County, Tex. 1962. 17185
Soil survey, Texas County, Okla. 1961. 16619
Soil survey, Thomas County, Nebr. 1965. 15606
Soil survey, Thurston County, Wash. 1958. 17531
Soil survey, Tift County, Ga. 1959. 11949
Soil survey, Tillamook area, Oreg. 1964. 16717
Soil survey, Tippah County, Miss. 1966. 15195
Soil survey, Tippecanoe County, Ind. 1959. 12929
Soil survey, Tolland County, Conn. 1966. 11707
Soil survey, Tompkins County, N.Y. 1965. 15915
Soil survey, Treasure County, Mont. 1967. 15319
Soil survey, Tri-county area, N.Dak. 1966. 16251
Soil survey, Trout Creek watershed, Colo. 1961. 11653
Soil survey, Tucker County [and] part of northern Randolph County, W.Va. 1967. 17616
Soil survey, Twiggs County, Ga. 1963. 11950
Soil survey, upper Flathead Valley area, Mont. 1960. 15316
Soil survey, Van Buren County, Iowa. 1962. 14000
Soil survey, Wabash County, Ill. 1964. 12532
Soil survey, Wabasha County, Minn. 1965. 15121
Soil survey, Walla Walla County, Wash. 1964. 17537
Soil survey, Walton County, Ga. 1964. 11951
Soil survey, Warren County, Miss. 1964. 15196
Soil survey, Waseca County, Minn. 1965. 15127
Soil survey, Washington County, Fla. 1965. 11860
Soil survey, Washington County, Md. 1962. 14371
Soil survey, Washington County, Miss. 1961. 15197
Soil survey, Washington County, Nebr. 1964. 15618
Soil survey, Washington County, Tenn. 1958. 17086
Soil survey, Watauga County, N.C. [1958] 16220
Soil survey, Wayne County, Ga. 1965. 11952
Soil survey, Wibaux County, Mont. 1958. 15320
Soil survey, Wichita County, Kans. 1965. 14209
Soil survey, Wilbarger County, Tex. 1962. 17186

Soil survey, Williamson County, Tenn. 1964. 17087
Soil survey, Wood County, Ohio. 1966. 16467
Soil survey, Woodward County, Okla. 1963. 16621
Soil survey, Yadkin County, N.C. 1962. 16221
Soil survey, Yoakum County, Tex. 1964. 17187
Soil survey, York County, Pa. 1963. 16806
Soil survey, York County, S.C. 1965. 16996
Soil survey, Zuni Mountain area, N.Mex. 1967. 15824

U.S. *Treasury Dept. Bureau of Statistics.*
Territorial development of the United States. [1901] 4508

U.S. *Treaties, etc., 1841–1845 (Tyler)*
Maps of the boundary between the United States and the British possessions in North America. 1842. [Reprod.] 1908. 10474

U.S. *War Dept.*
Atlas containing maps of Chicago River. [1900] 1510
Atlas of battlefields of Chickamauga, Chattanooga, and vicinity. 1900–1901. 1355
Atlas of the Battlefield of Antietam. 1904. 1354
Atlas of the War of the Rebellion. 1892. 10683
Atlas to accompany the Official Records of the Union and Confederate armies. 1891–95. 1353
Internal improvements. [1825–43] 1377
Military maps illustrating the operations of the Armies of the Potomac & James. [1869] 3688
Official atlas of the Civil War. [1958] 10684
Reconnoissance of the Mississippi & Ohio Rivers. [1875] 1325

U.S. *War Dept General Staff.*
Atlas of the world battle fronts. [1945] 5903
Geographical divisions for the administration of certain war activities. [1917?] 10702
Order of battle maps: Operations in Italy. [1946] 8958
——— Operations in Sicily. [1946] 8959

U.S. *Waterways Experiment Station, Vicksburg, Miss.*
Geological investigations of the Atchafalaya Basin. 1952. 14292

U.S. *Weather Bureau.*
Airway meteorological atlas for the United States. 1941. 10504
Atlas of climatic charts of the oceans. 1938. 5397
Climatic charts of the Unites States. 1904. 4493
Climatology of selected harbors. 1961. 10593
Evaporation maps for the United States. 1959. 10505
North Atlantic tropical cyclones; tracks ... of hurricanes and tropical storms, 1886–1958. 1959. 10284
Rainfall and snow of the United States. 1894. 1360

Rainfall-frequency atlas of the Hawaiian Islands. 1962. 11984
[River and Flood Forecasting Service. 1941] 10763
Summary of international meteorological observations. 1893. 1359
Surface currents of the Great Lakes. 1895. 10333
10–millibar synoptic weather maps. 1959. 10285

U.S. *Work Projects Administration. Alabama.*
Real property survey ... Bessemer, Ala. [1940] 11209

U.S. *Work Projects Administration. California.*
Housing survey covering portions of the city of Los Angeles, Calif. [1940] 11540
1939 real property survey, San Francisco, Calif. [1940] 11591

U.S. *Work Projects Administration. Florida.*
Real property survey [St. Petersburg, Fla. 1940] 11925

U.S. *Work Projects Administration. Illinois.*
Report of the Chicago Land Use Survey. [1942–43] 12650

U.S. *Work Projects Administration. Indiana.*
Real property and land use survey, Fort Wayne, Ind. [1939] 12961
Real property survey, Gary, Ind. [1936] 12968

U.S. *Work Projects Administration. Kentucky.*
Real property survey ... of Louisville, Ky. [1939] 14254

U.S. *Work Projects Administration. Minnesota.*
Atlas of the city of Minneapolis, Minn. 1941. 15153
Census tract maps of the city of St. Paul. [1938] 15165

U.S. *Work Projects Administration. Ohio.*
Real property inventory, Columbus, Ohio. [1936] 16520
Real property inventory maps, Sandusky, Ohio. [1939] 16556
Real property survey of Cincinnati and environs. [1941] 16490

U.S. *Work Projects Administration. Oregon.*
W.P.A. traffic survey ... of Portland, Oreg. [1939] 16741

U.S. *Work Projects Administration. Tennessee.*
Real property inventory and low income housing area survey, Knoxville, Tenn. [1939] 17099

U.S. *Work Projects Administration. Virginia.*
Real property survey; land use survey maps, Alexandria, Va. 1939–[40] 17362

U.S. *Work Projects Administration. Washington (State)*
Real property survey, Seattle, Wash. 1940. 17568

U.S. Accurate Map Company.
Rapid street location map of Indianapolis, Ind. 1965.   12983

United States Express Company.
Express and railway guide. [1895]   4512

Universal History.
Maps and charts to the modern part of the Universal History. 1766.   639

Universal Map and Drafting Company.
Official sectional maps of Tarrant County, Tex. [1966]   17184

Universal Reference Company.
Reference atlas of Manhattan. 1910.   385

Universities' Mission to Central Africa.
Universities' Mission to Central Africa Atlas. 1903.   10086

Unwin, William Jordan, 1811–1877.
Homerton college atlas. 1863.   330

Unz, and Company.
Atlas of New York City and the metropolitan district. 1916.   4951

Updegraff, Allan Eugene, 1883–
Literary Digest atlas of the new Europe. 6th ed. 1923.   7804
———— 7th ed. 1925.   7805

Uruguay. *Comisión de Estudios del Puerto de Montevideo.*
[Puerto de Montevideo. 1898]   18403

Uruguay. *Servicio de Hidrografía.*
Rio San Salvador. 1954.   18405
Rio Santa Lucía. 1940.   18406
———— 1955.   18407

Ustrîâlov, Nikolaĭ Gerasimovich, 1805–1870.
Карты, планы и снимки къ первымъ тремъ томамъ Исторіи царствованія Петра Великаго. [Maps, plans, and reproductions in connection with the first 3 volumes of the History of Peter the Great.] 1858–63.   4056

Vacani, Camillo, *Baron,* **1784–1862.**
[Atlante topografico-militare per servire alla storia delle campagne e degl'Italiani in Ispagna al MDCCCVIII al MDCCCXIII. 1823]   3130

Världsatlas. 1934.

Valck, Gerard, 1626–1720.
Nova totius geographica telluris projectio. [1720?]   562
———— [1748?]   605

Valck, Gerard, *and* **Schenk, Pieter, 1660–1718 or 1719.**
Atlantis sylloge compendiosa. 1709.   4276
Atlas anglois. 1715.   4001

Valette, John De La.
See De La Valette, John.

Vállalat, Kartográfiai.
See Kartográfiai Vállalat.

Vallancey, Charles, 1721–1812.
Military survey of Ireland. [1776] MS.   8231

Vallardi, Francesco, 1809–1895.
Atlante corografico, orografico, idrografico e storico dell'Italia. [1867–97]   3063, 3064

Vallemont, Pierre Le Lorrain, *abbé* de, 1649—1721.
Atlante portatile. [1748]   5980

Vallot, Joseph, 1854–1925.
Évolution de la cartographie de la Savoie et du Mont Blanc ... Atlas. 1922.   8489

Valuev, Petr Aleksandrovich, *Graf,* **1814–1890.**
Temperatur-Verhältnisse des Russischen Reiches. 1880.   9211
———— 1881.   9212

Van Antwerp, Bragg and Company.
Eclectic atlas ... of the United States. [1881]   1411

Van Campen, Savillion.
Our country, from 1800 to 1900. 1900.   10640

Van der Essen, Léon, 1883–
See Essen, Léon van der, 1883–

Van Horne, Thomas Budd, 1821–1895.
History of the Army of the Cumberland. 1875.   4519

Van Royen, William, 1900–
Atlas of the world's resources. v. 1–2. 1952–54.   5470

Van Schaik's Large print atlas for South Africa.
20th ed. 1952.   7529

Van Schaik's New large print atlas for South Africa.
1946.   7246

Vancouver, George, 1757–1798.
Voyage de découvertes à l'Océan Pacifique du Nord. Atlas. [1799]   198, 1219
Voyage of discovery to the North Pacific Ocean. Atlas 1798.   197, 1218

Vandall, Paul Ernest, 1920–
Atlas of Essex County [Ont. 1965]   10416

Völkischer Beobachter.
    Landstrassen-Atlas von Deutschland. 1935.   8611
    —— [2. verb. Aufl.] 1936.   8612
    —— [3. Aufl.] 1936.   8613

Völter, Daniel, 1814–1865.
    Schul–Atlas. [1840]   6090

Vogel, Carl, 1828–1897.
    Karte des Deutschen Reichs. [1891–93]   8687
    —— 1907.   8691

Vogel, Josef.
    Karte spricht! 30 bunte Bildkarten zur
    Erdkunde unseres Vaterlandes. 2. Aufl.
    [1933]   8555

Voigt, L.
    See Brunner, Anton, *and* Voigt, L.

Voigts, Heinrich, 1895–
    See Hagemann, Ernst, 1899–   *and* Voigts,
    Heinrich.

Volckmar, F.
    Atlas universal. 1906.   3383
    —— 1913.   6366
    Universal-Atlas. 1907.   331

Volk und Reich Verlag, *Berlin.*
    Handatlas für die Hitler–Jugend. 1939.   6992

Volkmann, Erich Otto, 1879–1938.
    Strategischer Atlas zum Weltkrieg. [1937]   5851

Volz, Wihelm Theodor August Hermann, 1870–1958.
    National structure of the population of Upper-
    Silesia. 1921.   8812
    Völkische Struktur Oberschlesiens. 1921.   8813

Volz, Wilhelm Theodor August Hermann, *and* Schwalm, Hans.
    Deutsche Ostgrenze. [Atlas. 1929]   8523

Voogt, Claes Jansz, *d.* 1696.
    Nieuwe groote lichtende zee-fakkel. 1782.
           1170, 3660
    Nieuwe groote ligtende zee-fakkel. 3. deel.
    [1717?]   7860
    Nueva, y grande relumbrante antorcha de la
    mar. [1700?]   530
    See also Loon, Joannes van, *and* Voogt, Claes
    Jansz.

Voorhies, Stephen J.
    Map of the subway system of New York.
    1947.   16073

Vorel, Stanislav.
    Kladsko. 1948.   8815

Vose, J. W., and Company.
    Atlas of the city of Syracuse, Onondaga
    County, N.Y. 1892.   2329

Vries, T. de.
    Europa en de landen; notitie-atlas. 8. druk.
    [1947]   7743
    Indië en de werelddelen. Notitie-atlas. 8.
    druk. [194–]   5768
    Nederland en de provincies. 12. druk. [194–]   9052

Vsesoiuznyi Kartograficheskii Trest.
    Атлас промымленности СССCP на начало
    2-й пятилетки. [Atlas of the industries of
    the USSR at the beginning of the 2d 5-year
    plan] 1934.   9269

Vuillemin, Alexandre A., *b.* 1812.
    Atlas universel de géographie. 1847.   6105
    France et ses colonies. Atlas illustré. 1851.   3002
    —— 1854.   4027
    —— 1873.   8467
    —— [1882]   3007

Vuillemin, Alexandre, *and others.*
    Nouvel atlas illustre. 1890.   3008

Wachter, Alfred Oscar, 1825–
    La guerre de 1870–1871. Atlas. [1872–73]   2984

Waghenaer, Luc Janszoon, *fl.* 1550.
    Mariners mirrovr. [1588]   3981
    Speculum nauticum super naiugatione Maris
    Occidentalis confectum. 1586.   3980
    Spieghel der zeevaerdt. 1585.   5165

Wagner, A. C., Company.
    Detailed motor book ... North-central Illinois.
    [1922]   10779
    Official simplified guide with dissected map,
    Cleveland [Ohio] and suburbs. 1921.   16501

Wagner, Emil, 1859–
    Atlas de poche de la Suisse. [1907]   3157
    Tasche-Atlas der Schweiz, politisch, statistisch.
    3. Aufl. [191–]   9449

Wagner, Hermann, 1840–1929.
    See Sydow, Emil von, 1812–1873, *and*
    Wagner, Hermann, 1840–1929.

Wagner, Reinhold.
    [Geschichte der Belagerung von Strassburg ...
    1870 ... Atlas. 1874–78]   8508

Waite, J. F., Publishing Company.
    New international office and family atlas.
    [1896]   1016

Walckenaer, Charles Athanase, *Baron,* 1771–1852.
    Atlas de la géographie ancienne historique et
    comparée des Gaules. 1839.   2958

Waldsemüller, Martin, 1470–1521?
Älteste Karte mit dem Namen Amerika.
1903.   5794

Waldsmith, Arnold J., 1907–
Dolph-Stewart atlas of Jacksonville ... Fla.
1938.   11884
Dolph-Stewart lot and block atlas of Jacksonville, Fla.   1940.   11885
—— 1942.   11886

Walker, A. H.
Atlas of Bergen County, N.J. [1876]   2152

Walker, Charles.
See Walker, John, 1786 or 7–1873, *and*
Walker, Charles.

Walker, Edwin Lesley, 1911–
See Scott, Marlin Elmer, 1908–   *and*
Walker, Edwin Lesley, 1911–

Walker, Eric Anderson, 1886–
Historical atlas of South Africa.   1922.   10161

**Walker, George Hiram, *and* Jewett, Clarence
Frederick, 1852–1909.**
Columbia and Montour Counties, Pa.   1876.
                                                  2471, 2491
County atlas of Tioga, Pa.   1875.   2497

Walker, George Hiram, and Company.
Atlas, city of Everett, Middlesex County,
Mass.   1896.   1880
Atlas of Attleboro'town Mass.   1880.   1850
Atlas of Barnstable County, Mass.   1880.   1806
Atlas of Brookfield, West Brookfield and
North Brookfield towns, Mass.   1885.
                                            1868, 1920, 1947
Atlas of Essex County, Mass.   1884.   1813
Atlas of Fall River City, Mass.   1883.   1882
Atlas of Greenfield Town, Mass.   1884.   1886
Atlas of Holyoke City, Mass.   1884.   1892
Atlas of Malden City, Mass.   1885.   1899
Atlas of Middlesex County, Mass.   1889.   1819
—— 1906–1908.   1820
Atlas of New Bedford City, Mass.   1881.   1912
Atlas of Northampton City, Mass.   1884.   1917
Atlas of Plymouth County, Mass.   1879.   1824
Atlas of Springfield City, Mass.   1882.   1940
Atlas of Taunton City, Mass.   1881.   1944
Atlas of city of Beverly, Essex County, Mass.
1897.   1853
—— 1907.   1855
Atlas of the city of Malden, Middlesex County,
Mass.   1897.   1900
Atlas of the town of Hull, Plymouth County,
and part of the Jerusalem Road, Norfolk
County, Mass.   1895.   1893
Atlas of the town of Melrose, Middlesex
County, Mass.   1899.   1908

Atlas of the town of Milton, Norfolk County,
Mass.   1896.   1910
—— 1905.   1823, 14500
Atlas of Westfield Town, Mass.   1884.   1948

Walker, H. B.
New international atlas.   1913.   4401

Walker, John, 1759–1830.
Atlas to Walker's Geography.   1797.   689
—— 1802.   3536
Universal atlas.   1816.   6038
—— 1822.   6048

**Walker, John, 1786 or 7–1873, *and* Walker,
Charles.**
British atlas.   1838–[39]   8131
—— 1848.   8133

Walker, John, and Company.
Slate–paper outline atlas.   [19—?]   5769

Walker, Oscar W.
Atlas of Gardner Town, Mass.   1886.   1884
Atlas of Massachusetts.   1891.   1802
—— 1894.   1803
—— 1900.   1804
—— 1904.   1805
—— 1909.   3768

Walker, Oscar W., and Company.
Atlas of Winchendon Town, Mass.   1886.   1952

Walker, Sarah Sue.
Oregon coast county maps.   1947.   16649

Walker and Miles.
New standard atlas of the Dominion of
Canada.   1875.   1237

Walker Lithograph and Publishing Company.
Atlas of Barnstable County, Mass.   [1910]
          3769, 3772, 3773, 3776–3778, 3780, 3782,
          3784, 3786, 3790–3792, 3794, 3795, 3799
Atlas of the towns of Braintree and Wey-
mouth, Norfolk County, Mass.   1909.
                                                  3774, 3798
Atlas of the towns of Needham, Dover,
Westwood, Millis, and Medfield, Norfolk
County, Mass.   1909.   3779, 3787–3789, 3797
Atlas of the towns of Topsfield, Ipswich,
Essex, Hamilton and Wenham, Essex
County, Mass.   1910.
                          3781, 3783, 3785, 3793, 3796

Wall, William G., *b.* 1792.
[Hudson River portfolio.   1828]   4958

Wall, Mann and Hall.
Illustrated atlas of Noble County, Ohio.
1879.   2406

Wallace, J. B., *and* Shillington, T.
Empire city lot book, being a complete atlas of

Manhattan Island north of Forty-Second
Street. [1873]   2295

Walleczek, Erich, *and* Gamerith, Hermann.
Drau von Lienz bis Marburg. [1905?]   7844
Mur von Tamsweg bis Radkersburg. [1950?]   7865
Salzach von Krimml bis zur Mündung.
[1950?]   7884

Walleczek, Erich, *and* Pranzl, Sepp.
Österreichischer Faltbootführer ... Traun von
Koppenbrüllerhöhle bis zur Mündung.
[1950?]   7935

Walleczek, Erich, *and* Styx, Kurt.
Österreichischer Faltbootführer ... Enns von
Radstadt bis zur Mündung. [1950?]   7934

Walling, Henry Francis, 1825–1888.
Atlas of the Dominion of Canada. 1875.   1238
Atlas of the State of Michigan. [1873]   1960
Atlas of the State of Ohio. 1868.
    1389, 2346, 16376
Atlas of the State of Wisconsin. [1876]   2633
Tackabury's Atlas of the Dominion of
Canada. 1875.   10357
—— 1876.   4481
See also Campbell, Robert Allen, *and* Walling,
Henry Francis, 1825–1888.
See also Martenet, Simon J., 1832–1892,
Walling, Henry Francis, 1825–1888, *and*
Gray, Ormando Willis.

Walling, Henry Francis, *and* Gray, Ormando Willis.
New topographical atlas of the State of Ohio.
1872.   2347
New topographical atlas of the State of Pennsylvania. 1872.   2453
Official topographical atlas of Massachusetts.
1871.   1800, 14398, 14399

**Walling, Henry Francis, *and* Hitchcock, Charles
Henry, 1836–1919.**
Atlas of the State of New Hampshire. [1877]   2136

Wallis, John.
New atlas of France. 1794.   8460

Walser, Gabriel, 1695–1776.
Schweitzer-Geographie. 1770.   4067

Walsh, John B.
Atlas of Auglaize County [Ohio] 1898.   16382

Walter, Thomas U.
Quadrangle, Birmingham [Ala.] Map book of
business district. 1914.   4536

Walton, B. J.
Truckers escrot. [1961]   10936

Walujew, P. A.
See Valuev, Petr Aleksandrovich, *Graf*, 1814–
1890.

Wand, Otto, 1879–1949.
See Muris, Oswald, 1884–1964, *and* Wand,
Otto, 1879–1949.

Wander-Atlas der Zürcher Illustrierten. [1934–48]   9454

Wang, Shou-ch'êng, 1895–
Chung-kuo fên shêng hsiang t'u. [Detailed
provincial atlas of China. 1942]   9580

Wang, Shu-shih.
Chung-kuo li shih ti t'u. [Historical atlas of
China] 1953.   9526

Wang, Wên-shao, 1830–1908.
Kuei-chou t'ung shêng ti yü tsung t'u fên t'u
ch'üan han. [Complete county and city atlas
of Kweichow Province. 1892] MS.   9658

War atlas for Americans. 1944.   5904

Warajiya.
Osaka-shi kubun chizu; poketto-gata. [Osaka
City ward maps; pocket edition. 1956]   9945
Saishin Tōkyō-to kubun chizu. [New ward
atlas of Metropolitan Tokyo. 1958?]   9992
Tōkyō-to kubun chizuchō. [Tokyo ward atlas.
1958]   9993

Ward, *Lady* Emily Elizabeth Swinburne.
Six views of the most important towns ... of
Mexico. 1829.   5116

Ward, Harold Bernard, 1889–
Octovue map of the world. 1st ed. 1943.   7166

Ward and Company.
Miniature atlas. 1857.   825

Ward, Lock and Company.
Handy atlas and world gazetteer. 1908.   3586
Multum in parvo atlas of the world. 1925.   6601
Touring atlas of Great Britain & Ireland.
[1925]   8031

Ward Lock's Handy world atlas and gazetteer.
[1950]   7383

Ward, Marcus.
Shilling atlas. [187–?]   6170

Warden Company.
Atlas of Kay County, Okla. 1921.   16607

Warman, Henry J.
Alpha map transparencies—Mid-continental
U.S.A. 1964.   10569
—— 1967.   10570
Alpha map transparencies—North America.
1967.   10291
Alpha map transparencies—South America.
1966.   18188

Warne, Frederick, and Company.
Everyway motoring atlas of the British Isles.
[193–] 8033
Handy world atlas and gazetteer. [1903] 6312
Junior atlas. New ed. 1868. 332

Warnecke, Rudolf, 1885–
105 Karten ... Haus und Hof in der Nieder-
deutschen Sprache. 1939. 8585

Warner, George E., ca. 1826–1917.
See Beers, Frederick W., Warner, George E,
and others.
See also Beers, Frederick W., Leavenworth,
A., Warner, George E., *and others.*

**Warner, George E., and Foote, Charles M., 1849–
1899.**
Atlas of Grant County, Wis. 1877. 2646
Plat book of Allamakee County, Iowa.
1886. 1642
Plat book of Buchanan County, Iowa. 1886. 1648
Plat book of Clayton County, Iowa. 1886. 1653
Plat book of Fayette County, Iowa. 1879. 1661
Plat book of Houston County, Minn. 1878. 2021
Plat book of Howard County, Iowa. 1886. 1671
Plat book of Iowa County, Iowa. 1886. 1674
Plat book of Marshall County, Iowa. 1885. 1686
Plat book of Olmstead County, Minn. 1878. 2031
Plat book of Otter Tail County, Minn. 1884. 2033
Plat book of Winneshiek County, Iowa.
1886. 1707

Warner and Beers.
Atlas of Bond County and the State of Illinois.
1875. 1516
Atlas of Bureau County and the State of
Illinois. 1875. 1520
Atlas of De Witt County and the State of
Illinois. 1875. 1528
Atlas of Grundy County and the State of
Illinois. 1874. 1535
Atlas of Henry County and the State of
Illinois. 1875. 1537
Atlas of La Salle County and the State of
Illinois. 1876. 1544
Atlas of McLean County and the State of
Illinois. 1874. 1546
Atlas of Macon County and the State of
Illinois. 1874. 1548
Atlas of Macoupin County and the State of
Illinois. 1875. 1550
Atlas of Moultrie County and the State of
Illinois. 1875. 1556
Atlas of Piatt County and the State of Illinois.
1875. 1560, 4586
Atlas of Shelby County and the State of
Illinois. 1875. 1566
Atlas of Stark County and the State of Illinois.
1873. 1568
Atlas of the State of Illinois. 1876. 1513
Atlas of Whiteside County and the State of
Illinois. 1872. 1576

Atlas of Woodford County, and the State of
Illinois. 1874. 1580
Illustrated historical atlas of St. Clair Co., Ill.
1874. 12481

Warner and Higgins.
Atlas of Edgar County and the State of Illinois.
1870. 1530

Warner, Higgins and Beers.
Atlas of Logan County and the State of Illinois.
1873. 12353
Atlas of the State of Illinois. 1871. 1512
Atlas of Warren County and the State of
Illinois. 1872. 1574

Warp Publishing Company.
Atlas of Kearney County, Nebr. 1946. 15486

Warre, *Sir* Henry James, 1819–1898.
Sketches in North America and the Oregon
Territory. [1848] 4470, 4471

**Warren, Jule Benjamin, 1887– and Denmark,
L. Polk.**
North Carolina atlas. 1947. 16210
—— 1952. 16211

Warren, William, 1806–1879.
Atlas to Warren's System of geography.
1843. 333

Warsaw. Instytut Geologiczny.
Atlas géologique de Pologne. [1956] 9141

Wartmann, Hermann, 1835–
Atlas über die Entwicklung von Industrie und
Handel der Schweiz. 1873. 3146

Washburn, Delos Cuyler, 1868–
Map of Ambridge, Pa. [1931] 16816

Washburn Leader, *Washburn, N.Dak.*
McLean County atlas, N.Dak. [1937] 16295

Washington *(State) Dept. of Agriculture.*
Atlas of Washington agriculture. 1963. 17406

Washington *(State) Dept. of Highways.*
County maps, prepared by the Highway Planning Division. [1958] 17415
General highway and transportation maps.
[1941] 17412

Washington *(State) Secretary of State.*
King County legislative district maps. [1965] 17470
Legislative district maps. [1965] 17404
Pierce County legislative district maps.
[1965] 17503
Political maps showing congressional, legis-
lative and judicial districts. [1946] 17405
Spokane County legislative district maps.
[1965] 17523

Washington (State) State Advertising Commission.
Official sectional guide to your vacation in
Washington State. [1950]   17420
—— [1955]   17423

Washington (State) State Aeronautics Commission.
Washington flight maps. 1948.   17407

Washington Post.
Standard war atlas with marginal index.
[1898]   4217

Wąsowicz, Józef, 1900–1964.
See Romer, Eugeniusz, 1871–1954, *and*
Wąsowicz, Józef, 1900–1964.

Wasserwanderbuch. 1953.   8675
—— [3. verb. und erweiterte Ausg. 1954]   8676

Watering places of Great Britain. 1831.   5196

Watson, Gaylord.
New and complete illustrated atlas. [1885]   929
New commercial, county and railroad atlas
of the United States and Dominion of
Canada. 1875.   11034
New commercial, county and railroad atlas of
the United States and territories, and British
provinces. [1875]   1392
New indexed family atlas of the United States.
1883.   915, 1414

Waucomont, Th. *and others.*
Atlas moderne. [1950]   7431

Waupaca Abstract and Loan Company.
Plat book of Waupaca County, Wis. 1912.   3935a

Wauters, Alphonse Guillaume Ghislain, 1817–1898.
Atlas pittoresque des chemins de fer de la
Belgique. 1840.   7957

Webb Publishing Company.
Atlas and farm directory … Barron County,
Wis. 1914.   5081
Atlas and farm directory … Benton County,
Minn. [1914]   4775
Atlas and farm directory … Buffalo County,
Wis. 1914.   5082
Atlas and farm directory … Chippewa
County, Minn. 1914.   4778
Atlas and farm directory … Crawford
County, Wis. 1914.   5085
Atlas and farm directory … Dakota
County, Minn. 1916.   4780
Atlas and farm directory … Dodge County,
Minn. 1914.   4781
Atlas and farm directory … Grant County,
Minn. 1914.   4786
Atlas and farm directory … Green Lake
County, Wis. [1914]   5088
Atlas and farm directory … Jackson County,
Wis. [1914]   5090

Atlas and farm directory … Juneau County,
Wis. 1914.   5092
Atlas and farm directory … Kandiyohi
County, Minn. 1915.   4791
Atlas and farm directory … Lincoln County,
Minn. 1915.   4795
Atlas and farm directory … Mille Lacs
County, Minn. [1914]   4799
Atlas and farm directory … Clayton County,
Iowa. 1914.   4631
Atlas and farm directory … Fillmore County,
Minn. 1915.   4783
Atlas and farm directory … Lyon County,
Minn. 1914.   4796
Atlas and farm directory … Redwood County,
Minn. 1914.   4806
Atlas and farm directory … Trempealeau
County, Wis. 1914.   5106
Atlas and farm directory … Vernon County,
Wis. [1915]   5107
Atlas and farm directory … Winneshiek
County, Iowa. 1915.   4665
Atlas and farm directory … Pipestone County,
Minn. [1914]   4804
Atlas and farm directory … Renville County,
Minn. 1913.   4807
Atlas and farm directory … Rice County,
Minn. 1915.   4808
Atlas and farm directory … Sherburne
County, Minn. 1914.   4812
Atlas and farm directory … Steele County,
Minn. 1914.   4814
Atlas and farm directory … Traverse County,
Minn. [1915]   4816
Atlas and farm directory … Wabasha County,
Minn. [1915]   4817
Atlas and farm directory … Waseca County,
Minn. [1914]   4818
Atlas and farm directory … Watonwan
County, Minn. 1915.   4820
Atlas and farm directory … Waushara
County, Wis. [1914]   5110
Atlas and farm directory … Wright County,
Minn. 1915.   4823
Atlas and farm directory … Nicollet County,
Minn. 1913.   4801
Atlas and farm directory … of Todd County,
Minn. [1914]   4815
Atlas and farmers' directory … Kanabec
County, Minn. 1915.   4790
Atlas and farmers' directory … Mower
County, Minn. 1915.   4800
Atlas and farmers' directory … of Polk
County, Minn. 1915.   4805
Atlas and farmers' directory … Wilkin
County, Minn. 1915.   4821
Atlas and farmers' directory of Anoka
County, and the eleven northern townships
of Hennepin County, Minn. 1914.   4774, 4787
Atlas and farmers' directory of Brown County,
Minn. 1914.   4777
Atlas and farmers' directory of Faribault
County, Minn. 1913.   4782

Atlas and farmers' directory of Goodhue County, Minn. 1914.   4785

Atlas and farmers' directory of Isanti County, Minn. 1914.   4788

Atlas and farmers' directory of Lac Qui Parle County, Minn. 1913.   4793

Atlas and farmers' directory of McLeod County, Minn. 1914.   4797

Atlas and farmers' directory of Meeker County, Minn. 1913.   4798

Atlas and farmers' directory of Olmstead County, Minn. 1914.   4803

Atlas and farmers' directory of St. Croix County, Wis. 1914.   5103

Atlas and farmers' directory of Scott County, Minn. 1913.   4811

Atlas and farmers' directory of Sibley County, Minn. 1914.   4813

Atlas and farmers' directory of Winona County, Minn. 1914.   4822

Farmers atlas ... with complete survey in township plats, Freeborn County, Minn. 1913.   4784

Farmers atlas ... with complete survey in township plats, Le Sueur County, Minn. 1912.   4794

Farmers atlas ... with complete survey in township plats, Washington County, Minn. 1912.   4819

Farmers atlas ... with complete survey in township plats, Yellow Medicine County, Minn. 1913.   4824

Weber, H. L., *and* Swingley, C. D.
The 1894 atlas of Crawford County, Ohio. 1894.   2366

Weber, Richard, *and* Korbe, Carl.
Kartenskizzen zum Weltkrieg. 1944.   5852

Wedell, Rudolph von.
Historisch-geographischer Hand-Atlas. 2. Aufl. [1843]   157

Weeden, John W.
East Greenwich and Potowmut ... [R.I.] 1964.   16952

East Greenwich, No. Kingstown, and Potowomut street map [R.I.] 1963.   16954

Providence, Cranston, and Warwick street maps. 1964.   16971

Rhode Island and nearby Massachusetts; street maps. 1967.   16948

Rhode Island map calendar. 1962.   16946

South and west Rhode Island street maps. 1966.   16947

Street maps: Johnston, No. Providence ... [R.I.] 1963.   16951

Street maps: Providence, East Providence ... [R.I.] 1965.   16972

Warwick street map [R.I.] 1963.   16976

Wei, Shêng-ho.
Chi-lin shêng hsing chêng ch'üan t'u. [Admin-

istrative atlas of the Province of Chi-lin. 1927]   9650

Weidmüller, Wilhelm.
Hiematkarten für die Volksschulen in München. [1956]   8871

Weigand, Gustav Ludwig, 1860–1930.
Linguistischer Atlas des Dacorumänischen Sprachgebietes. 1898–1909.   3096, 4054, 9207

Weigel, J. A. G.
See Schneider, Adam Gottlieb, *and* Weigel, J. A. G.

Weigel, Johann Christoph.
Atlas portatilis. 1720.   5967
—— 3. ed. 1745.   5978

Weijnen, Antonius Angelus, 1909–
Dialect-atlas von Noord-Brabant. 1952.   7956

Weiland, Carl Ferdinand, *d.* 1847.
Allgemeiner Hand–Atlas. [1848]   6107
[Atlas von America. 1824–28]   1225

Weimar. Geographisches Institut.
See Geographisches Institut, *Weimar.*

Weinberg, Allen, *and* Fields, Dale.
Ward genealogy of the city and county of Philadelphia. [1958]   16886

Weinfeld, Ignacy, 1877–   *and others.*
Atlas statystyczny Polski. 1924–25.   9136

Weingaertner and Shumate.
Atlas of the city of St. Louis [Mo.] 1892.   15270

Weinlander, Paul, 1890–
Township plats of Washtenaw County, Mich. 1934.   14824

Weir, Thomas R.
Economic atlas of Manitoba. [1960]   10392

Weir, Walter Wallace, 1882–   *and* Storie, Raymond Earl, 1894–
Soils of Santa Clara County, Calif. 1947.   11476

Weiss, Johann Heinrich, 1759?–1826.
Atlas Suisse. 1786–1802.   3152

Weisse, Hildegard.
Indien; Entwicklung seiner Wirtschaft und Kultur. 1958.   9689

Welbanks, Wallace P.
Atlas of Duluth, Minn. 1912.   3817

Welfare Federation of Cleveland. *Research Dept.*
Health and welfare services by census tracts. 1951.   16510

What's the score in our neighborhoods? ...
Greater Cleveland [Ohio.   1948]   16506

Weller, Edward, *d.* 1884.
Atlas of Scripture geography.   [1883]   5374
Portable atlas of physical geography.   1871.   5780
Student's atlas of physical geography.   1873.   5781

Wells, Edward, 1667–1727.
New sett of maps.   1700.   531
—— 1718.   3479
—— [1719?]   3480
—— 1722.   564
—— [1738?]   3489, 4284, 5972

Wells, Jacob.
Series of globular maps.   1878.   6198

Wells Mail Advertising.
So you're new to the Island [Wash.] empire.
[1954]   17422

Wendelken and Company.
Atlas of the towns of Babylon, Islip, and south
part of Brookhaven in Suffolk County, N.Y.
1888.   2269

Wenschow, Karl, 1884–1947.
Atlas für höhere Lehranstalten.   [1950]   7432
Heimat-Atlas Fränkische Regierungsbezirke.
[1951]   8733
Heimat-Atlas Regierungsbezirk Schwaben.
[1950]   8732
Heimat-Atlas Regierungsbezirke Nieder-
bayern und Oberpfalz.   [1951]   8734
Heimat-Atlas Württemberg-Baden-Hohen-
zollern.   [1949]   8828
Heimatatlas Baden-Württemberg.   [1953]   8717
Weltatlas.   1947.   7289
—— [1948]   7333

Wenzel, Walter.
Wortatlas des Kreises Wetzlar.   1930.   8586

Werdenhagen, Johannes Angelius von, 1581–1652.
Rebvs pvblicis Hanseaticis.   [1641]   7645

Werner, Friedrich Bernhard, 1690–1778.
[Views of the cities of Europe.   1700–54] 2782, 7646

Werner, Oscar, 1849–
Katholischer Kirchen-Atlas.   1888.   90
Katholischer Missions-Atlas.   1885.   3339

Werner Company.
Peoples illustrated and descriptive family atlas.
[1895]   1006
Pocket atlas.   1896.   1444

Wesley, Edgar Bruce, 1891–
Denoyer-Geppert Atlas of American history.
[1957]   10641
Our United States: Its history in cartovues.
[1965]   10642

—— Its history in maps. [1st ed.   1956]   10643
—— [1st ed.   1957]   10644
—— [2d ed.   1961]   10645
—— [3d ed.   1965]   10646

West Bengal. *State Statistical Bureau.*
Statistical atlas, West Bengal.   1953.   9712

West Coast Plan Service.
Pinellas County, Fla., land atlas.   1957.   11848

West Virginia. *Dept. of Commerce.*
Economic atlas for West Virginia.   [1961]   17598
—— [1965]   17599

West Virginia. *Economic Development Agency.*
Economic atlas for West Virginia.   [1960–61]   17597

West Virginia. *State Road Commission.*
General county highway maps of West Virginia.   [1957]   17603
—— [1962]   17605
General highway county maps of West Virginia.   [1943]   17601
—— 1950.   17602
General highway map[s] ... West Virginia.
[1959]   17604
—— [1964]   17606
Transportation map[s] ... West Virginia.
[1940]   17600

Westermann, Georg.
Atlas.   Heimat und Welt.   1950.   7433
—— 1952.   7538
—— 1953.   7583
Atlas der Weltgeschichte.   13. Aufl.   [1923]   5580
Atlas der Weltwirtschaft.   [1928]   5476
Atlas für Berliner Schulen.   pt. 1.   [1950]   7434
Atlas für die Schulen in Schleswig–Holstein.
[1950]   7435
Lebensraum des Menschen.   1954.   7614
Polizei–Atlas.   [1928]   6692
Taschen Welt Atlas.   [1932]   6788
—— 5. Aufl.   [1935]   6865
Weltatlas.   9. Aufl.   [1922]   6509
—— 10. Aufl.   [1922]   6510
—— 12. Aufl.   [1922]   6511
—— 13. Aufl.   2 v.   [1923]   6536
—— 15. Aufl.   [1926]   6638
—— 26. Aufl.   [1928]   6693
—— 28. Aufl.   [1928]   6694

Westermanns Deutscher Reichs-Atlas.   [1935]   8697

Western Atlas Company.
Atlas of Lewis County, Mo.   1897.   2084

Western Map Company.
Freeway atlas ... Los Angeles and vicinity.
[1963]   11555

Western Publication Company.
Plat book of Woodward County, Okla.   1910.   3885

Western States Publishing Company.
County maps with publicity [Oregon] 1949.   16651
Presenting your atlas for Lane County, Oreg. 1951.   16696

Weston, William J.
Plat book of Gogebic County, Mich. 1910.   3802

Weston, William J., *and* Hancock, C. F.
Plat book of Houghton County, Mich. 1911.   3804

Wexford County, *Mich. Extension Service.*
Wexford County farm home locations. 1966.   14840

Wheaton, A., and Company.
Reference maps of the Far East. [1942?]   9494

Wheaton's Modern atlas of Africa. [1937]   10099

Wheaton's Modern teaching atlas. 1936.   6883

Wheeler, Eugenia A.
Minnesota. [1875]   2008

Wheeler, James Talboys, 1824–1897.
Analysis ... of the historical geography of the Old and New Testaments. 1853.   91

Whico Map and Publishing Company.
South Texas and Texas gulf coast. [1960]   17133

Whipple, Alphonso.
Fire insurance map of Carondelet, St. Louis, Mo. 1st ed. 1895.   15271
Fire insurance map of East St. Louis [Ill.] 1889.   12677
—— 3d ed. 1896.   12678
Fire insurance map of St. Louis, Mo. 1876.   15267
—— 1889–92.   15269
—— 1895–98.   15272
Fire insurance maps of Granite City ... Ill. 1898.   12687
Insurance maps, 2d series. [1874]   2062
—— [1876]   2063
Kirkwood, St. Louis County, Mo. 1897.   15261

Whitcombe and Tombs.
New war atlas. 2d ed. [1941]   5905

Whitcombe's Atlas of geography for New Zealand and Australian schools. 3d ed. [1943]   7133
—— 4th ed. [1946]   7227

White, David H.
Atlas of Pierce Co., Wash. 1928.   17498
Township maps of Pierce County, Wash. 1911.   17496

White, Henry Ernst, 1866–
Plat book of Starke County, Ind. [1925]   12915

White, J. E., *and others*.
World's atlas and educational guide. 1892.   979

White, M. Wood.
New county and district atlas of the State of West Virginia. 1873.   2627

Whitford, Adcook, Lix, and Ludgate Corporation.
Book of maps showing city of Syracuse by wards. 1929.   16171

Whiting, Daniel Powers, *d.* 1892.
Army portfolio. No. 1. [1847]   3687

Whitley, Paul Clyde, 1893–
Paul's Sectional map of Texas. [1934]   17142
—— [1936]   17144

Whitman and Howard.
Atlas of the towns of Revere and Winthrop, Suffolk County, Mass. 1906.   1930, 1955

Whitney, William H.
Union and Confederate campaigns in the lower Shenandoah Valley. 1883.   1356, 2605

Whittaker, G. *and* W. B.
Travellers pocket atlas ... England & Wales. 1823.   8101

Whittle, James, *ca.* 1757–1818.
See Laurie, Robert, ca. 1755–1836, *and* Whittle, James.

Wichtigsten Kriegs– und Feldzüge der Weltgeschichte. [2. Aufl. 1928]   5581

Widmer, Otmar, 1891–1962.
Pflanzengeographischer Welt–Atlas. 1940.   5383
—— 1941–[52]   5384

Wiechert, Otto.
Heimat-Atlas für Ostpreussen. [1936]   8765

Wieder, Frederik Caspar, 1874–1943.
Monumenta cartographica. 5 v. 1925–33.   5795

Wiener, Charles, 1851–1913.
See Spitzer, Frédéric, 1815–1890, *and* Wiener, Charles.

Wijk Roelandszoon, Jacobus van, 1781–1847.
See Bennet, Roelfo Gabriel, 1774–1829, *and* Wijk Roelandszoon, Jacobus van.

Wild, Heinrich, 1833–1902.
Regen-Verhältnisse des Russischen Reiches. 1887.   9213

Wild, J. C.
Panorama and views of Philadelphia. 1838.   5024

Wilgus, Alva Curtis, 1897–
Atlas of Hispanic American history. 1932.   18043
Historical atlas of Latin America. 1967.   18044
Latin America in maps, historic, geographic, economic. [1943]   18045

Wilhelm Sales Agency.
Rural route guide, Scott County [Iowa]
1953.   13913

Wilhelmshaven, Germany. Marineobservatorium.
Atlas der Gezeitenströme für das Gebiet der
Nordsee. 1939.   7871
—— 1943.   7872
Gezeiten und Gezeitenströme im Jadegebiet.
1939.   8878
Karten der Gezeitenströme für das Gebiet der
Insel Helgoland. 1941.   8876
Karten der Gezeitenströme für das Gebiet der
Isle of Wight. 1940.   7851
Karten der Gezeitenströme für das Gebiet des
Kanals. 1940.   7852
Karten der Gezeitenströme für den Eingang
zum Weissen Meer. 1942.   9298
Karten der Gezeitenströme für die Bucht von
St. Malo. 1941.   8511
Karten der Gezeitenströme ... für die Strasse
von Dover. 1940.   7843
Karten der Gezeitenströme für südliche
Nordsee, östlicher Teil. 1941.   7873
Karten der Gezeitenströme für die West- und
Nordküste Norwegens. 1943–44.   9115
Karten der harmonischen Gezeitenkonstanten
... für das Gebiet der Deutschen Bucht.
1939.   8877
Karten der harmonischen Gezeitenkonstanten
für das Gebiet der Biskaya-Bucht. Ausg.
A. 1944.   7834
—— Ausg. B. 1939.   7833
Karten der harmonischen Gezeitenkonstanten
für das Gebiet der Nordsee. Ausg. A.
1942.   7874
—— Ausg. B. 1939.   7875
Karten der harmonischen Gezeitenkonstanten
für das Gebiet der Nordwestafrikanischen
Gewässer. 1941.   10092
Karten der harmonischen Gezeitenkonstanten
für das Gebiet der Westbritischen Gewässer.
1939.   8070
—— 1942.   8071
Karten der harmonischen Gezeitenkonstanten
für das Gebiet des Kanals. Ausg. A. 1942.   7853
—— Ausg. C. 1939.   7854
Karten der harmonischen Gezeitenkonstanten
für die Gewässer vor der Ostküste der
Vereinigten Staaten. 1942.   10997
Karten der harmonischen Gezeitenkonstanten
für die Murman-Küste und das Weisse
Meer. 1942.   9298
Karten der harmonischen Gezeitenkonstanten
für die Ostcanadischen Gewässer. 1942.   10355
Karten der harmonischen Gezeitenkonstanten
für die Westibirischen Gewässer. 1942.   9321

Wilkes, Charles, 1798–1877.
Narrative of the United States exploring ex-
pedition during the years 1838–1842 ...
Atlas. 1844.   3245
United States exploring expedition, during the
years 1838–1842. Atlas. 1850–58.   3246

Wilkes Brothers Abstract Company.
Atlas of Washington County, Oreg. 1909.   3887

Wilkinson, James, 1757–1825.
Diagrams and plans ... of ... the principal
battles and military affairs treated of in
Memoirs of my own times. 1816.   1344

Wilkinson, Robert, *fl.* 1785–1825.
Atlas classica. [1797]   54
—— 1797–[1805]   3290
General atlas. 1794.   4301
—— 1800–1802.   696
—— 1800-[1803]   701
—— 1800-[1805]   6018
—— 1800-[1808?]   3532a

Will County, *Ill.*
Will County election district maps, excluding
Lockport Twp. 1962.   12561

Willard, Constance Beatrice, *and* Cobbe, Rosser W.
American library atlas of the world. [1911]   3634

Willard, Emma Hart, 1787–1870.
Atlas. 1826.   334
Series of maps to an Abridgement of the History of the United States. 1831.   10650
—— 1833.   10651
Series of maps to Willard's History of the
United States. 1828.   10647
—— 1829.   10648
—— [183–]   10649

Willard, R. C. *and* Robinson, Edward Kilburn, 1883–
Practical map exercises and syllabus in English
history. 1923.   8025

Willett, Charles Kenneth, 1905–
Lee County, Ill., atlas and plat book. [1935]   12344

Willetts, Jacob, 1785–1860.
[Atlas designed to illustrate Willetts' Geography. 1818]   6041
—— [1820]   6046
[Atlas of the world. 1814]   3384
—— [1820]   3385

William-Olsson, William Frits, 1902–
Economic map of Europe. 1953.   7658

Williams, Calvin S.
New general atlas. 1832.   6072

Williams, Clarence S.
Flight folders for round–the–world flight.
1942.   5339
Itinerary of round the world flight. 1942.   5340

Williams, Edgar, and Company.
Historical atlas map of Marion & Linn Counties, Oreg. 1878.   16706

Williams, John Jay, 1818–1904.
Maps illustrating the Isthmus of Tehuantepec. 1852.   2690

Williams, Phineas A.
Along the roads of Jamaica. [1952]   18176

Williams and Heintz Map Corporation.
Boating atlas of tidewater Virginia. 1962.   17335

Williams Atlas Company.
Atlas of Orange County [Fla.] 1963.   11841

Willis, Bailey, 1857–1949.
Research in China, 1903–1904. 1906.   3194

Willits, Walter W.
Farm atlas of Mecosta County, Mich. 1915.   4756

Wills, Leonard Johnston, 1884–
Palaeogeographical atlas of the British Isles. 1951.   8012
—— [1952]   8013

Willsden, S. Blake.
World's greatest war. 1917.   4250

Willsden, S. Blake, and Company.
World's greatest war. [1914]   4249

Wilm, Ludwig, *Ritter* von.
See Frobenius, Leo, 1873–1938, *and* Wilm, Ludwig, *Ritter* von.

Wilner, Merton Merriman, 1867–
New atlas of the world. 1919.   4450b, 6400

Wilson, Ellwood.
Map of village of Saranac Lake, N.Y. 1907.   16162

Wilson Engineering Company.
Hempstead County, Ark. [1964]   11295
Miller County, Ark. 1959.   11299
Texarkana, Ark. 1959.   11319

Wiltsch, Johann Elieser Theodor.
Kirchenhistorischer Atlas. 1843.   2785

Winfield, Charles H.
[History of the land titles of Hudson County, N.J. 1609–1871. Atlas. 1872]   15706

Winkler, Georg.
Atlas der Ost- und Südostfront. [191–]   7797

Winkler, Hubert, 1875–1941.
See Hannig, Emil, 1872–1955, *and* Winkler, Hubert, 1875–1941.

Winkler, Wilhelm, 1893–
Pfälzischer Geschichtsatlas. 1935.   8756

Winston, John C., Company.
Loose–leaf atlas of the world. [1928]   6695
—— [1931]   6769
Modern complete atlas of the world. [1932]   6789
New and complete atlas of the world. [1920]   6429
—— [1927]   6664
—— [1929]   6717
—— [1931]   6770
Perpetual loose–leaf atlas of the world. [1921]   6473

Winter, Albert.
See Loreck, Carl, *and* Winter, Albert.

Winterbotham, William, 1763–1829.
American atlas. 1796.   1216, 1366

Winterset Madisonian, *Winterset, Iowa*.
Atlas of Madison County, Iowa. [1943]   13674

Wirsing, Giselher, 1906– *and others*.
Krieg 1939/40 in Karten. [1940]   5906
—— 1939/41. [1942]   5907
War in maps, 1939/40. 1941.   5908

Wisconsin.
[County maps of Wisconsin showing flow of traffic] 1934.   17636

Wisconsin, *Defendant*.
State of Michigan, plaintiff, v. State of Wisconsin, defendant. [Suit . . . to determine the boundary between the States . . . 1925]   14554

Wisconsin. *Dept. of Agriculture*.
Wisconsin agriculture; a statistical atlas. [1928]   17631

Wisconsin. *Dept. of Agriculture (1915–1929)*.
Land economic inventory, Bayfield Co., Wis. 1928.   17662

Wisconsin. *Dept. of Agriculture and Markets*.
Land economic inventory, Douglas County, Wis. 1933.   17725
Land economic inventory, Juneau County, Wis. 1933.   17790
Land economic inventory Langlade County, Wis. 1933.   17816

Wisconsin. *Division of Land Economic Inventory*.
Sawyer County. [194–?]   17922
Wisconsin land inventory, Ashland County general cover map[s. 1936]   17653
Wisconsin land inventory land cover map[s] Barron County. [1939]   17657
Wisconsin land inventory land cover map[s] Burnett County. [1941]   17679
Wisconsin land inventory land cover map[s] Calumet County. [1939]   17685
Wisconsin land inventory land cover map[s] Columbia County. [1939]   17695
Wisconsin land inventory land cover map[s] Dane County. [1939]   17709

Atlas [Zeekaerten. 1675?]   485
Germania Inferior. [1690?]   9083
Theatrum ichnographicum omnium urbium
  et praecipuorum oppidorum Belgicarum
  XVII Provinciarum. [1700?]   4045, 9036
Theatrum praecipuarum totius Europae
  urbium. [1695?]   3964

With, Cläre.
Amerika, Länder und Völker. [1930]   10271
Indien. [1930]   9702
Japan. [1931]   9810
Niedersachsen. [1933]   8794

Witmer, A. R.
See Bridgens, H. F., Witmer, A. R., *and*
  others.

Witt, Werner, 1906–
Wirtschafts- und verkehrsgeographischer
  Atlas von Pommern. 1934.   8757

Die Woche, moderne illustrierte Zeitschrift, *Berlin.*
Kriegs Atlas der "Woche". [1914]   6374

Wölfle, Karl.
Hamburger Geschichtsatlas. [1926]   8859

Woerl, Joseph Edmund, 1803–1865.
Atlas über alle Theile der Erde. 5te. Aufl.
  1842.   6095
Carte de la France. [1833?]   5226

Wolff, Carl, 1838–1908.
Historischer Atlas. 1877.   158, 2796
See also Kiepert, Heinrich, 1818–1899, *and*
  Wolff, Carl.

Wolff, Julian, 1905–
Sherlockian atlas. 1952.   8022

Wolfgang, Abraham.
Atlas minor. [1689]   502

Wolfram, Georg Karl, 1858–1940 *and* Gley, Werner, 1902–
Elsass-Lothringischer Atlas. 1931.   8485

Wolverton, Chester, *and* Breou, Forsey.
Atlas of Monmouth County, N.J. 1889.   4914

Wona-Verlag.
Marsa–Taschen–Altas von westlichen Kriegs-
  schauplatz. v. 1, 3. [1915]   5853

Wonhaksaeng, *pseud.*
Tae Myong ilt'ong sanha to. [Atlas of China
  in the Ming period (1368–1644) 1721]   9548

Wood, Lyle Arthur, 1907–
Atlas, Beltrami County, Minn. 1942.   14930
Atlas of Pennington County [Minn. 1935]   15073
Koochiching County [Minn.] atlas. [1956]   15023

Wood, Paul L.
Atlas of the town of Ludlow, Mass. 1930.   14489

Wood Atlas Company
New atlas of Monroe County, Iowa. 1937.   13758

Woodbridge, William Channing, 1784–1845.
Larger atlas. [1822]   336
Modern atlas. [1824]   337
—— 4th ed. 1831.   340
—— New ed. [1831]   339
—— 5th ed. 1833.   6073
—— [1843]   343
School atlas. 5th ed. [1821]   335
—— [1826?]   6057
—— 1830.   6068
—— 14th ed. 1831.   338
—— Improved ed. 1833.   341
—— [16th ed.] 1835.   342

Woodman, Prentiss Mollen, 1846–1925.
Minnetonka map-directory. 1908.   2006a

Woodward, Horace Bolingbroke, 1848–1914.
Stanford's Geological atlas of Great Britain.
  1904.   2879
Standford's Geological atlas of Great Britain
  and Ireland. 2d ed. 1907.   2880
—— 3d ed. 1914.   5190
—— 4th ed. [1925]   8014
—— Photographic supplement. 1913.   5191

Woolman, Harry C.
See Rose, T. F., Woolman, Harry C., *and*
  Price, T. T.

Worcester, Joseph Emerson, 1784–1865.
Ancient, classical and Scripture atlas. [1850?] 5375
Historical atlas. New ed. 1827.   159
—— 3d ed. 1828.   4144
—— 1856.   5582
Modern atlas. [1845?]   6102
Worcester's Outline maps. [1829?]   210

Workman, B. A., *and others.*
Gestandaardiseerde Suid-Afrikaanse atlas.
  [1953]   7584
Standardised South African atlas. 1952.   7539
  [1953]   7585

World atlas. Atlas kieszonkowy. [1942?]   7121

World Missionary Conference. *Edinburgh.*
Statistical atlas of Christian missions. 1910. 3340

World Oil.
World Oil Atlas. 2 v. 1947–48.   5774

World Publishing Company, *Cleveland.*
New revised atlas of the world. 1936.   6899

Wright, C. H.
Illustrated historical atlas of Spencer County,
  Ind. 1896.   12912

Yeager-Klinge Company.
Atlas of the North Shore, Beverly to Magnolia, Essex Co., Mass. 1919.   14405

Yen, Tê-chih, *fl*. 1834.
Huang ch'ao nei fu yü yi t'u so mu pên. [Imperial atlas of the Ch'ing period. 1834]   9551

Yerkes, Charles S.
Insurance map of Chicago grain and malt elevators, warehouses, docks and freight depots. 1903.   12607
Insurance map of the Chicago grain elevators. 1894.   12597
Insurance map of the Chicago lumber districts. 2d rev. and enl. ed. 1895.   12600
Insurance map of the Chicago packing houses and Union Stock Yards. 1901.   12605
Insurance map of the Chicago ware houses and docks. 1895.   12601
Insurance map of the lumber districts of Minneapolis, Minn. 1894.   15149

Yoda, Yūho, 1864–1909.
Dai Shin teikoku bunshō seizu. [Detailed provincial atlas of the Ch'ing Empire. 1906]   9557

Yoshida, Otohiko.
Kaitei Nihon shōogyō chizu. [Revised business atlas of Japan. 1905]   9793
[Nihon Shō-gyō chi-dzu.—Business atlas of Japan. 1906]   3211

Yoshida, Tōgo, 1864–1918.
Dai Nohon dokushi chizu. [Atlas of Japanese history. 1940]   9797

Young, Alden W.
Map of village of Riverhead, town of Riverhead, L.I., N.Y. [1934]   16151

Young, Charles H.
Map of San Joaquin County, Calif. 1911.   11468

Young, Robert N., 1923–
See Griffin, Paul Francis, *and* Young, Robert N.

Young, V. J.
Jefferson County, Ill. 1956.   12289
Wayne County, Ill. 1959.   12544

Yü ti tsung t'u. [Atlas of China. MS. 1368–1644]   9536

Yugoslavia.
Annex to the Memorandum of the government of the Federative People's Republic of Yugoslavia. [1946]   9460
Cartes sur la structure ethnique de la Carinthie Slovène. [1946?]   7890
Cartes sur la structure ethnique de la Marche Julienne. [1946?]   9001
Maps relating to the ethnical structure of Slovenian Carinthia. [1946?]   7891
Maps relating to the ethnical structure of the Julian March. [1946?]   9002
Problème des 200.000 Yougoslaves en Autriche. 1947.   7892
Question of 200.000 Yugoslavs in Austria. 1947.   7893

Yunnan, China *(Province) Min chêng t'ing*.
Yün-nan shêng hsien shih chü kai k'uang t'u. [General atlas of the hsien, cities and bureaus of Yunnan Province. 1944]   9665

Yusuf Kamal, *Prince*, 1882–
Monumenta cartographica Africae et Aegypti. 1926–51.   10090

Z Map Company.
Atlas & map of Pittsburgh, Pa. 1952.   16912

Zaleski Falkenhagen, Piotr, 1809–1883.
See Bansemer, Jan Marcin, 1820–1840, *and* Zaleski Falkenhagen, Piotr, 1809–1883.

Zamyslovskii, Egor Egorovich, 1841–1896.
Учебный атласъ по русской исторіи. [School atlas on Russian history.] 1887.   4057

Zanichelli, Nicola.
Atlante geografico sintetico Zanichelli. 1951.   7493
Atlante geografico Zanichelli ad uso delle scuole. 1947.   7290
—— 1950.   7436, 7437

Zannoni, Giovanni Antonio, Rizzi-,
See Rizzi-Zannoni, Giovanni Antonio, 1736–1814.

Zaremba, Józef.
Atlas ziem odzyskanych ... Atlas of the new territories of Poland. 1947.   9137
—— Atlas of the recovered territories of Poland. 1947.   9138
—— Wyd. 2. 1947.   9139

Zatta, Antonio, *fl*. 1757–1797.
Atlante novissimo. 1779–[88]   650
—— 1779–[99]   651

Zatta, Antonio, *and* Zatta, Giacomo.
Nuovo atlante. 2. ed. 1799.   6014
—— 3. ed. 1800.   695

Zatta, Giacomo.
See Zatta, Antonio, *fl*. 1757–1797, *and* Zatta, Giacomo.

Zeeman, K.
See Bos, R., *and* Zeeman, K.

Zeichnungen als Beigabe zu der Festschrift zur Säcularfeier ... zu Celle. 1864.   8741

Zorn, Wolfgang.
Historischer Atlas von Bayerisch-Schwaben.
1955.   8727

Zorrilla de la Barra, Abraham.
Atlas pintoresco del Perú.   [1948]   18381

Zrimec, Stane, 1918–
Gospodarski atlas sveta.   1952.   5477

Zürich. *Vermessungsamt.*
Offizieller Plan von Zürich.   [1952]   9459

Zuev, Nikita Ivanovich, *d.* **1890.**
Историческій атласъ для древней, средней
и новой исторіи. Ч. I. [Historical atlas
for ancient, mediaeval and modern history.]
1867.   3325

Zutz, V. E.
Gregory County [S.Dak.] township maps.
1956.   17033